WORLD
ECONOMIC
DEVELOPMENT

WORLD ECONOMIC DEVELOPMENT

1979 and Beyond

Herman Kahn
with the Hudson Institute

Westview Press / Boulder, Colorado

Copyright © 1979 by Herman Kahn

Published in 1979 in the United States of America by
  Westview Press, Inc.
  5500 Central Avenue
  Boulder, Colorado 80301
  Frederick A. Praeger, Publisher

Library of Congress Catalog Card Number: 79-1737
ISBN: 0-89158-392-0

Printed and bound in the United States of America

Contents

PART I
FRAMEWORK, CONCEPTS, PERSPECTIVES

v

PART II
THE REAL WORLD

Tables and Figures

Preface

When the International Chamber of Commerce first began planning its 1978 Congress, we invited Herman Kahn and the Hudson Institute to play central roles in our proceedings. We expected that they would offer a stimulating perspective for our deliberations, but they have done a far bigger and better job than we had a right to expect. While Herman Kahn would be the first to acknowledge that much of the discussion is tentative and speculative, it has succeeded in providing us with such extraordinary and provocative concepts as the idea of the "agnostic use of history, analogies, and metaphors." This aids greatly in dealing with the real world in the absence of rigorous theories and complete and well-documented information. This is precisely the spirit of this book.

We are all aware that important new problems and prospects lie ahead. We also recognize that we must cope with them if we are to survive. Much is already known about some of these problems; and every bit of knowledge we have should certainly be used. However, many situations are so beclouded by ambiguity, insufficient data, or contradictory and confusing ideological polemics that the best we have to work with are theories of varying plausibility or even intuitions. Mr. Kahn explains in this book how, as practical people, we can go ahead even on such a basis.

I am also intrigued by Herman Kahn's concept that the late nineteenth and early twentieth centuries can be broken down into four periods, and especially by his identification of the years 1974 to 2000 or so as *L'époque de Malaise*. I am much heartened by his argument that natural social, political, and cultural forces are likely to slow the growth of both population and production long before the world encounters any fundamentally unmanageable or disastrous problems of supply, pollution, or other side effects of the "great transition" he envisages from pre-industrial to post-industrial society. I note his fear that these forces may be emerging too rapidly and prematurely—at least in the Advanced Capitalist nations. On the other hand, I particularly appreciate his imaginative projections of the new and exciting forms of social organization and patterns of life that he foresees as possible over the next century or so.

We were delighted to be able to use the special edition of World Economic Development as the focus of our deliberations at the twenty-sixth Congress of the ICC in Orlando in October 1978. The favorable reception Herman Kahn received at Orlando for his brilliant analysis testifies not only to his eloquence and persuasiveness but to the cogency and significance of his arguments for businessmen, policy makers, the educated public, and the entire international community. We are gratified that a wider audience will benefit from the publication of this edition, and we thank Herman Kahn and the Hudson Institute, for their contributions to the world's knowledge and comprehension of subjects that are as vitally important as they are poorly understood.

> *Ian MacGregor*
> President
> International Chamber of Commerce

Acknowledgments

This book examines the prospects for world economic development. It focuses primarily on the period from 1978 to 2000 and pays particular attention to the earlier part of that interval. Because the world has recently been in a chaotic state, it is especially difficult at present to talk about the next ten or twenty years. Not only do unsettled conditions cloud our vision, but they also generate events that could significantly alter the future. Furthermore, there is great confusion about what is currently happening. If I had spent more time in research and analysis before writing this book, it would have been possible to elaborate and clarify many ideas touched upon cursorily or even superficially, but the study would also probably have lagged behind events. It is precisely during the current period of uncertainty that this work may be of greatest value, although we also hope we say many things in this study of relatively permanent significance.

My willingness to publish the study sooner rather than later was increased by the generous offer of the International Chamber of Commerce to make a special edition of this book a basic document of their 1978 Annual Conference and to help support the necessary research both intellectually and financially. The special edition was prepared and distributed at the ICC convention in Orlando, Florida, in October 1978. Copies of the special ICC edition are available from the Hudson Institute. The present trade edition is a slimmer, less specialized, and hopefully more lucid and direct statement of the main ideas and issues laid out at greater length in the special edition.

Hudson Institute's Business and Society Program provided additional support through grants from the Ford Motor Company and the Olin and Scaife Foundations. Materials were also drawn from

Hudson's Corporate Environment Program, an ongoing effort supported by fifty major corporations.

This book reflects the contributions of many members of the Hudson Institute staff and of others. We are grateful to Paul Bracken, Bill Brown, Jack Cassidy, Thomas Dichter, Marie-Josée Drouin, Irv Leveson, Leon Martel, Thomas Pepper, John Phelps, Garrett Scalera, and Jimmy Wheeler for their contributions, helpful criticism, and useful suggestions; to Andrew Caranfil, Ruth Paul, Carl F. Plossl, Barbara Rovello, Lynne Salop, and Mildred Schneck for documentation and other information; to Marilee Martel, Carol Kahn Mathes, and Ernest Schneider for expert editorial assistance; to Marilee Martel for preparing the index; to Dr. Barnet Groten for a most thorough, perceptive, and useful critique; to Richard A. Lacey for copy editing the final draft; and to Daniel Raymond Stein for editing and serving as editorial consultant for both the special and the trade editions.

I am especially grateful to Paul Bracken for some of the material on Mexico; to Marie-Josée Drouin, who made helpful comments on the entire manuscript and who helped prepare the section on Canadian malaise; to Irv Leveson, who read the entire manuscript, offered many helpful suggestions, and made major contributions to the sections on affluent countries, malaise in the United States, and inflation; to Leon Martel, who contributed much of the section on malaise in the USSR and the Soviet bloc and who supervised and coordinated the production of both editions; to my old friend John Phelps for his dedicated assistance and advice; to Garrett Scalera, who was a major participant in the early phases of this book and who contributed heavily to Chapter 6 on South Korea, Taiwan, and Japan; and to Jimmy Wheeler, who made major contributions to the sections on inflation, malaise, international trade, and Japan. The section on cultural encounters and cultural reactions in Chapter 3 was revised by me and Thomas Dichter from materials first developed by Edmund Stillman and William Pfaff.

I would also like to express my appreciation to the many people who helped with various other parts of the book, especially those who initiated an earlier project from which this book developed. Hideaki Kase was going to be a co-author of this work until time and circumstances interfered. Perhaps most important, special thanks are due to our many friends in South Korea and Taiwan, particularly Kim Mahn-Je, the late Mason Yeh, and their associates and colleagues who first sparked our interest in doing the earlier project and thus the book. They taught us a great deal over the last few years from their first-hand experience with economic development.

Our gratitude goes to Maureen Pritchard, Vivian Hildebrandt, and Dorothy Worfolk for their tireless efforts in supervising the typing of the manuscript, with the able assistance of Kathleen Dymes, Helen Iadanza, Ilse Lehmeier, Anne Marsek, Rose Marie Martin, Betty McRobbie, Mary Mitchell, Jane Petrone, Carolann Roussel, Elaine Shelah, and Annie Small. We are also grateful to Kathryn Finch for her graphic work and to Adam McDonald and John Palka for logistic support.

The staff of Westview Press were both forbearing and helpful as we galloped to meet seemingly impossible deadlines for the special ICC edition. We wish to thank particularly Fred Praeger, publisher; Lynne Rienner, vice-president and executive editor; Rolla Rieder, vice-president, production; Lynn Lloyd, associate editor; and whomever helped them accomplish the miracle. They have continued to encourage and assist us throughout the preparation of this trade edition.

Like any social product, this book has drawn on the learning and labors of many individuals. Nonetheless, as the author, I bear full responsibility for its contents and will accept with pleasure any plaudits for its merits and with equanimity the inevitable slings and arrows for its flaws.

Herman Kahn

Introduction

A special edition of this book was prepared for the twenty-sixth Congress of the International Chamber of Commerce in October 1978 in Orlando, Florida. It is also part of a continuing series of Hudson Institute studies on "The Prospects for Mankind." The first volume of the study, *The Next 200 Years: A Scenario for America and the World*,[1] was sparked by the American Bicentennial, when it was natural to look 200 years ahead as well as 200 years back. That book argued that the 400-year period more or less centered on 1975 would mark a transition to a more or less stable (at least for a time) world society of unprecedented affluence—a period that might well turn out to be the most dramatic and significant in human history. Other studies in "The Prospects for Mankind" series take off from *The Next 200 Years* by examining current and short-term issues within this 400-year context.[2] Paralleling these is a series of studies of the economic, social, and political development of various countries.[3]

The Next 200 Years explored the theoretical feasibility of the proposition that while world population and gross world product cannot grow indefinitely at current rates, population should be able to increase by a factor of ten and gross world product by a factor of as much as one or two hundred without exceeding the intrinsic carrying capacity of the earth. However, we believe that the population and gross world product are likely to stabilize well below these levels— the population at about two or three times that of today and the gross world product at perhaps twenty or thirty times its present size. The book tried to make plausible our conclusion that natural social, political, and cultural forces were likely to slow the growth of both population and production long before the world encountered any fundamentally unmanageable problems of supply, pollution, or other side effects of the great 400-year transition.

The present volume examines the elements of change and

1

continuity in both the advanced and developing economies that are shaping this Great Transition. It examines some of the more immediate problems and issues associated with the process of economic growth. In some ways it is an application, elaboration, and continuation of *The Next 200 Years*. The themes of both books are summarized in the statement that opens the first book:

> . . . Two hundred years ago almost everywhere human beings were comparatively few, poor and at the mercy of the forces of nature, and 200 years from now, we expect, almost everywhere they will be numerous, rich and in control of the forces of nature.[4]

We still believe in that prediction—barring (an essential *caveat*) bad luck or bad management.

World Economic Development concludes that many widely accepted ideas about economic growth are outdated (if they were ever true), and that much of the pessimism that until recently has characterized the discussion of economic growth is unwarranted. Humanity should go ahead and take its chances despite the possibility of bad luck or bad management because the prospects are so exciting, because it is still probably safer to go ahead than to try to stop prematurely the growth process, and because it is impractical to do anything else. The attempt to "stop the world" might slow down the Advanced Capitalist nations for a while, but it would not change the historical trends much unless it created a disaster.[5]

While this prognosis may seem optimistic when contrasted with most current literature, much of it is simply realistic. Our long-range projections may have a helpful impact on morale and commitment, but we are not in the business of trying to create or sell positive attitudes. All our conclusions—optimistic and otherwise—are the results of our studies and considered judgments, and not of wishful thinking, political ideology, or an attempt to provide an inspirational message. We are not against such attempts; it is just not our business. (However, when our studies justify optimism, we are perfectly willing to use them to help raise morale and increase commitment.)

On the other hand, some of the short-run projections in this book may be regarded as pessimistic—and perhaps rightly so. Such projections could also become self-fulfilling prophecies. However, they seem to us much more likely to result in greater realism in evaluating current issues, and thus become self-defeating prophecies. Again, except under extraordinary circumstances, it is not our business to worry excessively about creating self-fulfilling or self-defeating prophecies through our objective studies and observations. Our basic purpose is to devise and exposit policies that create desirable prophecies, but this is unlikely to be feasible if there is too great concern about facing unpleasant possibilities.

The future will not be problem free. We do not even rule out the possibility of an overwhelming catastrophe (the most significant being a large nuclear war). However, the future we envision as most likely will be characterized by gradually diminishing economic growth as a result of what are often called "social limits." This is very different from drastically curbing growth to cope with (wildly exaggerated) supply and pollution crises, a solution often advocated by elites who are misinformed or misled by ideology and self-interest. The key long-term problems are more likely to be associated with personal affluence and affluent societies than with poor people and poor societies.

This book argues for rapid worldwide economic growth, for Third World industrialization, and for the use of advanced (or at least appropriate) technology. It suggests tactics and strategies to facilitate all of these objectives. We make no apologies for these positions. However, the desirability of increasing economic affluence and technological advancement is under such broad and intense attack today that some defense seems necessary. Indeed, so much smoke has been generated that many observers incorrectly believe there must be a raging fire.

This book is divided into two parts. Part I sets forth some general historical theories, concepts, and contexts that we feel provide useful background for understanding the current and future situations. Much of this material is controversial; about half of it is original; about half is borrowed. Even when we are skeptical about the material, we and many others have found that these theories, concepts, and contexts are extraordinarily useful to generate language, metaphors, analogies, and scenarios, as well as to explain and "predict" what is happening.

Part II focuses on many of the same ideas but in the current context and from a relatively narrow and concrete perspective. In Part II we are much more detailed, empirical, *ad hoc,* and contemporary. The bridge between the two parts occurs at the end of Chapter 4 of Part I in the section entitled "What Do We Really Believe? Summary and Recapitulation of Part I."

The appendix contains some detailed material on constructing quantitative scenario contexts too digressive to include in the text.

Notes

1. Herman Kahn, William Brown, and Leon Martel (New York: William Morrow, 1976).

2. *World Food Prospects and Agricultural Potential,* by Marylin Chou, David Harmon, Jr., Herman Kahn, and Sylvan Wittwer (New York: Praeger, 1977); *Long-Term Prospects for Developments in Space (A Scenario Approach),* by William M. Brown and Herman Kahn, HI-2638-RR, October 30, 1977; *Let There Be Energy: A Balanced Program for Today and Tomorrow,* by William M. Brown and Herman Kahn; *Trends in Nuclear Proliferation, 1975-1995: Projections, Problems, and Policy Options,* by Lewis A. Dunn and Herman Kahn, HI-2336/3-RR, May 15, 1976; and *Changing Dimensions of Proliferation Policy, 1975-1995,* by Lewis A. Dunn, HI-2497/2-RR.

3. *The Japanese Challenge,* by Herman Kahn and Thomas Pepper (New York: Thomas Y. Crowell, forthcoming, 1979); *The Future of the U.S. and Its Regions,* by Irving Leveson and Jane Newitt, HI-2816-RR, May 1978; *The Future of Brazil,* edited by William H. Overholt (Boulder, Colorado: Westview Press, 1978); and *The Future of Canada,* by Marie-Josee Drouin and B. Bruce-Briggs (Toronto: McLelland and Stewart, 1978). In progress are studies of Argentina, Australia, Brazil, Quebec, and Thailand. Paul Bracken's *The Future of Arizona* is in press (Boulder, Colorado: Westview Press, 1979).

4. *The Next 200 Years: A Scenario for America and the World* by Herman Kahn, William Brown, and Leon Martel (New York: William Morrow and Company, 1976), p. 1.

5. As noted earlier, the special ICC edition of *World Economic Development* was prepared for the Twenty-sixth Annual meeting of the International Chamber of Commerce in Orlando, Florida, in October 1978. As part of the proceedings of that meeting Prime Minister Lee Kuan Yew gave an excellent speech on "Extrapolating From the Singapore Experience." He discusses such significant issues as the comparative advantages and disadvantages of the developing and developed nations and the merits and demerits of market orientation versus government planning and intervention, with specific references to the experiences of the countries of Southeast Asia. His speech is part of the record of the ICC meeting, and we urge interested readers to obtain a copy. We quote the speech at several places in the present volume because of its great pertinence and interest.

Part I

Framework, Concepts, Perspectives

1

The Big Picture—
And Some Details

Watersheds of History

Excluding great religious events, there are two great watersheds of civilized history. The first was the agricultural revolution that started in the fertile crescent of the Middle East some ten thousand years ago and took about eight thousand years to spread around the world. The second was the Industrial Revolution. It can be argued that the first watershed, the agricultural revolution, created civilization—civic culture. It created a relatively high standard of living for elites and made possible the survival of many more people. However, it did not greatly change the standard of living of the world's masses. No agriculturally-based society ever dropped much below the equivalent of $100 GNP per capita or exceeded the equivalent of $500 per capita for any lengthy period.*

It was not until the Industrial Revolution began in Holland and England about two hundred years ago that a sustained growth occurred in the average level of income. Since then, the average income of about two-thirds of the population of the earth has increased by factors of from five to twenty. We suggest below that by the end of what we call the Great Transition, average world per capita income will increase from current levels by a factor of about ten. This

---

*All dollar figures in this book are quoted in the equivalent of fixed 1978 U.S. dollars. (We assumed a 7 percent inflation over 1977 dollars, which was the official estimate but may turn out to be low.) While this concept of a fixed United States dollar immutable over time and space stretches both imagination and theory to the limit, we judge it to have enough meaning and relevance to be useful. A 1978 dollar is 2/3 as valuable as a 1972 dollar and 4/9 as valuable as a 1958 dollar. We note this since so much data appear in fixed 1972 or 1958 dollars.

change and all that is associated with it will alter the basic character of world civilization.*

The Great Transition, which includes the Industrial Revolution, encompasses roughly the last two hundred years and the next two hundred years. Many of its aspects are not spread evenly over the entire four-hundred-year period; rather, they are mostly contained within the second half of the twentieth century—"the half century of rapid and worldwide transition." This period is so dramatic and so startling that we may usefully think of it as almost by itself encompassing the historical watershed we have called the Great Transition. Earlier and later periods of the Great Transition can be seen respectively as a sort of takeoff or preparatory period and an aftermath or consolidation period.

Figure 1.1 shows how dramatic one important aspect of this half century is. Many demographers feel that the curve reasonably describes the past, present, and future history of population growth. About 90 percent of the area below the curve and above 1 percent growth lies in the period from 1950 to 2000. We therefore argue that a world demographic transition is taking place, with population going from about 2.5 billion in 1950 to about 6 billion in 2000. While there may be another increase of a factor of two or three before population stabilizes (assuming current trends continue), the explosive so-called exponential growth will be over by the end of the twentieth century.

For almost ten millennia the total number of people in the world oscillated between 10 and 500 million, with a very slowly increasing long-term trend (less than 0.1 percent per year). Around the seventeenth century A.D. there was a dramatic increase in the rate of population growth, which became almost explosively rapid (about 1 percent) in the middle of the second half of the twentieth century. The rate probably peaked in the early 1970s at below 2 percent. It will almost certainly stay over 1 percent for the rest of the century. Most demographers believe that the rate will decline quite rapidly, dropping even faster than it rose until it reaches a fairly slow pace (a fraction of a percent) in another century or so. Barring some great change, world population eventually will again become relatively static.

One of the other dramatic events in the half century of rapid

---

*We often refer to the very long-term future, the centuries or millennia ahead. We do not pretend to predict these. Usually, these statements about the very long-term future simply show, looking at all current trends as well as we can, what we conclude will happen if these trends continue indefinitely.

9

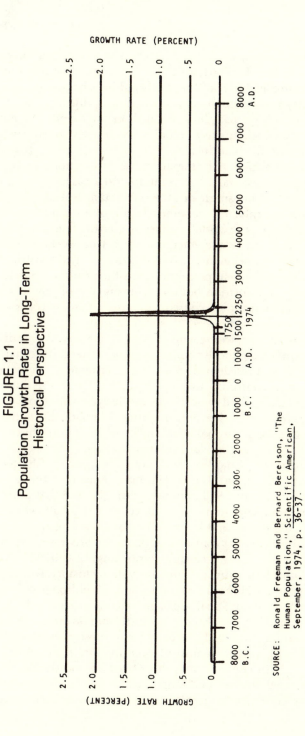

FIGURE 1.1
Population Growth Rate in Long-Term
Historical Perspective

GROWTH RATE (PERCENT)

SOURCE: Ronald Freeman and Bernard Berelson, "The
Human Population," Scientific American,
September, 1974, p. 36-37.

worldwide transition was the introduction of nuclear armaments and other weapons of mass destruction. While it is probably not yet true that all human life could be destroyed by a large nuclear war, this capability may be approaching and clearly illustrates the potential consequences of bad luck or bad management. As additional inherently dangerous technologies become developed, such potentialities seem likely to increase.

On the positive side, the scientific innovations in computers, communications, and other technological areas are equally or more significant.[1] Some single out the spectacular feat of space satellites and vehicles exploring the solar system—of human beings and their artifacts leaving the world's surface—as a truly dramatic new kind of event. Others stress the emergence of a true world economic and intellectual ecumene and universalization of the Industrial Revolution. A quite different perception puts the primary emphasis not so much on the transition but on the emergence of physical or social limits to growth and the consequent transformation to a "sustainable world economy"—however this may be defined.

To some degree, we are entering virgin territory. We are discussing a process affecting the dynamics of an industrial culture that in many respects is unprecedented in history. Fortunately, we believe that there is more continuity than discontinuity. If true, this improves our ability to understand these trends. We disagree with those who argue that useful comprehension requires a major breakthrough in sociological or anthropological theory or in philosophy or religion. We are not attempting such a breakthrough.

Teilhard de Chardin, William Thompson, Charles Reich, Marshall McLuhan, Willis Harmon, François Revel, Abraham Maslow, and Jonas Salk, among others, believe that a mystical or spiritual transformation is associated with this half century, and is driving the trends and forces.[2] We do not accept the concept of a mystical or spiritual transformation as the driving force, but we do agree that something exciting is happening. 1950 to 2000 is surely not just another half century in humanity's long history. During this half century the world should go from almost 2.5 billion people to about 6 billion; from about $2 trillion of gross world product to $15 trillion to $20 trillion; from mostly poor to mostly middle income or rich; from mostly rural to mostly urban; from mostly pre-industrial and illiterate to mostly industrial and literate; from mostly ill-fed, ill-housed, ill-clothed, and short-lived to mostly well-fed, well-housed, well-clothed, and long-lived.

The picture that has just been presented is one of relatively smooth development, the reaching of a goal, and roughly speaking, staying with that goal for the rest of history. This is most implausible because history is not likely to be like that for one, much less for many, millennia. History always shows change: rise and fall; reformation and counter-reformation; disruption and reconstitution; decline and renaissance; extension and diminution; other internal or external contradictions; or mutations causing conflict and change, defeat or victory. We do not dwell on such possibilities, though, for they are not relevant to our three immediate concerns: to present images of the next few centuries that reflect current and emerging trends, to analyze the present and the next decade or two, and to proffer some prescriptions for today.

One of our most important aims is to study some of the discontinuities within the continuities, and *vice versa*. We tend to emphasize continuities more than discontinuities because we believe that history is relatively continuous, that institutions and other social constructs are grown rather than created overnight, and that almost every aspect of tomorrow's society will have historical roots. If we slightly overemphasize the continuities, we offer a useful balance to the prolific literature that rejects and ignores the historical past to argue for a pervasive and sharp break—a viewpoint we consider almost totally unjustified.

In much the same way that the agricultural revolution spread around the world, the Industrial Revolution is also spreading and causing permanent changes in the quality and characteristics of human life. Instead of taking eight thousand years, however, this second diffusion is progressing with incredible speed and will probably be largely completed by the end of this century. Two more centuries should see almost all countries become post-industrial—or at least attain or pass the level of the current Advanced Capitalist nations.

The Great Transition

Images of the long-run future will hold true only if other things are more or less equal. If basic assumptions change, projects may have to change accordingly. But even if the images do not turn out to be valid, they can still be realistic—that is, providing a reasonable picture of the basic trends of our time. Thus, such images may still be useful as a context for short-range planning.[3]

The age-old question: "When will this accelerated economic and population growth end, and how?" often dominates discussion of longer-range planning. People have asked this since the beginning of the Industrial Revolution, with virtually all observers agreeing that such rapid expansion could not continue indefinitely; the high growth rates of the Industrial Revolution must represent a transitional period in history. However, there has been no agreement about when or how the transition will end, or where it will lead.

There have always been some people who expected the end would be disastrous. Until recent years this was a distinctly minority opinion, only occasionally in vogue. An increasing number of people—especially among literate and academic elites—has come to believe that rapid exponential growth may be humanity's greatest tragedy rather than its greatest triumph; that human beings are on the verge of a catastrophic collision with reality. Our view of the likely future is very different.

To characterize the economic changes that seem likely, we distinguish among primary, secondary, tertiary, and quaternary kinds of economic and quasi-economic activities.[4]

Primary activities are extractive—principally agriculture, mining, forestry, and fishing. A pre-industrial society focuses on these activities. Basically, the society is organized to "play games with and against nature."* Before the Industrial Revolution, for every person who lived in a city, perhaps twenty people labored elsewhere, supporting the city dwellers by pursuing primary activities.

The principal secondary activities are construction and manufacturing. The corresponding society is organized mostly to "play games with and against materials." The culture is primarily urban, characterized in our time by the nation-state and by a relatively sharp distinction between the city and the countryside.

---

*The term *playing games with or against nature* and other uses of game metaphors emerge from the extensive literature of gaming, simulation, and role playing. They should be thought of partly literally and partly metaphorically. The idea is that the major roles of the individual in a primary society involve activities that can be characterized as "interacting with and against nature" rather than, as in the other cases, "with and against materials," "with and against organizations," or "with and against communities." The word *game* introduces the concept that much as in a game, human economic activities are governed by many formal and informal rules and customs, and that rational tactics and strategies can be important in making more probable the achievement of desired goals. The inspiration for this terminology (and of the term *post-industrial*) comes from the American sociologist, Daniel Bell. See Daniel Bell, *The Coming of the Post-Industrial Society*, (New York: Basic Books, 1973).

Tertiary activities are services to primary, secondary, or other tertiary activities emphasized in an emerging post-industrial economy. These are services to society; hence the term *service economy*. Such services include transportation, communications, insurance, finance, management, engineering, merchandising, aesthetic design, advertising, many governmental activities, and much education and training. In emerging post-industrial societies, even those engaged in primary and secondary activities find themselves closer to white collar tertiary activities than to the traditional primary and secondary blue collar interactions with and against nature or materials. The society is organized to "play games with and against organizations." It is characterized by organizational and professional pluralism, particularly in the distribution of power and prestige and is probably more suburban than urban. Its business activities may be dominated more by transnational corporations than by purely national corporations or indigenous individual proprietorships. The emphasis is on the "knowledge" industries and the growth of bureaucratic and intellectual elites.

Early in the twenty-first century, a partial transition to a different kind of service economy should occur, at least in what we call the Advanced Capitalist countries.[5] This is what we call a quaternary or true post-industrial economy—a tentative concept subject to many *caveats*. Basically, it holds that primary, secondary, and tertiary activities will eventually constitute only a small part of human endeavors. The strictly economic tasks of furnishing the material and commercial needs and mechanical services of a society will require fewer and fewer people.

At the limit, these tasks will be carried out largely by highly automated equipment and complex computers. The small professional group needed to operate the equipment may not, despite its seeming critical importance, be the elite of their society just as

---

Some readers may be offended at our applying such a seemingly trivial word as *game* to the long record of human heroism and disaster. As noted above, the word *game* is not intended to detract from the seriousness or significance of the activities, but rather to relate them to the large and complex body of formalistic rules that govern human behavior and to the complex interplay of means and ends in purposive human actions. For a classic discussion of the role of play and games in human societies, see *Homo Ludens: A Study of the Play Element in Culture* by Johan Huizinga (London: Routledge, Kegan Paul, 1949). As we mention later, it is only in the quaternary society that the word *game* is likely to apply literally.

farmers, even big landholders, are not a very special elite in today's society. As the average income and welfare benefits increase, low-level service jobs will disappear, become high-level jobs, or become completely or partially voluntary. For example, full-time maids have already almost disappeared in the Advanced Capitalist countries.

Such high-level personal service roles as teacher, psychiatrist, doctor, author, priest, and public entertainer will increase. Both consumers and producers will pursue these activities for their own sakes—that is, for relatively non-economic or personal reasons and not because they contribute to the performance of primary or secondary activities. Much basic research would be included in this category. Means as well as ends will be evaluated in terms of their wider social, personal, and cultural implications, rather than by narrow cost-benefit calculations. An activity will be judged as much by what kind of people it produces and how it affects the individual and the community as by narrow profit and loss calculations. Economic and technical efficiency will be de-emphasized in favor of concepts of the good and the beautiful according to cultural and personal criteria.

Such a society can be characterized as playing games "with and against people, with and against communities, and perhaps with and against oneself." Indeed, the use of the word *game* will probably become less metaphoric and more literal.

This image of post-industrial society is not idiosyncratic. Many great thinkers speculating on what the Great Transition of the Industrial Revolution would bring have envisioned similar outcomes. Karl Marx's vision is probably the most renowned of these scenarios. Marx believed, as we do, that the Industrial Revolution would usher humanity into a new era. Although Marx first thought that only a violent revolution would remove the capitalists, he believed that the era after their demise would be far better than the past and that the ordinary human being would reach new heights surpassing those achieved by the elites in fifth century B.C. Athens or during the Italian Renaissance. Marx foresaw a society in the distant future where "nobody has one exclusive sphere of activity but each can become accomplished in any branch he wishes, (where) society regulates the general production and thus makes it possible for me to do one thing today and another tomorrow, to hunt in the morning, fish in the afternoon, rear cattle in the evening, criticize after dinner, just as I have a mind, without ever becoming hunter, fisherman, shepherd, or critic."[6]

J. M. Keynes put forth remarkably similar images of a rapid Great

Transition to a quaternary society in an essay published in 1930. Keynes clearly foresaw a better world where the values and priorities of the capitalist system would ultimately be rejected, and where humanity would be free to pursue nobler goals:

> I draw the conclusion that, assuming no important wars and no important increase in population, the economic problem may be solved, or be at least within sight of solution, within a hundred years. This means that the economic problem is not—if we look into the future—the permanent problem of the human race.
>
> I see us free, therefore, to return to some of the most sure and certain principles of religion and traditional virtue—that avarice is a vice, that the exaction of usury is a misdemeanour, and the love of money is detestable, that those who walk most truly in the paths of virtue and sane wisdom take least thought for the morrow. We shall once more value ends above means and prefer the good to the useful. We shall honour those who can teach us how to pluck the hour and the day virtuously and well, the delightful people who are capable of taking direct enjoyment in things, the lilies of the field who toil not, neither do they spin.
>
> But beware: The time for all this is not yet. For at least another hundred years we must pretend to ourselves and to everyone that fair is foul and foul is fair; for foul is useful and fair is not. Avarice and usury and precaution must be our Gods for a little longer still.[7]

In contrast with Marx and Keynes, our scenario does not anticipate a future utopia. We are skeptical or agnostic about this. Indeed, the world of one or two hundred years from now may not be a very happy place—at least by present standards. Instead of harmony, the future might be plagued by disorder and unrest or subjected to regimentation. The visions of both *1984* and *Brave New World* seem genuine possibilities, even if not inevitable or even likely.

A century from now, much relative poverty and perhaps even major pockets of absolute poverty will probably still persist. The arithmetic (but probably not geometric) gap between the richest 10 percent and the poorest 10 percent of the world's people will almost certainly be greater than today. But unless the future is marred by a major nuclear war or other disaster, almost all of humanity will be materially better off. The traditional grinding absolute poverty, famine, pestilence, disease and incapacity, illiteracy, and backbreaking toil, all of which have been humanity's lot throughout history, should be almost gone, and with luck for once and for all. What the majority of people will do in such a world is an open question and may be a serious problem.

The opportunities for both good and evil will be enormous. If all goes well, the centuries to come could well be when humanity's true history begins.

If, as seems reasonable, technology continues to advance and wealth accumulates and spreads throughout the world, the global society might eventually become largely post-economic as well as post-industrial. There is no intrinsic reason why consumer goods, such as the twenty-second century equivalents of houses, automobiles, and television sets, should not become almost infinitely durable. Very likely, rapid obsolescence or deterioration of many products would no longer occur. Industry's tasks would be limited to gradual replacement. Overall production might substantially decline as the world's people became satisfied with the existing stock of physical goods. And given the probable high level of automation, the workers required to maintain the stock might be only a small percentage of the world's population. Business, as we know it, might even disappear. (In a way this is exactly the social system or society which many in the New Class believe is coming, but at a much higher level of affluence and technology than they envisage. As we discuss in Chapter 3, our major quarrel with their vision is with its premature quality rather than with its contents.)

If these visions materialize, the quaternary culture would be strongly reminiscent of many aspects of the richer and more stable pre-industrial cultures that included many of these "mundane" activities:

- Reading, writing, painting, acting, composing, musicianship, arts and crafts—done for their own sake or as a part of a larger context.
- Tourism, games, contests, rituals, exhibitions, and performances.
- Gourmet cooking and eating, an aristocratic and formal style of life, Epicurean and family values (including visiting, entertaining, and "togetherness").
- Hunting, fishing, hiking, camping, jogging, boating, skiing, mountain climbing, scuba diving, gliding, and many new activities associated with advanced technology.
- Acquisition and mastery of many other non-vocational skills and hobbies.
- Improving property (motivated mainly by non-economic considerations) through gardening, upkeep, interior decorating, and the use of home-made artifacts and art.

- Conversation, discussion, debating, and politicking.
- Many other cultural and social activities.
- Elaborate multi-person "games" played for days, weeks, or months with the aid of computers and advanced communication systems—e.g., future versions of Diplomacy, Dungeons, and Dragons, etc. These could have both ceremonial and competitive aspects—be public spectacles or private entertainment.

There could also be activities of a sort usually judged as more significant, or at least less private, than those listed above:

- Public works and public projects—some done more for propaganda, morale, interest, amusement, ceremonial, or ritualistic reasons than for "cost-effective" economic or research objectives (e.g., the equivalent, in today's terms, of some space activities, some undersea exploration, much protection of the environment, and monumental architecture).
- Openly ceremonial, ritualistic, and aesthetic activities (often in specially created and elaborate structures and environments). Their purpose could include the evoking of images or feelings of splendor, pride, pomp, awe, and communal, ethnic, religious, or national unity or identity; oneness with nature and the universe, and various "explorations in inner space" or other forms of emotional or spiritual self-fulfillment.
- The creation of taboos, totems, demanding religions, traditions, and customs; arbitrary pressures, constraints, and demands; moral and social equivalents of war; some other pressures and risks, including those involved with some of the more bizarre forms of "discretionary behavior" and the "testing" of one's abilities and limitations.

Finally, the concept of quaternary culture includes mystical and "inner space" activities. Many writers on this subject assign a much higher role to these activities than we do, although we concede that they may be significant and perhaps even dominating.

This quaternary culture is already emerging in many Advanced Capitalist nations, largely among what we will call the New Class. In fact, one way of defining the New Class is as people who have mostly upper-middle class backgrounds and who have been raised in or live in a more or less quaternary culture or in the more analytical, aesthetic, symbolic, or intellectual parts of the tertiary sector. One of our major themes will be the social, intellectual, and cultural difficulties that the largely New Class quaternary culture will have in dealing with the more mundane and practical aspects of the world.

Some people may feel that this future quaternary economy is in some sense unreal—a bit like a play-world or a play-acting world. We do not deny this observation and emphasize that it may be very difficult to think of certain traditional issues seriously in this kind of quaternary economy. There may indeed be a lack of contact with traditional reality, which nonetheless may remain important, if only latently.

This transition would mark the completion of the Industrial Revolution, the second great watershed of human history. Still more distant societies will probably consider these centuries of industrialization to have marked humanity's journey from a world that was basically inhospitable to its few dwellers to one that was fully commanded and presumably enjoyed by its multitudes. Table 1.1, which divides man's economic history into five stages, summarizes this picture.

If we place ourselves in the year 5000 or so and look backward, we might recognize three stages separated by two narrow, almost instantaneous, periods of transition. The first stage is the period before 8000 B.C. of hunting bands and tribes. We might shorten the process we call *modernization* or the Great Transition—that is, from 1800 to 2200—into a single line at about the year 2000. From this perspective, that 400-year period might be seen as almost instantaneous termination of the so-called civilized era and the creation of something new. After all, the agricultural revolution is usually seen in a similar way, even though in fact it took thousands of years to spread around the world. Thus, from the perspective of the year 5000, our economic history might appear as shown in Table 1.2.

We do not have a good idea of what we mean by *post-industrial*. The term itself is negative, describing what will not be rather than what will be. There are, as Table 1.2 shows, many other possible terms. *Post-civilized* implies that our ideas of civilization have thus far been largely determined by traditional society, but they will no longer hold. *Post-economic* implies that the behavior of most human beings most of the time will not be simply determined by cost-effectiveness. For example, even today, whether an affluent American travels three hundred miles or three thousand miles to a vacation spot may not be much affected, much less determined by the distance or air

TABLE 1.1
Stages of Economic History

Date	Stage
	Hunting and Food Gathering (Pre-agricultural and usually primitive)
8000 B.C.	
	Basically Agricultural (Pre-industrial and usually civilized)
A.D. 1800	
	Various Stages of Industrialization (Or Modern and/or Technological)
A.D. 2000	
	Various Stages of Post-Industrial Emerge (But initially 3/4 of world still lives in poor, transitional, or industrial economies)
A.D. 2200	
	Transition Largely Completed to a Worldwide High Level Affluent Post-Industrial Economy

"Modernization" or The Great Transition

TABLE 1.2
Social Evolution

Emergence of First Humans			
2,000,000 Years of Hunting Bands, Food Gatherers, and Tribal Societies			
8000 B.C.			Transition due to Agricultural Revolution
10,000 Years of Traditional and Civilized Societies			
A.D. 2000			The Great Transition (What we call "modernization")
Post-Industrial	Post-Human	Post-Promethean	
Post-Civilized	Faustian	Godlike	
Post-Economic	Post-Faustian	Truly Religious (e.g. Neo-Deist)	
Truly Human	Promethean	Neo-Mystic	

fare. For all practical purposes, the person thinks of the two distances as about the same. Similarly, future income will be so high and costs so low that most individuals will be indifferent to the prices of their various options.

We do not know exactly what we mean by *truly human* and *post-human*, but they seem like usefully provocative phrases. *Faustian* connotes making a pact with the devil to gain power, wealth, and secular knowledge. (In the legend the devil eventually claims Faust's soul, but this need not happen; in fact it does not happen in Goethe's version.) *Promethean* is intended to emphasize knowledge and progress; no pact with the devil is involved, though of course Prometheus was grossly punished for his temerity in giving fire to humans by being bound to a rock and having his liver eternally gnawed by a vulture.

We do not claim to know much about the long-term outlook for humanity, except that we believe it will probably be incredibly affluent by current standards and that the accompanying technology can give the average individual capabilities that have previously been reserved for gods or magicians.

Why More Economic Growth?

Almost everybody agrees with Sophie Tucker, that "it is better to be rich than poor."* In discussing the possibilities of how affluence and technology can be used to improve human life we have increasingly been drawn to the concept, used in various current Hudson Institute studies, of what we call the Marriage of Machine and Garden.[8] The concept of the Garden comes out of some well-known American and European literature that extols the virgin forest and the rural, agrarian, or wilderness areas of North America that were formerly untouched and were often regarded as a refuge or earthly Garden of Eden for Europeans. At the same time, however, the United States is also the most technologically advanced nation in the world; hence the Machine.

Some historians suggest that it is useful to view American history as

---

*She actually said something like the following: "I've been rich and I've been poor and it is no great shakes to be rich, but, other things equal, I much prefer being rich." This goes along with the very general position that the rich are often miserable but they often have a great deal of freedom in choosing their misery. Perhaps more important, being rich often protects one from disasters or allows one to alleviate the effects.

a continual struggle between the pastoral, rural, or wilderness ideal and the rapid, almost ruthless, industrialization and urbanization of the continent. Sometimes the two themes fought; sometimes they merged into a single whole; sometimes they settled for an uneasy truce. We visualize the Garden society as a modernization of the rural, pastoral ideal, a possible future society whose ideology is directed toward maintaining a high quality of life but that shows little change and technological dynamism.[9] The Hudson Institute studies noted that a very attractive life style that might characterize almost any of the eventual possibilities of modernization would be such a marriage. It may also be a part of the transitional society that is still far from achieving the ultimate goals of modernization.

This is just one of a number of potentially attractive scenarios for the use of affluence and technology. Yet, incredibly, such scenarios or images of the future are increasingly rejected as unfeasible or even undesirable. The economic growth scenario, for example, seems to us attractive. Yet instead of enthusiasm for more economic growth, opposition to growth is mounting. Neo-Malthusians argue that the world's resources are insufficient to support continued expansion of gross world product and population. They contend that even if resources were available, pollution, ecological imbalance, or management problems would lead to disastrous consequences. We believe that we and others have answered this thesis effectively. Therefore, we do not deal with it further except to identify specific serious problems that could result from the limits-to-growth movement rather than from the finite size of the earth.*

Others argue that humanity's output is already adequate. These numerous opponents of growth believe that the transition to "the good and the beautiful" can be accomplished now. Actually, gross

---

*It should be noted, for example, that even the Club of Rome has changed (backed down?) from its original thesis. Thus, the Club of Rome no longer argues for any specific resource constraints or overwhelming pollution problems. Rather, it argues that the system as a whole is too complex or otherwise unmanageable, even if the various parts of it function acceptably. This may be correct, but supporting evidence has yet to be adduced. The Club of Rome often criticizes Hudson Institute studies for assuming that the system works overall and then demonstrating that this is not contradicted by any issue. This criticism may also be correct. We simply do not know if the system as a whole works, and as yet we have no valid models for testing to see if this is so. The Club of Rome maintains that it can make such tests by using its big computer models, but we deny their relevance to this order of question and believe we can demonstrate that in fact they are inapplicable.

world product will expand enormously as developing countries accumulate capital and technical expertise and become mass consumption countries. The world economy will first become super-industrial rather than post-industrial.* In 1978, for example, there were almost 300 million cars in a world of about 4.25 billion people. If current trends continue, there will be about a billion cars in the year 2000, but the number of people on earth should increase by less than 50 percent. A similar doubling or tripling (or more) can be expected for other consumer durables, as well as for the output of energy and other resources.†

It is this super-industrial aspect of our long-range scenario that is being most questioned today on grounds of both desirability and feasibility. We do not maintain that great tragedies cannot happen, including the collapse of civilization. We do argue that no basic technological and economic barriers preclude our scenario. Such barriers may exist, but they have not as yet been demonstrated. (Bad luck or bad management, of course, can always cause trouble.)

We firmly believe that despite the arguments put forward by people who would like to "stop the earth and get off," it is simply impractical to do so. Propensity to change may not be inherent in human nature, but it is firmly embedded in most contemporary cultures. People have almost everywhere become curious, future oriented, and dissatisfied with their conditions. They want more material goods and covet higher status and greater control of nature. Despite much propaganda to the contrary, they believe, almost

---

*This prospect of what we later call a super-industrial economy is discussed in detail in Chapter 5.

†We selected the example of the expansion in the number of cars deliberately. Many in the upper-middle class in affluent countries display today an almost manic animosity toward the car. Nevertheless, the car is likely, and correctly, to continue to be the preferred means for mass transportation in most of the world. See *The War Against the Automobile* (B. Bruce-Briggs, New York: Dutton, 1977). Perhaps even more threatening—or desirable, depending on one's perspective—is the prospect that the number of "tourist days" (days per year spent by tourists away from home) will go up by a factor of ten or more by the year 2000. The income and time available for tourism may go up by factors of five or more while the costs of travel drop and its convenience improves. Tourism will become available to the majority of humanity—not just to an affluent minority. The average quality of the experience may go down, but many more will enjoy it. And enough new and esoteric possibilities will still exist to permit the affluent minority to continue to have many exclusive pleasures. Chapter 5 elaborates on this.

certainly correctly, that it is technologically and economically possible for them to achieve these goals.

We are not arguing that humanity's desires are open-ended. But the rewards of economic growth and advanced technology—however flawed and problem-ridden—are not illusory. The social limits to growth are simply not, for the time being, likely to be as restrictive as much current discussion suggests. At least 90 percent of the world's population reject such arguments. As these people become more affluent and as their children adopt new values, their opposition to growth may increase—why not? As the world gets richer, the marginal utility of increased wealth will probably diminish. But we feel that we have taken account of this as well as we can by limiting in the Hudson standard scenarios (Chapter 2) gross world product to about $200 trillion, a factor of only twenty-five or so over today.

Even if much better arguments were advanced in favor of social limits to growth, most people are willing to take chances. It is probably a waste of time to think ideologically about stopping progress (much less social change) and foolish to regret that much of the physical environment and many established institutions must change. Much may be protected or preserved, and many aesthetic, environmental, and conservationist values may be furthered and enhanced. Nonetheless, some basic and irrevocable changes will occur. There will probably be many gradual changes in the direction of less "creative destruction" and slower growth.[10]

Serious discussion should start with some common-sense, widely-accepted assumptions about growth and change in order to waste less energy and time on utopian, ideological, or impractical issues. Eight of these sensible assumptions are:

1. Modernization in one form or another is now both natural and inevitable—though the rate may vary enormously and there may be hard core pockets of resistance. There is also much argument over what modernization means. (Many do not accept our definition that it is equivalent to participating in the Great Transition.)
2. Change always involves risk, pain, dislocation, and doubt. The objective should be to alleviate these symptoms rather than to eliminate them. It is especially wrong to increase the amount of pain by counterproductive digressions.
3. How change occurs is subject to some degree of intervention. Intervention may not always be knowledgeable and may not always achieve what it sets out to do, but it can be useful. It can also be counterproductive.

4. Nothing can prevent further change—for good or evil. Therefore, it is probably best to try to direct change towards the good or at least the less evil. This assumes that even if we cannot always agree on a long list of things we would like to have, we can usually agree on a long list of things we would like to avoid.

5. Modernization no longer means Americanization—or even Westernization—though much can still be learned from the West. Japan, South Korea, Taiwan, Singapore, Mexico, and Brazil may be more useful examples than some currently affluent countries. Each country will have to find its own way and will have to decide which mountain it will choose to climb, by what road, and with how much of the "old baggage and possessions" it wants to retain for sentimental or other reasons.

6. The trip will be much easier and safer if there is a relatively unified commitment to the trip and its objective and if skilled guidance and direction are available to help the travelers avoid becoming lost or trapped.

7. While not all the experience, pathbreaking, and equipment of those who have gone first is useful, much is and should be exploited.

8. It is simply untrue that there is no possibility of having an attractive, human, high quality, affluent technological society. In particular, there are likely to be many possible Marriages between Machine and Garden. There are also possibilities for other more urban-oriented ways in which humanity might use wealth and technology to design highly desirable life styles.

The Difference Space May Make

We suspect that some of our readers, even those who do not accept the usual limits to growth position, may be uncomfortable with our scenario and its fairy tale ending of the Marriage of Machine and Garden. To them, it probably does not seem reasonable that the long record of human history as a tale of tragedy, foolishness, and greatness will somehow change so drastically, even if the change might be for the better. Even those who accept the quaternary society or the Keynesian or Marxian images as technologically, politically, and culturally possible are likely to be dissatisfied. For them, history simply ends too soon. Does humanity really wish to "stagnate?" Will people really want to give up their games with and against nature, materials, and organizations?

Our guess is that not everybody will enjoy this future society. Some persons may want more economic progress or technological advancement (or other dynamism) than is likely to be attained by an early transformation to a largely quaternary culture. Many others, of course, will enjoy this post-industrial society most of the time, and some may enjoy it all of the time. We believe that most people could be reasonably happy living in and supporting an advanced and affluent (but neo-traditional) quaternary culture—or perhaps the mystics will be right and we will all regard our own or others' navels—or some other deeper and more significant form of spirituality or life of the mind will emerge.

Nevertheless, such a post-industrial society lacks the excitement, challenge, and opportunity that some of us have learned to value. A life of tradition, mysticism, spirituality, or of the intellect in this sense could seem inadequate. The excitement and dynamism of the Great Transition might then be remembered as part of a lost heroic age. Many ambitious people will undoubtedly want to contribute to goals that are larger than establishing and reinforcing the tenor of a rich and comfortable but ritualized and slowly changing life, however intrinsically interesting and absorbing this life might be. Unless all this potential energy and dynamism is strongly repressed or channeled into constructive activities and endeavors, it could create horrendous problems.

We suspect that outer space or other frontiers such as the ocean bed could become a major focus for restless people. The existence of a frontier would serve as a challenge to their dynamism, initiative, and entrepreneurship. It could also accommodate those individuals, families or groups who wish to progress faster or to achieve more— who like competition and growth.

The future role of outer space can be seen from three different perspectives: it will not have any crucial or dramatic effect within the next century or two; it will have an absolutely essential role in changing the world's prospects from basically neo-Malthusian to basically post-industrial; or it will complement and enlarge the possibilities for post-industrial society but will not be essential for such development.

We believe that the third perspective is by far the most reasonable and likely. In our view, early in the twenty-first century, space activities will play important and perhaps central psychological, material, and cultural roles in making earth a better and more interesting place. Initially, people in space are going to be preoccupied with the space equivalents of primary, secondary, and tertiary activities and will likely leave most quaternary activities to those who remain on earth. People in space habitats may be ingeniously creative, but relatively few of them will spend much time on artistic and cultural, mystical, spiritual, or purely intellectual pursuits.

In our view, the emergence of a largely post-industrial society need not end humanity's future economic and technological challenges. Rather, it could provide a base from which human beings might move outward into the solar system and possibly eventually into interstellar space. In any case, the openness, opportunities, and challenges of outer space may exert a profound and sustained influence on an otherwise excessively static or introspective society on earth. Even after the Great Transition has occurred, there may still be plenty of room for economic growth, technological dynamism, exploration, and innovation—either as ends in themselves or, more likely, as means to a greater end.[11]

The Multifold Trend and Macro-History

The Great Transition can be set into a larger context of the Basic Long-Term Multifold Trend of Western Culture (see Table 1.3). This trend goes back about a thousand years and is one of the most basic and enduring tendencies of Western culture. The Great Transition can be viewed as the culmination of the Multifold Trend. The Transition both changes the Trend in some fundamental ways and makes it more or less universal—in part through a semi-Europeanization or Westernization of the rest of the world and in part through external impact on the Multifold Trend itself.

The relatively desirable aspects of this Trend are embodied in the concept of progress that has dominated the last two or three hundred years. On the whole, and certainly before the Enlightenment in the seventeenth century, Western elites did not like the Multifold Trend. Even today, many consider "progress" in such areas as crime, violence, drugs, promiscuity, pornography, and other weakenings of traditional moral and legal standards to be objectionable. (In the short run, as explained below, we expect a slowing down or even reversal of these recent trends to take place in some countries.)

The Multifold Trend is best thought of as a single entity whose every aspect is both a cause and an effect—a driving force and a consequence. Listing the elements separately leads to arbitrary distinctions and categories; they should be thought of as aspects or

TABLE 1.3
The Basic Long-Term Multifold Trend

Some aspects of this trend go back a thousand years; except as noted, most go back several centuries. This trend is toward:

1. *Increasingly Sensate Culture* (empirical, this-worldly, secular, humanistic, pragmatic, manipulative, explicitly rational, utilitarian, contractual, epicurean, hedonistic, etc.) — recently an almost complete decline of the sacred and of "irrational" taboos, charismas, and authority structures
2. *Accumulation of Scientific and Technological Knowledge* — recently emergence of a genuine theoretical framework for the biological sciences; but social sciences are still in an early, largely empirical, and idealistic state
3. *Institutionalization of Technological Change,* especially research, development, innovation, and diffusion — recently a conscious emphasis on finding and creating synergisms and serendipities
4. *Increasing Role of Bourgeois, Bureaucratic, "Meritocratic" Elites* — recently emergence of intellectual and technocratic elites as a class; increasing literacy and education for everyone; the "knowledge industry" and "triumph" of theoretical knowledge
5. *Increasing Military Capability of Western Cultures* — recently issues of mass destruction, terrorism, and diffusion of advanced military technologies (both nuclear and conventional) to non-Western cultures
6. *Increasing Area of World Dominated or Greatly Influenced by Western Culture* — but recently the West is becoming more reticent; a consequent emphasis on synthesis with indigenous cultures and various "ethnic" revivals
7. *Increasing Affluence* — and recently more stress on egalitarianism
8. *Increasing Rate of World Population Growth* — until recently; this rate has probably passed its zenith, or soon will
9. *Urbanization* — and recently suburbanization and "urban sprawl"; soon the growth of megalopoli, "sun belts," and rural areas with urban infrastructure and amenities
10. *Increasing Recent Attention to Macro-Environmental Issues* (e.g., constraints set by finiteness of earth and limited capacity of various local and global reservoirs to accept pollution)
11. *Decreasing Importance of Primary and, Recently, Secondary Occupations* — soon a similar decline in tertiary occupations and an increasing emphasis on advanced, honorific, or desirable quaternary occupations and activities
12. *Emphasis on "Progress" and Future-Oriented Thinking, Discussion, and Planning* — recently, some retrogression in the technical quality of such activities; conscious and planned innovation and manipulative rationality (e.g., social engineering) increasingly applied to social, political, cultural, and economic worlds, as well as to shaping and exploiting the material world; increasing role of ritualistic, incomplete, or pseudo-rationality
13. *Increasing Universality of the Multifold Trend*
14. *Increasing Tempo of Change in All the Above* (which may, however, soon peak in many areas)

---

parts of a whole. The Multifold Trend affects every aspect and part of society: fine arts, truth systems, family relationships, government, performing arts, architecture, ethics and morality, music, law, economics, civic relationships, literature, and education.

The Multifold Trend, despite leading and lagging sectors, goes in one direction—at least on the average and over a long period of time. It should not, however, be thought of as a locomotive on a fixed straight railroad track leading inexorably to a final destination. We should allow for some curves, some switching back and forth, and even occasional changes in railroad lines. Or even more, to change metaphors, its movement resembles a river flowing down to the sea. If one closely examines a section of a river, eddies can make it difficult or impossible to discern which direction the river is flowing; one must look at the river as a whole or from a distance. The ebb and flow of the tide can, for a short time, even reverse the flow of the river.

Essentially the Multifold Trend describes a one-way process from very deep religiosity to total secularism. Many macro-historians believe that such a trend is more or less irreversible—or at least that any reversal will occur only after a "rise and fall of civilization" scenario has been completed. This thinking is typified by what we call Sorokin-Spengler or Toynbee-Quigley type scenarios.[12] The former can be outlined as follows:

1. Multifold Trend ends in late sensate chaos
2. Increasing polarization, conflict, and decadence
3. A weakening of the society's ability to defend itself
4. Crisis and collapse (often by invasion or revolution)
5. A new charismatic idea or religiosity emerges
6. Ordeal and catharsis as the new idea spreads
7. The new idea takes over, peaking in about half a millennium
8. New Multifold Trend (takes a millennium or so to run its course)

(This scenario fits Spengler's ideas more closely than Sorokin's, though both share many of the concepts.)

A simplistic Toynbee-Quigley type scenario can be outlined as follows:

1. Mixture of two cultures
2. Gestation of an "instrument of expansion"
3. The Expansion
4. Age of Conflict (warring states)

5. Universal empire and then some decay
6. A new instrument of expansion and repeat of two to six (or one to six)
7. Eventually a failure to generate a new instrument of expansion
8. Increased rigidity and decay
9. Successful invasion or revolution and destruction of the old society

In the Toynbee-Quigley scenario, a mixture of cultures creates a new culture that eventually leads to a new kind of dynamism. The mechanism that brings this about is called an *instrument of expansion*. Ability to wage war, for example, would be one such instrument. The expansion of a culture often takes place through the creation of "warring states" that belong to the same overall culture, yet fight among each other as well as with others. In a final age of conflict one of the states or a federation of states conquers or absorbs the other nations and creates a universal empire.

The conquering civilization, which appears to be at its peak of brilliance, power, and vitality, begins to show seeds of decay after a few centuries. The early Toynbee believed that at this point the culture was likely to succumb, but Quigley and the later Toynbee argue that a new instrument of expansion may emerge either through native creativity or through contact with another culture.[13] The civilization then goes through a similar scenario, perhaps several times. Finally a point will be reached where the universal empire is simultaneously decaying and subjected to an inner or outer attack (typically by what Toynbee calls the internal or external proletariat, or what we would think of as a revolution of the lower classes or an attack by invading barbarians). If such an attack occurs when the empire is very weak, it will collapse.

In almost all previous empires, overhead costs—maintenance of the army, the central government, and the elite or aristocracies— tended to get out of control. Sometimes, notably in China, this was accompanied by a huge population expansion that accelerated the depletion of natural resources in much the way that many neo-Malthusians believe is happening today. The combination of a rapidly expanding population and an expensive increasing overhead has almost always proved fatal. The universal empire becomes progessively weaker and often decadent, unable to prevail over its internal and external enemies. This last part of the Toynbee-Quigley scenario can include much of the Sorokin-Spengler scenario.

Today, barbarians from the steppes, mountains, or sea pose no threat to modern societies with their awesome capabilities for violence. (Indeed, the last barbarians, the Kazaks, were put down in 1890. But, as will be noted in Chapter 3, the United States nearly experienced a widespread Indian revolt in that same year.) Some people believe, however, that even though the overhead problem does not seem likely to occur again because modern societies are so highly productive, the current enormous increase in transfer payments so typical of the modern welfare state may play a similar disastrous role (see the discussion of creeping stagnation in Chapter 4).

We believe that there are increasing forces in contemporary Western societies that tend towards anarchy, chaos, nihilism, and decadence. Some persons and groups are struggling to create something new, more or less along the lines of the Sorokin-Spengler or Toynbee-Quigley scenarios; others seem to be interested only in destruction, believing a new and better culture will then automatically emerge. We argue that at the moment, Western culture, despite or perhaps because of the enormous dynamism of the Great Transition, does not have as much vitality, faith, loyalty, self-confidence, and high morale as it did from the fifteenth through the nineteenth centuries or even during the period 1886 to 1913, which we call *La Première Belle Epoque. (La Deuxième Belle Epoque,* 1948 to 1973, was almost as notable for the relatively low vitality and political morale that prevailed in most of the Affluent Capitalist countries as for their enormous economic and technological dynamism.)*

We tend to think of World War I as being the great divide, although most of the specific weaknesses and excesses now associated with the welfare state are post–World War II phenomena. We do not argue that a permissive welfare-oriented society *necessarily* brings about declining will, morale, patriotism, and so on, although there are often some connections. However, welfare and permissiveness do have a tendency to go too far in a modern context. The tendency of Affluent Capitalist democracies to live far beyond their means creates serious problems. They also increasingly tend to allow children, at least in much of the upper and upper-middle classes, to grow up with somewhat weak super-egos, little sense of maturity, and often an almost total lack of meaning and purpose for living conventional lives.[14] These things could presumably be corrected by more discipline, heightened responsibility, and some purely technical changes in upbringing and education. More simply, they could be

---

*Chapter 4 presents our ideas about these sub-periods of the twentieth century in detail.

corrected by ideological or religious revival or renewal. Indeed, such a movement now seems to be underway in a relatively weak form in some Western countries and in a somewhat stronger form in the United States.

About a dozen seminal macro-historians have studied the comprehensive issue of the rise and fall of civilizations. They all have found three basic phases in a culture, although they do not associate identical scenarios with the three phases. These similarities are shown in Table 1.4. These historians agree that if one examines all the aspects of the Multifold Trend and how they affect a society, one would almost always find that the fine arts are a leading sector for change. (We have argued in a recent study that, at present, this is less true in the United States.)[15] Table 1.5 lists the basic characteristics of art that correspond to each of the three phases of a culture. (We use Sorokin's terminology because it is relatively neutral. The others tend to carry connotations that we do not necessarily share, since we are agnostic or skeptical about many of the theories associated with various macro-historians.) We have added a "late sensate" stage to the list.

In Western culture the ideational stage lasted from the sixth century through the eleventh century. During that period there was no perspective painting because "God's eye is everywhere." The painted features on individual faces are usually unrecognizable because "God knows His own." The first picture by a serious artist in which we see even an element of the countryside is by a Flemish artist of the twelfth century—and it is the countryside seen through the window of a room in a monastery.

One can characterize the four stages of fine arts by suggesting that when a civilization is started, the purpose of the art is to enhance an idea—art for God's sake, or for the idea's sake. The second phase, the idealistic or integrated phase, served to improve human beings, to make them more noble, more heroic, more patriotic, more motivated, morally uplifted, better informed and so forth. In the third stage, we have art for art's sake. In the last stage, we have art as a revolution, as a happening, as a protest, or even art for no reason—pure chaos. What has happened has been well described by Daniel Bell:

> The last hundred years has seen an effort by antibourgeois culture to achieve autonomy from the social structure, first by a denial of bourgeois values in the realm of art, and second by carving out enclaves where the bohemian and avant-gardist could live a contrary style of life. By the turn of the century the avant-garde had succeeded in

TABLE 1.4
Cultural Phases in Macro-History[a]

Sorokin	Spengler, Toynbee, et al.	Sombart	Berdyaev
Ideational	Growth, Spring, Childhood	Ascetic-messianic	Barbaric-religious
Idealistic	Maturity, Summer	Harmonious	Medieval-Renaissance
Sensate	Autumn, Winter, Civilization, Decline	Heroic-Promethean	Humanistic-secular

There are, of course, always minor themes, reluctant or nominal conformers, undergrounds, holdovers, dropouts, dissenters, schismatics, heretics, unbelievers, and other deviants or exceptions. (These may be a majority of the population, still not very visible.)

[a]Pitirim Sorokin, *Social and Cultural Dynamics* (New York: Bedminster Press, 1962); for further details see Oswald Spengler, *The Decline of the West* (New York: Modern Library, 1969); Werner Sombart, *The Quintessence of Capitalism: A Study of the History and Psychology of the Modern Business Man*, translated by M. Epstein (New York: Dutton, 1915); and Nikolai Berdyaev, *The Meaning of History*, translated by George Reavey (London: 1923).

TABLE 1.5
Four Phases in the Fine Arts

Ideational	Idealistic or Integrated	Sensate	Late Sensate
Transcendental	Mixed style	Worldly Naturalistic	Underworldly Protest
Supersensory	Heroic	Realistic Visual	Revolt Overripe
Religious	Noble	Illusionistic Everyday	Extreme Sensation seeking
Symbolic	Uplifting	Amusing Interesting	Titillating Depraved
Allegoric	Sublime	Erotic Satirical	Faddish Violently novel
Static	Patriotic	Novel Eclectic	Exhibitionistic Debased
Worshipful	Moralistic	Syncretic Fashionable	Vulgar Ugly
Anonymous	Beautiful	Superb technique Impressionistic	Debunking Nihilistic
Traditional	Flattering	Materialistic	Pornographic
Immanent	Educational	Professional	Sadistic

establishing a "life-space" of its own, and by 1910-1930 it was on the offensive against traditional culture.

Today, in both doctrine and life-style, the antibourgeois has won. This triumph means that, in the culture today, anti-nominalism and anti-institutionalism rule. In the realm of art, on the level of esthetic doctrine, no one opposes the idea of boundless experiment, of unfettered freedom, of unconstrained sensibility, of impulse being superior to order, of the imagination being immune to merely rational criticism. There is no longer an avant-garde, because no one in our post-modern culture is on the side of order or tradition. There exists only a desire for the new.

The traditional bourgeois organization of life—its rationalism and sobriety—no longer has any defenders in the culture, nor does it have any established system of culture meanings or stylistic forms with any intellectual or cultural respectability. To assume, as some social critics do, that the technocratic mentality dominates the cultural order is to fly in the face of every bit of evidence at hand. What we have today is a radical disjunction of culture and social structure, and it is such disjunctions which historically have paved the way for more direct social revolutions.[16]

If one takes this assessment seriously (we believe the situation is more complex) one might be concerned about the United States, or at least about its high culture (that is, the visible culture in which most "serious" art is produced). As far as we can ascertain from professional art critics, art historians, and art dealers, the last heroic painting by an American artist was done in 1945. Almost all art produced in North America and western Europe today is sensate or late-sensate. This contrasts with the socialist realism of all the communist countries or the radical heroic art in much of Latin America.

In addition, various truth systems are associated with the phases. These are shown in Table 1.6. The idealistic truth system is a mixture of the ideational and sensate. If a society reaches a stage where late sensate truth systems prevail, it is in serious trouble. (This book is basically a sensate book, but early sensate—almost idealistic.) If United States or European truth systems follow the fine arts and we get into a situation where the average person, or perhaps just the average person in the high culture, has late-sensate truth systems, it will be most difficult to operate the system. It will become truly decadent and unable to cope with its problems.

Political Cycles

In a fascinating study of "cyclical" cultural change, Aristotle analyzed the constitutions and histories of Greek cities and put his results into a historical scheme that was similar to schemes known to almost every educated Greek, including Plato. Aristotle's scheme superficially looks much like the scenarios of our macro-historians, but it is on a different historical principle and scale. His cycle is measured by generations, not by millennia. (We have modified his arguments slightly to suit our needs—see Figure 1.2.)

Aristotle argued that a cycle starts with a Sacred King who has been selected or aided by the Gods. Many Greek cities were founded by heroic figures who became mythological—that is, Sacred Kings. Everybody either had or was supposed to have total faith in the Sacred

TABLE 1.6
Three Systems of Truth

Ideational	Sensate	Late Sensate
Revealed	Empirical	Cynical
Charismatic	Pragmatic	Disillusioned
Certain	Operational	Nihilistic
Dogmatic	Practical	Orwellian
Mystic	Worldly	Blasé
Intuitive	Scientific	Transient
Infallible	Skeptical	Superficial
Religious	Tentative	Weary
Supersensory	Fallible	Sophistry
Unworldly	Sensory	Formalistic
Salvational	Materialistic	Atheistic
Spiritual	Mechanistic	Trivial
Absolute	Relativistic	Changeable
Supernatural	Agnostic	Meaningless
Moral	Instrumental	Alienated
Emotional	Empirically or	Convenient
Mythic	Logically verifiable	Absolutely

King's right to rule. All persons presumably believed in the divine origins of the system. The members of the King's family or the priesthood eventually created a hereditary aristocracy that did not have the same total faith in the system as the people (perhaps because they observed the royal family too closely). They would not participate in the government unless they had a high degree of control over it. At this point, something resembling a theology is needed—a systematic attempt to rationalize a system that has lost some of its charisma and divine character. The theology may stem the tide, but it will not restore the original faith.

An oligarchy of wealth, talent, or military capability soon takes over from the aristocracy. An oligarchy needs greater freedom, more options, and more pluralism. It cannot command the same degree of faith and unity as a king or a hereditary priesthood. The appropriate faith for it, therefore, is some kind of deism. The system is still authoritarian and its legitimation is still based upon sacred concepts, but it is much more secular.

The next stage occurs when people begin to ask "Why shouldn't we

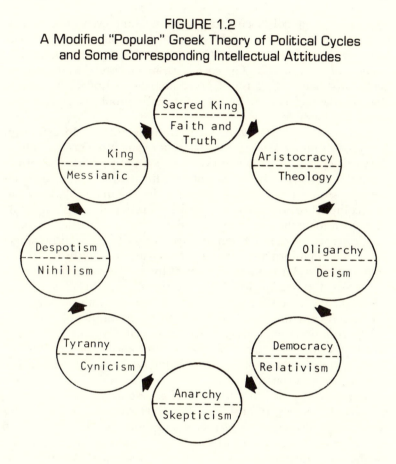

FIGURE 1.2
A Modified "Popular" Greek Theory of Political Cycles
and Some Corresponding Intellectual Attitudes

take over the government ourselves?" At this point, relativism seems to be the appropriate belief system. One person's system, one person's belief, one person's judgments are, until tested or otherwise invalidated, as good as any other. But more than a remnant remains of the old traditions and customs. Respect for authority, faith, and loyalty to the old beliefs are still evident.

One big problem with democracy is that it may erode into anarchy—a total rejection of all authority, a blocking of any action because of a multitude of pressure groups who are unwilling to compromise or work together. The appropriate belief system is skepticism. More and more people, particularly among the elite, challenge everything. There is no automatic authority, no source of legitimacy except plebiscites and elections—and even these may be challenged. There is much debate, diversion of effort, self-indulgence, and self-seeking. Order, justice, efficiency, and effectiveness are at low ebb. The society is, by our previous definition, decadent—that is, because of psychological, political, or cultural changes, the society is no longer able to solve problems it could have coped with previously.

Such a society eventually turns from skepticism to cynicism. Everybody's motives are suspect, and more and more people believe the worst of each other. Their cynicism is usually justified. Tyranny inevitably develops. (In Greek political theory, the tyrant was often the representative of the masses against the oligarchs.) Nothing can be accomplished unless force is used or threatened; people must be compelled to do the right thing or risk punishment or death. Serious public discussion of policy languishes. The leader may rely on others for advice and information, but no one can argue with the leader as a matter of right. He has a monopoly of force. The state, in fact, now represents nothing but force. Yet legitimacy, stability, and readily accepted rules are needed desperately. As Napoleon supposedly said, "We can do anything with bayonets except sit on them."

This situation leads to despotism. A new leader eventually emerges, sometimes with a messianic message of ideological renewal. One can go back to the old days or start something radically different. In any case, the cycle is started again.

Aristotle concluded that no form of government was clearly best, not even democracy. It must be understood that in many countries, a step towards democracy is also a step towards anarchy, tyranny, or despotism—or at least revolution or revolutionary coups. Democracy for the sake of democracy is ideology, not judgment. All too often, Americans assume that democracy is always the best solution, everywhere, at all times, for all nations. Also, all too often our government tends to exert pressures to put this dubious axiom into practice. Yet in the last 200 years democracy has only worked and survived more or less continuously in a handful of countries: Scandinavia, Holland, the United Kingdom, the United States, Canada, Australia, New Zealand, and Switzerland.

Aristotle's diagram and the supporting argument show that any automatic support of short-run moves to democracy is simply irresponsible. Whether or not an increase in civil liberties, an introduction of the ballot, or an introduction of political parties in any particular situation is progress toward long-run democracy is an open issue and cannot be judged by those who are ignorant of local conditions. These are not ideological problems. Democracies are grown, not created.

Macro-Historical Possibilities

Table 1.7 classifies six very different macro-historical possibilities. The Pelagian and Augustinian positions refer to two Christian monks who lived in the fourth century Roman Empire. Pelagius believed that human beings were intrinsically good, much like some contemporary child psychologists who believe that there are no bad children, only bad parents. Augustine believed that human beings were conceived in sin and were born with basic evil tendencies that had to be repressed or overcome. Although we tend to prefer the post-industrial Augustinian position, we are basically agnostic. We will, however, discuss elements of the Augustinian position in a way that should be useful and stimulating to believers as well as to agnostics in almost any of the positions.

Freud, while often considered a Pelagian, is actually perhaps the outstanding Augustinian of the twentieth century. Among other things, he pointed out that civilization is repression, and the child must be socialized at all costs, although he added that one might still wish to reduce the costs. America, which tends to be Pelagian, only seems to have heard the last remark, thus converting the outstanding Augustinian of the twentieth century into a Pelagian.[17]

The Agnostic Use of Information and Concepts

One of our major "methodological" tools is the agnostic use of information and concepts. To explain this tool, we begin by contrasting the academic and the practical styles, exaggerating the differences to heighten the contrast. Consider professor-student interactions. Normally professors exposit certain topics that they understand well, covering all the issues that are relevant from their perspective. Then the professors test the ability of students to understand and use the concepts by formulating clear-cut questions that have verifiable answers. Enough information has been supplied, or will be easily available using resources on campus, so that students can answer the questions satisfactorily. To the extent that any theoretical reasoning is used in answering the question, the theories are also available and are known to be relevant, valid, and complete. Finally, the students are given sufficient time to find and use whatever the information they need. Note that:

1. Proper background has been supplied in advance,
2. Questions are clearly formulated,

TABLE 1.7
Basically Different Views of Likely Socio-Economic Futures[a]

View of Man	Post-Industrial	Neo-Malthusian	Typical Macro-Historian (i.e., basic change in culture)
Pelagian	Infinite material progress for all, with increasing equality and justice on a business-as-usual basis (e.g., Utopian view of the enlightenment and industrial revolution) perhaps a Marxian type utopia or benevolent "1984" or "Brave New World" (e.g., Skinner's "Walden Two")	"Equilibrium" with economic equality and social justice and stability at low material standard of living (e.g., voluntary simplicity or Club of Rome utopia—or dystopia)	Concepts of Chardin, Harmon, Marcuse, Maslow, Reich, Revel, Thompson and various Western mystical and Buddhist sects towards a new social and spiritual world order
Augustinian	Some progress but increasing gaps; much economic technological growth; stratified, stabilized, centrally governed societies; order over justice; "1985 technological crises and Faustian choices" may force a less benevolent "1984" or "Brave New World"	Prometheus bound; humanity forever constrained by greed, scarcity, and catastrophic natural limits; totalitarian rule or Hobbesian state of nature combined with desperate struggle over finite resources; perhaps a catastrophic collapse and regression of world society	Typical macro-historian scenario of conquest and/or late sensate collapse, i.e., polarization, crisis, ordeal, catharsis, and then a new religiosity or ideology (see discussion of Sorokin-Spengler or Toynbee-Quigley scenarios)

[a] We are indebted to A. J. Wiener for creative suggestions on this chart. It is included here because it illustrates the range of viewpoints and possibilities in a very useful way. We do not discuss it systematically but only touch on some of the above possibilities in the next section and later. As the reader may have guessed, we are more Augustinian than Pelagian.

3. Adequate high quality information is available,
4. Adequate high quality theories are available,
5. Clear distinctions exist between right and wrong answers,
6. The time needed is available.

None of these conditions obtains in most situations studied by the Hudson Institute (or indeed in many real life situations). Decision makers have to make do with what they have available. This means that the questions are not precisely formulated; the answers are not verifiable; high quality data, adequate theories, and sufficient amounts of time are not likely to be available. In fact, the biggest issues may be "What is the question? How much time is available? What information and theories that are accessible are relevant? If these are contradictory or inconsistent, how do we deal with them?"

A similar situation is encountered when one looks at the differences between a professor's own doctoral thesis and most real world problems. In the thesis, the question or issue is almost always carefully and narrowly formulated to make it possible for the work to be original; enough time is allocated to make the work of publishable quality; and the dimensions and scope deliberately specialized to fall within one's normal field of interest or capability. In the real world, of course, the scope of the problems and quality of solution are determined by the existential context and time pressures are ignored at great peril.

It is a hopeless, even irrational illusion to expect real world business or political situations to be as neat and orderly as the problems presented in academic discussions. It is even more hopeless to expect to find high quality theorems and models that will be realistically applicable. And only rarely has all the relevant and available information been gathered. Business and political decision makers have to come up with reasonable solutions based mostly on low quality information and theories applied in situations where the questions are imprecisely or inaccurately formulated and where no one knows ahead of time whether the answers suggested are right or the politics devised will work. Controversy will continue even after the fact because there will be different interpretations of what actually occurred and why.

Sometimes decisions come up in such a way that additional study and analysis may be possible. But even then, decisions cannot be held up indefinitely. In most cases the additional analysis will probably not be decisive, particularly if the situation is changing rapidly. Indeed, a slow-moving study will often lag far behind events.

How, then, should one proceed? Presumably as people have always proceeded: by using their best judgments, intuitions, and guesses. Often the basic reasoning and methodology will be faulty if applied generally or inexpertly. Yet decision makers often arrive at good answers to the specific problems they have to deal with.

I have some experience with this situation in an area where most laymen would not expect these kinds of problems. As a theoretical physicist I worked closely with some of the best physicists of our generation. Contrary to popular impression, these scientists did not always work rigorously, nor were they as careful as their reputations and self-confidence would indicate—even in their own fields. They often put forth hypotheses as if they were mathematical theorems of universal validity, although it was easy to show that they weren't. Nevertheless, they rarely made errors in dealing with the practical applications of these hypotheses. Even though they thought of these theorems as universally applicable, the hypotheses had generally been developed out of very special problems. The scientists intuitively applied the theorems only to areas and under conditions where, in fact, they did fit. As a result, they almost always obtained correct or at least usable results, even though they claimed more for their theories than was actually provable.

Decision makers are often in much more precarious positions. They may have little available to them beyond experience in varied and not always relevant fields; theories that are often a synthesis of various anecdotes, metaphors, and analogues; and, sometimes, empathy with various important groups. Yet many competent, pragmatic decision makers have done very well. Throughout much of human history, leaders have used the same basic techniques. They intuitively understood the specific issues facing them so well that they could deal with them in an empirical, pragmatic *ad hoc* fashion; or they used some kind of theoretical framework to produce solutions that were quite reasonable; or they creatively exploited limited but perceptive observations.

Until quite recently, no scientific survey data existed, nor did much formal theory. More often than not, the theorists in economics and sociology do not originate their "inventions." Rather, they describe events that occurred before the theories were devised. The theorists' contributions were and are less inventions than descriptions of the actions of practical people in a more or less rational and comprehensible manner. Constructs or institutions emerge or are invented by very practical people and often become quite developed before the theoreticians even notice them. In recent years this has happened with the transnational corporations as a pervasive world force, the Eurodollar market, the rapid economic emergence of Japan and the New Industrial countries, and by and large, the current stagflation.

Our more or less agnostic use of information and concepts is intended to resemble but is not identical to the traditional pre-scientific way of proceeding. First, we are genuinely agnostic about many of the themes we use; we simply do not know whether they are correct or not, or if they are, we are not sure of the extent of their validity. It is therefore important to hedge against these theories being right without relying on their being right. Second, we are often willing to use these concepts as dramatic and pedagogically useful ways to explain or illustrate certain principles or facts. In many cases, sophisticated empirical or theoretical explanations can be used to show that the concepts do apply, but these are likely to be both confusing and complex. Sometimes relatively simple arguments are more persuasive, more heuristic, and thus more useful to the reader. Also, such materials may produce interesting scenarios, basic contexts, apt metaphors, significant hypotheses and a language that is both precise and rich. (Chapter 2 provides some of these scenarios, contexts, metaphors, hypotheses, and language.)

The Concept of the Six Degrees of Belief[18]

Because we are dealing with uncertain and controversial material, we find it very important to be consciously and intellectually aware of where we and others stand on many positions and issues. It is almost impossible for us to get along using a simple true-false dichotomy or even a trichotomy of true, uncertain, and false. In a sense, we are trying, in this kind of situation, to give our own and others' subjective positions, or the likelihood that a certain proposition is true, or that a certain policy will work—and our confidence in our own beliefs or others' attitudes toward our own beliefs. Using numbers giving estimates of these subjective probabilities and degrees of confidence, or other precise estimates and ranges, would give a misleading appearance of a non-existent precision and analytical clarity.

Our problem is like that of an individual studying the colors of a rainbow who wishes to relate these colors to other colors he notes in the environment around him. Our culture has decided to divide the rainbow into seven colors: red, orange, yellow, green, blue, violet, and indigo. All adult members of our society recognize, of course, that there are no sharp dividing lines. Not only are the boundaries indistinct or arbitrary, various shades other than those mentioned can be identified. In fact, every conceivable wave length of light between

4000 and 7600 angstrom units is available in the visible portion of the rainbow. But nothing would be sillier than saying we think of a certain shade such as orange as being precisely 6400 angstrom units— or even ranging between 6300 and 6500. We simply do not think like that; we cannot estimate that precisely what we mean by orange or any other color. We could say orange is in the region of 6400 angstrom units, but that would be unnecessary since the term orange exists and gives about the degree of precision we need. Furthermore, *orange* covers other mixtures or blends such as red and yellow that give the human eye the appearance of orange and which we wish to include in this category. We would also like our terminology not only to reflect our uncertainty about purity and wavelength, but also to have a little connotation as well as denotation—that is, to have some emotion and feeling about it.

We propose to do the same thing for degrees of belief. We argue that it is useful to distinguish at least six degrees of belief in a theory, a proposition, or a policy: atheism, agnosticism, skepticism, deism, Scotch verdict, and acceptance. For most purposes we find in these six degrees and some associated nuances a satisfactorily rich and precise vocabulary. Our usage of these words will be slightly idiosyncratic but it is close enough to the normal literary meaning so that readers who are not cognizant of the definitions that follow can still comprehend our use of these terms.

Most readers will be familiar with all but one of the above terms— *Scotch verdict.** In criminal proceedings in Scotland, the jury need not choose only between guilty or not guilty (the only two verdicts in most Western judicial systems) but may decide on a third verdict, "not proven." This means that the case against the defendant was very persuasive and for practical purposes (i.e., lending an individual money, hiring or firing a person, etc.) most laymen would probably accept the case presented by the prosecutor, but that it has not met the legal requirement of "beyond any reasonable doubt."

Note that we have largely used language derived from religious, metaphysical, and legal discussions. This is not surprising because it is exactly in these areas where the issue of proof and degree of belief has been most thoroughly explored and discussed in much the same way that interests us.

---

*Note to our Scottish readers. We follow the customary British English and American English usages of the term Scotch. No offense is intended and partisans should feel free to refer to this important concept as the Scottish or Scots verdict if they so desire.

Atheism, naturally, implies more or less total disbelief or rejection. The *agnostic* position is that one does not know whether to believe or not. If one has an agnostic position toward some relevant issue or data, one may wish to have contingent or complex plans that work if the alleged facts or theories are valid, but does not rely on them being so. By *skeptical* we mean the denotation and not the connotation of the term—that is, we are not implying a leaning toward disbelief or hostility. We use the word to mean that one is prepared to believe but has some doubts and therefore wishes more data, argumentation, or other evidence of validity. The *deist* position accepts that there is "something in the idea" but is not sure about specifics and degree of validity. There are some insights in the proposition being discussed but one is not prepared to endorse every item. A deist is more willing to base plans on the information than the agnostic or skeptic but is still not willing to rely on it being right.

The Scotch verdict often denotes what might be called an "almost proven" or "good enough for me" (or "good enough for our purposes") situation. It is for us probably the most important category, since in our considerations we often have information that we consider valid enough for public policy purposes or for decisions of most private individuals and yet may not quite approach rigorous academic or mathematical standards. Whether or not one is willing to go ahead on this "not proven" basis, the other side cannot argue that the position has been proven false or is unlikely to be untrue because the case is simply too plausible. This is an important aspect of the "not-proven" concept. Neither side may be able to force the other side—intellectually or morally—to accept its position, nor can it dismiss opposing views out of hand. The intellectual support behind most of the more complex or controversial decisions made in public policy or business is of the "not-proven" variety—good enough for the supporting group, taken seriously by individuals and most opponents, but not rigorously provable.*

---

*This concept of *Scotch verdict* is closely related to another concept that we have found extremely useful at the Hudson Institute, the concept of *surprise-free.* We argue a scenario or prediction can be surprise-free to one group and not to another group, so therefore the concept must be related to the people who hold it. We do *not* mean by surprise-free "most probable," "most likely," or "most important" (though these adjectives often apply). We simply mean that we would not be surprised if such a prediction turned out to be valid, or if such an event occurred. So two surprise-free projections can be inconsistent, since we would not be surprised if one *or* the other occurred. It

One can have a different kind of support than the Scotch verdict when decisions are made on the basis of a position accepted by some narrow professional group, academic school, public group, or even by the broad academic community or the general public. This could be "proven beyond a reasonable doubt" but also be more of an ideological or religious position held by its supporters. Or it could be even more *ad hoc* or idiosyncratic.

Acceptance does not normally mean validity, only that the group concerned does not question it. Often it just implies being consonant with the group's values, ideology, or even prejudices. This can apply to general academic as well as broad public acceptance of any concepts, theories, facts, or other information. Such acceptance is often so obvious, immediate, and widely shared that it is almost unperceived. Thus, acceptance is often too automatic to involve serious discussion or questions. One of the reasons for explicitly discussing many concepts is to cast doubt on some propositions that command widespread and automatic acceptance. Much public and private business is, of course, conducted on what is sometimes called "conventional wisdom." Of course, the conventional wisdom— widely accepted propositions—can also be valid, or at least more valid than positions held by its challengers.

An important purpose of this book is to make the reader more conscious of these intellectual and ideological underpinnings. This enterprise is not necessarily constructive. If we shake people's faith in certain concepts or assumptions, we may erode their confidence and commitment. Confidence and commitment are very important to success. However, more often than not, this is a risk we are willing to take.

Any attempt to base policies solely on rigorous studies and documentation is simply a recipe for inaction, not for improved policy making. Attempts to glide over this fact can lead to endless delays while pursuing more information, or attempts to obscure the "inadequacies in the information available" or the degree to which one is relying on uncertain information or personal judgments.

---

should be noted that most of the world's business is conducted on the basis of surprise-free projections, which may or may not include a validity equal to that of the Scotch verdict. The usefulness of this terminology is that it makes explicit what one believes about the projection and makes it simpler to advance and discuss these concepts systematically in either an academic or practical discussion. This is nothing new, except for this explicitness; however, this explicitness can be very important.

Obtaining the *appearance* of rigor and objectivity is a typical motive (conscious or unconscious) for devising or using a large-scale computer model. Such a model can create (at least sometimes) an illusion of universality and certainty. In most applications with which we are familiar such models have been a much less useful guide than the intuitive guesses and judgments of reasonably experienced or knowledgeable individuals. It can be even worse to attempt to base policy in a particular issue on evidence restricted to careful academic studies that leave out all that can be gained by the careful use of one's eyes, ears, intuition, and empathy.

We started our discussion by using the analogy of a rainbow. But every reader knows that one could not use the canonical colors of the rainbow in a simple way to describe the many characteristics of real world colors. First of all, as already noted, colors are often complex, made up of a mixture of other colors. They can vary in complexity, hue, intensity, and brightness as well as purity; the texture and finish of the surface makes a great deal of difference in their appearance; and so on.

It would be similarly simplistic for us to imply that the degrees of belief can be ordered in a simple way and described as neatly as we indicate below. We will, however, normally use a simple ordering because it will be more useful than not in most of the situations we discuss. However, we would like to be able to modify the simple question of degree by indicating that there are different kinds of attitudes even where the general category has been specified. We therefore suggest that the reader examine the following list and comments carefully.

1. *Atheism* (Disbelief)
   a. *Hostile Rejection:* Has absolutely no interest in position, no wish to discuss it, will not use the language, and is dismayed if the proposition is put forward.
   b. *Tolerant Rejection:* Does not believe but does not care if others believe.
   c. *Neutral Rejection:* Often a *technical or analytic rejection* held without emotion or passion.
   d. *Empathic Rejection:* Perfectly willing (or even prefers) to let other people believe; usually willing to discuss relevant issues seriously and empathically with them.
   e. *Metaphoric Acceptance:* Not only tolerant and willing to discuss relevant issues, but willing to use the same metaphors and images.

As examples of what we mean by the above, one might easily have each of these five attitudes, respectively, toward somebody's (a) acceptance of astrology or witchcraft; (b) belief in lucky days, charms, or numbers; (c) belief that there are (or are not) 3 trillion barrels of recoverable oil to be found in the next three decades; (d) belief in a religion one did not accept, but approved of or at least did not wish to challenge; and (e) willingness to talk about God, salvation, and heaven in much the same terms the believers do, with or without constantly making one's basic atheism clear.

2. *Agnosticism* (Does not know)
   a. *Disinterested Ignorance:* Could be thoughtful or considered; could be an issue that just never came up before—or at least one had not thought seriously about it and therefore had no position on it (perhaps does not even want to).
   b. *Cannot Be Known:* Very often an individual feels that a subject is simply unknowable, at least in the absence of divine revelation or an extraordinary breakthrough in theory or data; would be perfectly willing if he knew how to do it to increase his knowledge, but might feel that it is not possible to do so at least with the time and resources available.
   c. *Open Mind:* The person may well have a quite different attitude from the two indicated above. He wants to know and thinks he can know, but at the moment has not yet made up his mind.

3. *Skepticism* (Open to persuasion but has doubts—wants more evidence)
   a. *Friendly:* This is very close to the open-mind agnostic position, but leans much further toward belief.
   b. *Neutral:* Self-explanatory.
   c. *Hostile Skepticism:* While basically negative, takes possibility of believing seriously—perhaps because of official position or context—indeed, one may have to take the position that one is open-minded and prepared to be persuaded, but really be more of an agnostic or atheist than can be admitted.

4. *Deism:* One feels that there is something to the concept but is not sure what. In religion it can go all the way from

belief in a unique and supreme but unknown Being who is terribly interested in human beings to a clear concept that this Supreme Being (or Force) may exist but that we do not understand anything of its purposes or goals—if such anthropomorphic concepts apply at all. There can be a very large range in deist positions, but without any claim to many, if any, specific revelations. Deists do not accept much doctrine or dogma. We will often take a deist position, or something more, about the various historical theories discussed earlier (and later).

5. *Scotch Verdict* (Not proven, but most reasonable people will accept)
   a. *Legalistic or Moral Rejection:* Since the individual is not convicted one has to treat him as innocent even though many feel almost certain that he is guilty.
   b. *Grounds for Hedging or Great Care:* The information concerned cannot be ignored even if it is not good enough for "conviction." Certain limited or hedging actions should be taken.
   c. *Practically Accepted:* Will act largely as if issue has been decided.

   In almost all cases of Scotch verdict that interest us, our attitude will be of the last type (c). We understand that we have not quite proven the case and therefore we have to be cautious and even open-minded, but will still normally proceed as if there were proof.

6. *Acceptance*
   a. *Proven Beyond Reasonable Doubt:* This, of course, is a legal concept.
   b. *Professionally or Academically Acceptable:* Passes the technical standards of the profession. These may not be universal, but are accepted within the group concerned. What is proven to a physicist is often not proven to a mathematician.*

---

*The word *heuristic* is very interesting as it applies here. We once polled the Hudson Institute and found that half the staff thought the word heuristic was a common, ordinary word that could be used without explanation; the other half had not even heard of the word. What made the poll most interesting was, generally, speaking, that the people with the largest vocabularies, the most

    c. *Issue of Ideology or Religion:* One believes because it fits into his *weltanschauung,* his entire belief structure. It is easy for the individual or group concerned to believe. Perhaps he or they have had revelations.

    d. *General Acceptance by Community:* In this case the acceptance is usually so complete and automatic that it is uncritical. It is a bit like a fish in the water; the fish may not even know it is in water until it is taken out and put in air. So the general acceptance by the community can involve a low grade of proof, even though the proposition is accepted as being correct beyond any reasonable doubt. "The earth is flat" or "the sun goes around the earth" are good examples of "beyond reasonable doubt" in some intellectual milieu.

Notes

1. These include nuclear energy, electronics, lasers, aircraft, antibiotics, satellites for observation and communication, advanced space shuttles and space tugs, new materials (e.g., new metals, plastics, and artificial fibers), microbiology, high-yielding varieties of plants, other kinds of genetic engineering, and scientific and technological agriculture.

2. See, for example, Pierre Teilhard de Chardin, *The Appearance of Man* (New York: Harper & Row, 1956); Willis Harman, *An Incomplete Guide to the Future* (San Francisco: San Francisco Book Co., 1976); Abraham Maslow, *The Farther Reaches of Human Nature* (New York: Viking Press, 1971); Herbert Marshall McLuhan, *The Mechanical Bride: Folklore of Industrial Man* (London: Routledge and Kegan Paul, 1967); Charles Reich, *The Greening of America* (New York: Bantam, 1971); Jean Francqis Revel, *Without Marx or Jesus: The New American Revolution Has Begun* (Garden City, N.Y.: Doubleday, 1971); Jonas Salk, *The Survival of the Wisest* (New York: Harper & Row, 1973); and William Thompson, *Darkness and Scattered Light* (Garden City, N.Y.: Anchor Press, 1978).

3. Such images may often play the same role as diagrams in mathematical proofs. Any particular diagram is very specific and concrete, but the usefulness of the proof does not lie in its being applicable only to the specific and concrete diagram on which it was based. The specific diagram can, at the same time, both represent other diagrams and be unique. Of course, if the

---

literary people, had not heard of the word. A heuristic argument is an argument that is very persuasive but does not meet the standards of rigor of the audience. The concept is important in physics, mathematics, and some branches of sociology. The distinction is almost never made in English, humanities, language studies, and so on. In these areas, if the argument is plausible, it is usually good enough.

diagram has some serious defect, it may lead to misleading argument and erroneous proof. But even so, just going through the exercise can be useful, since doing so may reveal the defects of the diagram and therefore lead to better diagrams. Many of the scenarios in Chapter 2 function similarly to diagrams or pictures in other contexts.

4. Colin Clark is responsible for the first three distinctions; we added the fourth. See his *The Conditions of Economic Progress* (New York: St. Martin's Press, 1957), p. 491.

5. This terminology comes from Angus Maddison; see his "Phases of Capitalistic Development," *Quarterly Review*, Banca Nazionale del Lavorno, No. 121, June 1977.

6. Karl Marx and Frederick Engels, *The German Ideology* (New York: International Publishers, 1947), p. 22.

7. J. M. Keynes, "Economic Possibilities for Our Grandchildren," in *Essays in Persuasion* (New York: Norton, 1963), pp. 371-372.

8. Studies forthcoming: See *The Japanese Challenge* by Herman Kahn and Thomas Pepper (New York: Thomas Y. Crowell, 1979) and *The Future of Arizona* by Paul Bracken (Boulder: Westview, 1979).

9. For a good discussion of these issues, see Leo Marx, *The Machine in the Garden* (London, England: Oxford University Press, 1964).

10. *Creative destruction* is Joseph Schumpeter's phrase. It emphasizes that all economic innovations and growth, as in the biological world, involve much destruction and removal of the old. See his *Capitalism, Socialism, and Democracy*, Third Edition (New York: Harper & Row, 1950).

11. Another Hudson study explores various possible roles for space: William M. Brown and Herman Kahn, *Long-Term Prospects for Development in Space* (A Scenario Approach), HI-2638-RR (Croton-on-Hudson, New York: Hudson Institute, October 30, 1977).

12. Pitirim A. Sorokin, *Social and Cultural Dynamics* (New York: Bedminster, 1962); Oswald Spengler, *The Decline of the West* (New York: Modern Library, 1969); Carrol Quigley, *The Evolution of Civilizations* (New York: Macmillan, 1961); and Arnold Toynbee, *A Study of History* (New York: Oxford University Press, 1946).

13. Arnold J. Toynbee, *Mankind and Mother Earth: A Narrative History of the World* (New York: Oxford University Press, 1976).

14. We discuss our notions about child-rearing and about the more general problem of educated incapacity in Chapter 8.

15. *The Future of the U.S. and Its Regions*, Irving Leveson and Jane Newitt (Croton-on-Hudson, New York: HI-2816-RR, May 1978).

16. "The Cultural Contradictions of Capitalism," in Daniel Bell and Irving Kristol (eds.) *Capitalism Today* (New York: Basic Books, 1971), p. 48.

17. These views of Freud's, paraphrased above, are perhaps most forcefully stated in *Civilization and Its Discontents* (New York: W. W. Norton, 1961).

18. For additional discussion of the six degrees of belief and of related issues, see *Let There Be Energy* by William Brown and Herman Kahn (forthcoming).

2

Economic Growth: Contexts, Scenarios, Images

The Current Hostility to Economic Growth

Even many who accept the desirability of economic affluence and technological achievement have qualms about using the common measure of such progress—GNP (gross national product) per capita. Indeed, almost any *explicit* use of this index has become discredited in some academic and intellectual circles. *Explicit* is emphasized because, despite its many theoretical and practical defects, practically everybody includes GNP per capita in any serious judgment about a nation's economic affluence, technological advancement, and ability to produce for culturally desirable purposes. Furthermore, governments everywhere try to increase it. Even the zero-growth movement uses the GNP concept, if only negatively.

After an excessively optimistic phase early in the post–World War II period, the intellectual climate surrounding the concept of modernization through economic and technological advancement has, until recently, tended to be excessively pessimistic.[1] To the extent that the very legitimacy of the goal of development is now called into question, this negative climate has been strongly reinforced. It is a climate that can have pervasive, if often subtle, destructive effects.

Belief in the ultimate desirability of economic development and technological advancement is a powerful force for constructive efforts, especially for obtaining foreign and domestic political and moral support. Conversely, the belief that modernization is harmful, illegitimate, or largely a failure erodes national as well as international development efforts and undermines foreign aid programs designed to encourage, extend, and protect development. It also undermines the willingness to tolerate some of the bad effects of modernization for the good it produces.

53

These doubts and concerns, intensified by a new focus on pollution and quality of life issues, do not spring from failure or disasters in recent years. In fact, much of the disappointment and disillusionment comes from success. By its nature, success may create, reveal, or exacerbate many problems. Good results are taken for granted, while bad results are judged intolerable.

We have compared many of the costs of development with its benefits and are prepared to justify our support for what we call modernization. We are convinced that economic development, industrialization, and the application and use of intermediate and advanced technology will—by and large and under current conditions—be judged desirable by our culture and by most other cultures. Moreover, we believe that one need not share our enthusiasm for many of the things we advocate to recognize them as the preferred options at present. This does not imply that we are confident that the worldwide movement toward modernization must turn out well—only that it is a good gamble.

All consequences of modernization and progress will be neither wildly successful nor universally desirable. Even if they are beneficent in the medium run, the question of their capacities for good and evil over the long run still remains open. Despite these concerns, we give little credence to the negative attitudes toward economic growth so prevalent in recent years. Many of these activities are excessive, elitist, romantic, self-serving, or based on false information or absurd theories.

Indeed, self-interest and self-indulgence—especially the narrow biases and interests displayed by many upper and upper-middle class people in affluent countries—have dominated recent discussions of economic and social problems to a degree that is seldom acknowledged. This book focuses on three subgroups comprising what we call the Anti-Growth Triad.[2] Listed in order of increasing importance to our concerns, they are: (1) affluent radicals and reformers; (2) Thorstein Veblen's "leisure class"; and (3) a subgroup of upper-middle class intellectuals we refer to as neo-liberal members of the New Class.[3]

Members of the Anti-Growth Triad have typically enjoyed the benefits of economic growth and modernization since their childhood, but as adults they are now disillusioned with further growth for reasons that run the gamut from admirable to unreasonable to selfish. They try to discourage others from gaining what they have enjoyed and now disdain. Some of their points, such as possible misuses of affluence and advanced technology, are valid;

others are gratuitous or just wrong. Mostly, the Anti-Growth Triad seems likely to create diversions that greatly increase the costs and difficulties for the upwardly mobile but that are unlikely to change the basic trend of the world as a whole.

One can respect various philosophical rejections of affluence or technology as harmful to the human spirit, yet deny that these rejections have any universal validity. One may wholeheartedly endorse the concept embodied in many Eastern religions that "many mountains lead up to heaven" and "many roads go up each mountain" ("heaven" serving as a metaphor for an eventual post-industrial society of one kind or another), yet believe that not all molehills are mountains and not all roads lead to the top. We believe that most real mountains and paths do point to modernization. Therefore, the basic goals and strategies for much of the Third World and some of the developed world are reasonably clear.

Some observers have suggested that, since both the advocates of early or forced limits to growth and we believe in some limits, our debate is purely technical and the differences in our viewpoints hold little interest for the general public. Actually, the differences are fundamental. These introductory comments provide some background for our more detailed discussion in subsequent chapters.

The common concern that dangerous mistakes can result from rapid growth is definitely justified. (Table 2.1 summarizes some pros and cons of economic and technological growth.) As the economic and technological scale and pace of development have increased, the likelihood has also increased that major dangers can arise too suddenly to be dealt with in time to avoid disasters (e.g., the thalidomide and Minamata tragedies). Rapid growth may increase the possibility of serious imbalances (e.g., the existing world overcapacity in steel or a potential worldwide shortage of energy in the next decade or two), but it can also create situations that make it easier to deal with such imbalances. Industrial pollution, for example, reached high levels in some developed countries, but these countries have been able to use their resources and technological capabilities to avert disasters, if not all serious problems, by dramatically reducing the rate of pollution while there was still time.

The necessity for dealing with these kinds of problems has been widely recognized. Regulatory agencies have tightened their requirements, in some cases excessively. Effective programs to protect the environment have already been institutionalized in North America, Japan, Australia, and northwestern Europe. In the years to come, almost all highly industrialized nations are likely to have much less

TABLE 2.1
Some Pros and Cons of Economic and Technological Growth

	Basic Argument		Basic Caveat
1.	Affluence and technology are good things, both as ends and means.	1.	But not always and not everywhere—many bad aspects (e.g., often excessively encourages materialistic values).
2.	It is not good to be poor and primitive.	2.	Many important values are associated with Stoic, ascetic, Epicurean, or pre-industrial and traditional lifestyles.
3.	In any case, economic wealth and technical capability provide security and insurance[a]—and can be essential to survival.	3.	May also create excessive dependence on wealth and technology—can make life too easy and unchallenging, in any case not really essential unless competing in material terms with an "advanced" culture (either militarily or commercially).
4.	Provides a base for power and influence.	4.	To do bad as well as good—and as in 3 above, also creates a need for more power and influence, can also lead to arrogance, carelessness, and callousness.
5.	Gaps help make the poor rich.	5.	But not all of them, may damage their self respect and status, seduce them into giving up more than they gain, and lead to feelings of injustice, envy, guilt, and contempt.
6.	Rapid growth facilitates the Great Transition and early achievement of affluence.	6.	But can also be excessively destructive of existing values and assets and may even help precipitate the kind of disaster one is trying to insure against.
7.	Growth facilitates adaptation to change and fulfillment of economic aspirations.	7.	But it causes too rapid change and arouses excessive economic and other aspirations.
8.	Also allows for the provision of adequate infrastructure and welfare.	8.	Same comments as above (e.g., creates an excessive need for these).

[a]By "insurance" we include having economic and technological flexibility to react to problems, whether caused by people or nature (e.g., oil shock or climate changes), toughness of the system, and capability to prevent, influence, correct, or alleviate the impact of harmful events on oneself and others.

pollution than they now have, despite the widespread impression that these problems are getting worse. Pressures for high standards must be maintained, but here as elsewhere overly zealous crusaders have sometimes done more harm than good. This is a learning process automatically involving much waste motion and inefficiency, unfortunately tragically excessive at times. One reason for such excesses in coping with pollution is that many people are upset about dangers that are either exaggerated or already handled satisfactorily.

While the danger of mistakes, imbalances, and major new problems (many as yet unperceived) can be overstated, it should not be dismissed. The danger is serious enough to justify more effective study, planning, and research, including greater efforts to establish safeguards. However, we do not believe that the danger can be avoided or even significantly reduced by misguided attempts to mandate a lower rate of economic growth across the board.

The most sensible opponents of growth call for caution. They say, "Why take a chance?" or "Why not stop growth, at least in the developed world, until we are more sure of the consequences?" This position may seem reasonable enough, but generally it is motivated by a distaste for an ever-wealthier world. Many upper and upper-middle class people correctly perceive that while growth was helpful to them at one time, it now often hurts their personal and class interests.

Most lower income people in the developed world have their basic material needs satisfied (often through welfare programs), while many upper income people are satiated by a vast variety of material goods. The result is that an emotional appeal for a simpler and less materialistic way of life is gaining favor among many of the affluent, and the middle class is increasingly losing its motivation to strive for further economic gains. Few lower income people take this position; nor do most relatively wealthy people agree—at least not yet.

If opposition to growth were primarily a genuine appeal to caution, it could help reduce pollution and waste of resources and stimulate greater care in innovation and expansion. Unfortunately, however, when they are not pushing some narrow class or personal position, most opponents of growth often are excessively eager either to maintain the status quo or to "junk" the entire world economic system—or sometimes, paradoxically, both. The typical limits to growth advocates do not have a tenable middle ground position. If finite limits to growth do exist (because of insufficient resources or excessive pollution), then the proper focus for the world's economy

would be to curb growth to bring about a sustainable steady-state
economy as soon as possible. Such a world would have to maintain an
acceptable standard of living more or less indefinitely. This would
probably require a dramatic cut in production and consumption
levels in the developed world. It would also mean much less
willingness to protect uneconomic endangered species, ecology, and
the environment. Even a modified version of most resource limit
positions requires radical and immediate changes that would not
favor many of the shibboleths of "the environment" and "the
ecology." No genuinely poor society would even consider putting
aside 100,000,000 acres in Alaska or otherwise worry about preserving
in perpetuity pristine wildernesses almost equal to France in area, a
proposal that almost passed the U.S. Congress in 1978 and that remains very alive.

A fundamental tenet of modern Western culture until recently has
been that the secular trend of technological and industrial progress
will lead to better standards of living and a better quality of life for
more and more people. The anti-growth movement challenges this
concept. The idea of progress goes back about two or three hundred
years and is thus a relatively new idea in human affairs. There is no
overwhelming *a priori* reason to believe that it is necessarily correct.
Still, the concept became so firmly embedded in Western culture that
as recently as the mid-1960s, historians and social scientists believed
that the commitment to economic and technological progress was
virtually unchallengeable. After World War II the commitment was
globally recognized under the banner of the "revolution of rising
expectations." Few countries in the world have consciously and
explicitly resisted economic and technological progress as too
destructive of old and valued institutions and traditions.*

The belief that progress is inevitable and generally beneficial has
come to be considered as a "natural" world view. It is rarely regarded
as an artificial philosophy or ideology, except by the limits-to-growth
movement. We agree with the historian Sidney Pollard that:

> The idea of progress is, in this modern age, one of the most important
> ideas by which men live, not least because most hold it unconsciously
> and therefore unquestionably. It has been called the modern religion,

*Burma and Nepal are two exceptions. While China under Mao put ideology
ahead of economics in theory and practice, material progress was a high
second priority. In almost all other countries, at least lip service was paid to
economic development. We briefly discuss post-Mao developments in China
in Chapter 7.

and not unjustly so. Its character, its assumptions, have changed with time, and so has the influence exerted by it, but at present it is riding high, affecting the social attitudes and social actions of all of us.[4]

The Nature of the Challenge

Challenges to the concept of progress are not new. What is new is the effectiveness of today's challenge and its broad support by the upper-middle class and professional elites. These groups have an essentially modern outlook, have benefited most from technology and industrialization, and presumably understand and appreciate the modern industrial world. In the past, challenges to modernity have come from romantics, reactionaries, aristocrats, aesthetes, and various religious and ideological groups. Many of these people, too, have jumped on the Club of Rome bandwagon.[5] However, the basic impetus for the campaign against economic growth still comes from "modern," "progressive," and "enlightened" individuals and groups with much greater than average education and affluence.

The various attacks on and negative prognoses about current capitalist industrial cultures encompass many themes, old and new, most of which have some validity. The list below gives a sense of the variety of perspectives that the anti-growth movement draws upon to rationalize, exploit, and promulgate its message.

    I. Those who argue that the capitalist industrial culture is now historically obsolete and is or soon will be due for the trash heap of history:
- A. Older Marx, Lenin, old left generally
- B. Younger Marx, Marcuse, Reich, Revel, new left or humanist left generally
- C. Keynes (effect of affluence via compound interest)
- D. Schumpeter (the failure of success)
- E. Modern post-industrial formulations
  - 1. Some views of the service economy and knowledge society
  - 2. Maslow/Reich self-actualizing society
  - 3. Our view of some possible quaternary cultures
- F. Many macro-historicist prognoses (Spengler, Toynbee, Sorokin, etc.)

   II. Some miscellaneous traditional critiques:
- A. Anti-bourgeois/secular humanist criticism
- B. Reformist-welfare/humanist/conservationist groups
- C. Heroic/religious critique

      D. Technocratic/socialist/central planner critique
III. Other more modern critiques:
      A. The Galbraithian institutionalization analysis
      B. Arguments and perspectives based on the liberal crisis
      C. Moral deterioration possibility
      D. "Future Shock" thesis
      E. Zero growth/"anti-progress"/pollution/ecology perspective

For many people the anti-growth arguments prove the evils or impending collapse of the capitalist and private enterprise way of life. People who already believe, for other reasons, that the current system is wrong welcome supporting evidence from these new perspectives. Most of the diverse limits-to-growth arguments provide what purports to be "scientific evidence" for reforming our ways and reversing current trends. The combination of many disparate points of view strengthens opposition to growth. As a result, during the last decade the anti-growth syndrome has become dominant among intellectuals and educated elites all over the world, especially in the Affluent countries.

It is too early to judge the ultimate effect of this movement. However, unless the level and quality of the discussion of the issues is improved, the potential for ill is great. The recent recession has forced some re-evaluation of the future of economic development, but the reappraisal has been surprisingly incomplete. One explicit purpose of this book is to understand and promote the pro-growth position. We will, however, also give information on all sides of those issues about which we have anything useful to say.

The Gap Between the Rich and the Poor

Our basic context for worldwide economic growth is set forth in the following pages. Unlike others who discuss the popular concept of the "widening gap" between the rich and the poor, we focus on the positive aspects of the gap. The increasing disparity between average incomes in the richest and poorest nations is usually seen as an unalloyed evil to be overcome as rapidly as possible through enlightened policies by the advanced nations and international organizations. If this occurred because the poor were getting poorer, we would agree, but when it occurs at all, it is almost always because the rich are getting richer. This is not necessarily a bad thing for the poor, at least if they compare themselves with their own past or their own present rather than with a mythical theoretical gap.

In contrast, we view this gap as a basic "engine" of growth. It generates or supports most of the basic processes by which the poor are becoming rich, or at least less poor.[6] The great abundance of resources of the developed world—capital, management, technology, and large markets in which to sell—makes possible the incredibly rapid progress of most of the developing countries. Many of these poorer countries are also developing relatively autonomous capabilities at an increasing rate.

Current attitudes toward the gap illustrate the world view of many modern liberals. The dramatic increase in the disparity of per capita income between the wealthiest and poorest nations would have been a cause for self-congratulation by the fortunate wealthy nations at an earlier time in history—whether Roman, Greek, Chinese, or Indian. Indeed, when the colonial powers expanded their dominion, their affluence was largely accepted by all parties as a sign of their inherent superiority. Today, however, it is more a source of guilt than of pride for descendants of those same high morale colonialists. Yet such guilt is even less justified today than a hundred years ago.

It is still not widely understood that in light of eventual modernization colonial rule was likely to produce more advantages than disadvantages. Moreover, in much (but not all) of the Third World, the European expansion was more just and humane than most previous conquests by expanding cultures. Without condoning the evils of colonialism, one can nonetheless say that conquest is not an international crime invented by the European peoples. The poverty that exists in the Third World was not caused by European colonization, nor can the current problems of the Poor nations be solved by fostering a sense of guilt in the Rich nations. The affluent minority of humanity has a genuine responsibility to aid the poor, but largesse dispensed because of guilt is likely to produce counterproductive and self-righteous expectations and attitudes in developing countries.

The modern liberal view holds that an international system that perpetuates inequalities among nations is morally unacceptable. This attitude is indelibly Western in origin and is most prevalent among citizens of what we call the Atlantic Protestant culture area.*

---

*Scandinavia, Holland, United Kingdom, United States, Canada, Australia, and New Zealand.

As an enlightened modern American, the author has some sympathy with this view but does not expect that a relatively egalitarian world can be achieved in the near future either through violence or through an outpouring of generosity by the advanced countries.

It is one thing to wish the world were a better place, and quite another to make it happen in the very near future. World leaders who proclaim that closing the gap between the rich and poor countries is the most urgent task of our times should ask themselves how this can be done. This alluring goal simply cannot be approached, much less attained, in the next 100 years. The gap might close for the most rapidly developing countries, but from a practical standpoint, the arithmetic gap will almost surely widen for most of humanity. To anyone who assays the problem with a modicum of seriousness, this conclusion is virtually inescapable.

Actually, the world is doing a lot better than most people realize. Table 2.2 shows the current state of the world, with the countries of the world divided into three broad groups. Two of these groups, Communist Asia and the Middle Income countries, are about as rich as or richer than almost any society before the Industrial Revolution. Therefore, by historical standards, we have to think of them as Affluent. Nevertheless, by the standards of today, or at least by the standards of the Rich countries today, they do not appear to be wealthy at all but rather to be low income. If a country is Rich by the standards of the Poor and Poor by the standards of the Rich one is almost driven to the terminology Middle Income. We have, therefore, chosen this term. We think of the countries in Communist Asia as being on the border between the Poor and Middle Income countries, but normally we will include them in the Middle Income category. In any case, one can argue that almost half the world's population now lives in countries that have progressed enormously in acquiring wealth and have done so almost completely since World War II.

The progress since World War II has been most heartening. If we had written this book in 1950 we would have been forced to concede that there was no serious evidence that affluence was spreading from the West to other nations, with the possible exceptions of Japan and the Soviet Union. Even in those two countries, the standards of living were in fact low (about equal to the average of the Middle Income countries today). Furthermore, in 1950 there was a genuine question about Japan's ability to recover from World War II. The conventional prognosis was that Japan would become a huge Asian slum. As far as we can discover, nobody predicted anything close to what actually happened. Today, on the basis of the enormous progress during what

TABLE 2.2
Population Distribution among Country Groups

		Population (in billions)		Population (in billions)	Income Per Capita
Poor Countries	1.25 billion (29% of world)	{	Very Poor	1/4	$ 130
			Coping Poor	1.0	300
Middle Income Countries	2.0 billion (47% of world)	{	Communist Asia	1.0	500
			Transitional	1/2	500
			Mostly Developed	1/2	1,500
Affluent Countries	1.0 billion (24% of world)	{	Affluent Communist	1/3	4,000
			Affluent Market-Oriented (includes oil-rich)	2/3	8,000

Note: All sums are in "1978 dollars" (i.e., 2/3 of a 1972 dollar or 4/9 of a 1958 dollar). The percentages of 29, 47, and 24 given above are excessively precise but are reasonable estimates; the picture given is not misleading. However, one should note that there are many poor people living in Middle Income, and even some Affluent countries—and some Middle Income and Rich people live in the Poor countries.

we later call *La Deuxième Belle Epoque* (1948 to 1973), we must conclude that economic development is simply not a unique product of the West. Indeed, we will argue in later chapters that what we call the neo-Confucian cultures of Asia are actually better at economic development than the traditional Western cultures.

The Middle Income countries generally, and the neo-Confucian countries in particular, are in many cases closing the gap with the Rich countries, but this is usually ignored in most discussions. When people talk about "the gap" they are usually now talking about the gap between the 25 percent of the world that is Rich and the 30 percent that is Poor. This gap could only be closed in the near future by a massive reduction in the affluence of the developed countries and perhaps of the Middle Income countries as well. Over the next few decades capital investment would have to be shifted to the poorest of the Poor countries. The bulk of capital and consumer goods (except for bare necessities, produced in the developed countries) would have to be exported from the developed to the developing nations. If some of our conjectures are correct, something like this may happen to some degree as a result of "natural" forces. However, no political system is sufficiently totalitarian to deliberately and intensively implement such a program on a worldwide scale nor would any sensible people wish to do so.

If such a program could be put into effect, we doubt if it would lead, even in a generation, to the attainment of Western housing standards and educational levels in, say, Bangladesh, as measured by the drastically depressed standards that the West would then have. In short, the most commonly expressed economic goal—"closing the gap"—is absurd as a realistic world goal for the rest of the twentieth century. Moreover, the decrease or elimination of absolute poverty is clearly a higher priority task than the reduction of relative poverty. Maintaining, or even increasing the gap, may be the best way to accomplish this. As President Kennedy once said, "A rising tide floats all ships."

We do not expect anything comparable to the current large gaps to be the final outcome of the present world system, even given the presently widening gaps. To the contrary, we expect the gap in per capita income to be greatly lessened in a historically short period of time—100 or 200 years. This will occur so rapidly precisely because of the wide and still growing gap. The greater the difference in relative income between the Rich and the Poor countries, the greater the ability of the Poor countries to "take off" and the greater their potential growth rate. Rather than being a measurement of the basic problem, the widening gap is in reality a force for transferring the benefits of economic development to the poor. Once economic development starts, the gap facilitates it. As a result, many countries above the lowest levels have been experiencing very rapid growth; for them, the relative gap has declined.

The most that realistically could be achieved in the next decade or two would be to reduce the *rate* at which the gap is *widening*—hardly an inspiring goal. Should we actually set out to achieve it, the most likely result would be to delay the time when the Poor nations would become economically fully developed—and even more important, to delay a dramatic decrease in absolute poverty that now seems likely to occur during the next fifty years.

Our argument is summarized in Tables 2.3 and 2.4. Table 2.3 lists the basic theses and Table 2.4 indicates two groups of issues that face humanity and describes our knowledge of these issues. Nine issues are relatively understandable, and thus presumably surmountable or soluble; ten involve basic uncertainties and thus are potentially disastrous. We are convinced that the first group of issues is well enough understood to justify confidence in moving ahead. We obviously do not know everything we would like to know about them, hence the small question marks scattered among the check marks. The situation is similar to when President Kennedy committed the United States to a moon landing within ten years. We basically knew how to do it, but it took about $10 billion of research, development, tests, and evaluation to resolve the "details." The problems with economic growth are much more serious and the uncertainties greater. Many surprises and many difficulties will be encountered, but probably none that cannot be dealt with—at least not if they are largely in these nine areas.

The second group of issues, even with reasonably good management and luck, may still involve great potential for disaster. These ten issues are the most important now facing humanity. If they cannot be resolved successfully, it will be little consolation to know that the first nine can be. However, the first set rather than the second has generated most of the public controversy, discussion, and agitation in the developed world in recent years. We believe that these nine issues should not be treated as vehicles for crusades and rhetoric, but rather as technical and cultural problems to be handled in a professional or workmanlike manner. The emotion expended on these solvable issues is mostly wasted or counterproductive. The present volume, therefore, mainly addresses some of the ten more poorly comprehended issues.

TABLE 2.3
The Great Transition

A POSITIVE AND
REALISTIC IMAGE
OF HUMANITY'S
EARTH TREK

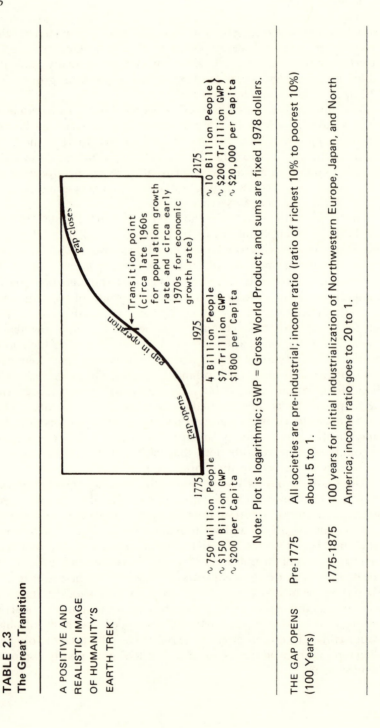

Note: Plot is logarithmic; GWP = Gross World Product; and sums are fixed 1978 dollars.

THE GAP OPENS (100 Years)	Pre-1775	All societies are pre-industrial; income ratio (ratio of richest 10% to poorest 10%) about 5 to 1.
	1775-1875	100 years for initial industrialization of Northwestern Europe, Japan, and North America; income ratio goes to 20 to 1.

TABLE 2.3 *(Cont.)*

THE GAP IN OPERATION (150 Years)	1875-1950	Emergence of mass consumption societies in Europe, Japan, and North America and start of worldwide industrialization.
	1950-1975	Most rapid economic and population growth in history; initial emergence of super-industrial economies,[a] technological crises, and many historic transitions, e.g., inflection points in world population and perhaps gross product curves (also first steps into space).
	1975-2000	Continued rapid growth in middle income countries but less so for rich countries; reduction in gap between rich and middle income countries.
	2000-2025	Emergence of post-industrial economies in most Western cultures, Japan, and perhaps USSR. Full development of super-industrial cultures and societies in advanced countries. First signs of a worldwide maturing economy. First serious moves to colonize space. Income ratio of 200 to 1.
THE GAP CLOSES (150 Years?)	2025-2175	Worldwide slowing down in population and economic growth rates (not only in percent but also in absolute numbers). As a result, it takes almost 150 years for emergence of post-industrial economies almost everywhere. (Perhaps also the establishment of an in-dependent solar system society.) Income ratios (on earth) 40 to 1 or less—perhaps much less.
	Post-2175	Post-industrial society stabilizes, ossifies, or the next development in humanity emerges.

[a]We distinguish among economy, institutions, culture, and society as follows: Economy—economic and technological activity; Institutions—laws and organizations; Culture—style, values, national character and attitudes; Society—the whole. Super-industrial economy refers to large size and scale of modern enterprise and the importance of its impact on the external social and physical environment. Post-industrial economy refers to a future very affluent economy that meets its industrial and materials needs with a small percent of its work force and economic effort. Presumably first the economy emerges, then the institutions, the culture, and finally a harmonious society.

TABLE 2.4
Two Kinds of Issues Facing Mankind

1. *Nine mostly understandable (and, presumably, surmountable) issues*

(These issues are at the center of current controversies and are thus very troublesome for the present and the immediate future. However, we believe there is—or could be—a surprisingly large consensus about their shape and possible solution. Thus, the current debate is misleading, and drains off intellectual energies that could better be devoted to the great issues below. At the same time much current discussion discourages practical steps by assuming their inadequacy. An effort should therefore be made to articulate this consensus and demonstrate the likely feasibility of solutions so that the issues can be addressed with higher morale and greater competency and, at the same time, more attention be given to the truly difficult issues of the future.)

1. Likelihood of peak in percent rate of growth of world population and GWP occurring and of the slowdown in rate of growth being caused more by "natural" limitation of demand than by shortage of supplies and space or by pollution.

2. Various demographic, locational, and income issues that occur during the transition.

3. Providing an adequate supply of food.

4. Transition from fossil fuels to "eternal" sources of energy.

5. Expanding base or capability for other resources.

6. Pollution, ecological, and environmental programs to provide clean air, clean water, and aesthetic landscapes.

7. An important and exciting role for space and advanced technology.

8. "Surprise-free" partial images of the future, including the likely emergence of first the super- and then the post-industrial economies.

9. The extraordinary capability and flexibility associated with coming levels of affluence and advanced technology.

TABLE 2.4 *(Cont.)*

2. *Ten poorly comprehended (and potentially disastrous) issues*

    (These are the great issues of the future. What they will be in general terms is sometimes clear, sometimes not; in any case the exact shape they will take, the degree of danger and problems involved, the opportunities presented, and the solutions required are terribly unclear.)

    1. Actual role for good or evil of science and advanced technology.
    2. Effects of bad luck and bad management.
    3. Effects of U.S. super-industrial economy on environment, society, and culture of U.S., and the world.
    4. Effects of U.S. post-industrial economy on environment, society, and culture of U.S., and the world.
    5. Parallel developments in other countries—including the likely dynamics of economic and technological development within and among various nations. We can group nations initially in seven categories (numbers in parentheses are millions of people): 1. Desperately Poor (215); 2. Coping Poor (950); 3. Communist Asia (925); 4. Transitional Society (500); 5. Mostly Developed (350); 6. Communist Europe (385); 7. "Capitalist Affluent" (675).
    6. Popular and Elite images of the present and future of these groups (by themselves and others) and the likely problems and opportunities caused by these images.
    7. Other issues relating to quality of life, attitudes, values, morals, morale, and cultural change for the above groups.
    8. Subsequent internal and external political, institutional, strategic and arms control issues, and control of violence generally.
    9. Complicated, complex, and subtle ecological and environmental issues.
    10. Stabilization or reversal of the long-term Multifold Trend of Western culture toward a sensate society—or its replacement by new sources of meaning and purpose.

Asymptotic (or S-shaped) versus Exponential Growth

In *The Next 200 Years*[7] we posited a somewhat more difficult situation than we thought would actually happen. We projected a world population in the twenty second century of almost fifteen billion people with a gross world product (in 1978 dollars) of almost $400 trillion. We now suggest what we believe are more realistic projections for one or two centuries hence: about 10 billion people and a gross world product of about $200 trillion. Our purpose in setting forth both projections was to have a picture of the long term, not so much because we expect the future world actually to resemble either image, but because we need to conjure up a sense of where current trends may lead.

We agree with those I call neo-Malthusians that growth will be limited. However, we have both fundamental and technical differences with their view. The basic premise of the neo-Malthusians' position is so simple and persuasive as to seem almost self-evident: The world's finite resources must eventually be depleted; the only question is how soon this will happen. Their model assumes a fixed pie confronting an exponentially growing demand. Growth is assumed to continue at roughly current rates until it runs into disastrous physical constraints.

If one accepts this, then the dangers posed by continuing growth are obviously great. However big the pie, it is being eaten. Even if the end point cannot be predicted precisely, an end is nevertheless inevitable. Furthermore, as the Club of Rome studies point out, when you are dealing with exponentials, the time available can rapidly become surprisingly short. Using up resources today means fewer are available for the poor today, and for everyone tomorrow. Even if one were firmly convinced that the thesis is wrong, the neo-Malthusian position should not be dismissed as unworthy of serious discussion. To do so would be like dismissing a religion or ideology that was sweeping the country merely because one did not accept its doctrine. Polls indicate that two-thirds of the American people have been strongly influenced by the neo-Malthusian view and share many of its tenets.[8]

We reject the fixed pie metaphor and argue that it is much more useful to think of the world's resources as a process or system for creating and exploiting various kinds of assets and using them in many different ways. Such a process is similar to a muscle; the more you use or exercise it, the stronger it gets and the more work it can do. While a muscle is finite and does not last forever if abused—and can even become damaged—it is much better to use the muscle prudently than to leave it idle.

This process has, of course, been happening over the years. The world has continually found not only new resources, but new kinds of resources and new ways to extract and use them. New technology, for example, has made it possible to exploit off-shore and Arctic oil supplies. Secondary and tertiary recovery from existing wells and production of oil from shale and tar sands are feasible and likely to become commercially viable. These resources may never be used because the world may turn to new sources of energy in much the same way that it shifted from wood to coal and from coal to oil. Indeed, a capability for transition to eternal and renewable sources of fuel in the twenty-first century can be predicted rather confidently, even though sufficient fossil fuels are available to last at least two centuries.[9] New sources and new kinds of resources arise from expanding use, not from standing still.

The basic question is how far this process can go. How much can our "resource muscle" be used without becoming abused? This depends partly on rates of growth and development of new technologies. It now seems clear that our known resources, even employing only *current* (or near current) technology, would be sufficient for many centuries to meet much more than even the relatively extreme levels of demands we posited. Within two or three decades new technologies will be developed so that the posited world of 10 billion people and 200 trillion dollars GWP (World A below) can be maintained forever. Furthermore, *all currently perceived and understood* problems of pollution could be dealt with, assuming reasonable management of the world's economies.

It is only because we are able to confidently make such strong statements—much stronger than we had envisaged when we started this study—that we are comfortable with the conclusion that resources and pollution are not likely, by themselves, to constitute crucial constraints on continued rapid economic growth. Instead, growth will taper off because of slackening demand, changed values, and changed attitudes. The latter constraint is now called, by ourselves as well as by our critics, *social limits to growth*, although we imply something quite different by this phrase than do most who use it.

It is a commonplace that few growth curves in nature can be exponential or "geometric" for very long. They tend instead to follow the so-called logistic or S shape, as illustrated by the two solid lines in Figure 2.1.

FIGURE 2.1
Alternate Futures

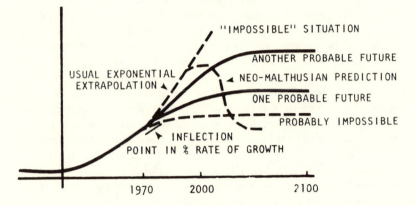

If there were no social limits to growth, humanity might well have continued the recent growth rates of 2 percent for population and 5 percent for GNP for many decades, perhaps even a century. The numbers then become truly mind-boggling, as Table 2.5 shows.

Figure 2.1 and Table 2.5 illustrate the heart of our disagreement with many current analyses. It is clear if one looks at a naive exponential growth picture such as the one given in Table 2.5, the world could get into trouble quite rapidly, especially if one assumes a constant growth rate to the year 2200. Nobody believes that the population of the world is then going to be 340 billion people, the gross product $500 quadrillion, and the per capita income $1,500,000. (Incidentally, we are in no sense prepared to say that those figures are actually impossible. Technology is such that it would not surprise us if, in fact, it was feasible. We just do not care. We and everybody else would be terribly frightened if this were a serious prospect.)*

The alternative that people usually assume is neo-Malthusian collapse. They then make a recommendation corresponding to the dotted line we call "Probably Impossible," which in effect says, "Try to stop the thing dead right now or even reduce the current situation."

---

*This issue provides the first of many examples of what we call educated incapacity. "Serious" studies have been done that assume, implicitly or explicitly, 5 percent growth for two centuries and then conclude that we will thus exceed the carrying capacity of the earth. In effect, these studies first concluded that the world could not accept a factor of 10 or 20,000 increase in the use of resources and then cried an alarm about *today's* use of resources.

TABLE 2.5
What If "Exponential" Growth of Population Continues at 2 Percent Per Year and GWP at 5 Percent Per Year?

	1975	Naive Extrapolation					Our Guess for Peaking Out
		2000	2025	2050	2100	2200	
World population (in billions of people)	4.0	6.5	11	18	48	340	10
Gross World Product (in trillions of 1978 dollars)	7.5	25	85	290	3,400	500,000	200
GWP/CAP (in thousands of 1978 dollars)	1.9	4	8	16	70	1,500	20

We suggest that very little analysis has been done on a world with 10 billion people, $20,000 per capita income, and $200 trillion gross product—a world we think of as perhaps "the most probable situation." It is at least surprise-free. And we believe that very little ingenuity soon demonstrates that as far as we know today this kind of a world does not present us with any extraordinarily difficult technological or economic problems, given reasonably good management. We tentatively conclude that even if the management is not good but not really bad, we could probably get from here to there, not necessarily smoothly and perhaps with a lot of tragedy on the way. However, one does not decrease the probability of tragedy by trying to rein in growth rapidly or forcibly. We presume that far and away the safest, most normal and reasonable path is to go along with what might be thought of as the "natural" path, where natural forces do the slowing down, not government programs. Obviously there are some places in the world—Latin America is probably one and India and China are probably others—where government programs designed to encourage population limitation are good things. The crucial methodological point is to stop thinking in terms of exponential curves but rather in terms of the so-called S-shaped curves discussed in the appendix.

This is definitely *not* to argue that resources should be wasted (although differing definitions of waste are possible) or that population and economic growth can continue unabated at current rates. The Club of Rome has correctly concluded that great caution is necessary because major problems lie ahead, some of which may require worldwide cooperation—or at least coordination of policies—to solve. If a higher degree of genuine cooperation were necessary, the problems might turn out to be insoluble. Our basic differences with the Club of Rome are over the underlying nature of the problems, their urgency and timing, how to deal with them, and the likely prognoses. While various forced and induced limitations on human activities will have important and even essential roles, these roles are still very limited and directed more to quality of life issues than to vital issues of survival. (As we get richer we desire and can afford cleaner air, cleaner water, and more aesthetic landscapes.)

Our belief, developed in *The Next 200 Years*, that there will be a turndown in the long-term rate of economic growth in the United States and in the world, does not stem from any fear of lack of energy or other resources or of inability to cope with pollution. These could eventually cause a slowdown, but it seemed to us then, as it does now, overwhelmingly likely that long before such physical constraints set serious limits on either population or economic growth, social and cultural factors would effectively intervene. The physical factors were almost irrelevant in practice. The system simply does not get very close to these limits. We also believe that these cultural and social factors are, on the whole, more or less "natural" and probably inevitable. However, as a policy matter, we argue that most of them should be at least slightly discouraged rather than enthusiastically encouraged so as to defer the time for the growth rate to turn down and also to diminish the rate at which the slowing down occurs. Specifically, we believe that any attempt to save non-renewable world resources just so that the grandchildren will not be deprived is almost laughably foolish—an example of educated incapacity rather than a manifestation of an intelligent concern for the grandchildren. (This does not apply to such things as wilderness areas and endangered species, although here too we believe that some excessive programs are being pursued.)

The key point is that the ability to handle the problems of the future will be aided much more than hurt by increasing the world's wealth and technological capabilities. Such increases will permit more flexibility and effectiveness. A wealthy society can afford more costly processes. It can cope with most of its problems and still build surpluses to insure against foreseen and unforeseen contingencies. It seems paradoxical to many people that the very problems that have been created by wealth and technology can also be solved by them, but this is not a genuine paradox. When one has wealth and technology without worrying about how to use them, problems are created. But the moment that serious concern arises over their actual and potential uses, the problems can usually be alleviated or prevented.

Technical solutions are generally more effective than strong limitations. For example, new cars coming off the assembly lines today generally produce about ten percent of the emissions that cars did in the late 1960s. It would be difficult to do anything equally effective simply by demanding limitations. Of course, it will take at least another ten years to replace the current car population with new models, but this is about as rapid as realities permit. And the future should bring even more effective designs, probably not using current types of combustion engines. By the end of the century, we expect to see the introduction of largely pollution-free transportation systems.

Many people who are concerned with the future see rapid population growth as the world's most pressing problem. Currently, the population is continuing to increase because the declines in birth rates that occur with industrialization and urbanization lag several decades behind declines in death rates. There is now fairly widespread agreement that this will lead to a population of about six billion by the end of the century, and almost everyone agrees that it is desirable for world population growth rates to top out soon. There is, however, little agreement on the maximum feasible world population limits.* Various methods of controlling birth rates are proving increasingly effective, but they may not be sufficient for the near future. To date, however, virtually every country that has industrialized and urbanized has also experienced reduced population growth. It therefore seems reasonable to expect that the faster the world develops economically, the faster population growth rates are likely to decline. From many points of view, they may have already declined too much in the developed countries. It should not be forgotten that different areas of the world have different problems, most of which will have to

---

*This is also a central issue. If one assumes that a crisis stage is reached at a world population of six billion or so, then there is clearly not enough time to rely on economic growth as the ultimate solution. However, there is little evidence that this assumption is correct. Nevertheless, we favor government encouraged birth control programs in mainland China, south and southeast Asia, and much of Africa and Latin America. Unless they prove much more effective in the future, such programs are unlikely to be a solution in themselves. A reasonable guess is that increased wealth and urbanization from continued economic growth are the keys. Also, it is hard to find persuasive arguments (as judged by most people) that the developed nations should, on the whole, pursue more stringent population limitations than they currently do. We are adherents of a *laissez-faire* policy, but if we advocated any policy at all, in many of these countries it would be to maintain or increase current birth rates.

be dealt with by the people most directly affected.

We believe, for example, that it is perfectly possible to have a world population of ten billion people one or two centuries hence that will not produce urban densities too high to be tolerable as judged by most current value systems and that will allow plenty of space for all needed activities.[10] While we have no idea of what the technology, wealth, values, and histories of the various areas of the world would be, we believe that life-or-death resource or population problems are unlikely to occur in any wealthy and technologically advanced nation.

From this perspective, the often-cited experiments with rats in a cage are irrelevant. It is true that rodent neuroses, illnesses, and aggressions build up rapidly when the density of rats is increased. But the issue of strain among human beings is much more closely related to the floor space per individual and the number of rooms per family than to the mathematical concept of the number of individuals per square mile. Since floor space and numbers of rooms can be made almost as large as one desires by multi-level buildings, the density problem can be dealt with readily.

If current trends are at all applicable it furthermore seems unlikely that future cities will approach the densities that were common in ancient walled cities. Classical Rome, for example, had more than 50,000 inhabitants per square mile; such modern cities as Paris also have more than 50,000 persons per square mile; and in the east side of Manhattan about fifty years ago, there were more than 100,000 persons per square mile. Unless for some reason the cultures concerned choose to build very densely settled cities, we do not expect any city of the year 2000 to reach these densities.

When people talk about conurbations or megalopoli, they mean the tendency of relatively high density areas around different cities to blend into a kind of supercity. However, it is very important to realize that most of these will resemble Westchester County more than Manhattan or Brooklyn. This county, in which the Hudson Institute is located, has about two thousand people per square mile and is generally considered one of the best places to live in the United States. It has several cities, including the large one of White Plains, but despite the population density basically the setting is rural-suburban. Although Westchester is considered part of the New York metropolitan area, few people driving around in the county would think of it as highly urbanized; yet it is. Most of the blacked-in areas set forth on maps showing the degree of urbanization in the United States are less densely settled than Westchester County.

On the other hand, some very large areas in such countries as India and China are likely to have quite high population densities—

though very likely not as great as Rome, Paris, or the east side of New York City. If future builders or authorities are at all ingenious and creative, these enormous conglomerations of human beings can have many advantages as well as drawbacks. The difficulties are obvious— e.g., most intra- and inter-urban movement will have to depend on mass transport, with private vehicles severely limited. However, enormous numbers of human beings make possible really satisfactory mass transport (e.g., with convenient, high frequency, 24-hour schedules) of various sorts and all kinds of other specialized facilities for a simple reason: these services will have plenty of customers, especially since living standards will be much higher than they are now.

But there are other difficulties. All of the open green spaces will have to be planned. Sparsely used recreation areas will be relatively distant. Presumably, some will want to get away from the mass of humanity—or they may be like the Japanese, who seem to like crowds. Indeed, these cultures will probably not produce people who will feel much pressure to get away from one another. These people will not be the traditional "teeming poor" of past Chinese or current Indian cities. They will instead have standards comparable to European living standards of today, even if they have lower (as may well happen) living standards than their contemporary European or "overseas" cultures. Surely such a projected future would be a great improvement over the current situation for all but some current elites and some other groups which are especially well-off today. Even if many citizens of the Advanced Capitalist nations would not like these huge Asian conurbations, the main issue is how the people concerned will feel about it. We would guess that they may feel very good.

In the balance of this chapter we turn to a more systematic and detailed presentation of some of the basic Hudson Institute scenarios and images of the future. These go beyond the specific issues of income level or population density discussed above to consider alternative possibilities under various conditions of growth for life styles, political systems, and patterns of international order.

THE FUTURE: SCENARIOS AND IMAGES

Chapter 1 examined certain aspects of the past and various theories of history to sense how the world might develop in the future. An extensive scholarly and popular literature on future prospects has informed a fairly broad worldwide public about much of the good or bad that the future may bring. However, with some important exceptions, this literature does not explore what we consider to be the most important socio-political and economic issues. Therefore, we will continue our "more or less agnostic use of concepts and information" and consider "artificial history" in the form of scenarios and more or less arbitrary contexts. In particular, we discuss how one might formulate images and scenarios for the short, medium, and long-term future of world economic development. We hope not only to improve our own discussion but also to encourage the more general and more appropriate use of scenarios and special contexts. (In Chapter 8 we discuss how private and public groups might use them, and some of their possible uses in planning and public information programs.)

Many groups already use these techniques. Indeed, in the last two decades the word *scenario* has become ubiquitous.[11] However, the deliberate formulation of long-term scenarios and other images of the future has usually been left to groups with political, ideological, or commercial interests—or to those just seeking entertainment. Thus, their results may be misleading or at least inappropriate for many of the purposes that interest us.

In addition, a fair number of scenarios display much "religious art," ideological nonsense, and what Daniel Bell has called "future schlock." Nonetheless, socioeconomic scenarios and scenario contexts can be useful. We would like to facilitate the process of developing them both by encouraging the use of specific scenarios and by making scenario writing easier, more unified, more systematic, and more creative and imaginative where appropriate. Some of the lack of interest in economic development today and the indifference or hostility to the impressive economic achievements of what both we and the *Economist* have called the NICs (New Industrial Countries) reflects ignorance and incomprehension of how exciting and beneficial these successes are and will be for the citizens of those countries and others as well.* This is true even if

---

*The *London Economist* listed eleven countries as NICs, including Brazil, South Korea, Taiwan, Spain, Portugal, and Greece. The reader might note that all six were under widespread political criticism and attack while they were accomplishing their "economic miracles." The first three are more or less still under attack. By American and most European standards, all six did have relatively oppressive political systems. But this was equally true of most of the other countries of the world—including many that were more or less directly comparable to the NICs. Therefore, one could argue that since these six countries were doing great things for the future, and even the present, of most of their people, and were not by and large much worse politically than most other countries in the world (even if not much better either), they should have been more praised and admired, or at least the good should have been balanced against the bad. It was relatively rare to find such balancing during

these "economic miracles" are flawed in various ways.

A similar situation has arisen recently about the possibilities of advanced technology. The dominant emphasis or fashion is on negative aspects and negative prospects and disasters. Yet today's many troubling issues and concerns should not overwhelm the promise that technology also holds for good.

The historical record shows that imaginative medium and long-term images of the future have often helped create such fashions—or the opposite.* But they can also place current priorities, problems, issues, or controversies into a more balanced and clearer perspective and provide useful and stimulating contexts for examining them. Shared images of the future can also contribute to a sense of community and nationality and can help create a sense of institutional meaning and purpose. In sum, they can create unity, commitment, high morale, and even a sense of manifest destiny or religious mission.

Such goals, however, should be pursued cautiously. The appearance or reality of fanaticism, trendy fashions, "pie in the sky" hopes, or other illusionary concepts can be counterproductive. Appropriate images, on the other hand, can be useful and inspiring. Plausible and exciting—or even just realistic—ten to fifty year projections may have desirable effects on day-to-day planning or short-term programs for many developing nations. The same is also true for realistic disaster scenarios—scenarios all wish to avoid.

The Basic Quantitative Scenario-Context (World A)

We are going to limit ourselves initially to what we call a surprise-free scenario. That is, we would not be surprised if something like this

---

the late 1960s or early 1970s. We will defer further discussion of these issues to Chapters 6 and 8.

The other five NICs were Mexico, Turkey, Yugoslavia, Singapore, and Hong Kong. While these were much less criticized, none of them, with the possible exception of Hong Kong, has the kind of constitutional guarantees and parliamentary institutions taken for granted in many Western countries as normal and universally applicable.

*It is not generally realized that Rachel Carson's *Silent Spring* (Boston: Houghton-Mifflin, 1962) is "only a scenario" and in no sense a serious analysis or projection of what was happening in 1962. The Club of Rome studies of both the Forrester and Meadows groups, would have been much more appropriately described—and used—as imaginative catastrophe scenarios than as serious projections.

scenario did not happen for the next decade or two, and perhaps even longer. We would be surprised if the world continued along the path suggested for several centuries.

We judge our scenario to be surprise-free, but that does not imply that it is probable. We could easily devise ten or twenty surprise-free scenarios, which implies that the probability of most of these scenarios is something less than .1 or .2. The world of the future is so rich in possibilities that many things could happen that would not surprise us. This is one of the major reasons why, unless they have some special interest, we do not examine systematically highly improbable or surprising events; there are simply too many to consider systematically. We always note when discussing surprise-free scenarios that "the most surprising thing that could happen would be no surprises." But there are so many ways in which surprises can occur that there is no possibility of investigating them systematically. Hence, the common criticism that organizations such as the Hudson Institute focus on surprise-free scenarios (even though they admit that surprises are inevitable) is a valid observation about a genuine weakness of these studies, but hardly a serious criticism of any specific study. We can do much to alleviate this problem, but whatever we do will be inadequate compared to what we would like.

We start with a basic and precise quantitative scenario that we call our "World A" or sometimes our "Guarded Optimism World," the context for much subsequent discussion. Our purpose is not to predict the future exactly, but to communicate exactly an image or a concept, even if we do not hold the image or concept as precisely as the specific numbers suggest. The scenario also supplies a precise framework that can be used as a backdrop for many issues or as a basis for elaborating concepts and possibilities.

We naturally wish to make our basic scenario for the future of the world correspond as closely as possible to the real world of 1978, the starting point of the scenario. The world is made up of many countries, each of which contributes its individual population and gross product to the world total. Thus we think of our world scenario as the sum of many country scenarios. For understanding, describing, and projecting the growth of countries as they enter into our world scenario we have found it especially useful and convenient to classify each country into one of six economic categories.[12] The figures in parentheses give the range of per capita gross (PCG) products included. The categories overlap to allow for some flexibility in assignment.

1. Very Poor (0-250)
2. Coping Poor (200-600)
3. Communist Asia (~ 500)*
4. Middle Income (400-4,000)†
5. Affluent Communist (~ 4,000)
6. Affluent Market-Oriented (3,500-10,000)‡

The above classifications are decided by the current levels of affluence of the countries concerned and also by our judgment of their likely immediate prospects.§ The six categories are described below.

1. Very Poor

Low income and no particular prospects of rapid growth (although in our Guarded Optimism World most of these countries do moderately well). The countries include about 250 million people and can be thought of, for the time being, as hard-core poor or at least as having severe development problems. Many of them have had declining levels of per capita income in the last few years. About one-third of the population (83 million) of the Very Poor category is in one country, Bangladesh. However, there are about twenty countries included in this category.

Most experts are now relatively negative about the prognoses of these Very Poor countries. Everybody recognizes that there is only a limited amount that the outside world can do for them. Basically, they have to pick themselves up by themselves, though outside aid can be quite helpful. The problem is similar to that of rehabilitating a

---

*The sign ~ means *approximately*.

†We sometimes divide this into two groups: Transitional (400-1,200) and Mostly Developed (1,000-4,000). We also sometimes include Communist Asia in an enlarged Middle Income group.

‡We could have called this category *Affluent Capitalist* or *Capitalist Affluent* but then the initials would have been the same as either category 5 or 3, respectively. Besides, *market-oriented* probably has a more accurate connotation for most of the countries concerned.

§In listing the countries in our six categories by geographic areas within each category, we include Mexico and the Central American and Caribbean countries in Latin America.

family that has resisted rehabilitation in the past—the prognosis is very poor.

We think the situation is not quite that bad in some of these countries. Some have had special problems in recent years (e.g., Bangladesh and Sri Lanka) that are much less intense now. In others, the quality of government has improved or seems likely to improve in the near future. Almost all now have so-called five year development plans, but most of them are just plans, not realistic programs. Indeed, some are more hopeful platitudes than serious programs. We assume in our Guarded Optimism World that this Very Poor group grows about 4 percent a year in gross product but does not slow down population growth rate very much (population grows by 2-1/3 percent). They therefore get a 1-1/3 percent increase in per capita income. This is not large, but is still optimistic, if not wildly so. There will be no great surprise if something like this happens, but there would be even less surprise if they did more poorly. These 250 million persons are about 6 percent of the world population, but they represent a most dramatic and serious problem, and perhaps a more strongly felt problem, than do the equally bad—and larger—pockets of poverty in the richer countries. The VP countries are: *Africa:* Benin, Burundi, Chad, Ethiopia, Guinea, Lesotho, Mali, Niger, Rwanda, Somalia, Upper Volta, and Zaire; *Asia and Middle East:* Afghanistan, Bangladesh, Bhutan, Burma, Maldives, and Nepal; *Latin America:* Haiti.

We estimate the above countries have a total gross product of about $40 billion, which is a little larger than World Bank figures, but might still be low if fully corrected for purchasing power.

2. Coping Poor

While quite poor, and with many problems, the Coping Poor countries also have assets and are indeed coping. As a result, they have reasonably good prospects in the medium or long-term future. They should average about 5 percent growth (3 percent per capita). This is much higher than their recent expansion but by no means impossible given a little luck and small improvement in management. India is a good example of one of these nations. Roughly two-thirds of the people classified as living in Coping Poor nations live in India. However, there are fourteen other countries in this category.

India is in many ways an industrial country. It has one of the largest railroad systems in the world and manufactures almost all of the parts and equipment needed for the railroad system. It has a large steel industry and has capabilities in such advanced technologies as computers, nuclear energy, and nuclear weapons. It cannot be regarded as a pre-industrial country. On the other hand, India is a Poor County, a condition that will probably persist for a long time. According to the *World Bank Atlas,* which used the average exchange rate of the last three years in making the calculations, India's per capita product is about $160. Other calculations that include the effects of internal prices and of non-market production and transactions estimate that the per capita product is more like $300.

The countries in this group: *Africa*: the Comoros Islands, Gambia, Kenya, Madagascar, Mauritania, Sudan, Tanzania, Uganda; *Middle East*: Yemen Arab Republic, Yemen People's Democratic Republic; *Asia*: India, Indonesia, Pakistan, Sri Lanka.

3. Communist Asia

Communist Asia, of course, consists mostly of the People's Republic of China, although we include Mongolia, North Korea, and the former states of Indochina (whose per capita income is much less than $500). Our estimate of about a billion people in Communist Asia in 1978 is well within the range of usual estimates, although slightly on the high side. (Taiwan is not included as part of the People's Republic of China, but is included in the next category as the Republic of China.)

4. Middle Income (or Capitalist Middle Income)

The Middle Income category includes a large range of nations, with a total population of about a billion. By historical standards, all of them are very affluent countries. However, by the standards of what we call the Affluent Market-Oriented countries, they are not well off. Hence the term Middle Income. If we use the *World Bank Atlas* for our estimates, their average income is very close to $1,000. Their growth rates vary enormously but tend to be between 5 and 10 percent. We will take 7 percent as a likely average for the near future, but expect a declining rate in the medium and long term. The assumption of an initial 7 percent is slightly optimistic, but the slowing-down assumption may be pessimistic for our Guarded Optimism World.

A little more than a third of the population of Middle Income nations live in the New Industrial Countries, sometimes called "Other Japans." The PCG of the New Industrial Countries is about $1,500. We expect this group to grow about 9 percent a year. The other two-thirds of the Middle Income population have about half of the PCG of the New Industrial Countries and about half their growth rate.

Rather than divide the Middle Income category into New

Industrial Countries and other Middle Incomes, we have sometimes found it useful to divide the Middle Income category into two subcategories we call Transitional and Mostly Developed. Each of these categories has roughly half a billion people. Mostly Developed includes most of the New Industrial Countries. The Transitional—the label perhaps reflects a certain amount of optimism—countries have substantially lower PCGs and expectations. The Mostly Developed Middle Income countries are: *Africa*: South Africa, Djibuti, Gabon; *Europe*: Spain, Greece, Portugal, Cyprus, Malta, Isle of Man, Gibraltar, Ireland, Albania, Bulgaria, Rumania, Yugoslavia; *Asia and Middle East*: Iran, Iraq, Hong Kong, Lebanon, Oman, Brunei, Singapore; *Latin America*: Mexico, Jamaica, Panama, Puerto Rico, Trinidad and Tobago, Guadeloupe, Barbados, Brazil, Argentina, Venezuela, Uruguay, Surinam, Netherlands Antilles; *Oceania*: American Samoa.

The Transitional Middle Income countries are: *Africa*: Nigeria, Egypt, Morocco, Algeria, Ghana, Mozambique, Cameroon, Rhodesia, Ivory Coast, Angola, Tunisia, Zambia, Senegal, Liberia, Lango, People's Republic of Botswana, Guinea-Bissau, Swaziland, Equatorial Guinea, Cape Verde Islands, Ceuta and Mellila, Sao Tome; *Asia and Middle East*: Mauritius, Seychelles Islands, Philippines, Thailand, South Korea, Malaysia, Syria, Republic of China (Taiwan), Jordan, Macao, Turkey; *Latin America*: Cuba, Guatemala, Dominican Republic, El Salvador, Honduras, Nicaragua, Costa Rica, Belize, St. Lucia, Grenada, Dominican Republic, Antigua, St. Kitts-Nevis-Anguilla, Colombia, Peru, Chile, Ecuador, Paraguay, Guyana, St. Vincent, Bolivia; *Oceania*: Papua New Guinea, Fiji, British Solomons, Western Samoa, Trust Territories of the Pacific, Tonga, New Hebrides.

5. *Affluent Communist*

This category has five countries: the Soviet Union, East Germany, Czechoslovakia, Poland, and Hungary. (The other European Communist countries are included a little misleadingly in the Middle Income category even though we occasionally call this category Capitalist Middle Income.) According to the *World Bank Atlas,* these countries should have about 337 million people in 1978 (we will round it off to 1/3 billion). Each of the above nations should be reasonably close (say within 25 percent) of the suggested PCG of $4,000. However, there is much controversy about the best numbers to use for the PCGs of these nations, particularly for the Soviet Union (the World Bank, for example, assumes that the PCG in the Soviet Union is closer to $3,000 than $4,000). We are more or less following various CIA and academic analyses in giving them about half the

PCG of the Affluent Market-Oriented nations. As we describe in Chapter 7, we expect the growth rates in these countries to continue to be relatively low—say 4 percent—rather than to return to the high growth rates of the post–World War II years.

6. Affluent Market-Oriented

We include here all of the rich members of OECD and of OPEC: *Europe*: West Germany, United Kingdom, Italy, France, Netherlands, Belgium, Sweden, Austria, Switzerland, Denmark, Finland, Norway, Luxemburg, Iceland; *North America*: The United States, Canada; *Asia and Middle East*: Japan; *Oceania*: Australia, New Zealand, New Caledonia; *Latin America*: Canal Zone; *Middle East*: Emirates, Israel, Kuwait, Saudi Arabia; *Others*: Bermuda and Virgin Islands.

These include about two-thirds of a billion people with an average PCG of $8,000 but in our World A, only a modest growth rate of about 4.0 percent from 1978 on, or about 80 percent of what they averaged from 1948 through 1973. If this estimate holds, most of these countries will not fully compensate for their low growth rates during the recent recession and thereafter.

Table 2.6 summarizes the basic demographic and economic indices of the six groups and of the world as a whole for 1978, the starting point of our scenarios for World A, discussed in this section, and also the data for 1985, 2000, and the final stable state (asymptote). Worlds B and C, discussed in the next section, have the same starting point.

We have deliberately chosen the starting points and the asymptotes in Table 2.6 to be integers and easy fractions to emphasize the roughness of the data. However, with the corrections already mentioned for the Coping Poor, the numbers reflect quite accurately the data in the *World Bank Atlas*, International Monetary Fund estimates, and various Congressional documents. Except for the relatively high GPs and PCGs for the Coping Poor, the reader can think of them as being representative of the data that is the basis of much current discussion.

In this book we envision current trends as leading to generally declining relative (percent) economic growth rates for the world in the future and a gradual leveling off of total population and gross product, even though we think in terms of a more populous and far more affluent future world.* We assume in these scenario contexts

---

*An important exception to our overall assumption of declining growth rates is the performance of nations in the Very Poor and Coping Poor categories in our World B, discussed in the next section.

TABLE 2.6
World A: Guarded Optimism Scenario Context[a]

	Very Poor	Coping Poor	Communist Asia	Middle Income	Affluent Communist	Affluent Market-Oriented	World
Population (in billions)							
1978	.250	1.000	1.000	1.000	.333	.667	4.250
1985	.296	1.143	1.104	1.217	.352	.701	4.807
2000	.402	1.455	1.303	1.694	.387	.769	5.9845
Asymptotic	1.000	2.750	1.750	3.000	.500	1.000	10.000
Per capita Gross Product (in 1978 $)							
1978	160.0	300.0	500.0	1,000	4,000	8,000	2,000.0
1985	196.4	369.0	780.0	1,318	4,945	9,622	2,394.5
2000	295.1	561.0	1,240.0	2,309	7,275	13,555	3,256.0
Asymptotic	4,000.0	8,000.0	16,000.0	32,000	20,000	40,000	20,000.0
Gross Product (in trillions of 1978 $)							
1978	.0400	.300	.500	1.000	1.333	5.333	8.5
1985	.0581	.421	.750	1.604	1.740	6.745	11.294
2000	.1186	.816	1.616	3.911	2.818	10.418	19.488
Asymptotic	4.0	22.0	28.0	96.0	10.0	40.0	200.0

[a]We have used, and set forth for mathematical convenience, a much higher level of accuracy than the data justify.

TABLE 2.7
Assumed "Asymptotic Values" of the Three Basic Variables

Category	VARIABLE Population (in billions)	PCG (in thousands)	GP (in trillions)
Very Poor	1	4	4
Coping Poor	2 - 3/4	8	22
Communist Asia	1 - 3/4	16	28
Middle Income	3	32	96
Affluent Communist	1/2	20	10
Affluent Market-Oriented	1	40	40
World	10	20	200

that these current trends continue indefinitely. In our quantitative scenarios we incorporate this leveling-off phenomenon by means of "asymptotic values" of population and product. For our purposes, an asymptote is a straight line that a quantity or variable (in this case, population and gross product) approaches as the time increases indefinitely. So we think of high but constant values of population and gross product in the distant future. These values are summarized in Table 2.7. This is not necessarily a prediction, but only a convenient way to incorporate current trends and ask what happens if they continued indefinitely.

We have used quotation marks around the term *asymptotic values* because they are not really estimates of the long-term futures of the countries concerned. Rather, they are numbers that we need in our equations and that play the role of an asymptotic value in these equations. We have to make such an assumption if we are to draw our characteristic S-shaped curves for each of the categories. These curves reflect some increase in absolute growth rates followed by an eventual leveling off. *There is no implication, except in the sense of being more or less surprise-free, that we are trying to project the very distant future as it would really occur.* Rather, we are suggesting that these asymptotic values reflect some of our current assumptions about the basic long-term dynamism, on the average, of each of these categories.

We will not be surprised if the projections over the next two or three decades calculated by using the assumptions in Tables 2.6 and 2.7 were not unreasonable, but not for much longer than two or three decades. We would be astounded if this categorization of the world continued indefinitely—if all the numbers came out even roughly right. We would not be shocked if some of them did. At the minimum, various nations will move in and out of the various categories, since some will grow faster or slower than the average. However, we do not wish to take account of this or other complications in the basic scenario we are setting forth; hence, our assumption that each category moves as a unit.

To emphasize this assumption, we will occasionally modify our terminology from Very Poor to Initially Very Poor, from Coping Poor to Initially Coping Poor, and so on. This is appropriate for another reason. All of the categories eventually get relatively rich; none stay so poor in our world that they can still be called Very Poor or even Coping Poor. However, because of the built-in assumptions they remain relatively poor—or at least less rich than the other categories.

In the real world, we expect many of these Poor nations will eventually pick up the techniques of economic growth. Indeed, we expect both the technology and the opportunities for rapid growth to become so available and so relatively easy to exploit that many of those societies that today find it most difficult to make this kind of adaptation will do so.

Our underlying assumptions for the asymptotic value table began with the notion that if current trends continued indefinitely, the Affluent Market-Oriented countries would eventually stabilize at about five times the current per capita income, which seems to be about as good a number as any other; there are many scenarios in which per capita income stabilizes at less, many others in which it stabilizes at more. The asymptotic values for the poor were basically determined by the requirement to have the asymptotic ratio of the richest to the poorest to a factor of ten—a large decrease from the current factor of sixty, but one that recognizes that the current cultures of these Very Poor countries, even with large but imaginable changes will not result in societies that could support a very high level of affluence. Such changes are not ruled out in a real world; but they are not part of the assumptions of World A. They will not occur in the next few decades. There is no other specific rationale for using a reduction of six in the income inequality. Indeed, we cannot produce any convincing rationale for any number except that it should be less than sixty and greater than two or three.

We believe that the Coping Poor should do about twice as well as the Very Poor. We then argue that Communist Asia should do twice as well as the Coping Poor. Continuing this argument, the Middle Income should do twice as well on the average as Communist Asia. This is not because Communist Asia might not be able to do much better (basically they are very competent societies, though they have many ideological, logistic, and administrative difficulties from the viewpoint of economic growth), but in World A they do not choose to do that well. As far as the Affluent Communist countries are concerned, they seem to be running into quite serious troubles today, as are the Affluent Market-Oriented. We decided to preserve, in the asymptotes, the ratio of the PCGs of Affluent Communist to the Affluent Market-Oriented (one to two), even though in the short run we give the former a higher growth rate.

We could produce a much weightier, more arcane, and perhaps more persuasive rationale for the above numbers. However, we would be stretching our ability to judge and sense the future, so we use the numbers suggested—our judgment of our most surprise-free projection—to illustrate what we mean by a Guarded Optimism World.

In terms of the quantitative models described in the Appendix, the values chosen for the asymptotes do not affect the initial rates of change. They will affect the point at which the curves begin to bend over. In fact, the formulas we use allow us to conveniently separate out the initial growth rates from the effects of the asymptotes we have chosen.*

We present in Figure 2.2 our growth curves for population, PCG and GP out to the year 2200 for our "Guarded Optimism World" or "World A." Below the growth curves we show how the relative (percent) growth rates decline. Table 2.6 lists values of the same variables for 1978, 1985, and 2000, and the asymptotic values, so that the reader can get a sense of what we mean by this basic scenario.

This kind of mathematical model for growth scenarios is often more useful for furnishing insights into prospective patterns and relationships than it is for exact predictions. Consider, for instance, how the relative PCGs might change in the future. We have built a certain dynamic into our model. Without asking whether or not the dynamic can be expected to hold in the real world in the next century or so, let us simply ask what would happen if the dynamic held. If we do this we can get the three curves shown in Figure 2.3.

---

*See Appendix for details.

FIGURE 2.2
World A (Curves for Whole World)

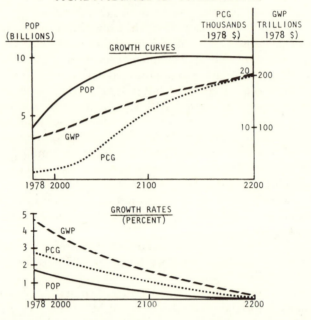

The top curve (as labeled) shows the ratio of the Affluent Market-Oriented group to the Very Poor group. (This is what people often mean by "the gap.") Sometimes, however, they may mean the second curve, which shows all the rich (including the Affluent Communist) divided by all the Poor (including the Coping Poor). We note that the Affluent Market-Oriented/Very Poor gap *increases* into the next century and then starts to decrease. We think of this as a very reasonable projection of the world although we would not place too much faith in the specific numbers (except perhaps for the next decade or two). It certainly would not surprise us if the peak occurred ten years earlier or ten years later. Of course, the further in the future, the less seriously we take the projection. To the extent the gap performs a role as an engine of development, this engine gets more powerful as far as the Poor are concerned. One of the things we will discuss is the possibility that the Middle Income countries will interact with the Poor countries in a novel way that seems likely to start soon and to increase over time.

Another use of this kind of scenario is to provide a straightforward, precise, simple and clear background on which one can "plant" or

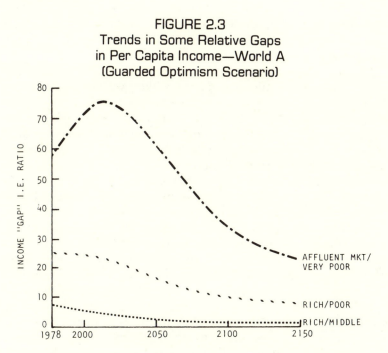

FIGURE 2.3
Trends in Some Relative Gaps
in Per Capita Income—World A
(Guarded Optimism Scenario)

"paint" all kinds of details. (This is why we call it a scenario context.) It may or may not be predictive, but it should be at least interesting and free from contradictions, so that one can comfortably use it. We set forth some other quantitative scenario contexts below, but we consider this one our base case, to be thought of both as illustrating many of our points and to make clear when we digress from this base case that we are considering alternative possibilities.*

Scenario-Contexts for High and Low Growth (Worlds B and C)

This section presents our assumptions and quantitative results for two variations of the basic scenario-context discussed in the preceding section. All three are basically "business-as-usual" and "more-of-the-same" worlds in which the dynamism of most of the nations concerned has peaked in the middle of the second half of the twentieth century. While they do well from then on, their growth rates gradually decrease. In two of the Worlds the Very Poor do much better than they have ever done, but still not extraordinarily well. The

---

*See Appendix for technical details.

Very Poor do well in World A, even better in World B, but badly or poorly in World C. The Coping Poor do at least moderately well in all three worlds.

World B, the high-growth case, reflects greater overall optimism about future economic growth. We make two changes from our World A assumptions: (1) we permit the relative growth rates of gross product (GP) of the Very Poor and Coping Poor categories to rise to 7 percent in the future, removing the restrictions that *all* relative growth rates must decline as in World A and C; and (2) we assume an asymptotic GWP of $400 trillion instead of $200 trillion, and all the asymptotic PCGs are doubled over World A.

World C is our pessimistic, low-growth case. Most affected for the worse in this world are the Poor and Middle Income categories (including Communist Asia) whose asymptotic PCGs are cut in half from World A. This reflects assumptions that, for this pessimistic case, the Poor grow only very slowly in the indefinite future, and the Middle Income groups fail to develop the potential that we give them in World A. The asymptotic GWP of World C is $125 trillion.

In Worlds B and C, we do not change our population assumptions from World A, although we recognize that most demographers today would argue that rapid urbanization and relatively rapid increases in PCG are likely to lead to relatively rapid declines in the birth rate. However, to the degree that the Poor countries remain very poor, unless we have actual starvation or other increases in the death rate caused by severe poverty, high population growth rates will very likely continue in the low growth world for a much longer time than in the other two worlds. This would, however, just exacerbate the difference in a way that is not very important for our considerations. We simply do not wish to consider this extra complication. Figure 2.4 and Figure 2.5 show the relative PCG "gaps" for Worlds B and C.

Some Basic Political, Cultural, and Social Contexts

Our basic interest in this book is in what we call modernization. In pursuing the various possibilities—and in describing some unlikely developments—we find it useful to posit some suggestive, if simplistic, societal milieus in which such modernization might take place. Each of these social milieus could be associated with a different Basic Quantitative Scenario-Context such as that exposited above, but, unless specified otherwise, we will normally assume the World A (Guarded Optimism) scenario for at least the rest of the century.

The range and complexity of possible future societal milieus are so

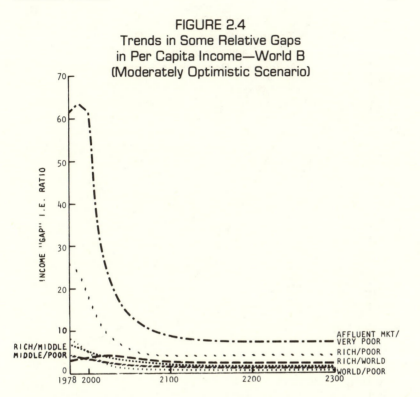

FIGURE 2.4
Trends in Some Relative Gaps
in Per Capita Income—World B
(Moderately Optimistic Scenario)

vast that futurologists find it hard to get a serious handle on them, despite all that has been written in this area. Therefore, we have first attempted to set forth a series of political, cultural, social, and technological themes containing various ideas and elements for scenario-contexts. We then put these themes in the order in which we expect they would attract attention to and investment in economic development and technological advancement. (This order is not necessarily rigorous. Also, some of the themes could change over time and lead to a reordering of the list.)

All of these themes are later elaborated in varying detail, ranging from a paragraph to a few pages. Yet, because of their brevity, even the lengthiest discussion necessarily lacks complexity and nuances. No model of an advanced society that is presented as simple, homogeneous, or ideologically unchanging over time can be highly plausible—particularly if technological changes continue to be dramatic. However, such simplicity has many advantages, enabling us to speculate about the effects of a large variety of socio-political

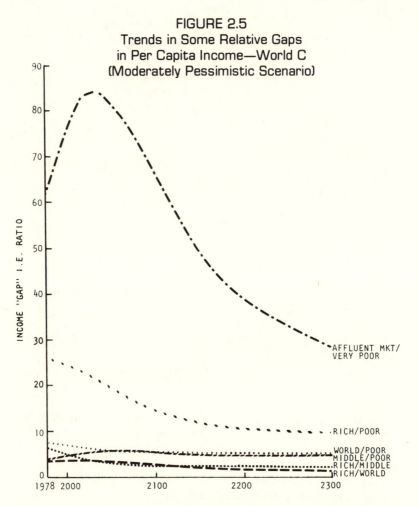

FIGURE 2.5
Trends in Some Relative Gaps
in Per Capita Income—World C
(Moderately Pessimistic Scenario)

trends and permitting the themes to be mixed together in various ways in varying proportions to produce more complex contexts and scenarios.

Five Basic Socio-Economic Themes

We set forth below five basic socio-economic themes (and a number of variations of each) that might characterize the whole world or a major part of it for some period of time. At any particular moment the real world will, of course, encompass a complex mixture of these and other themes. One purpose of the list is to describe the real world as such a mixture that presumably changes over time. Such descriptions are necessarily rough and aggregated; nonetheless they can be useful in an overview of history, even though they overlook or even mistakenly describe the direction of local tides, ripples, eddies, and even occasional storms and typhoons. In using these descriptions, the deliberate or unintentional omission of certain themes or theories may be as noteworthy as those that are considered.

There are at least six ways that one can use a theme: normatively, descriptively, as perspective, for scoring or measurement, as metaphor or analogy, and as an ingredient for scenarios. The most important function of these themes may be as aids in normative policy making. They can be used by various groups who want to promote policies, other developments, and trends that suit their goals. They can be used as a standard for judging or rating the world. And they can be used as a source of scenarios. One can ask what would happen if this theme or that were emphasized more, or if an attempt was made to change the evolving world to fit one theme or another. They can be used as images of the future or as elements of an ideology of the present. We elaborate on the themes and sub-themes listed below to help the reader to understand what we are talking about.

We label our five basic themes as follows:

1. *Efflorescent World Societies*[13]
   a. Intensively Darwinian Competition
   b. Relatively Cooperative and Benevolent
2. *Technological and Growth Oriented Worlds*
   a. "Normal Human Behavior" Guarded Optimism
      (Our World A—i.e., 2a and World A are identical)
   b. Moderate Optimism (Our World B)
   c. Guarded Pessimism (Our World C)
   d. Disaster Version
   e. Success Version (Marriage of Machine and Garden)
   f. A Skinnerian utopia[14]
3. *Relatively Competitive, Nationalistic, and Aggressive Worlds*
   a. Competent and Lucky
   b. More Destructive and Less Competent—or Just Unlucky
   c. Various Disaster Scenarios
4. *Various Low Growth Worlds*
   a. "Economic and Social Malaise" World (An Intensified Form of Our World C)
   b. "Small is Beautiful" (When Appropriate) World Society
   c. A (Competent) Triumph of Garden over Machine
      (i) OECD-wide
      (ii) Worldwide
   d. Troubled and Retrogressing World

    e. A Rigid Emphasis on Stability, Localism, and Risk
      Avoidance
        (i) OECD-wide
        (ii) Worldwide
    f. An Anti-Technological, Anti-Growth World
        (i) OECD-wide
        (ii) Worldwide
  5. *Specially Troubled, Retrogressing, or Catastrophic Worlds*

This list contains more cases than can be seriously addressed; even so we have had to make arbitrary selections and have not mentioned many interesting futures. We find such lists useful in deciding which themes to use or emphasize in subsequent scenarios, for noting explicitly and clearly some of the possibilities that are not pursued, and for contrasting the possibilities that are being discussed with those that are not.

We cannot address all the relevant political, cultural, and social issues within even a single context. But we can still put ourselves within different frameworks and then conjecture about the degree to which various issues will develop and be resolved and about how economic development and technological advancement may occur.

The Five Basic Context Themes and Their Variations

1. An Extreme Efflorescent Society

Humanity takes seriously the biblical injunction "to be fruitful and multiply." This objective is pursued with great determination and nearly complete disregard for the anti-growth values or other limits-to-growth positions and attitudes.[15] As long as the drive to be fruitful continues, huge investments are made in economic and scientific development. Society increasingly sponsors intensive research in biology as well as in hard technologies. As a result humanity's ability to modify and adapt plants and animals to local conditions and needs increases enormously. At the same time, there are active and effective attempts to eliminate or modify social mores, customs, and values that have outlived their usefulness by tending to make the society less competitive, dynamic, or adaptable than is desired.

Some strange developments could occur in an extreme efflorescent milieu. If a high level of artificial intelligence is created, for example, it might ultimately be necessary to decide whether the injunction "to be fruitful and multiply" extends to intelligent computers and robots. The eventual replacement of humans by machines cannot be ruled out (assuming that a sufficiently creative intelligence could be designed into self-producing machines). Whether this occurs or not, many other kinds of cyborgs and human-machine combinations of extraordinary intricacy and capability are likely to be created and used.

The main reason for mentioning this context and its two variations is to show that some extreme cases could occur that are quite different from those we will examine more closely. This context is also useful as a parody of what many of the anti-growth movements project as the logical (if not literal) outcome of the current world society. Despite being a parody, in many ways it corresponds temporarily to some high morale societies of the past. Indeed in some ways it resembles the expansion of the United States across North America during the eighteenth and nineteenth centuries. Yet even a discussion of these themes, except as parody or polemic exaggeration, is absent today because the efflorescent society concept and ideal is so inappropriate to our current high living standards, to our subdued dynamism, and to our increasing belief in and acceptance of anti-growth or limited-growth values. However, this could become more relevant, at least temporarily, if either outer space or some of the more currently hostile areas of the world are opened up to intensive human settlement and economic development. Given some of the new technologies that seem likely to appear, some aspects of this theme might reappear. We note briefly the following two variations:

1a. Intensive Darwinian Competition Version. This would be the most extreme version of the efflorescent society. The society would be absolutely ruthless in pursuing the goal "to be fruitful and multiply." In fact, the objective might be pursued with an almost manic determination. It might not be an unpleasant society for those who live in it and share its goals, but most people today (or at least those in reasonably successful and attractive societies) would find it distasteful if not horrible. However, it would still be regarded as an improvement by many in the present Third World.

1b. A Relatively Cooperative and Benevolent Version. Once again, humanity decides to be fruitful and multiply—to fill every habitable niche and corner of the universe with life of one sort or another, especially with preferred forms of human life. However, this culture avoids ruthlessness and maintains great concern for such values as safety, art, family, human rights, happiness, and cultural continuity. There may be a willingness to take big risks, but there is not a willingness to pay exorbitant prices. There is less willingness to discard as many older customs and values, or to be as callous with less competitive individuals or institutions, as in the Darwinian version. Much Darwinian selection and competition still occurs, but this process is tempered by a strong emphasis on cooperation and benevolence; the society cares for and protects its progeny. There is, however, still great emphasis on adaptation, and on social (and perhaps biological) engineering to facilitate such adaptation.

This theme is still far removed from anything suggested in this book as likely, but it is only a moderately extreme version of what we are suggesting. However, the differences are important, and we therefore list this scenario as another example (along with 1a) of what we are *not* recommending.

2. Technological and Growth Oriented Worlds

Despite the range of outcomes that are possible, not much happens in these growth-oriented themes. The nation-state retains a dominant but decreasing role in international relations and a high degree of loyalty and dynamism on the national level partly because there is no obvious replacement. A number of *ad hoc* international organizations could come into being and perform important functions, but there is no coalescence into anything like a genuine world government. There are no great disasters, wars, or catastrophic depressions.

We listed six versions of these worlds in the basic list:

a. "Normal Human Behavior" Guarded Optimism (Our World A—i.e., 2a and World A are identical)
b. Moderate Optimism (Our World B)
c. Guarded Pessimism (Our World C)
d. Disaster Version
e. Success Version (Marriage of Machine and Garden)
f. A Skinnerian utopia

This entire book focuses on our Worlds A, B, and C above. From the viewpoint of the dramatic events of the last two hundred years, not much happens in any of these three growth-oriented themes, at least as long as the world stays mostly in that theme. The makeup of the world looks much the same in the year 2000 and later as it does today. Some important *ad hoc* international organizations may emerge, but there is no real world government, any great disasters, wars, or depressions. Although there is great variation among the three themes, it is very much business as usual.

Growth-oriented worlds "d" and "e" are supposed to span the range from disaster to success. We probably do not spend enough time and enough space in this book on (d) and (c) scenarios. If our attitudes of several years ago had persisted, we probably would have focused much more attention on these disaster scenarios. Much has happened in the last two years to decrease the probability of economic disaster, but we remain concerned about it. Most of our disaster scenarios arise out of an inability to control inflation, but while we believe the likelihood of this inflation is still disturbingly high, the potentiality for disaster is somewhat less now.

There are obviously going to be many tensions and internal contradictions which could eventually easily lead to other worlds. Some of these changes may be more or less intentional as some leaders or groups actually try to go in the new direction. However, under current conditions we find it difficult to believe that any world leader or large group would consciously choose to break out of this relatively narrow range. Of course, the change could occur because of unintended acts, evolution, increasing internal contradictions, excessive strains and so on.

All these topics are covered in Part II at some length. We discuss the sixth technological growth oriented version below because many technocratic, scientific, or otherwise fuzzy liberals view it seriously in one form or another.

2f. A Skinnerian utopia. Behavioral science theories similar to those set forth by B. F. Skinner in such works as *Walden Two* and *Beyond Freedom and Dignity* turn out to be practical bases for highly technological and affluent societies. If so, societies might develop in which almost all individuals are relatively well balanced mentally, highly motivated, basically cooperative, and law abiding. At the same time, high levels of initiative, courage, daring, and dynamism are also maintained, along with necessary levels of aggression and competitiveness. If the latter qualities disturb the smooth functioning of the society they are effectively discouraged.

Many technological growth enthusiasts would choose this kind of society. Of course, whether it could work is an open issue at best. It may be completely impractical, at least for Western cultures. Or it might be practical in the West only in a society such as Orwell's in *1984* or Huxley's in *Brave New World,* rather than in the kind of democratic, individualistic, pluralistic society that most Western readers of this book and most potential members of such a society would prefer. In part it would be closer to many traditional Confucian values than to most Western values of the last two hundred years. We could much more easily imagine some of the neo-Confucian societies choosing such a world. (In some ways mainland China under Mao aspired to a form of this alternative.)

One extreme version of a Skinnerian utopia would not only accept scientific behavior control and modification, but would emphasize genetic manipulation, chemistry, surgery, and other scientific forms of behavioral modification, if and when they are developed. An intense process for monitoring immigrants and even nations would also exist in this (or perhaps any) Skinnerian society, presumably for positive reasons.

The society could easily have more than a touch of efflorescent world themes, but would probably not take them as seriously as the truly efflorescent worlds. It could also include many of the attitudes of the more humanistic societies described under low-growth worlds, especially since it is paternalistic. Rapid economic growth would not be an end in itself, but only a means to achieve a high standard of living and a high quality of life, however defined.

This Skinnerian-utopian society would probably place great value on knowledge—especially science and technology—but not necessarily on its widespread dissemination. Population growth would be desirable only as it fulfills other values. The culture would probably not be intrinsically hostile to growth because it would feel competent to cope with any likely increase in population economically and technologically and from many other viewpoints as well. The current widely-perceived threat that the world may be overwhelmed by excessive population growth would seem rather foolish, except perhaps in special situations where it might be a serious problem.

The first order of business in the Skinnerian-utopian world is an orderly, smooth-working society. Once this desirable state has been reached, some population limitation might occur because stability is then heavily emphasized. This plateau would be reached rather quickly, in ways similar to our projections that assume limits to growth are created by inefficient government bureaucracies and regulations, by various other societal inefficiencies, and by a diminished desire to attain enormous wealth. Both the government and society may decide relatively early that further rapid growth—or even the accumulation of wealth beyond what is needed for insurance against disasters and catastrophes—jeopardizes stability and creates more problems than it is worth. However, we would argue that most likely it would consider our World A as about right.

3. Relatively Competitive Nationalistic and Aggressive Worlds

Up to this point we have assumed a relatively even course of international relations: problems of politics and violence do not seriously affect economic development. For example, we mentioned our belief that the political map of the world will probably not change drastically for the next two or three decades. Possible exceptions are in the Middle East, the three divided states, and further problems in the Indochina area. However, even these seem less likely than they once did. It is difficult to find a twenty or thirty year period in the eighteenth and nineteenth centuries in which the map of the world was that stable.

Conceivably, international relations could deteriorate so far that many of the problems of the eighteenth and nineteenth centuries re-emerge. However, even if we had the same kind of intense domestic and foreign policy problems associated with the existing or emerging nation-states of those centuries, there would not necessarily be a comparably high level of international and domestic violence. The nuclear balance, for example, makes people much more cautious. Also, internal development still seems to be one of the most effective methods of increasing a nation's power and status as opposed to external aggression. Furthermore, there are genuine changes in the attitudes of most nations and peoples about conquests, repression, aggression, and similar activities.

We suggest, therefore, that there are two ways in which these worlds could deteriorate. One is that the world becomes very crisis prone but economic development is not affected greatly, at least in the two or three decades that most interest us. In the second, there are much more intense and dangerous kinds of competition that could make a big difference. This theme can be associated with the various degrees and rates of nuclear proliferation as well as with high levels of terrorism and intense national and international crises. In particular, about ten Third World countries seem to have overt or covert nuclear programs that provide an option to acquire nuclear weapons or a base for acquiring such an option.

The first version of this theme assumes that relatively few of these Third World countries actually exercise this option in the late 1980s or early 1990s, although they might before the end of this century. In the second version we assume that most or all of these countries do acquire nuclear weapons. Obviously, a large number of countries with nuclear weapons could change the characteristics of all kinds of crises as well as the problems posed by different kinds of terrorism.

3a. Competent and Lucky. There are conventional wars and revolutions and much more destructive behavior, neuroses, crime, terrorism, and other illegal activities than in category 2, but none of this is intense or frequent enough to disrupt basic economic and technological trends. Economic development and technological advance continue, although associated with more turbulence and even violence than today. However, there is, *de facto,* a high degree of world order and world trade.

Not only do the nations handle their affairs quite well, but they are also lucky. No major accidents occur that really make a difference. For example, if one had told any group of people in any previous period of time that the United States and the Soviet Union would have thousands of nuclear missiles available for instant action in literally a matter of minutes if not seconds, and that very few people would be nervous or seriously concerned that one of these nuclear devices might be launched by accident or unauthorized malice, they would be most surprised. For about two thousand years the concept of the Sword of Damocles has always been perceived as a most threatening situation. We now all live in exactly that situation. Yet most people believe that the thread with which the sword is held is really quite strong. In any case, they go about their day-to-day business more or less oblivious of this quite startling danger.

In this version the nation-state plays a much more aggressive role, but not to the point of jeopardizing the further development of a world market and international division of labor. World trade continues to increase, at least initially at a rate of more than 5 percent per annum. Economic growth and political stability is more like that of the United States in the nineteenth century (but without the Civil War), and unlike the violent events that occurred during the rise and fall of the Spanish and Portuguese empires, although such violent events are not completely ruled out.

This theme assumes that the world doesn't improve much over its current state. In fact, it deteriorates somewhat, partly because some of the rising nationalist states (e.g., China and Brazil), or perhaps several European nations, become relatively aggressive. Also terrorist organizations often work closely with sympathetic governments. This kind of cooperation is tolerated, which is a major part of the problem. Discretionary behavior is acceptable—at first because the world felt that it could afford to accept it. Society did not feel so threatened that it had to stop this kind of challenge and disturbance. Later, it found it could not.

Within nations, economic development and technological advance are similarly associated with turbulence and violence. However, even this is not on the scale we would have expected ten to twenty years ago because many countries have adjusted to the process of changing the old and absorbing the new and are able to manage the transition. Under current conditions, economic advance, while disturbing and disrupting, also has the potential for contributing to stability, whereas economic stagnation has a great potential for breeding disorder. In this world there is as much disorder as order.

3b. Much Like 3a. Above, But More Destructive and Less Competent—or Just Less Lucky. In this world international competition is even more likely to get out of hand, but doesn't quite explode into a continent-wide thermonuclear war—or into many small ones. (If it does, category 3b becomes inoperative and we move to another theme.) There are threats of war and perhaps some limited use of nuclear weapons. There is rapid, almost explosive nuclear proliferation.

In this theme, not only do the ten Third World countries mentioned exercise their nuclear option in the late 1980s and early 1990s, but some of the big powers help them to reach that point, perhaps because of political competition or perhaps for economic reasons. There is much competition among the powers and a growing attitude of "if we don't do this someone else will." One can imagine a country procuring nuclear weapons for itself and then exporting them to amortize their costs. Once the threshold for this process has been openly crossed, even Switzerland or Sweden could follow suit for the same reasons.

Although this theme plays a central role in some other Hudson studies, we do not discuss it at length here. Basically it suggests that violence does not remain potential and abstract but is exercised either as actual destruction or as intense threats of destruction. Every nation is obligated to take account of the possibility. No longer is nuclear war "unthinkable." Many countries acquire a low level of active defense for protection against simple missiles and simple aircraft attacks. None would work well against highly sophisticated or massive attacks, but that is not their main concern.

In some ways economic development can go faster in this world because the requirements of national security are so overwhelming and obvious. The traditional drive behind economic development becomes very relevant and strong. Countries and citizens are willing to sacrifice to achieve greater wealth to pay for national security requirements. The high level of violence is damaging and costly, but it also creates an extra willingness to work and to advance technology.

This world could, of course, be very dangerous. Modern technology creates all kinds of options for destructive techniques and tactics. If violence erupts at a sufficiently high level, it would greatly affect economic development and even technological advancement. If a large and very destructive war occurs, people might feel that they don't want to live with modern physics and modern technology any more; there could be a reversion to a strongly anti-technological and anti-growth economic world. This would occur either in a very intense and widespread way or only temporarily and locally. If only a few countries gave up modern science and technology, other countries would gain an advantage they might choose to exercise. In particular, they might choose to exercise it while the opportunity existed to prevent future problems from arising—i.e., to preempt the rearmament of those who had given up modern arms.

4. Various Low-Growth Worlds

All of the worlds we have been talking about are very high growth by the standards of most current discussion even though in many cases we think of them as relatively low growth (i.e., our C world). Thus many people believe that our usual projection for the end of the century—about six billion people and a gross world product of $15 trillion to $20 trillion—is simply going to strain the carrying capacity of the earth beyond feasible or desirable limits. We disagree strongly, but we believe it is useful to describe worlds in which the gross product is less than $15 trillion in the year 2000, and perhaps grows only slowly from then on. One reason for going through these cases is to explicitly indicate differences between what we discuss in this book and what other authors or groups are considering.

4a. Economic and Social Malaise. There seems to be an extraordinarily pervasive and continuing malaise in many OECD countries. At the Hudson Institute we used to argue that during the 1965 to 1975 decade the United States had gone into a malaise situation but had started to emerge during 1976 and 1977. We are less sure now that this emergence is occurring. In this world context full emergence does not occur; instead, there is a serious relapse. Business remains relatively unprofitable or too risky in the United States, Europe, and Japan, although not necessarily for the same reasons. In the near future there is a severe depression but not an economic collapse; recovery is slow and unsure—at least in the Advanced Capitalist nations.

In the same way in which *La Première Belle Epoque* (1886 to 1913) was followed by what we call *La Mauvaise Epoque* (1914 to 1947), we have a second good era (1948 to 1973) followed by a second bad era (say

1974 to 2000). In the first cycle the growth rates of the Advanced Capitalist nations went from 3.3 percent to 1.8 percent. The second period was a very bad one indeed, with two world wars, the Great Depression, two communist revolutions, the rise of world fascism, and many other unpleasant events. Presumably this kind of alternation could occur again. Indeed, many people think of this world as relatively realistic. Some would even include an economic collapse equivalent to the Great Depression.

4b. "Small-Is-Beautiful" (When Appropriate) World Society. This context is characterized by systematic serious attempts to limit, worldwide, the exploitation of the earth and its resources. While such exploitation is still promoted by those with professional or materialistic interests, their efforts are greatly restrained. There is little social encouragement of their activities. A negative or indifferent (but not necessarily hostile) attitude is usually displayed by the high culture towards those who engage in aggressive attempts at exploitation. Many projects are pursued, but the burden of proof for justifying the exploitation is on the advocates, who lack a large automatic constituency. The basic concept of this society is that "unless a satisfactory case can be made to the contrary, less is more." Environmental, work place, and financial regulations are all onerous.

This context could still attain a high level of technological advance, for example encouraging ventures into space to remove any polluting activities from the earth (e.g., nuclear power). Satellite solar power stations might conceivably become desirable to reduce environmental problems on earth. We believe both of these to be unlikely in the next two or three decades, primarily because terrestrial energy problems probably will not be sufficiently severe to justify such projects. However, such problems may seem sufficiently severe to enough people that space development as a locus for polluting or disturbing activities could be given a relatively high priority. In the meantime, there is not much general research and development on most esoteric technologies. Emphasis is mainly on "soft" technologies and technologies that help to enhance and protect the environment.

The main source of problems in this world would be the various conflicts that would develop between different kinds of ins and outs. There are at least three kinds of outs. The first kind includes those who are relatively poor or not quite as well off as they would like to be and who simply want greater dynamism than they would be offered. Second are those who see positive values in more dynamism, technological capability, and greater adventure. The third are those who would achieve greater power over other groups. All these could be willing to take aggressive actions if it seems profitable to do so.

This world may not have enough resources or advanced technologies to deal with the kinds of difficulties that could arise. But the main difficulty which makes this world implausible is that influential as the small-is-beautiful movement is, it seems absolutely inconceivable that it could affect seriously more than a few of the Advanced Capitalist nations. The Atlantic Protestant culture area and France might be affected to varying degrees, but this would simply mean that some Middle Income nations would probably work harder because they would now be spurred on by the concept that they could pass the Advanced Capitalist nations. Furthermore, the Advanced Capitalist nations would not be as competitive with them, so what the Middle Income nations lost in market and other driving forces supplied by the gap, they might gain from the reduced competition.

4c/1. Low Growth: A Competent OECD-Wide Triumph of Garden over Machine. In the industrialized countries, upper-middle class elites continue to feel that further economic growth interferes increasingly with their standard of living and their quality of life. These people, along with the Anti-growth Triad, feel this way with great intensity and seek to bring about no growth or very slow growth. They have disproportionate influence because they tend to control both the popular and prestigious media and to have great impact in education, government, and some religious groups.

One would assume that the outcome would be in many ways similar to that in category 4b except that there would be a much greater chance for backlash. People might well feel extreme animosity towards the groups that had forced slow growth on them in their own class interests and there would be much greater class bitterness, internal strife, and perhaps a counter-reformation movement trying to correct the excesses of the New Class and its allies. There would also be a national security problem if the rest of the world did not follow along.

4c/2. Low Growth: A Competent Triumph of Garden over Machine Worldwide. The non-OECD world quickly adopts much the same ideology as the OECD nations. Thus a malaise in development, or at least a lack of dynamism, continues for much longer and is much more widespread than it would be if it were limited to OECD countries. (For a while, this scenario looked almost plausible, but although many in the Third World pay lip service to limits-to-growth concepts and may cause many psychological and political problems, they are not likely to gain enough support.)

A competitive spirit eventually reappears and creates an increasingly dynamic attitude toward economic development. The timing of this eventual change to intense competition—especially from the non-OECD world—would determine the nature of the optimistic of pessimistic variations.

In an extreme version of this scenario, the basic historical analogy would be the Portuguese and Spanish empires, which initially expanded with great speed and success but tapered off relatively soon and then stagnated. In a less dramatic version, the current economic malaise in the OECD world continues for some decades. This greatly depletes the resources and opportunities otherwise available for worldwide economic development. However, in one reasonable and eventually optimistic outcome of this case, the more or less autonomous development of the Third World itself would help to pull the world out of its stagnation—perhaps violently.

4d. Low Growth: Troubled and Retrogressing World. Nothing really works right any more. The various nations perhaps start an escalating and eventually self-destructive program of protectionism and "exporting unemployment" by increasing tariffs and other barriers to imports, while ruthlessly cutting export prices and trying to dump their goods into other countries. Their hope is that they will at least benefit at the margin, even though on the average they are not meeting all costs. Their main goal is to reduce their unemployment.

Another possibility is that this world starts out more or less like the economic malaise scenario, but collapse occurs. This could be caused by a break in the chain of payments. For example, Italy, Brazil, or Mexico can no longer meet their payments and no one bails them out. Or, bailing out the defaulting country sets off a wild inflation that in turn results in a different kind of economic collapse.

Alternatively, the economist Kondratieff, turns out to be right in his prediction, and we hit the fifth peak in the price cycle. (Previous peaks were in 1790, 1820, 1870, 1920, and presumably in the 1970s. For a discussion, see Chapter 4.) The huge expansion from 1950 to 1975 has run its course and is followed by consolidation and regrouping. Since capital industries are overbuilt, there cannot be more steady progress until other sectors catch up. It could be argued that even if the Affluent Capitalist nations have overbuilt their capital structures, there is still an enormous demand by the Middle Income countries. These are now large enough to absorb substantial capital exports from the Affluent Capitalist nations—often in the form of turn-key projects—whole factories that repay their costs out of their products. This concept could work if these exports can be financed. One of the reasons that the recession from 1974 to 1975 was so mild in the United States and Japan was that these countries exported, respectively, about one-quarter and one-third of their exports to Third World countries other than OPEC nations. This was very important in maintaining their economic momentum and aiding their recovery. In one version of the low-growth scenario serious financing for such exports can no longer be arranged.

Another possibility for this scenario is that all the structural weaknesses, symptoms, and causes of the current malaise simply turn out to be bigger than expected. Cumulatively, there is a straw that breaks the camel's back. The societies could live with any small number of these extra costs and risks, but not with all of them.

4e. A Rigid Emphasis on Stability, Localism, and Risk Avoidance. The press and popular magazines tend to convey the impression that New Class anti-growth values (described in Chapter 3) will triumph soon. We believe that this is very unlikely within the next decade but could happen before the end of the century. If these values do prevail, a modern version of past societies run by aristocratic, educated elites could occur—something similar to the late Confucian era in Korea or China. An extreme, rigid opposition to change characterized such societies, especially opposition to changes that interfered with established institutions or customs. For example, prior to the twentieth century in China—a country which had a thousand-year-old tradition of ancestor worship—it was very difficult to built a railroad or a highway without disturbing cemeteries. To do so, therefore, it became necessary to call out the troops to quell public opposition.

In this context, we imagine that the OECD countries have many figurative cemeteries that are not to be disturbed—a general attitude that is basically hostile to innovation. As a result there is an enormous reduction in research and development, in new technologies, and in major new economic projects.

As always, there are at least two cases. In one, the OECD world is affected, and presumably the communist world or the Third World becomes overwhelmingly strong. In the second case, the entire world is affected by this emphasis on stability, localism, and risk avoidance, returning to a stagnating and probably a retrogressing economy. However, it might not be very dramatic. There could even be very small improvements in living standards such as occurred in the eighteenth and early nineteenth centuries. However, basically the current status quo would continue in most of the world except for those countries that could not control their population growth and would presumably then be faced with extraordinarily serious problems.

4f. Anti-Technological, Anti-Growth Worlds. There are many other events possible where a large portion of the world is hostile to technology alone or is hostile to both technology and economic growth. For example, certain religions could arise with this characteristic or there could be some disastrous events, either accidental or deliberate, that made increasing portions of the world take such a position. It is hard to imagine that this occurs to such an extent that by itself it really has a dramatic worldwide impact. This context assumes that this slowdown in technological advancement is pervasive and dramatic. People no longer acquiesce passively when some groups push their efforts; instead many take an active opposing role. Some of the more extreme attitudes are applied to scientific projects as well. There is a blanket objection to the potential for destruction brought about by any increase in human knowledge, the possible loss of values and environmental pollution in further economic progress, and potential effects on the quality of life or the habitability of earth. In other words, the Advanced Capitalist countries (OECD) are hostile to whatever new problems *might* be created and oppose the *unknown* risks that inevitably accompany any major innovations and new activities.

The slowdown is not likely to be permanent, however, since the Soviet Union or the newly emerging economic powers such as Brazil would continue to take an active interest in "progress" and carry on despite the non-efforts of the OECD world. The level of activities supported by the Soviets or the new emerging powers would be substantially below that which would occur if the OECD world chose to pursue these objectives, but they might lead the OECD countries to reconsider long-term development. Of course, if Japan were to return to a policy of growth, it would make a major immediate economic difference, and eventually a political difference as well.

Competition from somewhere in the world would eventually make the basic OECD posture intolerable—but this change may come in a traditional "too little too late" fashion or in another almost equally disastrous pattern of slow erosion, gradual withdrawal, unacceptable losses, and a violent return.

In this context, the world as a whole becomes enamored with the new attitudes. As the poorer countries become wealthier, they gravitate toward the culture models of the OECD world and settle for the new life style of these countries, which has become traditional. The slow growth is contagious psychologically, politically, and economically, and the masses are told that the slow growth is also inevitable. The lack of economic and technological progress is a matter of apprehension only among a dwindling number of people with "reactionary" *laissez-faire* and growth-oriented attitudes that are anathema to the dominant culture. Most people welcome the "stagnation" as a respite from the headlong change and turmoil of the Multifold Trend. They even believe that this is the only way to prevent Spengler-Sorokin or Toynbee-Quigley scenarios. This last kind of scenario is most likely to arise from a disastrous world experience such as a big war, nuclear accident, widespread ecological or environmental disaster, or other catastrophic experience.

5. Specially Troubled, Retrogressing, or Catastrophic Worlds

This is a catch-all category that includes all the disasters people worry about: drastic climate change in large areas of the world; a severe heating or cooling of the earth; perhaps a melting down of the ice caps in the northern hemisphere; destruction of the ozone layer; a serious ecological disaster with worldwide and permanent effects; new diseases that cause a catastrophic drop in grain production so that there is widespread starvation and disorganization; and so on. All topics we would consider as worldwide catastrophes are included in this category.

We do not believe that any of these have high probability, but because there are so many ways things can go wrong, we do not know—and cannot know—the total probability of things going seriously wrong in one of these ways. We include all these worlds in that group that we have defined as "very improbable situations" which would be digressive to examine systematically.

These improbable or far-fetched issues are taken increasingly seriously by many scientists and laymen. One of the fears that inevitably accompanies the development of what we call the super-industrial economy is that such possibilities become less improbable. We will defer all discussion of these possibilities to Chapter 5 on the emerging super-industrial economy. As the scale of human economic and technological activities increases, they are more likely to be the sources of such a disaster.

The discussion in the rest of this book is mostly restricted to technological and growth oriented worlds that are also relatively peaceful. We view these as the most probable worlds, but not so overwhelmingly probable that the other possibilities should be as de-emphasized as they are in this book. We do so here because of our focus of interest and of limitations of space. In a more complete treatment, at least the relatively competitive and aggressive worlds would also be considered quite seriously.

In this book, we will spend most of our time developing the Guarded Optimism World (World A) although we will occasionally digress to some of the other scenarios or contexts set forth above. The main reason we brought the latter to the attention of the reader was to emphasize the extensive range of possibilities that can occur, either conceptually or actually. Of course, our list is simplistic because it does not really describe the many mixtures, contradictions, and evolving changes that may occur. The world is going to be a rich place, and no simple description depending on a few themes or ideas or concepts is going to do it justice. On the other hand, there are normally dominant themes or dominant concepts that do describe much of what is happening or may happen. It is in this sense that we wish to use these themes, contexts, scenarios, and images in the rest of this book.

Notes

1. For an example, see our comparison in Chapter 8 of the annual address by Robert S. McNamara, president of the World Bank, "1977 Annual Meeting of the Boards of Governors; Summary Proceedings," pp. 9-35, with his previous addresses.

2. We use the phrase with apologies (and thanks) to Edith Efron, who has used *Adversary Triad* as a label for the scientists, neo-liberals, and lawyers who have played such an important role in many self-styled public interest movements. The terms New Crusaders and Secular Evangelists have been used. We discuss the Anti-Growth Triad again in chapter 3. There is a Hudson Institute research project on this subject.

3. The term *"New Class"* was coined by the Yugoslav political figure and writer Milovan Djilas to refer, in broadly similar ways, to the "intelligentsia" in communist countries. See his *The New Class* (New York: Praeger, 1957). In a way similar to our usage, it has been popularized by several people, especially Irving Kristol. We discuss and use the concept further in Chapters 3 and 8.

4. Sidney Pollard, *The Idea of Progress* (New York: Basic Books, 1968), pp. ix-x.

5. The Club of Rome sponsored the basic document of the movement: Donnella H. and Dennis L. Meadows, Jorgen Randers, and William W. Behrens III, *The Limits to Growth* (New York: Universe Books, 1972).

6. We discuss the gap again in Chapter 7 as part of a more detailed analysis of the problems and prospects of the Rich, the Middle Income, and the Poor countries.

7. *The Next 200 Years: A Scenario for America and the World,* by Herman Kahn, William Brown, and Leon Martel (New York: William Morrow and Company, 1976).

8. Louis Harris, "Majority Pessimistic on Reaching Ideal," *The Harris Survey,* December 25, 1975.

9. See the discussion of United States energy issues in Chapter 5 and the forthcoming *Let There Be Energy,* by Herman Kahn and William Brown.

10. For a more detailed analysis of such a projected population, see John Thomas and B. Bruce-Briggs, *Population Distribution in a Year 2100 World—An A Fortiori Case—20 Billion Population,* HI-1622/2-CC, May 5, 1972.

11. As near as I can tell the term *scenario* was first used in this sense in a group I worked with at the RAND Corporation. We deliberately chose the word to deglamorize the concept. In writing the scenarios for various situations we kept saying "Remember, it's only a scenario," the kind of thing that is produced by Hollywood writers both hacks and genuises. There is no *a priori* concept that a scenario should be taken seriously or that it is intended to reflect aspects of the real world. Some scenarios do; others do not. Scenarios are simply a more or less imaginative sequence of events that are put together so that each event forms a context for the other events and so that there is some continuity over time in the "narrative."

12. At the Hudson Institute we have extrapolated growth curves for population, gross product, and per capita gross product for a number of individual countries and for these six categories or groups of countries. Those curves are not included in the present book, although some of the calculations are used for the "gap" curves in this and the following section.

13. Efflorescent: a flowering, a blooming, or fulfillment. This concept was first suggested by Pat Gunkel.

14. B. F. Skinner, a Harvard behavioral psychologist, has written extensively on behavioristic models of the future. See Burrhus Frederick Skinner, *Beyond Freedom & Dignity* (New York: Knopf, 1971); and *Walden II* (New York: Macmillan Co., 1948).

15. See our discussion in Chapter 3 of the emergence of the Fourteen New Emphases for an elaboration of some of the current anti-growth values and attitudes.

3

Cultural Change and Economic Growth: The Emergence of the Fourteen New Emphases

Modernization and the Bourgeoisie

To achieve some grasp of the present or the future we start, as always, by turning to the past for a sense of what can happen. Many anthropologists have concluded that contacts between different societies are probably the most effective and surely the most common occasions for cultural change. Such contacts include small-scale military incursions, trade, and the arrival or return of individual foreign travelers (whether Marco Polos or ordinary tourists). We focus on the historical effects of the rise of the bourgeoisie and of industrialization on the West and on the subsequent effects of these events on other societies. If the industrialization was reasonably effective, we often refer to it as modernization or progress. In the past for most societies these three terms—industrialization, modernization, and progress—could be used more or less interchangeably. Another rough synonym used to be Westernization, but this no longer applies.

A culture can be influential without being modern. Chinese, Roman, and Byzantine cultures, for example, had enormous impact on the less sophisticated cultures they came in contact with as a natural result of their capabilities, sophistication, and size, not of their modernity. When the Jesuits visited China in the sixteenth century, they felt that in many ways Chinese culture was superior to Western culture, even if it was less modern. (The Jesuits also believed that China's lack of military prowess was a serious defect; even more serious was the absence of Christianity.)

There is much current discussion and controversy about what the concept of modernization should include. Some believe it ought to cover guarantees of civil rights, income redistribution, political rights, participation of women, parliamentary institutions, and many other institutions or attributes. We are willing to concede that any or all of these things may be desirable, but they are conceptually and empirically separate from modernization. Measuring the degree of modernization is difficult. However, using our concept of the Great Transition as the basic metaphor, modernization may be thought of as how far a society has come from pre-industrial or how far it still has to go to become post-industrial.[1]

Many people deplore the kinds of changes that occur when a traditional society modernizes. They talk about the breakdown of culture, are preoccupied with losses, and lament that things will never be the same again. Yet there is another side to this picture. For every loss there is usually a corresponding gain. Furthermore, change itself is unavoidable. All change (including modernization) involves the breaking of older cultural patterns and usually the adoption of new ones. This process is inherently painful in varying degrees because modernization involves changing people as well as artifacts, resources, and leadership.

Cultures are not changed by single events or causes, nor are there uniform reactions to change. Whether the reactions are severe or mild depends on many factors. Perhaps the most important single variable both historically and at present is the extent to which the intruding culture is perceived as a threat to personal, class, national, or religious interests. This sense of threat used to be sufficient to cause most cultures to choose the status quo. However, contemporary societies often deliberately seek cross-cultural change. Until recently, this urge was enhanced by the emergence and almost universal acceptance of the desirability of progress and also of many organizational, economic, and technological innovations. As a result of all these, modernization has become decreasingly difficult, even if not necessarily less painful. However, the consensus about the meaning and desirability of modernization, progress, and industrialization is now eroding.

Indeed, the current popularity of the anti-growth movement suggests that the acceptance of a notion of progress, like that of other ideas and values, may be transient. If so, the modernization process could become much more difficult or even stop prematurely. We do not believe that this would be desirable. If there can be a renewed consensus—and if the human duality of extreme recalcitrance and rigidity coupled with surprising adaptability is better understood— more ways may be found to facilitate cultural change. This may require making modernization exciting and fashionable once more.

Consider the following analogy. Suppose that in a psychological experiment small children who were learning to walk were placed in the doorway of a large room and asked to move ahead on their own feet. In one case, the children's mothers were allowed to stand passively in a doorway behind the children; in another, the child was placed in the doorway, pointed forward, and the door was closed behind the child. Those children who sensed their mothers standing behind them were able to walk ahead with far greater ease than those who sensed that no one was there.

Support and admiration by outsiders can play a similar positive role in economic development. Conversely, non-support, harping on the negative aspects of development, or ill-advised criticism of the country concerned without reference to its positive achievements can hinder modernization.

Western ambivalence toward modernization, even when there is approval of the goals, is clearly seen in Karl Marx. Marx disliked the bourgeoisie and many aspects of industrialization, but he accepted both as necessary and inevitable steps in the historical development of what we call the post-industrial society. Marx's perspective, argument, lucidity, passion, and drama retain their pertinence:

> The bourgeoisie has disclosed how it came to pass that the brutal display of vigor in the Middle Ages, which Reactionists so much admire, found its fitting complement in the most slothful indolence. *It has been the first to show what man's activity can bring about. It has accomplished wonders far surpassing Egyptian Pyramids, Roman aqueducts, and Gothic cathedrals; it has conducted expeditions that put in the shade all former Exoduses of nations and crusades.*
>
> The bourgeoisie cannot exist without constantly revolutionizing the instruments of production, and thereby the relations of production and with them the whole relations of society. Conservation of the old modes of production in unaltered form was, on the contrary, the first condition of existence for all earlier industrial classes. Constant revolutionizing of production, uninterrupted disturbance of all social conditions, everlasting uncertainty and agitation distinguish the bourgeois epoch from all earlier ones. *All fixed, fast-frozen relations, with their train of ancient and venerable prejudices and opinions, are swept away, all newly-formed ones become antiquated before they can ossify. All that is solid melts into air, all that is holy is profaned, and man is at last compelled to face with sober sense, his real conditions of life, and his relations with his kind.*
>
> The need of a constantly expanding market for its products chases the bourgeoisie over the whole surface of the globe. It must nestle everywhere, settle everywhere, establish connections everywhere.
>
> The bourgeoisie has through its exploitation of the world-market

given a cosmopolitan character to production and consumption in every country. To the great chagrin of Reactionists, it has drawn from under the feet of industry the national ground on which it stood. All old-established national industries have been destroyed or are daily being destroyed. They are dislodged by new industries, whose introduction becomes a life and death question for all civilized nations, by industries that no longer work up indigenous raw material, but raw material drawn from the remotest zones; industries whose products are consumed, not only at home, but in every quarter of the globe. In place of the old wants, satisfied by the productions of the country, we find new wants, requiring for their satisfaction the products of distant lands and clime. In place of the old local and national seclusion and self-sufficiency, we have intercourse in every direction, universal inter-dependence of nations. And as in material, so also in intellectual production. The intellectual creations of individual nations become common property. National one-sidedness and narrow-mindedness become more and more impossible, and from the numerous national and local literatures there arises a world-literature.

The bourgeoisie, by the rapid improvement of all instruments of production, by the immensely facilitated means of communication, draws all, even the most barbarian, nations into civilization. The cheap prices of its commodities are the heavy artillery with which it batters down all Chinese walls, with which it forces the barbarians' intensely obstinate hatred of foreigners to capitulate. *It compels all nations,* on pain of extinction *to adopt the bourgeois mode of production;* it compels them to introduce what it calls civilization into their midst, i.e., to become bourgeois themselves. In a word, *it creates a world after its own image.*

The bourgeoisie has subjected the country to the rule of the towns. It has created enormous cities, has greatly increased the urban population as compared with the rural, and has thus rescued a considerable part of the population from the idiocy of rural life. Just as it has made the country dependent on the towns, so it has made barbarian and semi-barbarian countries dependent on the civilized ones, nations of peasants on nations of bourgeois, the East on the West.

The bourgeoisie keeps more and more doing away with the scattered state of the population, of the means of production, and of property. It has agglomerated population, centralized means of production, and has concentrated property in a few hands. The necessary consequence of this was political centralization. Independent, or but loosely connected provinces, with separate interests, law, governments and systems of taxation, become lumped together in one nation, with one government, one code of laws, one national class-interest, one frontier and one customs-tariff.

The bourgeoisie, during its rule of scarce one hundred years, has created more massive and more colossal productive forces than have all preceding generations together. Subjection of Nature's forces to man, machinery, application of chemistry to industry and agriculture, steam-navigation, railways, electric telegraphs, clearing of whole continents for cultivation, canalization of rivers, whole populations conjured out of the ground—what earlier century had even a presentiment that such productive forces slumbered in the lap of social labor?[2]

Marx, along with many capitalist economists, seems to view acculturation as relatively simple, with much the same impact in all cultures and in all times. We now know that this is incorrect; different cultures and even different nations and groups within a culture are often affected quite differently by the rise of the bourgeoisie and by industrialization. Furthermore, there is at least as much continuity as change in societies undergoing industrialization. "Creative destruction" does occur, but there is also much evolution and just plain creation.

The Communist Manifesto was written in 1848. Since then, the bourgeoisie and capitalism have released more "massive and more colossal productive forces" than even Marx envisioned. Today the effects are almost as widespread and pervasive as Marx anticipated, but it was not until after World War II that industrialization spread worldwide. Furthermore, it is no longer solely Western or capitalist. Various socialist economies compete to furnish alternative patterns for industrialization even in the short run. Furthermore, neo-Confucian cultures seem to be better at industrialization, and perhaps modernization as well, than Western cultures.* There are truly many roads up each mountain and many mountains up to heaven. Modernization seems increasingly likely to take different paths in different societies.

During the early economic development of Russia and Japan, and in much of the early post–World War II literature on modernization, the idea was prevalent that progress was achieved by destroying the old society and starting afresh from a *tabula rasa*. The Soviet Union and mainland China are probably the most outstanding successes of this violent synthesis approach—at least if one looks at ends and does not count the costs. Yet some scholars have pointed out that modernization was well under way under the tsars and speculated that if this had continued even more might have been achieved than under the Soviets—and at much lower human and economic costs

---

*We develop this argument in several places below. See also Chapter 6 and Chapter 8.

and with the end result a much more desirable and attractive society. Indeed, mainland China began in 1978 to turn some of the clocks backward.

The violent synthesis approach also worked elsewhere, but usually only partially, inadequately, and without staying power. It was once commonplace to say that Kemal Ataturk modernized Turkey after World War I. Ataturk and his followers did achieve much, but Turkey still does not look very modern some fifty years later. Indeed, to the extent that Turkey is a modern nation, the real modernization occurred without much coercion during what we call *La Deuxième Belle Epoque* (1948 to 1973).* However, Ataturk did create some important preconditions.

It is no longer widely believed that a *tabula rasa* or resort to violent synthesis is a prerequisite for the successful industrialization of any of the current Middle Income countries. These societies have learned to exploit their strengths and alleviate their weaknesses and have launched themselves on the path to industrialization. We argue that *under current conditions* the neo-Confucian cultures have many strengths and relatively few weaknesses. Japan, South Korea, Taiwan, Hong Kong, Singapore, and the ethnic Chinese minorities in Malaysia and Thailand seem more adept at industrialization than the West. Mainland China, and perhaps Vietnam or North Korea will probably soon join this list, although the issue is still moot.

If industrialization is measured by gross national product per capita (GNP/CAP), Japan is almost certain to surpass the United States in a decade—or sooner. South Korea has a fair chance of duplicating this feat early in the twenty-first century. Many of the others may do so in the long run. The People's Republic of China will probably not do this well as long as it values its announced goal of the creation of a "new man" more than it does GNP/CAP. The new "revisionist" regime of Hua Kuo-feng and Teng Hsiao-ping is clearly willing to make many changes to facilitate production. However, any stark and fundamental confrontation between socialist ideology and production goals could still run into trouble if motivated by the slogan "ideology and production, but ideology before production" if not now, then in the future.

In the past, Confucian cultures were appraised quite differently. For more than a hundred years, from the early 1800s to the early 1900s, China's industrialization was hindered by its rigidly anti-modern

---

*See Chapter 4 for a detailed discussion of the four sub-periods of the twentieth century.

culture. Even after the revolution of 1911, this cultural legacy, the political and social disorder, World War I, the global depression in the late 1930s, and the Japanese invasion continued to hinder development. However, the old rigidities and blocs have eroded and the cultural legacy is now positive. Since 1945, almost every neo-Confucian culture has, in its own way, been highly skillful at industrialization. The conventional wisdom of the late nineteenth and early twentieth centuries that the Chinese simply could not learn how to industrialize has been turned inside out to read, "The Chinese can industrialize under any and all circumstances."

When the old molds of the different subcultures of the Sinic area were sufficiently modified (but not destroyed), each could begin to choose its own path to industrialization. The Confucian culture area contrasts with the Indian culture area, which in some ways has had almost as brilliant and long a past as the Chinese. Europeans traditionally thought of the Indian continent as an area of great riches. For about two thousand years, trade with India drained the Mediterranean world and Europe of gold and silver because Europeans had little to offer the Indians in return for their jewels, silks, and spices. Yet until recently, Indian subcultures have been spectacular failures at modernization; there is no country in the Indian culture area whose per capita income is much over $300.[3]

Two thirds of the world's poor live in the Indian culture area; the rest live in parts of Latin America (usually in Amerindian culture areas), in tribal Africa, or in resource-poor countries in North Africa and the Middle East. We argue later that all of these areas should do reasonably well in the long run, but we do not expect a remarkable reversal of past experience comparable to that in the Confucian cultures. Some parts of Latin America and Africa may do well. These will probably come from among those countries that have already attained Middle Income status.

It was often assumed in the past that industrialization was best accomplished through parliamentary institutions and the free market. This seemed to be the lesson of the English, Dutch, and American experiences. But when Germany, soon followed by Russia, also began to industrialize with great skill and rapidity, some doubts appeared. During the period we call *La Première Belle Epoque* (1886 through 1913), for example, tsarist Russia grew at an average of about 5 percent per year. When Japan modernized, it became obvious that authoritarian regimes with a relatively mixed economy could also do well. Finally, as the dramatic accomplishments of the Soviet Union and the People's Republic of China became clear, the idea gained ground that only totalitarian regimes could modernize effectively and rapidly.

Such reasoning ignores both the early and the even more impressive later successes of various democratic and authoritarian regimes. It also exaggerates the admittedly impressive achievements of the Soviet Union and the People's Republic of China. The Soviet Union probably had little choice but to follow a severe authoritarian or totalitarian pattern. Any attempt to create parliamentary democracy in Russia would likely have been as short-lived as was the Kerensky government.

For most countries, something between the democratic and totalitarian models seems appropriate for development. Any shade between those two extremes may suit different countries under different circumstances. We prefer democracy, just as we tend to prefer a relatively free market and private enterprise to socialism and the welfare state, even for poor countries. Yet we are not rigid on this point. Hong Kong is one of the best examples of an intelligently run free market economy, while Singapore is a well-run welfare-oriented economy with much more socialist state intervention. Both countries have done magnificently. However, our ideological preference notwithstanding, Singapore has done a better job. And Taiwan and South Korea (which are in between) also seem to utilize state intervention, planning, and overall guidance with great skill.

The concept "many mountains to heaven and many roads up each mountain" is a valid recipe for modernization. Of course, the small-is-beautiful or voluntary-simplicity adherents may ask, "Why do we have to climb mountains? We prefer the foothills." We would not argue with them if they are sincere in what they say and are not an elitist minority group trying to impose its will. Many people have lived in the foothills and lived quite well.* It is difficult to imagine a more impressive society in some ways than Athens in the fifth century B.C. Of course, the Athenian culture was based on slavery, but possibly it could have been achieved without slaves and with only a minimum use of technology. By our definition, unless a culture uses

---

*We include in the term "living in the foothills" what is sometimes called the mastery of inner space and the more extreme anti-technology, spiritual, or aesthetic commune movements—i.e., almost all the contexts of themes discussed under Low Growth Worlds in Chapter 2. All of these have goals that could be called modernization—but it is such a different kind of movement from that traditionally associated with the term that a different expression is preferable even if one of these movements turns out to be the wave of the future.

technology at least as a way station, it is not modern no matter how brilliant it may be. The concept of modernization is inextricably bound up with the industrial revolution, with increasing affluence, and with advancing technology.

Most readers of this book are familiar with the argument of Max Weber that the Protestant ethic was extremely useful in promoting the rise and spread of modernization.[4] Most readers, however, will be much less familiar with the notion that has gradually emerged in the last two decades that societies based upon the Confucian ethic may in many ways be superior to the West in the pursuit of industrialization, affluence, and modernization. Let us see what some of the strengths of the Confucian ethic are in the modern world.

The Confucian Ethic

The Confucian ethic includes two quite different but connected sets of issues. First and perhaps foremost, Confucian societies uniformly promote in the individual and the family sobriety, a high value on education, a desire for accomplishment in various skills (particularly academic and cultural), and seriousness about tasks, job, family, and obligations. A properly trained member of a Confucian culture will be hardworking, responsible, skillful, and (within the assigned or understood limits) ambitious and creative in helping the group (extended family, community, or company). There is much less emphasis on advancing individual (selfish) interests.

In some ways, the capacity for purposive and efficient communal and organizational activities and efforts is even more important in the modern world than the personal qualities, although both are important. Smoothly fitting, harmonious human relations in an organization are greatly encouraged in most neo-Confucian societies. This is partly because of a sense of hierarchy but even more because of a sense of complementarity of relations that is much stronger in Confucian than in Western societies.

The anthropologist Chie Nakane has pointed out that in Western societies there is a great tendency for "like to join like" in unions, student federations, women's groups, men's clubs, youth movements, economic classes, and so on.[5] This tends to set one group in society against another: students against teachers, employees against employers, youths against parents, and so on. In the Confucian hierarchic society, the emphasis is on cooperation among complementary elements, much as in the family (which is in fact the usual paradigm or model in a Confucian culture). The husband and wife work together and cooperate in raising the children; each has different assigned duties and responsibilities, as do the older and younger siblings and the grandparents. There is emphasis on fairness and equity, but it is fairness and equity in the institutional context, not for the individual as an individual. Synergism—complementarity and cooperation among parts of a whole—are emphasized, not equality and interchangeability. The major identification is with one's role in the organization or other institutional structure, whether it be the family, the business firm, or a bureau in the government.

Since the crucial issues in a modern society increasingly revolve around these equity issues and on making organizations work well, the neo-Confucian cultures have great advantages. As opposed to the earlier Protestant ethic, the modern Confucian ethic is superbly designed to create and foster loyalty, dedication, responsibility, and commitment and to intensify identification with the organization and one's role in the organization. All this makes the economy and society operate much more smoothly than one whose principles of identification and association tend to lead to egalitarianism, to disunity, to confrontation, and to excessive compensation or repression.

A society that emphasizes a like-to-like type of identification works out reasonably well as long as there is enough hierarchy, discipline, control, or motivation within the society to restrain excessive tendencies to egalitarianism, anarchy, self-indulgence, and so on. But as the society becomes more affluent and secular, there is less motivation, reduced commitment, more privatization, and increasingly impersonal and automatic welfare. Interest in group politics, group and individual selfishness, egoism, intergroup antagonisms, and perhaps even intergroup warfare all tend to increase. It becomes the old versus the young, insiders versus outsiders, men versus women, students versus teachers, and—most important of all—employees against employers. The tendencies toward anarchy, rivalry, and payoffs to the politically powerful or the organized militants become excessive and out of control.

For all these reasons we believe that both aspects of the Confucian ethic—the creation of dedicated, motivated, responsible, and educated individuals and the enhanced sense of commitment, organizational identity, and loyalty to various institutions—will result in all the neo-Confucian societies having at least potentially higher growth rates than other cultures. We will argue in Chapter 6 that three neo-

Confucian societies—Japan, South Korea, and Taiwan—are now doing very well indeed, but for quite different reasons. Japan, of course, is in some ways still the most formal and hierarchic modern society and has retained many of its other traditions. South Korea has traditionally been more Confucian than Confucian China. Even under the Japanese occupation and during the post war turmoil it did not lose this characteristic. Taiwan tries to be the cultural and political heir of traditional Confucian China and consciously prizes its Confucian heritage. However, among Confucian societies, Taiwan is one of the most individualistic and competitive.

The Issue of Culturism and Neo-Culturism

There is great concern in the world with racism, sexism, excessive nationalism, and other "isms" that are believed to create undesirable, if not immoral, attitudes. We define *culturism* as the belief that culture is rather sticky and difficult to change in any basic fashion, although it can often be modified. Culturism assumes that various cultures differ not only in their aesthetic tastes, customs, values, and traditions, but also in their abilities to cope with various kinds of problems and situations. Specifically, cultures differ in their capacities for modernization either in their indigenous setting or in various foreign settings. We believe that this ability to modernize often depends upon time and place. Sometimes what are relatively minor changes from the viewpoint of the basic culture can make huge differences. (It is as a result of such relatively small changes that neo-Confucian cultures are now probably more adept at modernization than Western cultures.)

We think of ourselves as culturists or perhaps neo-culturists. The prefix *neo-* is appropriate because we believe in the basic adaptability of cultures as well as their tendency to resist basic changes, and we believe that under modern conditions it is going to be increasingly easy for almost every culture to modernize.

We do not think of cultures as genetically determined. We would be very surprised if the existence of any significant genetic element in determining the variations among most, and perhaps among all, cultures is established. We do not, however, deny the theoretical possibility of such an element. In principle there is no reason why some psychological dispositions might not be genetic. But we know of no persuasive evidence for the existence of genetically determined cultural differences.

Our point is simple. Different cultures socialize children differently. Even with a relatively unitary culture, child rearing practices vary over time, place, and class. These child rearing practices and the other existing institutions strongly affect the performance of the culture. Because it is easy to visualize the political and ideological abuse of such a belief as neo-culturism, there is a tendency to deny or ignore important cultural differences that significantly affect the behavior of individuals and nations. We argue that it is difficult if not impossible to understand the kinds of issues we are discussing unless one is a neo-culturist. We are not cultural determinists, but we do believe in the strong influence of culture.

We are also cultural relativists. At least for most cultures, we believe that the notion of one culture as generally superior to another culture has no particular meaning except from a specific perspective and by specific criteria that often depend on time and place as much as on the cultures being compared. We do not argue that all cultures are equally good but only that all cultures have good and bad points, especially if judged from their own perspectives, and often if judged from other perspectives as well.

This doctrine could be dangerous. Many believe it translates easily into racism, excessive nationalism, or other unpleasant attitudes. We believe that under current conditions most of this concern is excessive. Such attitudes are not caused by a distortion of neo-culturist doctrines but *vice versa*. The nationalism, racism, or other attitude already exists, and then "observations" about different cultures are used to rationalize them.

Whether or not one accepts our analysis of *why* neo-Confucian cultures are so competent in industrialization, the impressive data that support the final thesis are overwhelming. The performance of the People's Republic of China; of both North and South Korea; of Japan, Taiwan, Hong Kong, and Singapore; and of the various Chinese ethnic groups in Malaysia, Thailand, Indonesia, and the Philippines, discloses extraordinary talent (at least in the last twenty-five years) for economic development and for learning about and using modern technology. For example, the North Vietnamese operated one of the most complicated air defense networks in history more or less by themselves (once instructed by the Soviets), and the American army found that the South Vietnamese, if properly motivated, often went through training school in about half the time required by Americans. We do not gloss over the enormous differences among these neo-Confucian cultures. They vary almost as much as do European cultures. But all of them seem amenable to modernization under current conditions.

We are aware that excessive emphasis on this kind of doctrine may lead to problems, even if it doesn't turn into racism or nationalism. It might but normally does not lead to a feeling of inferiority by other cultures. Most people have a remarkable ability to live with these kinds of differences and function well unless the demonstration and discussion is more flagrant and invidious than seems likely to occur.

The converse, however, is less true. It is likely, for example, that members of neo-Confucian cultures will get a sense of superiority, whether cultural, racial, or nationalistic. We do not think it is bad for Westerners or others to understand and accept our cultural arguments. We do believe that Japanese society, South Korean society, and to a lesser extent other neo-Confucian minorities around the world may become arrogant and self-satisfied in ways that would be unpleasant if not dangerous. Some Confucian societies have a long history of cultural arrogance, self-confidence, and self-respect. When limited, this is extremely constructive and healthy, but it is easily carried to an excess that includes contempt for other cultures or practices. We noted in recent travels in these neo-Confucian societies they have begun to accept their "cultural superiority" with great ease. Indeed, many want to carry it a bit further than we feel is either useful or justifiable.

Such feelings of superiority have existed at one time or another in almost all groups, cultures, and nations, including the French, the English, the Germans, the Japanese, and the Americans. (An American congressman early in the twentieth century said, "Someday Shanghai will arrive at the cultural level of Cincinnati"; Napoleon called the British "a nation of shopkeepers.") It seems to us there is a very good chance of a revival of contempt for the West and particularly for the Americans. (Attitudes of superiority can also have ideological, religious, or other roots. Thus, East Germany and the Soviet Union tend to despise the West as materialistic, hedonistic, and decadent.)

In many ways Western cultures appear decadent—at least from any traditionalist perspective. Young people appear, superficially, to be less patriotic than their parents and grandparents and also distinctly less willing to make sacrifices for the public interest or even their own careers (except as part of a trendy fashion such as environmentalism). They are distinctly less willing to accept military training or any kind of onerous task or discipline, no matter how valid or important the local or national need. There is extreme hedonism, self-indulgence, decadence, and vice. There is general concern in all of the neo-Confucian societies, the Soviet Union, and East Germany, that some of these "diseases of the West" be kept away from their own people. In this respect, the current Western campaign in favor of human rights may backfire badly because in many Confucian societies it looks like a campaign for selfish, self-indulgent, and reckless individualism and egoism.[6]

CULTURAL ENCOUNTERS AND RAPID CULTURAL CHANGE

One of our goals in this book is to understand the impact of various forms and aspects of modernization on the more than 150 different nations that now exist. Many of these nations are themselves highly complex societies with numerous diverse subcultures, subgroups, and social classes that also vary in their reactions to the various pressures and inducements. We wish to enlarge the perceptions of our readers about the diversity of possible cultural encounters and the varied patterns of reactions to those encounters.

We are particularly interested in contacts between two groups, societies, or cultures, when one is clearly superior to the other in some important competitive area such as agriculture, industry, technology, military prowess, or organizational ability. Even if the superiority is recognized by both sides, there is often much disagreement about its source. Some of the confusion that accompanies such contacts often arises from this disagreement. There is also often disagreement about the value of this superiority and thus in the willingness of various groups to undergo changes to gain similar advantages.

To facilitate this understanding and enlargement we will discuss briefly a large number of examples taken from the ancient world and the recent past. We find in them many useful analogies to the impact of the West on non-Western cultures, to the overall impact of modernization, and to how the introduction of new values affects cultures. These examples are particularly valuable because many are at least partly familiar. Because our descriptions are sketchy, these examples may seem bizarre, irrelevant to what is going on today. However, we believe every example has a contemporary analogue and is useful in understanding today's world, particularly the reactions that are irrational or that involve magical and symbolic elements that must be understood in their own terms.

We have borrowed a paradigm and much supporting material from two colleagues to facilitate discussion of these relatively subtle and unfamiliar issues.[7] This paradigm suggests four basic kinds of reaction patterns—acceptance or rejection either with or without violence (see Table 3.1). We classify rejection as either rational or non-rational, but use three categories for acceptance or synthesis: talismanic, semi-talismanic, and rational.

Non-Violent Rejection of the Intruding Culture

Rational

The Pharisees "separatists" earned their name because they vigorously opposed Hellenistic customs. Scholars seem to agree that the *New Testament* view of the Pharisees as arrogant and tendentious is misleading. By rejecting Greco-Roman culture, they gave up any chance to achieve political ends by working through the existing system. The Pharisees were not particularly violent or demented. They tried to minimize their contact with the Greco-Roman culture because they felt they had more to lose than to gain from an exchange. They simply preferred their own way of life. As the historian Ralph Marcus notes, their messianic hope amounted to a "bold and original program" for the promotion of treasured values and customs, despite a hostile foreign rule.[8]

The Slavophiles were a rather homogenous group of well-to-do intellectuals who flourished in Russian society in the 1840s and 1850s. They felt that their mission was to define Russia's historical role and its place in the world in terms of Russia's relationship to the West. Slavophile theories emphasized that "organic togetherness" was the ideal human condition and that ancient Slavic society and culture epitomized this ideal. Their reactions to the West were an amalgam of fear, insecurity, and arrogance based on a sense that Russia was too good for the West, and a belief that the West would destroy the Russian soul. Tolstoy shared these views. Slavophiles believed that Russia could match from its unique historical resources anything the West could offer. Solzhenitsyn today has many elements in common with the Slavophiles.

Gandhi's rejection of the West was based on the major precepts of Hinduism, his religion. He strongly believed that one's life should be ordered only by those wants that can be satisfied through physical labor by the individual. In an extreme form, this belief in self-sufficiency was as much psychological as religious. Gandhi reacted negatively to the West's dependence on mechanical tech-

TABLE 3.1
Reaction to Cultural Change

I. *Nonviolent Rejection of Intruding Culture*
  A. *Rational*
    Pharisees
    Slavophiles (Tolstoyan)
    Gandhi
    Latin Amerindians
    Négritude
    Dutch Guiana Bush Negroes
  B. *"Apocalyptic"*
    Essenes
    South African "Zionists"

II. *Violent Rejection of Intruding Culture*
  A. *"Austere" and Largely Rational*
    Maccabeans
    Bar Kochba
    Wahabis
    Sepoy Rebellion
  B. *"Manic"*
    Zealots
    Some American Indian Uprisings
    Boxers
    Mau-Mau

III. *Nonviolent Synthesis with Intruding Culture*
  A. *"Talismanic" (or Magical)*
    "Rice Christians"
  B. *Semi-Talismanic*
    Primitive Christians (Gnostics)
    "Afro-Asian Socialism" (Pacific, as in Burma, Ceylon, India, etc.)
  C. *Rational*
    Sadducees
    Brahmo-Samaj
    Meiji Japan (1880-1900)

IV. *Violent Synthesis with Intruding Culture*
  A. *"Talismanic" (or Magical)*
    Tai-Ping
    Lumpa
  B. *Semi-Talismanic*
    Bolsheviks
    Maoists
    India
  C. *Rational*
    Black Muslims

nology and to its money economy. He thought these would cause more dissatisfaction, lack of confidence, and suffering among his fellow Indians than the poverty they were already experiencing. He was not a modernizer, although many of his followers were.

Gandhi's approach was rational. He neither blindly rejected the West's intrusion nor simply advocated reactionary conservatism. He believed strongly that human existence is a journey of "ceaseless growth," but he saw this growth as spiritual rather than material, a progression from violence and selfishness to non-violence and simplicity. Like the Slavophiles, Gandhi was trying to protect his culture and tradition from Western intrusion. Many adherents of so-called Buddhist economics (e.g., Schumacher) are Gandhian in trying to find alternative kinds of growth.

In discussing *Latin Amerindians*, a sharp distinction must be made between the Amerindian and and the Mestizo. The Mestizo usually speaks Spanish and is poor, but is basically part of the predominant Western modernizing culture. If you ask a Mestizo why he wears sandals, he is likely to reply that he wears sandals because he is poor. An Amerindian would say it's because he wants to keep his feet close to Mother Earth. These different responses symbolize different relationships to the Westernizing cultures. The Amerindian's reaction emphasizes his cultural belief that poverty has some intrinsic value. It is an affirmation of his way of life. The Amerindian does not, therefore, seem to have much potential for change or growth on the Slavophile model.

The term *Négritude* was coined in 1935 by Aimé Césaire, a black from Martinique. Négritude represented a movement in the then French dominated West Indies and West Africa that considerably predated the black power and the black-is-beautiful movements in the United States. The similarities are obvious. Both movements emphasize the integrity and importance of blackness. The Negritude movement was an intellectual response to the French policies of assimilation. Césaire deliberately selected the term *Négritude* with its pejorative connotation to stimulate a re-evaluation of blackness and black people, not so much by whites as by the blacks themselves. In 1959 he redefined *Négritude* as follows:

> . . . the consciousness of being black, the simple recognition . . . of one's destiny as a black person, of one's history and of one's culture.

At an earlier date, Césaire expressed the spirit of the reaction to French policy in a poignant poem:

Mercy! Mercy for our omniscient conquerors
Hurray for those who never invented anything
Hurray for those who never explored anything
Hurray for those who never conquered anything
Hurray for joy
Hurray for love
Hurray for the pain of incarnate tears.[9]

The poem's deliberate exaggeration shocks the reader out of what Césaire probably thought of as a blind acceptance of the French policy of assimilation. His attitude was less a matter of hostility to people who invented, explored, and conquered than a plea for the resurrection of blackness as an identity of genuine value. Thus, "Hurray for joy, for pain and tears."

The Dutch Guiana (Surinam) Bush Negroes are descendents of African slaves brought to Surinam in the seventeenth century. In the nineteenth century they rebelled against their masters and escaped into the jungle. To this day, the group, estimated at about forty thousand, remains quite independent. They speak variations of African languages, and continue a separate existence both physically and culturally. They understand the differences between themselves and more modern urban cultures and prefer what they have. They seem to live well on their own terms and clearly prefer their life in the jungle to what we would regard as a more "civilized" life. This preference seems genuine rather than a result of a lack of knowledge about or experience with alternative life styles. Surinam has a 200-year history of changing control by the British, French, and Dutch. The domination by different Western powers may have exacerbated the anti-Western, pro-tradition reaction of the Bush Negroes.

During *La Deuxième Belle Epoque* (1948 to 1973) this type of rational rejection of modernization and Western culture was rare. "Rational" rejection occurs almost exclusively among upper-middle class elites in Western cultures. The quotation marks around rational refer more to the seemingly calm and reasonable tone of the arguments than to the substance of most of these discussions. Many people of this persuasion who now live in communes or have dropped into a life of "voluntary simplicity" can be correctly categorized as rationally rejecting much of Western culture—at least for a time.*

"Apocalyptic"

This non-violent rejection of the intruding culture is characterized

---

*The recruits come almost overwhelmingly from upper-middle class families and would normally belong to what we call the New Class.

by a totally religious revelation. Similar behavior by an individual might be considered pathological; by a community, it is more often simply counterproductive (at least from the viewpoint of those who have not received the "divine revelation").

The *Essenes* seceded from the main Jewish community in the first century A.D. in protest against the policies and practices of the Maccabees. They fled into the wilderness, lived a semi-monastic life, and believed that their community would be proclaimed the true Israel in the dawning of the Messianic age. This almost total withdrawal (many of these communities practiced chastity) and equally total commitment to the coming of the Messiah represent an extreme reaction to the Greco-Roman intrusion.

The origins of the *South African "Zionist"* or *"Spirit"* churches are similar to those of the Baptist churches of southern blacks in nineteenth century America. Both used the church simultaneously as a method of assimilation and even more as a way to preserve and defend their own culture in the face of white domination. The South African Zionist churches are highly apocalyptic, emphasizing a mandate received by a prophet in dreams, visions, or resurrection experiences. They expound a strict and austere ethic that includes taboos on alcohol, tobacco, and most Western medicines. Especially in the early days of these "Spirit" churches (from 1908 to the 1920s), their increasing membership was stimulated by a desire for religious and political autonomy. It is significant that the church spread into Rhodesia in the 1920s via migrant workers returning from jobs in white-dominated industries in South Africa.

We are inclined to believe that much of the hippie and drug culture of the late 1960s in the Atlantic Protestant culture area could be categorized as an apocalyptic cultural withdrawal. We expect to see more apocalyptic withdrawal movements in the future, but with fewer destructive effects on the disciples.*

Violent Rejection of the Intruding Culture

"Austere" and Largely Rational

The *Maccabeans* were a group of Jews led by two brothers who rebelled against the Syrian rule of Antiochus IV in the second century B.C. This was a time when Jews were coming to see that their cultural identity inhered far more in their religion than in their political and social forms. The revolt of the Maccabeans, which took the form of highly successful guerilla warfare, was in direct reaction to the

---

*Scandinavia, Holland, England, United States, Canada, and Australia were the sources of almost all the hippies of the late 1960s.

proscription of central aspects of Jewish religion, notably the right of circumcision. The Greeks and the Romans thought of circumcision as an absolutely unthinkable deformation of the human body, much as we would look upon scarring the human face. Since they emphasized and admired nudity, circumcision seemed ludicrous as well as barbarous. To Jews, however, circumcision marks the covenant of God with Abraham and is probably the single most important ritual of the Jewish religion. So it was natural that they would revolt against the "humanistic and humanitarian" Roman laws barring circumcision. The Maccabeans were competent people; they were probably the first non-Greeks who regularly defeated a phalanx.

The *Wahabis* of Nejd (Arabia) were a puritanical Muslim sect that appeared in the interior of Arabia in the early eighteenth century. Between 1803 and 1813 the Wahabis were active militarily, preserving and defending the orthodoxy of their religion against any foreign non-Muslim influence. The current Saudi Arabian dynasty is directly descended from the Wahabi line of kings and still attempts to preserve much of this heritage.

In many ways, the Muslim religion rejects Europeanization. Some of the Muslim hostility to the Israelis can be thought of as a reaction against a European intrusion. Indeed, until recently, Muslim representatives at the United Nations often referred to Israel as a "Western incursion." Most Muslim communities are still religious. No open agnostics or atheists presently govern any Muslim country except Turkey, which has been an aggressively secular state since Ataturk. For all practical purposes, countries such as Iran and Malaysia are also secular states, but they pay at least lip service to Muslim precepts. However, many of the less well-educated are fundamentalist in their attitudes, particularly in Iran.

We do not expect to see much of this violent rational rejection in the modern world, although some would argue that many of the various terrorist groups or violent demonstration movements are best appraised from this perspective. The former are clearly closer to the "manic" movements we are about to discuss; the latter we judge to be closer to the nonviolent but somewhat talismanic rejection with many elements of semi-talismanic synthesis. There are also many rational elements of rational reform and protest that in effect are really a synthesis.

"Manic"

The *Zealots*, a Jewish Palestinian sect of the first century A.D., were uncompromising in their opposition to Rome. Turning to terrorism and assassination, they were known as "Sicarii" (dagger men) because they used hidden daggers to kill people they deemed friendly to Rome. It was a "normal" event for the Zealots to fight to the last man, woman, and child to defend their fortresses, as they did at Masada. The common practice of the Zealots was to draw lots if they lost their fortresses. The men who lost killed the others and then committed suicide.

Many "manic" groups of this kind (but not the Zealots) believed that they were immune to the weapons of their enemies. Thus, the Boxers, the Mau Maus, and some American Indian tribes thought that enemy bullets could not hurt them. In a sense, these groups became crazed by their extremism.

The last of the serious *American Indian uprisings* was planned in 1890. Many different tribes participated in a big gathering on one of the reservations. They had a "talking cross," a practice that involved advancing their cause by using the magic of the enemy. They believed that the uprising would make the railroad disappear and the buffalo return. One of the most interesting Indian uprisings was the caste war in Yucatán, where the local population fought for about twenty years against the Spanish. (They also had a talking cross.) A scholar who studied this group visited Yucatán much later. When he tried to get information about uprisings, nobody could tell him anything. Eventually he went deep into the jungle where he found a group of people waiting for him. They asked, "Where are the rifles?" He replied, "What do you mean?" Evidently, it had been prophesied 100 years earlier that an Englishman would bring rifles a century later. "You are an Englishman; 100 years have passed; where are the rifles?" That these people were in some sense still waiting is significant. They were not militant, but it probably would not have been difficult to touch off another rebellion.

Cultures, customs, or beliefs may become misunderstood under adverse circumstances and over time. Whole nations, sub-groups, and sub-cultural entities have reacted to cultural intrusions in ways that seem pathological or "manic." The reactions vary greatly: often they are far from rational; sometimes they may be rational but very different from what might be expected. Each culture responds uniquely, reflecting different aspects of its particular experience: a complex of memories, legends, grievances from the long- or short-range past, environmental conditions, local literature, and the lives of the individual men and women.

The *Boxers* was the name that foreigners gave to what became an officially supported peasant uprising in China in 1900 whose purpose was to oust all foreigners. The Chinese name means "righteous and harmonious fists." The Boxers believed that their rituals gave them supernatural powers, including immunity to bullets. They were fiercely aggressive against Western influences, killing suspected Chinese Christians on sight and burning churches and foreign residences. They believed that Chinese poverty and all other problems were the direct results of Western contact. The Boxers were explicitly committed to total destruction of the Western presence in China. (China's troubles, in fact, were caused by Malthusian pressures and the decadence of the Manchu governors.)

The *Mau Mau,* the name given to a movement of the Kikuyu tribe of Kenya, was a complex amalgam of religious, inter-tribal, and anti-colonial sentiments during the late 1940s and early 1950s. The movement's origin, however, can be traced back to the first decades of the century and the Kikuyu's long-stifled grievances against white settlers who claimed large tracts of ancient tribal lands. The extreme tactics of the Mau Mau included the horrifying display of dismembered bodies in full public view as warnings of the group's fervor and commitment. Initiates were forced to violate some of the most sacred taboos of their tribe. Having done so, they were symbolically dead men—cut off from the past—and thus resurrected as totally committed to the Mau Mau cause.

Non-Violent Synthesis with the Intruding Culture

"Talismanic" (or magical)

The *Rice Christians* of Asia are often thought of as beggars who spent their time at or near the Christian missions to get handouts of free rice. Actually, they clung to the missions because they saw the West as triumphant; to them the Christian church was the heart of the West. They suspected that this superiority was because of some magical quality that inhered in Christianity. They were, therefore, more interested in magic than rice.

Semi-Talismanic

The primitive Christians *(Gnostics)* constituted a theological movement that reached its peak in the first and second centuries A.D. They believed that passage to heaven was possible only by the use of a special kind of knowledge *(gnosis)* that we characterize as semi-magical. They refuted the traditional Christian concept that belief alone can bring salvation; instead, one must *know.* In a sense the

Gnostics were early examples of what Eric Hoffer calls the "true believers." They believed they understood Christianity better than the Christians.

The semi-magical, somewhat simplistic approach to a new cultural form has many parallels in recent history, particularly in much of post–World War II *Afro-Asian socialism.* Afro-Asian visitors to the United States were often rather patronizing about the "primitive" capitalist system they found here. In their eyes, the United States had a crazy anarchy of markets, while their homelands were blessed with a modern rational socialist planning system.

There is a succinct example in the American play *Raisin in the Sun.* In the play a chauffeur thinks that the essence of being a businessman is to sit in the back of the car while the chauffeur sits in the front. He has no idea that something else happens when the businessman leaves the car, enters his office, and makes use of certain skills. Much of the passion for modernity in the Third World resembles an almost magical belief that merely by taking on some visible outward forms of modernity (much as did the Rice Christians from the church missions), one automatically becomes modern. Similarly, many of the solar energy enthusiasts appeal to magical elements and use incantations in their periodic demonstrations (e.g., Solar Day in June 1978). We take this to be more play than real, but perhaps not.

Rational

The *Sadducees* (ca. 130 B.C. to A.D. 70) were a predominantly aristocratic, wealthy Jewish sect. They were eager to compromise with their pagan Roman rulers and found it easy to assimilate Hellenistic values and attitudes. They even underwent painful operations to remove the appearance of having been circumcised (necessary if they were to compete in the Greco-Roman games). Nevertheless, the Sadducees were highly religious; their lives were bound up with the Temple. Some of them understood that an outward change in appearance does not affect the inner man, while others felt that a change in appearance was the essence of assimilation.

The *Brahmo-Samaj* was an intellectual circle established in 1828 by Rammohan Ray in Calcutta. The group was composed of a number of intellectually bold Bengali Hindu scholars who helped establish the first private modern higher educational institutions in India. Their efforts were clearly a direct result of contact with the West; they espoused Christian ethics and Western educational methods but did not want any part of Christian theology. They strongly preached a return to a monotheistic and Upanishadic Hinduism purged of the abuses of traditional idolatry that they regarded as backward and corrupt. The Brahmo-Samaj, much like other groups of intellectuals in non-Western countries, attempted to combine the best aspects of both worlds.

Meiji Japan (1868 to 1912) began a period of intense borrowing from the West comparable to an earlier borrowing by Japan from China. Remnants of military rule and feudalism were abolished, and a strong Western style centralized bureaucratic government was built under the able leadership of the Meiji emperor. During this time Japan became a modern world power. Rapid industrialization took place, and transformations occurred in science, education, philosophy, art, and literature. Yet Japan retained its distinctive Japanese identity. In fact, the slogan "Western Science, Japanese Spirit," was used, a variation of the earlier slogan, "Chinese Knowledge, Japanese Spirit."

Violent Synthesis with the Intruding Culture

"Talismanic" (or Magical)

The *Tai-Ping* rebellion, which took place between 1850 and 1864 in China, was basically a reaction to foreign intrusion. The rebellion was led by Hung Hsiu Ch'uan who called his movement "the Heavenly Kingdom of Great Peace." Hung had failed the civil service examination and became discouraged and sick. When he recovered, he received a divine revelation that he was the younger brother of Christ. He borrowed elements of Christian doctrine (along with pre-Manchu native elements) to form the ideological basis for the rebellion during which 20 to 40 million people died.

The *Cao-Dai* is an eclectic, strongly nationalistic modern Vietnamese religious sect whose believers see it as the world's most perfect religion. Borrowing elements of religious doctrine from Taoism, Buddhism, Confucianism, and Catholicism, it includes among its pantheon of saints Buddha, Confucius, Jesus, Joan of Arc, Victor Hugo, and Sun Yat Sen. The sect was started in 1926 by a Vietnamese civil servant working for the French administration; he claimed to have received a revelation from God during a seance. In the late 1960s Cao-Dai was reported to have over 100,000 adherents.

The *Lumpa* church is a tribal religious movement in Zambia and Central Africa. The church was begun in 1953 by an African woman named Alice Lenshina who, according to the church doctrine, died and returned to life with God's commandment to save the Africans from witchcraft, sorcery, and sickness. She was widely accepted and by 1960 could claim over 50,000 church members. The church ethics outlawed magic, witchcraft, divorce, polygamy, beer drinking, and many traditional tribal customs. Instead, the church established well organized, clean villages which the government of Zambia considered illegal. Alice Lenshina was arrested in 1971, and the church has declined since then. Alice Lenshina also claimed to be a reincarnated younger sister of the reigning Queen of England—hence her name, a corruption of *Elizabeth Regina.*

Semi-Talismanic

We consider Bolshevism, Maoism, post–1930 Japanese political state Shintoism, and Afro-Asian militant socialism to be semi-talismanic because all share a seldom-recognized strong magical element. In varying degrees, these movements or periods of history made gigantic strides towards modernization in relatively short periods of time against enormous cultural and physical obstacles. But some of the practices of these movements, normally classified as active forms of education and rational indoctrination, also constitute ritualistic and religious propaganda.

An example can be cited from *Maoism* in the early days of the revolution in China. The communists would enter a village and accuse its most senior and respected leader or landlord of the most awful crimes. They then pressed the village for a vote on the leader's guilt or innocence, a vote that often resulted in his execution. This was, in part at least, a ritual killing of the past—a magical element with great potential for changing the orientation of a culture. (It also made the villagers into active accomplices in the revolution.) The stories of Mao swimming across the Yangtze and the incredible ubiquity of the *Little Red Book* indicate a conscious recognition of this magical element in what is essentially Mao's deification. This deification created a mythical hero (or Sacred King) for the purpose of moving a mass of people and giving them a contact point—a locus of faith. This enormously facilitates the painful process of breaking with the past.

In some areas of the world, resorting to magical methods may be necessary to move a nation forward by unleashing energies and sweeping aside obstacles. Such methods may or may not be creative and constructive and aid in introducing useful and permanent institutions. The extent to which people relate to and even yearn for some mixture of this magical violence is remarkable. The sacred cows of India are an interesting example. They are not as serious an economic burden for India as many people think; they are probably a cause of backwardness, though not a major one. But even if the sacred cows were a crucial hindrance to progress, it is clear that no rational movement could remove this obstacle. The intense political, religious, and cultural opposition to such a change could only be overcome by a movement combining magic, charisma, and other superrational elements.

Rational

Finally, we include relatively violent attempts to adapt other cultural forms and ideas to a local culture. These attempts are basically rational rather than magical, but the rationality is based on the idea that large groups of people will take on elements of another culture only if forced to do so. Perhaps certain areas of the world cannot be modernized without introducing charismatic concepts. But such concepts are not sufficient; the country's leaders must be tough. We do not believe that high levels of coercion must be maintained for long periods. Indeed, under current conditions there seems little need in any country to go beyond a moderately coercive and authoritarian society. We believe that once development is started, it behaves like compound interest obtained by judicious investment in technology and capital goods. In most cases, at least under current conditions, this can be done without much violence.

An example is the *Black Muslim* movement in the United States, which has been extraordinarily successful in modernizing people at the bottom of black American society. Most Black Muslim recruits came from federal and state prisons; many were immigrants from the South to the North who were unsuccessful and dropped to the bottom of Northern society. A young black drug addict who joined the Black Muslim system had a much better chance of recovery than with the more orthodox methods used by white society. As Muhammed Ali kept explaining in his talks at Yale and Harvard, people outside the Black Muslims could not understand the movement as long as they thought of it as a political movement; it was a religious movement. At present the Black Muslims have dropped their racial hatred and more irrational elements because, as their new leader put it, "It is no longer necessary for us to use those techniques to lift our people."

We close with the Black Muslims because our emphasis is on the need for a genuine effort to capture and harness the minds and hearts of people. In a sense, development policy must become a "religious" matter in many countries today—particularly in some of those we have described as Very Poor. We do not mean to argue that economic infrastructure, political activity, and planning of concrete programs should be neglected. But we do believe that development can be most successful if these concerns are communicated to people at the level of human psyche where matters of identity and existential meaning are galvanized. The world's major religions—certainly in their formative stages—recognized this. It is in this broad sense that we cautiously use the term *religious* in connection with economic development.

The emergence of new values is one common cultural reaction to the impact of modernization, both in traditional or nonliterate cultures and in complex, literate, and relatively technologically advanced societies. We now turn to a more detailed examination of changing patterns of values in American society and other Advanced Capitalist nations as they make the Great Transition from pre-industrial to post-industrial. We call this change in patterns of value and behavior the rise of the New Emphases. We identify fourteen of these New Emphases. They are most clearly exemplified in the beliefs, behavior, and life style of those who comprise what we call the neo-liberal New Class.

SOME CURRENT CULTURAL CONTRADICTIONS OF ECONOMIC GROWTH: THE NEW EMPHASES

The world is now at a critical point in the history of economic growth and modernization. In the Advanced Capitalist nations, the growth orientation of Western societies, a relatively unquestioned guiding light for the last two centuries, is under direct challenge by advocates of limits to growth and by other groups. At the same time the Middle Income and some of the Poor nations are in a takeoff stage.

Thus, many of the values that underlie growth are now being challenged by the wealthy—possibly with decisive effects for the wealthy. It is too early to predict reliably how much confusion this will cause in the developing nations, but we think that while it will lower the potential growth rate of almost all nations and create some real problems in special cases, it will not change overall trends much. In some cases it will add to the incentives to grow; the prospect of catching up becomes easier and more exciting.

Economic historians have always identified a clear correlation between past economic growth and such underlying cultural elements as the "Thirteen Traditional Levers" listed in Table 3.4. The traditional values embodied in these societal levers and binders are still held by a majority of the American people—perhaps even by

most of the working and middle classes in the United States, Western
Europe, and Japan. However, a relatively "new" emerging set of
emphases is becoming increasingly influential and threatens to slow
or even stop economic growth in the Affluent Market-Oriented
countries. These New Emphases are listed in Table 3.2. Although the
values and preferences outlined there have existed for a long time,
they are now beginning to play a much more intensive, pervasive, and
overwhelming role.

A quick glance may not reveal just how critical their relationship is
to economic growth, but a closer look almost certainly will. It makes a
difference whether these Fourteen New Emphases are held as a
"discretionary choice" (caused by changes in levels of affluence or
awareness or other changes in the world external to the individual), or
because of preferential values and moral imperatives. Whatever their
source and intensity, the New Emphases can create the "cultural
contradictions" referred to in the title of this section.[10] Indeed, growth
as we have known it in Western history would not have begun or
continued if these New Emphases had existed previously as strongly
and widely held values.

We are not arguing that they are all to be deplored. Most are clearly
desirable, at least in moderation. Many adjustments are certainly and
undeniably necessary if growth is to evolve healthily. Eventually
economic growth may cease, but this will probably occur when
economic activity reaches a plateau at a very high level or when our
culture enters some other stage of history. The question of whether
the New Emphases are desirable is not clear-cut; rather, it is mostly a
matter of timing, intensity, tactics, and other subtle distinctions.

We expect that as more nations move into—or further up—the
declining part of the S-shaped curves for population and gross
product, the conflict between the "new" culture exemplified by the
New Emphases and the traditional culture will grow in intensity and
scope. (As always, this is both cause and effect. The New Emphases
aid or force the decline in the rates of growth and the erosion in
dynamism; this in turn reinforces the New Emphases.) We therefore
now turn to a discussion of the important issue of the social limits to
growth. This discussion will provide the necessary context for our
subsequent detailed description of each of the Fourteen New
Emphases.

The Social Limits to Growth

An expanding literature devoted to the so-called social limits to

TABLE 3.2
Fourteen "New" Emphases and Trends in U.S. Values

1. *Selective Risk Avoidance* (Innovators, entrepreneurs, businessmen, and "do-ers" generally must bear all risks and the burden of proof as if only they and not society as well benefited from their profits and efforts)
2. *Localism* ("ins" vs. "outs," no local disturbance or risks because of needs of external world)
3. *Comfort, Safety, Leisure, and Health Regulations* (often to be mandated by government regulation—sometimes approaching "health and safety authoritarianism")
4. *Protection of Environment and Ecology* (at almost any cost to the economy or other programs)
5. *Loss of Nerve, Will, Optimism, Confidence, and Morale* (at least about economic progress and technological advancement)
6. *Public Welfare and Social Justice* (life must be made to be "fair"—equality in result, not of opportunity—justice should not be blind)
7. *Happiness and Hedonism* (as explicit and direct goals in life)
8. *General Anti-Technology, Anti-Economic Development, Anti-Middle Class Attitudes* ("small-is-better" and "limits-to-growth" movements, but enormous resources can be allocated or great economic costs accepted to further Points 1-7 above)
9. *Increasing Social Control and "Overall Planning" of the Economy* (but mostly with New Class values and attitudes and by "input-output" theorists)
10. *Regulatory Attitudes That Are Adversary or Indifferent to the Welfare of Business* (the productivity and profitability of business are taken for granted)
11. *"Modern" Family and Social Values and a De-emphasis of Many Traditional (Survival and Square) Values*
12. *Concern With Self* (often accompanied by an emphasis on mystic or transcendental attitudes and values or an expression of the "me generation")
13. *New Rites, Ceremonies, and Celebrations* (both against and instead of traditional ones)
14. *New Sources of Meaning and Purpose; of Status and Prestige*

growth holds, we believe correctly, that the main limits on economic growth will be caused by decreasing marginal utility for more production per capita and by increased difficulties resulting from the Fourteen New Emphases. Both should lead to a gradual de-emphasis on the production of material goods—or even to a deliberate negative emphasis including hostile attitudes toward innovation, genuine antipathy to business, extreme opposition to Schumpeter's "creative destruction," fear of technology, and so on. Even though we share some of the ideas and values of the New Emphases, when we judge that they are being carried to excesses we refer to "putting sand in the gears."

All of this has been discussed for a long time, but until recently it has not been understood that a diminishing drive for growth, increasing emphasis on other values, and a greater tolerance for sand in the gears might be caused by a near crusade against growth by certain elite groups rather than by the general public. Indeed, such a crusade is often carried out *against* the public's wishes and deeply held interests. We did not fully grasp the extent and speed with which these new attitudes could become influential, but we now expect that a relatively few influential opponents of growth will exert an increasing leverage that will hinder the operation of business in our society.[11]

There is a reasonable basis for the current, much advertised lack of business confidence. It follows that at this critical juncture society should not add any more sand to the gears than is absolutely necessary. In particular, the Fourteen New Emphases seem to be having an extraordinary impact on the costs and risks of doing business in almost all advanced affluent countries. We use the United States (and, subsequently, Japan) as the major referent for discussion of these trends because we are better informed about recent American and Japanese experience. However, we are convinced that these New Emphases represent important social limits to growth in all the affluent OECD nations. Something similar to the Fourteen New Emphases may well turn out to be a basic internal contradiction of capitalism. As capitalist countries become rich, these Emphases may emerge as powerful forces that, if given sufficient priority, eventually slow down or stop further economic growth and perhaps technological advancement as well.

Very different attitudes ranging across a broad spectrum can be adopted toward these Emphases. At least six different attitudes can be discerned. (In discussing these attitudes, we will use attitude toward ecology and environment as a typical issue.)

Traditional Attitudes

1. *A Matter of Indifference.* The traditional attitude of Western culture and of the Jewish, Muslim, and Christian religions is that nature exists to be used or conquered. In harsh climates or environments it is often thought of more as an enemy than as a friend. Whenever ecological values have clashed with other important values, the latter have normally been given priority. The *Old Testament* gives human beings "dominion over the fish of the sea, and over the fowl of the air, and over the cattle, and over all the earth and over every creeping thing that creepeth upon the earth." Neither the *Koran* nor the *New Testament* stresses ecological values for their own sake.[12]

2. *A Discretionary Choice.* These are "more or less" changes in priorities caused by increased affluence, changing awareness and information, technological and social innovations, and other new pressures or opportunities. Relatively narrow cost/benefit criteria can be very important in affecting these choices. People are now seldom really indifferent to the environment, but, until recently, few have felt rich enough to sacrifice much to preserve it. The Advanced Capitalist nations are now so well off by historical standards that clean air, clean water, and aesthetic landscapes are being given much higher priority than previously. However, for most people in most places, they still don't come ahead of enhancing prosperity and security.

3. *A Preferential Value.* These are basic changes in likes and dislikes, tastes, attitudes, values, and customs. For example, French people have traditionally placed a much higher value on taking an annual vacation away from home than have Americans. But younger Americans tend to be closer to the French in this respect than they are to their own parents. Both would make sacrifices for vacations which would be considered ridiculous by the older American.

Emerging Attitudes

4. *Proper or Meritorious Behavior.* More than a preferential value but less than a moral imperative. A good example of proper behavior is the pressure not to pick your nose in public or to belch after a meal. (The latter, of course, varies among cultures; in China belching after a meal shows proper appreciation for its high quality.) It is obviously not immoral

to belch or pick your nose, but it does show that you have been badly raised if you do so; they are "wrong" things to do. Meritorious or proper behavior is also not a moral issue. For example, in many religions, one is supposed to give 10 percent of his income to charity. A practitioner of the religion is under no compulsion to give more than 10 percent, but it is meritorious to do so; it is good behavior and one gets credit for it. We believe that the attitude that will eventually be adopted by most Americans toward the Fourteen New Emphases will place them in the category of proper or meritorious behavior. They will be more than preferential choices but less than moral imperatives or matters of central importance.

5. *Matter of Central Importance* (e.g., *An Issue of Physical Survival; Grave Hazard to Health, Economic, Cultural, or Other Values; or An Issue of Psychic Survival; Aesthetic Imperative*). Many people argue that the New Emphases may not be moral imperatives but that they are still very important for other reasons, so much so that they simply do not wish (or cannot) live in a world in which the relevant New Emphases are not given an appropriate priority. Sometimes their reasons are romantic, sometimes stylistic, sometimes semi-religious. Much of the small-is-beautiful movement or the current emphasis on solar energy partake of this perspective, as do many of those who are participating in the current revolt against the "excessive materialism" of our culture.

Sometimes this belief is held as a literal issue of survival for one or another of the New Emphases (a currently common one is preserving the environment). Often people who really take the moral position given below understand that others do not share their moral values; therefore they switch to the survival issue as more persuasive. Still others take the attitude that the society has become too unpleasant in one way or another; therefore survival is not worthwhile. Even if one did not take such an extreme position, one could still feel it is of the utmost importance that current developments be checked or changed, that the New Emphases be emphasized. Many people who so view preserving the environment are also convinced that they are living in an era of limited resources. Surprisingly, most of these people do not note that in many cases preserving just the appearance of the environment (as in strip mining) does not raise any survival issue but is instead a luxury that can only be indulged by a society with excess resources. Whether or not they make this mistake they typically argue that all ecosystems should be protected, either because they are unique or are part of a larger whole whose interactions are never completely known. They think of the ecosystem as similar to a watch; any interference with the inner works is likely to be disastrous.

6. *Moral, Ideological or Religious Imperative.* Does not allow for give-and-take bargaining, easy compromise, or normal narrow cost-benefit analysis. It is often thought that the issues are obvious and controversies are often thought of as being conflicts between morally secure positions based on higher values and positions that are morally indifferent, or based on lower or vulgar values.

The attitude of discretionary choice is basic. Once a person has many material goods, the marginal utility of having more of them usually goes down and he will not work as hard to get more. Also consider what happens when the welfare state expands. People are still concerned with basic needs, but they depend less on their own efforts because they know the state will provide. They can thus afford to put less emphasis on fending for themselves, on savings, and on insurance. Poor people usually do not object much to pollution if it means more jobs. Richer people feel they can afford to have clean air and clean water, even if it costs them something. None of these new attitudes necessarily represents a change in available information (e.g., attitudes toward some food additives). For most older adults in the United States, these changing conditions are more important than any change in values.

However, changing values *per se* are important for many people—particularly younger groups. As parents become better off they tend to shift the emphasis in the training and education of their children away from economic growth toward other values, many of which are either indifferent or hostile to economic growth. These children grow up with few direct experiences that emphasize and reinforce many of the work-oriented, advancement-oriented, survival-oriented values of their parents. Sometimes the new values are held as moral imperatives rather than as strongly felt preferences that do not raise issues of right and wrong. The difference between preferential values and moral imperatives is important.

Assume that an individual informs the authorities that he or she intends to kill two people a year, but offers to make up for this by turning over to the state enough money to save at least twelve lives a year (perhaps by preventing other murders or by better health and safety precautions). The net effect would be to save ten lives a year. Thus, the self-appointed killer argues persuasively (and inaccurately) that if the authorities care about human life, they will surely accept the offer. However, the injunction against murder is an absolute moral imperative and not just a preference. The state simply will not bargain about the issue. It is not interested in this kind of cost-effectiveness analysis. It wants instead to make clear that murder is an abhorrent crime that will not be tolerated.

Let us assume now that an individual goes to the authorities and says he or she would like to dump a certain amount of pollutants into a river because it is convenient for a specific operation to do so. The person offers to give the state enough money for every pound of pollutants dumped to enable the state to remove or prevent the spread of two pounds of pollutants elsewhere in the river. Therefore, the more the person dumps, the cleaner the river. Almost everybody who is interested in a clean river will accept this offer. Those who hold traditional values will say if we are affluent enough to afford clean water, then let us have it. Those who value clean water over economic growth will also accept the offer even when they are relatively poor. Only those who feel too poor to afford clean water and would therefore prefer that the money be applied to "more urgent tasks" and those who think of preventing pollution as a moral imperative (perhaps almost as strong as that against murder) will find the proposition unacceptable. However, many of these people will not accept an offer to save ten other rivers for permission to dirty one river. They see this as a moral rather than a cost-effectiveness issue.

The Anti-Growth Triad

The most intense support for the New Emphases comes from the upper and upper-middle classes. Within this group there are three subgroups that advocate the New Emphases with a special, indeed in some cases an almost manic crusading zeal. These subgroups we labeled in Chapter 2 the *Anti-Growth Triad*. We sometimes refer to the more extreme members of the Triad as *Crusaders for the New Values* or *Secular Evangelists*. To elaborate our earlier discussion, we see the Anti-Growth Triad as composed of:

1. *Affluent Reformers (or Radicals)*. It is a familiar paradox of politics that members of the upper classes and the aristocracy often lead or work with reformist or even revolutionary groups, sometimes even attacking the society that has been so

benevolent to them—at least in material terms and status. Such people are sometimes referred to pejoratively but accurately as "parlor pinks," "limousine liberals," or devotees of "radical chic." Some, however, genuinely dedicate themselves to these movements in a competent and effective way. (Friedrich Engels and Franklin Roosevelt are good examples.)

2. *Thorstein Veblen's "Leisure Class."* According to Veblen:

> The leisure class is in great measure sheltered from the stress of those economic exigencies which prevail in any modern, highly organized industrial community. The exigencies of the struggle for the means of life are less exacting for this class than for any other; and as a consequence of this privileged position we should expect to find it one of the least responsive of the classes of society to the demands which the situation makes for a further growth of institutions and a readjustment to an altered industrial situation.[13]

The leisure class normally does not have to make "agonizing compromises" because of economic or occupational pressures or to associate closely with the middle class or working class. This is truer today than it was at the end of the century—and also applies to the other two members of the Triad.

3. *Neo-Liberal Members of the New Class.* We will consider the New Class first. Mainly of upper-middle class origin, the New Class derives its status and occupation from possession of considerable education. Its members actually earn their livings through their linguistic, symbolic, analytic, aesthetic, and academic professional skills. They are more or less intellectual or artistic—or are dropouts from such a life into bohemian or voluntary simplicity life styles. The New Class comprises a large part of academia, the media, most "public interest" groups, and many philanthropic, public service, and social service organizations—all of which not only have been growing in size, but are gaining influence in the Western industrial countries and in Japan. While it is not easy to define the New Class precisely, it was once equally difficult to delineate the aristocracy, the bourgeoisie, and the proletariat with great clarity. Each of these classes also contains important sub-classes, new arrivals, and dropouts. Initial analysis suggests that the New Class can be defined in terms of:

• high, or potentially high (i.e., students) formal education;

- professional occupational status, with an emphasis on the "soft" sciences and arts;
- high (but not the highest) income, often derived from professional activities or non-market sources (government or non-profit salaries, grants, and contracts); and
- relative youth.

The last criterion is important. Because the New Class is "emerging," its attributes should be most obvious among the young. In this connection, Karl Marx's insight that a class does not exist unless it is self-conscious is instructive. This kind of consciousness has appeared only recently among members of the New Class. Some intellectuals and bureaucrats have always behaved like the New Class, but perhaps only within the past decade have its members become numerous enough to achieve the critical mass to break out of a subordination to other groups and stike out on their own.[14]

Who Is in the New Class and What Are They Up To?

The New Class is a cultural, social, and economic concept rather than a political, ideological, or ethnic concept. Nevertheless, in the United States it can be conveniently divided into five main political groups. A relatively large group, perhaps about a third of the New Class, has traditional liberal attitudes. These people largely agree with or follow in the tradition of Roosevelt, Truman, Stevenson, Jackson, Meany, and Humphrey. (They should not be confused with so-called nineteenth century liberals who espoused the *laissez-faire* economics of Adam Smith.)

A second group, probably not as large, but at the moment much more self-confident and active, is now frequently called neo-liberal. These people are heavily influenced by the counterculture of the late 1960s. They provided much of the constituency for Eugene McCarthy and George McGovern and almost all of the active members and supporters of such public interest groups as the Sierra Club, Common Cause, and Nader's Raiders.

The remaining third or so of the New Class can be divided into three fairly equal groups: traditional conservatives, neo-conservatives, and the more or less humanist left. Speechwriters for Reagan and Goldwater or the staff of the *National Review* would be typical traditional conservatives. The neo-conservatives would typically include such people as Irving Kristol, Daniel Bell, Nathan Glazer, and James Q. Wilson. The magazine *The Public Interest* is almost a trade journal of the neo-conservatives (and one of the best sources for high quality discussions about United States domestic issues).* Traditional conservatives tend not to trust neo-conservatives because the traditional conservatives cannot always predict their reactions or stands on specific issues. Important differences in values and positions often distinguish these two groups.

The humanist left tends to be closer to the traditional liberals than to the neo-liberals, but they are much more radical in their politics and much more concerned with "human" than with material issues—i.e., with preserving spontaneity, creativity, and "doing your own thing" rather than with trade unionism, social security, income redistribution, or regulation of the stock market.

At the moment, neo-conservatives are relatively "in," and the influence exerted by neo-liberal members of the New Class is no longer as pervasive as it once was. In the 1976 United States presidential election, for example, neither party emphasized neo-liberal New Class issues except for those with very wide acceptance, such as environmental protection. (More than 90 percent of the American public are for protection of the environment—but only at reasonable cost and with reasonable tactics and objectives.) Yet the neo-liberals of the New Class still tend to be extremely important because of their domination of middle-level regulatory agency staff positions, their highly effective use of the law and the courts, their tremendous influence in the media, and their skilled use of public interest organizations, demonstrations, and lobbying campaigns.† Furthermore, barring unexpected events we believe that the neo-liberals will return to the center of the political stage in the early or mid-1980s.

---

*Almost all other organizations with the term "public interest" on their mastheads are largely dominated by the Anti-Growth Triad.

†For example, when President Carter took office in 1976 he appointed about a hundred people who could be characterized as neo-liberal New Class. Almost all were appointed to middle level administrative positions that do not require senatorial confirmation. In most cases the people appointed could not have gained senatorial confirmation if they had been proposed for higher level jobs that require such confirmation. The President did this in part to see to it that these New Class values and attitudes achieved official representation in the governmental decision-making process and in part because he seemed to have thought of many of these persons as objective, although this was clearly incorrect. For a good discussion of many of these appointments see "Nader's Invaders Are Inside the Gate," by Juan Cameron, *Fortune*, October 1977, 252-262.

A strong case can be made that in the late 1960s and early 1970s, the humanist left and the neo-liberal members of the United States New Class, taken together, largely controlled or dominated the following groups and institutions: the humanities and social science faculties of almost all leading universities (both private and public), professional schools, and teachers colleges; most national media organizations (i.e., the influential daily newspapers, most of the periodical press, the book publishing industry, the commercial television networks, recording, films, and most educational media); the fine arts; the establishment foundations and other nonprofit eleemosynary institutions concerned with influencing public opinion; many research organizations; a large part of the staffs of liberal congressmen; the federal social welfare bureaucracy; and the apparatus of the new governmental regulating agencies.

While this domination has weakened, neo-liberal values and sensibilities are continuing to penetrate additional United States institutions and groups, including natural science faculties, business schools, rank and file school teachers, state and local government bureaucracies, the clergy, advertising, trade union staffs, salaried professionals of all kinds, and even business corporations, especially in departments of public relations, long-range planning, and internal education. Private companies have increasingly adopted the expedient of hiring people of this type precisely because they have verbal and analytic skills. Sometimes these people are co-opted by the companies they work for.

The New Class is likely to be in staff rather than line or substantive positions and to produce or deal in ideas or words, holding their jobs because of analytic and literary skills. They are not usually involved in the commercial and administrative aspects of an operation. Thus we do not think of the chief executive officers of these organizations as New Class people. By using the phrase "largely controls or dominates," we mean that they set the basic tone of an organization and its basic policies toward the information it deals with.

Given the "counter-reformation" movement of great strength that developed in the middle and late 1970s, the immediate future role of the neo-liberal New Class movement is in some doubt. (Indeed, this chapter is part of this counter-reformation movement.) By this we do not mean that the size of the neo-liberal New Class will decline markedly, but only that their morale, specific substantive positions, and "excessive" influence may be greatly changed in the next decade or two—depending in part on the outcome of the current debate about their values and goals. Indeed, the neo-liberal New Class is increasingly adopting something between a veneer and reality of modifying their extreme position of taking every issue as a moral imperative of central importance. Some of them, at least, are beginning to apply a test of cost-benefit analysis, or at least are going through the motions of doing so. As a result, they no longer appear to be fanatics. (This does not, however, apply nearly as much to the neo-liberals on congressional staffs—at least as yet.)

Many articles are being published about the neo-liberals and neo-conservatives. Most of these articles are about the excesses of the neo-liberals, the extraordinary resurgence of the conservatives, and sometimes about the excesses of the neo-conservatives as well. There is not as yet any consensus. It would seem that the intellectual argument is now being won by the neo-conservatives. For the first time in American politics since Alexander Hamilton and the Federalist Papers, conservative viewpoints and programs are displaying an intellectual ability and a capacity for scholarship that used to be almost the exclusive property of the liberals. Of course, many of these neo-conservatives would think of themselves as liberals, but the basic points they espouse—the inevitability of inequality, the need for tradition, the importance of patriotism, the suspicion of general principles or sweeping reforms, the intractability of human nature—are all basically associated with a conservative philosophy.[15] (The current emphasis, of course, is on neo-conservative rather than on conservative.)

For some time we have expected compromises resulting from changing emphases and shifting values eventually to lead to a leveling-off or plateau of economic growth—perhaps until something new intervenes—long before the world encountered physical limits (resource shortages or pollution), that might prevent further growth. But we underrated the degree of hostility to growth that would be displayed by the leading edge of the opposition movement. Instead of encouraging or tolerating a gradual shift to values that are hostile or indifferent to growth, the New Class, or certain parts of it, is taking a much more activist and political role—espousing low growth directly as a value in itself (indeed sometimes as a moral imperative) or as an urgent necessity, often throwing sand in the gears of the whole system and in any case impeding it, we believe, too suddenly and too violently. To use Marxist terms, we do not really challenge their historic role, but we do fear that they are going too far too fast.

Why do they do this? We believe that this is best understood by thinking of their position as arising out of a very intense change of values—so intense that it is better thought of as the creation of "moral imperatives." The neo-liberal New Class in fact takes many of the Fourteen New Emphases as moral imperatives. Many people in the Anti-Growth Triad think of the New Emphases as a form of modernization more in tune with current realities than traditional concepts of modernization, i.e., economic development and technological advancement. In the very long run (fifty or so years from now), they may be correct, but we believe that they are, to say the least, premature.

Many New Class people, particularly the neo-liberals, sense that further economic development works against their interests. For example, as the size of the upper-middle class increases, dilution of the benefits of being upper-middle class occurs, as does increased competition for these benefits. Furthermore, increased affluence decreases the availability of many other benefits, such as competent, inexpensive services (e.g., maids). Consequently, the upper-middle class finds itself threatened if, with further modernization, large numbers of people move into the upper-middle class or become affluent enough to crowd them.

Recent books have discussed these phenomena in some detail, but often from a misleading perspective, by assuming that the interests of the existing upper-middle class are the same as everyone else's. They do not recognize that middle class individuals who move up benefit from substantial improvements in their standards of living. Those who have already achieved the higher status feel that they lose something when others join them, a loss usually greatly exaggerated. What is in reality little more than an annoyance hardly justifies the "Third Dismal Theorem" coined by E. J. Mishan: "The more science, technology, and the gross national product grow, the more nasty, brutish, vile and precarious become human existence."[16]

Most analysts concerned with the future of the developed nations believe that in the next century New Class "brain workers" of all political complexions will play central roles in influencing the direction of the societies they live in. If so, much of this influence seems likely to be in the direction of the Fourteen New Emphases. Additional support for neo-liberal positions will come from the rich and from the leisure class, as well as from the upper-middle class generally—indeed, from all groups who believe they gain from maintaining the status quo and slow growth. It will also come from those who are genuinely concerned about specific issues. (The two groups often overlap.) Thus, support for any of the New Emphases can in various circumstances, come from a wider constituency than the Anti-Growth Triad. We turn now to a discussion of each of the Fourteen New Emphases.

The Fourteen New Emphases Elaborated

1. *Selective Risk Avoidance*

This is possibly the most important of the New Emphases, and is to some degree shared by everyone. Many new projects and activities are in fact potentially too big or too dangerous to be viewed with equanimity. Few reasonable people, for example, would favor another dramatic breakthrough in weapons technology such as that which made multi-megaton bombs readily available to techno- logically advanced nations (especially since the number of such nations is growing rapidly). Similarly, little rejoicing is likely when the ability to design children genetically is attained.

One result of these genuinely and almost universally distinctive possibilities is an increased awareness of this kind of issue. We now seem to be trying to decrease many kinds of risks that our society has been willing to accept in the past—trying both to lessen the chance that something will go wrong and to compensate much more fully if things do go wrong. Many of these dangers are purely hypothetical, but they are taken seriously—perhaps too seriously.

No one disputes the need for special efforts to decrease or eliminate new and unevaluated risks. But this attitude persists even if these potential innovations are associated with relatively small disutilities and what would otherwise be very desirable projects. There is an almost overwhelming tendency, at least among the Anti-Growth Triad, to feel that not doing anything is acceptable, since it doesn't change the status quo. By contrast, the risks of doing something positive by innovation and creativity cannot really be evaluated, even when they look favorable. Such attempts to choose between sins of omission and sins of commission affect many aspects of our lives, from medical practice to drilling for oil to construction of nuclear reactors. The New Emphasis on averting risk probably results as much from a sharply decreased willingness by the Anti-Growth Triad to tolerate risks or costs in the service of national economic or political goals as from the enlarged dangers. Indeed, opposition to these risks of commission often camouflages ideological and po- litical class interests. Triad members oppose or doubt the desir- ability of many traditional societal goals. They feel outraged if asked to accept risks on behalf of goals they think of as unwise, depraved.

counterproductive, or obsolete.*

It is not surprising that regulatory authorities and courts much prefer risks of omission to those of commission, especially if personnel of these agencies are themselves members of the neo-liberal New Class or for other reasons feel ambivalent or hostile toward growth goals. As a result, in the absence of corrective forces, the system has already reached a point where it is being increasingly counterproductive—where errors of omission overwhelm excessively feared errors of commission, even from the perspective of many who fear these potential errors.

Among the candidates for obsessive or excessive public concern are various risks associated with environmental protection, unemployment, health, safety, business failure, price and quality of consumer goods, major financial investments, old age, and sickness. All these problems undoubtedly deserve attention, but we believe that many current programs have been pushed to the point of very small or even negative returns, and that most current proposals would make matters worse.

In some cases, the risks really are so dramatic that extreme caution is clearly called for, e.g., manipulating the genetic inheritance of microbes and viruses, the construction of some kinds of nuclear reactors, or the stockpiling of nuclear weapons. Such technologies raise the possibility of unprecedented or unknown dangers in a most alarming fashion—even if little verifiable damage has yet occurred. Risks can in fact be even more alarming if the only indication of danger comes from theoretical calculations involving unreliable

---

*Many members of the environmental movement believe they should not be blamed if cynical people who are trying to preserve the status quo base their arguments on environmental arguments or exploit regulations and laws promulgated to protect the environment for their own purposes. Environmentalists should understand that such uses and abuses of their concepts, regulations, and practices are inevitable. They should accept that this cost (the fact that they have made these tactics so feasible and respectable) should be included. Even when these environmental concepts are sincerely held, one characteristic of the New Class of all political persuasions is a great need to feel self-righteous and, particularly when young, to pursue "higher causes." This is as much a matter of "play" and perhaps even of "growing up" as of serious commitment. There is nothing intrinsically wrong with this, but when it causes unnecessary problems and costs to people who are trying to earn a living or complete important projects, it can easily go too far. None of the above suggests that environmental protection should be neglected, only that costs and risks calculations be done more objectively and less relatively.

assumptions. The uncertainty itself is frightening, and the idea of government or business "playing" with such risks or being callously indifferent to them can be terrifying.

This problem cannot be solved simply by saying that it is better to be safe than sorry. This is the point we wish to emphasize by the phrase, *selective risk avoidance.* The New Class is often perfectly willing to risk the economy, foreign policy, economic growth, high productivity, jobs, and so on. Furthermore, they do not put much value on the important degree of safety that is attained by having a large economic surplus or advanced technological capability to cope with the many problems of the future, whether these are caused by humanity or nature, by ourselves or by others. It is only by emphasizing certain risks and more or less ignoring others that they can claim that it is better to be safe than sorry. A better test would be to ask what would happen to the society as a whole if the standards they suggest were universally applied—a sort of Kantian Categorical Imperative type of premise and test.

Prudence can easily be carried to self-defeating levels—and can also take the form of being callously indifferent to benign possibilities and urgent needs. For example, many medical experts now believe that the cost time, and other difficulties involved in introducing new drugs for general use have become excessive. Not only are many useful remedies never approved or have their approval excessively delayed, but regulations and red tape are so deterring that many potentially useful drugs are abandoned in advance by the companies concerned. It is often pointed out that aspirin, one of the most useful drugs, could probably not be approved today because of its many side effects. The potential contribution of the drug industry in the United States is so curtailed and delayed that many people throughout the world, as well as in America, are paying a price in increased sickness and suffering.[17]

Many other programs of "risk avoidance" seem to have been carried beyond any useful benefit-cost ratio to the point where they have become counterproductive, i.e., where the risk one is trying to avoid is being increased rather than decreased. Thus, malpractice suits in the United States—which are supposed to protect and reimburse patients—are now actually causing so-called "defensive medicine" to be practiced that reduces the quality of medical care while raising its cost. Damages assessed by courts have become so high as to make liability insurance rates a serious block to improved health care. A similar effect is behind one of the major objections of the automobile industry to such safety devices as air bags; the product liability potentialities become horrendous.

As some people become more affluent they may well wish to take fewer risks for the sake of traditional societal goals even as they take more personal risks for their own sake, perhaps to make up for the lack of challenge in their daily lives. It is significant that many Americans are courting increasingly greater physical risks by skiing on dangerous slopes, skin diving to great depths, hang-gliding, and so forth. This seeming paradox is not strange. As society as a whole backs away from risk-taking, many individuals compensate by creating personal excitement, challenges, and tests in the form of extreme physical daring (the number of deaths from these so-called thrill-seeking activities has dramatically increased in recent years).[18] These individuals enjoy placing themselves in an unforgiving environment (as opposed to their usual environment, where nothing is lost if one makes a mistake). This need on the part of some people to test themselves is not a justification for public authorities to be reckless, but it does suggest that some uncompromising and unreasonably protective attitudes and measures should be critically re-examined.

2. Localism

In the Affluent Capitalist countries, local communities increasingly display striking caution and even resistance toward economic development or new projects that involve any local inconvenience, even if the region or the nation as a whole would gain from them. For example, almost everyone benefits by having highways, moderate income housing, factories, and power plants somewhere in the region, but almost everyone loses something by having them located next door.

This localism used to be an important characteristic of underdeveloped nations. It now occurs increasingly in the developed countries as well, at least in those communities where the majority (or an influential minority) has already achieved ample material success and is essentially satisfied with things as they are. There is increasing hostility to being disturbed to promote further economic growth—particularly if this growth is to benefit others. In addition, if people move into communities they like, they usually do not want to see their communities changed—even if the changes are inevitable accompaniments of what would otherwise be desirable growth.

Until the last decade, this conflict has not been severe enough in the United States and most developed countries to prevent needed regional facilities from being constructed or to prevent outsiders from moving where they wished. However, recently a series of events and attitudes has greatly strengthened the hand of local obstructionists, making it more difficult to initiate important projects and to install the infrastructure and facilities needed for rapid economic development. In the United States and elsewhere, tax equalization, revenue sharing, and other legislative or judicial acts that uncouple local revenues from local economic activity have reduced the financial incentives of local people for more development. But most important is the moral support for local opposition to specific projects that is supplied by the general worldwide attack on the morality and desirability of economic growth. This support displays the following attitudes and behavior:

- *Disillusionment with progress.* "You can't fight progress" is no longer an unanswerable argument.
- *Limits-to-growth movement.* It is your duty to fight "progress"; it is not selfish to do so.
- *Environmentalism.* While everything pollutes in some way, why should we suffer from other people pursuing their private or community interests? Many environmental enthusiasts would like to operate the United States like a large museum set in a wilderness preserve.
- *Anti-auto, anti-noise, anti-traffic agitation.* Especially acute now because so many in the upper-middle class are irrationally hostile to the automobile and to such technical innovations as supersonic aircraft.
- *Community control.* In the United States, where much of the motivation for more community control came from the anti-poverty program, this concept did little for the poor, but middle class communities were able to seize upon and use it with a vengeance.
- *Widespread disillusionment with governmental and business leadership.* It is increasingly believed that these elites either do not know what they are doing or have not given adequate attention to the public interest.
- *Greater acceptance of discretionary behavior.** You can "fight

---

*The term "discretionary behavior" is meant to be analogous with the concept of discretionary income. This is income that a family can spend in almost any way it wishes, without jeopardizing its current or future prospects. Similarly, our current society will tolerate a rather large range of behavior which, if the society were operating under crisis or austere condi-

city hall" or other parts of the traditional establishment and get away from it.*

- *Flaccid and sometimes stupid leadership by the establishment.* Not only can you fight city hall and get away with it, you can often win even when you have a bad case if you are willing to work at it or make a big fuss. This is particularly true because the "city hall crowd" is often incompetent at this kind of contest.

- *Growing affluence.* Economic growth and a large tax base are no longer needed as much as they once were to supply needed local revenues and jobs—at least not for the upper-middle class and the rich (i.e., not for the Anti-Growth Triad).

- *Increasing selfishness.* People are more willing to espouse their class or personal interests openly or to hide them under a very thin veneer of promoting the public interest—or are more easily persuaded that they are acting in the larger public interest and for higher values and not for narrow class or private reasons. They seem to be more hypocritical or self-deluded about many growth issues. (To the extent that this occurs because of the recent anti-growth intellectual fashions and similar trendy attitudes, the recent recession, many backlashes, and the "counter-reformation" movement are making many in the Anti-Growth Triad at least aware of accusations of self-interest, hypocrisy, and self-delusion. This may yet lead to a serious re-examination of basic premises and a decrease in their self-righteousness. It has already led to what we called above "the reality or veneer" of moderating extreme

---

tions, would be judged as totally unacceptable. Excessive toleration of discretionary behavior is characteristic of the last stages of a *Belle Epoque* period (such as Europe from 1886 to 1913) and perhaps in the 1960s and 1970s. In fact, it can be argued that this excessive tolerance causes a *Belle Epoque* period to erode. See Chapter 4 for further discussion of this point.

*The phrase "You can't fight city hall" is traditional in many United States cities. It implies that sensible people work with or accept the local government's ideas. Opposing them was so difficult at one time that doing so was like running into a stone wall. Furthermore, causing trouble to city hall created concern that angered officials might retaliate—or at least not cooperate on future issues. We use "city hall" as a metaphor for any part of the establishment once considered too powerful or dangerous to provoke or cross, but that no longer appears so fearsome or potent—or, sometimes, even competent.

positions as moral imperatives or of central importance with regard to many endangered species and environmental issues.)

As we describe in Chapter 6, localism has become an almost overwhelming problem in Japan, in part because of the moral support given by the limits-to-growth movement.

3. Comfort, Safety, Leisure, Health, and Vocational "Self-Actualization"

Poor or ambitious people are often happy to work long hours at relatively dangerous, dirty, dull, or otherwise onerous tasks just because they have to earn a living. This is often not understood by the New Class. An outstanding characteristic of the New Class (and not just of the neo-liberals in it) is the expectation that such sacrifices are not necessary to make a living. They differ so much in this respect from most of the working and middle classes that one of their defining characteristics could be their belief that every human being is entitled to "meaningful" and attractive work of his choice to be done in a pleasant, safe, and otherwise benign environment.

As a result of the influence of trade unions, rising levels of affluence, and the New Class, many Affluent Capitalist countries have or will soon have standards that will make it unreasonable or illegal for anybody to give up much in the way of comfort, safety, or health to earn a living, even if desperately anxious to do so. "Job enrichment" may be imposed on many who only want a reasonable salary, fair treatment, physically acceptable work conditions, and such traditional fringe benefits as pensions and job security. Furthermore, middle management and top executives as well as the poor will become less ambitious and demand more leisure than has been customary. Executives who take three-day weekends (leave early Friday and return late Monday)—or two-month vacations in the summer—are less likely to initiate high-risk projects that require almost daily concern and observation. This has been a problem in some European countries and is becoming one in some parts of the United States.

Unions or regulatory agencies often promulgate safety and health measures that are not really needed or effective but are expensive. Such measures can increase business costs enormously without actually contributing much to the nominal values their advocates claim to be furthering. This process can be particularly destructive if the customary rules of the game for business are subject to sudden and arbitrary, almost capricious changes. Such changes can damage morale and confidence and make businesses excessively conscious of uncertainties. This uncertainty can be worse than full knowledge of how bad a situation really is. The latter allows for planning to deal with the situation; the former can cause prolonged discussion, indecision, and deferred investments. In the United States recently this has affected capital investment in new plants as opposed to improving or enlarging existing plants with new equipment. Faced with the many current uncertainties, corporate appropriation committees tend to prefer the latter alternative and to adopt a "wait and see" attitude toward more ambitious, long-term, and risky commitments. Given the genuine uncertainties that always exist, it can be quite difficult to restore confidence once it is destroyed. This is especially true if the tax laws are also weighted against risk taking.

4. Protection of Environment and Ecology

Much of the recent extraordinary concern about the environment and ecology is legitimate and in the public interest. Much that we would judge to be extreme also reflects worthy, if idiosyncratic, values. But much is disingenuous in that it really reflects hidden values or motives and disguises localism or other narrow personal, ideological, political, or class interests that would otherwise be too naked and blatant and therefore neither acceptable nor effective. A selfish concern for one's own quality of life, together with an almost total lack of concern for that of others, is often presented as an altruistic concern for the environment, ecology, or other "higher values."[19] This portrayal can develop a life of its own and become completely out of control, particularly if awareness of personal and class interests has been suppressed. Conscious hypocrisy or customary political rhetoric can be less destructive since they normally do not lead their practitioners to believe that "We walk with God" or that "Our side is defending higher values."

Until quite recently, most leaders of the environmental and ecological movement showed minimal interest in the cost of their demands. As a result, they sometimes pursue legitimate objectives too far. This lack of responsibility is diminishing somewhat in the United States and Japan but much less so in Europe. Thus, the first-year delay in the Alaska pipeline, which is usually attributed to opposition by the Sierra Club and its collaborators and allies, was probably justified. The pipeline was badly designed and would have caused large-scale unnecessary damage to the environment that could have been avoided at relatively little cost, except for the cost of the delay itself. However, some critics of the delay pointed out that since there are 100,000 square miles of tundra in Alaska, no matter how much damage the pipeline causes, plenty of undamaged tundra would remain. However one feels about this, it is clear that the case for redesigning the pipeline was reasonably good. It should have been and was satisfactorily redesigned. However, subsequent unnecessary delays cost the United States at least $20 billion in foreign exchange, many billions in unnecessary construction costs, and even more in unquantifiable costs. This is simply too much to pay unnecessarily.

A country cannot operate without causing damage somewhere. Everything cannot be preserved everywhere all the time. One solution, for the United States at least, would be to think of various areas as falling into the seven categories shown in Table 3.3. It is not necessary to classify every part of the country in the near future, but it would be wise to start the process at both ends—by protecting pristine areas and making allowances for "national dumps." If this is done properly, it should be possible to protect the environment more effectively, at least as far as most Americans are concerned, and with less interference and expense to economic projects, public recreation, and many important cultural values.[20]

5. Loss of Nerve, Will, Optimism, Confidence, and Morale About "Progress"

Loss of nerve is widespread. Even the most dedicated enthusiasts of economic growth and technological advancement tend to have some twinges of concern about where we are going and what may go wrong. They and others are troubled, for example, about such things as psychedelic drugs, electronic pleasure machines, cancer-inducing substances in the environment, man-made climate changes, and modern weapons technology. Even advocates of deterrence by so-called Mutual Assured Destruction are concerned about the possibility of accidental or unintended wars. Almost all knowledgeable people are worried about some of the potential products of the hybrid sciences with the prefix "bio." And more than a few feel that the "management of complexity and change" is itself becoming unmanageable.*

This fear of current and future developments inevitably and justifiably causes some erosion of will, optimism, and confidence in continued economic development—even with an increased awareness of the need to proceed with caution. This leads to slower

---

*For details, see the discussion in Chapter 5 "Growing Pains," particularly the discussion on the emerging problem-prone super-industrial economy.

TABLE 3.3
Proposed Land Use Categories

Specially Protected Areas	A:	Only minimal interference to environment and minimal risk of damage are tolerated
	B:	An almost full restoration or equally acceptable substitute is practical and there is little or no perceived degradation in the medium- and long-run, but temporary disturbance is acceptable
Normal Areas	C:	Almost any "improvement" and most reasonable changes which the local community will accept are allowable
	D:	Adequate but not necessarily complete restoration or substitution, but no changes that are widely regarded as eyesores
	E:	Economic restoration or substitution encouraged or even subsidized—some degradation or change tolerated but no dramatic destruction
Degradable Areas	F:	Same as "E" but some eyesores and waiving of standards are permitted for specially valuable or needed projects
	G:	"National Dumps"[a] of various sorts (perhaps as part of a controlled waste management and economic development program)

[a]We often use the term "National Industrial Resource Park" as a relatively inoffensive term for "G areas." But so many environmentalists think of this as a deliberate euphemism to disguise "legalized rape of the environment" that we must explain further. The metaphor of "legalized rape," despite its popularity, is a very bad one for this issue. All humans may be equal in the eyes of God, but when we look at the enormous variety of environments with which nature presents us—forest, desert, mountain, sea, tough, vulnerable, highly resilient, and remarkably impressionable—to name but a few broad differences—it is hard to conceive of the need for such "equal" protection of all the varieties of environment without first noting their differences. Mere existence makes a human precious; the same is not true of every acre.

economic growth and less rapid technological advancement—and properly so. Although we share many of these concerns, we argue that this erosion of will sometimes approaches pathological dimensions that are almost certainly counterproductive. Public and private decision makers, engineers, and scientists should undoubtedly be prudent, but they should not discard common sense. "Selective risk-taking" is still risk-taking. Caution should not be carried beyond a point where the cost-benefit ratio is too high.

Some of the main adverse effects of anti-growth propaganda and gloom about the future manifest themselves subtly in such things as career choices, the attitudes of bureaucrats and voters, and willingness to compromise personal or family values. Even judges read newspapers and watch television, and their decisions are affected by the fashions or concerns reflected—especially those who lean toward neo-liberal positions. Perhaps the worst problems arise in the schools. Much of the United States education establishment stresses anti-growth attitudes to the point where they may well dominate the education of many young people long after extremist anti-growth positions have lost their credibility among knowledgeable people. Unnecessary hostility against progress—or just an excessive loss of "nerve, will, optimism, confidence, and morale" among so many of the young—may cost our society dearly in both the short run and the long run.

6. Public Welfare and Social Justice (Including Equality of Result—or Even Nominal Egalitarianism)

The direct budgeted cost of welfare and social justice is an important issue. It alone could slow down economic growth and technological advancement. Between 1965 and 1975 there was a near doubling of personnel and tripling of costs of many municipal programs in the United States, while the useful output of these programs fell dramatically—particularly in programs supposed to further public welfare and social justice. These results undoubtedly were a major disappointment to those who introduced the programs.* We focus on some of the more subtle psychological and

---

*The disillusionment was so great that in the 1976 election two slogans became popular with both the left and the right in the southwest United States: "Be happy you are not getting as much government as you are paying for," and "Please don't do anything for me this year, I am still trying to recover from what you did for me last year." And both presidential candidates ran against "Washington" and big government. The passage of Proposition 13 in California in 1978 may have initiated a trend toward the grass roots implementation of these sentiments.

cultural considerations.

The first occurs when "everybody feels that the state owes him or her a living" (or knows it will ultimately provide), or when relief and welfare compete with private industry in economic incentives. This not only affects those on relief or welfare, but simultaneously reduces the need for others to gain financial and vocational security. Failure becomes less frightening. All of this has many good aspects, but it also reduces motivation and the commitment to work and to succeed. We have little to add to the current extensive literature on such issues except to comment on the difference between equality of opportunity and equality of result.

Only recently has a high degree of legally protected equality of opportunity been achieved in the United States by bringing many undesirable discriminatory practices under a reasonable degree of control. Many of the discriminatory practices that still exist exert little practical force because equally attractive opportunities are open to the group being discriminated against. Now, however, many programs of reverse discrimination and consequent lowering of standards are attempting to correct what are called historical disadvantages. These clearly exist, but imbalance in results is not necessarily evidence of immoral discrimination or even of a condition urgently needing correction by quotas (or goals, a well-known euphemism for quotas). For example, before World War II an overwhelming majority of the top theoretical physicists were Jewish or had Jewish family backgrounds, but this did not reflect special bias by institutions in favor of Jewish physicists. In fact, just the opposite seems to have been true. Similarly, people of Irish descent were disproportionately represented in the New York City police force at one time. And more boys than girls seem to get into trouble in school.

Our point is that numerically lopsided ethnic representation is not *a priori* evidence that a problem even exists, much less one that needs active corrective intervention by the state, or even that the causal conditions were undesirable. Furthermore, it can be extremely difficult and costly to correct a historical legacy by inappropriate reverse discrimination. However, a low level of reverse discrimination in many situations, and a high level of reverse discrimination in certain specific areas, can be reasonable and acceptable. An example is visible and favorable presentation of minority groups on television, where the image of the entire community is affected by what it sees.

In general, we cannot afford for very many years a lowering of performance in school, business, and government by forcing markedly reduced standards of entry (thereby also lowering motivation for many deserving aspirants). Giving a few extra points on an examination (as is often done for veterans) is much more acceptable than quotas or goals that simply tend to degrade standards uncontrollably or much too far. To disrupt a community by forced long-distance busing to bad schools is, and should be, anathema (as opposed to open schools, voluntary busing, general improvement of schools, and in some situations, improved "magnet" schools).

The main issue is not just the direct loss of productivity that occurs when one is forced to accept applicants who are inadequately trained or skilled. It is the overall decline, particularly in the school system and civil service, but also in general standards and self-images, which occurs when excessive efforts are made "not to penalize various minority groups with racist tests or standards," and to have, instead, what become, in effect, rigid quotas or goals.

A certain contradiction sometimes occurs in the ethnic conscious-ness movement. On the one hand, some of these people decry any attempt to "force" acculturation on the grounds that it is cultural aggression. On the other hand, they point to any differences of income as positive proof of discrimination. But it is obvious that in a basically Anglo-Saxon capitalistic society, unless people acculturate, they must pay a price in loss of opportunity and promotion. This is not discrimination. Acculturation is needed to perform one's job successfully and to succeed in the new environment. Most parents in the United States would prefer their children to acculturate, thereby improving their job and career prospects. This would also seem to be in the national interest. And despite much rhetoric to the contrary, the children involved are not in a position to make a meaningful choice. (To the extent that they are able to do so, they usually have the same long-term objectives as their parents.)

7. Happiness and Hedonism

To a degree unprecedented in any previous culture, young people in much of the United States and Europe and increasingly in Japan are taught that their goal in life should be personal happiness, to be achieved by direct efforts. Yet throughout history, people have either not worried much about personal happiness or have been taught that it would be achieved as a reasonable and likely by-product of some other pursuit—a rewarding vocation, well-paying job, harmonious family life, difficult achievements, honorable success, and so on.*

---

*The term *pursuit of happiness* in the Declaration of Independence actually has the connotation of freedom of religious choice and freedom to pursue those goals that bring about personal happiness as a by-product.

Many societies have not even recognized personal happiness as an important value. For example, Pitirim Sorokin noted that in Western culture the search for happiness on earth does not appear as an issue in any written record that has come down from European writers from the sixth through tenth centuries.[21] We would argue that the current emphasis on the legitimacy, need, and even obligation to search for happiness not only causes much unhappiness, but also results in lowered economic performance by the individuals concerned—and probably in more consumption and less saving. It can also lead to a situation in which all values except those of the extreme secular humanist tend to be degraded or ignored.

Overemphasis on the search for happiness can easily lead to hedonism, which is not the same as happiness. Hedonistic cultures are prone to excessively promiscuous sex, drugs, drink, and other vices. All of these may appear as short-cuts to happiness and in some ways probably are, if only temporarily. But most readers will presumably agree with the author that a major focus on vice is unsatisfactory from the viewpoint of either the individual or society.

8. General Anti-Technology, Anti-Economic Development, Anti-Materialistic, Anti-Bourgeois Attitudes

It is useful, in discussing these issues, to keep in mind the following argument. Concede for the moment that the modern nation-state creates and entails much that is distasteful or destructive. But also concede that it is one of the most effective institutions ever devised to achieve the following goals: defense and offense; economic growth; gaining influence over others, both internally and externally; carrying out big projects; and finally, generating a distinct charisma (nationalism) of its own. If one cares nothing for these goals or thinks of them as undesirable, then one might well think of the large modern nation-state as a mistake and think instead that small is beautiful. On the other hand, if one appreciates these goals as either means or ends, then the adage may be counterproductive.

One set of arguments for technology, economic development, large centralized projects, materialism, and bourgeois attitudes rests on how much they contribute to the same goals as those of the nation-state, either directly or through the society as a whole. Among these goals are safety and security. The main argument historically for all of these goals has not been the standard of living or quality of life but the need to have economic surplus and technological-organizational capabilities to deal with known and unknown dangers and enemies. This need exists even if economic progress contributes to creating these problems. This set of arguments, however, is overly defensive, even if it does justify support for more growth and technology and some retention or reinforcement of materialistic attitudes. All these goals have intrinsic positive values that are important for many people.

9. Increasing Social Control and Overall Planning of the Economy by the New Class

The view that "that government governs best which governs least" *(laissez-faire)* and "leave to the government things that only a government can do, or which the government clearly does best," is increasingly being replaced, at least among the neo-liberal elements of the New Class, by the view that the government should take an active and positive role toward almost every aspect of society. Indeed, government is asked to achieve ends that most twentieth century capitalistic democracies have not normally considered the government's business. It is sometimes argued that the government should promote most of the Fourteen New Emphases, either by direct sanctions or by internalizing the costs and benefits of various activities, so that business corporations and others have to take account of them.

There would presumably be a broad consensus that government-mandated protection of the environment is needed, and wide acceptance if the government pursued this objectively, realistically, efficiently, and with limited and practical goals. The first problem is that most planners simply do not know how difficult it is to plan comprehensively, completely, or effectively. They do not realize how unreliable, old, and incomplete the data are; how misleading, simplistic, and controversial the theories are; and how superficial and naive the basic models are—no matter how sophisticated they may seem to the lay public (and sometimes to their designers) mathematically and computationally. Finally, and most important, they do not know how controversial many of the explicit (and even more the implicit or unconscious) goals and objectives are.

The genuine issue is seldom "should there be planning or not?" but instead "at what level should the planning be done and who should do it?" For example, broad guidelines and general rules can be laid down for zoning and developing an area, but the actual detailed planning is better done by builders, contractors, developers, and by the individuals who buy the homes. The number of planning hours involved would be greater than if a centralized planning authority attempted to carry out the same program. Furthermore, since the planning is done by people who have a genuine personal commitment and stake in the outcome, the quality and intensity of planning are likely to be much better.

The more sophisticated socialist economies are moving toward increasing use of market forces. The trend is for central authorities to keep control of broad strategic decisions while allowing a good deal of detail, tactics, and even some strategic choices to be worked out—or guided—by the price mechanism.

So-called indicative planning seems unlikely to work well in countries such as the United States and Canada. Despite the claim that this method works in Japan and in France, these nations do much less planning than is often assumed, and there is more facade than force behind what planning exists. Furthermore, and perhaps most important, this planning is done by cadres who form a separate and distinct group that has gained the confidence of businessmen and much of the population. It is almost inconceivable that a similar group could take over this function in the United States— particularly not a group formed from the "best universities" in this country.

Few American businessmen would accept the idea that government officials drawn from academia understand what is going on better than they do themselves, even if their counterparts in Japan and France sometimes do; and both groups may well be justified in their judgment. Many American businessmen would agree with William F. Buckley, Jr., who said, "I'd rather be governed by the first 100 names in the Boston telephone book than by the Harvard faculty," or President Truman's comment about Rhodes scholar Senator Fulbright: "There goes the best argument ever seen for the land grant college." We would argue that in the United States, these attitudes are perfectly reasonable, not Yahooism.

In fact, neo-liberal members of the New Class who agitate for national planning reveal their naiveté when they refuse to admit even to themselves that they are really talking about national planning formulated by themselves and for themselves. If they expected the planning would be designed and implemented by an opposition group (e.g., conservatives or neo-conservatives), they would certainly oppose it. Under current conditions, however, they are confident that they can dominate or strongly influence the planning agencies.

They may well be right. Given their "educated incapacity" in practical affairs and their obvious ideological, social, and political biases, we would oppose the increase in their influence that would occur if formal bureaucratic national planning were instituted.[22] We would oppose it especially if their increased influence occurred as a perfectly "natural" and acceptable fact, since neo-liberal New Class people are disproportionately represented among those who make big mathematical or other elaborate economic models. There is nothing sinister about the disproportion, but it strongly influences the substance and agendas of the programs that are emphasized.

10. Regulatory Attitudes That Are Adversary or Indifferent to the Welfare of Business

Judges in higher courts and staffs of regulatory agencies in Atlantic Protestant culture area countries strongly hold many of the New Emphases. The government might promote its new programs in ways that are cooperative and conciliatory towards the existing system and that preserve confidence in the reliability of the rules and the fairness of the decisions. The bureaucracy might display ingenuity, creativity, and common sense when clashes occur— arriving at a genuine synthesis and compromise—by paying attention to such issues as economic and technological efficiency, practicability, the need for businessmen to operate in a relatively predictable environment, and the existence of other growth-oriented attitudes, goals, and values.

In many Affluent Capitalist countries, however, the agencies concerned, as well as the legislators and some of the voters and leaders, are actively hostile toward the existing system and toward many traditional values. As a result, they introduce these New Emphases in such a way as almost deliberately and consciously to increase the destructive impact of their rules, regulations, and other innovations. People who identify strongly with the New Emphases tend to have closed minds and hostile attitudes towards the current system. Even the less ideological exponents of regulation tend to dismiss complaints or suggestions that originate from the business and technological communities as griping or unjustified cries of "wolf."

Perhaps the most difficult problem to cope with today is the uncertainty created by the changing regulatory environment. Such uncertainty can be more detrimental to new projects, or even to continued operations, than bad news. If something that could not be foreseen happens, the proponents or management of the project cannot be blamed. But if there is apprehension about the possibility of trouble and it occurs, then great annoyance will be directed at those who went ahead anyway. Furthermore, if a utility plans on a new billion-dollar generating plant and it is held up for two or three years by an environmental protection group (at an added cost of $10 to $100 million dollars a year), the additional expenses may not have been allowed for by the business—or worse, not allowed by the regulatory authorities to be part of the base for calculating rates. From both a personal and business point of view, the proponents of the project or its managers may feel that this kind of loss is more to be avoided than a much greater but predictable increase in costs that can be planned, approved, and budgeted. The latter costs do not threaten the business by the possibility of not being recompensed; nor do they raise the spectre of charges of mismanagement or incompetence.

11. *"Modern" Family and Social Values and De-emphasis of Many Traditional Values*

This cluster of positions is characterized by such terms as *togetherness, permissiveness,* and *parents and children (or teachers and students) being friends and companions,* and the need for *thorough, continuous, and systematic two-way communication of each side's basic hopes and fears.* One problem with these attitudes is that they tend to destroy the authority of parents, teachers, and others who should be respected. Friendship and fraternization may be desirable, but experience has shown that unless the "officer class" is extraordinarily competent, discipline and leadership (e.g., authority) require a certain separation from the "enlisted personnel."

It would be better if officers and authorities did not need such artifice, but experience suggests that it is risky for most organizations and institutions to try to get along without it. If one tries to explain this today to young people who have little grasp of the idea of authority, one must first point out what authority is. It is not the same as coercion—that is, the use of power rather than authority. Nor is it a matter of persuasion, dependent upon having articulate and well-reasoned arguments. Authority is not even having and exerting leadership, which is a function of personality, capability, and charisma. It is also not a matter of controlling reward and punishment, though this helps (as do all of the above attributes of having power, personal leadership qualities, and the ability to be persuasive). Authority is the right to be heard and taken seriously, simply because of *who* one is: a parent, a teacher, an athletic coach, an officer, or whoever.

The idea can be illustrated by the example of two athletic teams. They are identical, except that one follows the orders of the team member who is wearing a red arm band. The other has a much more flexible rule: whoever is best qualified at the moment (i.e., whoever feels he or she is in the best position to make the judgment) calls the signals. The first system leads to unity and disciplined effort, while the second produces, except in very special situations, endless conflicts and even anarchy. Under normal conditions, the first team is almost certain to do much better than the second.

In designing institutions, it is important that everybody know where to turn for instruction and for leadership. This equivalent of the red arm band (i.e., the specialness of the wearer) must be taken seriously. Too much "fraternization" should be discouraged. It is, of course, preferable that the designated individual have both the reality and the appearance of being competent, knowledgeable, and possessing good judgment. Indeed, if the person does not, the institution may fail or the person concerned will find his or her authority eroding (or replaced). In reality, parents, teachers, and officers, on the average, have much relevant experience and usually know important things. If the system is to work, it should not be necessary for each of them to establish credentials every time the need for advice or a decision arises.

However, this issue of authority is only one of many recent changes in values. More important, partly because it is more widespread, may be the change in vocational values illustrated by a shift in the content of typical American soap operas. Fifty years ago, when one listened to these shows on the radio, an employee who drove himself to the point of getting an ulcer in the interests of advancement or the best interests of the company was considered a hero wounded in the battle for success. Such an employee deserved greater honor than the "unwounded." Today the same individual would be portrayed as a compulsive neurotic with twisted values who needs mental therapy. In the old-style soap operas, whenever a conflict occurred between job and family or between success and friendship, the conflict was usually resolved in favor of the job or success; if not, tragedy ensued. Today the reverse is true. Unless the conflict is resolved in favor of the family or friendship, a tragedy follows.

The Thirteen Traditional Levers listed in Table 3.4 have been the basis of middle class American values since the beginning of the republic and are similar to the traditional value systems of most Affluent Capitalist nations. Today, many of them are almost the exact antithesis of the modern family values referred to above. They are all under challenge, particularly by upper-middle class liberal groups.

Many people do not realize that it is possible, in principle, to reconcile placing a high priority on both the Thirteen Traditional

Levers and on most of the Fourteen New Emphases. The problem is not so much an intrinsic conflict but that the same people who accept the New Emphases most eagerly and intensely tend also to have value systems and goals other than those associated with the Thirteen Traditional Levers. Sometimes they are actively hostile rather than just indifferent toward almost all of them, even when they do not conflict with the Fourteen New Emphases.

12. Concern with Self (Often Accompanied by an Emphasis on Mystic or Transcendental Attitudes and Values or an Expression of the "Me Generation")

Young people in Western countries and in Japan are increasingly preoccupied with such questions as: "What are my feelings about this?" "Am I listening to my inner self?" "Am I growing?" "How am I being changed?" and so on. At one extreme, this vocabulary and attitude can reflect a kind of "inner space" consciousness that is often also a conscious attempt to imitate Indian culture—a culture which has yet to show much talent for economic development, regardless of its achievements in other areas.*

This New Emphasis is not necessarily unhealthy; indeed, it may be admirable. But such contemplation and preoccupation with one's self can clearly be at odds with the traditional inner-directed attitudes associated with duty, self-sacrifice, the work ethic, and achievement—all spurred by competition and advancement orientation—or even in competition with the other-directed attitudes described by the eminent sociologist David Riesman in *The Lonely Crowd*, attitudes which can also lead to social cooperation and discipline in getting things done.[23] This focus of interest on inner space and consciousness—or just on one's feelings as a central issue—can weaken traditional values and can lead to very undesirable levels of self-indulgence, illusion, and narcissism.

13. New Rites, Ceremonies, and Celebrations

All peoples at all times need ritual and ceremony. What is new is that the society no longer fulfills this need for the neo-liberal New Class. To a great degree, particularly for the neo-liberal New Class,

---

*Indian mystical religions and cults are fashionable at present. While much of this seems a kind of faddism and a variation of the "me generation" focusing attention on itself, some of it seems to reflect a serious trend that could have a significant impact on Western culture—and eventually on economic growth, scientific research, and advanced technology.

TABLE 3.4
The Thirteen Traditional Levers

1. Religion, tradition, or authority. Automatic and perhaps unthinking, respect for the legacy of the past, for continuity, for the existing "social contract," and for persons in authority (e.g., parents and teachers).

2. Biological and physical realities (e.g., respect for and acceptance as more or less normal and to some degree inevitable of the pressures and dangers of the physical environment, the frailty of life and health, the more tragic aspects of the human condition, and the basic and natural "unfairness" of any feasible social order and of life itself, etc.).

3. Defense of frontiers (territoriality).

4. Earning a living—obtaining the five guarantees Chinese communes often explicitly promise to their members: 1) adequate food, 2) adequate clothes, 3) adequate shelter, 4) adequate medical care, and 5) adequate funeral expenses. Sometimes they add: 6) adequate education and 7) adequate pregnancy leave and expenses.

5. Defense (by the nation, business, or family) of vital strategic and economic interests.

6. Defense (again, by the nation, business or family) of vital political, moral, and morale interests.[a]

7. Other appeals to economic or technological rationality and efficiency.

8. The "manly" emphasis—in adolescence: team sports, heroic figures, aggressive and competitive activities, rebellion against "female roles"; in adulthood: playing an adult male role (similarly, a womanly emphasis).

9. The "Puritan ethic" (deferred gratification, work-orientation, advancement-orientation, sublimation of sexual desires, sobriety, good work habits, etc.).

10. A high (perhaps almost total) loyalty, commitment, or identification with nation, state, city, clan, village, extended family, or secret society.

11. The "martial" virtues—duty, patriotism, honor, heroism, glory, courage, loyalty, and pride.

12. Other sublimation or repression of sexual, aggressive, aesthetic, or "other instincts."

13. Other "irrational" or restricting taboos, rituals, totems, myths, customs, and charismas.

---

[a]Many of those who oppose the Thirteen Traditional Levers would be willing to allow almost any excesses in the defense by a minority or dissident group of its vital political, morale, and moral interests, at least if they are sympathetic with this group's view of its vital interests. They do not, however, allow this privilege to the nation, the business firm, the WASP family, or the square individual.

contemporary society has gone out of its way to downgrade the significance of ritual and ceremony. An example of the demythologizing of ritual and ceremony is the current American practice of moving holidays to a Monday or Friday to make a three-day weekend. This is clearly convenient and practical but diminishes the sacred, dramatic, or patriotic significance of the holiday. (Of course, if it has already lost this quality, the change is a symptom, not a cause; it is a recognition that the holiday has been demythologized.) All religions and cultures have understood that a holiday means: *This day is different . . . on this day we. . . .* Then comes something important and different such as sacrifice, celebration, fasting, going to church. The loss of the sense of the sacred or of almost any sense of religion in many of the churches of what we call the "transcendental creeds," which are largely upper-middle class, and even more New Class, also reflects this New Emphasis.

14. New Sources of Meaning and Purpose; of Status and Prestige

Pride and status are also needs in all cultures and times. What is new is that the modern affluent countries no longer fulfill these needs in many of their upper-middle class young. Or sometimes the paths suggested to achieve status and pride encourage neo-liberal extremism. Today many teachers and parents admire the young person who has the spunk not to focus on a prosaic everyday career but who goes out and does some important public service—even before he or she has attained or achieved much material success (e.g., the many people who have achieved short cuts to fame or fortune or both through various movements based on one or more of the New Emphases). This is much more prevalent in the Atlantic Protestant culture area, particularly the United States, than in the other Affluent Capitalist countries. In the past, of course, the upper-middle class and the middle class were marked off from the society as a whole by their characteristic dress and manners. Anyone could tell they were different from a worker or aristocrat. Today it is the workers or ex-workers who in their newly won respectability tend to dress in normal business attire while the upper-middle class increasingly apes the costumes of the poorest workers, feeling totally confident that they will not be mistaken for poor workers because they dress even more sloppily and with a somewhat different style than the few workers who still wear such clothes. In effect, wearing ragged blue jeans (which the worker wouldn't be caught dead wearing) has become the new sign and proof that one is *not* working class.

B. Bruce-Briggs made up a list while he was with the Hudson

Institute of the differences in life style between what might be thought of as the New Class and the middle class. We give a slightly revised version below:

Traditionalist	*Progressive*
Hunting	Bird Watching
Camping	Back Packing
Domestic Cars	Foreign Cars
Big Cars	Small Cars
Contemporary Homes	Avant Garde Homes
New Homes	Restorations
Flashy Jewelry	Artistic Jewelry
Furs	Leather
Spectator Sports	Cultural Events
Power Boats	Sail Boats
Motorcycling	Bicycling
Carpentry	Handicrafts
Marching Bands	Chamber Ensembles
Hereditary Societies	Discussion Groups
National Guard	Reform Politics
Color TV	Hi Fi Stereo

Obviously there will be many exceptions and anomalies, but we believe that by and large the list holds. Members of the New Class reading the list will immediately recognize the often amused contempt that they or most of their colleagues will have for the activities of the middle class. The contempt is no longer reciprocated, although before World War II it was—as exemplified in almost any Marx brothers movie or the comic strip "Bringing Up Father." The middle class has learned to tolerate and even respect the leisure activities of the upper-middle class and of the New Class. Unfortunately, there is no reciprocal courtesy.

We have discussed the Fourteen New Emphases from the viewpoint of someone who is largely unsympathetic to them or is at least against their being pursued with excessive zeal. As society changes, the emergence of new value systems and emphases such as these is to be expected. Furthermore, someone who does not share or even completely disagrees with most of these New Emphases could still agree that our society as a whole might benefit from having some people believe in them and exert pressure on their behalf. It is generally true that things that are everybody's business tend to be nobody's business—they can be dominated by narrow special interests. To achieve balanced results on issues of this kind, it can be useful for advocates of New Emphases to create strong pressures. The pressures might be counterproductive if pursued to excess, but very useful in counterbalancing the potentially excessive influence of opposite interest groups. If both groups tend to be too narrow and extreme (and usually motivated—at least in part—by self-interest), then a more balanced synthesis should result.

Assuming that such a synthesis is desirable, and agreeing that changes in our value systems are both inevitable and desirable, we still argue that on the whole, the Fourteen New Emphases are currently having more of a negative than a positive impact. This is true partly because the emphases are held with such ferocious intensity by so many members of what we have called the neo-liberal New Class. Unlike the upper-middle class generally (which often holds the same New Emphases), these people do not realize that they are serving narrow class and private interests at least as much as they serve the general good. We believe that this lack of self-awareness by the neo-liberal New Class creates highly destructive results in the emergence and implementation of the New Emphases.

This lack of self-awareness is also a major active ingredient in translating these New Emphases into premature limits to growth, limits that we call social because they inhere in values and attitudes, and not in actual physical limitations. The New Emphases, in and of themselves, need not necessarily translate into severe limitation of growth, for most of them can be synthesized with the Thirteen Traditional Levers. The others can be satisfactorily addressed if the controversy is only with those who hold the New Emphases because of "externalities" or "preferential values." It is only when they are held as moral imperatives by people who do not realize that they are using them to serve their private interests that the advocacy becomes so dangerous to the rest of society.

Some of the great strength of the "true believers" comes because they are leading a movement that represents much more than a narrow minority of the upper-middle class. As people become more affluent and feel safer, their interests move from the bare necessities of political survival and economic growth to other values. In the long run, as we come to recognize our own potential to change our lives, this will probably be good. Changes in externalities do make an immediate difference, and it is likely that new preferential values will also eventually emerge. We must adjust to both of these, even if we do not think of them as moral imperatives. Where highly reliable behavior and intense commitment are needed or useful, it is not necessarily bad if they emerge as consequences of deeply held moral imperatives. But during the interim period, when confusion and irrationality are present, we must proceed with some sense of balance, avoiding premature visions of utopia or apocalypse. We must find enough grace to concede that there may be much lasting value in old traditions. Economic growth and advanced technology are not logically synonymous with destruction; they are necessary for our well-being and even our survival. They are to be approached with a healthy degree of caution, to be sure, but also with hope and enthusiasm. If we are dominated instead by fear, the result could be a sort of paralysis that would not help anyone.

Notes

1. "Distance," of course, is used here partly as a metaphor and partly as an analogy. In any case, the concept is complex. See Chapter 8 for a more extended discussion of the metaphor and other issues related to modernization.

2. Karl Marx, *The Communist Manifesto* (Chicago: Henry Regnery, 1963), seventh printing, pp. 19-23 (emphasis added).

3. This figure is based on a high ICP-type estimate. The results of phase 1 of the United Nations International Comparison Project (ICP) were published in 1975 in Irving B. Kravis, Zoltan Kenessey, Alan Heston, and Robert Summers, *A System of International Comparison of Gross Product and Purchasing Power* (Baltimore & London: The Johns Hopkins University Press, 1975).

4. Max Weber, *The Protestant Ethic and the Spirit of Capitalism,* translated by Talcott Parsons (New York: Charles Scribner's Sons, 1930).

5. Chie Nakane, *Japanese Society* (Berkeley, Calif.: University of California Press, 1970).

6. A number of visitors to the Soviet Union have reported that Solzhenitsyn is often (very incorrectly) so regarded.

7. Edmund Stillman and William Pfaff are the colleagues. Toynbee exerted a strong influence on them and on the author of this book. Historians, of course, differ in their interpretations of what actually happened and why. We do not discuss these controversies.

8. "The Hellenistic Age," in *Great Ages and Ideas of the Jewish People* (New York: Random House, 1956). Burma's rejection of modernization for many years is similar. To some extent, Saudi Arabia also behaved this way.

9. From *Cahier d'un Retour Au Pays Natale,* as quoted in Colin Legum, *Pan-Africanism* (New York: Praeger, 1962), p. 93.

10. The term is adapted from Daniel Bell's *The Cultural Contradictions of Capitalism* (New York: Basic Books, 1976). Bell's book focuses mainly on

numbers three and six of our New Emphases. Bell treats systematically and creatively many of the issues treated briefly in this chapter.

11. See the chart in Chapter 4 of what we call "New Costs and Risks for U.S. Business." Many of these were either nonexistent a decade ago or have become much more extreme and exaggerated than they used to be. Most of these issues or trends are accidental or unplanned. Some, even though they entail significant costs and risks, are desirable if implemented in a reasonable fashion. But the people who crusade for these reforms often have very narrow ideological or class interests and consequently do not understand or even care about the problems they create. In some cases their tactics are actually counterproductive. Thus, they can cause a backlash that leads to an excessive rejection of their values and programs. Alternatively, the tactics can be really designed to accomplish the reformers' hidden agendas or real objectives, which may include self-serving, prejudicial, or ideological goals.

12. See Lynn White, "The Historical Roots of our Ecological Crises," *Science Magazine,* March 10, 1967, p. 1203.

13. Thorstein Veblen, *The Theory of the Leisure Class* (New York: Viking Press, 1958), p. 137.

14. We have borrowed and revised some materials from an unpublished Hudson paper by B. Bruce-Briggs and from a Hudson study by Thomas Dichter on the New Class scheduled for publication in 1979.

15. See, for example, the excellent (if partisan) article by the liberal economist Robert Lekachman, "Proposition 13 and the New Conservatism," *Change,* September 1978, pp. 22-27. Lekachman notes that "[the] contemporary mood is signalized in particular by the great success of *The Public Interest* . . . [Until] the advent of this journal, American liberals and moderate radicals very nearly monopolized the pages of the intellectual media," (pp. 24, 25).

16. Taken from Leonard Silk's review of Mishan's book, *The Economic Growth Debate* (London & Reading, Mass.: George Allen & Unwin, 1977) in *The New York Times Book Review,* February 5, 1978, p. 12. Mr. Silk, a business columnist for *The New York Times,* cites Mishan's remark with great approval.

17. For many examples of such counterproductive activities and attitudes, see "Of Mites and Men," by William Tucker, *Harper's,* August, 1978, pp. 43-58.

18. According to *Newsweek,* August 18, 1975, three of the most dangerous new recreational activities are: 1) hang-gliding (virtually invented in 1970, the sport claimed eighty-five lives by 1975 and boasted 25,000 enthusiasts); 2) white water canoeing (one small stretch on Virginia's Shenandoah River claimed seven lives in a thirteen-week period in 1975); and 3) cave diving, which in 1974 claimed twenty-five lives. *Newsweek* quoted a young Los Angeles lawyer who regularly engaged in the three different "thrill" sports as saying: "I constantly test myself against powerful forces but at least I'm leading an exciting life." See also "How to Fulfill Your Death Wish," *Esquire,* August 15, 1978, p. 67.

19. For examples, see William Tucker, "Environmentalism and the Leisure Class," *Harper's*, December 1977, pp. 49-80.

20. These possibilities are discussed in *Let There Be Energy* by William Brown and Herman Kahn (forthcoming).

21. Pitirim Sorokin, *Man and Society in Calamity: The Effects of War, Revolution, Famine, Pestilence Upon Human Mind, Behavior, Social Organization and Cultural Life* (New York: Greenwood Press, 1968).

22. See Chapter 8 for additional discussion of planning.

23. David Riesman, Reuel Denny, and Nathan Glazer, *The Lonely Crowd* (New Haven: Yale University Press, 1976).

4

A Speculative Overview
of the Current Situation

During the two great watersheds of world economic development—the agricultural revolution and The Great Transition—the
world changed from hunting and food gathering tribal communities
to traditional civic societies governed by elites living in cities, and
during the period still continuing, most or all traditional societies are
changing from pre-industrial to post-industrial. Both transformations are probably equally deep and profound, but we expect the
second to occur twenty times faster than the first. The agricultural
revolution started about ten thousand years ago and took almost eight
thousand years to diffuse around the world. The Great Transition
started about two hundred years ago with the Industrial Revolution
and should take about four hundred years to complete. Sometime in
the twenty-second century most societies should be fully or nearly
post-industrial.

Many of the quantitative phenomena associated with this Great
Transition are best described by S-shaped curves, most of which will
reach their highest rate of increase during the last half of the twentieth
century. This period will "break the back of the job" but not complete
it. Even partial completion will take another century or so, despite the
attitude of many (particularly neo-liberal New Class members and
some small-is-beautiful advocates) that the job of economic
development is essentially finished as far as their personal and
familial objectives are concerned, and that it is time to turn to other
issues. We agree that we must turn to other issues, but we must still
involve ourselves with many of the old issues as well.

Four Sub-Periods of the Twentieth Century

Partly on empirical evidence and partly on theoretical grounds, we
divide the twentieth century into four sub-periods, all of which are on

the steep part of the S-shaped curve, but each of which also has specific characteristics of its own. Table 4.1 summarizes some basic characteristics of each sub-period.

Our overall sense of what is happening was set forth almost 500 years ago by Niccolo Machiavelli in his *Florentine History.*

> It may be observed that provinces, amid the vicissitudes to which they are subject, pass from order into confusion, and afterward recur to a state of order again; for the nature of mundane affairs not allowing them to continue in an even course, when they have arrived at their greatest perfection, they soon begin to decline. In the same manner, having been reduced by disorder and sunk to their utmost state of depression, unable to descend lower, they, of necessity, reascend; and thus from good they gradually decline to evil, valour produces peace; peace, repose; repose, disorder; disorder, ruin; so from disorder order springs; from order virtue, and from this glory and good fortune.[1]

In discussing how the above process has worked in the twentieth century, we focus initially on the sixteen nations Angus Maddison has called the Advanced Capitalist nations (ACNs): the United States, United Kingdom, Germany, Italy, Japan, Belgium, France, Netherlands, Canada, Australia, Switzerland, Austria, Sweden, Denmark, Norway, and Finland.[2]

In the first three-quarters of the twentieth century, the Advanced Capitalist nations went through three distinct phases of alternating higher and slower growth. They now seem to have started another period of slower growth, entered by some ACNs in the mid-1960s and by others in the mid-1970s. The current period of slower growth seems likely to persist for many years and to have important implications for social change. We provisionally assume the existence of this fourth period and tentatively assign the year 2000 as its nominal ending. This date is chosen as much on aesthetic as on analytic grounds. (However, one version of the Kondratieff theory, discussed below in this chapter, suggests a thirty-five year period, or about 2010, for the turning point.)

The combined gross domestic product of the ACNs grew at an average rate of 2.8 percent per year between 1870 and 1976, with great variations during that time. Output rose by an average rate of 2.5 percent per year from 1870 to 1886, a pace never previously attained, but slightly under the average for 1870 to 1976. This growth rate was driven by many technological innovations, relatively large capital movements, and agricultural development of the American Great Plains.

Growth rates accelerated even more in the period we call *La Première Belle Epoque* (1886 to 1914), averaging 3.3 percent. These twenty-eight years saw more than a doubling of gross domestic product of the Advanced Capitalist nations. Nothing comparable had even before occurred. It is not surprising that these years came to be known as *La Belle Epoque*. (We added a *Première* to the well-known phrase to distinguish it clearly from *La Deuxième Belle Epoque*.)

The industrialized nations thereafter entered a long period (1914 to 1947) of slower growth, two World Wars, the Great Depression, and such severe political troubles as the two great communist revolutions and the rise and fall of fascism.[3] During these thirty-four years, the output of the sixteen ACNs rose at an average rate of only 1.8 percent, slightly over half the rate during *La Première Belle Epoque*. World trade grew at only .5 percent a year. These average rates of growth were not bad compared to those during the eighteenth century and even during the first half of the nineteenth century, but they represented a pronounced drop from those during *La Première Belle Epoque*. This lessened growth rate and the many economic and other crises of those years richly entitle the period 1914 to 1947 to the appelation *La Mauvaise Epoque*, at least by the standard of either *Belle Epoque* period.

The late 1940s ushered in an unprecedented boom that lasted a quarter of a century. Output in the ACNs rose at a sustained average rate of 4.9 percent during the twenty-six years from 1948 through 1973. By that time, the production of the ACNs (with a current population of almost two-thirds of a billion) had almost quadrupled. Comecon (the Soviet Union and the six communist East European nations, current population 0.4 billion) did even better, as did those nations with about two-thirds of the world's poor. As a result, almost 50 percent of humanity now lives in Middle Income countries. The world as a whole averaged an annual 5 percent growth in gross world product during the boom period. World trade grew by the fantastic average rate of 7.5 percent annually. In the latter half of the period, the big transnational corporations (TNCs) grew at a dizzying ten percent a year. In brief, the world had experienced *La Deuxième Belle Epoque*.

During 1974 to 1978 the Advanced Capitalist nations struggled to respond to sharply higher energy costs, soaring inflation, international economic imbalances, and excess productive capacity within relatively adverse psychological, social, cultural, and political contexts. Average growth of the ACNs fell below two percent, but we expect it will improve soon. Over the next two or three decades it

TABLE 4.1
The Four Sub-Periods of the Twentieth Century

	Duration[a]	Average Economic Growth Rate of ACNs[b]	Other Economic Growth	Some Outstanding General Characteristics of the Period
1 *La Belle Epoque* (The Good Era)	1886 thru 1913 (28 years)	3.3%	Russia also takes off, ROW[c] stagnant	Creation of a "spectacular gap" between the ACNs and the rest of the world
2 *La Mauvaise Epoque* (The Bad Era) or The Era of Instability	1914 thru 1947 (34 years)	1.8	But Soviet Union 5-10%, ROW still stagnant	Two world wars, the great depression, rise and fall of fascism, two great communist revolutions, emergence of two superpowers
3 *La Deuxième Belle Epoque* (The Second Good Era)	1948 thru 1973 (26 years)	4.9	Middle Income nations take off and grow 5-10%	Cold war, decolonization, emergence of Middle Income nations, emergence of Japan as second or third greatest economy, emergence of New Class limits to growth concepts and ideologies. Many S-shaped curves reach their maximum percent growth rate

| 4 *L'époque de Malaise?* (The Era of Malaise?) | 1974 thru 2000? (27 years) | 3.5 | Comecon[d] is about 4% (perhaps less) but middle income nations continue | Further emergence of Middle Income nations, great potential for violence and disorder, vulnerable national and world economic systems—but less than 30% of the world lives in "poor nations" |

[a]The dating is somewhat different from that of Angus Maddison, who uses 1870-1913, 1914-1949, 1950-1970, and 1971 on. We dropped 1870-1885 (which had only a 2.3 percent average growth rate but did see many important technological innovations in Europe and North America and also a worldwide flow of capital) and moved the other dates around to maximize the lengths of the two *Belle Epoques* and the differences in growth rates between them and the other periods. This periodization is more useful to us and more consistent with much of our later argument.

[b]ACNs—Advanced Capitalist Nations.

[c]ROW—Rest of World.

[d]Comecon—the Soviet Union and the six Communist Eastern European nations.

should average about two-thirds the rate of *La Deuxième Belle Epoque.* These decades, we believe, will best be characterized by the sobriquet *L'époque de Malaise*—where *malaise* means not being really sick, but not being really well either. We do not expect this label to hold for the Poor or Middle Income nations. On the contrary, we expect most of these countries to do well. However, we expect Comecon to do only slightly better than the ACNs.

Figure 4.1 shows the aggregate gross domestic product (GDP) of the sixteen Advanced Capitalist nations from the takeoff period through the four major sub-periods of the twentieth century. (More detailed breakdowns and discussions for individual ACNs are presented in Chapter 7.)

La Première Belle Epoque (1886 to 1913)

Much of the modern industrial world emerged during this period. Peter Drucker has pointed out that all of the industrialized countries and almost all the specific industries that dominated the first two-thirds of the twentieth century had emerged by 1914.[4] In some ways this was the golden age of the ACNs. They had all adopted relatively modern outlooks, but they still had deep roots in traditional faiths and beliefs and had high morale about their economic and social systems. We are not likely to see a comparable period of such high self-confidence and sheer energy again, at least not for the bourgeoisie in the ACNs. However, one can see something like this in South Korea and to a lesser extent in Taiwan.

La Première Belle Epoque was filled with contradictions. In France there was an outbreak of behavior that most people thought of as extreme decadence: open homosexuality, drug use, immoral co-habitation, and other flagrant violations of middle class norms—in brief, a revolt against the bourgeoisie. The movement was mostly limited to the *avant-garde*, who marched under the slogan *épater les bourgeois*—"shock the bourgeoisie." What emerged is what we have called *discretionary behavior*: terrorism, nihilism, anarchism, other violent or extreme political movements, and much individual idiosyncratic behavior. We argue later that such behavior is likely to be typical of any long, prosperous, and safe period in which good things are taken for granted and problems and inequities are increasingly regarded as anomalous and intolerable. It is also likely to occur when there is a rapid erosion of traditional standards because of changed child-rearing practices and effective negative propaganda from alienated or counterculture groups.*

---

*We discuss some of these problems in the United States in Personal Notes 1 and 2 in Chapter 8.

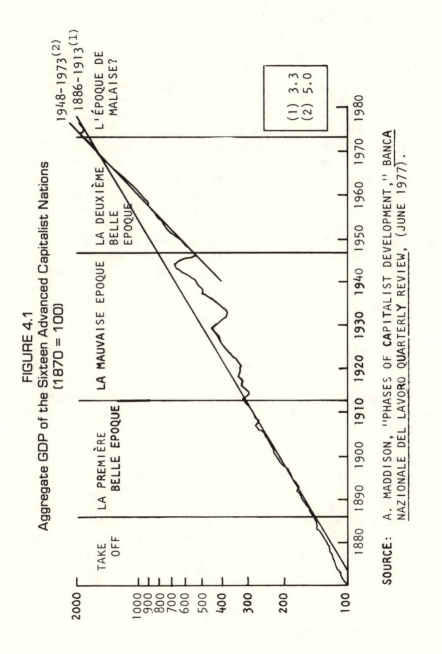

FIGURE 4.1

Aggregate GDP of the Sixteen Advanced Capitalist Nations
(1870 = 100)

SOURCE: A. MADDISON, "PHASES OF CAPITALIST DEVELOPMENT," BANCA NAZIONALE DEL LAVORO QUARTERLY REVIEW, (JUNE 1977).

La Mauvaise Epoque (1914 to 1947)

La Mauvaise Epoque began with World War I, a war that initiated so many far-reaching changes as to represent the great divide of Western culture. The high morale and simple faith and confidence in the capitalist system shared by so much of the bourgeoisie (and many others) during *La Première Belle Epoque* would never be seen again. The energy, dedication, patriotism, commitment, and heroism displayed by soldiers and civilians alike during World War I were not accidental. They were qualities, however, which were abused by the governments concerned. There is little doubt that either side would have gained greatly by accepting a negotiated defeat at almost any time during the war rather than pushing on year after year in pursuit of victory. This choice of sacrifice over prudence and rationality is both impressive and depressing.

World War I is far and away the most extreme example of what Kondratieff calls *peak wars*.[5] From start to finish, it was driven less by rational aims than by internal dynamics and momentum. It was an "unnecessary war" in the sense that its goals could either have been achieved by other means or were disproportionate to the risks undertaken and the damage done. This was not true of World War II. It was genuinely important to resist and even to destroy Nazism, and this could probably have been done only through a war.

During *La Mauvaise Epoque* the international economy and the international power system were managed very badly. World War I so thoroughly disillusioned people about once-acceptable calculations of national power and concern with national prestige that they subsequently refused to take precautions that would be considered elementary even today. There was, at least rhetorically, too much dependence on the League of Nations and on such ineffectual gestures as the Kellogg-Briand anti-war pact. Many aspects of current NATO planning are seriously deficient and even illusionary (NATO's membership coincides roughly with the ACNs). Still, most of the time post–World War II defense planning and thinking have been far better than the sheer bungling and counterproductive utopian efforts of the inter-war period. Furthermore, the United Nations is not idealized as if it were a functioning world government, even though it comes closer to performing this role than the League of Nations ever did.

Economic management during these years—particularly by the United States, England, and France—was also extraordinarily incompetent. There are almost no current French and British actions that can be compared with the futile and inept attempts in the 1920s to preserve the gold standard and "protect" the franc and the pound. Washington has done nothing in recent years that compares with the disastrous Smoot-Hawley Tariff of 1930. This tariff not only touched off an avalanche of beggar-thy-neighbor policies among the nations of the world, but also made demagogic nonsense of the American attempts to collect the war debts by preventing the Europeans from shipping their manufactured goods to the United States—the only possible means of payment. Practically all important economists in the United States signed a public appeal condemning the Smoot-Hawley Tariff.*

The United States economy at that time had many weaknesses that simply do not exist today. These weaknesses often resulted from relatively unsophisticated practices and institutions, such as three-year mortgages that were payable in a lump sum rather than over the twenty or more years of fixed payments that is the current practice. During the Great Depression, therefore, roughly one-third of all United States mortgages came due every year, with calamitous results. Unemployment insurance, federal insurance of banks, the Securities Exchange Commission, and many other reforms and institutions had not yet come into existence. The domestic and international economic system today is both much tougher and subject to much less abuse of certain kinds. However, we argue that with sufficiently bad luck or bad management, a calamitous economic crash remains possible.

La Deuxième Belle Epoque (1948 to 1973)

This is the period that we believe has just ended. In *The Year 2000* we argued that such a period started in 1952 (an excessively parochial

---

*Near unanimity among the economists does not necessarily mean that they are right, but it should be taken seriously. The same kind of unanimity seems to have characterized almost all American economists who made predictions or projections about the immediate post–World War II period. They agreed that it would be marked by a more or less catastrophic depression. One can argue that if President Truman had followed much of their advice, such a depression might well have occurred. And almost nobody seems to have foreseen that anything like *La Deuxième Belle Epoque* would occur. Practically everybody thought that *La Mauvaise Epoque* would more or less continue. (Perhaps even more important in deepening and lengthening the United States Great Depression was the ineptness of the Federal Reserve authorities in more or less inadvertently allowing the money supply to collapse.)

American view tied to the end of the Korean War).[6] In *Things to Come* we argued that *La Deuxième Belle Epoque* came to a temporary halt for the United States in 1965, but that high growth rates would resume for the United States and for the world when the Vietnam War was over and would continue through the early or mid-1980s.[7] This was incorrect, but with proper management *La Deuxième Belle Epoque* could probably have continued through the early or mid-1980s (as we suggested in *The Next 200 Years*).[8] But it now seems clear that *La Deuxième Belle Epoque* ended in the early 1970s and will not resume unless very good measures comparable to those described in Part II are adopted and turn out to be even more effective than we expect. More likely, such expedients, even if successful, will fail to reproduce—at least for the ACNs—the economic dynamism of *La Deuxième Belle Epoque*. However, they might come close.

Despite its considerable failings and blemishes, the period was highly successful. For the first time, the Third World joined in the process of rapid economic development; almost two-thirds of the Third World countries benefited greatly. The fruits of the Industrial Revolution "trickled down" from the original Advanced Capitalist nations and the Soviet Union.[9]

Most people were probably surprised at our assertion in Chapter 2 that less than 30 percent of the world should be judged as living in Poor Nations and about 47 percent can be judged as living in Middle Income nations. We think this categorization is quite reasonable. The average income in the latter nations ($400 to $3500 per capita) would seem rich by traditional standards even if poor by the standards of those who are wealthy today. This would therefore seem to be a pretty good definition of Middle Income. We will have more to say about this in Chapters 7 and 8.

For the ACNs as a group, every year was a growth year during *La Deuxième Belle Epoque*. Even in bad years their average total growth in gross product did not decline below 1 percent. By contrast, annual growth rates were negative in nine years of *La Mauvaise Epoque*. And during the first two years of *L'époque de Malaise*, the growth rates were .01 and -1 percent. A quarter century of uniformly good (or at worst mediocre) years created great strains and imbalances in the economic and social practices of most ACNs. An unrealistic level of confidence emerged. Some aspects of this are summarized by the phrase "revolution of rising expectations"—now often corrected to the "revolution of *lowered* rising expectations."*

During *la Deuxième Belle Epoque* there were no blatant abuses of government power in the ACNs comparable to those of Hitler and Stalin (Mao Tse-tung may have come close, but China was not an ACN), no world wars, and no economic crashes or other historical disasters such as plagues or bloody revolutions. Not surprisingly, a widespread feeling emerged that the ACNs need no longer take seriously the Four Horsemen of the Apocalypse (War, Famine, Plague, and Insurrection). Even more unrealistic and damaging, institutions and infrastructures that had been created and maintained at great cost were regarded as being quite natural. Simultaneously, many idealistic and unrealistic young members of the upper-middle class began to think of the defects and costs of society as intolerable evils that should not be endured, not realizing that all institutions have defects and limitations.[10] Such psychological, political, cultural, and social issues can have strong impacts on long-run economic performance.

La Déuxième Belle Epoque displayed even more extreme forms of discretionary behavior than did *La Première Belle Epoque*, particularly in the Atlantic Protestant culture area. We believe it will be harder to purge the system of this behavior and the attendant attitudes than it was earlier. For one thing, disastrous as World War I and the Great Depression were, they did have some healthy and cathartic after-effects that served to eliminate certain counterproductive attitudes and values that had built up. Nothing like this seems likely to occur in the years ahead. Even if *L'époque de Malaise* does occur, it is not likely to force reality testing on many in the New Class and their allies and co-belligerents. The United States malaise apparently started in the mid 1960s, and many aspects apparently bottomed out, at least temporarily, around the mid 1970s. The United States may thus have anticipated the general malaise by about a decade and may have passed through part of its "crisis" stage. We discuss this further in Chapters 5 and 8.

---

*Actually, poll data in many countries indicate that there are now widespread expectations of declining living standards as well as of a declining quality of life. Both expectations are probably wrong. The phrases "lowered rising expectations" (but still *rising* expectations) as far as the currently Affluent nations are concerned and "rapidly increasing rising expectations" for the Middle Income countries would describe a reasonably probable future.

L'époque de Malaise (1974 to 2000?)

We are uncertain whether *La Deuxième Belle Epoque* has really ended and if so, when. We are also uncertain whether an identifiable new period with relatively clear and definite characteristics will emerge. The description of this fourth period, therefore, involves a bold prediction; it is always dangerous to extrapolate from a record of only three or four years, even if the prediction is supplemented by a theory.

If *L'époque de Malaise* does materialize, it will probably display some very complex and contradictory trends. Certain well-designed programs could alleviate much of the social, political, and psychological malaise we anticipate, but we don't expect such programs to materialize either early or effectively. (The ameliorative programs are, however, more likely in the economic area than in others.)

L'époque de Malaise will be evident in most ACNs, in the Soviet Union, and perhaps in much of the rest of Comecon. In many developing countries, despite slower growth in industrialized nations since 1973, there has been rather unexpected continued strong growth. The Middle Income developing countries continued to show strong growth during 1973 to 1976 despite the oil price rise, recession, and various manifestations of malaise in the ACNs and elsewhere.

If history repeats itself, *L'époque de Malaise* should continue to the end of the century and perhaps beyond. However, one new factor— the rapid growth of the developing nations—could help lift the industrialized nations out of the doldrums relatively quickly this time. Furthermore, Japan may also show renewed high growth and thus make a big difference.[11] Finally, the mere fact that *L'époque de Malaise* does not involve nearly as dramatic a change in prospects as *La Mauvaise Epoque* could be significant.

The productivity slowdown in the United States appears to have been partially caused by increased environmental, safety, and other kinds of regulation. Many of these and other practices and trends that increase business costs and risks are associated with the Fourteen New Emphases. Others are tied to such special technical factors as the adverse effects of the tax treatment of illusory gains from inflation.

The United States seriously attempted to control inflation in the early 1970s. Several European countries were willing to tolerate high inflation because of their great concern about unemployment. While the economic stimulus carried the West European expansion, it produced some serious problems for them during 1976 to 1978, when the United States was on the road to recovery from the 1975 recession. This and other factors helped the United States launch a relatively early and sustained recovery.[12]

Since strong economic growth continued in western Europe through 1973, the pressures of slower income growth were not important until the petro-dollar era began in 1974. However, a growing number of signs of a European malaise began to emerge even before then. These developments seemed to signal the emergence of a new era that was in part a result of the excesses of past growth and in part a result of the immediate attempts to learn to live with slower growth. However, the malaise itself diminished growth. In any case, *L'époque de Malaise* is apparently now well under way.

Before discussing this period and the various possibilities inherent in it, we offer some generalizations about any "long upswing" such as a *Belle Epoque*, particularly during a relatively secular period such as occurs at the end of the long-term Multifold Trend.

A Generalized Long Upswing (A Typical *Belle Epoque* from Start to Finish)[13]

We present now a fairly generalized description of how a *belle époque* period may create in the long run many internal contradictions and other strains. This discussion, while rooted in the historical realities of both *Belles Epoques*, is deliberately cast in abstract and general terms. However, this abstract structure corresponds closely enough to the events (particularly during *La Deuxième Belle Epoque*) that we can use it as a partial paradigm of what actually happened. Viewing it as an archetype, we can apply the essential ideas to many countries, whereas if we were trying to summarize the historical record, we would need a different story for each situation. (Thus we ignore World War II for the time being.) The fifteen points that follow are a phase-by-phase account of the evolution of our archetypical long upswing.

1. A Sobering Context

The economy has just passed through a long ten-to-thirty-year period of stagnation, or slow and uncertain growth, the kind of growth that might follow a serious extended depression or occur in a society with serious institutional or structural problems that prevent economic dynamism. Until the problems are alleviated, much hesitation and political instability are likely.

Jobs and a sense of security and stablity have been scarce and are much sought after. Where conditions are at all acceptable, conservatism in politics and business are prized. However, there is also widespread awareness that the system has grave defects. Many people feel disinherited, alienated, or unjustly treated. Others feel sympathetic to the less fortunate. Thus, radicalism and pressures for income redistribution, welfare, and other reforms are strong.

Excessive productive capacity persists and may even increase for a time. Despite growing obsolescence of much existing capital stock, relatively little investment is made in new capital facilities or in replacing existing plants. There is little or no exploitation of new technologies. Economically, a highly competitive situation exists. Wages and other costs are generally depressed, with wages probably depressed more than other costs. Where increased production is required, therefore, the preference is to use more labor and to make do with existing equipment and plant rather than make major new investments that might not turn out well. (This may be the basic explanation for the recent large rise in the United States employment figures with relatively little rise in GNP.)

The propensity to save grows. Savings become more valuable because of an accompanying price deflation (or decelerating inflation) and because people feel they need a cushion or insurance. Unused new technologies and relatively idle savings accumulate.

Cautious, disciplined, prudent personal behavior is seen as desirable. Such behavior is reinforced by the school, family, church, neighborhood, and other institutions. There is increasing public and private enthusiasm and support for work, advancement, achievement, personal and organizational discipline, and other business-oriented values and attitudes. Most social institutions are anxious to support expansion and investment. Toleration of the ideological and bureaucratic difficulties that are so common today decrease. Voluntary dropouts from society tend to look more like failures than like romantic and glamorous revolutionaries and trail-blazers.

The swing back to "square values" and "square behavior" is, however, incomplete and irregular. It will take time for this reaction to attain the level and intensity it once had, if it ever does. More likely, a new synthesis with strong and clearly demarcated values and behaviors of its own will eventually emerge.

2. A Slow Revival

In time, the continued deterioration and obsolescence of existing plants erodes excess production capacity. Some new technologies and needs are too attractive to ignore, and some investment therefore starts. Finally, a new generation begins to mature that has greatly lowered expectations, is less "shell-shocked" than its predecessors, and is more willing to operate in the prevailing conditions and make personal sacrifices, accept vocational commitments, take risks, and appreciate available opportunities.

3. A Turning Point

Opportunities for new investment open up as obsolete and worn-out equipment and facilities are replaced and new activities are undertaken. A short "profitable" war or other stimulus to economic activity may occur. Such "trough wars" tend to be relatively nondivisive and popular. Otherwise, given the prevailing caution and prudence, they would not be allowed to happen or would soon be terminated by some kind of compromise.

As activity is stimulated and demand increases, momentum and confidence build up. Demand greatly increases for both replacement and expansion of the capital goods sector, resulting in a backlog of orders. Experienced and competent labor begins to be fully employed. Wages and salaries begin to rise. This cycle stimulates further the retirement of inefficient and obsolete equipment and plants and provides an additional basis for a substantial revival of demand for both consumer and capital goods.

All this occurs at a relatively low and sustainable level. A guarded optimism emerges, but there is little initial willingness to take big risks; speculation is restrained. The economy is still responsive to management by fiscal or monetary measures, so that economists and others gain confidence in the government's ability to successfully manage the system. (Some—perhaps most—of the post–World War II success of Keynesian economics may have resulted from this effect.)

4. Many Feel There is a Clear Sustained Upswing Starting

Income and profits rise, savings accumulate, credit expands, and assets increase in value. All this provides even more capital for expansion. While many feel the expansion will slow down or abort, it proceeds quite well, partly because a relatively disciplined and experienced work force is available and both business and government are helpful. Many cautious investors appear and much accumulated technology is exploited. New inventions and innovations are encouraged. Demand for new (and old) projects and products sharply increases. Many new enterprises or practices are conceived, adopted, started, financed, implemented, and many succeed. Despite good prospects and available capital, most entrepreneurs maintain their conservatism and push only justifiable projects.

5. *An Expansion Psychology Begins to Develop*

Expansion leads to more expansion (i.e., steel mills are built to supply steel to build still more mills). Some double and triple ordering occurs; backlogs build up to very high levels. There may be temporary bottlenecks and some short and shallow recessions, but recovery is generally quick and the economy resilient.

Because of the general prosperity, there is great pressure to increase government programs; counter-pressure is relatively small. The prosperity also causes the government to become less concerned with keeping the money supply tight or doing other things that might dampen the financial exuberance. As a result, costs begin to increase and inflation starts to become a serious problem. The inflation, however, is largely unanticipated. This means that large transfers of income go to business, government, and creditors generally. Furthermore, because so much of the economy is not practically or formally indexed, the impact of any inflationary spurt is absorbed rapidly and without much notice. Those who gain wealth or income greatly enjoy it, while those who lose do not yet seem to notice it much. The monetary illusion is maintained, and the inflation therefore acts largely as an additional spur to the expansion.[14] One reason for the high success rate is that caution and skepticism are still prevalent; there is little or no speculative fever.

6. *Full Confidence Is Restored*

By now the system is clearly in an expansionary phase. Almost everybody believes it. Labor and other costs increase, the inflation accelerates but remains moderate. At this point, everyone is conscious of the increase but not used to it. Employers and purchasers resist increases. Despite their confidence, workers and sellers are not militant. Furthermore, even low rates of inflation are frightening. Monetary and fiscal authorities are highly sensitive to it. (Later they will raise their estimate of what constitutes an "acceptable rate of inflation.")[15]

An intensive search for new technologies and other new opportunities gets under way. Companies are eager to replace obsolete equipment so they can use capital instead of increasingly expensive labor.

7. La Belle Epoque *Psychology Emerges*

After a decade or two of good times, good will, optimism, and confidence, a clear *belle époque* psychology emerges. This psychology unleashes enormous energy and dynamism but also leads to a great increase in discretionary behavior and to various other countervailing forces and trends that will soon decrease momentum for growth. But, for the moment, countervailing trends have more prominent political and social than economic effects.

Despite these negative trends, confidence in the future remains high. Indeed, confidence and optimism replace cautious calculation and skeptical analysis and begin to play an important role in inspiring the business community and other sources of economic growth and investment. The number of failures caused by over-confidence, over-extension, or poor management increases, but the failures have little effect on the overall positive climate. In fact, typical price-earnings ratios of many stocks double or triple for about a decade. At the same time, higher taxes, increased government transfers of income, a growing government bureaucracy, and more government regulations render the long-term business climate increasingly negative. However, these developments are not taken very seriously. The inflation finally begins to take off. In many cases this relieves debtors of much of the burden of their accumulated debts and many ill-advised projects succeed. Thus the erosion of basic institutions spurs speculation and risk taking, at least for a while.

8. Emergence of Discretionary Behavior as a Norm

A generally lax attitude develops towards many traditional values, particularly in the homes and churches of the upper-middle class. People begin to take affluence and prosperity for granted. Discretionary behavior becomes extreme and destructive. It is reinforced by anti-bourgeois, anti-business, anti-Philistine, anti-materialistic attitudes and social movements. However, most of the extreme forms of protest are limited to vulnerable or marginal types of people.[16]

9. Resilience of Economy (or Apparent Good Management by Government)

During the two or three decades after the bottom of the trough, three to five "business cycle" fluctuations occur, and perhaps one or two Kuznets cycles.[17] All the recessions are shallow and the recoveries swift and complete. Figure 4.2 illustrates this.

Toward the end of the period, however, some erosion occurs. The "Phillips curve" begins to deteriorate, the recessions get deeper, and the recoveries become slower and less complete. However, confidence persists that government can manage the economy. It is not realized

198

FIGURE 4.2
Business Cycles During an Upswing

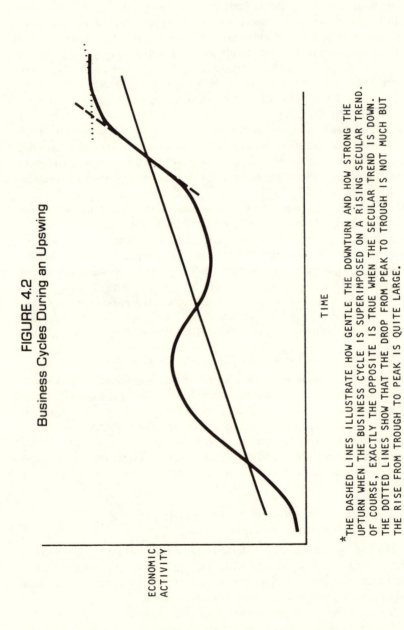

ECONOMIC
ACTIVITY

TIME

*THE DASHED LINES ILLUSTRATE HOW GENTLE THE DOWNTURN AND HOW STRONG THE
UPTURN WHEN THE BUSINESS CYCLE IS SUPERIMPOSED ON A RISING SECULAR TREND.
OF COURSE, EXACTLY THE OPPOSITE IS TRUE WHEN THE SECULAR TREND IS DOWN.
THE DOTTED LINES SHOW THAT THE DROP FROM PEAK TO TROUGH IS NOT MUCH BUT
THE RISE FROM TROUGH TO PEAK IS QUITE LARGE.

that during a long upswing normal recession cycles have abnormally flat bottoms and sharp expansions, but that the reverse normally occurs if the basic period is one of a slowing down in the rate of expansion.

10. Confidence Peaks Even While Extraordinary Strains and Excesses Appear

A "peak war" or some other disturbing event or series of events emerges and is pursued with excessive zeal, partly because excess energy is available and there is little spirit of caution or prudence to induce a willingness to compromise or cut losses. Indeed, incompetence and over-confidence have built up, and much of the society's thinking is based on illusions and lessened reality testing.

Inflation begins to be a serious social and political problem, and the financial structure becomes increasingly dependent on debt and speculative values. At the same time, other societal strains appear as a result of the long period of success and prosperity. Pelagian attitudes prevail almost everywhere.

11. Extremist Discretionary Behavior and Polarization of Society

Many excessive expectations have been created and not met. Disturbing events and policies proliferate. Toleration for injustice or inequality decreases. Upper and upper-middle class elites are looking for causes. There is much dissension, polarization, recrimination, and disillusionment. A general outburst of extremist discretionary behavior against the system is led by an articulate upper-middle class. This outburst is tolerated because social customs, values, and attitudes reflect the belief that society is basically safe, secure, and stable. This belief, while still strong, begins to erode under the influence of events. There is a noticeable shift in attitudes from Pelagian to Augustinian. Change is visible in all aspects of the culture and begins to affect the general lifestyle. Diverse sub-cultures arise, some explicitly experimental or bohemian. The adversary (or counterculture) flourishes.

Financial speculation becomes rife and is increasingly based on fads, self-fulfilling prophecies, "discounting the hereafter," and Ponzi schemes (i.e., dividends that are not paid out of real profits but out of capital or by concealed or open income transfers). Price levels soar. High costs and expensive rigidities become built-in vested interests in many public and private institutions.

Upper-middle class young people, who were raised in a protected affluent environment and a more or less idealistic atmosphere (and thus take their benefits and comforts for granted), increasingly reject the rampant materialism. They tend to have extremely unrealistic expectations and dismiss the idea that every system has weaknesses and injustices. Their early "boy scout," "Santa Claus," or "Sunday School" socialization is not naturally and gradually eroded by the slings and arrows of growing up. It either persists or is abruptly and catastrophically challenged by extremely disillusioning experiences. New searches by subcultures and experimental groups for "meaning and purpose" emerge. The basic concepts of what was called the *avant garde* in the early 1920s and late 1960s become popular. These notions as summarized by Malcolm Cowley include: the idea of salvation by the child; the idea of self-expression, the idea of paganism; the idea of living for the moment; the idea of liberty; the idea of female equality; the idea of psychological adjustment; and the idea of changing place.[18]

12. Eventually Comes a Day of Reckoning

A relatively serious depression, military defeat, or other debacle finally occurs. Recovery is slow and erratic. There is worldwide excess capacity rather than orders for expansion of plants. Even normal replacement of plants is not undertaken. The minimal ordering of new equipment that still occurs is undertaken cautiously, mostly for the short run instead of the long run. Other aspects of the society— confidence and respect for the system, personal pressures to do a good job, etc.—are also slow to recover. Basic anti-business, anti-bourgeois, anti-Philistine attitudes are remarkably persistent. They handicap business, either directly or through the creation or toleration of many specific regulatory and tax problems, and undermine consumer confidence. Upper-middle class youth once again begin to appreciate square goals, if not square values. The rapid cultural change of the last period of the upswing retains momentum but slows.

13. Recovery Proceeds, but Erratically

In the economy, excessive stimulation, excessive reform ("excessive" given the weakness of the patient) or other mistakes tend to occur. These could cause a new and deeper depression. Political alliances change; ideological "reshuffling" occurs. Reactionary, revisionist, extreme, and moderate camps emerge within former alliance blocs.

14. A Troubled Period of Transition and 'Sobering Up'

Either an *époque de malaise* occurs or the system collapses, depending on how many mistakes and excesses have occurred. The depth and duration of the malaise or collapse depends to some extent on the mistakes that come after it.

A new mood of seriousness, pessimism, and skepticism eventually takes over. Radical, politically moderate, or reactionary movements emerge; perhaps all three appear. There is a renewed focus on political and cultural issues. Both new and old institutions, values, goals are attacked—often savagely, intensely, articulately, and competently. However, the old values, formerly explicated and defended by people who were not used to doing so, are now much better defended by people who have had to relearn fundamentals.

A counter-reformation, building up for some time, also begins to emerge, emphasizing square values or a new synthesis. What also emerges is a greater sensitivity to the internally developed endogenous social, cultural, and economic problems that came to the fore during the past cycle. This provides some synthesis between the reformation and the counter-reformation. The "sobering-up," for the time being, is superficial; many groups continue to push increasingly inappropriate programs and trends.

15. Full Emergence of a New Synthesis Between the Reformation and the Counter-Reformation

A prolonged counter-reformation temporarily comes to the fore, but its influence is incomplete. For a while it coexists with the reformation. Finally, there is some synthesis between the old and the new, as "new" cultural meanings become unconsciously held and form a new "traditional culture." Thus, the ground is prepared for a new long upswing as the energies of the population are released to go about "business-as-usual" once again, though at the next level of the spiral (or the slide).

The Concept of Creeping Stagnation

Civilized societies have existed for more than ten thousand years, but it wasn't until the end of the eighteenth century that any society was able to support sustained technological and economic growth. We still only partially understand why none of the other societies ever "took off." One likely reason is that in all of them there were many social inhibitions to growth and technological advancement that effectively stifled promising developments. Indeed, in our society economic growth, and perhaps technological advancement as well, may also slow down because of the previously described social limits to growth and the Fourteen New Emphases.

Creeping stagnation is a way station to this slowdown. We believe that this condition exists in many European countries, to some degree in Canada and Australia, and to a lesser but more dramatic extent in the United States. It is more dramatic in the United States because of the prominence of the Anti-Growth Triad and their activities.

A society may ostensibly consider economic growth as one of its important goals but at the same time institute other measures or allow other trends to occur that largely stifle economic growth. The adjective *creeping* indicates that this stifling may be done in small steps and slow degrees and that the society may never have made a deliberate and conscious choice to so limit economic growth. Rather, such a society would have adopted a number of measures that ultimately led to a sharp decrease in the rate of growth, even though at no point was a clear-cut choice to achieve this change actually formulated and approved. Indeed, had such a choice been clearly presented, it would almost certainly have been rejected.

The concept of creeping stagnation also includes the increased possibility of economic insecurity, economic crisis, or other economic instability that could cause a society not only to slow down but to collapse. Again, this applies only if the measures taken were not consciously chosen with these risks in mind. Creeping stagnation does not include measures that everybody can see would cause tremendous problems. Such measures are usually withdrawn or corrected before they can do their potential damage.[19]

The most important causes of the current state of creeping stagnation emerged during the last half of *La Deuxième Belle Epoque*. We believe most of the ACNs show a definite erosion of prudence, efficiency, discipline, behavioral standards, the work ethic, advancement orientation, and the like. We also believe that if the long upswing comes close to the end of the thousand-year Multifold Trend (a period in which affluence has grown enormously in the ACNs and in which sensate values have replaced older ideational and idealistic values), the effects of the long swing are much more pronounced than if the swing begins at an earlier time. (This is one reason the effects were stronger in *La Deuxième Belle Epoque* than in *La Première Belle Epoque*.)

There is another important effect we call "the poverty of affluence." This involves the difficulty that the *nouveau riche*, whether nations or individuals, have in adjusting to their new-found affluence and living within their greatly increased means. The ACNs desperately need a "revolution of lessened rising expectations"—the notion that expectations can still rise, but not as rapidly as they have.

Equally important is an understanding of the significance of the New Emphases. As we get richer, we naturally turn our priorities and attention to issues other than just earning money and being efficient about using resources. The richer we are, the cleaner we wish the air and the water to be and the more we desire improved conditions for our work and leisure activities. We do so not because these are matters of life and death but because these are good things to have and we value them.

Finally, there is the whole problem described in Chapter 3 of cultural change and the confusion and "strange" reactions that accompany rapid cultural change. These are occurring today as we go through the most rapid part of The Great Transition. The intrusion of both the super-industrial and the post-industrial economies and the concomitant emergence of the Fourteen New Emphases have the impact of introducing a new culture.

All of the above issues influence creeping stagnation, but the New Emphases and cultural change have the greatest impact. Under current conditions, we institute these new values and new concepts unskillfully, sometimes even incompetently, and occasionally in an extremist almost talismanic and semi-rational fashion. The recent Sun Day in the United States exemplifies this. It almost certainly did not contribute much to the short- or medium-run solution to our energy problems. Indeed, it may have hurt instead, but it was great fun and politics for many and a quasi-religious experience for a few.

Denison has recently estimated that the costs of regulation in the United States have resulted in a lowering of the size of the nonrestricted business sector in 1975 by about 1.5 percent.[20] We argue that his estimates are very low. He focuses on the costs that are actually incurred by industry but does not take the less tangible factors fully into account, including the effect of discouragement, the investments and projects that simply don't happen because people don't wish to undertake them under the new conditions, and the huge costs associated with inactivity enforced by government.[21]

Consider the issue of the government slowing down the licensing of coal lands for exploitation. At present, about two-thirds of the coal operators of America are earning a high "economic rent," that is, income derived from owning relatively desirable coal mines. The spot price of coal has risen more than oil, increasing by a factor of six or so. (This is a rough estimate because the price depends so much on the quality of the coal, where it comes from, where it is delivered, when and how the contract was negotiated, and so on.) The increase has been so spectacular not because it is physically difficult to open up productive coal mines, but because so many of the fields are currently unavailable for exploitation. They are either on government lands (almost totally unavailable since 1971) or cannot be opened because of government regulations. As a result, the United States has to pay high prices to operate a number of marginal mines to meet the demand. This has driven the price up enormously in a country which has literally enough cheap coal to supply the entire world for centuries, given some technological advances.

Consider the current proposal to put aside an area in Alaska (the area is almost the size of France) as a relatively untouched wilderness. The plan would also make it extremely difficult to develop the rest of Alaska. Yet Alaska may be as rich in resources as Siberia or Western Australia. What would have happened to the Soviet Union or Australia if their "mostly untouched" areas had been put aside as wilderness sanctuaries or if the thirteen American colonies had tried to preserve the forests of Kentucky and Pennsylvania? If one treats such potential resource areas as sacred treasures in a museum, one is not going to have much economic growth.

Or consider the use of costly tactics to introduce new standards and concepts. Even when the tactics are reasonable, they are still costly and should be avoided when possible. An example is the Clean Air Act of 1970, in which Congress mandated that the United States auto industry meet certain levels of anti-pollution performance by 1975; a date chosen arbitrarily (i.e., the magic of the number five as opposed to four or six).[22] Most experts were reasonably sure that the industry would not be able to reach the suggested performance levels by that time.[23] But the United States Congress believed that setting an extremely stringent deadline would shake the industry out of its complacency—"hold industry's feet to the fire." Of course, if one does this too often, industry's feet will be burned, as has happened. We believe that one reason the auto industry had such a bad year in 1974 was that many Americans bought cars in 1973 to avoid buying them in 1974. They felt, correctly, that the 1974 cars would be poorly designed because of the makeshift arrangements the automobile industry would have to use to meet the Congressional requirements. The result was overly expensive cars with relatively poor performance (about 10 to 20 percent less mileage than a better design available in a year or two would provide).

If this correctly describes consumer behavior, Congress saw to it that the United States had the worst of all worlds. The over-buying in 1973 helped to fuel the inflation even further, while the under-buying in 1974 and 1975 presumably helped to deepen the recession. This is an isolated incident that partly represents just bad luck. The over-buying could have occurred in a recession year and the under-buying in a period of inflationary expectations. There are, however, more fundamental possibilities that are worth mentioning. Let us start with the now well-known "Laffer Curve."

Laffer and His Curves

Arthur Laffer has noted that "there are always two rates that produce the same revenue," as illustrated in Figure 4.3. Figure 4.3 shows the amount of taxable revenue that is raised as the government collects more and more taxes. It is a purely conceptual curve, since the exact curve would depend very much on the exact measures the government uses to raise taxes, the history that preceded the government's effort, and many other factors.

The Laffer Curve indicates, perhaps simplistically but persuasively and correctly, that in principle if the government had a zero tax rate (assuming government could still operate) no revenue would be produced. As the government increases its tax rate, the revenue increases until it reaches a peak. At this point the tax collection interferes so much with the operation of the legal monetary economy that the actual revenue begins to drop with further increases. Even though the tax rates are high, the volume of reported taxable activities drops even more rapidly. Taxable activities go underground (become illegal), involve barter operations, take on other aspects of a subsistence economy, or simply cease because of the high costs and risks of lessened return created by the government's taxes. We note this point by r_m on the curve. The points r_1 and r_2 illustrate that both a higher and a lower rate of taxation would then produce exactly the same revenue.

The dotted curve illustrates the highly plausible hypothesis that the GNP would be above zero even if there were no taxes (and therefore no formal government), that it would rise to a peak (which for most economies probably occurs far before the point r_m), and would then fall gradually as the tax rates increase. At the end point, when no taxes are being collected, one would still have an economy of sorts, but it would be operating at a very low level.

Initially, the activities of government usually improve the operation of the economy because the government is performing essential or economically productive functions. But at some point after the government has begun to take very large amounts of the gross national product, this diversion begins to depress the GNP even if it still produces (for a while) increased tax collections. While

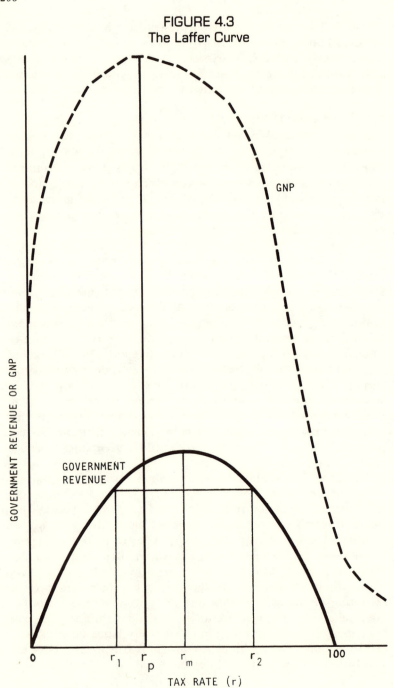

FIGURE 4.3
The Laffer Curve

reasonable persons may disagree about the quantitative impact of any specific rate of taxes or the usefulness of revenues that go through governmental channels, almost all would agree that at some point the funds that pass through government hands are likely to be less effective in creating incentives for growth or to be efficiently invested than if left in private hands.

Laffer believes that almost all the Affluent Capitalist governments have set their tax rates so high as to pass r_m, the point of maximum return, not to mention r_p. Therefore, the easiest way for these governments to increase their tax revenue, at least in the medium and long run, would be to lower the tax rate. We suspect that he is right or close to being right. Obviously, the magnitudes depend on specific aspects of past and current government behavior that have tended to be associated with a higher take. Furthermore, a return to higher GNP may be far from instantaneous.

Our basic hypothesis is that except for Japan, governments of the ACNs have pushed this process about as far as it can go. The pressures to do so have been high, particularly in a period of long upswing (that is, *La Deuxième Belle Epoque*). Only recently have the opposing forces or counterpressures been stimulated and become organized into effective political forces.[24]

While the government might take a narrow view of the situation and wish to operate at the point r_m, it would be better if it operated at some point between r_m and r_p, particularly if instead of just focusing on GNP, it focused on increasing the rate of growth. Many of the government's aims that it expects to achieve by taxing and redistributing income could be better achieved through a higher rate of economic growth. This would be true at least for reducing absolute deprivation (as opposed to reducing relative deprivation). If r_p is well below r_m, it behooves the governments to stay well on the lower side of r_m. Clearly, a government should be willing to lose a little on taxes to gain a lot on GNP.

This entire discussion is conceptual. Tax issues are highly complicated affairs; effects are only fully developed over time; and there are so many other issues that affect the discussion that we do not believe, even conceptually, that the above discussion can be made into a rigorous argument. However, the principle is correct and must be taken into account.

If one accepts the idea that a country may, in principle, be operating past point r_m or even if one only accepts the possibility of operating too far past the point r_p, there should be deep concern about current tax rates in the ACNs. There is, however, no implication that a lowering of tax rates would always result in an immediate increase of revenue or of the rate of growth of GNP. However, we suspect that under current conditions this is likely to be true in many countries of the world. We do not believe that the conditions are quite as good as they were, say, in 1920 and 1962 in the United States when tax cuts by presidents Harding and Kennedy respectively were remarkably effective in both stimulating the growth of the United States economy and increasing tax collections. (We assume a cause and effect relationship that is widely accepted, although, like almost all interpretations of real world events, it too has been challenged). A number of quantitative approaches have been tried to make the above arguments more precise and therefore more persuasive.[25] As far as we can tell, these quantitative analyses are not much more persuasive than our intuitive judgment or that of most readers.

There are many other costs, associated with overly high taxes. Perhaps the most important is a general lowering of standards. In the United Kingdom, to take an extreme example, the tax rates in the higher brackets are 98 percent of the unearned income and 83 percent of the earned income. In a time of peace, in a country at least nominally capitalist, this is a bizarre absurdity. It simply forces everybody in these brackets to spend much time, energy, and thought on legal and illegal methods of tax evasion. Almost nobody is willing to accept that kind of clearly punitive taxation as being, under normal circumstances, a reasonable prerogative of the government. It is morally and politically akin to a minority group being singled out by a hostile government. People who pay these taxes honestly will surely not feel any sense of pride of citizenship in doing so.

New Costs and Risks for United States Business

Table 4.2 lists what we call "New Costs and Risks" for United States business. The list gives many of the reasons (most of which are relatively new in emphasis or character) why we may continue to have creeping stagnation in the United States—at least in terms of investment in new facilities and in other innovations that require making large commitments.

Kondratieff Theory

Earlier in this chapter we discussed a long-run cyclical theory of socio-economic behavior based as much upon psychological and cultural as on material factors. There are several long cycle economic theories. Two of the most important are probably those of Simon Kuznets and of Richard Easterlin on the effect of population fluctuations on economic behavior.[26] The work of these two theorists is widely accepted. Much less accepted but in some ways more relevant to our discussion is the work of the Russian economist Nikolai D. Kondratieff.[27] He made a study of a number of price movements in Western economies going back to about 1790. The price movements for the United States are reproduced in Figure 4.4. Kondratieff noticed what he took to be two and one-half long waves from the late 1880s to the mid-1920s, and he predicted that a third wave would peak during the late 1920s, to be followed by a depression. Partly because of this prediction, he was taken very seriously by Joseph Schumpeter and some other noted economists.

After enjoying a certain vogue, Kondratieff's ideas were challenged, and his theory subsequently dropped out of favor. Interest in Kondratieff's long waves has revived in recent years, sometimes modified by various new consideratons. Notably, Jay Forrester of M.I.T. and Walter Rostow of the University of Texas are directing active current research programs based upon their versions of the Kondratieff theory.[28] Forrester focuses on leads and lags generated by the interplay between the capital goods industries and the consumer goods industries, while Rostow concentrates on the leads and lags generated by the interplay between commodities and industrial products. Both make dire predictions about the immediate future, but for somewhat different reasons. Forrester argues that the capital goods sector has been overbuilt worldwide; therefore he foresees a long period of excess capacity and deflationary pressures—in effect, the fourth Kondratieff downswing. We argue that there is almost no question that something like Forrester's analysis holds for the world steel industry today. Many industries have built up, worldwide, a huge excess capacity in exactly the way he describes and may have work it off in much the way he suggests. When we discuss situations comparable to that in the steel industry we will refer to them as Forrester-Kondratieff type depressions, or downswing situations.

Rostow argues that contemporary Kondratieff theorists have been misled by the pervasive inflation and that the proper index to look at is not the price of commodities but the ratio of the price of commodities to manufactured goods. This ratio has been depressed since 1950. In effect, Rostow is arguing that the fifth Kondratieff downswing has already occurred; that because of their relatively low prices there has not been sufficient expansion in commodities production; and that it takes about two or three decades to get enough

TABLE 4.2 *(Cont.)*

IV. Government Fiscal and Monetary Policies
  A. Social Security and energy taxes
  B. Tax reform
  C. Oil leases
  D. Other tax issues
  E. Temptation to "excessive" stimulation, welfare, income redistribution
  F. Structural deterioration
    1. Phillips curve
    2. Business cycle
  G. Lack of clear and predictable system for capital budget decisions
  H. Fear of shifts in central bank policy and possible politicization
  I. Tendency to use policy to offset real adjustment to changing conditions rather than aid adjustment

V. Domestic Issues: education, law and order, municipal services and costs, minority problems and issues, population shifts, and other urban problems. Irrational commitment to various equity issues without reference to cost

VI. International Trade and Finance Issues
  A. Possibility of "beggar thy neighbor" policies
  B. Foreign debts
  C. Vulnerability of U.S. and Eurodollar banks
  D. European malaise
  E. Canadian and Japanese malaise
  F. Increased Soviet strength
  G. OPEC and Middle East issues
  H. General growth in economic interdependence
  I. Flexible exchange rates
  J. Developed-Less Developed country relations

FIGURE 4.4
U.S. Wholesale Price Index, 1750-1976

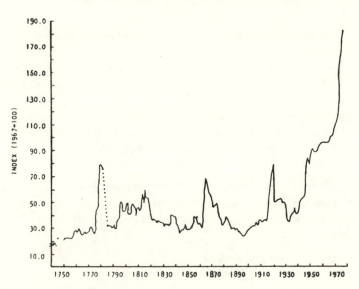

*THE READER SHOULD NOTE THE APPARENT EXISTENCE OF FOUR "TROUGHS" ABOUT 1790, 1845, 1895, AND 1930 (I.E., ABOUT 45 TO 55 YEARS APART) AND FOUR PEAKS ABOUT 1815, 1865, 1920, AND 1975 (I.E., ABOUT 50 TO 55 YEARS APART). IT IS THE APPARENT REGULARITY OF THESE PEAKS AND TROUGHS WHICH SUPPLY THE BASIS FOR SEVERAL THEORIES OF A LONG CYCLE OF ABOUT 50 YEARS DURATION.

SOURCE: U.S. DEPARTMENT OF COMMERCE, HISTORICAL STATISTICS OF THE UNITED STATES (COLONIAL TIMES TO 1790) AND ECONOMIC REPORT OF THE PRESIDENT, 1977.

investment into commodities production to correct this imbalance. Thus, Rostow expects that this lag of investment in commodities production will bring about various resource scarcities (and presumably high commodities prices and inflationary pressures). We agree that something like this has clearly occurred in the energy industry. We will refer to this as a Rostow-Kondratieff type problem, which also takes two or three decades to improve.

The two theories are contradictory if one thinks of Kondratieff theory as being an overall theory of the entire world economy. However, one could argue that different parts of the world economy are going through different phases or forms of the cycle. Whether or not one wishes to take this approach, there is certainly some tension between these two versions of the Kondratieff theory, Forrester's fourth downswing and Rostow's fifth upswing. We argue for including, at least in the current situation, a psycho-social or institutional perspective such as was presented in the section on the long upswing. From this point of view we have just finished a long upswing and are due for a downswing, but we do not draw any necessary implication of a long series of up and down cycles, although we do not rule such a series out either. (We should also mention another version of Kondratieff—that of Schumpeter. He believed that the cycles were touched off and supported by periods of intense and pervasive technological innovation followed by long periods of consolidation.)[29]

The original author of the theory, Kondratieff, cannot comment on the various versions of his theory. In fact, he did not try to explain the price movements he described at all but simply argued that the empirical evidence was sufficiently convincing to prove the existence of such waves. He also noticed a connection between the troughs and peaks of these waves and various European wars. In particular, the bottom of each wave often more or less coincided with a relatively small and profitable war that helped get things started again, while the apogee was characterized by what he called a *peak war*. The latter was very destructive and divisive, almost as if the society had an excess of energy, dynamism, and ruthlessness that it could not contain.

Trough wars, in effect, helped get things started again and were followed by a twenty or thirty year period of rising prices during which almost everything worked well: the system was competent, resilient, enthusiastic, recuperative, and flexible. Finally, however, a number of stresses and strains built up more or less as we indicate in our long upswing, but the system got overconfident and ruthless and finally a "peak war" was precipitated. In theory, the extreme exacerbation of the peak war more or less damages the system; at the same time prices are pushed to extremely high levels. The subsequent collapse and deflation generates a period of declining or low (stable) prices for the next fifteen to twenty-five years.

Figure 4.5 summarizes how one might try to fit the United States into this theory of trough and peak wars by showing the United States wholesale price index from 1750 to 1976 and marking Kondratieff troughs, peaks, and (theoretically) associated waves. World War II does not fit into the scheme. From Kondratieff's economic perspective, World War II can best be thought of as "Hitler's war," caused almost completely by political issues exploited by an evil genius. One can think of the effects of World War II as analogous to a pendulum hit by a shock. This blow might cause a premature termination of one cycle (roughly Rostow's scheme), a higher amplitude (roughly Forrester's scheme), or some mixture of both. Figure 4.5 (see arrows) suggests that World War II changed the amplitude of the cycle, not its length. The lower curve indicates how price movements might have appeared without the effects of the war on the trend. This interpretation comes closer to Forrester's perspective than that of Rostow.

In effect, our long upswing is similar to the Forrester and Rostow models. However, we add an important psychological and cultural component, at least for what might be taken as the fourth Kondratieff upswing. This component may not have been very strong in the first two Kondratieff upswings, but has become more important because the upswings are now occurring at the end of the long-term Multifold Trend.*

We expect all the problems described to last a few decades unless something quite dramatic happens. We suggest in Part II that such dramatic events could arise from Japan or the Middle Income countries. In effect, we think that a selective application of what

---

*Some readers might be concerned that we are some type of Kondratieff cultist. While interest in his theory has increased in recent years, we share the common academic position to the extent of being at least agnostic about the general theory. However, we are not at all agnostic about believing that the current worldwide problem of overcapacity in steel is extraordinarily close to the kind of thing that has been modeled by Forrester; that the problem of the energy industry is close to the description given by Rostow in his version of Kondratieff's theory; that a good view of the general malaise that the Advanced Capitalist nations are suffering today is closely related to what we just called the psychosocial version of long swings; and that the Middle Income nations are entering a long upward swing for reasons clearly described by Schumpeter's concept of exploiting existing technological opportunities.

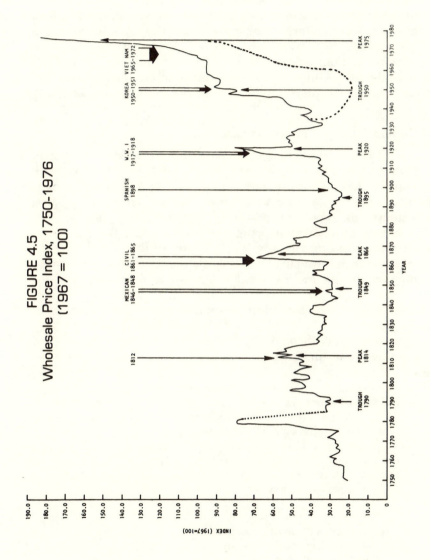

FIGURE 4.5
Wholesale Price Index, 1750-1976
(1967 = 100)

might be called Kondratieff type mechanisms deserves at least a Scotch verdict of not proven but highly plausible, to use the terminology of Chapter 1. Our scheme about the United States wars or Kondratieff's discussion of the European wars deserves at least tolerant atheism. One should not be upset at such phrases as trough war and peak war even if one does not accept that there was some inter-connection between these wars and the long cycles. We ourselves are inclined to take an almost deist position with regard to the last; there is something in it but we are not quite sure what it is.

Current Western Cultural Trends

This entire book reflects our belief that the Atlantic Protestant culture area is prone to what we call *educated incapacity*, mixed with much wishful and illusionary thinking. We have argued that many citizens of these countries tend to make overly sanguine, if not naive, assumptions about the practical possibilities for good or even competent government in many areas of the world. Other Europeans are less optimistic and also less Pelagian (in this case the two go together) than most citizens of the Atlantic Protestant culture area. But even they are less realistic (and less Augustinian) than they used to be. We have also pointed to tendencies in Western culture towards anarchy, terrorism, and nihilism—in effect, towards a breakdown of society.

No wonder William Butler Yeats' chilling vision "The Second Coming" seems increasingly apt:

> Turning and turning in the widening gyre
> The falcon cannot hear the falconer;
> Things fall apart; the center cannot hold;
> Mere anarchy is loosed upon the world.
> The blood-dimmed tide is loosed, and everywhere
> The ceremony of innocence is drowned;
> The best lack all conviction, while the worst
> Are full of passionate intensity.
>
> Surely some revelation is at hand;
> Surely the Second Coming is at hand. . . .
> The darkness drops again; but now I know
> That twenty centuries of stony sleep
> Were vexed to a nightmare by a rocking cradle,
> And what rough beast, its hour come round at last,
> Slouches toward Bethlehem to be born?[30]

While Yeats' warning comes from the right, the feeling that such fears are justified now encompasses the whole ideological spectrum.

This problem does not arise from any actual experience of economic, technological, or safety failure of our society (though there is much discussion of the possibility of such failures), but instead from a deep-seated cultural failure. Can anything be done about this? We believe so.

Perhaps the single most important thing that could be done would be to substitute reasonably accurate positive images of the future for the depressing images that now prevail, especially in the Advanced Capitalist nations. It is hard to find a leading school or university in these countries that did not at one time or another favor limiting economic growth; almost all still preach the Fourteen New Emphases as received doctrine. While some of these Emphases may be desirable, many upper-middle class elites in the affluent countries are pursuing them with irrational intensity. We believe that other approaches to these problems would be much more constructive and might make an enormous difference in the future of our society. We discuss this topic further in Chapters 5 and 8. Some of the suggestions we put forth in those chapters are practical; others are overtly polemical and intended to stimulate the imagination.

The growth of terrorist movements in many places is no accident. Indeed, it is an almost inevitable result of excessive Pelagianism combined with specific historical events. From our perspective it is especially noteworthy that terrorist movements in almost every Western country draw mainly from young upper-middle class people or at least from university students. It is a movement associated with excessive and naive expectations. In West Germany it has also been stimulated by the erosion or destruction of the father as a symbol of authority and a general rejection of pre–World War II politics and ideology. In Italy, the frustrations caused by the dramatic and systematic ineptness of the national government have also played a role. The Weathermen (later stylishly renamed the Weatherpeople) in the United States have tended to come from families with substantially higher incomes than those of the average student at the high status universities that these young people frequently attended. We think of many of these young terrorists more as spoiled brats than as young idealists who have had their expectations frustrated—although both perceptions have some validity. In any case, there is an inadequate super-ego; the children have not been properly socialized, and there has been a lack of leadership by responsible, mature adults. While this phenomenon is fully consistent with the Long-Term

Multifold Trend, it can be more directly attributed to *La Deuxième Belle Epoque*. After twenty-six years, relatively good times were taken for granted; bad things became intolerable.

The effect of almost two decades of these widespread, systematic, and effective attacks on our culture should not be underestimated. The adversary culture and the counterculture have taken their toll. However, the consequences of the anti-growth movement may be even more serious. The children of our privileged classes are led to believe that in our society the rich get richer and the poor get poorer, and that this crime is perpetrated by exploiting the defenseless, plundering the planet of precious resources, polluting the environment, and sometimes by poisoning the food with dangerous additives. The whole is compounded by business indulging in rapacious, unethical, and even illegal behavior as a matter of course. They are taught, furthermore, that this process is leading, perhaps inexorably, to disaster. From this point of view the emphasis by many American businessmen on teaching America that "profit is not a dirty word" is almost laughable. They are being accused of murder, poisoning, genocide, debauching the public, despoiling the environment, and robbing the poor and the grandchildren!

It is, for example, almost never mentioned in any school course I have seen on food that, except for lung cancer, the age-specific incidence of cancer has gone down. (Cancer of the lung is presumably caused by smoking, which does seem to be a genuine problem.) The reason that deaths by cancer have gone up is less because of an increase in carcinogens in food and the environment, and more because of increased longevity; people are no longer dying at younger ages of other diseases. Carcinogens may have increased in food and the environment but not sufficiently to negate the increasingly positive qualities of the overall physical and social environment.

At one time, the United States was probably the worst offender in indoctrinating its upper-middle class young against its own society. One reason was the impact of the Vietnam War. But even about such issues as world starvation, pollution, and limiting growth, some completely indefensible programs are promoted. For example, the World Council of Churches once conducted a systematic campaign urging that Americans eat less meat in order to provide more grain for the starving people of India. As it happens, plenty of grain was then (and remains) available at about $250 a ton—not at about $100 per ton. If a few Americans eat less meat, this price is not affected significantly, so the campaign would not increase the grain supply for Indians. The issue was purely financial. The Indians needed about 10 million tons of grain, and the question was who was going to pay for it. When the World Council of Churches was repeatedly confronted with this fact, they finally changed their campaign: eat less meat to show your moral solidarity with Indians; then take the money you save and send it to the Indians so they can buy more grain. This is a difficult way to raise money in the United States for any cause. Obviously the purpose of the exercise had nothing to do with the Indians. It had to do with trying to make Americans feel guilty for living well.

An even more dramatic technique for doing this is the following example much used in American schools. The United States has about 6 percent (approximately one-sixteenth) of the world's population. The metaphor used to describe the world is that sixteen men are in a raft. One (the American) has ten barrels of water; the others are dying of thirst. The American intends to take a public bath in each barrel, one per day. The American believes he owns the water because he earned it, but the others think he stole it. Since he is a decent fellow, he gives the others a cup of water a day. His policy is obviously stupid, counterproductive, and immoral—stupid because the American will soon run out of water for himself; counter-productive because he is almost guaranteeing a revolt in which the water will forcibly be taken away from him; the immorality needs no comment.

This picture has nothing to do with reality. As we have already pointed out, about 25 percent of the world is Affluent today; another 45 percent is Middle Income; and only 30 percent can be considered Poor. Furthermore, the outstanding supplier of "water" (i.e., grain) to the world is the United States, and much of it is supplied at concessionary prices. Finally, the issue is not one of the "ethics of a lifeboat," where water is not available at any price, but the exact opposite: grain is plentiful everywhere at a reasonable price. The issue is almost purely a question of why the thirty percent have not jumped on the development train, despite the many opportunities available during *La Deuxième Belle Epoque.* They may need help, and some help by outside private and public organizations and individuals should be supplied. But basically the solution lies in increased productivity by the countries concerned.

What Do We Really Believe?
Summary and Recapitulation of Part I

We stated that we do not believe there is any validity in the simple limits-to-growth position that claims that we are running out of many critical resources or that we cannot deal satisfactorily with current pollution problems. Such language as "energy-scarce world," a special emphasis on "renewable resources," or the belief that the high-consumption society is immoral because it uses up resources that will be needed by "the grandchildren" are all notions that can be dismissed—at least as worldwide problems, if not always locally. We remain willing to examine evidence that suggests these concepts are relevant, but so far we have found none. Much of our argument holds up even if there were such physical limits to growth. However, the notion of adequate long-run availability of resources (at least to a modern technological society that is also moderately well-managed) is basic to most of our considerations.

We briefly described a number of historical contexts and concepts, some purely descriptive, others based on much theory and research. All dealt with the "big picture" in the most generous or ominous sense of the phrase. It is an effort to fill a void; most contemporary discussions lack a broad canvas for sketching detailed arguments. We do not expect our readers to accept our various pictures as necessarily accurate. We do think that they should know these contexts exist, that some competent people believe in them, and that they offer useful and often interesting perspectives from which to view current events. We also defined and elaborated the "more or less agnostic use" of information and concepts and the six degrees of belief. Except for the Multifold Trend, we are agnostic to deist about most of the material in Chapter 1. The Multifold Trend does seem to characterize most Western cultures for the last thousand years and now applies to most cultures throughout the world.

In Chapter 2 we formulated and discussed various scenarios and contexts for the future development of the world economy. Some are very possible, or at least "surprise-free;" others reveal unlikely possibilities that are nonetheless instructive or theoretically illuminating. We indicate a large range of possible outcomes, but there is clearly no way to explore these alternative futures systematically. One can only select and discuss interesting examples. This chapter continues to furnish a backdrop for more detailed discussions and to provide a kind of artificial history. We believe that what we call our World A or Guarded Optimism World is a most useful scenario context for discussing many detailed issues. The five themes and their sub-variations, also described in this chapter, give a range of perspectives on what might happen and on what is happening in the world. Even more important, these themes include many things that are not being recommended and that we do not think will happen. Yet, if one listens to much current discussion, one would think that these themes are either being recommended or are occurring. We find having these themes identified and available a most useful capability in making our discussion more precise and communicative, despite some accompanying artificiality and arbitrariness.

Chapter 3 examined what is in some ways the main topic of this book: rapid cultural change and various reactions to cultural encounters. The Hudson Institute at one time held regular seminars on the Vietnam War; they opened with about two hours of Bible study. Our purpose was to familiarize seminar participants with the Essenes, Zealots, Maccabeans, Pharisees, and other Biblical groups because each had an interesting analog in the Vietnamese context. Unless one understands the enormous diversity displayed by subcultures in their reactions to certain situations, one lacks a real sense of what has happened and can happen in the world.

In effect Part I tries to compensate for the almost complete absence of a shared literature among most contemporary educated readers. Almost every culture in the past has been able to operate in the context of a literature almost all its members have read, understand, and are familiar with. It was easy to make detailed references to this shared background. For example, every participant in the United States Constitutional Convention of 1789 had probably read the *King James Bible,* most or all of Shakespeare, Milton's *Paradise Lost,* Plutarch's *Lives,* and other Greek and Roman classics. Although *The Wealth of Nations* and *The Decline and Fall of the Roman Empire* were published in 1776, every delegate had certainly read them or was familiar with their arguments. To some degree, Part I should provide our readers with such a common frame of reference. This can be almost as useful to explicate disagreement as to built concurrence.

Chapter 3 introduced a central theme of the book: under current conditions, extraordinarily important social limits to growth, including the Fourteen New Emphases, are emerging in every Affluent Capitalist economy and, unless dealt with reasonably, are likely to develop rapidly and perhaps even too rapidly. Without suggesting that these limits are necessarily undesirable in the long run, we argued that their premature emergence is counterproductive. We think of them as cultural contradictions of economic growth. The social-limits-to-growth movement has also become a problem in the developing world. This movement causes confusing signals to be communicated to elites in the developing countries, to attendees at international conferences, to students from the developing world enrolled at universities in developed nations, and to various progressive and liberal groups. The elites as a result are often unsure whether economic progress is being promoted as a goal to be sought after, an evil to be avoided, or a weakness that one lives with but controls.

Another major theme in Part I was modernization, defined as the transition from what we call pre-industrial to what we call post-industrial. Although we do not regard modernization and industrialization as identical, we argue that they overlap for most countries, at least for a time. It would be difficult to make the transition to post-industrial without passing through a period of industrialization, but some resource-rich countries might conceivably do so.

Part I ends with Chapter 4, which started by defining our concept of the four basic socio-economic periods of the twentieth century: *La Première Belle Epoque, La Mauvaise Epoque, La Deuxième Belle Epoque,* and *L'époque de Malaise.* We believe that *La Deuxième Belle Epoque* has just ended and *L'époque de Malaise* has commenced. This is probably the best context from which to view much that is happening on the world scene. We qualified this by pointing out that the Middle Income nations and the Coping Poor are less likely to be affected by the malaise than the Affluent Capitalist and Affluent Communist nations. We defined malaise as "not feeling well"—i.e., one is not quite sick but not really well either. (However, one who has malaise may be much more prone to serious sickness.)

We take seriously the concept of the long upswing and (paradoxically) the general eroding effect such a period has on morale, commitment, seriousness, and discipline in the Advanced Capitalist nations; its effects on the Communist, Middle Income, and Poor nations exist, but are much less pronounced. The high expected growth of the Middle Income nations, if it occurs, will present the ACNs with both markets and competitors. Particularly if we accept the Forrester-Kondratieff or Schumpeter-Kondratieff concepts, the Middle Income nations may provide all-important markets for excess capacity (Forrester-Kondratieff diagnosis) or opportunities to exploit new technologies (Schumpeter-Kondratieff diagnosis). As will be discussed below, the Japanese economy may also be able to ameliorate these long-term effects to some degree.

We take seriously the idea that we seem to be entering an epoch of malaise that could easily be converted into *La Deuxième Mauvaise Epoque;* that a New Class exists in all the Affluent nations (but in different forms in capitalist and communist nations); and the Fourteen New Emphases are part of an emergent new ideology and to some degree a new culture that is rapidly affecting traditional industrial culture, economy, and institutions. This impact raises many of the kinds of issues discussed in Chapter 3 on cultural change and economic growth.

Part II is largely self-contained, although it uses much of the language and many of the concepts and theories of Part I. Part I can be thought of as formulating, elaborating, enriching, and promulgating various perspectives for the arguments in Part II. It precedes Part II for pedagogic and literary rather than logical reasons. The language and concepts of Part I facilitate the discussion and comprehension of Part II.

Part II opens with Chapter 5 on "growing pains." It describes the emerging super-industrial economy and focuses on both the good and bad aspects of the next two decades or so, elucidating some of the more important reasons for hope and fear. Chapter 6 describes two countries that are doing very well, South Korea and Taiwan, and one that is doing fairly well, Japan, and discusses some tactics they have used to develop rapidly. The first two provide an extraordinarily useful contrast with the ACNs as examples of high morale, commitment, and good management—a contrast between relatively healthy developing societies, despite their political and other problems, and developed societies that seem less healthy, despite their affluence and more democratic institutions.

Chapter 5 includes a systematic discussion of some institutional issues, focusing on malaise as a reasonable description of the current situation of the ACNs and Comecon, whether or not one accepts the periodization of the twentieth century into four *époques.* Chapter 5 also discusses inflation, which contributes to the *malaise* and arises out of the *malaise,* but is nonetheless a separate phenomenon.

Our expectation of a period of malaise is only a hypothesis—a hypothesis that could be too optimistic as well as too pessimistic. Thus we may be right about the forces leading to malaise but may have underestimated their strength. If so, *L'époque de Malaise* could easily be transformed into *La Deuxième Mauvaise Epoque,* something resembling the traumas and catastrophes of the period 1914 to 1947. From this perspective, the potentially harmful consequences of modern technology, particularly weapons of mass destruction and their likely rapid proliferation, can only be viewed with the gravest apprehension.

Chapter 7 includes some additional discussion and personal observations about the Affluent, the Middle Income, and the Poor nations in the context set forth in the study as a whole.

Many readers who are skeptical about grand generalizations or artificial typologies put forth in Part I may be less skeptical about the relatively specific points made in most of Part II. Indeed, they may consider our discussion of such current world economic problems as stagflation, interdependence, energy, money, debt, confidence, and morale, and the examples furnished by South Korea, Taiwan, and Japan to be the substantive heart of this book. But we believe that the controversial and philosophical material in Part I is equally and probably more important.

We end Part II with Chapter 8, which expresses our views on various issues and policies. This chapter delineates what we think of as the most important "lessons" of this book, describes some potentially useful programs for dealing with the future, and permits us to elucidate some personal preferences and animadversions.

Notes

1. Niccolo Machiavelli, *Florentine History*, translated by T. Bedingfeld, (New York: AMS Press, 1905).

2. For recent quantitative information in this section we drew heavily on Maddison's "Phases of Capitalistic Development," *Quarterly Review*, Banca Nazionale del Lavoro, No. 121, June 1977.

3. Although the communist revolution in China did not attain its final victory until 1949, we include it in this period because most of the events that produced the victory belong in *La Mauvaise Epoque* rather than the succeeding period.

4. Peter Drucker, *The Age of Discontinuity* (New York: Harper & Row, 1969).

5. The concept of *peak wars* that are divisive and costly and *trough wars* that are milder and typically for profit is an element of the Kondratieff Cycle, an attempt to explain long term cycles in prices (and perhaps output) lasting about 50 years. N. D. Kondratieff, "The Long Waves in Economic Life," *The Review of Economics and Statistics* 17, no. 6 (November 1935):105-15. See also discussion below.

6. H. Kahn and A. J. Wiener (New York: Macmillan, 1957).

7. H. Kahn and B. Bruce-Briggs (New York: Macmillan, 1972).

8. H. Kahn, W. Brown, and L. Martel (New York: Morrow, 1976).

9. See Table 2.2 in Chapter 2 for a numerical breakdown of population distribution and income per capita among country groups.

10. We discuss this further in Chapter 8.

11. Japan's problems and prospects are discussed in Chapter 6. For a more extended discussion see Herman Kahn and Thomas Pepper, *The Japanese Challenge* (New York: Thomas Y. Crowell, 1979).

12. Problems of malaise and inflation in the United States are discussed in Chapter 5.

13. The word *typical* refers as much to the inherent plausibility of the description as to the two historical *Belles Epoques*. Perhaps *archetypical* would be a better term. Though we have tried to be plausible, the extent to which our abstract structure corresponds to the actual events is necessarily often controversial. We think of this section as setting forth a paradigm of a long upswing. We can then ask how much the two *Belles Epoques* corres-to it, and assess the analytic and predictive value of our archetype.

14. See Chapter 5 for an extended discussion of inflation.

15. A curious exchange on this issue of "acceptable rate of inflation" appeared in *Newsweek:*

> [QUESTION]: Legend has it, Professor Samuelson, that successive editions of your textbook kept raising the inflation rate you saw as "tolerable," until finally you stopped giving a figure. How has your thinking evolved?
>
> SAMUELSON: My textbook, like most others, has been warning for 25 years that our mixed economy doesn't know how to command price stability with efficient full employment. In the 1950s, I specified lower and lower inflation rates as "tolerable." But once we put the Eisenhower slack years behind us, the need to compromise with more uncomfortable rates of inflation has, in my opinion, grown.
>
> A rate of price rise between 5 and 7 percent, provided it is not accelerating, is uncomfortable but it is viable. Compared to the alternatives of wage and price controls or contrived stagnation, this 1970s way of life seems preferable.

One gathers from the above that Samuelson believes when the inflationary pressures are low (e.g., in the 1950s) the tolerable rate is low; when the pressures are high, the tolerable rate is high. But this is paying lip service to inflation. It is also an attitude shared by most Keynesians.

16. The restless young, the alienated, the disillusioned, the frustrated, the seekers of "meaning and purpose," various "true believers," and those in the middle and upper classes whose status or income stayed constant or was reduced, while the status or income of almost all around them rose.

17. These cycles are fifteen to twenty-five year fluctuations in growth, usually associated with long periods of construction activity. The theory was developed by Simon Kuznets of Harvard University. Simon Kuznets, *Capital in the American Economy: Its Formation and Financing* (Princeton, New Jersey: Princeton University Press, 1961).

18. Malcolm Cowley, *Exile's Return* (New York: Viking Press, 1951), pp. 59-60.

19. For example, in 1977 the United States Department of Transportation tentatively decided that all American cars should have air bags in 1979. Air bags are clearly unpopular or at least viewed with some skepticism by many

Americans. These people will not buy a car with an air bag until they see how it works out. One can assume that perhaps a fourth of the American car purchasers would defer their purchase of a car. This enormous drop in car sales, at a critical point in the economic cycle, would almost certainly precipitate an economic crisis. This was realized and the decision to force air bags on all cars was postponed.

There is a similar issue pending that we hope will have been resolved by the time this book is published. Under the Clean Air Act of 1977 any region in the United States that is not in conformity with environmental regulations of the EPA by July 1, 1979, and does not have a written agreement with the EPA on how to achieve such conformity, will not be allowed to put up any buildings that might pollute the atmosphere. They will not even be allowed to offset the new pollution by buying out current pollution—as is often done today. In something like half the country, almost all commercial and industrial construction will have to stop. Again, if there is such a dramatic cut in investment it would have an immediate and dramatic effect on the business cycle, probably forcing a collapse or at least a crisis.

20. By 1975, growth in output per unit of input was reduced by 0.35 percentage points—about one-fifth of historical growth. See Edward F. Denison, "Effects of Selected Changes in the Institutional and Human Environment Upon Output per Unit of Input," *Survey of Current Business* 58, no. 1 (January 1978):22.

21. Some of these are charted in Table 4.2 "New Costs and Risks."

22. Readers who do not understand why 1975 was chosen over 1974 or 1976 should count their fingers and toes.

23. There is some controversy about this, especially since some Japanese automobile manufacturers seemed to have attained the mandated performance. However, the main reason for the timetable was not its feasibility but the feeling by many congressmen that the industry simply would not take pressures seriously unless they were hurt quite severely. They may have been right.

24. The passage in 1978 of Proposition 13 in California and new tax revolts in Denmark and France are symptoms of the underlying unrest.

25. Jude Wanniski, *The Way the World Works* (New York: Basic Books, 1978); Arthur B. Laffer, "Unemployment and Taxes," *National Review* 29, no. 4 (February 4, 1978):48-50.

26. Simon Kuznets, *Capital in the American Economy* (New York: National Bureau of Economic Research, 1961). Richard Easterlin, *Population, Labor Force and Long Swings in Economic Growth* (New York: Columbia University Press, 1968); Richard Easterlin, Michael Wachter, and Susan Wachter, "The Passing of the Kuznets Cycle: Is There Life After Death?" paper presented at the annual meeting of the American Economic Association, December 28, 1977.

27. Nikolai D. Kondratieff, "The Long Waves in Economic Life," *The Review of Economics and Statistics* 17, no. 6 (November 1936):105-115.

28. Jay Forrester, "How the Long-Wave Theory May Explain the

Sluggishness in Capital Formation," *Financier*, September 1977, pp. 34-38; Jay Forrester and Nathaniel Mass, "Understanding the Changing Bases for Economic Growth in the United States," *U.S. Economic Growth from 1976 to 1986: Prospects, Problems and Patterns, Volume 6, Forecasts for Long-Run Economic Growth*, U.S. Congress.

29. J. A. Schumpeter, *Business Cycles* (New York: McGraw-Hill, 1939).

30. William Butler Yeats, *Later Poems* (New York: Macmillan, 1928), pp. 346-347.

Part II
The Real World

5

Growing Pains: The Emerging Super-Industrial Economy, Malaise, and Inflation

THE EMERGING SUPER-INDUSTRIAL ECONOMY

In this chapter we discuss major trends and problems of the existing world economy. We use the theories, concepts, metaphors, and analogies developed in Part I to enrich rather than to support our discussion. We start with one of our most important concepts: the imminent emergence of a worldwide super-industrial economy in which projects are on such a large scale that the external or unintentional effects (what economists call "externalities") can become even more important than the primary (or intended) products. If the impact of the super-industrial economy on the social and physical environment is not controlled, it is pervasive and perhaps destructive.

There are two kinds of super-industrial economies: *problem prone* and *problem controlled.* A problem-prone economy exists when the super-industrial economy first emerges (as it is doing now in much of the world) and the externalities are new, unclear, and difficult to control. The results include inadequate or inappropriate technology and poor design and operation. When and if these external impacts are satisfactorily controlled or alleviated, the super-industrial economy becomes problem controlled.

Being super-industrial may not always entail large inputs. Thus, less than 3 percent of the work force (labor actually on farms) produces more than 95 percent of the foods and fibers the United States needs. (The labor that supports agriculture by providing various farm inputs belongs to the industrial or service sectors.) Therefore, we think of the United States as having a post-agricultural economy. However, considering the gigantic scale of United States agriculture and the impact it has on the American social, political, economic, and physical environments, the United States appears to be both post-agricultural and super-agricultural. It should be noted that in principle an economy can have any combination: neither, either, or both. However, if it is both, then the super-industrial aspect must be problem controlled or it would not be truly post-industrial.

We believe that problem-prone super-industrial economies are emerging quite rapidly throughout the world—certainly more rapidly than are post-industrial economies. This is one reason for the current widespread concern about energy, resources, and the environment. Another is that the post-industrial economy has emerged sufficiently to create a large group of people (upper-middle class generally and neo-liberal New Class specifically) who are more or less post-industrial and hypersensitive to the difficulties created by industrialization. Many of these difficulties are pseudo-problems—problems that do not exist at all or are problems only for this group.

The number of people engaged in secondary-type economic activities in the ACNs is now constant or even diminishing, but is not diminishing elsewhere. However, this is not the real issue. It is the output of goods and the potential side effects, not the input of men or resources, that makes an enterprise part of the super-industrial economy. Because of the rapid advance of the Middle Income countries—and to a lesser degree of the Poor countries—the secondary sector is growing rapidly in numbers of people engaged and even more rapidly in output. While the growth rate of gross world product has probably already peaked at about 5 percent (the peak rate of the smoothed-out curve), the absolute growth rate of the worldwide secondary sector has probably not yet peaked and probably will not do so much before this century's end—if then. (This assumes that *L'époque de Malaise* continues without degenerating into *La Deuxième Mauvaise Epoque.*)

Table 5.1 summarizes some aspects of this emerging super-industrial economy. This table may deeply concern many readers who feel that we can scarcely handle our present problems, let alone what many will regard as an approaching mess. Originally we were going to call this chapter "Current Assets and Positive Trends," based on our view that almost every item in Table 5.1 is an asset. We soon realized that the Anti-Growth Triad would interpret almost every item mentioned as a horrendous problem. Our view is that all of these items probably will create problems, but most of them are still worth encouraging.

We are concerned about the emerging problem-prone super-industrial economy, but we also believe that much of the

TABLE 5.1
The Likely Emerging "Problem-Prone" Super-Industrial Economy
(1980-2000?)

1. *Scope:* More or less worldwide
2. *Annual Production:* GWP $10-20 trillion, 25-50 billion barrels of liquid fuel, 1-2 billion tons of steel, 30-60 million cars, 1.5-3.0 billion tons of grains, etc.
3. *Rate of Growth of GWP:* 4.0% or less per annum (down from the 5% of La Deuxième Belle Epoque)
4. *Population:* 4.5 to 6.0 billion
5. *Population Growth Rate:* 1.5% ± .3% per annum (down from almost 2% of the early 1970s)
6. *Volume of World Trade:* $1-3 trillion of exports (1978 dollars)
7. *Externalities:* Issues of environment and location can no longer be ignored—external costs must usually be internalized and may dominate other issues
8. *Size of Business Organization:* Largest will have $10-100 billion in gross receipts, and/or 500,000 to 1,000,000 employees—many worldwide organizations with $5-10 billion in gross receipts and more than 100,000 employees
9. *Size of Project:* Super-ports, super-industrial plants, $.02-2 trillion synthetic fuel industry, North Sea development, James Bay, Alcan Project, other Arctic pipelines, etc.
10. *Size of Equipment:* 1,000,000 lb. plane; 10,000,000 lb. space platform; 1,000 mile transmission line; 5 kilometer antenna arrays in orbit; 2,000 megawatt electric power plants; perhaps 1,000,000 ton tankers; 50 to 200,000 bbl/day synthetic fuel plants
11. *World Use of Energy:* 300-1000 q/year ($q = 10^{15}$ B.T.U.s)
12. *Probable Inflection Point:* (In Percent Growth Rates) Passed in early 70s for both world population and GWP
13. *Typical Problems:* (See 1985 Technological Crises, Fourteen New Emphases, and Worldwide Labor Imbalance)
14. *Typical Opportunities for "God, Gold, and Glory":* (or Honor, Riches, and Fame)[a] See rest of this chapter and discussion on Futurology Ideologies and the Paneqole Program in Chapter 8

[a]This is the secular form of "God, Gold, and Glory." The phrase was used in a well-known speech by Napoleon to the French Army just before they invaded Italy. "God, Gold, and Glory" refers, of course, to the motivations of the sixteenth and seventeenth century explorers and adventurers.

environmental, ecological and anti-pollution movement has been premature, although in part usefully premature. At the moment, the intense contrary publicity notwithstanding, relatively little damage is being done by industrial activities worldwide. Except for heavy metal and similar industries and certain special areas and problems, few industrial and related activities should be regarded as creating a current crisis. However, the potentialities for damage are great now and will increase sharply in the next decade or two.

Fortunately, the institutions, techniques, and attitudes needed for effective control have been appearing for some time, and their rate of appearance and ability to cope are also accelerating. It is likely that we will soon see significant changes in our culture to correspond to these new institutions. (Some of these will probably correspond to some versions of the Fourteen New Emphases or the Marriage of Machine and Garden.) In this sense, the order that we suggested in Chapters 1 and 2—first the super-industrial economy, then the institutions, and then the culture before we achieve a harmonious society—is partially reversed. The institutions are emerging and the culture changing at about the same time as, or even before, the new economy has fully emerged.

Many people will consider the assertion that current industrial activities are doing relatively little damage to be remarkably callous if not downright stupid. There are some simple tests for getting a perspective on this issue. One is whether the industrial activity changes the amount that a life insurance company or health insurance group plans to charge for this policy. Most people agree that, on the average, an insurance company will be at least as concerned about those issues and as careful as the individuals affected. If this is the test, then except for such things as heavy metals, heavy smoking, and some specialized industrial problems, by and large the rate charged for health or life insurance in the ACNs does not vary appreciably either by geographic area or for most occupations and activities associated with technology and indus-trialization.

The automobile is a clear exception. In the United States, about fifty thousand people a year are killed in automobile accidents and about a million more are injured. The automobile's external impacts are very high, not only on life and health but also on the physical structure of society. But this is judged by most Americans to be an acceptable cost for this highly convenient and useful mode of transportation. However an almost manic hatred for the automobile has developed among upper-middle class elites in almost all the

Affluent countries. Nevertheless, we believe the automobile age is still young. Today there are about three hundred million cars in the world; we expect this number to be doubled or tripled by the end of the century. Car owners are still members of an exclusive club, but this club will markedly less exclusive in the near future. We also believe that as more working class and middle class people obtain and use automobiles, there will be increasing tendencies for upper-middle class elites to disdain the automobile and the supposed passion "squares" have for personal vehicles. This hostility is partly created by obvious disutilities associated with traffic jams and pollution, both of which seem to be decreasing in many countries, but are less tolerated than in the past. The main issues, however, are class-related—including not only tastes and values, but social status and class identification.[1]

We are not sure that the automobile will be as well-controlled as will most other manifestations of economic development and technological advancement. We are reasonably sure that most of the cars manufactured at the end of the century will be more or less pollution-free—at least those intended for use in areas in the ACNs with pollution problems. We also believe that many but not all of the problems of accidents and excessive traffic jams in the ACNs will be greatly alleviated. Technology or institutional arrangements may develop to cut traffic fatalities significantly.[2]

In most other cases we expect technological developments similar to those that have already occurred with elevator doors. Fifty years ago it was not uncommon to see people who had sustained severe injuries, perhaps even the loss of a hand or foot, because they had been trapped in a closing elevator door. Today, such injuries are almost non-existent. Elevator doors have sensors, close softly, and if anything is caught in the doors they will not close. A similar technology is developing to cope with the accidental swallowing of poisons or medicines by young children. Medicine bottles are now designed so that young children cannot open them. More and more we expect society to take a paternalistic, nurturing attitude towards its vulnerable members.

But this also creates a problem. If we always treat children and young adults as fragile, we know they will be badly raised. The young are actually quite tough and require challenges—even some hardships—for full development. Excessively safe, paternalistic, forgiving environments can be disastrous. The problem of the future, at least in the Affluent countries, is more likely to be one of excessive coddling than the currently popular Anti-Growth Triad image of an excessively cruel, callous, destructive society constructed by rapacious businessmen out to make a profit at any cost. We suggest that in only two or three decades, the physical problems of the super-industrial economy will have been largely alleviated in the Affluent countries and prevented or largely alleviated in most of the developing countries. However, this process will create other social and psychological problems.

There are three important reasons to believe that physical problems of this kind will be relatively manageable. First, and most important, we are already developing the necessary advanced technologies. Second, implied by the first, we are paying great attention to these problems by allocating resources and making restrictions. We argue that at present too much attention is being devoted to these issues. It is not cost-effective in dealing with actual current dangers but is probably good training and education for the problems of the near future. This attention encourages research and planning and might lead to much prevention as well as to cure.[3]

Third, the Affluent countries of the world have already passed the all-important inflection point in their growth rates. Economic growth will continue at a high rate and may increase in absolute terms, but it will decrease in percentage terms. This is already making many problems easier to deal with, and *eventually* should do so for almost all of them. We believe these problems will peak out in the mid-1980s. Confusion and apprehension about this are among the underpinnings of the present malaise.

A Technological Crisis in 1985?

The concept of a 1985 technological crisis seems to have first been proposed by one of the most intelligent and wisest men who ever lived—the late mathematician John von Neumann. He suggested in 1955 that:

> The great globe itself is in a rapidly maturing crisis—a crisis attributable to the fact that the environment in which technological progress must occur has become both undersized and underorganized. . . .
>
> In the first half of this century . . . this safety . . . was essentially a matter of geographical and political *Lebensraum:* an ever broader geographical scope for technological activities, combined with an even broader political integration of the world. Within this expanding framework it was possible to accommodate the major tensions created by technological progress.

Now this safety mechanism is being sharply inhibited; literally and figuratively, we are running out of room. At long last, we begin to feel the effects of the finite, actual size of the earth in a critical way.

Thus the crisis does not arise from accidental events or human errors. It is inherent in technology's relation to geography on the one hand and to political organization on the other . . . in the years between now and 1980 the crisis will probably develop far beyond all earlier patterns. When or how it will end—or to what state of affairs it will yield— nobody can say.[4]

Many analysts at the RAND Corporation were impressed with this viewpoint. Reprints of the entire article were subsequently distributed at about half the seminars held at the Hudson Institute in the 1960s. This led to a list of about seventy problems (lumped together as "the 1985 Technological Crisis") that seemed to us to illustrate some likely future concerns.[5]

By contrast, consider the following passage from the Annual Report for 1978 of the President's Council of Economic Advisers:

Social regulation of the market place has arisen in response to pervasive problems that have affected nearly all Americans at work and at home. In 1976 one of every 11 workers in private industry suffered from an accident or illness related to the job; *4,500 workers lost their lives from such causes.* The Bureau of Labor Statistics estimated that over 39 million workdays were lost in the private sector in 1976 because of nonfatal occupational illness or accidents and *in the mining and construction trades, workers on the average lost more than one workday per year because of accidents and illness occasioned by the job.* Because of the uncertain links between occupational hazards and illness, data that are readily available may well understate the problems.

Environmental problems are even more pervasive. Air pollution, produced by numerous industrial processes and the operation of transportation vehicles, has been clearly linked to many different illnesses. Adverse water quality has also proved to be dangerous. *A recent study made by the Environmental Protection Agency (EPA) found the water of 80 cities to contain chemicals that are known to cause cancer in animals.* To these known problems must be added the rapid growth in the use of pesticides and possibly toxic chemicals, which continues to outstrip current knowledge about their long-run effects.[6]

Anybody reading the above, knowing how seriously it is taken and aware of the enormous efforts made to cope with the problems described, might assume that the United States faced some kind of intense crisis, perhaps the crisis von Neumann was talking about. In fact, the issues mentioned have arisen not because of increased danger, but mostly because today we are much richer and more sensitive than we used to be; as a result we have much higher standards. In a way the point in the quotation about the mining and construction trades (which are admittedly dangerous occupations), "workers on the average lost more than one workday per year because of accidents and illness occasioned by the job," puts the problem the Council of Economic Advisers is worrying about into proper perspective. Hardly any society in history would have thought an occupation critically dangerous in which only one day a year at work is lost.

Take another seemingly extreme problem: 4,500 workers lost their lives from occupational hazards. A problem involving this many human deaths must be taken seriously, but the number must also be kept in perspective. The United States had 90 million workers in 1976; 4,500 deaths is 5 per 100,000 workers. Since the death rate in the United States is about 900 per 100,000, this increases the death rate by about .5 percent. This affects the premium for life insurance, but just barely. The cancer problem mentioned almost certainly does not affect life insurance rates in any area. This is not to say that such a problem could not arise, only that the problem described is almost certainly not as frightening as it probably appears to most readers. It is a serious problem worth attention and concern, but not fear and trembling.

We are not trying to denigrate the importance of the problems. If there is a dramatic situation with only one life at risk, everybody will be concerned, and properly so. The problems mentioned are matters the government should work on seriously, but the hubbub occurs in part because the health services concerned do not appear to have many higher priority problems to work on. If they do, they should work on them instead. Most important, the level of the problem is one that we associate with partial success, not with total failure. That is exactly why these problems have come to the fore—because, as a result of success, more urgent and critical prior problems have receded. While young people can get cancer or circulatory problems, these are generally diseases of older people rather than of the young. Because contagious diseases are now so well controlled, many now live long enough to become prone to the health problems of older age.

If one evaluates the impact of much modern activity on the environment not as a vital health issue or as the cause of a serious reduction in life expectancy, but aesthetically, then the "crisis" has been with us for a long time—from the earliest cities. Almost every realistic description of ancient walled cities or of the cities of the eighteenth and nineteenth centuries in Europe and the United States emphasizes what aesthetic horrors they were both for the average person (e.g., slaves or workers) and often for the higher classes as well. By the year 2000 or soon after, it seems likely that northwest Europe, North America, and Japan will meet reasonable goals for clean air, clean water, and aesthetic landscapes, while producing at two or three times their current rates. This fantastic feat will owe less to limitation (though limitation will play an important role) than to affluence, advanced technology, and proper design and operation.

One could argue that current efforts are in many ways five to ten years premature, at least in their excessive costs and disruption. The United States is saddling itself with economic and social costs that are too great. For example, in coping with our energy problems, the use of energy is excessively hindered by some current attempts to clean up the environment, and its production is even more greatly hindered. The effect is to slow down economic development more than we should at a time when it would be most helpful to speed it up. However, it would be a mistake to try to deal with an emerging problem-prone super-industrial economy by fine tuning and close scheduling. Therefore, on the whole, we believe that things have been timed reasonably well. We incur excess costs and other mistakes because the movement is premature and often has excessive and emotionally determined priorities. Yet these costs are probably small compared to those that will be avoided. If the effort were much more restrained, the necessary learning, educational effort, institutions, personnel, and proved and reliable technology would appear a decade or two later, and we might have to be prodded into action by actual rather than fictitious disasters.[7]

We are not sure that our optimism in believing that these problems will be largely solved in the ACNs should be extended to the world as a whole. Many areas will have a much different attitude towards these issues. While we do not believe the entire world will suffer because of a lack of cooperation of any significant portion of it, certain areas could present serious local difficulties. And, of course, many of the things that the Anti-Growth Triad objects to the most (such as "tourist pollution," i.e., the middle class invading their playing grounds and refusing to work for them as reliable and inexpensive servants and employees) are going to be worse than ever before.

The emerging super-industrial society—exciting and yet threatening—is a key to one of our major themes. Those who are frightened, terrified, disgusted, intimidated, aggravated, or annoyed by the emerging problem-prone super-industrial economy are bound to have low morale. As much as they fight the change, there is little they can do to stop the worldwide movement. They can cause serious costs and other problems for their local areas or even countries, but they are not going to stop development in the Middle Income and Poor countries—and probably not in most of the Affluent countries. Therefore, those who think that the coming society is going to strain the earth beyond its carrying capacity are especially depressed.

Those who participate in the protest movement in order to fill in the idle hours and to get together with other like-minded young people—i.e., as part of the process of growing up—will enjoy themselves even if they do not win the war, but only a battle here and there. And those who simply want to alleviate the process, the genuine conservationists, will gain most of their aims in Japan, North America, and northwest Europe.

The vast majority of people in the world share our vision of a complicated, complex, probably somewhat dangerous transition period which, on the whole and always barring bad luck or bad management, will be marked by rising living standards and less rather than more sacrifice. Eventually almost all of the problems will be dealt with satisfactorily, at least by middle-class standards, and true post-industrial society will emerge. Once we learn to deal with the various manifestations of the super-industrial society and control its effects so that its unintended impacts on the social and physical environment are no longer as significant as its intended impacts, then it will no longer be problem prone. It will resemble a modern water supply or sewage system, needing only professional attention to create and maintain high performance.

The potential for feasible technological fixes or solutions to important issues such as energy, pollution, safety, and health should not be underestimated, although it frequently is. The astonishing history of science and technology in the nineteenth and twentieth centuries shows that solutions to the physical needs of society have usually become rapidly available when those needs were perceived as urgent and feasible. Whether for armaments, commerce, exploration, travel, or recreation, technology and affluence delivered remarkable solutions within reasonable time periods. (We concede that conclusion may well not apply to the arms-control or genetic manipulation problems.)

An examination of the efforts now being made indicates that one or more technological solutions will become available for pollution, traffic, resource, ecology, and similar problems. These solutions will usually require time and money to develop and install. For example, little doubt exists that coal-fired power plants can reduce their emissions by a factor of ten or more. However, retrofitting the existing facilities to meet this goal is costly, ponderous, and some times not feasible. Even for new facilities the costs might be deemed exorbitant at the suggested standards if the construction must be based upon present reliable designs. However, a number of promising new technologies (such as fluidized-bed combustion or the use of solvent-refined coal) are expected to become commercial within a decade. After that occurs, the problem of excessive emission of pollutants from new electric power generation facilities, will largely vanish. The older, more difficult facilities will be tolerated, retrofitted, or phased out. Unfortunately, the time required for large changes is often measured in decades if practical technological fixes are the preferred solution.

The complaint is often heard that new technologies only breed new problems that require still further solutions. Although this argument in its pure form seems to suggest that technology should not have been invented in the first place, we argue that this judgment usually ignores the net gain created. Indeed, increasingly the gains are taken for granted, and only the losses are considered. In some cases, however, the complaint has merit. In the past, technologists were asked to produce steel mills and automobiles when few constraints existed on the emission of pollutants. Are the industrialists to be blamed for this "oversight"? or the politicians? or the bankers? Hardly! In most cases the problem was not so bad or the less offending technology not so good that society (for example, consumers) was willing to pay for the less offending technology.

The careless discard of pollutants has, when not specifically restrained by law or custom, always been customary behavior. Therefore, society must set its standards as it desires—and can afford—and expect nothing more. If we in the United States were somewhat lax in this respect prior to the mid-1960s, we are now making up for lost time. Much has been accomplished; with one or two exceptions, the problems are no longer getting worse. The alternative technologies are becoming better, the affluence is greater, and standards are rising rapidly. The new technologies will be used to meet the new standards that have been and are being set.

In another twenty years or so, the problems will not all have been resolved, but much progress will have been made, the outlook for the future will be favorable, and the strident environmental movement is likely to have substantially receded. By then, new procedures will have become routine, including those that will keep professional attention focused upon possible new threats from the emerging super-industrial projects. This is a relatively new development that will surely become permanent. Technology will assume its proper role as a servant of the people, not a master—a role an affluent and technologically capable society can both demand and afford.

Having outlined the broad dimensions of the emerging worldwide super-industrial economy, we now turn attention to more detailed discussions of specific prospects and problems that we believe will accompany the super-industrial economy. First, we examine benefits and possible detriments of the new technologies that are an integral part of the super-industrial economy. Then we turn our attention to energy problems. Finally, we will discuss briefly three different but significant aspects of the emerging super-industrial economy: transnational corporations, the nascent Pacific Basin Trading Investment area, and the world impact of tourism.

New Technologies

We are optimistic about the long-term future for much the same reason we are most apprehensive: technological advancement. Even though its funding is probably slowing down slightly, applied technology is still proceeding at an incredibly rapid rate in a large number of laboratories using disciplines that have only been partially exploited. While most of these new technologies are benign, some are threatening.

Until the atomic bomb was invented, it was hard to find a technology so threatening that most people would feel that the bad would outweigh the good in a very simple and direct way: more people would be killed, injured, or would suffer from physical abuse of some kind than would benefit from the new technology. We are not including the subtle philosophic, psychological, and cultural damage that technology and science do. Copernicus, Marx, Freud, Pavlov, Einstein, and the originators of quantum mechanics have all affected people's self-images and psyches. In one way, technology uplifted humanity to the rank of a Prometheus, a Faust, or even a God; in another way it downgraded humanity from images of God located in the center of the universe to programmed devices of chemistry and physics located in an insignificant corner of the universe.

In its capabilities for simple straightforward death and destruction and for creating really new ways in which human creations can get out of control, nuclear energy was the first item out of Pandora's Box. But as in the Pandora myth, we must not leave hope locked up in the box. We must balance the positive aspects against the negative.

Table 5.2 lists a dozen technologies that are likely in the next two or three decades to develop to an extraordinary degree. All of them are now being developed and some will appear in the near future.

We note in Table 5.3 the pace of development in space-related technologies, giving a picture of the tremendous growth of high technology areas. It would be a major digression to expatiate at length about all the items listed in Tables 5.2 and 5.3. Suffice it to say that all of these rapidly developing technologies offer exciting benefits in the near term. Readers interested in possible developments in outer space are referred to *Long-Term Prospects for Development in Space* by William M. Brown and Herman Kahn.[8] We also elaborated at greater length on the new technologies in the special ICC edition of *World Economic Development*.

Energy Issues[9]

What about the energy needed for the super-industrial society? Scientists and engineers are generally agreed that a sufficient research and development effort will make available before the year 2000 several new technologies that can provide the world with nearly unlimited and economical quantities of clean energy from renewable or inexhaustible resources. The technologically advanced nations could obtain most of their energy requirements from these sources by the year 2025. Some of these sources would also be feasible for many developing nations. Furthermore, conventional and currently unconventional fossil fuels will last for centuries. Thus, if the appropriate decisions are made, our grandchildren will not be plaugued by an energy crisis. In addition, if we relieve the pressure on the traditional fuel supplies by shifting rapidly to the advanced technologies, then more "natural" oil and gas would be available to less developed nations.

Many questions will remain about the long-term environmental effects of various energy technologies, but they do not seem at the moment to pose any imminent or inevitable danger to the world. The potential for such dangers will be further reduced if we can make at least a partial shift to non-fossil energy sources early in the twenty-first century. Therefore, increased use of our indigenous fossil fuel resources for the next twenty-five years or so will not be tantamount to

TABLE 5.2
Rapidly Developing Technologies

---

1. New and Very Abundant Sources of Gaseous and Liquid Fuels
2. Other Inexhaustible and Relatively Inexpensive Energy Sources
3. "Pollution-Free" Industries and Transportation Systems[a]
4. Finding and Extracting Mineral Resources
5. Conventional Agriculture, Unconventional Agriculture, and Artificial Foods
6. Materials Progress in Fibers, Foams, Composites, Ceramics, Crystals, Polymers, Adhesives
7. Human-Machine Communications and Capabilities

A. Hardware in Year 2000	*Factor of Improvement*
• Operating Speed	10–10^3
• Storage Capacity	10^5–10^{10}
• Reliability	10^3–?
• Information Transfer Rate	10^3–10^5

B. Software in Year 2000	*Factor of Improvement*
• Data Compression	2–1000
• Programmer Productivity	10–100
• Voice Communication	?
• Automatic Programming	?

8. Automation: Improved Machines
                Tele-operators
                Robots
                Intelligent Robots
9. Bio-engineering and Genetic Engineering in Agriculture and Animal Husbandry[b]
10. Other Hyphenated Sciences (Bio-physics, Bio-chemistry)
11. Ultrasensitive Sensors for Use in Satellites and Elsewhere
12. Other "Exponential Growth" in Space-Based Commercial Ventures

---

[a]Nothing is completely pollution-free, but most people will consider these virtually pollution-free.

[b]We are deliberately leaving out applications to humans, since so many of these have aspects that are seen by many people, including myself, as threatening.

TABLE 5.3
Examples of Progress in Space Technology

System	1960	1975	1990	2000
1. Launch Vehicle: Payload Capacity (lbs.)	25	250,000	10^6 (Reusable)	2×10^6 (Reusable)
2. Communication Satellite (Channels)	15 (Low Orbit)	15,000 (Synchronous)	100,000 (Synch)	10^6 (Synch)
3. Communication (Mars to Earth) Bits/Sec	8	10^5	10^7	10^9
4. Man Days/Mission	.1	250	10^5	5×10^5
5. Resolution (km)	5 (Low Orbit)	.1 (Low Orbit)	.05 (Geosynchronous Orbit)	.02 (Geosynchronous Orbit)
6. Data Storage	15 Pages (.5 Megabits)	2,000 Books (20 Gigabits) (300 Pages/Book)	1/2 Library of Congress (8,000 Gigabits)	10 Library of Congress
7. Energy Storage (kw hrs./lbs.)	.02	40	800	1,200
8. Active Circuits/cu. in.	4	120,000	5×10^8	$10^{10} - 10^{12}$
9. Space-Borne Computer Speed (Operations/Second)	$.002 \times 10^6$	$.5 \times 10^6$	30×10^6	$100\text{-}1000 \times 10^6$
10. Cost of Launching ($/lb. to Earth Orbit)	10,000	250	25-50	10-30
11. Position Error (meters)	1,000	50	.1	.02
12. Failures/HR/Megabits	10^{-2}	10^{-4}	10^{-6}	$10^{-7} - 10^{-8}$

Source: William Brown and Herman Kahn, *Long-Term Prospects for Developments in Space (A Scenario Approach)*, HI-2638-RR (Croton-on-Hudson, N.Y.: 1977), p. 75.

robbing the poor or our grandchildren, nor will it endanger the world—particularly if we begin immediately to design appropriate long-term programs. One long-range program that could be quite useful as a hedge against the many uncertainties and as a bargaining point would be the institution of a contingent $200 billion synthetic fuel program by the United States.[10] One reason why this hedge is desirable is that the cost of the fuel produced by such a program, if we correct the normal calculation for inflation effects, is more likely to be in the range of $8 to $16 a barrel than the usually quoted $15 to $30. (This is clearly shown in Table 5.9 on page 311.)

A great many favorable things could happen that would make us want to change the contemplated synthetic fuels program in one way or another. Thus, it would also be irresponsible to commit our society *irrevocably* to spending $200 billion on such a program. Some of the many possibilities for good luck are:

1. "Unexpected" success in *energy conservation* through increased efficiency (by improved operation or design) and savings (i.e., foregone consumption), both probably induced mostly by higher prices and mandatory legislation rather than by exhortation.
2. Unexpected success in *conventional oil and gas production* (i.e., good luck, assisted by changed price expectations, improving technology, and more expeditious and rational regulatory procedures).
3. *Technological breakthroughs* in finding and producing conventional oil and gas (e.g., in analytical and technical means for exploration, drilling, and production).
4. *Successful accelerated development worldwide* of many known energy resources: Alaskan hydrocarbon resources, Venezuelan and Canadian heavy oils and tar sands, increased production in many non-OPEC Third World countries, rapidly growing Soviet and/or Chinese fuel exports, and a general movement by Europe and Japan toward greater use of coal and nuclear power.
5. Many *changes in OPEC practices* (including United States-Saudi agreements, perhaps following a "settlement" of the Arab-Israeli conflict)—or just much greater and more reliable Saudi Arabian production.
6. *Unexpectedly early exploitation of long-range technologies:* e.g., from GEOSOLFUS[11] sources, substitutes for or startling improvement in internal combustion engines, several ad-

vances such as the Wanlass motor, new technologies for use of clean-burning inexpensive coal in small units, very efficient power generators (e.g., MHD), etc.

7. Competitive conventional *fuels from unconventional sources:* I. *Natural Gas*—(a) from the geopressurized zones of the Gulf Coast, (b) from coal deposits, (c) from the tight sand formations of the Rocky Mountains, (d) from Devonian and other Eastern shales. II. *Oil*—(a) by improved tertiary recovery and (b) from the deep sea (operation below 1,000 feet).

8. *Unconventional production*—e.g., *in situ* techniques for the extraction of gas and oil from solid fossil fuels: coal, oil and gas shales, and tar sands; or major technological breakthroughs in the manufacture of synthetic fuels from any source.

9. *Novel and/or controversial institutional and technological developments or innovations* (a general consensus in favor of nuclear power, a return to free market economics, the development of inexpensive processes for exploitation of methane hydrates, artificial photosynthesis to produce hydrogen cheaply, etc.).

10. A "natural" (non-energy related) *slowdown in economic growth* or emergence of a successful movement toward "soft" technologies, or voluntary simplicity.

Any of these contingencies could potentially make an enormous difference in the energy picture. It seems perfectly reasonable that, if proper programs were followed, each of these ten classes of events would have one chance in ten of emerging as a significant option by 1990 and at least one chance in five by the year 2000. If so, while it may make sense to ignore each, we simply cannot afford to ignore them as a group. There is only one chance in three that none of them will emerge by 1990 and only one in ten that none would emerge by the year 2000. Looking back from the vantage point of the year 2000, it is exactly these events that are likely to have been crucial for the energy needs of humanity. Nevertheless, for a *secure* program we have concluded that it is important to emphasize a brute force mid-term solution to the pressing problem of excessive fuel imports: the creation of a large synthetic fuel industry based initially on current technology, much of which stems from World War II. However, during the next several years increased knowledge and experience with "conventional" production of synthetic fuels or the developments stemming from these ten contingencies could lead to a significant modification of the brute force program—or indeed any program. This approach would be re-evaluated frequently to take advantage of all favorable events, and it is hedged against unfavorable developments.*

Under appropriate leadership the Congress and the American people are not likely to be led astray by the mere possibility of good luck. The difficult and potentially expensive decisions that prudence requires could still be made. No one expects motor vehicle drivers to go without insurance because they might not have an accident. Nor do we encourage owners of well-constructed "fire-proof" buildings not to buy fire insurance. If our own energy future is to be secure, we have to be equally cautious. (In trying to enact a domestic United States energy program, it is widely recognized that it was the administration that was unreasonable, rather than the Congress.)

The Transnational Corporations (TNCs)†

One of the main reasons why *La Deuxième Belle Epoque* was so dynamic was the almost totally unexpected and extraordinary growth and diffusion of transnational corporations, or TNCs. TNCs were already playing a major role in world affairs before many in the academic and media communities noticed what was happening. Today there is a plethora of books, studies, and discussions about the transnational corporation. We will confine ourselves to a few observations.

First, we do not think that their growth rate has topped out, although we do believe the American transnational corporations will no longer have the extremely dominant role that they had during *La Deuxième Belle Epoque*, a role that they shared with corporations of

---

*As of late 1978, the data coming in suggested that numbers 1, 2, 7, and 10 were already happening, making a fuel crisis caused by pressures on supply capacity in the late or early 1980s relatively unlikely. The most likely current scenario for such a crisis would be the emergence of excessive optimism, causing all expensive programs to be canceled and thus resulting in a self-defeating prophecy.

†We employ the United Nations usage of *transnational* rather than *multinational*. We ourselves use *multinational* to mean multinational in ownership, operation, or management while we use *transnational* simply to imply that a company operates across national borders. The latter may not be any different otherwise from a company that operates in its home country.

other nations of the Atlantic Protestant culture area. During *La Deuxième Belle Epoque,* an enormously high percent of dynamic transnational corporations, particularly in the European Economic Community but also worldwide, were American, English, Dutch, or Swedish in origin. It was these companies and not French, West German, Belgian, or Italian companies that exploited the benefits of the creation of the European Economic Community. Companies based in the latter countries have now also begun to expand their transnational activities.

Even more important is the growth of Japanese transnational corporations and, recently, of the South Korean trading companies. There are also government or private TNCs from Venezuela, Brazil, Iran, Canada, Saudi Arabia, Hong Kong, Taiwan, and Singapore that are increasingly achieving a worldwide presence. Therefore, when we talk about the growth of the transnational corporation it should be clear, while not denigrating the role of the Atlantic Protestant culture areas, that their former relative monopoly is going to be successfully breached. This is one reason why the TNCs will grow so fast.

Additional reasons for the growth of TNCs include:

1. Continuation of world peace, relative political stability, and worldwide economic growth (even if it is more like 4 percent than 5). However, there will not only be a slowing down of the growth of the developed world but an even greater slowing down of the growth of the TNC operations in the developed world. This will result in more interest in the developing world and a rapid growth of some operations of current TNCs and new competitors in the developing world.

2. There may be some growth of protectionism that will put greater pressure on the TNCs in the future than in the past to get beyond barriers to trade.

3. In the past, TNCs were often accused but were mostly innocent of locating plants away from the home country to exploit less expensive labor and then re-export back to the home country or to other high cost areas. But this will become increasingly important and is extraordinarily useful for the world as a whole, although it may or may not hurt specific industries in the home country. This is one of the reasons we expect continuation of high growth rates in the Middle Income countries; the TNCs will help to expand their GNP for export purposes.

4. Increasing importance of economies of scale, large amounts of capital, competent managements, advances in new technology, and skilled marketing. As we point out below, these are just a few of a large number of tasks for which the transnational corporation is almost ideally suited.

5. Continuing decrease in transportation and communication costs.

6. Momentum from current investment and experience. A number of companies have learned how to operate worldwide and are continually looking for opportunities to do so. A number of others wish to imitate their experience. Again, since the greatest opportunities are likely to be in these Middle Income countries, the action also is likely to be in them.

7. No pervasive or effective interference from political authorities. There is enormous and pervasive criticism, and presumably much of it will continue. However, in many countries of the world, particularly Latin America, the Mediterranean area, and Southeast Asia, there is increasing tolerance at the practical level for the transnational corporation and a greater understanding of the important things they can do than existed a few years ago. It seems likely that for many countries of the world the transnational corporation could become effective in at least the ten areas shown in Table 5.4.

The controversy in the 1970s over the alleged payoffs made by Lockheed and other international businesses raised criticism of these giant organizations to the highest level in years. Such criticisms are not new and often have their historical roots in critiques that were leveled against the capitalists and the free enterprise system in the early stages of the Industrial Revolution. Yet most people today would agree that there is very little abuse by the TNCs comparable to kinds of things that the big corporations did in America in the nineteenth century. Even those abuses were not created by the capitalist system, but were simply a continuation of kinds of things that have always existed. It is the standards that are higher today in almost all systems.

Almost all countries in the world are willing to accept those TNC ventures where there is a clear transfer of an advanced technology. We will discuss in Chapter 7 the distinction between technology transfer, which is the ability to produce advanced items, and what we call the transfer of the use of technology. The latter tends to be much more important if much less glamorous than the former. For the transfer of

TABLE 5.4

Major Areas Where Transnational Corporations May Become the Dominant Agents

1. Raising, investing, and reallocating capital
2. Creating and managing organizations
3. Innovating, adopting, perfecting, and transferring technology
4. Distribution, maintenance, marketing, and sales (including financing)
5. Furnishing both local elites (and many in the home country as well) with suitable—perhaps ideal—career choices
6. Educating and upgrading both blue collar and white collar labor (and elites)
7. In many areas, and in the not-too-distant future, serving as a major source of local savings and taxes and in furnishing skilled cadres (i.e. graduates) of all kinds to the local economy (including the future local competition of the TNC)
8. Facilitating the creation of vertical organizations or vertical arrangements which allow for the smooth, reliable, and effective progression of goods from one stage of production to another. While, in many cases, such organization is a negation of the classical free market, it is still a very efficient and useful method of stable and growing production
9. These vertical organizations are also very effective ways of exploiting the comparative advantages of both peoples and areas. They literally can "put it all together" while supplying all the missing elements
10. Finally, and almost by themselves, providing both a market and a mechanism for satellite services and industries that can stimulate indigenous local development much more effectively than most aid programs

the use of technology, very often the TNC does not really play such a critical role, although it remains important.

A lopsided focus on acquiring the capability to manufacture everything from steel to trucks or even to produce drugs and computers has resulted in the countless purchase of plants that do not do their function properly, or are not competitive internationally, or whose products cannot even be marketed domestically in a protected market. Yet if one looks at the real impact of these goods on the country, in many cases it is their *use*, not the fact that they are produced indigenously, that makes the big difference to the development of the country. One has to have steel, fertilizer, drugs, and computers; one does not have to produce them.

It is nice, however, to produce them internally for a number of reasons. Here again, the transnational corporation can be very useful. It tends to be able to estimate the costs of the market a great deal better than the indigenous country. And if it is investing its own money or even the time and attention of its officials it will likely avoid boondoggles. TNCs make mistakes, but a lot less often than do inexperienced and politically motivated government officials. The TNC has to make the plant work and in so doing provides side benefits for the host country. For instance, a transnational company must do more than merely build a factory: It must see to it that equipment is obtained and properly used; it must use modern accounting systems and marketing systems; frequently it must train the consumer or customer in how to use its products. This may require first sending in technical personnel, including scientists; in the medium and long run it involves training indigenous people or making such training available to them.

This is a reverse brain drain. Hundreds of thousands of people have been exported from the developed world to the less developed world and had their skills used for the benefits of the less developed world in roles and places in which they had a great deal of leverage. The impact is many orders of magnitude greater than that of such things as the Peace Corps. Of course, in most people's judgment these activities and personnel get much less moral credit because the effort is being undertaken for profit and not out of some altruistic motive. But we would argue that results are what is important, not intentions. Furthermore, there is moral credit in doing a good job under difficult circumstances. Part of the psychological and social payoff of such a job comes from helping a less developed country industrialize.

The Likely Emergence of a Pacific Basin
Trading Investment Area

We discussed in Part I just how exciting the last two or three decades have been and how all kinds of variables either peaked or would soon peak, possibly for the rest of history. We also expect another fascinating change. The center of dynamism that used to be in the Mediterranean, at least for Western culture, and which then moved to northwest Europe and to the North Atlantic, is now moving (and has already partly moved) to the Pacific Basin. By Pacific Basin we do not mean just the countries that border on the Pacific Ocean, but rather we mean the members of what we call a Trading Investment Area or TIA.* In effect, the Pacific Ocean, which was once a great barrier, now becomes the world's greatest connector. It is cheaper to ship cars from Tokyo to Los Angeles than from Detroit. Furthermore, the new communication and computer technologies make it possible to operate in a very diffused fashion. Finally, the extra long-range or supersonic aircraft, particularly if outfitted with sleeping accommodations, make personal transportation quite convenient.

We believe that a Pacific Trading Investment Area will come into being in the early 1980s among countries that border or focus attention on the Pacific Basin. The pillars of this Trading Investment Area will be the four developed countries of the United States, Japan, Canada, and Australia. The most exciting countries are likely to be Brazil, Mexico, and what we call the smaller neo-Confucian cultures.† They will be workshops, super-dynamic areas where things are really happening.

We think of this economic community as having a basic growth rate (excluding the United States, Canada, and Australia) of well over 5 percent. The United States, Canada, and Australia, with 4 percent rates or less in the early 1980s will drag the growth rate down. We assume that Japan will also be slowing down but will still be over 5 percent. The main point is that there will likely be enormous growth in two dynamic areas: in Mexico, Brazil, Venezuela, and maybe Argentina and Chile; and in the neo-Confucian cultures.

It is still an open issue how well Indonesia does. But we are very hopeful that this will be the one Indian culture that really surges

---

*A Trading Investment Area is defined as a group of countries all of whom send half their foreign trade to other members of the group or who receive half their foreign trade from other members of the group, all of whom invest their foreign investments with other members of the group, and all of whom receive half their foreign investments from other members of the group. It is almost an economic community by itself.

†To distinguish them from the large neo-Confucian cultures of Japan and mainland China. The smaller neo-Confucian cultures are South Korea, Taiwan, Hong Kong, Singapore, and to a decreasing degree (because of the declining percent of ethnic Chinese, whether they have been mostly assimilated, as in Thailand, or mostly not, as in Malaysia and the Philippines), Malaysia, Thailand, and the Philippines.

ahead. (Thailand is also an Indian culture which we hope will surge ahead, but the spearhead there seems likely to be borne by a more or less assimilated Chinese ethnic minority, though clearly the Thais participate in and run the show.) It would probably be best for the Indonesians if they learned how to give fuller rein to the talents of their Chinese ethnic minority than they have been doing recently. We also suspect the Philippines will do quite well particularly because so many Filipinos seem to share the passion for education that the Chinese culture does, and also, and perhaps more important, if the current apparent good management—at least of the economy— continues.

The second big Trading Investment Area, Western Europe and North Africa, seems likely to move its center from the northwest to "Mediterranea" (the nations bordering on the Mediterranean Sea), mostly the northern part. (In many ways this resembles the sunbelt shift in the United States—and also involves more than just climatic variations.) The Middle East can probably be taken as belonging to both TIAs or neither—the economic trade associated with oil and the concomitant trade and investment somewhat distort our categories. This Mediterranean TIA seems to us to be less likely to be quite as dynamic as the Pacific Basin area, but it should have growth rates of 4-5 percent, which except for *La Deuxième Belle Epoque* is very high indeed.

This is one of those situations where nothing succeeds like success so long as there is not excessive speculation and overbuilding (and that, of course, can easily happen). We make a distinction here between what is called a conflagration and a fire storm. In a conflagration, when a number of small fires join together the ratio of the area to the perimeter increases and the fire proceeds much more efficiently and may well burn intensely and have great staying power. In a fire storm, the fire creates its own environment such that, in effect, it feeds on itself creating a big draft of forced air, which really makes it consume everything very rapidly, but it does not last very long.

An analogy with the Pacific Basin is to imagine building a hotel for tourism. It becomes extremely profitable because of unexpected additional traffic by commercial travelers. Or building a hotel for commercial travelers becomes extremely profitable because of the extra income from tourism. This kind of synergism happens over and over again with almost every investment. It is healthy and contributes to the staying power of the growth. The analogy with the fire storm would be if the hotel is incredibly successful mainly because most of the guests were staying there while arranging to build their own hotels. This could only mean boom-bust.

Guest Workers and Marginal Input Organizations

One important current problem that is likely to intensify between now and the end of the century is a general labor shortage in filling lower paid jobs in the developed world and a huge excess of labor in much of the Third World. Indeed, the more successful the developed world the greater this issue of a shortage of labor in lower paid jobs will become. As a society gets more and more affluent, fewer and fewer of its members care to, or find it necessary to, work at menial, unskilled, dreary, dull, dirty, or onerous work of any sort. There are many persons in the Third World who would risk their lives for the opportunity to work at these jobs at salaries lower than those readily available in the Advanced Capitalist nations. We think something like this will soon be happening also for many of the Middle Income nations. On the whole these guest laborers do not take away jobs from the indigenous population. They often make jobs by filling in the low paid jobs at the bottom of some kind of industrial structure, thus supporting a number of middle level and high level jobs. Or they enable construction projects or other activities to get done (which without them would be prohibitively costly) and which in turn generate jobs for the affluent society. Or they do work that is not done at all if they don't do it.

This shortage of low paid workers and undone low level labor can be combined with very high unemployment rates. In a book written about fifteen years ago, my co-author and I suggested that there might be as much as 10 to 20 percent unemployment in the year 2000 in the United States, not because of a failure of the economic system but because of its success.[12] This unemployment would be so-called "frictional" unemployment—unemployed who think of themselves as in the labor market but not seriously so; they are between jobs, seasonal laborers, "looking around," and so on.

There are four or five ways to handle this problem in the Advanced Capitalist nations. The most obvious is to import labor from abroad. Or, similarly, the entrepreneurs and the businessmen in the Affluent world could establish subsidiaries or subcontract work that could no longer be done economically in their own country to be done abroad—a typical activity of the TNCs. The products are then re-imported. This is what is done with what the Americans call the "border industries" of Mexico, where factories located anywhere in

Mexico receive inputs from the United States, process them, and send the products back to the United States. These processed re-imported exports pay tariffs only on the value added in Mexico. On the whole this has been the basic strategy of the United States and Japan. The United States sends work to South Korea, to Taiwan, to Latin America, and elsewhere. The Japanese do the same with South Korea and Taiwan. The Japanese also export MIOs (Marginal Input Organizations) with second-hand Japanese equipment and Japanese ownership and management.[13] This is sometimes done in part as a joint venture with a national of the country receiving the MIOs.

One can import guest laborers and treat them more or less as citizens, as was done in much of western Europe. Or the guest laborers can be imported just as needed and kept in the country just that long and no longer, as Switzerland does with much labor imported from Italy. Or the guest laborers can be imported for very specific types of labor and then returned home, as is done on the South Korean construction jobs in the Middle East.

We believe that it would be very useful to the world to pursue the third kind of tactic for dealing with this problem. We do not oppose the first two under all circumstances, but we believe that for most countries the third tactic is unquestionably the best. We understand immediately that there will be criticisms about "indentured labor," but there is no reason why these criticisms should be valid. Often, the critics simply do not understand what is going on. For example, we often hear that Mexican immigrants will swim the Rio Grande river, walk the desert on foot, and risk their lives to get these jobs. It is then argued that we should prevent them from doing this because they are going to be exploited. They may be badly treated in the United States, but clearly they much prefer the ability to earn about ten times the going salary in Mexico, even if under onerous conditions. We believe that they are probably right in making this choice. There may be all kinds of reasons why the United States does not want the Mexicans to do this, but we should not be hypocritical and say it is for the benefit of the Mexicans themselves. They are surely better judges of this than we are.

World Impact of Tourism

The term *tourist* has had several definitions over time. We follow the United Nations definition that includes people traveling for business, family, mission, or meeting purposes, as well as for pleasure and education. The United Nations term thus is almost synonymous with *traveler* and covers travel for any purpose outside military and related activities.

There are several characteristics of tourism that make it of particular importance in its economic impact. In most of *La Deuxième Belle Epoque* and in most countries tourism income has grown at a greater rate than has gross domestic product. Furthermore, tourism-related industries are labor-intensive but require relatively few highly trained individuals. Thus, the tourist industry has been growing rapidly and has provided numerous jobs for relatively untrained individuals of the kind who form the bulk of the world labor force.

To put the industry in economic perspective, we estimate that more than 5 percent of the gross world product (or over $400 billion) will be spent on domestic and international travel in 1978. This is much more than is spent on armaments worldwide, and it is growing at more than twice the rate. While less than 20 percent of the tourist dollar is spent internationally, tourism clearly has been and is a major growth industry with worldwide economic impact.

Historically, tourism on this scale is essentially a phenomenon of *La Deuxième Belle Epoque* but seems likely to grow spectacularly even during *L'époque de Malaise.* It has been shaped by the development of rapid mass transportation and the tremendous increase in discretionary income and leisure for great numbers of people in many parts of the world. In times past, travel was restricted largely to commerce, religious pilgrimages, and military campaigns. Travel for pleasure was for the most part the prerogative of the wealthy. Today, nearly anyone in Western nations and an increasing number of people in developing countries can and do travel. For example, about 25 million Americans are expected to travel abroad in 1978, spending $10-$15 billion. In return, more than 20 million foreign visitors are expected to spend almost ten billion dollars in the United States in 1978—perhaps more if the dollar continues to decline. These numbers are expected to grow about 10 percent a year, at least for a while. This could increase tourism by a factor of five or so by the end of the century. The World Bank expects tourism to grow at only one and one-half to two times the rate of world GNP, but this could easily turn out to be a low estimate. In any event, tourism will become an increasingly important industry, probably the most important world export in terms of number of dollars (even eventually exceeding oil) and also in many countries the most important domestic industry.

It is difficult to determine how much money is spent on travel and tourism, directly and indirectly. Certain obvious factors such as transportation, hotels, meals, and recreational activities can be checked, but even these are often difficult to ascertain. Indirect sales such as clothing purchases, sport equipment, and new cars bought or old ones tuned up are much harder to document. In any case, the total expenditures associated with tourism are almost certainly higher than those usually published. Tourism is usually estimated to generate approximately 7 percent of the United States gross national product (making it the third largest industry) and is fourth in export terms (i.e., spending by foreign visitors). In many other nations, tourism is even more important. It is, for example, the major industry in Spain. By the year 2000, tourism may be the largest industry in the world and will have great impact in many areas, mostly in the Third World, that today have very little income from tourism.

Until recently, in many countries, tourism *per se* was not really considered an industry. The various tourist-related enterprises tended to look upon themselves as unique to their fields and not associated with other dissimilar ones. Thus, the airlines, car rental companies, bus lines, and railroads considered themselves to be in the business of moving people and things. The hotels and motels considered themselves in the lodging business. Restaurants and fast-food chains were concerned with serving food. Except where the interests of one spilled over into another's fields, (e.g., when airlines acquired hotels) there was little intercourse among the constituent industries that formed the overall industry labeled tourist.

This is increasingly changing. Component industries have begun to recognize their roles in the larger picture and information has been exchanged. Almost everywhere, cooperation and joint planning among the member companies in the tourist industry are beginning and the trend is expected to continue and accelerate in the future. Such collective action may well make tourism more convenient and attractive and thus accelerate the growth of the industry beyond present projections. This could be especially important for many Middle Income and Poor countries.

Other factors likely to contribute to the tourism increase include: discount fares; proliferation of travel agencies throughout the world; greater use of the automobile, the prime tourism travel medium; reduced communication costs and greater system integration; greater availability of data on travel, lodging, food, etc.; control of diarrhea as a factor in traveling, and so on. Thus, it seems that tourism is likely to continue to increase for the foreseeable future.

One probable long-range limiting factor to continued growth of tourism is population. Although population continues to increase, it does so at a declining rate. This is bound to have a long-term effect on the growth of tourism. An anticipated shift in population percentage by age groups will also have an effect, although not necessarily a retarding one, as the population bulge moves up the age scale with time. Another limitation is overcrowding. This more than anything else is likely to endanger the proper development of new areas. Eventually an inflection point (of percent rate of tourism growth) will be reached, after which the growth rate will slow. Many believe that this inflection point has already been reached, but we disagree.

We believe the growth in discretionary income, leisure time, and the inexpensiveness and convenience of travel and communication should more than cancel the effects of the slower growth in population. All of these "improvements" that will accompany economic development will enable increasing numbers of people to travel. That they will do so seems clear, if past history is a criterion. In the period since the end of World War II, traditional travelers, the upper-middle class and upper class members who alone could afford to do so, have been superseded by people whose ancestors seldom traveled far from their home towns and villages. Thus, we find the ubiquitous Japanese, cameras in hand, visiting all parts of the world in increasing numbers; almost a million will visit the United States in 1978. Former coolies from Singapore turn up at the Louvre in Paris. Expansion of airline service in the Pacific makes it not only possible but quite reasonable to visit South Sea islands formerly accessible only through literature and movies. That people are availing themselves of such opportunities is evidenced by the past and projected future growth of air traffic in Asia and Oceania. As developing countries expand their economies, more of their citizens will find themselves able to travel, and presumably will do so.

Some possible impediments to tourism growth could come about over time. Major upheavals such as war or world depression would, of course, radically alter the scenario. Barring some such cataclysmic development, other factors could also slow down the anticipated growth. Government action such as that taken by Brazil in 1976, which requires a substantial ($1,200) one-year, no-interest deposit before a resident is permitted to travel abroad is no help. Another favorite tactic of governments is to limit severely the amount of money citizens can take out of the country. Tedious or discourteous entry and exit procedures at ports of entry often serve to discourage visitors. Local hostility can have pronounced negative effects on tourism. St. Croix, in the United States Virgin Islands, had not recovered by 1978 from racially motivated murders of white tourists in the early 1970s. The repercussions seriously damaged tourism in the entire Caribbean, since people tend to lump all the islands into the same package.

The great virtue of tourism is that, almost by itself, it can act as an important channel for trickle-down—either across national borders or within a nation. It is both labor intensive and uses much low quality labor. We expect to see the tourist industry play a major role in the emerging super-industrial economy.

MALAISE AND INSTITUTIONAL PROBLEMS

The world economy, like each national economy, has at least three distinct components: production, consumption, and institutions.

The production component includes the intrinsic capability of the available technology, capital, existing plants, resources, and manpower (including management) to continue and expand output. The production component of the world economy appears to be in a very good state. Those who worry about basic or intractable raw material shortages, or even intractable pollution effects, are almost certainly wrong so far as the current issues are concerned.

The consumption component centers around whether there is a market for the goods. Can they be sold? This is not so much a question of people's needs or even wants, but of demand. Demand implies a willingness and an ability to pay for a product. The sale of the products can be financed. Maladjustments in the capacity between supply and demand are sometimes called structural problems. Examples are the current over-dependence on oil and the worldwide over-capacity in steel. None of these problems is as serious as is often believed, nor would they be as difficult to deal with if the third component—institutions—were in a more satisfactory state.

The effectiveness of a given economy and of the world economy also depends on its institutions. Are the legal, financial, economic, social, cultural, political, and other institutions of a society capable of utilizing the society's productive capabilities to satisfy consumer demands? How strong are the motivations and commitments of businessmen, workers, and consumers? Is the atmosphere and general milieu conducive to savings and investment? Are the governmental and private decision makers competent? At the moment, the answers to these and other questions are at best mixed, and often surprisingly negative, at least for the Affluent countries.

Institutional economics is a classic subject, but it has been relatively neglected in recent years. It lacks any genuine unifying theory, but its perspective is nevertheless useful, as the following discussion illustrates. For example, almost every society that has undergone rapid economic growth has been characterized during that period by sobriety of dress and behavior of businessmen—at least during business hours. This has been true of the British, Dutch, American, Japanese, and is true today of the South Koreans and Taiwanese. Such symbolic behavior can demonstrate commitment, reinforce a sense of fraternity, and even maintain or strengthen Protestant and neo-Confucian ethics. Econometric models often ignore this kind of data, even though the erosion or reinforcement of customs brought about by such behavior can have more consequential effects than the data ordinarily used by computerized models.

Our approach to institutional issues is practical and focuses on recent and current events. Without appealing to the speculative discussions in Part I, we argue that to some degree major economic institutions of the world (at least those of the ACNs) were "damaged" during the decade from 1965 to 1975. Faith in currency and in financial instruments generally was seriously undermined; inflation was institutionalized; and many things that once went easily and smoothly are now accomplished with great difficulty, if at all. Most important, there has been an erosion of traditional values and attitudes.

Institutionalized inflation is the most obvious sign that the system is malfunctioning. However, the loss of respect for institutions and the lack of effective leadership able to make constructive ideological commitments and inspire confidence in the system is more insidious. Part of the problem is the role of the current elites. The normal role of the elites in society is for some members and subgroups to furnish leadership, morale, and creative ideas, while others furnish critiques or hostile analysis. The former has not been occurring much recently.

One whole class of important concerns usually left out of economic analysis includes the many subtle ways in which faith (or lack of faith) in the value of money (the "money illusion") can affect an economic society. For example, during World War II, the German government found that, by and large, German workers could not be motivated to make sacrifices in exchange for money. This was mainly because of their memories of the runaway post–World War I inflation. Instead, German workers had to be given immediate material rewards, which in turn necessitated a guns and butter economy. By contrast, Americans were quite willing to accept pieces of paper that promised postwar goods for work performed during the war. A good part of the high wages and salaries paid during the war was saved for use later, because the collective American memory was that wars are followed by depression, a time when money is very valuable.

Faith in a reasonably fixed value for a nation's currency is extraordinarily important in making the economy work smoothly. This is true both from the point of view of objective calculations of profit and loss and risk, and in terms of the psychology of the individual and society. This asset, however, does not normally appear in any balance sheets.

In addition to its function as a mechanism of exchange and a store of value, currency also serves as a unit of measure. A person who tried to run a physics laboratory where temperatures were changing rapidly would, of course, correct the measuring instruments accordingly. Something analogous has to be done with money to correct for the effects of inflation if we are either to understand the many numbers that we collect or if various monetary contracts and instruments are to function properly. Unfortunately, unlike in a physics lab, how the correction is done affects the way the economy works. Calculations and contracts are often corrected in ways that are unnecessarily misleading and distorting. Furthermore, the corrections that work reasonably well in the early phase of an inflation often become increasingly misleading or counter-productive as the inflation continues or increases.

It is especially disquieting that so many economists underestimate the negative impact of institutionalized inflation under current conditions for many countries. They do so partly because they think that it has more or less been corrected by current high interest rates, indexed contracts, and various new institutions such as 8 percent wage increases plus 2 percent increases in productivity. They believe that this results in a predictable 6 percent inflation whose effects are really much the same as 2 percent wage increases and no inflation. We disagree, but will defer most of the discussion to the next section of this chapter.

The enormous virtues of a free market are based on the premise that the free market calculations make sense. If they do not, if they are distorted, then the free market simply does not function properly. This alone can create conditions that fit our definition of *malaise*. Economic activity is such a pervasive part of our society that if it functions badly because its basic mechanisms have introduced windfall profits and losses and other distortions through an arbitrary, capricious, and uncertain process, then we cannot expect the rest of the system to function well either.

United States Malaise

A group that is going downhill tends to be resentful and often makes invidious comparisons that make it feel even worse. To some degree this has been happening to the United States, but perhaps less so than would occur in most countries undergoing the same international decline. At the end of World War II, the United States produced about 50 percent of the world's gross product. Recovery in Europe and Asia changed this abnormal condition quite rapidly. At the present, the United States has about 25 percent of the gross world product; by the end of the century we believe it will have about 20 percent. This is clearly a kind of decline—at first rapid, but now slowing down.

Part of the decline was inevitable, and part of it has to do with the relatively poor performance of the United States economy. This relative decline and some aspects of the poor economic performance are illustrated by Figures 5.1 and 5.2. They show that particularly poor United States productivity increases in the late 1960s seem to have stayed poor for about a decade and that since the mid-1960s, actual productivity in the private non-farm business sector has fallen below the trend followed since 1950. What all this adds up to is that the United States economy is not as special as it used to be. This could depress some Americans. But while Americans lose something in their pride in being American by this development, it is not a severe loss.

Another factor contributing to United States malaise is the very great shock to its self esteem resulting from the Vietnam War. We believe that many events of the war have been misinterpreted and misunderstood. However, whatever the interpretation, the war was a severe blow to United States status, morale, pride, and self-confidence.

There is also a pervasive myth—not entirely groundless—that the United States was once a quasi-Roman republic that was virtuous, dignified, self-reliant, tough, hard, austere, and puritanical, but is now becoming decadent, as shown in part by the precipitous decline of the dollar. Many Americans seem to be natural macro-historians, favoring the concept that societies can become decadent, that civilizations rise and fall.

A good case could be made for malaise just by looking at the above national picture. However, we would like to focus on additional domestic issues, beginning with the issue of confidence in United States institutions, and with what might be called the trend toward alienation and a feeling of powerlessness among the American

FIGURE 5.1
Real GNP Per Employed Civilian in Six Countries,
1950-1974
(as a Fraction of U.S.)

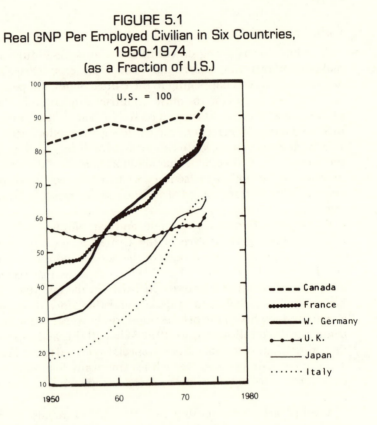

U.S. = 100

Canada
France
W. Germany
U.K.
Japan
Italy

1950   60   70   1980

people. A series of Harris surveys provides the main data. (See Tables 5.5 and 5.6.) There are two ways to interpret the results of these polls. One is that the answers reflect something wrong with the American people. The other is that the American people are responding (perhaps accurately) to the question, "What has been wrong with your leadership?" We believe that both interpretations are plausible. Confidence and admiration often have little to do with real performance. Thus, even if the American leadership behaved badly and were scored accordingly, this might be as much accident as cause and effect. We believe that the score is partly a cause and partly an effect of the malaise. Whether or not the American people understood what was happening, the survey results actually reflect fairly good judgments about what was happening, as we will try to document.

Crime and Misunderstood "Middle America" Issues

Some of the official data on the United States situation are

FIGURE 5.2
Annual Rates of Productivity Increase
in Manufacturing, 1967-1977

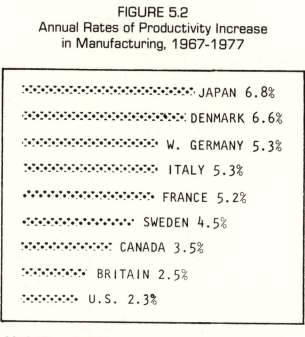

SOURCE: BUREAU OF LABOR STATISTICS,
PRODUCED IN NEWSWEEK, MAY 29,
1978, P. 79.

illustrated by Figure 5.4. We will start with crime, but we focus on the homicide figure because all other crime data are subject to much controversy. Figure 5.4 shows that in the 1930s the homicide rate rose steadily until the middle of the Great Depression, then dropped steadily until the United States entered World War II. There was a peak during the war (not surprising), followed by a resumption of the decline. The most remarkable thing about the world after World War II is that almost every big city in the developed world and most cities in the less developed countries became relatively safe. Some port cities had a few unsafe neighborhoods, but basically almost everywhere in the world one could walk reasonably safely, day or night.

The first country to change in this respect was the United States. The upturn in crime has been described lucidly by the eminent American political scientist, James Q. Wilson:

Early in the decade of the 1960s, this country began the longest

FIGURE 5.3
Productivity in the Private
Nonfarm Business Economy

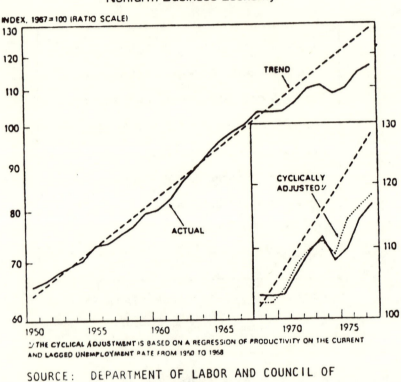

INDEX, 1967 = 100 (RATIO SCALE)

/ THE CYCLICAL ADJUSTMENT IS BASED ON A REGRESSION OF PRODUCTIVITY ON THE CURRENT
AND LAGGED UNEMPLOYMENT RATE FROM 1950 TO 1968

SOURCE: DEPARTMENT OF LABOR AND COUNCIL OF
           ECONOMIC ADVISERS.

sustained period of prosperity since World War II. A great array of programs aimed at the young, the poor, and the deprived were mounted. Though these efforts were not made primarily out of a desire to reduce crime, they were wholly consistent with—indeed, in their aggregate money levels, wildly exceeded—the policy prescription that a thoughtful citizen worried about crime would have offered at the beginning of the decade. Crime soared. It did not just increase a little; it rose at a faster rate and to higher levels than at any time since the 1930s and, in some categories, to higher levels than any experienced in this century. The mood of contentment and confidence in which the decade began was shattered.[14]

Wilson is talking only about crime, but something similar was

FIGURE 5.4
The U.S. Criminal Justice System

The charts below show that the enormous increase in crime is not an illusion. This is true despite a tendency during the 1960s among some upper middle class circles to believe that law and order were code words for anti-black sentiments, rather than expressing a genuine concern with a very real and pressing problem.

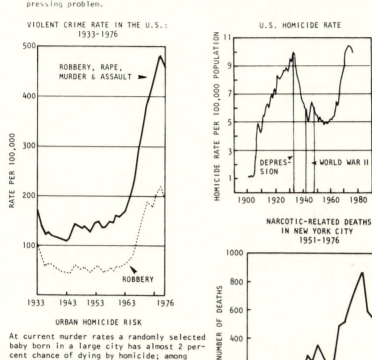

VIOLENT CRIME RATE IN THE U.S.:
1933-1976

ROBBERY, RAPE, MURDER & ASSAULT →

ROBBERY

U.S. HOMICIDE RATE

DEPRESSION ← WORLD WAR II

NARCOTIC-RELATED DEATHS
IN NEW YORK CITY
1951-1976

URBAN HOMICIDE RISK

At current murder rates a randomly selected baby born in a large city has almost 2 percent chance of dying by homicide; among males the figure is 3 percent.

Environment	Risk of Death in Combat or by Homicide
U.S. soldier in WW I	1.1% (combat)
U.S. soldier in WW II	1.8% (combat)
U.S. soldier in Vietnam	0.5% (combat)
Urban male born in 1972	3.0% (homicide)

SOURCE: NEW YORK CITY DEPT. OF HEALTH.

TABLE 5.5
Loss of Confidence During the Last Decade—Trend in Alienation and Powerlessness Felt by the American People

Agree with Statement	1966	1968	1972	1974	1976	1977 Jan.	Nov.	Changes 1966-1976	Change from 1976 to Nov. 1977
The Rich Get Richer and the Poor Get Poorer	45%	54%	68%	79%	77%	78%	77%	+32%	0%
What You Think Doesn't Count Much Any More	37	42	53	60	64	57	61	+24	-3
People Running the Country Don't Really Care What Happens to You	26	36	50	63	61	55	60	+34	-1
Felt Left Out of Things Going on Around You	9	12	25	32	42	39	35	+26	-7
Average Feeling Alienation and Powerlessness	29	36	49	59	61	n.a.	n.a.	n.a.	n.a.

Source: Louis Harris, *The Harris Survey*, January 5, 1978.

TABLE 5.6
Loss of Confidence During the Last Decade—Trend of Confidence in Leadership of Key U.S. Institutions

Great Deal of Confidence	1966	1972	1973	1974	1976	Change: 1966 - 1976	1976	Change: 1976-1977
Big Companies	55%	27%	29%	21%	16%	-32%	23	+ 7
Military	62	35	40	33	23	-31	31	+ 8
Medicine	72	48	57	50	42	-17	55	+13
Colleges	61	33	44	40	31	-20	41	+10
TV News	25	17	41	31	28	+ 5	30	+ 2
Religion	41	30	36	32	24	- 7	34	+10
Supreme Court	51	28	33	40	22	-20	31	+ 9
Press	29	18	30	25	20	-10	19	- 1
Law Firms	—	—	24	18	12	—	16	+ 4
Organized Labor	22	15	20	18	10	- 7	15	+ 5
Congress	42	21	29	18	9	-27	15	+ 6
Executive	41	27	19	28	11	-18	23	+12

Source: Louis Harris, *The Harris Survey*, January 5, 1978.

happening in almost every sector of American life. To quote Wilson again, "it all began about 1963. That was the year, to over-dramatize a bit, that the decade began to fall apart."[15]

By 1965 the slogan *law and order* had come into great prominence. Yet, for about five years after 1965 the literate media (*The New York Times, The Washington Post, Time, Newsweek, The Atlantic Monthly, Harper's, The New York Review*, etc.), except when they had an occasional and usually neo-conservative guest writer, almost continuously accepted that this slogan was a code word for anti-black attitudes and did not reflect a genuine concern about crime. This assertion seems to have been almost completely untrue. No demagogues we could identify actually used this slogan as a code word. Normally, they told you where they stood on social issues and then talked about law and order. Many blacks in northern cities also consistently put law and order as the top issue in their lives. Presumably they could not be using these as code words. This implication of bigotry was typical of what might be thought of as the reverse bigotry of the liberal New Class and the media it dominated during this period. This misinterpretation of their feelings severely aggravated many middle class and working people. It was partly responsible for their friendliness towards George Wallace and their animosity towards what Wallace called the "briefcase-carrying pinheads."

Law and order is only one of twelve "Middle America" issues (Table 5.7) that the elite-dominated media continually portrayed in terms of bigotry, even though most Americans were reacting to those issues in perfectly reasonable ways. Law and order was not a code term for anti-black sentiment, but rather a genuine cry of alarm over the enormous increase in crime. Nor is the opposition to busing particularly based on bigotry. Almost every American city now will accept court-ordered desegregation as long as it does not mean busing children long distances to bad schools.*

Average Americans were aware of some degree of bigotry in their attitudes, but it was equally clear to them that this had little to do with their actions or voting behavior. In this situation the concepts behind English libel laws should apply. Under English libel laws, if one says something nasty about an individual and has no particular reason for saying it, and it turns out the nasty thing was untrue, the offender has

---

*Similarly, the United States gun culture is not an expression of sado-masochism, latent homosexuality, pornography, or violence, but is in fact a quite acceptable and even admirable way of life. See the discussion in Personal Notes 1 and 2 in Chapter 8.

TABLE 5.7
Misunderstood "Middle America" Issues

1. Law and order
2. Busing
3. Basic attitude toward blacks
4. Gun laws and other gun issues
5. Pornography issues
6. Sex education in public schools
7. School tax revolt
8. Attitudes toward flag, religion, fighting words, etc.
9. Attitudes toward violent protest and participatory democracy
10. Hypocrisy
11. Graft versus corruption
12. Backlash against blacks

to pay damages. If it turns out the nasty thing was true, the offender has to pay triple damages on the quite reasonable grounds that the truth hurts more than a falsehood; it is much more difficult to answer or correct. This was very much the attitude of average Americans. As long as they kept their bigotry to themselves, it was nobody's business. But to find that perfectly legitimate concerns were taken as examples of bigotry simply infuriated Americans, increased their dissatisfaction and alienation that showed up so dramatically in the poll data, and thus further increased malaise.

Consider municipal services. During this period of rising prosperity and increasing slackness, the number of people employed in municipal services doubled, the costs tended to triple, and the output tended to halve. This was as true for the educational system as for the fire department, the street cleaners, or almost any other municipal service that can be assessed. Figures 5.5 and 5.6 give a sense of what happened in the United States educational system.

Economic and Ideological Issues

Another factor that figures largely in the United States malaise and is largely overlooked except by the affected group is that the real take-home pay of the average worker has remained fairly constant since about 1962. This was especially depressing because in the same period almost every other group in America—the poor, the rich, the upper-middle class, the intellectuals—did quite well. Not only has the

FIGURE 5.5
Total Expenditures Per Pupil in Average
Daily Attendance in Public Schools
1929-1930 to 1976-1977
(constant 1976-1977 dollars)

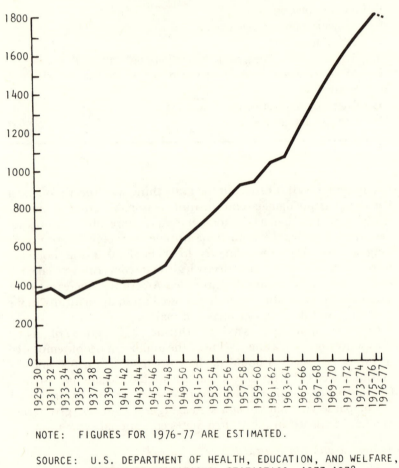

NOTE: FIGURES FOR 1976-77 ARE ESTIMATED.

SOURCE: U.S. DEPARTMENT OF HEALTH, EDUCATION, AND WELFARE,
          DIGEST OF EDUCATIONAL STATISTICS: 1977-1978.

FIGURE 5.6
Mean Scholastic Aptitude Test
(SAT) Scores for All Candidates

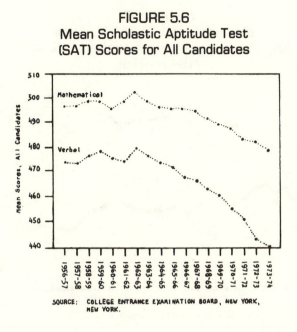

SOURCE: COLLEGE ENTRANCE EXAMINATION BOARD, NEW YORK, NEW YORK.

American worker not been doing well, but this fact has gone relatively unnoticed by everyone else, which further aggravates the situation. (In the late 1970s the family income often increased, but this was because another member of the family had joined the work force.)

Even though real take-home pay has not been increasing, compensation for workers (which includes fringe benefits—many of which the worker does not value) has increased dangerously, while corporate profits have decreased—a very unhealthy state for the business community. (See Figure 5.7.)

Figure 5.8 sums up the most important symptom of the American business establishment's malaise. It is a graph of the so-called Q value estimating prospects of American business. The stock market's valuation of the business as recorded by the price of the stock on the exchange is divided by the real depreciated value of the business—its replacement value.[16] It shows that, on the average, American businesses are valued at about half replacement value, which means that many are valued at less than half of the replacement value. This is one reason for the popularity of takeover bids; one can buy a concern at twice the stock market value and still have a bargain. This

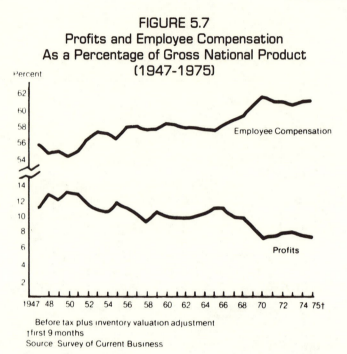

FIGURE 5.7
Profits and Employee Compensation
As a Percentage of Gross National Product
(1947-1975)

Before tax plus inventory valuation adjustment
†first 9 months
Source Survey of Current Business

is depressing to potential investors, since it implies an average value of a stock market investment is worth fifty cents on the dollar.

Another group severely affected by malaise are black teenagers, whose unemployment rates have been climbing since the mid-1950s and show increasing disparity in comparison with white teenagers. The high rate of black teenage unemployment is frequently attributed to short-term causes, most recently the recession of the mid-1970s, but as Figure 5.9 shows, female black teenage unemployment actually peaked in 1970 and male black teenage unemployment peaked in 1973.

What is especially depressing is the lack of effective action by the United States government. The increase in black adolescent unemployment began in the early 1960s. It apparently stems from a number of causes, some of which can be summarized by saying that there have been failures of church, school, neighborhood, and family. We believe that if any one of these influences could be greatly improved, a dramatic difference in the unemployment figures would result. We also feel that it is easiest for the government to work

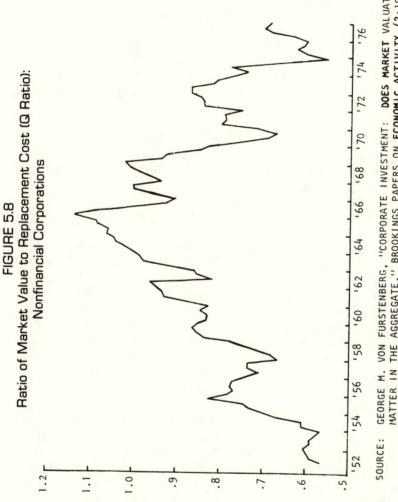

FIGURE 5.8

Ratio of Market Value to Replacement Cost (Q Ratio):
Nonfinancial Corporations

SOURCE: GEORGE M. VON FURSTENBERG, "CORPORATE INVESTMENT: **DOES MARKET** VALUATION
MATTER IN THE AGGREGATE," BROOKINGS PAPERS ON **ECONOMIC ACTIVITY** (2:1977)
PP. 351-55.

through the schools. The fact is that we know as a practical matter how to handle this problem.[17]

Unfortunately, when one visits the Departments of Health, Education and Welfare in Washington, D.C., one finds their interest in intervention almost completely centered on such issues as "improving" racial balance on school faculties and increasing the number of female principals. The former is not only totally irrelevant to the problems of the children, but does not seem to be particularly desired by either the black or white faculty members. The latter is of some importance to the teachers, but again has very little to do with the current dramatic problems of teenage unemployment.

In fact, about the only thing the federal government has done is to raise the minimum wage laws, now regarded as contributing to a major fraction of the black adolescent unemployment. Shockingly, the administration knew about this adverse effect when they increased the minimum wage; most experts still believe it to be true.

Even though many people claim to feel strongly about this issue, it is clear that no current program will do any good, and many current programs will worsen the situation.[18]

Let us examine some prevailing ideological issues that are of significant concern to a broad cross section of the country's population. Table 5.8 shows some psychic tensions from which many people in almost all the Affluent Capitalist countries suffer. In effect, modern secular societies do not encourage deep roots and the sense of security and safety that people really want. Another problem, most evident in the *weltanschauung* of the New Class, but affecting everybody, is general failure of nerve and reaction against growth and progress. People are frightened by modern technology and its potentially destructive products—from emotions programmed by a computer to nuclear weapons. Furthermore, given the kind of egalitarianism in our system, there is an increasing intolerance, notably by intellectuals in upper classes but to a degree by everybody, of the existence of "irrational," indefensible, and unjust inequities.

Another problem in our society is the enormous and intense spotlight on various societal failures. Even when the issues are not trivial (and they frequently are) the spotlight blows them up and, in effect, presents society as a whole as corrupt, indefensible, self-seeking, and so on. More than ever before the headlines attack the pillars of the establishment—the big corporations, Washington bureaucrats, the government—so that it is almost impossible to have any respect for the system.

These are just a few of the issues that are bothering the American

FIGURE 5.9
Unemployment Rates of 18 and 19 Year Olds by Age, Sex,
and Race, 1948-1977

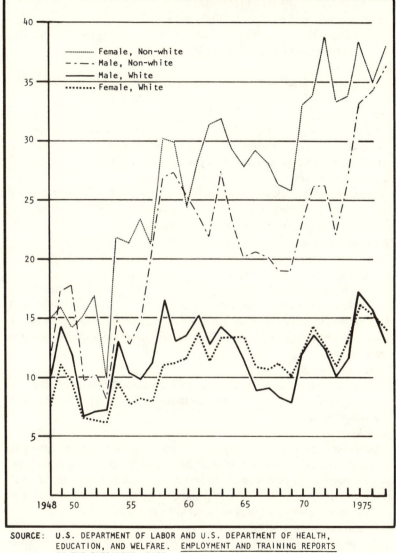

SOURCE: U.S. DEPARTMENT OF LABOR AND U.S. DEPARTMENT OF HEALTH,
EDUCATION, AND WELFARE. EMPLOYMENT AND TRAINING REPORTS
OF THE PRESIDENT, 1977.

TABLE 5.8
Some Psychic Tensions

A Search for "Meaning and Purpose" ("Existential Dread"):
Men are increasingly without comforting rituals, assured value systems, or fulfilling enterprises and activities.

Excessive Freedom from Constraints and Levers:
Excessive lack of structure and forced reality-testing lead to illusions, fads, destructive experiments with alternative life-styles, etc.

Rootlessness:
Unprecedented social and physical mobility and unprecedented weakness of familial, cultural, social, and economic ties.

Anomie:
Much modern work and even other daily activities appear fragmentary, uncreative, or meaningless, providing no responsible individual relationship to the result or any other enduring satisfactions.

Sense of Impotence:
The system often seems infinite in potentiality and power, yet for many individuals, the centers and levers of power seem hopelessly remote—at least as long as they stay in established channels.

Failure of Nerve:
Fear of nuclear war, civilian violence, erosion of standards, growth of anarchistic behavior and nihilistic sentiments, other upsetting changes— even technological progress no longer seems very beneficial—indeed general reaction against growth and progress—a further reaction against rationalist values of modern science and technology: against economic and administrative bureaucracies; and organized hierarchy, order, and tradition.

Eroded Self Image:
An effect of modern technology and theories, Copernicus, Darwin, Freud, Pavlov, Skinner, and the pervasive view of man as a cybernetic machine or automaton.

Pervasive Sense of Guilt:
Unrealistic expectations and subsequent frustration, disillusionment, and alienation, lowered tolerance by intellectuals and upper classes generally for the existence of "irrational," "indefensible," and "unjust" inequities—complicated in many nations by upper and upper-middle class "guilt complexes" and anti-anti-left ideologies.

Exaggeration of Societal Failures:
A harsh and dramatic spotlight on such issues as racial discrimination and racist practices, persistent poverty, white collar and business corruption, dangerous food additives, pollution, urban difficulties of various sorts. The spotlight causes an overemphasis and distortion of these issues.

people. The issues differ in intensity and duration, but they combine to make people feel vulnerable about themselves, about their society, and about its institutions. The result is malaise.

Another source of United States malaise, previously discussed, is extreme ineptness in dealing with the so-called energy crisis—an ineptness so extreme that it would raise fundamental questions about the system if the situation were typical. It is almost impossible to find any sacrifice by the United States government to improve the use or supply of energy, despite its "program." A widespread joke is that United States policy favors the use of coal (because the country has so much coal), but with two *caveats*—it should not be mined and it should not be burned. Sadly, this is a description of just what is happening. There are a number of incredibly serious deficiencies in the United States energy policy. For example, the following situation prevailed five years after the October War:

1. No reduction of red tape for building nuclear reactors (it still takes about thirteen years—it used to take five or less).
2. No clear policy on radioactive waste disposal, although the problem has existed since 1945 and does not really appear to be excessively difficult.
3. No real priority or urgency for use of coal.
4. No viable land use concept for strip mining.
5. Incredible delays in exploiting the outer continental shelf and Alaska for oil drilling.
6. No leases given on United States government-owned coal lands since 1971.
7. No commercial synthetic fuel plants (using shale or coal) have been programmed in the United States.
8. Oil and gas priced well below market value, in some cases extraordinarily so.
9. Totally unjustified price controls on unconventional gas.
10. An elaborate system of entitlements and multi-level pricing that has persisted long enough so that great efforts go into exploiting idiosyncrasies of the laws and regulations and not in improving efficiency and allocation of resources.
11. Regulatory, legal, and political impediments to nearly all new energy projects (supply, transportation, and use) reach historic highs.
12. An artificial glut of oil in California allowed to discourage drilling in Alaska and California.
13. No United States encouragement of Mexican oil and gas projects.

14. Encouragement and sympathy given to some of the more manic aspects of the solar power movement.

Hopefully, some of the above will have changed by the time this book appears. Few people assuming that the energy problem would continue would have said in October 1973 that more than five years after the October War the United States would not have started to address seriously most of the above issues, yet would be subsidizing oil consumption by about $30 billion a year.[19]

Finally, a few words about New York City's recurrent problems and current contribution to United States malaise. I have been on many platforms where speakers have said, "As New York City goes, so goes the nation." I have always corrected them, saying, "As New York City goes, so go Newark and Yonkers." In fact, I have been informed recently that both Newark and Yonkers have done a better job than New York City has in putting their fiscal houses in order. Not only is it disheartening to hear that as New York City goes, so goes the United States, it is simply not necessarily true.

Although New York City has begun to put its house in order, one can still find an enormous number of practices that would simply not be tolerated in any reasonably well managed city, particularly one that has been on the verge of bankruptcy and still desperately depends upon help from the national government. Suffice to say that New York City's problems were completely predictable. When I was a member of the Scott Commission looking into New York City's tangled affairs, we predicted bankruptcy for the city, though we didn't think the crisis would come so quickly. We also noted New Yorkers were unworried because they were confident that the federal government would bail them out.

For readers who wish to get a sense of just how badly a place can be run and how totally incompetent municipal management can become, I recommend highly Chapter 5 of *A Time For Truth* by William E. Simon.[20] Mr. Simon was a first-hand observer of and participant in the sorry events he chronicles, and his rendition is persuasive and perceptive. Among other salient observations, he makes it clear that New York's near bankruptcy was not mainly because of its welfare costs or other charitable activities. The big costs involved were subsidies by the city to its middle class residents and to city employees. For example, city employees' fringe benefits were twice the national average, a sum of money in itself sufficient to create a huge deficit. Simon notes:

. . . If one analyzes New York's fiscal crisis in terms of its real, not its mythic, elements, one sees plainly that nothing has destroyed New York's finances but the liberal political formula. Using the "poor" as a compulsive pretext, New York politicians formed a working coalition with a portion of the middle class to run the city for their mutual benefit at the expense of the productive population. And inevitably that productive population has slowly withdrawn, gradually destroying the city's economic base.[21]

Simon cites a passage from the last budget message of the redoubtable Mayor Robert F. Wagner, Jr., who declared in 1965, "I do not propose to permit our fiscal problems to set the limits of our commitments to meet the essential needs of the people of our city."[22] If this means anything at all, it implies that Mayor Wagner (and his successors) was willing to become bankrupt simply to meet needs far this side of desperate.

New York City has yet (as of late 1978) to pare its budget in any serious way. As we already noted, municipal services in the United States are already ridiculously expensive, and New York's costs are astronomical. For example, New York was spending three times more per capita than any other United States city with a population of more than one million. During the period when other city budgets doubled, New York's increased by three and a half times.

Let it be recorded that I am a New York City enthusiast. I like New York City; it is a good place to live and to visit. It has a sharp edge that makes it exciting, even if it is not a festival. Yet nothing would be more depressing or malaise-inducing than if the wave of the future of the United States were to be New York City in its recent diminished state. And nothing could contribute more to the United States going downhill rapidly than if such a perception were to be true. But it is not. Fortunately, New York City is unique in its problems as well as in its virtues. And the fact that New York City survives and seems to be showing signs of recovery, however faint, is testimony to the underlying strength of the system.

European Malaise

European malaise, while much less spectacular than United States malaise, is probably deeper and more fundamental. Europeans have never really recovered from World War II except economically. Even in the 1970s Europeans felt, "We have gone so far but have now somehow lost our way. Where shall we go in the future?" European society seemed fragile. It appeared impossible to ask any sector to sacrifice without a revolt. The general fear of terrorism in Italy, in West Germany, and in other countries exacerbated these feelings. Frequently unwilling to face up to many issues without United States leadership, even in situations in which it could clearly go ahead on its own, Europe also experienced enormous complaints about the same leadership.

European countries far exceed the United States and Japan in the percent of gross national product passing through government hands—another factor contributing to European malaise—an example of what we call the "poverty of affluence." Imagine a relatively poor country where citizens demand more roads, more hospitals, more education, more money spent on protection of the environment and so forth. In almost all cases, the government's answer is straightforward and persuasive: "We do not have the money." But in most modern industrial countries during the last decade or two this response has simply not been credible, and correctly so, particularly if the government was willing to "borrow now and pay later." Claimants could then argue that there was enough money to satisfy their urgent cause, indeed, enough for almost all reasonable demands from any significant group. Yet there is never enough money to implement all requests immediately; the total budget for any year must be restricted to "reasonable levels," however defined. The government must argue, "Priorities have to be set. Over the next decade or two we will do many of these things. However, some claimants must wait their turn. Some programs will come early; some will come later."*

Under modern political circumstances many groups get angrier at this "yes, but not now" answer than they would at simply being rejected. Everybody understands when resources are severely limited. It is quite different to be told, "You must wait in line behind other

---

*The theory of the poverty of affluence is very useful. We employ it to cover a number of different things. First and foremost, it includes the concept that the upper-middle class and some of the upper-class elites tend to live worse as everybody in the country gets richer. This is shown by lack of services, the disappearance of live-in maids, and the like. Second, the middle and lower classes start to compete with the upper classes for beaches, roads, and the like because everyone has a car. They also compete for the good schools. In effect, the lower classes crowd the upper—sometimes physically, as in traffic jams that are unavoidable no matter what your class if you wish to travel by car, and sometimes symbolically. Third, the whole concept of wealth disappears

people," or that someone has set "arbitrary" limits (and all such limits appear arbitrary to the hostile) on the amount of borrowing. These issues of priorities are among the most intractable and difficult to analyze reasonably. It is even more difficult to get the analysis accepted, partly because it invariably contains arbitrary or dubious elements.

In many ways this issue of the poverty of affluence has become dominant. It interacts, of course, with the so-called revolution of rising entitlements. People feel morally entitled to more services, more subsidies, or even more direct transfer payments from the government. Proponents increasingly think of the expansion of such programs almost as an absolute good—indeed, almost as a way of testing the moral worth and modernity of the country. (We discuss in Chapter 8 how unfair it is for the currently Affluent countries to criticize the Poor for not putting more resources into public social welfare programs than the Affluent countries did at a corresponding stage of development.) But even though an Affluent country can afford a high level of transfer payments, it cannot afford as much as demanded. There will also be growing objections from taxpayers and producers to this transfer of resources.

The situation is complicated by the excessively cautious (even puritanical) fiscal conservatives who always argued not only that almost any specific "luxury" is unnecessary, but also that the country or community is—or soon will be—living beyond its income and in dire danger of bankruptcy. These spokesmen usually only succeed in discrediting their cause and confusing the issue. Other observers are certain to point out, again at almost any level of expenditure, that income is not only ample but will grow. They argue that it is therefore only reasonable and just to utilize these resources, at least for high-priority needs and perhaps also to distribute the national income more fairly. In most countries Keynesian arguments will be

---

in the welfare state. It's not a matter of life and death anymore. There are so many free services in the world, so many back-ups and so on, you get nothing like the extremes of poverty and wealth experienced in earlier centuries. Finally, there is the issue of the *nouveau riche* and irresponsibility. The *nouveau riche* don't know what they can afford. They are not used to spending money. Also, there is a certain lack of responsibility in a country that is newly wealthy and holds the theory that spending is good for the country. At this point, we are using the poverty of affluence concept to refer to the last phenomenon, but, where appropriate, we use the concept for the others as well.

cited to suggest that redistribution or spending are necessary for the economic and financial health of the economy. We strongly believe that during a period of stagflation and anticipated inflation, this argument is wrong.

It is quite difficult to prevent inflation in a poverty of affluence situation. Thus, if a country has not been suffering from inflation, or at least if most people are not anticipating an inflation, and there is some inflationary force, the government is sorely tempted to increase the money supply and accommodate the inflation rather than accept even modest increases in unemployment and bankruptcies or even reduced wages and profits.

Another factor contributing to European malaise has been the increase in wages during the recent inflation, illustrated in Figure 5.10. The experience of almost every European country has been depressing. Only in France have some of these increases been matched by increases in productivity. In the long run, of course, increases in hourly earnings have to be based on productivity. But with the partial exception of France, the increases shown in these graphs were due to the bargaining power of labor. The societies concerned were unable to keep costs down during a period when it was terribly important to do so, feeling that labor could not be controlled. This is no longer as true, but while the feeling lasted it contributed to the doom and gloom atmosphere.

The stagnation part of much of the European stagflation illustrates Jay Forrester's argument that the Kondratieff cycle results from excessive expansion in the capital goods industries, despite the tendency to blame everything on OPEC. Furthermore, the European economies are obligated to accept even greater social security and welfare expenses than is the United States. In addition, they are bedeviled by rules that make it almost impossible for them to control their payrolls.

In general it appears that Europe will continue its high costs and rigidities and simply accept lower growth rates. Many Europeans argue that lower growth rates are not acceptable politically; it is politically essential to decrease unemployment drastically. If so, the Europeans are in very serious trouble, because it seems unlikely that they will be able to do this to a significant degree. On the other hand, we guess that there will be much less general political unrest than is feared. It may well be that the lack of interesting and stimulating opportunities for many young people will show up in increased terrorism that might touch off serious crises, but it seems unlikely that this will force the society to become drastically more authoritarian. Aside from terrorism, it seems unlikely that there will be enough political unrest to lead to extravagant radical or extremist actions or programs.

Assuming the above is correct (a big assumption), the basic projection is the one suggested by Forrester: until the excess capacity is worked off, stagnation will continue. The prognosis seems to be for a continuation of malaise rather than an erosion to *La Deuxième Mauvaise Epoque.*

All this is complicated by the psychological effects of the long upswing, particularly on younger people. We would argue that the growing upper-middle class malaise and alienation combined with the various limits-to-growth attitudes may end up causing more unrest than unemployment does. In fact, one of the reasons for stagflation is the emergence of the limits-to-growth and anti-technology attitudes and movements. These are both extremely important and extremely complex, and underlie a good many of the other phenomena that we are talking about. Even though Europe is the birthplace of the Industrial Revolution, and to a great degree the source of modern technology and science, Europeans have always been much more ambivalent about industrialization than the newer powers such as the United States, the Soviet Union, and Japan. Many Europeans distrust and fear American and Russian technology. They often wish to participate fully in the process, yet simultaneously have a strong feeling that this is the wrong road to take.

Europe is a complicated place. The list on page 59 of opponents of economic growth and technological advancement applies with much greater intensity to Europe than to most other parts of the world. These movements find much more support than a naive or uninformed person would expect and can cause more serious problems than even most experts imagine. Certainly they seem likely to lead to many counterproductive—or at least costly—activities and counterproductive or costly legislation. Perhaps these will not be as extensive and extreme as in the United States (where they threaten to make the system inoperative), but they can make cost-cutting and increased efficiency more difficult. Both of these are important in getting the European economies out of the stagflation era.

Another unsettling factor in the European scene was the annual OPEC price-setting drama. Concern over this has been greatly alleviated by the recent so-called oil glut and the increasing realization among Europeans that at least in day-to-day actions, OPEC is greatly affected by supply and demand. There is also the realization that the OPEC cartel is more like a price leadership or

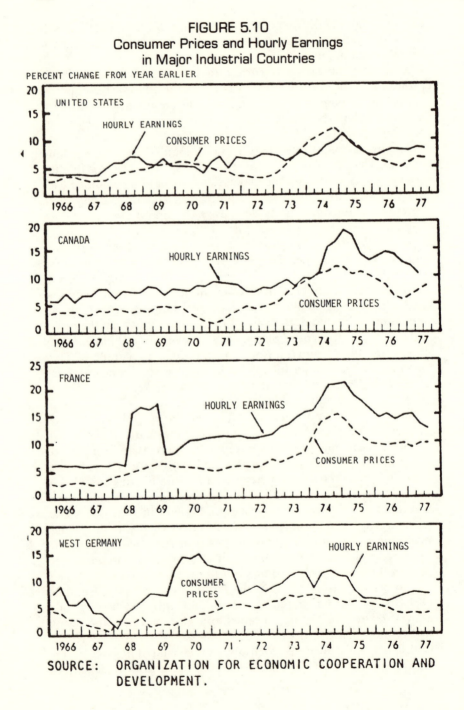

FIGURE 5.10
Consumer Prices and Hourly Earnings
in Major Industrial Countries

SOURCE: ORGANIZATION FOR ECONOMIC COOPERATION AND DEVELOPMENT.

FIGURE 5.10 (continued)

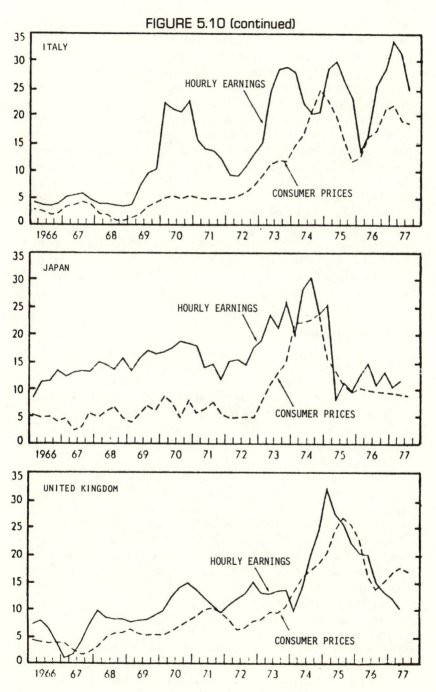

loose cartel situation than a tight monopoly whose policy is to maximize its total net income. However, since almost every respectable study predicts (probably incorrectly) tight oil supplies in the mid-1980s, the real price possibly doubling, apprehension over future OPEC misbehavior is very strong. If this widely accepted scenario is correct, the bargaining power of the Saudis over the world as a whole and over Europe in particular would increase enormously.

The Europeans are also particularly uncertain about their own political leadership. There is, at present, no European of any great distinction who speaks for Europe as a whole or even very much for his own country. While the discussion of the lack of legitimacy of political leadership in Europe seems overstated because to some degree close elections are perfectly normal and even inevitable in the democratic process as it is played out in the European nations, it is abnormal not to have any outstanding statesmen at all. If we define a statesman as a person who is willing, on many important issues, to accept political losses in the cause of principle or long-term considerations, then legitimate statesmen are, indeed, very few.

Canadian Malaise

The most vivid exemplification of contemporary Canadian malaise is that most Canadians are pessimistic about the future. Much of the Canadian governmental and intellectual establishment views the future through the blinders imposed by the limits-to-growth hypothesis. They not only believe that the whole world will be forced to slow down its economic growth because it is running out of natural resources, but that Canada too—despite its abundant resources—will have to proceed with great caution.[23]

The pervasiveness of limits-to-growth thinking in Canada is illustrated by the fact that a "conservor society" thesis is currently being developed in public discussions and workshops held throughout the country with the support of the Canadian government. The thesis assumes that Canada will be facing a crunch in natural resources before the end of the century and may have to return to labor-intensive industries and a lower standard of living. This is reinforced by fear of a shortage of capital.

Another example of Canada's malaise is the continuing sense of United States cultural and economic domination. It is often said that Canadians have an inferiority complex *vis-à-vis* the United States. This is no longer as true as it has been historically, but notions such as intellectual colonialism and cultural colonialism continue to dominate the Canadian debate over United States–Canadian relations. Any serious divergence between the United States and

Canada about economic policy or performance profoundly affects Canadian morale. For example, the faltering Canadian dollar is much more than a sign of Canada's lack of competitiveness or balance of payments problems or current political uncertainty. It is an event that contributes significantly to a loss of morale, for the United States is the traditional yardstick. Any divergence from the United States is felt much more deeply in Canada than it would be in any European country.

Perhaps the most important of the economic sources of malaise is the loss of competitiveness of Canadian manufacturers in world markets, especially in United States markets. Canadians fear that they will be unable to hold onto traditional markets, not only in the manufacturing sector—where the Canadian competitive position has already eroded—but also in the resource sector. This is inconsistent with the idea that the world is running out of resources, but few notice the contradiction. Recent cutbacks in nickel production, for example, illustrate this problem. It is increasingly felt that because of high wages, low productivity, and militant unions, buyers are looking elsewhere to obtain resources and Canada's traditional edge will erode over the next decade. The loss of competitiveness, combined with the pessimism *vis-à-vis* American corporations in Canada, has resulted in the standard observation that Canada is becoming not a branch planned economy, but a warehouse economy. This contributes to the malaise about the economic future of the country. A further aspect of malaise is the waning of Canada's once positive international image. Canada is still respected for its political and economic achievements, but not to the extent that it was twenty years ago.

The labor situation in Canada is another source of malaise. Though Canada has recently improved in this respect, in 1976 it had the world's second worst strike record and, after Italy, the highest number of work days lost to strikes. However, unions in the public sector continue to be militant, and unions in certain provinces (British Columbia and Quebec) still exercise great political clout. Labor relations remain tense and tenuous at best, and there is some fear that the situation could deteriorate in the next few years.

An additional source of malaise is the predicted high level of capital outflow. Canada used to be the net recipient of long-term direct investment. Since the mid-1970s this trend has reversed and Canadians are now investing more abroad than foreigners do in Canada. Part of this trend is the high level of investment in real estate in the United States. It has been said that the Canadian flag is more visible in Florida than it is in certain parts of Canada; this may soon be true in California as well. This partly reflects the well-documented sunbelt shift. Since Canada has no true sunbelt, Canadians tend to buy retirement or vacation homes in the United States.

However, since the outflow of capital—and particularly the boom in real estate investment in the United States—has increased substantially in the past year, one can also speculate that it reflects the political uncertainty that clouds the country at the present time about the status of Quebec. The issue is much more than a purely linguistic question; it raises the whole problem of federal-provincial relations. Since it is seen as a broad constitutional problem, it is not expected that the issue will be solved rapidly. The uncertainty it has raised about the sharing of power between the federal and provincial governments is leading Canadians to seek investment opportunities abroad and to make contingency plans in case they are not pleased with the outcome of the current negotiations.

Finally, perhaps the most important source of malaise is the feeling that Canada lacks strong leadership. The whole issue of the role of government in Canadian society is now being questioned. One of the distinctive differences between Canada and the United States is in the attitude toward government. Canadians have been much more receptive to having government play an important role in their economy and therefore have accepted the proliferation of crown corporations competing with private corporations. However, government spending now accounts for 43 percent of the GNP, and some Canadians are beginning to think the government may be playing too large a role. The concern is with more than just the size of government; it is also with its efficiency and with confidence in politicians as such.

Malaise in the East: The USSR and the Bloc

The symptoms of malaise are also evident in the Soviet Union and the countries of the East European Bloc. While different from the symptoms of malaise in the West, they are equally pervasive and are growing in importance. In the USSR, these symptoms are evident in slower economic growth, domestic social and cultural problems, and a number of problems relating to the international situation.

The Soviet Union has historically been able to achieve rapid economic growth—motivated in large part by the desire for a substantial military capability—through a strategy of accelerated industrialization based on the enforced mobilization of capital and labor. However, this strategy now seems to have run its course, leading to a virtually unavoidable decline in the economic growth rate.

The anticipated slowdown will result from several factors. First, the current trend of slower annual increases in productivity is virtually guaranteed by planned reductions in factor inputs including capital, the chief input for boosting productivity since Stalin's time.[24] In addition to falling productivity, two other important trends are also likely to slow Soviet economic growth. One is the certain slowdown in the growth of the labor force; the other is the growing scarcity of low cost raw materials, possibly including energy supplies. Let us examine the labor problem first.

Because of the combination of wartime losses of persons of marriageable age and the industrialization-induced trend toward smaller families, birth rates in the USSR began to decline during the 1950s and have been falling since. This decline is compounded by the bottoming out of the reservoir of surplus farm labor from which additional workers traditionally have been drawn. Short of heavy investments in agricultural machinery, it is unlikely that Soviet agriculture can manage with less than the 25 percent or so of the labor force that it currently utilizes, a force increasingly made up of elderly, unskilled workers.

Equally serious for the future economic growth of the USSR is the increasing scarcity of low cost raw materials, especially energy supplies. The economic growth of the USSR to date has rested mainly on the ready availability of inexpensive supplies of hydrocarbons located principally in the Urals-Volga region, which is convenient to Russia's major industrial concentrations. These oil and natural gas fields have been exploited with little attention to conservation techniques that would lengthen field life and maximize long-term production.

In oil extraction the principal production method has been the widespread use of water injection, a technique that produces a high initial flow at low investment cost but also damages oil reservoirs and reduces the amount of crude ultimately recoverable. In 1976, for the first time since World War II, the Soviet oil industry experienced a decline in its annual increment of petroleum output. While the Soviet Union has massive energy resources, it has serious economic and technological problems in finding and exploiting new oil and in transporting coal or gas. It seems likely that the maintenance of current levels—let alone planned increases—of energy production by the USSR will require allocations of investment capital and labor well beyond those now projected.

On the other hand, official reserves of natural gas in the Soviet Union are now over 1000 trillion cubic feet—the energy equivalent of the 170 billion barrels that is normally suggested as official Saudi Arabian reserves. It is hard to believe that the Soviets would not exploit this reserve adequately. We guess that their gas output will grow by at least 6 percent a year, more than enough to make up any shortfall in petroleum production, assuming they do a reasonably good job in petroleum as well.

The Soviets seem to have real problems in building pipelines of adequate quality. They have the steel and the engineering ability. It is mostly a question of quality. We assume that, if necessary, they ought to be able to do it, but this is by no means certain.

The Soviet press is already carrying articles critical of falling production levels, and almost daily there are new estimates of rapidly rising costs for hydrocarbons. Since energy consumption in the USSR has grown historically at roughly the same rate as economic growth, and since the Soviet Union is likely to be even less flexible at conservation than the West, Soviet leaders will be forced to make serious sacrifices to produce and transport energy or import whatever is necessary for economic growth.

Another factor that could significantly affect the future course of economic growth in the Soviet Union and deepen this symptom of current malaise is increased and unsatisfied consumer demand. Increasing industrial development and exposure to other mass consumption societies will stimulate consumer expectations. Remarkably, the Soviet Union has avoided spirals of rising expectations for consumer goods and has always been able to channel economic surplus to military and heavy industrial investments. However, the need for Western technology and its associated skills and the relative openness during détente have made the Soviet population more aware of modern consumer expectations. Eastern Europe's recent past is likely to be the Soviet Union's future. If so, the USSR can look forward to not only the revolution of rising expectations but possibly also to its own versions of the youth revolutions, the cultural revolution, and the sexual revolution. Moreover, increased authoritarianism and repression to insulate Soviet society from Western "decadence" is likely to increase malaise even if supported by the majority of the population.

An important social factor has been the fragmentation brought about by economic modernization in the more advanced societies in Eastern Europe. As in all societies, economic growth has increased the size and sophistication of the working class and the bureaucratization of the communist parties has meant looser ties to the workers. The result is a working class where self-consciousness and ability to assert its demands against the official hierarchy are increasing. Eventually, Soviet communism may face an ironic confrontation between communist political authority and the inexorable rise of an assertive working class.

Finally, a number of international problems contribute to malaise in the USSR. Among these are: (1) the crisis of the Soviet Empire in Eastern Europe, where Soviet hegemony is increasingly viewed as illegitimate; (2) the independence and hostility of the Chinese communists; (3) the rise of Western Eurocommunists whose increasingly successful, more open and pluralist, and above all increasingly independent parties are attracting East Europeans and gradually fostering alliances between East and West European communist parties; (4) continued inability, despite many temporary or limited gains, to replace its chief rival, the United States, in the many areas of the world where it has sought to challenge United States influence; and (5) a growing feeling that the Soviet form of communist ideology is not really the wave of the future.

Summary

In this section on malaise, we have argued that for somewhat different reasons, both the Affluent Capitalist nations and the Affluent Communist nations are running into serious problems. We have not discussed each nation separately, but we would argue that these problems are remarkably consistent, even though the causes and the symptoms may vary from country to country. We do not want to be metaphysical about this and argue that this coincidence must lie in something deep. It may be sufficient simply to say that after twenty-five good years it is time to have some bad ones. All kinds of bad habits developed during the twenty-five good years. Furthermore, after twenty-five good years, the old techniques no longer work. New techniques are needed, and the new techniques have not yet been devised.

The argument is very persuasive that the rich are not likely to be as well off for the next twenty-five years as they were from 1948 to 1973. As Chapter 7 makes clear, the same does not seem to be true of the Middle Income nations. It is true that in the past, the growth of the Middle Income nations depended very much upon the prosperity of the Rich nations but more and more the growth of the Middle Income nations is indigenous and relatively dependent on their own resources. While they have to export to the Rich countries, the intensity of the drive behind the essential line of exports is so great that almost no matter what the difficulties, the Middle Income nations will be able to cope. They will do better if there are fewer difficulties, and they will do worse if there are more difficulties, but it is a question of better or worse rather than of life or death. To some degree this is also true of the Poor countries, but for them the flexibility, the skills, the competencies, the drive, and the aggressiveness are all lacking or at least are not as strong as in many of the Middle Income nations. Therefore, the basic milieu and atmosphere can dominate the results more than in the Middle Income countries. Also, it is more of a matter of life and death for the Poor countries. We discuss all this further in Chapter 7.

INFLATION AND INFLATION CORRECTION

We indicated earlier that perhaps the single most important symptom of the current malaise (and an important cause as well) is stagflation—or at least the persistent inflation. If the inflation were controlled the malaise would not disappear, but it would certainly be sharply decreased for many groups and a number of other aspects of the malaise would be diminished. We have a classic vicious circle: many of the institutional problems that cause the malaise intensify and perpetuate the inflation, which in turn compounds the institutional problems and intensifies the malaise.

The current highly complex inflation has been extensively discussed for more than a decade. Our outline of Kondratieff theory noted that before World War II prices went up and down in long cycles. But, unlike all the other wars, there was no deflation after World War II. The ACNs got accustomed to a low inflation in the 1950s, but it did not persist. During the 1960s, when inflation rates began to rise and the dollar overhang started to be embarrassing, everybody slowly understood that something very threatening was happening.

There is now an extensive if controversial literature on the cause and control of inflation, its costs, and the various means to reduce or correct for these costs. We do not wish to review systematically these controversies, but we would like to make a few specialized points.

There is a great difference in the effects of an inflation depending on the degree to which it is anticipated, on the rapidity of various responses even when it was not anticipated, and on the kinds of action taken in response to either the anticipation or the actuality. If it is unanticipated and "money illusion" is widely held (the belief that money has a relatively fixed value), then some groups may not immediately insist on increased compensation to offset the effects of higher prices. (They may not have enough power or militancy.) If this occurs, there is an enormous transfer of wealth from creditors to debtors and from the private economy to the government. If the inflation is relatively anticipated, the transfer could go either way because there will have been uncertainty about the rate of inflation. Who gains and who loses will also depend on a number of other factors, such as the impact of taxes. Finally, if the inflation is over-anticipated, it makes the system more vulnerable to an inflation explosion, but it also tends to reverse the income transfer that occurs if there is under-anticipation.

Inflation, however, does more than just transfer income. It increases risks; it creates distortions; it decreases the efficiency of the system; it erodes morale, integrity, and discipline; and it destroys faith and confidence. How inflation expectations and corrections are built into the system determines the type and magnitude of losses, the specific pattern of wealth transfers, the erosion of values, and the distortion of attitudes. Before discussing these issues, we will examine—in a one-sided and simplified fashion—some of the theoretical causes, dynamics, and effects of inflation.

Monetarist Theories of Inflation Simplified

This simplified discussion attempts to explain just enough of these complex issues to our less-informed readers so that they will understand our position sufficiently for our purposes, even if they do not fully understand all the implications and nuances of the theory. We will illustrate our remarks with examples taken from the United States experience.

We start with the basic equation of monetary theory:

$$GNP = MV$$

In this equation, M is the total quantity of money available to spenders, and V is velocity, that is, the average number of times per year they spend it, or turn it over. The product is the total value of transactions, which is proportional to the GNP. Since V is normally defined by dividing the gross national product by M, we can take the proportional constant as equal to 1.

There is disagreement about the best definition of money. The most common versions are known as M_1 and M_2. M_1 is simply the sum total of the cash in the hands of the public and the total of demand deposits (the value of checking accounts in commercial banks). In March 1978 this consisted of $90 billion of currency and $250 billion of deposits, for a total of $340 billion. M_2 is M_1 plus the total amount of savings deposits in commercial banks. As of March 1978 this equaled a total of $820 billion.*

Many monetary experts think of M and V as being fundamental and the GNP as being a derived quantity—at least in the short run. That is, if M is the amount of the money (as defined in various ways)

---

*V_1 (the velocity of M_1) currently equals about 5.9 and has been increasing steadily for the past twenty years or so, while V_2 has remained roughly constant at about 2.2.

available to potential spenders, and V describes the rate at which these potential spenders turn the money over, then in this process of spending the money they create immediate short-run demand for gross national product. If there is enough capacity, this demand creates the physical output of gross national product. A greater demand for some goods or services than can be easily produced, creates upward pressure on prices, making the numerical value of the GNP increase more than the physical volume. The result is inflation. If the demand is too low there is surplus capacity or surplus product, which creates unsold products and services, which in turn create downward pressure on prices.

If one thinks of V as being relatively constant (or at least predictable) in the short run, then one can vary the value of the GNP, as measured in monetary terms, by varying the quantity of money. As indicated, the GNP can vary either because the actual physical output of goods and services changes or because the price level changes. The basic monetarist concept is that both can and probably will change but under different conditions. If the country is operating below capacity, an increase in money will probably induce an increase in the physical output of goods and services. This output increase will be followed by a rise in prices if the average expansion in the money supply exceeded average growth in production. If there is some strain on capacity, the price level will rise more rapidly. Monetarists argue that inflation is basically a monetary phenomenon dependent upon money supply or, in some circumstances, its velocity.

Recent experience in the major industrial countries strongly supports this simple view of the impact of money growth on output and price changes. This experience suggests the following sequence. Recessions are attacked by an expansion of aggregate demand, in turn stimulated by a combination of budget deficits and monetary expansion. For a short while output expands. Eventually, price rises follow, placing monetary authorities in an uncomfortable position. To prevent downward pressures, they are forced to further increase monetary growth. The underlying trend inflation rate rises to new levels after some delay. If the authorities then react sharply to the higher trend rate of inflation, the economy is pushed into a recession. Expansionary policy is then needed again to return to economy to full employment. However, each stop-go cycle of the economy starts at a higher trend rate of inflation, and pushes that rate higher in a ratchet-like fashion.

The close fashion between monetary growth and trend inflation can be seen for the United States in a simple chart prepared by Allan Meltzer reproduced in Figure 5.11. What this chart suggests is that the average rate of monetary growth for the past three years provides a

FIGURE 5.11
How Money Growth Affects Prices

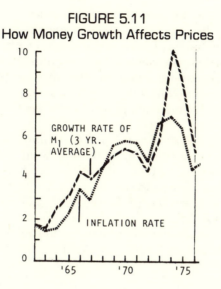

good rule of thumb estimate for the current trend rate of inflation. Furthermore, this suggests that wringing inflation out of the system would require steady and persistent declines in the growth rate of the money supply.

This concept is not as simple as it looks. Indeed, it is in some ways counterintuitive (as opposed to various cost-push and some demand-pull theories). We will elaborate it with an example. Assume that there is an increase in the cost of imported oil. Does that not automatically cause an inflation? The Monetarist would say no and argue that if the government kept the money supply fixed, the first effect of the price increase would be to force all economic actors to allocate a fixed level of purchasing power between imported oil and all other goods and services. Since the demand for oil is inflexible (at least in the short and medium run), more money is allocated to oil purchases, and there is then a decrease in purchasing power for other goods and services.* Eventually this will result in reduced production of the other goods and services. The ultimate effect would be a readjustment (usually painful) of the price level of other commodities so that average prices remain about the same.

There is great pressure on the government not to force that

---

*If the oil is imported this represents a real rise in costs to the country. It does, of course, induce a decrease in the standard of living or in savings. If the oil is domestic, it may just be a transfer of income to the owners of the oil and the average standard of living or savings is not necessarily affected.

readjustment. Usually, the government prefers some inflation—which diffuses the pain over a large number of people and over a longer time—so that very few people, if any, notice it at any one time. Furthermore, if there is a widely held money illusion, then most of the people concerned won't even know that they are hurt. Therefore, rather than accept a painful deflation, the government will expand the money supply to maintain purchasing power for the other goods and services.*

An increase in the price of oil does cause immediate inflationary pressure since prices tend to have downward inflexibility, but whether or not these pressures materialize depends on whether or not monetary policy accommodates it (i.e., is "permissive"). This position is now widely accepted, even by so-called Keynesians who tend to emphasize the stimulating or depressing effect of fiscal deficits and surpluses on economic activity and to downplay the importance of monetary conditions.† There are a number of differences between

---

*There is an interesting connection between the Keynesian and Monetarist theories. It turns out that very often the easiest way for the government to get more money into circulation is to run a deficit, issue bonds to pay for the deficit, and sell the bonds to the Federal Reserve in such a way as to create money. For a number of reasons, this is considered much better than just printing money. On the other hand, this is also the easiest way to finance a deficit. Thus, in practice, there may be no differences in the policies of the Keynesians and the Monetarists. They only differ in their interpretations of what is happening. However under current conditions, the so-called deficit that the American government is running is really not a deficit from the viewpoint of a genuine increase in the real value of the government's debt, but is a deficit only from the viewpoint of how it is financed in the sense of the creation of more money. Therefore, one can think in some sense of the current deficit as being more in line with Monetarist theories than with Keynesian theories.

†One can caricature Keynesian macro-economic theory as a simple investigation of aggregate demand. Keynes observed that under certain conditions it is possible for an economy to achieve a reasonably stable equilibrium at less than full employment of labor and capital resources. Given this possibility, a central government could push the economy to full employment of its resources by providing sufficient aggregate demand to induce multiple rounds of spending in the private economy. The primary tool by which governments were to influence aggregate demand was a budget surplus or deficit. An extension of this simple theory took the position that, in a severe depression, expectations about the future were so bad that monetary policy could not influence aggregate demand, leaving fiscal policy as the only possible macro-economic tool.

people who think of themselves as "mainly Monetarist" and as "mainly Keynesian" that strongly influence the analysis of inflation. These usually include:

1. Importance of quantity of money vs. interest rates
2. Size of gap between actual and potential GNP and employment
3. Importance of alleviating inflation vs. alleviating unemployment
4. Basic stickiness of prices and wages to downward pressures, the country's willingness to endure such downward pressures, and the costs of such downward pressures
5. Usefulness and practicality of various income policies (and especially of jawboning or various watered down forms of price and/or wage restraint)
6. Practicality and importance of fine tuning to avoid recessions
7. Importance of business profitability and of a positive political, legal, and social environment for business

The first point indicates that Keynesians tend to believe that the cost of money (that is, its interest) is much more likely to affect investment and buying decisions than the actual quantity of money (or near money) available to various purchasers or potential investors. Positions on this are consistent with each side's basic perspective. However, on the second point there is no equally logical connection between being a Keynesian and tending both to estimate potential GNP and potential employment on the high side and to think of the economy as being less than fully employed. Most Keynesians seem to do both. Monetarists tend to feel that the gap is smaller and inflationary pressures closer (or greater).

The two schools also tend, at the moment, to differ considerably—partly as a value judgment and partly because they differ on the estimate of its consequences—on the relative importance of reducing inflation or reducing unemployment. From the factual point of view, Keynesians almost always feel that prices and wages are very sticky and the country would be unwilling to endure the hardships connected with maintaining deflationary pressures over a long period of time. They usually feel that these measures would be ineffective and the consequences severe and unfairly distributed. Monetarists tend to feel that the country is (or could be) made much more willing to accept these hardships, which in any case they do not believe would be as great as the Keynesians estimate. They also tend to assess the alleged unfairness as either inevitable, bad luck, or exaggerated. Furthermore, they view inflation as equally likely to be unfair.

Some of the reasons for downside rigidity of prices and wages include:

1. Labor unions, welfare, unemployment insurance; multiple workers per family, and general affluence: all increase the ability and willingness of workers to resist pay cuts
2. Administered prices, "oligopolies" and other collusions among businessmen (and sometimes labor or government) that reduce competitive forces
3. Federally mandated rigidities that buttress 1 and 2 above:
   a. Price floors and supports
   b. Regulated monopolies
   c. Pro-union and "closed shop" regulations
   d. Import restrictions
   e. Minimum wage and mandated fringe benefits
   f. Various items on "Costs and Risks" table (p. 210)
4. Various built in escalators (i.e., built-in allowances for estimated inflation whether it occurs or not) in wage contracts, loans, much legislation, etc. that put upward pressures on wages and prices
5. Fear of price controls encourages business to raise or maintain list prices and inhibits price cutting (no one is willing to risk being stuck with low prices when controls are put in)
6. Increasing share of GNP going to government that is relatively unresponsive to market pressures
7. Other effects of inflationary expectations such as general slackness, carelessness, waste, and greater willingness to raise prices on any excuse.

The first three points are reasonably self-explanatory. Whenever one has a contractual obligation that includes a built-in fixed inflation correction (point 4), then one side has a vested interest in the inflation occurring and resists any pressures towards decreasing it. High fixed interest rates on bonds, for example, could become extremely onerous to the debtor if the inflation decreased. Similarly, the effect of the mandated increase in minimum wages in the United States in 1977 could raise wage costs and unemployment exorbitantly if there is low inflation. Furthermore, during any inflationary period there is great concern among businesses that price or wage controls may be imposed (point 5). Consequently, list prices are often set excessively high (and discounted unofficially) so that in the event, businesses will not be caught in a trap. This occurred in 1975 and 1976 and seems to be happening again in 1978.* It is difficult in an inflationary period to make accurate estimates and calculations. Owners and operators have the feeling that if prices and costs go up, the market will (immediately or eventually) accept them. This belief reduces the pressure to keep costs down. Furthermore, numerous costs cannot be kept down. All one can do is slow down the rate of increase, which is not as glamorous or as measurable a task as keeping down costs if the price level is fixed. Furthermore, in a long inflationary period, balance-of-payment problems become exaggerated and corrective measures become less effective.

Returning to our survey of the basic differences between the Monetarists and the Keynesians, even though the Monetarists tend to feel that prices are relatively flexible downwards, they usually don't believe in jaw-boning or other incomes policies. They regard the Keynesian tendency toward this to be a mark of their basically illusionary approach to economic issues. We tend to agree. For example, at a time when there was very little jaw-boning by either Nixon or Ford, American unions were quite responsible about wage increases, which barely kept pace with inflation. After talking to many union leaders, it seems clear that they might not have been so responsible if they had been jaw-boned. They were perfectly willing to restrain their wage requests to maintain the number of jobs and not to rock the boat. But if they had been singled out by the president to sacrifice the union members' interests for the sake of a larger whole, they coult not have afforded to go along. They would rather have been criticized for irresponsible behavior by outsiders than to risk the suspicion of union members that they were either currying favor with the administration or showing a lack of courage in representing the interests of their members.

At one time there was sharp disagreement between the two schools

---

*Many American businessmen believe that in 1975 and 1976, the United States economy was operated much like a huge Persian bazaar. Businessmen had to call up all over the country to get competing unofficial quotations on prices, and there was a good deal of haggling. This also occurs during normal times, but there was a huge increase in this kind of "price behavior." Businessmen everywhere were fearful of being caught with their "prices down." They even felt that it was worth losing a little business today, if necessary, to prevent this from happening. All this enormously decreases the efficiency of markets.

on the practicality and rewards of fine-tuning to avoid recessions. There has been such disillusionment with fine tuning that almost no one now claims that the economics profession has the skills to perform this wonder. During *La Deuxième Belle Epoque* most Keynesians felt that they had learned how to operate a nation's economy without any serious recessions. We believe that their policy successes were really the results of being in an upswing phase and thus being able to exploit the resiliency, flexibility, and toughness that is associated with such a *Belle Epoque*. Nevertheless, many Keynesians view the recent failures as a result of limited understanding of "supply side" shocks. This and recent policy statements suggest that the notion of "tuning," whether fine or coarse, is not dead.

Keynesian and Monetarist positions in theory come much closer together as the basic elements of each are studied and integrated into a systematic body of thought. In practice, the basic philosophical differences remain.* Keynesians take the position that government can and should intervene in economic affairs to improve overall welfare. Monetarists tend to argue that, in general, government intervention is counterproductive. Only when large and obvious gains and losses are at stake should market forces be interfered with. Regardless of the name put on policies from these two schools, these differences continue to exist.

We believe that it is terribly important—partly for the sake of balance and discipline—to have both perceived and real "down-side risks" in the system. A recession is the expression of such down-side risks. As such it can be a healthy and inevitable part of a growing dynamic capitalist economy. It allows or forces needed readjustments and consolidations of the various segments of the economy and it reestablishes financial and labor discipline. Occasional recessions are necessary to: (1) "teach lessons" on prudence, discipline, and care; (2) facilitate "creative destruction" (including the squeezing and elimination of marginal activities); (3) allow for adjustments in lagging sectors and a slowing down or using up of capacity in excessively leading sectors; (4) allow for assessment and reevaluation; (5) restore (or maintain) labor discipline; and (6) put other pressures on costs, waste, and inflationary trends. If it accomplishes all these

---

*It is important to note that Keynes' position is closer to what we have called the Monetarist school than to what we are calling here the Keynesian school. We will, however, continue to associate the post-war mainstream position with Keynes' name, as is the common practice.

things, then the GNP "lost" in a recession because the economy is operating below capacity can be an acceptable price for maintaining a healthy competitive system. It is not waste, but upkeep.

Recessions can not only be useful, but, under modern conditions, they are much less painful than they used to be—particularly the mild ones. It is therefore likely that a well-managed economy will—and should—have mild but relatively frequent recessions.

The economy has some similarities to an area prone to earthquakes. Relatively moderate earthquakes relieve strains and decrease the chance for a really big earthquake. Furthermore, they remind residents of the problem, encourage them to build better or elsewhere, and damage rather than demolish weak structures. Painful as this is, it is not as painful as total destruction. If, however, moderate earthquakes do not occur fairly often, then when one does occur it has to relieve all the accumulated stresses. This may be very disruptive indeed. In the same way, any attempt to operate a growing and dynamic capitalist economy without even occasional moderate downs (or at least growth recessions), as well as ups, is likely to face similar problems. Real economies and societies simply do not progress smoothly and without interruption, even during a *Belle Epoque*.

One of the problems with the capitalist system is that it depends enormously on business and consumers not only having confidence in the short-term prospects of the systems described in Chapter 3, when we discussed the New Emphases and Traditional Values, but also having great confidence that the rules will not be changed. For example, we have already mentioned that, once businessmen become afraid that price controls may be instituted, they have a strong tendency to keep their prices up and to hire and hoard certain kinds of manpower. Thus, even if the price controls worked during the period when they were needed, they leave a legacy that causes problems for a long time to come. This fear of the government changing the rules is justified. Often the government does not realize how poor its performance has been.

Consider, for example, the pattern in the steel industry. When demand is high and times are good pressure eventually builds up on steel capacity. This tends to occur late in the cycle. At this point, the government becomes very concerned with keeping prices down. Steel is a basic commodity, so a lot of pressure is put on the steel industry not to raise its prices. If the industry is making what the government says are reasonable profits the government can often be quite successful in applying this pressure. However, later on, when times are bad and the steel industry is losing money, the government tells them they ought to modernize. In effect what the government is saying is "heads you're even; tails you lose." Any industry must make a lot of money when the times are good to balance the times when they are bad.

This has simply not been allowed in the United States. In 1973, the Japanese steel industry was able to sell steel to the United States at more than 50 percent over the going price that the United States steel companies could charge. The import of steel was not under price controls. Under these circumstances the Japanese were able to build up quite comfortable profit averages that were very helpful during the bad days.

What makes the above kinds of situations worse is that people do not even realize the government has had this set of policies. Everyone was so concerned with keeping prices down when there was high demand for steel and so unconcerned about business when prices were low, that no one realizes that the steel industry is forced to play this no-win game. It is remarkable that the economists have been just as shortsighted as the government. Neither takes a long view and asks about the long-term consequences of policies and programs.

The basic trends over the last twenty years are clearly indicated by Figure 5.12. We used to think of inflation in the United States as being about 1 percent or so; it is interesting to note that when the Eisenhower guidelines were put in, the inflation that year was less than 1 percent. Today we are asked to tolerate and live with 5 percent inflation as normal. As described later, we personally do not believe that this is likely to be satisfactory in a country such as the United States, though such countries as Argentina have recently felt that 100 percent inflation was normal (at one point they reached a rate of 900 percent).

Costs and Distortions Caused by Inflation

Inflation imposes a wide spectrum of costs and distortions on economic activity. Specific details of these distortions vary from country to country, but the broad impacts remain the same. Most of our examples are drawn from the economy of the United States.

Consider a government paying a nominal 7 percent interest on long-term bonds (one can think of this as 2 percent real interest rate and 5 percent inflation premium). This correction for inflation really represents a repayment on principal; that is, it makes up for the fact that even though the face value of the bond is nominally the same, its

305

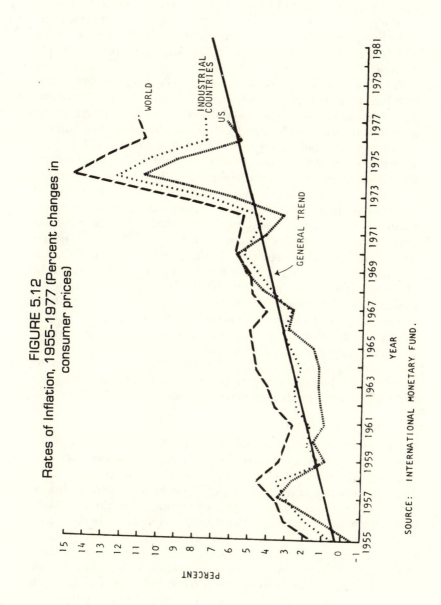

FIGURE 5.12
Rates of Inflation, 1955-1977 (Percent changes in consumer prices)

SOURCE: INTERNATIONAL MONETARY FUND.

real value goes down by 5 percent a year. The extra 5 percent that the bond holder collects simply corrects for this decrease in the real value of the bond. Because of the persistent money illusion, few people have understood or noticed most of the consequences of this simple concept.

The United States government, for example, has a net debt of over $700 billion. If there is an inflation of 7 percent, the real value of this debt goes down by about $50 billion. This means that if the government issues an additional $50 billion of notes and bonds, it has not increased its obligation in real terms but simply held its own. This also means that the nominal deficit should be decreased by about $50 billion, so that a nominal deficit of $50 billion in 1978 represented no real increase in debt. However, such inflationary refinancing of the debt has a hidden revenue benefit to the government, since interest income is taxed. If, however, one is concerned about the impact of government activity on financial markets, the current deficit (including off-budget agencies) is the relevant magnitude upon which to focus because it represents the net claim on the current flow of funds. Thus, the nominal deficit is also important when considering the impact of government on inflation. Since a significant portion of the deficit is financed by an increase in stock of money, an increase in the nominal deficit can represent a sharp monetary expansion in the economy.

The impact of inflation on the effective length of maturity and the treatment of nominal interest payments on operating (and tax deductible) costs can distort incentives enormously.

Housing as an Example

One example of how a badly corrected long-term inflation can distort the operation of the American economy was evident in the housing industry in 1978. Some said that the industry had recovered, but this was not entirely accurate. Demand for expensive homes boomed in 1978; it had been at an all-time high since 1976, while the rest of the housing market has remained pretty much in the doldrums. This boom in expensive homes is easily explained. During most of this period mortgages could be obtained for about 9 percent (or about 3 percent real interest and a 6 percent correction for inflation). People who make annual incomes of over $50,000 and reside in states with income taxes can often deduct more than 6 percent of their 9 percent mortgages from their income tax. This means that the cost of the interest to them is only 3 percent or less—at a time when the inflation rate is anticipated to be 6 percent. Thus they are borrowing at a negative real interest rate of more than 3 percent. This is very pleasant.

If inflation reaches 8 or 9 percent—a not unlikely prospect—then an equally pleasant capital gain will also be available. The value of the house will go up and the market value of the mortgage will go down so the total equity is greatly increased. The value of the house is likely to go up by more than the average inflation (recent experience shows that housing prices rise by about 5 percent more than the average inflation). Furthermore, confidence in this kind of "speculation" is heightened by the fact that, as a result of such negative interest rates, housing has proved to be good investment in the United States for the last twenty-five years. One has the impression that this kind of venture is not really a speculation but is actually a conservative investment—in fact, probably the only conservative investment available for protecting oneself from the ravages of inflation.[25]

The housing boom has become so intense that it was officially estimated in 1977 that about 20 percent of the buying of expensive homes in California was speculative. The buyer did not intend to live in the house at all but just bought it for resale. And the estimate of 20 percent was actually conservative in the sense that there was probably some speculative element in almost all buying of expensive homes, since the new owners believed that their investment would appreciate rapidly and thus willingly invested in and borrowed much more for the property than they normally would.

At the same time that the boom in expensive homes was occurring, relatively inexpensive housing stayed in a slump. People of modest means were unable to make the monthly installment mortgage payments which, because of inflation, were at least $100 greater than they would otherwise be. The interest rates included a hedge of about 6 percent against anticipated future inflation—which is actually an early payment on principal, showing up as increased equity in the house. Such extra payment transforms the traditional twenty-five-year mortgage into what is more or less a twelve-year mortgage since it in effect involves a more rapid repayment of principal. If the inflation continues at 6 percent a year, the value of the house doubles, and after about twelve years the buyer's equity in the house reaches 80 to 90 percent. It was this cash flow problem associated with such a rapid buildup of equity that caused the slump in low-cost housing. The usual view that it was caused by high prices is probably incorrect. The ratio of the price of inexpensive homes (not the average price, but the price of the kind of house people with incomes of $15,000 to $20,000 per year would normally buy) to family income was not that far from normal mainly because more wives were working. The cause of the slump was the disappearance of a true twenty-five-year mortgage. In this sense the huge increase in the costs of new homes gives an exaggerated picture of how fast prices have been rising and reflects the distortion of the market.

For a while, the situation was similar for a third category of United States housing: multiple dwellings. Potential investors in rental housing look for a return of 10 to 15 percent discounted cash flow after taxes, and they also want to reinvest earnings to make similar profits. If earnings are tied up in the increased value of the housing, they cannot be reinvested.

A different method of correcting for the inflation can be less distorting. For a brief example, we will make a suggestion that is probably impractical but illustrates our point. Assume that both the borrower and lender of a mortgage simply decide how much of the interest is real and how much is inflationary. Then, instead of adding the inflationary component to the regular interest rate, they simply index the principal of the mortgage. That is, they estimate that the mortgage will go up by 6 percent a year and say, "Let us increase the nominal value of the mortgage by 6 percent each year. This way the real value of the mortgage will be unchanged, and we will pay 3 percent of the new nominal value of the mortgage each year in interest."

Assume that the government does not allow that part of the interest rate indexed to the principal to be deducted as an expense. After all, it is not really an interest expense but is simply a correction to make up for the falling value of the dollar. In this case the cash flow problems of the lower income people will be greatly reduced because of the reduction of the size of their month payments. As a result, there would be an immediate increase in the construction of lower-priced houses. The enormous subsidy being given to the richer part of the community (which in some ways is desirable since it counteracts the excessive progressiveness of the tax system) is basically illegitimate because it is a subsidy which is not given by legislation.

The above arrangement would be satisfactory if the value of housing were to go up by about the same rate as inflation and the nominal increase in the mortgage was not subject to income tax. The major difficulty with doing this would be if the inflation varied over time, but this is not much different from the current situation where the correction is made on the interest. However, if one wished to improve this situation one could change the value of the mortgage not by a fixed rate but by a variable rate depending upon what actually happened to the various indices. This involves another problem. Which index does one choose? (These difficulties do not arise from our decision to use indexing of the principal but simply from our attempt to deal explicitly with the problem. The same difficulties arise in every other way of dealing with the problem, but usually they are glossed over or decided by the market's assessment of whatever way is chosen.) Let us assume that one uses the GNP deflator. For a number of reasons it is probably superior to the Consumer Price Index or the Wholesale Price Index, although it does not reflect directly the impact of inflation on the consumer's purchasing ability (presumably the Consumer Price Index would be better here) nor does it directly reflect the cost of building homes (presumably the Wholesale Price Index would be better here, or an index based upon wholesale prices and the cost of labor in the building industry).

What happens if the indices for houses in some areas are different from the general indices, particularly if it turns out that the housing does not go up as fast as the general inflation so that the protection offered by the value of the house will not really protect the lender? The actual experience, of course, has usually been the reverse, although not in all areas. Presumably the proper thing to do in areas where housing values seem unlikely to keep pace with inflation is to have shorter-term mortgages. The build up of equity in the house will then go much faster.

The purpose of discussing these inflation issues is to indicate just how distorting inflation can be in areas familiar to most readers (and, in any case, easy to understand) and how, if one addresses some of the problems directly, one may be able to deal with them.

Other Distortions

The problems are pervasive. Thus, in mid-1978, utilities paid about 9 percent on their bonds; one can think of this as 3 percent or so genuine interest and 6 percent or so as a correction for inflation. But the utilities and other companies are permitted to deduct the interest paid on bonds as a business expense; in effect, they are being permitted to deduct repayment on principal. Whether this profits the utility or not depends upon bookkeeping methods, regulations, and other institutional arrangements. Generally, however, there is no advantage to the utilities. Even though the replacement value of their plant may be increasing by 10 percent a year, they are not permitted to use this increase for rate setting. This means that the full 9 percent interest on their bonds is pushed through to the consumer as if it were an operating cost, causing very high operating costs in the short run (in the longer run there is a corresponding underpayment).

It would be more rational for utility companies to charge only 3 percent of the 9 percent interest as an operating cost (i.e., only real interest). Utility rates would then be lower than now, and would gradually increase over time and be more acceptable since customer income would rise at approximately the same rate if inflation is roughly the same for both. Such a change would require inflation correction for other parts of the balance sheet since partial correction may be worse than none at all.

Another distortion caused by inflation shows up in the proposal to buy natural gas from Algeria for four dollars per thousand cubic feet. This looks cheaper than expanding United States plants because capital costs are carried at full value, plus a 9 percent cost for interest. Imports or conservation, therefore, look cheap by comparison.

This problem is acute in the synthetic fuel industry. Almost all recent studies discuss at great length the cost of operating a plant to produce synthetic petroleum from coal or oil shale. This estimate is usually three dollars to ten dollars per barrel. Capital costs are estimated at thirty to ninety dollars per barrel per year of capacity. However, these studies devote no more than a couple of pages to converting this capital cost to an additional operating cost. In reality this conversion dominates the cost of output in any capital-intensive industry such as synthetic fuels and should be discussed and analyzed at great length. Table 5.9, from a Hudson Institute study, provides a dramatic example of the impact of inflation under various accounting schemes for capital cost conversion.

Normal business calculations yield capital costs per barrel ranging from thirteen to twenty-five dollars depending on assumptions. Treating the synthetic fuel industry as a utility and correcting for inflation reduces the cost to between six and seven dollars a barrel. Additional adjustments can reduce capital costs even further. At an extreme, capital cost can be reduced to about 10 percent of the high figure calculated using standard business assumptions. Many of the adjustments developed in Table 5.9 represent *ad hoc* adjustments for ongoing inflation and would be less important in a non-inflationary environment.

Extreme distortions of economic decision making, shown in the above examples, strongly support the argument that inflation must be either reduced or corrected, at least in key sectors. Entire industries could not operate today if they were not permitted to index the price of raw material in contracts and build cost-of-living escalator clauses

TABLE 5.9

Alternative Methods of Calculating Capital Costs/bbl. for a $1 Billion, 50,000-bbl./Day Synthetic Fuels Plant

	Return on Investment and Interest	Amortization (years)	Annual Capital Charges[a] or % of Investment	Capital Costs/bbl.[b]	
				300 Days[c]	330 Days[c]
Normal Business	15% R.O.I.	15	32.1	24.4	22.2
	15% R.O.I.	20	31.0	23.3	21.2
	10% R.O.I.	20	21.7	14.5	13.2
Normal Utility	1/3– 2% R.O.I. 2/3– 9% INT.	20	15.8	10.4	9.45
Add Inflation-Correction[d]	1/3– 7% R.O.I. 2/3– 4% INT.	20	10.39	6.92	6.29
Add GOCO (Government Owned and Contractor Operated)	3% INT.	20	6.72	4.48	4.07
	3% INT.	30	5.12	3.41	3.10
	2% INT.	30	4.46	2.97	2.70
	2% INT.	40	3.66	2.44	2.22

[a] Includes depreciation, interest, profit, taxes.

[b] Operating and other costs should be added to this.

[c] Assumed operating days/year.

[d] Correct 12 percent return on investment and 9 percent interest of Normal Utility for an assumed inflation of 5 percent to put calculation in real time.

Source: William M. Brown and Herman Kahn, *Suggestions for a Phase-II Energy Program* (Hudson Institute. A report prepared for the United States Energy Research and Development Administration, September 1977), p. 58.

into wage agreements. The "buyer" and "seller" simply would not be able to come to an agreement on the rate of inflation if they had to predict it years in advance and then be stuck with their predictions if they turned out to be wrong. If the private sector were forbidden to write indexed contracts, however, the collapse of these industries would be attributed to many other factors. In fact, only inflation (plus the legal restraint on contracts) would have been the real cause. Businessmen have invented indexing whenever it was absolutely necessary. Political pressure groups have used indexing for such things as Social Security payments. This is not to argue that all forms of indexing are beneficial, but only that it may be essential in certain key sectors and that the pressure to extend the number of activities indexed increases the longer or higher the inflation.

The Anticipation of Inflation

Let us examine the simplest case: no inflation is anticipated, but some occurs. If money illusion is maintained, people on a fixed income (in dollars) or who have various assets (denominated in fixed monetary terms) do not feel any great sense of loss. Yet a wealth transfer is taking place and two groups are gaining: debtors and the government. The gain to debtors is obvious. They repay loans with currency that represents a lower command over real goods than when the loan was issued. But the government gains in at least five ways from an unanticipated inflation:

1. As a debtor and disburser of fixed payments (pensions, welfare, rent, long term purchase contracts, interest and principal on the national debt, etc.)
2. As an employer (paying largely fixed wages)
3. As a recipient of seigniorage profits (can be considered as a debasement of currency or a tax on cash balances)
4. As a tax collector (brackets are moved downward in real terms; depreciation allowances are understated, nominal inventory gains, and high [i.e., inflation-corrected] interest rates all result in taxation of illusory income)
5. As a permissive umpire and bargainer, i.e., as a supporter of satisfaction and contentment (e.g., can exploit money illusion) and a reluctant appeaser of squeaking wheels and strong or activist pressure groups (e.g., advocates of full employment, high farm prices, public works programs, social welfare, etc.)

Many of these gains are eliminated or reduced, however, when inflation comes to be largely anticipated.

The first two gains cited above are self-explanatory, despite the large numbers. We have already mentioned that the United States government today has a net debt of about $700 billion. If inflation is 1 percent greater than anticipated, it "cancels" about $7 billion of this debt. The government's 1976 pension and welfare bill was nearly $154 billion, and its civilian wage bill was $42 billion—a grand total of about $200 billion. An additional 1 percent inflation, if not corrected for, would have saved the government $2 billion a year.

The third gain on the chart, debasement of the currency, is the traditional explanation for governmental induced inflation. These profits can also be quite high. On the United States stock of currency in circulation ($100 billion), each 1 percent of inflation gives the government about $1 billion in profit (assuming a purely domestic monetary inflation).

To the extent that a government collects progressive income taxes or capital gains taxes, it may gain enormously in an inflationary environment. Inflation moves the tax brackets downward (that is, relatively low income people are moved into higher brackets). If industry is on a FIFO accounting system (which most of the American industry was in the late 1960s and early 1970s), the increasing value of inventory is taxed. Finally, if industry is not allowed to deduct the correct amount of depreciation on its capital assets, profits are overstated. Such illusionary "accounting" gains are one of the worst aspects of inflation. A large jump in these taxes is induced only because the accounting system does not take account of the inflation. A tax of this sort can harm the net worth of a company and distort all kinds of transactions and relations.

An example will serve to illustrate the importance of inflation distortions on corporate balance sheets. Figure 5.13 estimates real retained earnings for non-financial United States corporations. If the balance sheets were corrected for illusionary monetary profits and understated depreciation, from 1967 to 1978 United States non-financial corporations paid dividends at such a rate as to create serious liquidity problems, thus reducing growth potential. It is most improbable that the boards of directors of many United States corporations would authorize dividends that would decrease growth potential for many years in sequence, but many must have done so unwittingly.

Perhaps the most important gain to the government is the last point. The government is always under pressure to spend more than

FIGURE 5.13
Nonfinancial Corporations: Earnings and Dividends

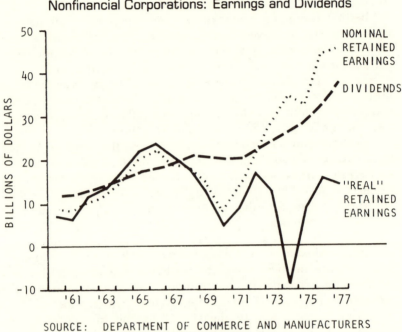

SOURCE: DEPARTMENT OF COMMERCE AND MANUFACTURERS
HANOVER TRUST COMPANY.

it has. It can painfully compromise by saying no to various interest groups, but this is often difficult. It is much easier to give the appearance of providing something to everybody. If the government finances this generosity by higher taxes or by selling bonds to the general public, diverting the public's purchasing power and savings to the government, this need not cause inflation, but it might create political difficulties since it explicitly "crowds out" certain types of private spending. The government is much more willing to accommodate these pressures by a permissive monetary policy that does cause inflation.

In general, as noted in point five, the government can exploit money illusion as long as it lasts and create satisfaction and contentment. That is, if the people who hold bonds, pensions, etc., do not notice or do not strongly object to losses in the value of their savings, and if those who gain are satisfied, it makes for a reasonably happy country in which business can be very prosperous.

If inflation is largely anticipated, almost all of the above gains are

TABLE 5.10
Average Maturity of Marketable Interest-Bearing
U.S. Public Debt, 1955-1977

Year	Years	Months
1955	5	10
1960	4	4
1965	5	4
1970	3	8
1975	3	0
1977	2	11

Source: U.S. Bureau of the Census, *Statistical Abstract of the United States: 1973,* 94th Edition (Washington, D.C., 1973); 98th Edition (Washington, D.C., 1977); *Economic Report of the President* (Washington, D.C., 1978).

eliminated or reduced except for the government's seigniorage profits. The government now loses more often than it gains. For example, by and large, people not only insist on an interest premium if they anticipate inflation, they also expect an additional premium because of the risk of further inflation. Thus, when inflation expectations were about 5 percent, long-term United States bonds were going for 8 percent, or at least 1 percent over what they would have gone for without the risk of inflation. (Actually, most people did not really expect an average inflation of 5 percent to continue for the full maturity, but they feared a burst of inflation that could wipe out a good percentage of the value of the bonds.)

It is true that the government still profits on short-term money. Taking advantage of these short-term benefits imposes the expense of having to shorten the average maturity of the debt. Table 5.10 shows how much United States government maturities have decreased in the past twenty years. This is an enormous disutility for the Federal Reserve Board, the Treasury, and United States monetary policy in general.

As an employer, the government is likely to find that it must give raises larger than those which just correct for inflation. Typically, it faces much increased militancy by its labor force both because of unionization and because of the increasing number of votes represented by government employees. However, most governments have yet to modify tax rules to adjust for inflation. Thus, they still gain enormously from the downward movement of progressive tax brackets, inflated capital gains, understated depreciation, and taxation of inflation-corrected interest income.

Many firms have adjusted their behavior where possible to correct for inflation distortions. For example, most United States firms have shifted from FIFO to LIFO accounting if there was any serious chance of large taxes upon illusionary inventory profits. More important, there is now much more tax evasion, tax avoidance, growth in the so-called underground economy, and a general depression of business. All these seriously depress tax collections.

Once people become militant, the major problems for the government are political. Inflation is now almost universally considered much more of a problem than unemployment. This has been true for most of the last five years but was not recognized by many people in positions of power, particularly liberal members of the New Class. These persons were so traumatized directly or indirectly by the Great Depression that until recently they could not imagine themselves arguing that inflation is more important than unemployment. Nevertheless, at various points during the recent recession, even the unemployed in the United States felt that inflation was the more serious problem. Most of those who were employed felt so even more strongly. As one congressman said, "Ten percent of the people in my district suffer from unemployment, but one hundred percent suffer from the inflation." As a result, most Western governments are as likely—or more likely—to lose an election because there is excessive inflation as because there is excess unemployment. The government can no longer think of inflation as creating satisfaction and contentment. The exact opposite happens.

One of the main reasons we think that governments may bring inflation under control is that in many countries of the world it is politically disastrous for inflation to get out of control.

Inflation Correction by Private Indexing

Money illusion cannot last forever. While many individuals may take a long time to react to a 1 to 2 percent inflation, they do not want to suffer this loss if they can avoid it. Reaction to a 2 to 3 percent inflation is much quicker and may make the system quite unstable. Eventually, both government and private employees will insist on higher salary increases; savers and investors will want higher returns, and so forth. There are two very different ways of correcting for inflation. One we call *pre-set*, which tries to estimate future inflation and then write the estimated correction into contracts ahead of time.

The other we call *ad hoc*, where one observes atual inflation and adjusts contracts based upon some index (the consumer price index, the wholesale price index, the GNP deflator, etc.).

It is often extremely important to use *ad hoc* indexing rather than the pre-set form. The rate of inflation is uncertain, and it may simply be too expensive and risky for both sides to hedge against this uncertainty. Consider for example, a twenty-year raw material contract. If mine owners wish to be protected from future inflation by a pre-set escalating contract, they would presumably insist on something like 6 to 8 percent. The buyers simply could not afford to guarantee more than 3 or 4 percent because they cannot lock themselves into a contract where they would lose a great deal of money if inflation fell much below 5 percent. It would be very difficult for these two sides to get together. If this market were forbidden by law to write *ad hoc* indexed contracts (or the law or custom simply didn't allow for such a contract), very likely the raw materials industry would collapse. Theorists would then produce a large number of multiple explanations for the collapse. Only the inability to index contracts would be correct.*

A similar situation could occur with long-range contracts for labor. It would not normally be possible for a labor union today to sign a three-year contract that had a fixed inflation correction of less than say 7 percent. The employer would probably not be willing to give much more than 3 or 4 percent, making it almost impossible to reach an agreement. Once again, many would insist on multiple causes for the militancy of labor and the recalcitrance of employers. However, the basic problem would be institutional—the inability to write a contract that was based upon an appropriate index.

Probably the worst defect of a pre-set indexing is that it creates a vested interest in continuing inflation. Consider, for example, a government bond that has a fixed interest rate of 8 percent for twenty-five years and is not recallable. If the inflation happens to go to zero, the interest rate on this bond is at least 5 percent more than it should be and represents a very high debt service cost. If a government had a large stock of such bonds outstanding there would be heavy pressure

---

*We prefer multiple explanations for most phenomena and are suspicious of single-cause explanations, but sometimes we recognize that a single cause is correct. It is terribly important to understand when this is so. The general bias against the seeming simplicity and narrowmindedness of those who argue for single causes of complex phenomena mitigates against even experts recognizing the single cause when it actually occurs.

to maintain inflation at least as high as the average inflation premium built into this debt.

Yet sometimes the appropriate index does not exist for *ad hoc* indexing. It is now generally recognized that the so-called cost of living index in most countries has exaggerated inflation so far as the country as a whole is concerned, because it focuses so much attention on urban prices. In the United States, the wholesale price index has been even worse because it double and triple counts many items (e.g., energy) and usually registers list prices, not transaction costs. The GNP deflator, though perhaps a better index for many purposes, it is not considered appropriate by either labor or employers.

Use of an appropriately specified index is very important. Indexing does create an inflation magnification effect and an incorrect index can cause a runaway explosion. In any system where indexing is an important element in private and public contrasts, provision of a well-constructed index by the authorities is imperative.

Furthermore, how the indexing is carried out can make a big difference. Consider a mortgage for a home. One can index either the principal or the interest rate, with quite different results from the viewpoint of the cash flow, and perhaps taxes, of the lender and the borrowers. We have already discussed how this change in the cash flow can make an enormous difference in the ability of various groups to conduct their business.

The Index Magnifier

Let us assume that: (1) some fraction R of all final transactions are indexed by some *ad hoc* system that works perfectly and that the rest of the economy is unindexed;[26] (2) inflation correction occurs every month; (3) a shock occurs that raises the index by some proportion S; and (4) there is a permissive monetary policy by the government so that there is no attempt to restrain the price level but just to accommodate these inflationary pressures without increasing them. Nominal GNP (Y_0) would then rise to $[Y_0(1+S)]$ if the structure of the GNP remains unchanged. At the end of the first month the total GNP would rise to $[Y_0(1+S)(1+SR)]$ because of indexing. Monetary officials, of course, will increase the money supply so that there is no monetary stringency.[27] The next month, since prices went up the previous month, nominal income would go up again—this time to $[Y_0(1+S)(1+SR)(1+SR^2)]$. One can develop the following equation to describe nominal income at any point in time.

$$Y_n = Y_0 \prod_1^n (1+SR^{n-1})$$

If the infinite product is permitted to converge on a new equilibrium, assuming no change in the level or structure of real income, one can approximate the rise in nominal income by[28]

$$Y\infty = Y_o \cdot e^{\frac{S}{1-R}}$$

Table 5.11 shows how inflation is magnified by indexing. If the economy is fully indexed (i.e., R becomes 1), the product does not converge and one would have a system prone to inflation explosion in which no shocks are ever damped out (at least in our very simple model). Since cash, cash balances in checking accounts, and other short-term debts are almost never indexed or indexed only in a very limited *ad hoc* fashion, this probably limits magnification to five or six even in an "almost fully indexed system." Moreover, the magnification is a measurement of the suffering imposed on the unindexed portion of the economy. The effect of the indexing is to shift the cost of the inflation to that part of the economy that is still measuring its income and wealth in relatively fixed terms. It has to accept more of a real income loss than it would if the rest of the economy were not indexed. In that sense, partial indexing is very unfair. However, no method of indexing is likely to be completely accurate. For a number of reasons the effects of the inflation are not uniform even if there are no such things as taxes or maturities of debt instruments to worry about. These make the situation much worse.

Indexing can be very useful, in fact essential, in certain areas. Yet universal indexing could be a disaster if it were simple-minded and automatic.

TABLE 5.11

Inflation Magnification Example: Nominal Income After Full Adjustment ($Y\infty$) (original level = 100)

R \ S	.01	.05	.1
.1	101.1	105.7	111.8
.5	102.0	110.5	122.1
.9	110.5	164.9	271.8

$Y\infty = Y_o e^{\frac{S}{1-R}}$

R = Proportion of income transactions fully indexed

Y_o = Assumed initial income level = 100

S = Proportion inflation shock

$Y\infty$ = Ultimate income level after the inflation shock has worked through the magnification process

Official Government Indexing

If used appropriately, official indexing can accomplish the following:

1. Increase downward flexibility of prices, wages, interest rates, and otherwise facilitate a soft landing from an ongoing inflation
2. Reduce the need to guess the inflation rate, reduce both expectations and adjustments to inflation, and restore faith and credibility in money and contracts
3. Prevent inflationary gains to government and others
4. Serve ends of *relative* social justice, business stability, and equity (at least the inequities are chosen by the government)
5. Prevent disastrous "anti-inflationary reactions" to a near inflation by a population that has already been made "allergic" or at least educated
6. Encourage savings and mobilize capital
7. Make accounting, decision making, and discussion realistic
8. Be done gradually or selectively

Under current conditions the most important issues may be numbers one and two. Point one makes it possible to use indexing to facilitate coming down from an ongoing institutionalized inflation; point two makes it possible to live with it.

Indexing is not a panacea. Indeed, it can be very dangerous. Inappropriate indexing can:

1. Try to compensate for the uncompensable, e.g., hide a real increase in the price of oil, or a change in international competitiveness
2. Destroy certain automatic compensatory measures that normally mitigate an inflationary shock and add automatic compensatory measures that increase the effect of an inflation or inflationary shock (i.e., increase the magnification factor)
3. Eliminate important lags, austerities, and political pressures
4. Destroy important utilities associated with "money illusion"
5. Cause the degree of inflation to be even more politically motivated and in effect create a new area for "bungling government interference" and for making the simple complex
6. Shift a magnified burden to the unindexed or less indexed groups

Inflation Trends

Various socio-economic explanations of inflation stress the militancy of interest groups and the consequences of their activities for the wage-price spiral. A better term than militancy might be "aggressive income bargaining" among various groups, especially industry and labor. Since World War II, both groups have had growing confidence in the government's capability to maintain full employment. For this reason, they were relatively unconcerned about the rather gradual inflation rates of most of the postwar period since they permitted wages and prices to be adjusted readily. Aggressive income bargaining put pressure on the government to provide accommodating policy, and the government acquiesced. Thus, pressure group militancy, although certainly an element, cannot be looked upon as *the* major cause of inflation. (However, the inflation itself can increase the militancy of various groups and cause over-anticipation of inflation, as well as great pressures toward inflation.)

Other factors at least as important include lessening public concern about the size of government debt, spending, and the use of deficits. This decreased concern occurred throughout the 1960s when the desire for the government to assume new obligations was accompanied by a rising tide of expectations in societies that were becoming more pluralistic. The phenomenon was initially confined to the United States and the United Kingdom, but it gradually spread throughout the industrialized world. A strong conviction emerged that economic growth is not only possible, but that the government can guarantee stable economic activity and that material well being will improve in the future. It can thus be argued that political attitudes underwent a dramatic transformation.

Major power groups after the war accepted the paternalistic role of government. In some countries this was new. Among the primary factors behind this acceptance were the changes in social values (especially rising concern about equity and income distribution problems) and the new attitude toward full employment. Both labor and management now supported government efforts to maintain full employment, which tended to create greater stability in industrial relations. Given this dramatic expansion in government obligations, the government emerged as the major consumer or allocator of resources in the Advanced Capitalist nations. The percentage of GNP spent by the government has steadily increased in all but a few of the ACNs.

As a consumer, the government has a very low level of resistance to price increases; it responds poorly to the market mechanism. Furthermore, a shift has occurred away from government expenditures that contribute in some way to capital formation toward transfer and consumption payments that are much less contributory. This shift reflects changing social attitudes toward the proper role of government.

Government's growing role as a consumer parallels its role as an employer. Government wages must be somewhat higher than the national average to expand government relative to private employment. If, as is generally supposed, government employee productivity growth lies below that in the private sector, average national wage growth will rise while average national productivity growth will fall. The net result is, of course, inflationary pressure unless restrained by tight monetary policy.

The high costs of compliance to the swelling mass of detailed governmental rules and regulations have demonstrated inflationary potential in most industrial countries. In addition, after World War II, the major industrial countries never really returned to normal peacetime military activity levels. For example, the United States maintained very high military budgets in comparison with pre-war levels (Korea, Cold War, Vietnam).

These changes in social attitudes and the role of government have added to claims on national output. The willingness of governments to finance these growing claims, often by deficits, permitted these new social attitudes to have inflationary consequences. Each claim has an inherent inflationary bias but becomes inflationary only if financed. (For an illustration, refer back to Figure 5.11.)

This evolution of social attitudes and the government's response are perhaps the central factors behind the upward drift of inflation rates after World War II, but they do not explain the price explosion of the early 1970s. (See Figure 5.12.) For this one must look at the international dimension of inflation. The inflation explosion of the early 1970s has a unique set of characteristics. Table 5.12 lists several factors that by themselves would have been somewhat inflationary. Together, they created a sharp inflationary burst. None of these factors represented problems easily handled by domestic policy. Adjustment to each required a real income loss to most countries, or at least the urban sectors of those countries. Governments were not willing to force rapid adjustment on their domestic sectors, and given the breakdown of the old fixed exchange rate system the proper mix of domestic and international policies was unclear. In addition, the impact of policy interdependencies among industrial countries was

TABLE 5.12
Elements Contributing to the 1970s Inflation Explosion

1. Coincidence of exogenous shocks and resultant similar policy responses (OPEC, crop failures, etc.).
2. Coincidence of business cycles in major countries (partly induced by policy responses to shocks).
3. Breakdown of old international monetary order and lagged response to massive U.S. deficits.
4. Convergence of rates of productivity growth among industrial countries over the 1960s without appropriate terms of trade change via either the exchange rates or domestic prices.
5. Accelerated change in a number of the socioeconomic factors contributing to the post-war inflation trend.

vastly underestimated. The net effect was an inflationary boom that both domestic and international institutions were unable to resist.

The International Monetary Fund (IMF) and other major international institutions were set up during and after World War II as a result of the same types of pressures that were felt by domestic governmental institutions. One of the major aims of the IMF, for example, is to permit domestic governments to maintain full employment and economic growth. There was little concern about inflation in this context because in the past, inflation had been temporary and usually limited to one or two countries at a time. Moreover, known tools of the economic art could cope with it. Since there was practially no concern over inflation when the IMF was formed, it had no built-in safeguards against it. Indeed, at the time of its founding, it was feared that the IMF might be deflationary.

As the international monetary system evolved into a *de facto* dollar standard, it acquired a severe inflationary bias. A fixed exchange rate system based on one or more key currencies provides little discipline for—and some would argue that it encourages—policies in the key currency countries that create a balance-of-payments deficit. As long as the surplus (non-key currency) countries are willing to hold the volume of funds represented by the key currency country deficits, the system operates well.* The United States deficits during the late 1950s

---

*Here we refer to private individuals and firms as well as governmental authorities.

and early 1960s manifested the desire of the major trading nations (both private and public entities) to acquire and hold dollars. However, the massive deficits of the late 1960s far exceeded the reserve and transactions demand of foreign entities for United States dollars.

One can associate the large deficits with improper financing of the joint Vietnam War–Great Society package. And one can link the collapse of the fixed exchange rate system to its inability to adapt to this inflationary pressure. The maintenance of fixed exchange rates under the Bretton Woods agreement, combined with the inability of the United States to devalue the dollar, the unwillingness of other countries to increase the value of their currencies, and the growth of the productive ability of West Europe and Japan produced a structural loss of competitiveness by the United States during the period. Under the circumstances, these United States deficits could only have been adjusted to if surplus countries had been willing to inflate incomes and prices at home. Since they were not prepared to do so, this resulted in great pressure on the entire Bretton Woods system, which ultimately led to its demise.

Recent interest in the one-world model for explaining world inflation by excessive monetary expansion reflects the observation that such high rates of inflation are impossible in the absence of liquidity growth. It is generally argued that the liquidity growth leads and causes the inflation. The argument is quite true, but it ignores the institutional changes, biases, and weaknesses that set the stage for excessive liquidity growth. Simple monetary restraint to cure the upward drifting base inflation rate without modifying the institutional problems is doomed to failure.

Most of the effects of this burst of inflation have washed through the system. Yet inflation rates in most countries remain high and in many cases are rising. On close examination, the basic factors underlying the upward trend of inflation show no sign of fading away. Looking at the recent operations of government trying to adjust to various shocks, we find that they have not significantly changed how they go about their business. There are still many politically powerful conflicting claims on output, and governments still tend to be much involved in issues of equity and income distribution. By necessity, the government's role in these areas continues to expand, reflecting, if anything, expanded concern with social issues by the electorate.

One can speculate about what kind of government measures would stimulate a further lowering of inflation rates. If the factors mentioned above continue to have an inflationary bias, one cannot expect inflation rates to fall significantly below trend unless something fundamental changes. This something is the approach to solving social and ethical questions. Since a wealthy economy is going to want to cope with these issues, the question is how a government goes about doing so. Correction of inflationary bias requires innovative program design and a recognition of the true cost of the various programs taken in the aggregate.

The implications of this long-term rise in the inflation rate raise questions as to the sensitivity of an economy to external shocks. Higher inflation rates appear to render an economy more sensitive to them. It is clear that such shocks had dramatic effects on all economies in the early 1970s. The expectation of inflation has a much stronger influence than many economists concede, although most now agree that the burst of inflation since the early 1970s has created expectations of more inflation. These expectations are unlikely to change unless there are some major changes in the socio-economic structure. Since World War II, the expectation of slowing rising rates of inflation has been incorporated into the very fabric of society. Inflationary expectations are fundamental to the whole argument. Eradicating them is a formidable task.

These remarks have deliberately ignored the dramatic differences in inflation rates among the industrialized countries. For example, West Germany and Japan have largely controlled their inflation, and probably at less cost than their critics estimate. They provide useful examples of what can be done.

Notes

1. In the United States, most upper-middle class intellectuals would prefer being caught in almost any embarrassing situation rather than be seen driving a new Cadillac or new Lincoln. This is not because they associate these superior cars with wealth and power. They associate them with the Mafia, the successful Jewish contractor, the newly wealthy square black— and who wants to be associated with any of these? One result is anti-automobile campaigns under the guise of pursuing other objectives, e.g., some of the current energy conservation programs that mandate small cars.

2. One should be quite careful in trying to force these issues. For example, we would argue that it is almost certain that in the next four to five years there will be a revolt against the stringent weight regulations to be imposed on American made cars. Most middle class Americans insist their cars be usable in recreation and leisure time pursuits: to visit relatives and friends, to go on picnics, or to go camping. A large car is essential for such purposes,

particularly if you plan to take along three children, the dog, and such indispensable accessories as grandmothers and a bicycle. It may well turn out that the automobile companies will lose hundreds of millions or billions of dollars in investments that are currently mandated by law but that will almost certainly be changed in the next five to ten years, especially if EPA standards prove too onerous or if there is substantial improvement in energy prospects. In that case, the environmental restrictions will be met easily by large cars. Furthermore, some Americans are already evading the forced move to smaller cars by using light trucks, which are even less energy efficient and more polluting than "family size" cars.

3. It can also, however, lock a society into measures that are simply counterproductive or excessively expensive. In such cases the alarmists often create self-fulfilling prophecies. I know of no person who knows anything about the subject who believes that saccharine or cyclamates are dangerous from the viewpoint of changing the rates on one's insurance policy. Whether or not they pose some measurable risk is an open issue. Obviously if there is one chance in ten thousand over a lifetime of injury and there are some 4 billion people at risk there are going to be 400,000 injured people—and that's a lot of people. Nevertheless, it is not the kind of risk that most people take seriously. I myself would be quite surprised if the actual risk is as high as one in ten thousand. I have no objection to the government banning things that might kill or harm 400,000 people a year, so long as the ban does not inconvenience or hurt important groups to any substantial extent. I believe the ban on cyclamates and saccharine will do precisely that.

For those who are interested, the enormous fuss raised about the effect of flourocarbons on the ozone layer is quite legitimate from one point of view. However, even the alarmists do not think that the increased ultraviolet radiation would be as dangerous as spending a couple of weeks at the beach or moving to a higher altitude.

4. "Can We Survive Technology?" by John von Neumann, in *Fortune*, June 1955.

5. Herman Kahn and B. Bruce-Briggs, *Things To Come: Thinking About the 70s and 80s* (New York: Macmillan, 1972), pp. 210-213; and Herman Kahn, William Brown, and Leon Martel, with the assistance of the Hudson Institute, *The Next 200 Years: A Scenario for America and the World* (New York: William Morrow and Company, 1976), pp. 185-187.

6. Economic Report of the President, Washington, United States Government Printing Office, 1978, p. 209. (Emphasis ours.)

7. See, for example, *Silent Spring* by Rachel Carson (Boston: Houghton-Mifflin, 1962). This book was more fiction than fact; yet it was taken as gospel. More than anything else it seems to have triggered the whole environmental-ecological movement. A silent spring of the sort Mrs. Carson suggested never existed and probably never would have occurred as a serious general problem even under a bad situation—at least not as a norm. I suspect that history will judge its impact to be constructive, but I forgive many of my technological and scientific friends for frothing at the mouth whenever they

see approving references to it. Two excellent articles by William Tucker place Carson and the movement she inspired in a broader context: "Environmentalism and Leisure Class," *Harper's*, December 1977; and "Of Mites and Men," *Harper's*, August, 1978.

8. HI-2638-RR, October 30, 1977.

9. For a detailed and comprehensive statement of our views about energy problems see *Let There Be Energy* by William Brown and Herman Kahn (forthcoming).

10. See William Brown and Herman Kahn, *Suggestions for a Phase-II National Energy Policy* (Croton-on-Hudson, N.Y.: Hudson Institute, HI-2698/2-RR, November 1977).

11. GEOSOLFUS: The major "external" or renewable energy sources: *geo*thermal, *sol*ar, and *fus*ion. Advanced fission reactors (or the ability to extract uranium economically from low-grade ores or sea water) could also be considered to be inexhaustible. *Solar* includes indirect uses of the sun's energy: wind power, bioconversion, ocean thermal gradient, etc.

12. Herman Kahn and Anthony J. Wiener, *The Year 2000* (New York: Macmillan Co., 1967), p. 196.

13. See Kahn, Brown, and Martel, *The Next 200 Years*.

14. James Q. Wilson, *Thinking About Crime* (New York: Basic Books, 1975), p. 4.

15. Ibid., p. 5.

16. This definition is simplified. A more sophisticated definition would include various adjustments to account for bond financing and closely held firms. See George M. Von Furstenberg, "Corporate Investment: Does Market Valuation Matter in the Aggregate?" *Brookings Papers on Economic Activity* (2:1977), pp. 351-55.

17. See Frank Armbruster, *Our Children's Crippled Future* (New York: Quadrangle, 1978).

18. The reader who examines the graph in Figure 5.9 will note that in the 1950s black adolescent unemployment was not much higher than white adolescent unemployment. Over the next fifteen or twenty years, unemployment among black adolescents rose steadily to the extraordinary levels that it has reached today—and it reached these extraordinary levels before the 1970s recession. There are a number of causes for this, but basically it is a result of mismanagement. It cannot be changed in a year or two.

It is terribly important that something be done about this situation. Present programs are not only inadequate and inefficient but sometimes grossly disgraceful. For example, there has been a summer employment program in which the young people enrolled in effect had "no show" jobs. They were required to appear only to pick up their checks. Finally, an official in the large city where this was occurring became indignant and created public pressure for a change. The net result of the furor was that now the youngsters show up—but spend their time on the job playing cards and watching television. As a result, the program makes them less employable, rather than more. At the Hudson Institute we believe that practical programs exist, some of which have been proved effective in practice, to improve the situation in the short, medium, and long terms. It is past time that we started implementing these programs.

19. The United States average price is about $9; world price landed on United States shores is about $14. This makes the United States average price about $5 below the world price. Since the United States uses about 6 billion barrels a year, this is, in effect, a $30 billion subsidy for the consumption of oil.

20. William E. Simon, *A Time for Truth* (New York: Reader's Digest Press and McGraw-Hill Book Company, 1978).

21. Ibid., p. 142.

22. Ibid., p. 143.

23. See *Canada Has a Future* by Marie-Josée Drouin with Barry Bruce-Briggs (Toronto: McClelland and Stewart, Ltd., 1978).

24. United States Central Intelligence Agency, *Soviet Economic Problems and Prospects* (ER77-10436U, July 1977).

25. I have been very bothered by this. As far as I could tell in 1978, almost every well-off person that I knew of or could check on was fully invested in housing or the equivalent and consciously trying to take advantage of this negative interest rate. However, when I was young I was taught what at that time was called the Eleventh Commandment: "when everybody else is on the bandwagon it is the time to get off." I feel that the Eleventh Commandment is a very sound principle, and yet I don't feel that it applies at this time in this particular case. I rather expect that most of the people concerned will in fact make money—at least for a while. Clearly, it should mean that at some point we will see a huge over-building of expensive homes.

One thing that alleviates the problem is that the government has stepped in very firmly to try to prevent speculation (buying homes by people who have no intention of living in them, but only for resale). Moreover, the implicit speculation by homeowners is not as bad as it might be because, if the bottom falls out of the market, most home owners will hold onto their homes if at all possible and there probably will not be the catastrophic dumpings that would occur in other types of markets. Furthermore, if the inflation moderates, unless there has been a catastrophic drop in values, most home owners will be able to renegotiate their mortgages. This last, however, is by no means certain.

26. In this context, "unindexed" means without adjustment for inflation. This may occur because a sector is too economically weak to obtain a proportional adjustment in compensation or because it has a money illusion, believing itself to be unhurt by the price rise. The importance of such groups would be expected to diminish over time. A group that keeps pace with inflation without a formal contractual arrangement is considered indexed.

27. We are also, of course, assuming a credit system where all flows take place instantly and there are no lags in the effects of increases in money supply or other such real world complications.

28. This approximation overestimates the multiplier, with the error larger the greater is R and S.

6

Two and One-Half Heroes of Development: South Korea, Taiwan, and Japan

South Korea, Taiwan, and Japan exemplify the special relationship between the neo-Confucian cultures and the rapid emergence of a super-industrial world economy. Despite severe initial handicaps, all three have, in their own ways, successfully exploited *La Deuxième Belle Epoque*. Up to now, the first two have successfully—indeed superbly—adapted to *L'époque de Malaise*. Japan has done moderately well but is bedeviled with various institutional problems and a pronounced loss in effective leadership. South Korea and Taiwan also illustrate why we think the Middle Income countries, especially the New Industrial countries, will continue to grow rapidly.

The achievements of all three are now beginning to be taken for granted. It is often forgotten that conventional wisdom held that they were all considered almost hopeless cases and that their prosperity depended upon the continued prosperity of the Affluent countries. The current relatively high morale, commitment, and managerial and economic competence of the first two also provide a stark and useful contrast with what is going on in almost all of the Advanced Capitalist nations—including Japan.[1]

One of the most impressive achievements in all three countries is that their rapid growth has been accompanied by an increasingly egalitarian income distribution, a feat many economists previously considered impossible for a non-communist developing nation. Almost all their populations have contributed to the national achievement and have shared in the gains. All three have unquestionably been "heroes" of development. Principally by good management and hard work, they have lifted themselves from abject poverty to middle income levels in less than a decade. South Korea and Taiwan also deserve to be singled out to balance some of the criticism that has been leveled at them.

These two nations are now within a decade or so of becoming fully mature industrial economies. Along with some of the other rapidly growing Middle Income nations they should soon become full-fledged members of the Affluent group of nations. They will be the first new nations to make this transition since the early starters, the industrial nations of today. In this sense, South Korea and Taiwan clearly illustrate the Great Transition.

Although it is well understood that Taiwan and South Korea have done spectacularly well during their takeoff, especially between the early 1960s and early 1970s, it is less generally realized just how well they have done during the difficult recession environment of the last five years. Both are resource-poor nations with export-oriented economies. They were especially hard pressed in a world economic environment where resource prices sky-rocketed and trade fell. Thus, their performances during this difficult period are even more spectacular than the figures in Table 6.1 indicate.

Like the rest of the world, Japan, South Korea, and Taiwan were strongly affected by world inflation. In Japan and Taiwan, inflation got out of control. Both governments then instituted very severe and unpopular measures which succeeded in restraining inflation, but also precipitously depressed their growth rate. Both countries accepted these costs as the only way to curb the inflation. I believe that their analysis and value judgments were correct.

South Korea chose to accept the costs of a higher rate of inflation to maintain the pace of economic growth and, by devaluating their currency by 25 percent, to maintain export growth (presumably at the sacrifice of higher inflation rates). In retrospect, it can be argued that the Koreans "gambled" (i.e., took a well-thought-out, calculated risk) that the recession would not prove unusually deep or protracted. Had it been much worse than it was, they might have fared badly indeed. The South Koreans also managed to maintain a rapid pace of growth by rapidly and aggressively moving into new areas, especially overseas construction projects in the Middle East. They demonstrated their "flexibility," a particularly impressive aspect of their economies. They also followed sufficiently cautious fiscal and monetary policies to prevent an explosive inflation—even though the money supply and demand for goods was greatly inflated by overseas earnings. As a result the South Koreans averaged 8.5 percent growth in the two recession years of 1974 and 1975, and averaged about 13 percent in the next three years.

Whether it was the South Koreans or the Taiwanese and Japanese who pursued the best strategy is moot. The important point is that all three have both done extremely well in a particularly adverse

TABLE 6.1
Economic Growth and Inflation Rates: South Korea, Taiwan, and Japan[a]

	Japan		South Korea		Taiwan	
	Real Growth	Inflation	Real Growth	Inflation	Real Growth	Inflation
1963	10.5	7.8	8.8	19.7	8.5	3.2
1964	13.1	3.7	8.6	27.8	11.4	10.6
1965	5.1	6.7	6.0	15.0	10.4	7.2
1966	9.8	4.9	12.0	11.8	7.8	9.0
1967	12.9	4.1	7.2	11.1	10.4	10.7
1968	13.4	5.3	12.8	11.1	8.9	7.9
1969	10.7	5.3	15.2	10.0	8.6	5.1
1970	10.9	7.6	8.6	12.8	10.8	3.9
1971	7.4	6.2	9.8	12.1	11.7	2.8
1972	9.1	4.4	7.3	11.9	12.0	3.0
1973	9.8	11.8	16.4	3.1	11.9	8.2
1974	-1.3	24.3	8.3	23.8	0.6	47.5
1975	2.5	11.9	8.8	26.3	2.4	5.2
1976	6.0	9.3	15.3	15.4	11.5	2.5
1977	5.1	8.1	10.3	10.1	8.1	6.3
1978[b]	5 to 7	5 to 7	14 to 15	10 to 12	10 to 11	6 to 7

Left margin annotations: STILL LA DEUXIÈME BELLE EPOQUE (adjacent to 1966–1970); L'EPOQUE DE MALAISE (adjacent to 1975–1977).

[a] IMF, International Financial Statistics, May 1976, May 1977, and April 1978. 1977 growth and inflation rates provided by New York Representative Office.

[b] Estimates based on ROC and ROK government projections after first quarter, 1978. Initial official estimates were ROK 10 to 11% and 11%, ROC 8.8%, 5.4%.

Note: Japanese forecasts based on projections from various institutions reported in *Management Japan*, Vol. 11, No. 1 (Spring 1978) p. 25.

environment, mostly by good management. Had the South Koreans believed it useful or necessary to cut their inflation rate more sharply at the cost of their growth rate, they would have done so. The decision not to do so was a conscious choice not dictated by political fears or political weakness. The high growth rates of the two NICs during the last few years resulted from a readiness to act decisively, to cut losses, and to adapt to changing conditions more than anything else. Had either country followed a business-as-usual policy, the results almost certainly would have been disastrous. This is, roughly, what the Japanese did. But we will discuss the Japanese reaction after first examining South Korea and Taiwan in more detail.

South Korea and Taiwan

As examples of economic development, South Korea and Taiwan deserve attention from three perspectives.

First, their experience tends to highlight the key factors in economic development, including a balance between the political and the non-political, between the old and the new, and the importance of human versus material resources. Despite severe initial political and economic problems both have achieved rapid economic growth without great natural resources, indigenous capital, or advanced technology. Their success can be specifically attributed to cultural factors favoring development, excellent management of the economy, the favorable international and technological climate for growth during *La Deuxième Belle Epoque,* foreign aid, and, quite simply, hard work and dedication.

Second, these economies are prototypes for other developing nations. The literature on economic development often seems preoccupied with the problems and failures of developing nations. There is much that can be learned from mistakes and difficulties, but even more can be gained from studying successes pointing out the available opportunities. We increasingly believe that these two economies also have some important lessons for the Affluent countries.

We think of these two economies (and the pre-oil shock Japanese economy) as somewhat analogous in economic development to the Carnot cycle in engineering—a thermodynamically efficient cycle that shows what a perfect engine can do. Engineers measure other cycles against it to see how much improvement is theoretically available. In this sense South Korea, Taiwan, and pre-oil shock Japan can be considered about as economically and technologically efficient as developing nations can reasonably be. This is not to say that they do or did everything flawlessly, that all aspects of their societies invite emulation, or that other developing countries can simply copy them. We do believe, however, that all three economies hold useful lessons. South Korea and Taiwan typify other developing nations in important ways. (Yet there are also differences. I have already noted that neo-Confucian cultures enjoy advantages over many other cultures and that South Korea and Taiwan were under great external pressures not to make any serious mistakes.)

A third reason for being especially interested in these countries is that the very rapidity of their development tends to telescope the development process, thereby dramatizing many characteristics that are normally obscured. Like a time-lapse film of a growing plant, speeding things up can reveal characteristics of the growth process that might otherwise escape notice. Twenty-five years ago all three countries had very poor traditional agricultural economies (even the Japanese were basically rural). Today South Korea and Taiwan are transitional economies, soon to be reclassified as "mostly developed," and in the next five or ten years Japan will pass the United States in per capita income. In another twenty-five years South Korea and Taiwan should both be mass consumption nations. What has taken Japan a hundred years to achieve—and other nations two hundred—South Korea and Taiwan are likely to achieve in fifty. Thus, they dramatize and highlight the four-hundred-year transition period that we expect will lead to a new post-industrial world order.

The development experience of all three indicates how important it was for them to focus initially on overall economic growth rather than redistribution of income as the basic development strategy.* The initial growth was particularly impressive because it brought with it early and almost as a by-product a more egalitarian distribution of income and wealth than is found in most other countries. Some socialist states have achieved a more egalitarian distribution of income and wealth, but only at great economic and human costs.

All three have dramatically increased wealth and living standards at all levels of their societies. This has been widely recognized for the

---

*Japan and Taiwan, and to a lesser extent South Korea, of course, were partial exceptions to this since they have had quite extensive land redistribution programs and special programs to favor and assist the farmer. (South Korea has had the latter only since the *Saemaul*—rural development—program was introduced in 1970.)

Japanese economy (though today many Japanese feel hard pressed financially) but not so widely for the South Korean and Taiwanese. The basic point about Taiwan was stated concisely and well in a recent World Bank study:

> The record of the Taiwanese economy between 1950 and 1970 indicates the coexistence of high and rising growth rates, the gradual elimination of under-employment, and an apparent improvement in the size distribution of income. Taiwan thus may constitute one of the very few exceptions to the somber findings of Kuznets and Adelman who, on the basis of time series and cross-sectional evidence, found a prevailing U-shaped relationship between growth and distribution over time. Taiwan thus points to the possibility that there may be no necessary conflict in other countries, even in the short term, between growth and income distribution. The generally observed U-shaped relationship must be viewed as not inevitable in nature, but subject to control by man.*

The same characteristic has also been observed in South Korean experience:

> In the post–World War II economic history of South Korea may be seen a development process that benefited not only the upper- and middle-income groups, but also the poorest members of society, whose welfare was substantially raised. This process had three distinct phases. First came a phase lasting from 1945 to 1952, in which assets were redistributed but there were no major dynamic changes; second was a dynamic asset redistribution phase, from 1953 to 1963; and the third phase, from 1964 onwards, was a redistribution-cum-asset-value-realization phase, that still continues.[2]

Taiwanese and South Korean Development as Both Typical and Atypical

The three nations have done so spectacularly well for so many years

---

*Hollis Chenery, *et al.*, *Redistribution With Growth* (New York: Oxford University Press, 1975), p. 285. We would argue, however that, while the last sentence is largely correct, the spectacular performance of South Korea and Taiwan depended on the very special circumstances of having neo-Confucian relatively homogeneous cultures and very unforgiving external political environments that made achieving good government, having a high commitment to economic growth, and good management relatively easy—or at least necessary for survival. The two countries also had extraordinarily competent and versatile work forces.

that their performance is now often taken for granted or construed as so exceptional as to be *sui generis*—a tautology, in that the experience of every nation is unique. In the sense that the neo-Confucian culture that they typify appears to be *today* significantly more suited to economic development than any other, it is extremely unlikely that their success could be equaled by many nations. But it does not follow that they are thereby more exceptional than many other nations, including some often singled out as models of development or modernization. On the contrary, South Korea and Taiwan are in many ways quite typical—much more so than is Japan. From our point of view they have the added advantage of illustrating through their atypicalities some of the "myths" about or misleading or misunderstood aspects of the development process.

Measured by the attention they have been given in the literature on economic development (especially as models), the two most prominent nations are China and India. Important in population (containing respectively about half of the Middle Income population and about two-thirds of the Coping Poor) and gigantic in area as well, these unquestionably merit special and extensive attention. But it is not all clear that these continent-sized nations are appropriate examples for other developing nations. They are exceptional, perhaps more exceptional, than the extraordinarily successful city-states of Singapore and Hong Kong. India, for example, has sixteen official languages and about seventy major languages or dialects. In mainland China, virtually every province has its own distinct spoken language, even though the written language is the same. Both countries have a multitude of racial and cultural differences while offering, because of their geographic and demographic size, market possibilities for economies of scale that are out of the question for the great majority of developing nations.

Basic limitations also exist in relating current development experience to that of earlier eras. The developing countries of the past (today's developed countries) were for the most part major or great powers fifty or one hundred years ago. With the exception of Japan, they were all Western peoples, representing the technologically most advanced and militarily strongest nations of their time. By the beginning of this century they had divided most of the rest of the world among them. The modernization and industrialization of their domestic economies was directly related to expansion of their empires, territories, and spheres of influence as they sought to insure adequate supplies of raw materials and markets for their finished goods. Their motivation was enhancement of national power and prestige; their means included military aggrandizement and colonial empire-building as important additions to internal economic development and normal trade.

In contrast, there are over one hundred developing nations today. With the exception of China and India, and possibly Brazil and Indonesia, none could be classified as great or potentially great powers. For the most part, they are new nations, often created artificially out of colonies dismembered in the post–World War II period. Their governments are commonly run by military strongmen or juntas unrelated or only indirectly related to traditional sources of legitimate power. They are quasi-democratic or authoritarian, greatly concerned with the problem of legitimacy, and commonly plagued by coups. In the non-communist sphere, they are neither bound by nor do they bind others by "unequal treaties."[3] Technologically, their economies are very backward compared to the developed countries. Unlike their predecessors, these are small new nations struggling to catch up in a world still dominated militarily, politically, technologically, and economically by the traditional great powers.

Perhaps of equal importance is the tremendous change that has taken place in the world economy in the last twenty-five years. A nation industrializing in the late 1970s and 1980s had options that were nonexistent fifty years ago. First, the scale of the world economy has dramatically increased. Amounts of capital, levels of demand, and new technological advances enable projects that would have been feasible only in the developed world to become increasingly feasible for the developing world. Second, manufacturing industries that were once limited to the developed economies are increasingly moving to the developing economies for economic reasons. "New" industries such as electronics are providing opportunities for developed and developing economies alike. New institutions and sources of capital (foreign aid, grants, loans, the World Bank, regional and local development banks, and even more important now commercial banks, multinational corporations, and the Singapore and Eurodollar markets) have been created. In sum, a new nation developing in the late 1970s and 1980s is doing so in a world changing so rapidly, and already so different from the past, that the lessons of the old developed countries are hardly a fair guide for the problem and choices that lie ahead.

In this context the recent experiences of South Korea and Taiwan may be viewed as relatively typical. Both are small nations created out of former colonies after World War II. Taiwan at that time had 6 million people (now about 16 million) and South Korea 20 million (now about 34 million). Both are non-Western in race and culture and had belonged to Japan rather than to a Western power; hence they had possibly the least direct exposure to Western culture of any colonies. As former colonies, each had some infrastructure left from the colonial period but had economies directly tied to Japan (about 99 percent of exports). They had virtually no preparation for self-rule, although Taiwan came to be governed by a well-educated and experienced elite from the mainland. Both had primarily rural economies whose exports were almost totally primary commodities. They had traditional feudal land ownership systems of absentee landlords and tenant farmers. Per capita income was a few hundred dollars, and there were no bright prospects for capital formation. Understandably, at the end of the war, both were considered all but hopeless cases. No one seriously thought that they could become significant, viable economies on their own.

At least in terms of today's popular image of developing countries, these characteristics would tend to underline the apparent hopelessness of their situations. Both were already densely populated by world standards and faced both massive immigration problems and very high population growth rates; today Taiwan is the most densely populated and South Korea the third most densely populated country in the world. Neither had any significant natural resources. Both had largely subsistence economies, had suffered considerable damage in World War II, and had independence rudely thrust upon them, followed by major complications.

Their problems were further aggravated by major inflows of refugees—and for South Korea, by involvement in a devastating war. Before 1945 the exports of both countries were managed exclusively by repatriated Japanese nationals. Exports then virtually collapsed. The sudden liberation precluded an orderly transition period. When Taiwan became a remnant of the Republic of China, its limited resources were immediately used to support Chiang Kai-shek's military campaigns.

After the defeat on the mainland, about two million mainland Chinese fled to Taiwan, swelling the population to about eight million and creating severe internal strains between the Taiwanese Chinese and the new arrivals. There was even concern that an open conflict would break out between the two groups. Severe riots occurred in 1947. The prospects that an integrated Taiwanese society would emerge and successfully develop the economy seemed dim. The industry of Taiwan was damaged during the war, and severe strains had been put on its limited economy to support the losing

Japanese effort. Taiwan had few resources to cope with such a large immigration.

South Korea's achievements are even more impressive. When Japanese rule came abruptly to an end, South Korea's population was sixteen million. Within a year, the figure swelled by 21 percent as Korean forced laborers were repatriated from abroad and refugees poured in from the north. At the same time, some seven hundred thousand Japanese civilians and seventy thousand Japanese civil servants left, depriving the government and the economy of any continuity or preparation for self-management. The division of Korea, the first in over twelve hundred years, was itself traumatic. It deprived the south of the major coal deposits that were a basic source of South Korean wealth—of virtually all of its heavy industry and of almost all of its developed power capacity. Industrial production after the war fell to about 15 percent of that in 1944.

The American occupation authorities seemed unable to cope with anything beyond the basic problems of an orderly transition of refugees from abroad and repatriation of Japanese. They provided little financial or managerial help for Koreans, who were attempting to establish their first self-government in thirty-five years. After the liberation, Japanese-owned facilities were turned over to the United States military, who were ill-prepared to administer the transformation of these industrial assets, many of which were badly damaged by vandalism or poor maintenance.

Hardly had South Korea begun to get back on its feet when it was all but totally destroyed by war. During 1950 the North Koreans fought down the peninsula and then were driven back above the thirty-eighth parallel. Seoul was almost wiped out, changing hands four times. Almost one million South Korean civilians and an estimated three hundred twenty thousand soldiers were killed. Property damage, estimated at $2 billion, ruined almost the entire infrastructure of the country. After the Korean war, South Korea had to start again from scratch. In addition, it faced a heavy defense burden and the necessity of coping with a real external danger which continues to the present day. If these countries had not developed, they would have had a plethora of persuasive excuses with which to "explain" their lack of progress. What requires explaining is, "How did they do it?"

Pathways to Economic Growth

How did these seemingly helpless countries, with relatively few natural resources, transform themselves into two of the world's most successful economies in so short a period? Certainly some specific tangible factors, particularly the unusually large amounts of American foreign aid and military spending, played key roles. But these were much less important than the policies implemented by the respective governments and by intangible cultural factors.[4] Even their difficulties can be seen in retrospect to have been advantages. The continuing danger to each country clearly acted as a spur for a shared internal effort and justified the sacrifices needed for independence and development. This factor is not unique in history. The belief that the survival of the nation itself was at stake is usually considered the primary motivation behind the rapid and extraordinarily successful development of Japan in the early Meiji period. This was also true for the Soviet Union and, to some extent, the other Advanced Capitalist nations. However, this motivation was very unusual in the post–World War II era.

Cultural advantages are hard to pin down, but we believe that they were central to success. Both countries have homogenous populations that share, in their separate ways, a neo-Confucian culture. Despite the initial conflict between the Taiwanese Chinese and the mainlanders and the differences in their spoken languages, all Taiwanese share a written language and cultural heritage. The Republic of China in Taiwan has consistently stressed that it is the only legitimate protector of the revered traditional Chinese culture. This has served to bind together all of the population.

To say that Chinese culture has always been well-suited to industrial development is an oversimplification. China was at first hostile to industrialization in all its forms. What has made the economic development of these countries particularly successful is that they, like Japan, have managed to assimilate the old with the new. The strains brought about by exposure to the outside world and the difficulties of war and independence destroyed specific characteristics of the traditional culture without destroying the culture itself.*

China continually resisted encroachment by the West, permitting

---

*In Confucian China for example, the scholar was the most prestigious individual in the hierarchy; followed by the landed peasant, the backbone of the society; followed by the artisan; the businessman and the merchant were at the lowest level. The scholar today still enjoys great prestige, but the businessman has risen to a level comparable to that enjoyed by bureaucrats in Confucian China. Large business organizations are closely tied to the government officialdom and clearly distinguishable from small merchants in these dualistic economies. In both South Korea and Taiwan, but more in the former than the latter, even lesser merchants have relatively high status if they are reasonably successful.

Western influence only under pressure. Japan, after initially accepting the Portuguese and the Christian religion, closed itself off under the Tokugawa Shogunate for a period of about 250 years, until it too was forced to accept modernization to preserve itself. Korea became known as the hermit kingdom because it tried to protect its ancient culture from modernization. Traditional Chinese Confucian culture, in its various forms and to varying degrees, has been hostile to modernization and to changes caused by Western thinking.

Korea in particular, and China to a lesser degree, resisted much more strongly than Japan. Historically, Japan has been much more receptive than China to outside ideas, although not to outsiders. Even during Japan's 250-year period of officially-imposed insularity, many Japanese intellectuals readily accepted considerable seepage of ideas—especially technological ideas. In the years immediately preceding and immediately following the Meiji restoration, the Japanese educated classes were generally eager to accept foreign thought. Many Japanese wanted to go even further; the first Japanese minister to Washington, for instance, seriously urged intermarriage between Japanese and Westerners, a suggestion that would have been inconceivable in Korea. In both Japan and Korea intermarriage symbolizes a complete "de-Japanization and acceptance of a new civilization"; in China it symbolizes the absorption of the foreigner into the superior Chinese culture.

We want to stress two points about this cultural issue. First, many aspects of traditional culture that have survived in South Korea and Taiwan have been preserved for their own sakes and not because they are directly useful for economic development. Indeed, some that may be averse to development have nonetheless been deliberately retained; it is by no means true that either country has ruthlessly sacrificed everything that stood in the way of economic development. Second, many aspects of traditional culture, such as mythology and the sense of heritage, have simply defied eradication.[5]

Most of the elements of the traditional Confucian culture that would tend to restrict modernization and economic growth had been seriously eroding in both South Korea and Taiwan since the time of Japanese colonization. Conditions in both countries immediately after independence therefore permitted radical changes in land and business ownership and in managerial elites. Most of the productive land in Korea had been owned by the Japanese; it became available for Korean ownership after independence, thereby facilitating land reform. The American authorities also exerted pressures which may have been decisive.

The Japanese occupation of Korea eroded the credibility of the Korean king and his court, making a return to traditional Korean governmental patterns almost impossible. In addition, a Japanese preference for the lower-rank nobility, particularly professional bureaucrats, over the old establishment created a climate favoring upward mobility after the war, at least for the middle class. Korean Christians (then about 3.5 percent of the population) and intellectuals who were educated overseas in exile during the occupation had an extremely important impact.

The situation in Taiwan was comparable. The abandonment of Taiwan by Japan and the sudden influx of a "foreign" leadership from the mainland were factors that made land reform much more feasible than in most new countries. Land reform gave tremendous initial impetus to economic growth. The establishment of small farms and the elimination of tenant farmers in favor of small landholders, when done competently, has repeatedly been an important factor in stimulating agricultural development in the early stages of modernization. (The impact of land reform in Iran, for example, has been almost as profound but left a much greater legacy of bitterness among the mullahs and other traditionalists.)

The substitution of collectivization for land reform is extremely ineffective by comparison. Collectivization is met by resistance from small landholders in virtually all countries where it is attempted. Countries that might have carried out effective land reform have not done so, often because of the popularity of socialist thinking, both in socialist countries and among many Western and Westernized intellectuals.[6]

In the economic development literature of the last two decades, land reform has often been viewed primarily as a device to redistribute existing assets. Our view is that land reform can be much more than this. It can also be an endorsement of free enterprise, a means to provide upward mobility for the masses, and a pathway to the creation of that most stable political system—one based upon a large number of independent freeholders. Because agricultural improvement is the backbone of economic development and modernization in most economies, it is even more important than small-scale free enterprise—what we refer to as Marginal Input Organizations, or MIOs. In principle, both play the same role. Successful farming requires entrepreneurship, modern technology, and investment. Since farming is a business, it is not surprising that agricultural productivity is overwhelmingly greater in Taiwan and South Korea than it is in mainland China and North Korea.

Like all devastating wars, the Korean War broke down barriers and facilitated upward mobility and the redistribution of income. In itself, this of course did not guarantee that South Korea would do well or in any sense compensate for the incredible suffering and destruction wrought by the war. The war destroyed South Korea's most important physical assets and created about five million refugees. It was followed by rampant inflation, estimated at 500 percent between 1953 and 1957. For the first time, the military became established as the most important element in the society. However, the war also shattered the established order and opened opportunities for people from all segments of the society.

South Korea's early postwar economic recovery was not nearly as impressive as the spectacular growth that began with the *coup* that brought President Park to power in 1961, but it was impressive nonetheless. Industrial production rose between 1953 and 1958 by almost 14 percent a year, and the overall rise in GNP during this period was about 5.5 percent. However, the economy had little sense of direction and the political leadership was corrupt. Disquiet grew among those not in power; the masses continued to live desperately poor lives. During these years even economic aid was a mixed blessing. While aid kept people alive, the large imports of grain were disincentives to improving Korea's own agriculture. The South Korean economy was certainly not about to take off. It looked instead as if it would remain hopelessly dependent upon United States assistance for decades to come. The dramatic changes in the economy occurred soon after President Park's rise to power.

The South Korean Takeoff

Most of the specific policies implemented by the Park regime in its initial stages were not extremely successful. Yet the regime brought a sudden, dramatic increase in economic growth. In our opinion, the increase resulted from political stability and a favorable climate for economic development. Park had the military firmly under control, and the military virtually monopolized power in South Korea. By contrast, Syngman Rhee never completely controlled this key group and had lost what control he had before leaving office. From the initial announcement of the *coup d'état*, the slogan of the Park regime was "economic development first." And the tough policies that were implemented shortly after the *coup* reinforced the credibility of this slogan despite intermittent failures.

Some of the Park's most important measures were designed to aid the farmers. Within the first year agricultural credit at low interest was expanded thirty times from pre-1961 levels, and the government took over a considerable portion of the high interest debt. At the same time, the government levied heavy fines against many big business-men of the Rhee era in an effort to break up fortunes created by corrupt practices and to rechannel funds into productive industrial development. Additionally, the government promulgated a drastic currency reform in 1962, and severely curbed political demonstrations and related activities that had hindered economic activity.

These actions took place in the context of an earlier alliance between the military and the students, who at that time (and currently) looked to the military as agents of reform. As inflation and other severe economic problems persisted, the military government lost some of its reformist credibility but retained its reputation for getting things done. From this perspective, political stability and willingness to make tough policy decisions proved more important than the specific measures themselves.

The Park regime was free from dogma or ideology and willing to learn from its mistakes. Initially favoring the existing economic strategy of import substitution, it soon shifted to an outward-looking policy favoring export promotion. This proved to be the most important single change instituted by the Park government. Both Taiwan and South Korea are now considered classic examples of successful export-oriented or outward-looking economic growth. The key South Korean economic policy measures were instituted in 1964: increased incentives to exporters by means of preferential loans; income tax reductions; indirect tax exemptions; and devalua-tion of the *won* by almost 50 percent.[7] Korea went on a floating exchange rate in early 1965.

Although the economic measures were central we wish to stress those aspects of the outward-looking strategy that cannot be directly classified as economic. They have received less attention, but we believe that they were equally significant. One of these was the recognition of Japan in 1964, thus permitting close trade relations between the two countries.

This step required considerable courage and was highly criticized by many Korean intellectuals. The Rhee regime used anti-Japanese sentiment as the primary basis for developing national unity, second in importance only to the all-important question of surviving the North Korean threat. Although Japan made considerable investment in Korea in the colonial period and instituted practices that greatly facilitated economic development, it had been a brutal colonial master. In the 1930s Japan tried to integrate Korea and Taiwan totally into the Japanese nation, but as second-class citizens.

Anti-Japanese sentiment was thus deep-seated in Korea, particularly among the educated elites, many of whom had been in exile before independence. These elites composed the backbone of the pre-Park South Korean government and business establishment. President Park's decision to recognize Japan and reduce tension and ill-will between the two neighbors was farsighted. He recognized that Japan would in the medium-run and long-run become South Korea's most important trading partner. It was, in a sense, an "anti-anti-colonial policy." (We discuss in Chapter 7 how the Ivory Coast has also used anti-anti-colonial policies to further economic development.)

Another factor contributing to growth was that the government began not by building industries or worrying about foreign ownership (direct foreign investment was virtually non-existent), but by looking abroad to see what Korea itself might do, thus following the basic strategy of Meiji Japan. An important part of this approach, for example, was the establishment in 1964 of the government-subsidized Korea Trade Promotion Corporation (KOTRA). KOTRA was given a charter to promote Korean exports abroad and to conduct market research to see what industries or businesses Koreans should go into.

The turning point for South Korean exports occurred in 1963. The import substitution policy had led to the development of manufacturing industries to provide consumer goods for the South Korean people. However, when foreign assistance declined in the late 1950s, demand declined, and manufacturers found themselves with substantial unused capacity. In 1963 manufacturers (particularly in textiles) turned abroad, and exports jumped from less than $10 million to about $40 million. At the same time, the government removed restrictions on imports of intermediate goods, enabling manufacturers to use their foreign exchange earnings for new investment. With government stimulation, growth mushroomed.

The South Korean economy has been primarily dynamically reactive, actively and aggressively looking for areas where South Korea has a comparative international economic advantage. From this perspective, the strategy can be described as one of flexible growth capable of reacting rapidly and effectively to changes in the world environment. The driving force behind this strategy has been what might be called super growth industries. These did not exist ten years ago but are now capable of expanding by 50 or 100 percent or more per year because they operate in an area where the country has a definite comparative advantage.

Perhaps the single most impressive example of this flexibility has been the spectacular recent expansion of the overseas construction business. South Korea began to export construction services in 1967 at a total value of about $11 million. With the onset of the oil crisis, South Korea (the third largest importer of oil in the developing world) used this rapidly growing capability and considerable experience in operating overseas to go directly to the Middle East in an attempt to try to balance its huge deficit with OPEC. As a result, construction exports almost doubled in 1974 and in 1975 totaled more than $800 million, more than 50 percent over the original goal, which had itself seemed incredibly ambitious. South Korean business in the Middle East, in terms of contracts signed, rose from about $88 million in 1974 to about $733 million in 1975, representing over 90 percent of total overseas contracts. As of the period from January to August 1976, construction contracts totaling perhaps $1.5 billion were signed in the Middle East.[8] They have more than doubled since then.

South Korea's construction exports are by no means limited to this area. South Korean overseas contractors are doing or planning extensive business in southeast Asia, the Pacific region, Africa, and Latin America. These construction companies, like other super growth industries in Korea, operate essentially as transnationals in competition with companies from the most advanced countries.

Some Useful South Korean and Taiwanese Strategies and Tactics

The strategy of flexibility begins with a focus on marketing, searching out new opportunities where the comparative advantages can be exploited. This strategy merits study by other developing countries, most of which lack this important insight and perhaps the capability as well. Taiwan has an even greater involvement in the international market than South Korea; in fact, Taiwan's international trade (sum of its imports and exports) exceeds its gross national product. While these two countries may well be particularly suited to the development of this "flexibility," South Korea and Taiwan in practice simply adopted many policies and organizational models from others, something any country can do. For example, KOTRA was essentially patterned after JETRO in Japan. In principle, there seems to be no reason why other countries could not follow suit to an appropriate extent.

KOTRA is but one of many government-sponsored organizations designed to aid domestic manufacturers. Others include the productivity centers of South Korea and Taiwan that serve as both watchdogs and helpers, deliberately attempting to improve the quality of the nation's output. South Korea and Taiwan patterned themselves on the Japanese model (as has Singapore). As examples, they are of greater relevance because both countries, unlike Japan, entered their takeoff stages during the post–World War II period, and both of them are small nations lacking large internal markets or market potential.

Economic growth in all developing countries, including South Korea and Taiwan, is basically a catch-up rather than a pioneering phenomenon. For most, the initial focus can not be on trying to establish a balanced economy or on setting up a complete industrial structure on a small scale, but on export. In this respect, their development greatly differs from Japan whose catch-up growth from the Meiji Era onward focused primarily on the internal economy. But developing internationally competitive industries is essential for them, much more than for Japan either in the past or today.

Dramatic changes in international transport and communications have made direct involvement with the international economy possible. In contrast with Japan, which sent a handful of government-sponsored advisers abroad a century ago to observe and adapt what they saw, South Korea and Taiwan have operated in an extremely decentralized fashion. Their principal means of communication has been through self-motivated and self-sponsored private citizens from a wide variety of backgrounds and interests. Thus, the super growth industries of these countries were by and large not funded, determined, or controlled by the government. Rather, the government provided information, protection, financial incentives, and a stable, generally favorable investment climate. Aside from traditional monopolies, the government has retained control in industries considered important to the ultimate growth of the economy but insufficiently profitable for private investors to risk their capital. These include certain heavy and chemical industries into which these countries are not moving on a private basis. Thus, the "infant industries" in both economies have not been expected to provide foreign exchange, but to provide materials necessary for the long run, such as steel. As these businesses prosper, they are being gradually sold to the private sector (e.g., South Korea is now opening fifty government-owned industries to private investment).

Nationally Created Industries

The experiences of South Korea and Taiwan support our assertion in Chapter 5 that the value of the bourgeoisie in creating an industrialized society has not diminished since Marx wrote about it. It is no longer a question of public versus private ownership, nor is it a classic conflict between capitalism and socialism. It is rather a question of inefficiency versus efficiency. The examples we have cited above are government-created organizations that behave as if they were privately created corporations. These are characteristic not only of South Korea and Taiwan, but of a number of other developing countries, including Singapore. They are also directly comparable to public corporations created in Japan in the early days of Meiji, and to some extent to those in other advanced countries including even the United States (e.g., TVA). How well they perform (e.g., one can compare and contrast Brazilian or Malaysian or Indonesian public "capitalist" corporations with, say, Indian, Algerian, Ghanian, socialist ones) appears to be directly related to the degree that they are run as private operations as much as to any social or cultural factors.

The Pohang Steel Mill, for example, is a wholly owned government venture representing South Korea's first attempt in modern steel manufacture. It was initially conceived as a one-million-ton-per-year facility. Pohang managed to turn a profit for the first year, even though a capacity of this size for a modern integrated steel mill is generally thought to be inefficient by international standards. (It must be admitted that it benefited by steel price increases when it started production in 1973.) Pohang has since expanded to 2.5 million tons a year and has been preparing to double that capacity in 1979. This expansion was authorized by the government, but the contract for it was being competed for by private companies (particularly Hyundai) as well as by Pohang.

Pohang illustrates the principle of running a government corporation under much the same conditions as a private corporation. It has special preferences in terms of financial guarantees, and its initial capital is put up by the government. But if it fails to perform, not only is its management subject to immediate change, but its mandate may be given to a private enterprise with a better proposal or record. This way of operating—which exists also in Taiwan (e.g., the China Petroleum Corporation or China Shipbuilding Corporation), to a great degree in Brazil, and to a lesser degree in most other developing countries—can be sharply contrasted with government industries in such advanced countries as England, where inefficiency because of political pressures and a lack of a truly competitive environment is notorious. Even in the advanced countries where inefficiency can be "afforded," there are increasing pressures for change. An example is French Prime Minister Barre's program proposed in the late 1970s to reconstitute France's national industries on an internationally competitive basis.

One of the key characteristics of nationally created industries in South Korea and Taiwan that sharply differentiate them from those of the developed world is that they have been created out of nothing, as opposed to having been consolidated out of old and declining private businesses. And they represent a trend *towards* private enterprise rather than *from* private towards public enterprise. Simplistically, both types could be described as socialist enterprises; in reality they are miles apart.

Since the early postwar period, international development experts have recommended creating capital markets by transforming publicly created businesses into private entities by selling off government ownership, both to improve performance and to stimulate private local ownership. One of the best examples of how this is being done today is the Retser Engineering Company (RSEA) of Taiwan established in 1956 by the Republic of China government in Taiwan. Established by the Vocational Assistance Commission and seen initially as a means for constructively employing retired military personnel, this company focused extensively on welfare programs ranging from medical care to vocational education. RSEA was given as its first job building of the east-west cross-island highway that bisects the mountainous backbone of Taiwan through the northern part of the island. It began with twenty-two pieces of old construction equipment, a capital of $300,000 and three thousand unskilled workers.

After two decades this company has evolved into Taiwan's largest heavy construction enterprise. It employs more than twelve thousand men (of whom more than fourteen hundred are engineers), uses more than seven thousand pieces of modern equipment, and has sales of well over $1 billion. As RSEA has grown and diversified, it has become international and has pioneered in Taiwan's overseas projects. It was involved in all of the Ten Major Projects of Taiwan, and will be involved in the Twelve New Major Projects designed to replace these as a goal, as well as in international operations, particularly in the Middle East. It is still a "welfare-oriented" company, but it has reached a degree of prestige where it can be selective when reviewing applications from both retiring military personnel and civilians. The company reflects the country. It is upwardly mobile, and its current plans call for transformation to a truly private multinational company by selling half its stock to private investors.

In discussing the Japanese, South Korean, and Taiwanese development experiences we have deliberately avoided the word *model* to emphasize that the economies of all countries are unique. The term *development model* is overused in the literature of economic development and encourages a tendency to overgeneralize and to focus only on broad strategic approaches instead of conveying equally the crucial details on how to go about the job. It is important to have concrete and inspiring images of what some countries have done and how they did it, but the images are not always relevant to a specific local situation. Focusing on overall "models" often distracts attention from the essential task of adapting general concepts to particular localities. And this, of course, may make the difference between success and failure.

Rather than give a balanced picture of the South Korean or Taiwanese development experience we present here just a few specific aspects of South Korean and Taiwanese development that illustrate points we have been making. We also think that experiences are generally transferable and thus merit detailed study as working parts of any overall models used by decision makers in developing countries. If properly adapted to local conditions, several of these concepts could become the basis of a strategy for development.

In such areas as land reform and national planning, very detailed studies are available, but industrial parks and the *Saemaul*, for example, receive little attention in the literature on economic development. They seem to have little romantic appeal and are of no more than marginal interest to most professional economists and planners.

On the other hand, we have found that these are precisely the kind of specific and practical programs that development officials are most interested in. Officials from a number of countries are actively studying them on an informal basis reflecting grapevine communications rather than open publicity. This neglect is unfortunate because such ideas could be of considerable practical importance to many countries that know nothing of them. We believe that "comprehensive industrial park development" in particular may turn out to be one of the most important new tactics for industrialization to have appeared in the last two decades, both for the developing nations and for many developed nations.

The "Industrial Park Strategy" for Economic Development

Setting aside land for industrial use by creating so-called industrial parks has been a common practice for many years. They have been refined to such a degree in the last decade, particularly by Singapore, Taiwan, and South Korea, that the parks themselves can be regarded as a basic strategy for industrialization. If properly run, they can make it easy for a foreign or domestic entrepreneur to set up and operate a new activity—or expand an old one—with a minimum of hassle, red tape, cultural problems, and the like. Industrial parks in Taiwan and South Korea have also been combined with comprehensive development schemes to include all aspects of urban or regional development and have been specialized to meet specific needs. They have become central elements of national and regional plans.

The industrial park strategy for economic development offers key advantages for both slow and for fast growth countries such as South Korea, Taiwan, and Singapore. By simplifying bureaucratic procedures, cutting red tape, and decentralizing in an organized way many of the diverse requirements for industrialization, it greatly reduces the risk that bottlenecks will disrupt or slow down growth.

The first and most famous modern industrial park is Jurong Town in Singapore. This project began in 1961 when the government established the Jurong Town Corporation, which subsequently developed factory sites and infrastructure, including ports, warehouses, water, electrical and communication requirements, roads and rail connections, as well as housing and educational, social, and recreational facilities (including a huge Japanese garden and an eighteen-hole golf course). The town is in every sense a city in itself, developed in planned phases. The first phase, completed in 1968, totaled 3,650 acres; it has since been expanded to 14,000 acres and includes 600 factories and housing, shopping, office, and educational and recreational facilities for a total of 75,000 workers and their families. Land in the Jurong complex has been set aside for heavy industry, light industry, and special industrial activities. The Jurong Town Corporation has expanded its activities to include, for example, two free trade zones; it has thus become a key planning and operational organization for Singapore, along with the Housing Development Board and the Singapore Port Authority.

The Free Trade Zone (or Export Processing Zone—EPZ) can be the key element in this kind of planning in itself. Its obvious objective is to attract foreign investment exclusively for export. Although free trade zones have existed in Europe since the 1950s, the concept of developing one as a comprehensive industrial park originated in Taiwan. In 1965, the government of the Republic of China in Taiwan passed a law establishing EPZs; the first was set up in Kaohsiung in 1966. The initial 68-hectare area was intended for 120 companies but was quickly filled. Over 160 factories now operate there.

The success of this first effort led to the development of two more zones, one at Nantze, eleven miles north of Kaohsiung, and another in Taichung. By September 1975, more than 260 factories were operating in these three EPZs, employing over 62,000 workers. The total capitalization came to about $160 million. Of this, about $105 million was outright foreign investment, about $16 million overseas Chinese investment, and about $29 million joint ventures; the rest was local investment. The total value of exports from these zones was over $500 million in 1974, about 10 percent of all exports.

Taiwan has played a key role in assisting other nations to establish their own EPZs. For example, South Korea, the Philippines, and Mauritius developed zones after studying operations in Taiwan and Taiwanese officials have gone to Liberia, Thailand, Indonesia, Senegal, Costa Rica, Jordan, and other countries to help them prepare feasibility studies.

A Free Trade Zone is typically set up under a state-owned development corporation. The corporation purchases a certain amount of land, ranging from 60 acres for Taichung (Taiwan) to 600 acres for Masan (South Korea), to 1,700 acres for Mareveles (Philippines). Importation of capital equipment and raw materials is duty free, and all products, or a specified major proportion of production (for example, 90 percent of production for the Malaysian zones), must be exported. Labor-intensive light industries are usually preferred. Land is generally leased for long periods (often sixty to ninety years). Investors can either build factories or lease or buy them ready-made. Zone authorities develop most of the necessary infrastructure, including housing, banking and medical facilities, and provide a planned labor force. In South Korea, for example, special accommodations were developed for foreigners, including commissaries.

South Korea and Taiwan have expanded the industrial park concept well beyond the Export Processing Zone. South Korean industrial parks can be placed into at least three additional categories. First are export industrial estates where a considerable proportion of goods (up to 30 percent) can be sold domestically. Five of these estates are located around Seoul and over two hundred firms operate in them. Second are several industrial estates that range from Ulsan on the coast (about 6,500 acres designed for heavy industry) to Gumi in the interior (121 acres designed specifically for electronics) which are intended to rationalize supporting infrastructure (e.g., power and water supply, as well as labor). Third are local industrial estates established at 11 different sites throughout the country. They range in size from 98 to 980 acres and are intended to spur regional industrialization as part of the overall rural development program (the *Saemaul* program) and are designed to take advantage of local labor which is unemployed or underemployed, and not incidentally to slow the urbanization process.

Perhaps the most important single factor in setting up the parks is the acquisition of land at an early stage for reasonable and stable prices. In Japan, for example, land prices were rising at about 15 percent a year until 1971 when the Tanaka Plan was announced; they then started to rise by 30 percent or more annually until strict laws on land transactions sharply and perhaps dangerously curbed the development of new land. In South Korea, this problem would be already much worse in the absence of a carefully thought out program. For example, land prices tripled in 1972 in six major cities without tax control. Between October 1972 and July 1973 cities showed an average 13 percent land price increase (compared to 41.2 percent increase in rural and other areas where the Property Speculation Control Law tax does not apply).

The efficiencies that can be achieved with an industrial park strategy of development represent advantages that may lead to their playing an important role in worldwide development in the future. In particular, they may help to alleviate one of the most important problems of the last two decades, an increasing shortage of low-skilled, low-cost labor in the advanced countries, and an increasing labor surplus in the developing world. This situation, which has become less acute in the recent recession years but which, from our analysis, represents a basic long-term trend, has resulted in high rates of unemployment and underemployment, particularly in the poor or very poor nations where birth rates remain high.

With the notable exception of Japan, which is only now beginning to face a serious labor shortage, the Advanced nations have dealt with this problem primarily by importing labor, either internally or from less developed regions. For example, major regional migrations from the rural southern and New England states in the United States have taken place during the last decade at the same time as major shifts of labor-intensive industries from the highly industrialized East and Midwest to these same areas. At the same time, an estimated 8 or 9 million illegal immigrants plus an annual inflow of about 300,000 legal immigrants have entered the United States. Similarly, an estimated 8 to 10 million "guest laborers" from poorer areas of Europe, such as Greece or Algeria, have migrated to the industrialized northwest and regional shifts (e.g., southern to northern Italy and Germany) have taken place.

Despite the severe personal hardships and social problems associated with this, on balance it has been at least as useful for the laborers and their countries as for the employers and theirs. Much criticism is leveled at the exploitation of foreign workers, who are typically paid less than citizens of the host country. The point often ignored is that these workers, who are willing to leave their families, travel far, and endure poor living conditions, obviously do not consider themselves exploited. On the contrary, they see themselves as exploiting a great opportunity. For example, any number of Mexican "wetbacks" have repeatedly been caught crossing the Rio Grande while attempting to re-enter the United States. Many foreign laborers in Europe desperately try to remain there under almost any conditions. And even in South Africa the guards at the border are there to keep people out, not to prevent them from leaving. For such labor-exporting countries as Algeria, Spain, Greece, Turkey, and Finland, the money remitted home by overseas laborers has played an extremely important development role by providing a key source of foreign exchange and by training workers. South Korean coal miners, for example, who have gone abroad (principally to West Germany), virtually never work in the Korean coal mines once they return. They usually take higher-skilled jobs or use their savings to go into business for themselves.

This seems likely to continue, probably at an accelerated rate, as income gaps continue to grow, higher birth rates continue in poor nations, regional differences within the advanced countries decline, and new nations enter the ranks of fully industrialized economies. Likewise, the problems that accompany foreign workers in host countries seem likely to get worse, or at least come under greater international criticism.

We believe that the industrial park strategy of development, and EPZs in particular, may play an important role by facilitating a new emphasis on moving work to available labor rather than the other way around. Within fifteen or twenty years there may be far more people employed in EPZs than there are foreign workers in the advanced countries. For a country like Japan, for example, which is extremely reluctant to import foreign workers on a large scale, major investments in low-cost labor enterprises located in EPZs would seem a likely method to alleviate shortages of low-cost labor and, in fact, this appears to be a real pattern.[9]

Of course, this may not happen. If developing nations choose not to take advantage of EPZs, or if they establish them but change the rules or even nationalize the businesses, industrial parks may remain fairly limited. However, we expect that, as more countries establish such zones, it will be harder for any one country to back out. The costs of losing or even greatly jeopardizing the successful employment of workers in hundreds of factories would be drastic for the host country.

Land Reform in Taiwan

The land reform program sponsored by the Republic of China government in Taiwan is among the most successful ever carried out. Although the initial response in South Korea was also impressive, programs to stimulate agricultural development were neglected and this sector lagged badly until suddenly stimulated by the program described in the next section. In Taiwan, as in South Korea, Japan, and other countries that have succeeded at land reform, a major disruption followed that undermined the power of the traditional landowners. Taiwan's Land to the Tiller program has often been considered the most effective in the world and, along with the aspects of its "economic miracle," was often heralded as such a decade or so ago. But it must be admitted that Taiwan's success (like that of South Korea and postwar Japan) largely resulted from the absence of political opposition by major landowners. From this perspective, Iran's more limited success is more impressive or at least more "heroic." The one major obstacle to reform situations, great power held by traditional landlords, was absent because political power in Taiwan resided exclusively in immigrants from the mainland who held no land.

During the war years, Taiwan's agricultural infrastructure had been damaged by natural causes and neglect. Holdings under cultivation were reduced by about 30 percent between 1937 and 1946. After more than 2 million Chinese immigrated to the island in 1949, there was little option but to restore agriculture to meet immediate food shortages. In addition, major land holdings left by the Japanese were available for redistribution. The principal crop in Taiwan is rice, which is labor-intensive and lends itself to relatively small holdings (as opposed to plantations or grain farming), so parceling out small plots made economic sense. Finally, initial land reform programs and agricultural modernization programs had been carried out by the Japanese in Taiwan (as in South Korea), so that the indigenous farmers were much better prepared than "traditional" farmers in many developing nations were to operate their own establishments.

Having made clear that it is not likely that other countries could carry out directly comparable programs, we single out Taiwan's land reform program because we believe it clearly illustrates certain basic and generalizable points. Taiwan's land reform program was carried out in three stages:

1. In 1949 the rent paid by farmers was reduced to a flat 37.5 percent, compared with about 50 percent paid previously, and in some cases up to 70 percent, under the Japanese.
2. In 1951 the government released public land, most of which had been held by the Japanese, to tenant farmers who were able to purchase it on credit, to be paid through twenty semi-annual installments, at a price roughly equivalent to two and one half times the annual crop yield.
3. In 1953 the government initiated a "land-to-tiller" program (more or less simultaneously with its first four-year economic plan), under which private land holdings were limited to either three hectares of paddy or six hectares of dry land. The government purchased existing land holdings from the landlords, re-selling them to tenant farmers under the same terms as before. The landlords, in turn, were given 70 percent of the price in commodity (rice and sweet potato) bonds, redeemable in twenty semi-annual installments with 4 percent interest, and the rest of the price in stock in state-owned enterprises.

As a result of this program, nearly two hundred thousand farmers purchased public lands, and about three hundred thousand farmers purchased lands they had formerly rented. Approximately 90 percent of the land under cultivation became owner-farmed. Several measures that accompanied the land reform program served to increase agricultural productivity and provide foreign exchange. In conjunction with the American aid program under the Joint Commission for Rural Reconstruction, massive technical and significant financial assistance was provided to farmers in a wide variety of areas—plant industry, forestry, fisheries, irrigation—and in various services such as credit, cooperative programs, and health programs. Even though United States aid to Taiwan was terminated in 1965 the

Joint Commission has continued to play a key role, providing information to farmers, coordinating local programs with international programs, and carrying out considerable research. The Commission, which is a joint United States-Taiwan organization, has enjoyed considerable independence from the established bureaucracies and has therefore often been effective in ways which would be hard for a Ministry of Agriculture to duplicate. It has, for example, been able to sidestep official policy and act as a direct channel of international information for farmers. In this sense, it could be thought of as a model program for integrating indigenous farm policies in a developing nation with international aid programs by expanding the fund of knowledge and technology.

In addition, the Republic of China government in Taiwan introduced programs that reduced the effect of inflation on farmers. For example, in the early days of land reform, the government established a "paddy-rice and fertilizer barter system" that made farmers independent of the world price of rice while enabling the government to obtain large supplies of rice which could be used to stabilize food prices even without a government monopoly. Since then, agricultural productivity has increased steadily, principally through improved technology and diversification. Although cultivated land barely increased (about 4 percent between 1950 and 1975) and the number of agricultural workers has increased relatively little in the last two decades as the labor force has been used to supply the rapidly growing industrial sector; yet throughout the period, growth in farm output has been steady, averaging about 4.7 percent between 1951 and 1960 and about 4.2 percent between 1960 and 1970 (it roughly tripled between 1953 and 1975). The increasingly intensive use of chemical fertilizers has been, as one would expect, a most important factor in improving output. But the biggest change was the rapid increase in livestock which has averaged over 9 percent a year in the postwar era. What these changes reflect is both impressive programs to educate the farmers and incentives to increase investment.

Considering the rapid population growth, the low initial income and educational bases (though not low relative to other developing countries), and the fact that most of this preceded the major advances of the "green revolution," Taiwanese land reform stands as a uniquely impressive achievement. The *Saemaul* program, described below, has provided even more dramatic results but has not been more impressive. The rapidity of change in the South Korean agricultural sector is analogous to sudden spurts of growth in an economy after a recession—it is a catch-up phenomenon. South Korean agriculture was just waiting for a new deal. When it came, the agricultural sector jumped in a way that reflected latent potential as much as anything else.

Blessed with good land and a moderately favorable climate, Taiwanese farmers are able to triple-crop and sometimes quadruple-crop in increasingly diversified agricultural production. As a result, the value of rice production dropped from a prewar average of half of the total to about a third by the late 1960s; sugar cane and other special crops dropped from about a quarter to a tenth; and fruit and vegetable production increased by about 6 percent. Without a major increase in total land, Taiwan has been able to increase its total agricultural output 1.6 times by 1974 over that of 1950 to 1952, and its production of rice from 4.5 tons per acre in 1950 to about 7.5 tons in the early 1970s.

Taiwan's achievement also illustrates the importance of agriculture in economic development even when industrial production has had the basic priority. Interestingly, new agricultural problems in Taiwan are arising from the problem of limited land. It is unlikely that significant increases in output per man can be achieved unless the average size of the farm is greatly increased. In other words, Taiwan has *outgrown* its land reform and must now initiate a movement toward larger holdings. If one were to extrapolate the same situation to other countries, one could envision trying to deal with it through a pre-planned phased land reform breakup of the landlord-tenant system, leading initially to small holdings and eventually to large-scale, modern, highly technical "business" firms. Inefficient small farms are becoming an increasingly acute problem in Taiwan, and it will be interesting to observe how the Taiwanese cope with the "reverse land reform" problem.

Taiwan is an excellent illustration of how a tight land reform program can be carried out with little suffering. One can directly compare this to the many massive and usually showy reforms carried out by communist states. Quite apart from humanitarian considerations, such measures deprive a country of its most capable farmers. The end result is communal farms that have yet to prove themselves nearly as efficient as privately owned farms. Taiwan's experience tends to illustrate that giving the "land to the tiller" can be an extraordinarily effective way to increase agricultural production, at least in the medium term, while simultaneously raising rural income and thus incorporating the rural populations into a mass consumption economy. It also illustrates that success in this area can depend as much on developing products that are intentionally competitive and focusing on modern techniques and methods as on success in the industrial sector.

South Korea's Saemaul *Movement*

The *Saemaul* movement (or new community movement) in South Korea provides an interesting contrast to Taiwan's agricultural promotion efforts. Until recently, South Korea had given much less attention to rural development than had Taiwan. In 1970, realizing something must be done to stimulate this relatively stagnant sector (which was nevertheless growing at an average of about 5 percent per year) the South Korean government conceived the *Saemaul* program and launched it on a modest scale the following year. Its most interesting aspect is that it is as much a "spiritual revitalization" program as an economic program. It is also a completely national program involving all South Koreans, urban and rural, rich and poor. To a sophisticated Western observer (or Western-educated Korean) the "pep rally" approach appears merely propagandistic, and as a result it has been largely overlooked or ridiculed by outside observers. But the spectacular results that it has achieved in obtaining voluntary cooperation and initiative among Koreans make it clear that it has not been so regarded by them (or by visitors from other developing countries. The Malaysians at least—whose *Bumiputra* movement perhaps most clearly resembles *Saemaul*—have been studying it carefully.)

From our point of view it is most interesting and impressive for the very reasons it is criticized. We see it as an effort comparable to mainland China's effort to create a "New Man" or, in this case, at least a "Modern Man" out of a traditional peasant or urban laborer. But rather than trying to do this by threats and coercion, it is being done by persuading them that it is worth changing, by providing the knowledge and tools they need, and by encouraging them to make the transition through their own initiatives.

We believe that the key to the *Saemaul* program's success has been its focus on self-help, in contrast to many government giveaway rural reform programs (like Mexico's) which failed. Implementing it was also handled brilliantly. Essentially, the government categorized the country's thirty four thousand villages, selecting eight thousand initially where it thought the program would be *most* likely to succeed. This also became a source of early criticism, since it was obvious that these represented the least challenge and least needed assistance. But that was just the point; the secret to gaining the cooperation from the more skeptical or less ambitious villages was demonstrating that the program could work.

The program started modestly enough. The first target villages were each offered 335 bags of cement on the condition that they be used for community improvement purposes (e.g., drinking water facilities, communal laundry areas, common compost piles, etc.). Understandably, this unprecedented beneficence on the part of the central government was greeted with suspicion and in some cases rejected outright. The cost to the government was about $8 million; the value of completed projects was estimated at about $25 million. Not a very large scale, but very successful. In 1972, over sixteen thousand villages participated, and the government provided material and financing worth about $42 million to stimulate projects worth about $200 million covering both infrastructure and income generating projects with much of the government contribution being tied to local investment (i.e., matching grants) and all of it tied to local labor investment. The success of the *Saemaul* program must be attributed in large part to an effective leadership training program. Each participating village sent a representative to a national training center (there are one central and ten regional centers) to learn about the program. The high morale and idealistic environment they were exposed to might be likened to a Peace Corps training program where the people to be helped are one's own friends and family. This has resulted in new community consciousness. Although this example is a model case, it is by no means unique or exaggerated. Thousands of comparable cases demonstrate a degree of change as great as any brought about by socialist revolutions in a comparable period.

In 1974, a major new step was taken with the decision to extend the *Saemaul* program to include the entire country. There was no special community consciousness in urban areas, and the results have apparently been mixed, but it has by no means failed, already having produced notable results. One of its most controversial aspects was the decision to involve everyone from the president on down. Every South Korean citizen must now spend several weeks a year participating in an indoctrination program. As one could expect, this has not been exactly popular among the well-to-do and the well-educated. Nor do the cynical find any shortage of political propagandizing or self-serving praise of the current government. Participation in the indoctrination programs is certainly not volunatry, and an openly cynical participant does not go unnoticed.

Is this an unwarranted curtailment of the citizen's human rights or an abuse of political freedom by the party (or strongman) in power? Many of the liberal New Class would argue that it is, while making any number of excuses for excesses in socialist countries that are orders of magnitude greater. We would argue it is not. In principle it is no different from the requirement most nations have that young persons must serve their country for a year or two in the military, or, in some cases, in alternative national programs. And we argue that forcing white collar city dwellers to participate is a plus, that it is an example of a constructive way of stressing the principle that all persons are equal under law.

The measurable results of the *Saemaul* program indicate such spectacular success that it is impossible for any open-minded person to criticize it other than by nit-picking. Instead, the critics have ignored it. So far as we know, there have been no major articles about it in the prestige mass-media journals, although they have devoted considerable attention and space to "alleged" political abuses and favorable attention to comparable socialist schemes. Part of the reason for this is that the South Korean government itself has not tried to focus international attention on it, typically referring to it as a uniquely Korean program that cannot be fairly evaluated or emulated by foreigners (which in itself tends to create suspicion). But the main reason is that the typical sophisticated foreign observer simply does not comprehend what the stated and observable accomplishments mean. Economic development and the heroic achievements these people are making simply do not "turn them on."

Some Japanese Institutional Problems[10]

We now turn to the current Japanese situation. We argue that Japan is an outstanding current example of a nation suffering from severe institutional problems. Japan's urgent domestic demands are great. The Japanese have pressing needs for transportation, housing, infrastructure, recreational facilities, environmental protection, pollution control, and so on. They have much excess productive capacity that can be employed to meet these needs. They have the ability to finance the necessary programs and the willingness, both as a society and as private individuals, to pay for this financing (in part out of capacity created by further economic growth). And yet they seem to be totally unable to put the package together. Their institutions are not working as well as they should be. This is why, at least for the time being we have begun, with some sadness, to refer to Japan as a "half hero" of development.[11]

The Japanese are not normally thought of as having this sort of institutional problem. Rather, Japan is usually portrayed as one of the most effective societies in history in undertaking purposive communal actions and achieving consensual goals. Without question, Japan has been the most successful example of economic growth during *La Deuxième Belle Epoque.* Its GNP grew by about a factor of 10 in real terms, 2.5 times higher than the world average. Since 1973 the Japanese economy has grown more slowly, but nonetheless at rates that are still as high or higher than those of any other Advanced Capitalist nation.

Nevertheless, Japan's recovery so far has been lackadaisical. Japanese confidence in a genuine and sustainable recovery from the 1974-75 recession and in the country's future prospects remains stubbornly weak. The economy has genuinely critical problems: continuing excess capacity, slack domestic demand, relatively high levels of unemployment and underemployment, great pressures on certain industries to export at almost any cost, growing foreign criticism and alarm, and an increasing need for massive industrial restructuring. However, Japan's current lack of confidence runs much deeper than would appear justified by these factors alone. In fact, Japan's current economic morale is lower than at any time since immediately after World War II. This is one reason the Japanese do not seem able themselves to create or conceive of any satisfactory solution to their problems.

Rather than espousing a creative and open outlook, Japan is experiencing a substantial disillusionment with and a strong backlash against the very notion of economic growth. There is also a loss of societal meaning and purpose. Japan has more or less achieved the single most important goal it has been seeking for more than a hundred years. It has caught up to the West in enough significant ways that that goal itself no longer stands out as a vision of the future. With no model to follow and no design of its own, the country is drifting not only economically but also socially, politically, and culturally.

Success—Japanese Style

The subtitle of the book on which this discussion of Japanese institutional problems is based, *The Success and Failure of Economic Success,* is a much debated topic in Japan. Since World War II more than any other major power, including West Germany, Japan has emphasized the economic aspects of its society. In effect, the postwar Japanese made economic growth into a religion that, until the late

1960s, was both popular and successful. Its strength was reinforced by a genuine liking for the benefits of economic growth. But when the benefits began to be taken for granted, the costs and problems were emphasized, and it became possible to attack the whole concept of growth from a variety of perspectives—economic, physical, psychological, aesthetic, and even moral.

Disillusionment with growth spread surprisingly rapidly throughout Japanese society and grew to remarkable proportions. By the late 1960s and early 1970s, anti-growth attitudes and assumptions had become trendy and fashionable in many Affluent countries. These attitudes were expressed with the greatest intensity and effectiveness in Japan. In May 1970, the *Asahi*, the Japan's largest circulation newspaper, launched a *"kutabre GNP"* (down with GNP) movement, which both reflected the spreading mood and stimulated it further. The 1973 "oil shock"—the Japanese introduced the phrase into international parlance—seemed to confirm the anti-growth position, making further growth appear unfeasible as well as undesirable.

There was also a reaction against the overconfidence of the early 1970s when, for the first time since World War II, (and perhaps for the first time since the Meiji restoration) the Japanese felt a sense of leeway, safety, and security about the future. They had begun to travel abroad and to spend money on themselves. Then the roof fell in—or at least appeared to. In part, many Japanese felt that in some obscure way they had been tricked into overconfidence. They more or less made a silent vow of "never again . . ." There followed a five year period when, with two or three exceptions, we were unable to find any senior Japanese scholar, businessman, or government official who was willing to make a strong public defense of economic growth. This was quite different from the West, where even at the height of the anti-growth movement there were many articulate and effective defenders of growth. However, as the economic malaise that followed the "oil shock" continued without end, the Japanese public and elites began to re-examine anti-growth attitudes.

Even at this writing it is difficult to find in Japan the kind of enthusastic or dedicated defense of economic growth that is not uncommon in Western intellectual, business, and government circles. However, the emphasis on the effects of the general discussion on broad limits to growth should not lead to confusion about the real sources of the current malaise. These lie in the current problems afflicting Japan's economy, the pervasive sense of being adrift, and the need to restructure the economy to cope with long term trends in the labor force and the market.

This concern about the economy—both short term and long term—and the perception of a general loss of meaning and purpose is not restricted to the Japanese themselves, to say nothing of "paranoid" or "hypochondriac" Japanese. Even so seasoned and sober an outsider as Peter Drucker said recently, "For the first time in twenty years I left Japan not wholly confident about the country's future."[12]

The Limitations of Business-as-Usual

Given how widespread these beliefs are, we might correctly suppose that such lack of confidence is reasonable, at least for some sectors of the economy and from the viewpoint of some elements of Japanese society. Granting this, is some sort of economy-wide malaise inevitable? And if inevitable, is it likely to be temporary, or will it linger long enough or be deep enough to affect adversely the medium or long-term future of the country? We believe the answers to both questions are negative, but we concede that such a pervasive lack of confidence and low morale might well produce a series of self-fulfilling prophecies, leading in turn to a series of missed opportunities. Furthermore, the current situation does have many crisis-prone elements, and a continuation of inadequate policies could lead to a disaster. Whether or not there is a disaster, to continue current policies will have very unpleasant adverse consequences. Table 6.2 lists some of the likely outcomes of a business-as-usual approach.

There has been much concern expressed in the Advanced Capitalist nations about the growth of Japanese exports and, recently, about the enormous Japanese trade surpluses. We argue that in many ways the problem is even worse than the discussion indicates, at least if the usual assumptions are made. Most Japanese manufacturing companies have very large debt-equity ratios and therefore have to make large fixed payments on principal and interest whether they operate their facilities at full or part capacity. Because of the lifetime employment system, much of the wage bill is also a fixed cost whether or not the facilities are operated. Most of the plants are modern so that there is almost no possibility of their being scrapped or retired. Under these circumstances, the manufacturer is almost forced to produce and sell at almost any cost—in effect, to dump. Despite current export growth, most Japanese industries are still operating at about 80 percent capacity. Furthermore, this seems to be a genuine surplus capacity because, unlike many other countries, Japanese industries

TABLE 6.2

Consequences of a Business-as-Usual Approach

A. *Domestic Economic Consequences*
   1. Slow erosion of excess capacity
   2. Relatively low business confidence (and relatively low profits)
   3. Inadequate capital investment
   4. Level or slowly decreasing unemployment and underemployment
   5. Low consumer confidence, only a slow upturn in expenditures
   6. Continued high government deficits

B. *International Consequences*
   1. Continued pressure to export
   2. Rising yen
   3. Increasingly crisis-prone external pressures

C. *Other Domestic Consequences*
   1. Inadequate infrastructure (for the next ten to twenty years)
   2. Inadequate housing (for the next ten to twenty years)
   3. Delays in "fixing" pollution, etc.
   4. Pressure toward costly welfare orientation
   5. Gradually increasing xenophobia
   6. Ineffective counters to localism (e.g., more Narita Airport-style controversies)

---

normally operate at close to 100 percent capacity. If a Japanese manufacturer is frozen out of some markets, the manufacturer has to focus greater attention on other markets. If regulations are implemented to prevent exporting, the Japanese manufacturer is under great pressure to evade those regulations.

Under current conditions Japanese manufacturers usually prefer selling to the home market where they now generally get higher prices than abroad. However, also because of current circumstances, the home market is simply not large enough. Furthermore, it seems unlikely that there will be a revival of spending by either consumers or businessmen because the lack of confidence that prevents such spending seems based upon relatively firm and continuing conditions. Under these circumstances, Keynesian-stimulation policies simply will not work. If the government spends additional money, some goods may be sold but few, if any, additional people will be hired, little demand is created for increased capacity. Hence, there is almost no multiplier effect. All of this has created an intense interest in export trade. However, because of the rise in the yen, this export trade is increasingly unprofitable.

While Japan must export enough to pay for imported raw materials, a high level of exports is not a life-or-death matter for the Japanese economy as a whole. However, it can easily be a matter of great urgency for individual Japanese companies, so they naturally fight to keep their export markets as long as possible. Furthermore, despite more than adequate exports to pay for essential imports, many business and government leaders retain the traditional Japanese view that manufacturing exports are sacrosanct because Japan has to import so many of its raw materials. This stems, in turn, from a more fundamental fear, dating back more than a century, that Japan will either be overwhelmed by foreigners or be cut off from supplies of essential raw materials. Even today, many Japanese continue to see their success as fundamentally illusory. They lack confidence that the normal workings of the world trading system will provide them with raw materials—even if they have the money to pay for them, or the ingredients needed to convince others to lend them the money. Paradoxically, their excessive fear causes them to follow a policy that might destroy the very trading system on which they are so dependent.

Despite contracting or very slowly expanding world markets, exports have been pushed so hard that there has been growing foreign opposition. This opposition is becoming so intense and bitter that by itself it threatens the stability of the international trading system. There is a legacy of hostility—and fear—toward the Japanese among many in Europe and the United States and an increasingly general feeling that the Japanese have benefited more than anybody else from the international trading system yet have done little to help make it work well. Negative and hostile feelings are also held, for quite different reasons, by the Japanese who believe that they have been very successful in beating the West at its own game and now the West is trying to change the rules. The Japanese feel that they are successful because of their propensity to work hard, to save, and to invest huge sums and because they are clever, dedicated, creative, and willing to take great risks. They therefore feel entitled to success, but believe that the West is trying, by sheer force and unfair tactics, to keep them down.

Even if the Japanese had behaved impeccably, the pervasiveness, intensity, and success of the Japanese trade offensive would still have aroused great animosity and some jealousy. Many Japanese recognize that animosity, fear, and jealousy are normal concomitants of success.

They also recognize that many of these negative attitudes have been caused or exacerbated by unnecessarily provocative or aggravating Japanese commercial practices. Nevertheless, even these Japanese often feel that Japan is being treated unfairly.

There is no chance that the Japanese government will commit political suicide to please Washington or Europe. The early demands by the United States, now much moderated, that they allow their meat industry to disappear in the near future, or force a collapse of agricultural prices on their farmers, or make other drastic adjustments in the middle of a recession seem to them the equivalent of committing political suicide, as well as being excessively disrupting and damaging to important groups in Japan. Such demands simply demonstrated how unreasonable the United States could be. In fact, sometimes the United States demands appeared, whether justly or not, to be spectacularly unreasonable. For example, the United States told Japan it must grow by 7 or 8 percent a year. Many Japanese would have loved to do this but didn't know how to do so without touching off—or risking—an unacceptable inflation and deficits. Even then, the growth might not occur because both the inflation and the deficits would themselves weaken business and consumer confidence. Furthermore, many also believed if they risked a surge of inflation, the resulting backlash might further depress growth rates. The Japanese perceive the United States as hypocritical in claiming it is running a trade deficit to help out the rest of the world. (As far as I know, almost nobody believed this claim.) Yet United States rhetoric, in effect, often argued that Americans were good guys courageously doing their share while the Japanese bad guys intentionally shirked their responsibilities. (Most of the rest of the world believed that the United States was callously or self-indulgently running a huge trade deficit for reasons unrelated to any world interests—and that if such interests were served it was purely accidental.)

The Japanese press began to ask, "How would the United States feel if the Japanese came to the United States and said it must grow by 7 percent a year to eliminate domestic black unemployment, and to help the rest of the world?" Such a demand would be unbelievably silly, but no sillier than some of the demands the United States seemed to be making in a public and humiliating fashion. Finally, the Japanese noted that the Germans refused the United States' demands, clearly and sharply—and the United States accepted this refusal meekly. Why should they be treated worse than the Germans? Something "racist" must be involved. This feeling that United States policies are more or less "racist" was further intensified by the seemingly inexplicable and widely publicized decision not to sell surplus Alaskan oil to Japan in return for other oil from the Middle East to supply the American east coast. Instead, some of the oil now goes around South America to the east coast at great expense. Furthermore, the west coast surplus had caused a slow-down in drilling in both California and Alaska, thus contributing to possible national and world shortages. To almost no one in the oil business did this make sense, but it remained United States policy in 1979.

Despite the intense pressures the United States put on Japan, there was simply nothing that Japan could do (if restricted to normal policy options) that would change the situation very much in the short run, unless it was willing to bankrupt overnight such industries as meat and rice, and severely damage textile, toy, shoe, and other industries. Not unreasonably, Japan refused to do so in the middle of a recession. Furthermore, in almost every case, the people in the industry at risk tended to be Liberal Democratic Party (LDP) voters. And the LDP was simply too precariously perched in power to incur the anger of these people and lose their votes.

The United States pressed the Japanese so hard mainly out of a sense of aggravation, annoyance, and even revenge. In particular, the American negotiators believed that unless the Japanese "bled" a little bit, Congress would be so aggravated that they would pass excessively protective legislation. Therefore, it was important to subject the Japanese to some demonstrable suffering simply because of the United States' internal political situation. Many Japanese understood this, but it did not make them feel better.

A Modest Proposal—Our Yonzensō Plan

From a practical point of view, the situation seemed in early 1979 to be getting worse rather than better. We believe that there is a relatively simple and almost obvious solution. The most remarkable thing about this solution is that the Japanese once grasped the situation quite well, but they no longer seem able to do so. Japanese planners previously understood that Japan had to change its engine of growth every ten years or so, as indicated in Figure 6.1 Had this strategy continued on schedule, Japan would in all likelihood have proceeded along the growth path labeled "optimal" in Figure 6.2. The dotted lines in Figure 6.2 show actual Japanese growth rates since the late 1960s; the solid lines are the path we believe the economy could and should have taken. The latter would not mean a continually high or rising growth rate; in fact, it implies a steadily declining growth rate (as shown in the insert). Thus, by the end of the century, Japan's

FIGURE 6.1
Five States of Japanese Postwar Economic Growth

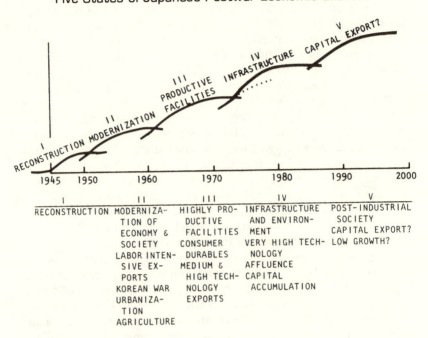

I	II	III	IV	V
RECONSTRUCTION	MODERNIZA- TION OF ECONOMY & SOCIETY LABOR INTEN- SIVE EX- PORTS KOREAN WAR URBANIZA- TION AGRICULTURE	HIGHLY PRO- DUCTIVE FACILITIES CONSUMER DURABLES MEDIUM & HIGH TECH- NOLOGY EXPORTS	INFRASTRUCTURE AND ENVIRON- MENT VERY HIGH TECH- NOLOGY AFFLUENCE CAPITAL ACCUMULATION	POST-INDUSTRIAL SOCIETY CAPITAL EXPORT? LOW GROWTH?

growth rate would conform to the historical growth rates of other Advanced Capitalist nations.

Unfortunately, the actual investment policies followed since the late 1960s (despite government rhetoric and paper plans to the contrary) have continued to emphasize highly productive facilities and infrastructure. As we noted above, this has led to a situation in which many businesses are stuck with so much excess capacity that they simply have no incentive to invest in either expansion or replacement. At the same time, they are under increasing pressure to produce even if there is no reasonable domestic or foreign market.

One possible alternative might be to adopt what we call in *The Japanese Challenge* the *Yonzensō* program.[13] We include in this concept a comprehensive program of infrastructure development designed to more than double the real wealth of the country in a decade or so and to stimulate business investment early in the effort. The program would be formulated and explained so that most

FIGURE 6.2
Illustrative Growth Pattern

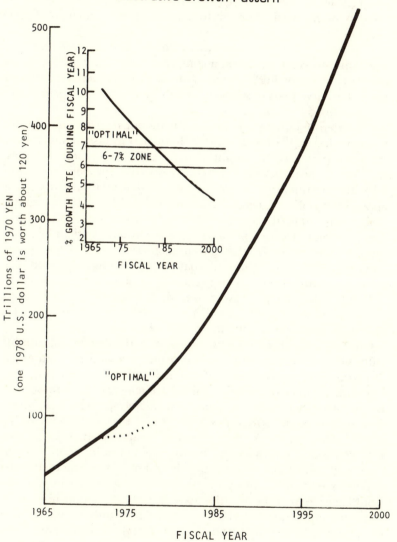

businessmen would judge that their current excess capacity could be rapidly put to use. This would then be an inducement to build new capacity. If businessmen refused to jump on the bandwagon, the program would obviously be less successful. High levels of excess capacity might persist, though for a much shorter time than if there were no *Yonzensō* program.

A *Yonzensō* program involves a different kind of revision of the economic structure, based on a comprehensive plan with an initial catch-up phase of high *average* annual growth (perhaps 10 to 12 percent) for five years or so and then stable growth of 5 to 7 percent for a decade or so.[14]

A *Yonzensō* Japan evokes an inspiring but realistic and credible vision including deliberate efforts to build new infrastructure, to raise the growth rate of the country temporarily by exploiting excess capacity, to use imports to deal with prospective bottlenecks and thus alleviate inflationary pressures, and to facilitate all the above steps by appropriate political, legal, social, and public information programs designed to dramatize the idea. If this plan were successful, Japan would be more worried by shortages and bottlenecks than by excess capacity. However, in the current depressed state of the world economy, it is easy to import whatever goods might be needed to alleviate shortages or bottlenecks caused by a "boom," and any boom-induced inflationary pressure would then be greatly mitigated. Presumably Japan would be willing to increase imports to meet such shortages and bottom out; and it might have to.

One big issue in a *Yonzensō* program is the degree and rapidity with which private industry and consumers would respond to the program with investments and purchases of their own. One ideal situation could be described as follows. The program is announced. Businessmen believe in it; many immediately perceive that unless they start expanding capacity quite soon, they will begin losing market shares in two or three years to companies that do expand. Under these circumstances, businessmen would soon become interested both in hiring more people and in commiting themselves to new investments. If this process worked, the government probably would have to institute deflationary-type policies that put downward pressures on the rate of hiring and of new investment. Among other things, it might raise interest rates and run a relatively tight monetary policy. The government might also encourage the use of foreign-exchange reserves to finance increased imports. As already noted, the Japanese should be prepared to buy as much abroad as needed to prevent bottlenecks and to keep prices down. This should begin early enough in the program so that everyone knows the government stands ready to curtail inflationary pressures. Japan would not necessarily have to run a negative balance of trade or current account, although either of these possibilities might occur and both should be allowed for.

The question is how high the growth rate would have to be to bring about a self-fulfilling prophecy of increased investment. It is new investment based on expectations of adequate levels of new demands that is the key element missing from Japan's current more or less conventional economic restructuring policy. Even with a 7 percent growth rate Japan would not run out of excess capacity fast enough to stimulate adequate levels of new investment, at least not for the next three to four years. This is why a 7 to 9 percent growth rate might well turn into a self-defeating, rather than a self-fulfilling prophecy. In other words, in many sectors the more businessmen invested, the more excess capacity they would create—at least for several years. However, at a sufficiently high overall growth rate, a self-fulfilling prophecy becomes plausible and effective in most sectors of the economy. We estimate that this rate would be somewhere between 10 and 12 percent, but it need not continue at that level for very long. Although this high growth is best thought of as a temporary catch-up phenomenon, it should be sufficient to inspire businessmen in most sectors to invest because they would calculate a need for new capacity in the near future and good long-term prospects. If the program worked, enough growth would be stimulated quickly enough to make this new capacity necessary at about the time it came on line, and the long-term (1985-1995) growth rate of 6 percent or so would be enough to make the long-term prospects seem reasonable. Table 6.3 summarizes the program.

Japan as an Archetypal Advanced Capitalist Nation

Many countries would benefit if the Japanese government accepts and promulgates the concepts of the Great Transition, the emergence of a post-industrial society, and the general idea that affluence and technology can be used to create a better life for almost everybody. However, most of the specifics of the *Yonzensō* program would probably be feasible only in Japan. Thus, although there is great excess capacity in much of Europe, there are no large unmet needs demanding enough to make the society as a whole (or very many individuals) willing to meet the costs or to sacrifice and finance programs to meet them. Nor would those societies be willing to risk touching off an inflation to fulfill these unmet needs.

The United States has, in many ways, even larger unmet needs than many of the European countries, but it also has inflationary pressures

TABLE 6.3
The Yonzensō Program (both a set of goals and various tactics, and strategic means to achieve these goals)

Goals:
One goal is to make Japan a much richer country, in terms of consumer welfare and the domestic purchasing power of the yen. Another is to initiate a long term program of "marriage between machine and garden." A third goal is to create adequate nationwide transportation and communications networks.

Tactics:
One tactic to achieve these goals is a temporary increase in the growth rate in a context that creates a self-fulfilling prophecy, causing businessmen to invest and making these investments pay off as they meet (real) new demand. Another tactic is to create opportunities for convenient and reasonably priced housing (and other consumer amenities) and create the necessary consumer confidence so that advantage will be taken of these opportunities.

Elements of the Program:
1. Ten-year program of infrastructure investment over and above existing plans. Stimulus of roughly ¥5 trillion ($25 billion converted at ¥200/$) a year for at least three years. But this stimulus by itself is not the key to the program; the key is the atmosphere in which this stimulus occurs.
2. Government commitment to a minimum spending schedule for, say, three years—an unprecedented move that would help spur confidence.
3. At the same time, an equally strong government commitment to standby anti-inflationary steps, such as encouragement of imports to prevent bottlenecks and keep prices down; also a standby tax increase to help prevent over-shooting after the program takes off.
4. A list of projects, but with latitude for local initiative, on a matching fund basis.
5. Personal commitment by the prime minister, the cabinet, and senior civil servants to a "national purpose" program.
6. Widespread dissemination of the concept that technology and affluence can be used initially to create a high quality of life and eventually create a satisfactory post-industrial society.
7. Other tactics and strategies to generate excitement and commitment.

---

greater than theirs. Furthermore, except for a few industries, the United States does not have much excess capacity. We are convinced that the United States already has full employment as far as the business cycle is concerned, and is more likely than not to have a new wave of inflation. The under-developed countries, of course, have many great needs but they simply do not have the financial capacity to finance them, nor the potential capacity to lift businesses up by their bootstraps any more rapidly than they are doing. In addition, even to the extent that they can in principle do so, the most appropriate programs for them involve reforms that are somewhat different from those suggested in the *Yonzensō* program.

Many of the problems the Japanese face are much the same as those faced by other advanced countries, but in the Japanese case, events are so telescoped as to disclose much new information—similar to what happens when a film of a slowly-moving process is speeded up. Consider, as examples, some restructuring issues. First and foremost, is the impact of increased productivity and affluence. As the Advanced Capitalist nations become more affluent and productive, and the Japanese more so than other countries, firms are forced to pay higher salaries to their workers. Eventually the situation gets to the point where it is no longer economical to use these high salaried workers to produce low value-added goods. It is still possible in many countries to save the jobs of the higher paid people and the management by importing inexpensive workers from abroad to accomplish the low value-added production, but there is absolutely no willingness in Japan to do this and decreasing willingness in other countries. Cheap textiles, shoes, toys, and consumer electronics are examples of the kinds of products involved. Japan has a bigger problem than most countries because it has such a homogeneous population. Thus, as soon as a few lower paid workers achieve higher salaries, almost all of them do. The process is not stretched out as in the United States, which has many minority, disadvantaged, and other groups who not only have relatively low productivity and low wages, but vary greatly in useable capabilities and proneness to enter the work force.

Adjusting to the rising level of productivity and wages is a natural process, but can be quite painful even in the best of times. However, when times are bad and the economy is shaky, bankruptcies and closings can touch off a snowballing response. Further, the displaced workers have much greater difficulty in finding new jobs and it is not easy to find new uses or investments for the displaced capital. Finally, there is often a common belief, especially during such periods, that the foreigners who are claiming comparative advantage may well be doing so merely as a pretext for efforts to shift the burden of recession from their country to another—so-called beggar-thy-neighbor policies. By the same token, a policy of keeping a nation's currency artificially low, say by 10 percent, is equivalent to a 10 percent tariff on imports, and a 10 percent subsidy to exporters.[15]

All this is complicated by competitive pressures from the rapid development and expansion of the New Industrial countries. Even if there had not been any increase in affluence and productivity in the Advanced Capitalist nations, the New Industrial countries would be taking away their foreign markets and pressing on their domestic markets. Under the current conditions, of course, the felt pressures are much more painful and severe. This pain does not make the need for restructuring any less. In any case it seems likely that the development of these New Industrial countries—and other Middle Income and even Poor countries—is going to be maintained or even accelerated. Further, the New Industrial countries at least are increasingly going to compete with the Advanced Capitalist nations in more and more advanced industries. And, while on the whole this will be good for both sides, specific industries or sectors may undergo some very painful experiences. Another process that is going to cause a real need for restructuring in Japan and other Advanced Capitalist nations— again, probably more so in Japan than in most—is the increasing level of education. In Japan, this seems likely to reach a point where the overwhelming majority of high school graduates will attend college.

We believe the Japanese will handle such problems by having more off-shore procurement, overseas investment, and a huge expansion in the tertiary and quaternary sectors for both domestic and foreign consumption. We have long predicted that there might be special problems in the construction field, because one cannot procure infrastructure and buildings off-shore. We have therefore suggested that the Japanese might wish to use temporary foreign laborers in this area in much the same way several Persian Gulf nations do, sending the workers home when the contract is completed.

The need for the above restructuring is one reason why the Japanese will have to become very outward looking economically, even if not socially and politically. This seems to be the easiest and possibly the only way in which they can have a very high standard of living, and supply sufficient jobs—at home and abroad—for their highly educated population.

Another long-range restructuring that seems likely to be important in all the Advanced Capitalist nations, with additional strength in Japan, results from the changing age structure of the population. Much attention has been focused on these demographic changes and the problems they cause, but few persuasive solutions have been suggested. These problems will resolve themselves one way or another and they cause important changes, but it is not clear that other than the most obvious advance preparations have to be made. In Japan, where both buildings and service personnel are likely to be very expensive, one can imagine many well-off older people living abroad at least part of the year where they can live in luxury at lesser cost—perhaps time-sharing their accommodations with relatives and strangers. This issue of changing age structure is further complicated in Japan because of lifetime employment, but the ensuing difficulties have probably been exaggerated. Thus, the wage differentials in respect to age alone (as opposed to skill and experience) in Japanese factories are not as high as many believe.

Almost all of these kinds of events and changes are occurring more or less in the same way in all of the Advanced Capitalist nations. All these countries need to focus more attention on advanced skills and technology, on professional and other highly paid services, on high value-added products, and on importing low paid, less-skilled labor or the products of such labor. The paradox of "the poverty of affluence" affects Japan much as it affects other Advanced Capitalist nations.

A Confused and Confusing Discussion

Japan's decreased effectiveness in dealing with various problems stems in part from its success (as it does in many of the Advanced Capitalist nations). Some of this was inevitable. However, the Japanese have been so successful that they are getting careless. Thus, they have seen how they can continually run large trade surpluses without bringing on serious retribution—at least so far. In general, they worry much less than they used to about whether they are making mistakes. One such current mistake is to retain—almost unchallenged—many habits and attitudes that served Japan so well for a century, but are no longer appropriate for a period when the country is affluent. Thus, the trade surpluses are a product both of the traditional attitude that an export surplus was essential for prosperity and the more recent one that any problems caused by Japan's trade surplus will be solved by the United States or by someone else.

The Japanese in reality have other choices. Instead of seeking insurance through restricting imports (whether by official policy or by customs and habits that linger on even after the policy has changed), Japan would obtain more insurance by increasing its imports, thereby improving the export prospects of other countries, who in turn could buy more Japanese exports. Indeed, if Japanese imports went up, other countries would have no objection to increased Japanese exports. Furthermore, if at some point Japan had to cut back on exports, and felt a need then to cut back on imports, it could easily do so by cutting out luxury imports and continuing to bring in essential goods. For a country as rich as Japan, increased imports lead to a decrease in risks. Japan and its trading partners would live better, prosper more, and build up a greater margin of safety against untoward events.

The main current difficulty in Japan is the absence of serious discussion that would serve to clarify the issues. The problem is not that the Japanese do not realize what their problems are; they are often quite clear about them. In most cases, however, they perceive no solutions for these problems. For example, they want more housing and better transportation but do not see how these can be attained. Indeed, they conclude that there is no way to attain them. In some cases they have misunderstood the causes of their problems. We argue, however, that the key ingredient currently missing is an overall vision, framework, or perspective toward the future—a framework in which priorities and other policies can be formulated and discussed. In such an overall context, different programs can reinforce each other rather than fight with each other and cause confusion.

It is equally important for the Japanese—and for others—to have a proper perspective on the world economy, to understand that the world is not running out of resources, to realize that pollution and environmental problems can be handled to the satisfaction of most people, and to recognize that affluence and technology are more or less desirable and can be made even more desirable by the proper use of the capabilities one gets from being affluent and technologically advanced. While the future is always uncertain and to some degree dangerous, many of the dangers of our current era arise less from the issues raised in the limits-to-growth debate than by the classic issues—the possibility of war, the possibility of decadence, the possibility of unexpected natural events, the possibility of being displaced, surpassed, or overwhelmed by competition. To underestimate these dangers, and overestimate issues raised by the limits-to-growth debate, is itself a danger. An important part of understanding what the real issues are in the Japanese economy is thus an identification of the issues that are false. Doing so is probably more important in Japan than elsewhere, because the discussion in Japan has been so confused and distorted in recent years.

A Tough Society

Japan has changed so much in the last twenty-five years that many observers assume that this incredibly rapid rate of change is itself a major issue. They ask, "How can any society adjust so fast to such a high rate of change?" In our view, however, Japanese society has adjusted relatively well to rapid change, and is basically capable of continuing to do so. When one looks at the low level of crime in Japanese cities and Japan's relative political stability, it is hard to see why people worry so much about the rapid rate of change *per se*. Japan obviously must deal with serious problems, but these problems are not creating the sort of seething cauldron that might superficially appear to exist if one looks only at such sensational events as the Red Army highjackings, the student attacks on Narita Airport, or the many (and usually orderly) political demonstrations that take place near government ministries in downtown Tokyo. These events are symptoms of unrest but in no sense do they represent a great mass of explosive problems. Japan actually has fewer such problems than many other countries. The kinds of problems that one might lump together under "future shock" are being dealt with adequately in Japan, by and large. We disagree with the conclusion drawn by many distinguished observers who think that Japanese society is unusually vulnerable to severe pressures.

Rapid change does, of course, bring about stresses but the remarkable stability of postwar Japan stems from cohesive forces and institutional strengths that have enabled the country to cope remarkably successfully with the cultural problems induced by rapid change. We feel it is incorrect to imply that the Japan of today could easily collapse, snap, or become pathologically deranged. Japan faces serious problems, but the existence of problems hardly means that the entire Japanese nation is "fragile" and may fall apart if not handled with care.[16]

If Japan actually succeeds in putting together a program that elicits the widespread support of its citizens, so that it can effect change rapidly in much the way we summarized above, it might make a real difference to the entire world's short-run prospects. Rather than having a $20 billion trade surplus, Japan's surplus might narrow to zero, or even seem negative for a period of time. This would not hurt Japan. Japanese exports and imports would likely both go up, imports more than exports because there would be less opposition to

Japanese exports under these circumstances. However, Japan has so much excess capacity in some areas that exports in these areas would continue or even expand. But it would be important for the Japanese not to build excess capacity that could not be maintained after the basic program had peaked. They should import things like cement rather than build more cement factories. An increase of Japanese growth rates from 7 percent to 12 percent, plus a rather strong stimulation of the rest of the world because of the increase in Japanese imports (and to some degree because of their exports as well) might raise the world growth rate by close to 1 percent. This could mean at least a temporary return to something close to *La Deuxième Belle Epoque*.[17]

Problems and Prospects for the Heroes

In saying that such countries as South Korea, Taiwan, Singapore, and Hong Kong—and perhaps soon again Japan—could be thought of as exemplifying a "Carnot cycle" in economic development we are overstating the case because even in these countries growth is not trouble free. Seoul, for example, has grown to a monstrous size—7 million persons out of a total population of 35 million according to the 1975 census—and as a result, South Korean society has been seriously disrupted. Taiwan has probably not been as disrupted as South Korea, but it also pays the many costs of the passing of traditional culture and its replacement by modern culture. In terms of national character, young people in both countries have displayed an unswerving dedication to make a success of themselves. In Taiwan, they have to choose a school whether they like the subject or not. As for the amenities of life, there is no question that most people in both countries are living much better in almost every way. In that sense, the passing of the old, while in some ways regretted, did not represent much of a hardship. The pollution from automobiles in the capital city is much more acceptable to many South Koreans and Taiwanese than are what some people think of as the wholesome emanations from animal wastes on a farm.

We do not believe that either South Korea or Taiwan is likely to have problems of the "failure of success" like the Japanese. Both are small countries with national security problems, and there is no way they are going to believe or feel that economic development was a mistake. They are also genuinely export-dependent, while the Japanese are not. This means they have to stay quick on their feet;

they cannot fool around. (The Japanese export industries, however, are still very well run.) And finally, they are not as insular as the Japanese. Both are much more outward looking, and are developing (the South Koreans especially) cosmopolitan globally-oriented businessmen.

This does not mean they cannot get into trouble. In 1978 South Korea was so confident that one worried that it might be overconfident. Their confidence was based on the extraordinary average of over 10 percent growth right through the worldwide recession. Taiwan was much less confident and is much less likely to become overconfident. However, Taiwan may have a problem that could become quite serious: the government is probably too used to intervening in the economy more than is currently needed. To some degree this intervention tends to pre-empt the possibility of the same programs being carried out by private industry. We would argue that probably the best thing that the Taiwanese government could do for its own economy would be to exercise somewhat less control and display more openness, and to allow or even encourage big businesses and big farming to develop. The latter policy would be held by many to violate the three principles of Sun Yat-sen but would seem to be almost inevitable if Taiwan is to reach its full potential.[18]

Whether or not the three societies we have discussed do as well as we believe they could do, all three have made important breakthroughs. The Japanese have achieved a level of affluence and technology that makes them almost invulnerable—at least for a while—to both mismanagement and bad luck. The South Koreans and the Taiwanese have gone far enough toward advanced technology and high productivity that an increasing part of their growth can be relatively autonomous. However, they have such great flexibility that they could do well even under rather poor conditions. In particular, the growing concern in many countries that the mainland Chinese may begin to export competitive products that would take away their markets, is probably not such a great problem to the Taiwanese and South Koreans. It seems likely that as these exports from mainland China develop, if they do at all, these two countries can keep ahead of the game in both technology and quality. Obviously, all three countries will undergo problems because they are forcing other countries to more rapid structural adjustments that these other countries wish to undertake, but it does not seem likely that these problems will be overwhelming. All in all, South Korea, Taiwan, and Japan have to some degree made it.

Notes

1. I should probably admit to a bias in favor of the five neo-Confucian countries of Japan, South Korea, Taiwan, Hong Kong, and Singapore. I visit almost all of them regularly. While each has some problems and defects, I almost always find my trips to them both enjoyable and inspiring. These countries have provided a remarkable contrast to most of the other areas of the world that I visit (though only the last four do so now). In these countries, I find it quite difficult if not almost impossible to make a very obvious suggestion to fix some egregiously dumb (i.e., counterproductive) technological or economic practice—dumb, as viewed from the society's current interests. In sharp contrast, it requires little effort to find many instances where such recommendations are appropriate in almost every other part of the world I visit. Furthermore, I often find rather general agreement that these specific dumb practices should be eliminated, reduced, or changed. But when I ask, "Why, then, isn't the change made?" the reply is invariably, "Politics." Additional questioning reveals that there has been no real attempt to balance the political costs against the costs of the "dumb policy." The latter costs are often perceived but not felt by the government—or no longer felt.

These neo-Confucian nations seem to have an extraordinary and attractive political philosophy that is quite different from that of most other countries. If something is being done that is obviously against the national interest, obviously counterproductive, obviously harmful—then they stop doing it. This is such a refreshing concept, so new, so creative, so vibrant with good possibilities that I just cannot help but admire the areas where it is practiced. (Of course, none of this applies across the board, but only to technological and economic issues that are not politically explosive.) I hope the reader will excuse my almost childlike enthusiasm for these countries, but I have spent many years in trying to make various policies more rational; it is nice to know that others are pursuing the same goal and even putting it into practice.

Lee Kuan Yew, prime minister of Singapore, described the situation of his country in 1965 after it separated from the Federation of Malaysia. "Suddenly, my colleagues and I found ourselves in a Singapore independent and on its own. On our island of 224 square miles were two million people . . . The question was how to make a living, how to survive. This was not a theoretical problem in the economics of development. It was a matter of life and death for two million people. The realities of the world of 1965 had to be faced. The sole objective was survival," (1978 speech to ICC Convention, Orlando, pp. 9-10). Just as Singapore, the other neo-Confucian countries had the same enormous advantage; all were grimly aware that they were poised on the edge of a precipice and none of them could survive a serious economic setback or faulty decision. Each also wanted to build up as much insurance and surplus as fast as possible. Furthermore, each government took great pleasure and satisfaction in observing the rapidly improving living standards of its people. Here again, Samuel Johnson's famous remark is appropriate—imminence of destruction does tend to concentrate the mind wonderfully. And this may well be the reason why Japan no longer performs so well. It does not have to.

2. Hollis Chenery, et al., *Redistribution with Growth*, p. 280. The coming to power of President Park in 1961 played a crucial role in creating and maintaining the third stage.

3. Although some argue that at least until recently they have been "victimized" by unfavorable terms of trade dictated by the developed nations. Whether true or false, it is a much different (and much smaller) thing than the unequal treaties of the past.

4. Foreign aid was unquestionably a major factor during the early stages. However, its importance declined dramatically in about a decade for both countries, so that its total impact was relatively minor. For example, foreign aid represented 83 percent of the total investment in South Korea in 1961. By the early 1970s it was less than 5 percent. It was effective government policies that made possible this transition from dependence on to independence of foreign aid. South Korea and Taiwan are rightfully often considered as the two best examples of the effective use of economic aid in the developing world. See *United States Aid to Taiwan: A Study of Foreign Aid, Self-Help, and Development* by Neil Herman Jacoby (New York: Praeger, 1967) for an excellent discussion.

5. How loyalty to the family as a basic cultural value interplays with economic development in neo-Confucian cultures illustrates both points. Such family loyalty has been traditional in China and Korea and remains a dominant influence in those countries. Loyalty to the family not only tends to inhibit nationalism (which played such an important role in the economic development of France and Germany) but also tends to promote corruption and nepotism. In contrast, in Japan loyalty is to the group, and this has played no small role in the success of Japan's huge trading firms. There are no trading firms of comparable size in Taiwan, although there are about fifteen hundred international firms there, because large companies tend to disintegrate as their more capable employees split off to go into business for themselves. The Republic of China government in Taiwan has not yet succeeded in creating this almost unique institution, although it has tried and is currently setting up a government-owned version. South Korea has succeeded in creating large trading companies through governmental action, despite the Korean preference for small, family-centered industries.

Perhaps a more important distinction that merits further study is that all of the major (i.e., the top five or six) trading firms in South Korea are a part of conglomerate business empires (or, conversely, all of the major business empires have trading firms) very similar to Japan's *zaibatsu*. Their origin as private family empires closely tied to, directed, and influenced by the government is particularly striking. Like their counterparts in Japan, each is a kind of mini-national industrial structure. Company functions usually include various manufacturing capabilities (light and, recently, heavy); international trading; perhaps shipping; insurance; etc. Unlike their Japanese counterparts, they do not include banking as a key function. This reflects a basic difference in these nations' economic structures and orientation. Japan, of course, is not an "export-led" economy, and the great proportion of its investment has been internally generated. For most developing countries, South Korea's variation on Japan's *zaibatsu* pattern offers an instructive example to successful adaptation.

6. Algeria is an excellent example. When it suddenly gained independence, Algeria had at its disposal large amounts of land formerly owned by the French colonists. Nevertheless, the government neither distributed the land effectively nor provided a climate conducive to agricultural development. It created worker-managed farms from the colonial holdings and left private farms alone. But the threat of nationalism remains, and it has inhibited private holders; the communal farms, as one would expect, have proven to be inefficient. The result is that agriculture—probably the nation's most important resource from the point of view of improving the lot of the people and at least as vital as the oil and gas—has been allowed to deteriorate.

7. The specific measures taken by the South Korean government at this time are well worth study. For a concise presentation, see David C. Cole and P. N. Lyman, *Korean Development* (Cambridge, Mass.: Harvard University Press, 1971), Chapter 4, or Wontag Hong and Anne Kruger, *Trade and Development in Korea* (Seoul City, South Korea: Korea Development Institute, 1975) Chapter 1.

8. "Muscle Power," *Time,* August 9, 1976.

9. The impact of Japan in this respect should not be underestimated. From direct overseas investments of a few hundred million dollars a decade ago, it has gone to about 20 billion dollars today and estimates by MITI are for 80 to 90 billion dollars by 1985. About 40 percent of this should be in manufacturing industries in LDCs, and perhaps their EPZs—an immense sum!

10. This section draws heavily on *The Japanese Challenge: The Success and Failure of Economic Success* by Herman Kahn and Thomas Pepper (New York: Thomas Y. Crowell, 1979). This book has been published in Japanese under the title *Soredomo Nihon Wa Seichō Suru: Hikanbyō Dasshutsu so Susume* (Tokyo: Simul Press, 1978). The longer book, of course, discusses many more issues. In particular, it develops more comprehensively the argument adumbrated in this section and presents in much greater detail our recommendations for future policies to return Japan to the status of a full-fledged "hero of development." The Japanese edition was an overnight bestseller, which pleases us greatly. It also seems to have touched off a serious discussion in Japanese government, academic, and business circles. It is too early to ascertain whether or not it will have a serious impact on policy. It is also too early to have received useful criticisms. Nonetheless, because our analysis of Japan focuses on institutional problems we decided it was appropriate to summarize our argument here. We assume, of course, that our insights are reasonably valid and therefore the Japanese could do much better than they are doing. Some of our critics will certainly maintain that the Japanese are doing as well as could be done and we are basically incorrect.

11. The remarkable competency and farsightedness that marked Japanese

economic policy making during most of the previous hundred years had begun to erode by the time of the celebration of the one hundredth anniversary of the Meiji restoration in 1978. It was almost as if they felt that two hundred years of excellent policy making was enough. Actually, it is probably not a coincidence that the Japanese began to lose their ability just about the time Japan got affluent enough so that policy was no longer a life and death matter.

12. Peter Drucker, "Japan: The Problems of Success," *Foreign Affairs*, April 1978, vol. 56, no. 3, p. 578.

13. *Yonzensō* refers to a revision of what the Japanese call *Sanzensō*, an abbreviation of the official title of the Third National Comprehensive Plan. (*San* means three, and *yon* means four.) Our proposed revision would change the emphasis of the program from its present abstract and politically constrained approach to a more creative and open one and, in particular, to an effort to remove various legal, social, and political barriers to the rapid and effective implementation of specific programs in housing, road construction, power plant development, and improved rail and air transportation networks. We have not actually devised a Fourth National Comprehensive Plan, but have simply suggested why and how a revision of the Third National Comprehensive Plan might be justified. (We apologize to the readers for forcing the word *Yonzensō* on them, but we need a special word to refer to this particular combination of both means and ends.)

14. The catch-up is central to the whole concept. Thus, in the United States the economy grew at an annual rate of over 8 percent in the second quarter of 1978, but we think of the U.S. as a country that is much more likely to grow between 3 and 5 percent than 8 percent. The 8 percent growth rate was possible because of the zero growth rate in the first quarter. In the same way, we now think that the Japanese economy is really a 6 to 7 percent economy, but because it has this huge excess capacity (some of it created as a result of relatively low growth since 1973), it can for a time catch up. Thus we think of the high-growth period envisioned in the *Yonzensō* program as being temporary, but important.

15. Exporters from the country get 10 percent more when they translate their foreign sales into local currency, while the foreign exporters to the country lose 10 percent when they make the corresponding transactions.

16. For a contrary view, see Zbigniew Brzezinski, *The Fragile Blossom: Crisis and Change in Japan* (New York: Harper & Row, 1972).

17. See Kahn and Pepper, *The Japanese Challenge*, op. cit. for a detailed statement of our proposal and the supporting evidence and argumentation.

18. Sun Yat-sen's "Three Principles of the People" were nationalism (the liberation of China from foreigners), democracy (government by and for the people), and livelihood (economic security for all the people). Variously interpreted by his successors, these principles form a central element in the ideology of the Republic of China government on Taiwan.

More on the Rich, the Middle Income, and the Poor Countries

The Growth of the Advanced Capitalist Nations in the Twentieth Century

We argued in Chapter 4 that there are four perspectives associated with a Kondratieff type of interpretation of the current persistent worldwide economic malaise in the Affluent Capitalist nations. The Rostow-Kondratieff perspective includes the concept of relative underdevelopment of commodity production because of a long period of relatively low prices (as compared to manufactured goods) and suggests that it will take a couple of decades or so to make this up. In the Forrester-Kondratieff interpretation there is great excess capacity in the capital goods industries because in the long upswing of *La Deuxième Belle Epoque* they have been providing for their own expansion as well as the expansion of the durable goods industries. Once this expansion tapers off, they do not even have replacement demand, since much of the plant and equipment is new.

The problems of the ACNs are also intensified by the growth of competitive capacity in the Middle Income countries and even some of the Poor countries. The Schumpeter-Kondratieff interpretation stresses that a period of consolidation and discovery must follow any long period of exploitation of existing technology. For the ACNs, there are no new technologies on the horizon that are likely to affect GNP dramatically in the next decade except mini- and microcomputers, space, communications, and their applications. However, as far as the Middle Income countries are concerned, it is exactly their ability to apply an enormous reservoir of new technology that seems likely to give them two or three decades of upswing.

Finally, there is what we called the institutional-Kondratieff perspective that appears especially plausible when applied to the last upswing or two. Certain additional behavioral consequences of the long upswing emerge in contemporary secular cultures that were not significant in the past heroic, religious, and disciplined cultures. The institutional-Kondratieff perspective argues that at the end of the long-term Multifold Trend a lengthy period of prosperity can be especially disastrous for discipline, structure, morals, morale, and individual and national character—at least as far as productivity and economic growth are concerned.

Whatever one's attitude toward these interpretive perspectives on long-term trends or cycles, the data on economic growth over the last century or so are interesting and deserve examination and comment. We showed the aggregated data or growth of gross domestic product on Table 4.2 of Chapter 4. The ten curves shown in Figures 7.1, 7.2, 7.3, and 7.4 portray the historical growth of gross product in ten of these Advanced Capitalist nations, mostly from 1860 to 1977, using data set forth by A. Maddison.[1] (We added the last two years of growth to his numbers.) We have also, for convenience, marked on each figure the periods into which we have divided the first 100 years. We will discuss these curves in much the same spirit that we did the material in Part I. Are there any particular trends that come to mind when one examines them? Do they have obvious explanations? We understand that this kind of approach can be misleading unless one has a plausible explanation of why the trends occurred, and even then one can be misled. Nevertheless, we pursue initially this "reasonable common-sense" approach and supplement it later with more analytical material.

Note that there are one, two, or three lines in each graph. These lines point out that generally speaking the curves that they are averaging are very closely aligned and that the curves smoothly hug the line in almost all cases. Each chart also displays the average slope of the line so that the reader can identify the actual rate of growth during the period in question.

It is sometimes argued that the staying power of the forces operating to produce the economic and technological aspects of the Multifold Trend can be seen by noting that, if one extrapolates the growth rates of *La Première Belle Epoque*, the ACNs had more or less recovered from the "lost growth" of *La Mauvaise Epoque* by the 1960s. Peter Drucker has often made the point that this occurred because the same technological and economic forces continued to be important.[2] We argue that this is reasonably correct for the Atlantic Protestant culture area countries but seems to be less true for the other groups. Also, the whole process appears to be subject in some countries to the unleashing of new productive forces and in others to the long-term topping-out forces we have discussed. All the countries have to face the change in conditions associated with the coming of *L'époque de Malaise.*

We begin with the United Kingdom, which more than any other country started the Industrial Revolution. The most remarkable thing about the United Kingdom is the basic long-run constancy of its growth rate. Line 1 tries to fit the 115 years of data not by passing the best (i.e., linear regression) fit through the curve, but by assuming that running a tangent along, or cutting a little into the peaks, gives a much better idea of the basic dynamic growth capability of the country. Line 1 has a 2.1 percent slope and fits the data from 1860 to 1914 extraordinarily well. However, there was "a GNP gap" between current production and the trend line. From this point of view, the United Kingdom by the end of *La Deuxième Belle Epoque* had made a recovery from an economic malaise that apparently set in after World War I and from which it did not start to recover until the end of World War II. Nor, despite the stimulation of *La Deuxième Belle Epoque,* did they overshoot the long-run (115 year) trend at all, as some other nations did. It would not be surprising if the United Kingdom settled down to a growth rate less than 3 percent. However, wage rates in the United Kingdom are now half those on the continent, so that it should be easy for English firms to become competitive. This is true for many American subsidiaries, but, unfortunately for relatively few indigenous firms.

The United Kingdom's growth behavior was not uncharacteristic of the Atlantic Protestant culture area countries. Figure 7.1 also shows the curve for Sweden. Sweden had a remarkably constant growth rate for the entire period, more constant than the United Kingdom's, perhaps because Sweden was much better managed during *La Mauvaise Epoque.* As a result, the economy was not as badly hit and the recovery not as steep.

Although the data are much less complete, the same concept would probably work quite well for Switzerland, also shown on Figure 7.1. The Swiss, unlike the Swedes, went through a very extended period of low growth in *La Mauvaise Epoque.* One is tempted to argue that their much better performance in *La Deuxième Belle Epoque* was basically because they had more catching up to do. If so, perhaps the Swedes, and perhaps also the other Advanced Capitalist nations, may now be in *L'époque de Malaise* or at least in a period of consolidation. This time, however, the Swedes may be in a poor position, given our judgment of their recent management, current attitudes, and current structural problems. One again assumes that with reasonably good

FIGURE 7.1
Total Output for the United Kingdom, Sweden, and Switzerland
(1913 = 100)

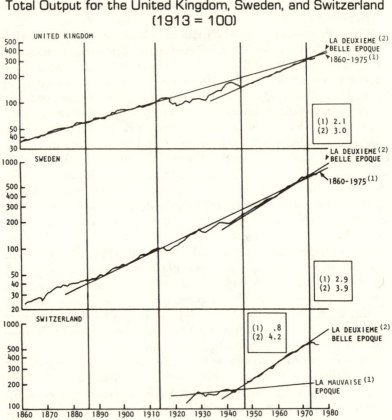

management this period may not be very bad for the Swiss (in the same way that *La Mauvaise Epoque* was not too bad for the Swedes).

These charts suggest the hypothesis that the economies have a sort of basic rate of growth and if they happen to lag behind, as England did, the catch-up is much faster. If they do not lag behind as much, as Sweden did, there is much less catch-up to be done and at not as fast a rate. We are in no sense advancing this as a theorem, but as a conjecture that probably has some validity, though we do not believe it is universally valid. In any case, this conjecture applies only to Atlantic Protestant culture area countries and perhaps to Switzerland. The Catholic countries took off much later than the Protestant countries took off and one now feels that once they get momentum up they may surpass the Protestant countries in GNP per capita. One

FIGURE 7.2
Total Output for the Federal Republic of Germany, Italy, and France

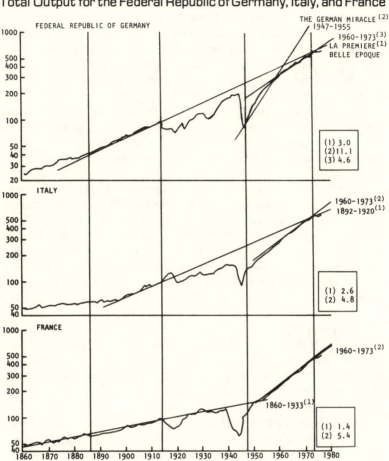

reason why this may occur is that when they grow, they are growing so rapidly they do not have enough time to change their national character to adjust to their new wealth. They do not get the same erosion of values that the Atlantic Protestant culture area countries do. Or perhaps it is simply that the Catholic culture is intrinsically less amenable to such erosion because of the greater strength of the family and of many other communal institutions. (We would like to re-emphasize that these are in no sense advanced as theories, but are conjectures and speculations.)

Figure 7.2 displays curves for West Germany, Italy, and France. We focus on West Germany. There are three trend lines on this chart. As always, the first is the projection of *La Première Belle Epoque.* It suggests that Germany may now be back to normal. The line shows again the ability (whether it is incidental or not) of the *La Première Belle Epoque* trend line to predict where the country will get to—or thereabouts. Instead of averaging the line over *La Deuxième Belle Epoque,* we broke it into two pieces: a catch-up period from 1949 to 1955, in which German GNP growth averaged 11.0 percent; and 1956 to 1978, in which it averaged 4.6 percent.

The catchup period is often called the German Miracle, which was the first of a number of economic miracles that attracted the world's attention during *La Deuxième Belle Epoque.* (The period includes at least a dozen other success stories, i.e., Japan and the eleven NICs.)

Since 1955, West German growth performance has been not as good as most people believe. In fact, it is exceeded by that of Italy, which in turn is surpassed by France. We have long felt that, under certain not implausible assumptions, the latter two countries might do very well indeed. We still think so, though in both cases there are a number of *caveats* associated with those not implausible assumptions having to do with the well-known political, administrative, and other national characteristics of the French and Italians. In particular, both nations have a tendency to throw away success. The Italians were busy doing so in the late 1970s. This is not to say that both nations did not perform well in the early stages of *L'époque de Malaise*—they did as well or better than almost any other Advanced Capitalist nation— even in such things as energy conservation. However, there is a kind of irresponsibility about both societies—particularly Italian soci- ety—that indicates real problems may arise.

Modern Italy is a little bit like two other "Italy-type" countries that at one point were doing very well and then collapsed. At the turn of the century two of the most promising nations of the world were Uruguay and Argentina. A common phrase was, "rich as an Argentine millionaire"; Uruguay was called "the Switzerland of Latin America." Both seem to have since collapsed for reasons not unlike those affecting Italy today.[3] Many factors caused the collapses, but we can single out for Argentina an inability to make the transfer to the impersonal corporate state, internal hostilities within Argentine society, and the cultural emphasis on familial relations and feuds. For Uruguay, one can argue that the dominant factor was the introduction, much too early and much too intensively, of the welfare state. All of these ills afflict Italy today, although to nowhere near the degree they affected these early successes in Latin America.

FIGURE 7.3
Total Output for Japan and Australia (1913 = 100)

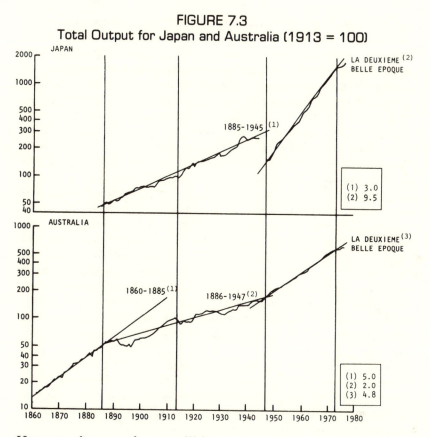

However, these trends may still be strong enough to prevent Italy's rapid growth in the future. In fact, they could bring about a collapse. I am not predicting this, only observing the possibility.

Without claiming too much for our analysis, we offer the following plausible explanation for the striking difference in the patterns of growth found in Japan, West Germany, France, and Italy. Each, but especially Japan and West Germany, was a relatively authoritarian power, was almost destroyed, and then recovered. Both Germany and Japan had quite high growth rates in *La Première Belle Epoque*, suffered disaster in World War II, and recovered afterward at a quite different pace from "normal." Furthermore, their basic growth rates were—and stayed—much higher than they had been in earlier periods. We associate this with a fundamental change in these societies, particularly in Japan but to a great degree in all the countries (except France, which was not initially as authoritarian), from authoritarian military states to ones less authoritarian, more democratic, and strongly business-oriented. Japan and West Germany are still disciplined societies, where, however, to a remarkable degree the government is of, by, and for enlightened businessmen or people deeply concerned about business success (e.g., West German unions). It should not surprise us that there is very rapid economic growth in a society where people cooperate with a sensible government and accept its leadership, respect the authorities, and are oriented toward business and private enterprise, and that has a broad-based business community that seeks profits through a high level of economic growth rather than by restricting the market.

In Italy and France—countries we normally consider more Latin in outlook—we find an almost equally pronounced change after World War II. Their economies did rather well. However, we are not as confident of their staying power as we are of West Germany's and of Japan's. Even West Germany, after early unusually high growth, slowed down so much that for the last fifteen years it has been surpassed in GNP growth by France by about 20 percent. However, we think that the long-term pattern will be slower growth in the Latin countries, but not as slow as in the Atlantic Protestant culture area nations. The effects of prosperity have been disorganizing and disorienting in these Latin countries in some but not all the ways described in Chapter 4 when we discussed sociopolitical effects associated with a long upswing in economic growth at the secular stage of the long-term Multifold Trend. In these countries religion, family, and tradition seemed to have prevented the development of an indigenous hippie-type culture.

The growth of the United States (Figure 7.4) has a somewhat different history from most of the other countries. The United States had a high rate of economic growth more or less continuously from 1880 until 1929 (or for fifteen years after *La Mauvaise Epoque* began), although there was a distinct difference between the two periods 1880 to 1895 and 1895 to 1929. Whether the high growth rate during the early part of *La Mauvaise Epoque* was because the United States was not damaged by the war or because of the tax cut put through by the secretary of treasury in the Harding administration just after the war, or whether it was due to other things is, and will remain, the subject of much discussion and controversy. The Great Depression hit the United States severely. While the United States had sustained growth from 1938 on, it never really recovered the momentum lost in the recession until the peak of World War II, when it barely hit the level of production that would have been extrapolated from the growth curves of *La Première Belle Epoque* (or even from 1880 to

FIGURE 7.4
Total Output for Canada and the United States (1913 = 100)

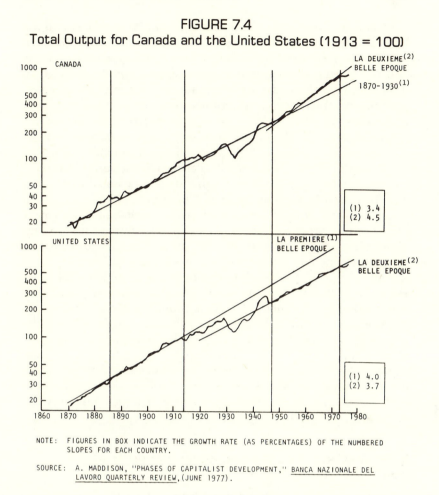

NOTE: FIGURES IN BOX INDICATE THE GROWTH RATE (AS PERCENTAGES) OF THE NUMBERED SLOPES FOR EACH COUNTRY.

SOURCE: A. MADDISON, "PHASES OF CAPITALIST DEVELOPMENT," BANCA NAZIONALE DEL LAVORO QUARTERLY REVIEW, (JUNE 1977).

1929). The United States record in *La Deuxième Belle Epoque* is not bad, but it clearly is not going to catch up with the trends established in the long period from 1880 to 1929.

Except for the many excesses committed under one of the most intensive and mismanaged government efforts at regulation that we know of in the West (as far as energy, environmental, ecological, health, safety, and similar regulation issues are concerned), the United States would appear to most observers, including us, as doing better today than many of the European ACNs. However, the United States also has many of the problems previously discussed under the heading of institutional-Kondratieff perspective.

Perhaps the verdict should be more mixed. We do know that the United States economy has managed to generate five million jobs in a two-year period from 1976 to 1978; this is quite impressive, but it is also associated with a lessened rate of increase in productivity. Also, the current revolt in the United States against excesses in taxes, government interference, government waste, and the excessive influence of the New Class seems likely to have some important constructive results. As a result of all of the above, we tend to think that the United States will have a relatively smooth voyage in *L'époque de Malaise*. However, this depends on the current backlash (against what we earlier called creeping stagnation and the new costs and risks) having a serious and constructive impact.

One positive sign is the more realistic approach to unemployment that currently prevails. Few serious or knowledgeable United States economists would today argue that the present 5.5 to 6 percent unemployment rate represents a basic systemwide problem. It is widely recognized that an arbitrary target such as the 4 percent of the Humphrey-Hawkins bill is unrealistic and that unemployment itself is comprised of a number of specific problems, mostly among the unemployed themselves. The remedies thus lie in fixing the unemployed, not in fixing the system. What is needed is a rifle, not a shotgun, approach; specific targeted programs rather than a broad stimulation of the economy. We believe on the basis of other studies, that such specific programs are very possible and could be done quite well. We see no signs, however, by and large, that such programs will be carried through under current conditions.

Why the ACNs Should Slow Down, But Not the MIs (Particularly Not the NICs)

We now take a closer look at what happened during *La Deuxième Belle Epoque* and why we argue in our Guarded Optimism Scenario that: (1) the growth rates of the Affluent nations will be substantially lower in the future; but (2) those of the Middle Income nations will probably continue at about the same level as the recent past, or at least are unlikely to increase or decrease very much; and (3) much the same is true for the Poor nations, except that some of the Very Poor ones may be able to get on the bus as well (however our Guarded Optimism Scenario is—relative to most expectations—quite optimistic about the Very Poor).

The exceptionally rapid growth that took place in the Affluent Capitalist nations during the period 1948 to 1973 stemmed from a number of sources, many of which no longer have significance for these countries. However, they are now likely to become significant for the Middle Income and Poor countries even during *L'époque de Malaise.* A rapid growth of markets stimulated dramatic gains in productivity because of economies of scale at a time when growth of markets and development of new technologies were mutually reinforcing. For most of the ACNs the bulk of the increase in market size was a catch-up phenomenon compensating for the losses of the war and the after-effects of the Great Depression. Equally important were dramatic increases in population, in domestic income per capita, and in the application of new technologies and related innovations. Increased demand for the outside world was only a fraction of the increase in domestic demand. None of these sources of stimulation appears likely to recur for some time (if ever) on the same scale for the ACNs, while something much like it will occur in the Middle Income nations.

Growth was also fostered by removal of international trade barriers and the creation of many new multinational trade and payment institutions to expand credit and facilitate movement of money, goods, and services. The Affluent nations could go much further in this direction, but not dramatically; most current attempts at reform are aimed at preventing abuses of the system and a regression in the world trading system. The world can still greatly improve trade relations of the Affluent with the other groups and trade relations among the other groups themselves, but is unlikely to do anything that has as big an impact on the Affluent as it did before 1973.

But interesting developments are opening up among the Middle Income nations and between the Middle Income and the Poor nations. While there has been much concern about the indebtedness of the Third World, it seems likely that as long as Third World prospects are attractive, there will be a steady and increasing flow of private funds to the more credit-worthy countries at rates that absolutely dwarf current and historical economic aid programs (with the possible exception of those of the immediate post–World War II period and the Marshall Plan). These sources of foreign funds are also likely to be supplemented by increasing savings rates in these same countries. As a result, we do not believe there should be any serious capital problems to limit their further economic growth. In fact, in many ways they should have fewer problems getting capital than the developed countries had at corresponding periods of their growth.

We are not saying that the banks making these loans are being prudent; we are saying that from the viewpoint of world economic development it is a good thing that they are doing this. Imagine, for example, that there was one chance in ten of a loan being defaulted within ten years. This would imply that the bank should be getting at least 15 percent real interest rates, and they are not; they are getting much less than this. But the risk that the banks run is not overwhelming; they have a small chance of serious injury and a large chance of doing well. In addition to the returns to the banks there is a great return to a large number of other peoples and many benefits which are simply not going to accrue to the lender. The banks, of course, are not doing this out of altruism; they are doing it because, one can almost say, they are "greedy for profits," but this is too strong.

A major cause of the recent growth of the ACNs was that Europe and Japan benefited from what the OECD has referred to as a technological and managerial gap between Europe and the United States. This provided great opportunities to raise productivity by importing knowledge along with more advanced equipment and then further improving productivity by improving management, often via the establishment of American transnational corporation subsidiaries or joint ventures in Europe. This technological and managerial backlog always existed. However, given the European and Japanese willingness and ability to absorb the new technologies and managerial techniques, the rapid expansion of world markets, and the relatively free international exchange of goods and capital, the opportunities created were enhanced and flourished.

Exactly this situation now exists among most of the Middle Income nations and to a much lesser extent among some of the Poor nations in their relationship to all of the ACNs, not just to the United States. Furthermore, the gross national product of capitalist Middle Income countries is about $1 trillion, or almost as large as the market of the ACNs in 1948. Considering their external market in the ACNs, their total effective market is in many ways larger. The size and current rate of growth implies that those Middle Income countries which have picked up the technique of growth could well have a *Belle Epoque* of their own as they close the gap between themselves and the ACNs. On the other hand, the technological and managerial gaps among Europe, Japan, and the United States have narrowed greatly. There is no sign that Europe will leap ahead of the United States, but Japan may.

Many of the productivity gains in the ACNs came from a movement of labor into more productive pursuits. The labor shift from agriculture yielded much productivity in France, Germany, Italy, and Japan; shifts from non-farm individual proprietorships to wage and salary employment were also significant in France, Italy, the Netherlands, and Norway. While these shifts could proceed further in the ACNs, only much smaller productivity gains will be available. The opportunities for growth by improved allocation of labor in the Middle Income nations and the Poor nations are actually larger than they ever were in the Affluent nations. The process has started and has gained great momentum in the NICs. We expect this to be the major source of growth in many Third World countries. While there is room for movement out of agriculture and non-farm self-employment in France, Italy, and Japan, they are unlikely to contribute even half as much to the growth rates of those countries as they did in the past. In the United States, the United Kingdom, Canada, and Germany any further shift from farms will have hardly any impact at all.[4]

Economic growth was stimulated also by exceptionally strong demand for consumer-durable goods. This in part reflected the pent-up demand from the Great Depression and World War II, plus growth associated with the automobile, increase in population, and the many new products developed or perfected in the early part of *La Deuxième Belle Epoque.* While the ACNs are ending this phase of economic growth, the Middle Income nations are just entering it.

While these products have been around a long time they are just being introduced to most of the consumers. And soon both higher income and consumer credit will be available to them. Savings and loan associations, for example, are now beginning to appear on a limited basis in many of these countries. The availability of products and credit will strengthen demand and reinforce opportunities for productivity growth.

In the Affluent countries, new products such as advanced communications equipment (automobile telephones, picture-phones, very large TV screens, videotape systems, home computers, and other electronic devices) and a variety of other new technologies may create new demand to support more moderate growth, but it is not likely to become large scale. Even where the potential market is large there is likely to be great technological success in bringing down the costs. (The already high levels of income make many such big ticket items easily affordable even at higher prices.) The result is that the demand has much less impact on national growth. Again, in Middle Income countries, the future availability of all these items means that at every level of income people will seek interesting and useful products to buy that they are likely to want, and for a very long time. All this helps motivate efforts to save and to produce more income, a serious problem in many

FIGURE 7.5
Growth Rates of Capital Stock Per Employee and Output Per Employee, Ten Industrial Countries, 1963-1974

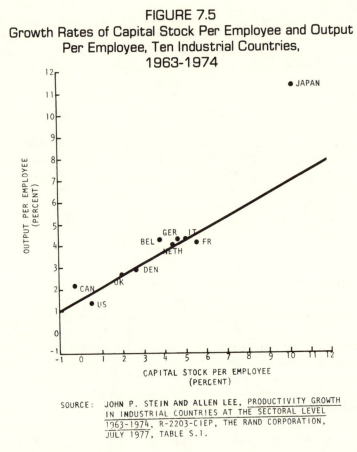

CAPITAL STOCK PER EMPLOYEE
(PERCENT)

SOURCE: JOHN P. STEIN AND ALLEN LEE, PRODUCTIVITY GROWTH IN INDUSTRIAL COUNTRIES AT THE SECTORAL LEVEL 1963-1974, R-2203-CIEP, THE RAND CORPORATION, JULY 1977, TABLE S.1.

Third World countries.

A major force behind the rapid rise in productivity in ACNs has been their high levels of capital investment. Figure 7.5 shows that the industrialized countries with the most rapid growth in plant and equipment per employee have tended to have the greatest increases in output per employee. This reflects not only the direct effects on productivity of more capital per worker, but also the greater improvements in technology introduced by the accompanying new machinery and plant and changes in production.[5]

We expect the effect of rising capital per worker to be even greater in Middle Income countries and in the Poor countries. In the Affluent countries, the effect of new investment is partly negated by the removal of old or obsolete equipment. In these Third World countries, new investment tends to generate new plant and equipment with much less retirement of all plant and equipment. Furthermore, the Poor countries do not have to move gradually through all the stages of technological development that occurred in the ACNs. Often, they can move directly into very modern technologies with large productivity gains. Some Middle Income countries have labor forces that are basically as efficient as any, and new equipment creates an output per worker almost equal to that of the ACNs—an enormous increase from the level that they had when working with obsolete equipment or not working at all.

One of the most important sources of past growth, the improvement in educational level of the labor force, almost has to slow down substantially in the United States, since the United States has already achieved an extraordinarily high level of education. (Yet important increases in learning beyond formal schooling may still occur among the many female, younger, and minority workers.) Many of the OECD countries have considerable room for increase in skills through education, but we doubt that they will pursue this tactic as far as the United States has (with the exception of Japan, which already is doing so). The advances caused by better education are potentially great in the Middle Income countries, particularly because many have already created a system that can provide the education and the students and effectively utilize the graduates.

Many of the Poor countries, unfortunately, already have "too many" people educated at a high level, in the sense that there are too few opportunities for these people. The resources and effort that went into educating them do not normally bring further economic growth. Sometimes this is also true in Middle Income countries, but decreasingly so—another reason why we expect them to continue or increase their recent rates of growth.

Presumably these are also some of the reasons why, as Stein and Lee point out, the industrial countries with the most rapid growth of both capital per worker and productivity tend to be those that initially had the lowest levels of efficiency and capital stock.[6] This convergence is made possible by the transfer of technology and illustrates how gaps generate more rapid development.

While many of the forces that operated during *La Deuxième Belle Epoque* will continue to be significant, their impact will not be the same on the Advanced Capitalist nations. However, given a reasonable international environment, they will operate very effectively on the Middle Income nations. Markets have been opened up that are already so large that it is most unlikely that the further opening and growth of markets will have a comparable impact on opportunities for already industrialized countries to achieve major improvements in efficiency. A main effect of further market growth will be to extend opportunities for a broader set of countries.

Where Does the United States Stand?

The United States is now out of step. During the last half of *La Deuxième Belle Epoque,* the Advanced Capitalist nations largely conformed in timing many major growth movements. They all generally advanced together from 1948 to 1973. During the early and middle parts of that period, an expansion in one country was often balanced by a recession in another. In the latter part of that period, these countries began to experience synchronous business cycles which intensified the later expansions and recessions. Luckily, it now looks as if the ACNs will no longer have such synchronized business cycles. Of course, for a while the OECD attempted to make them synchronous again by applying the "locomotive" theory promulgated at several of the summit conferences. According to this theory the West Germans and Japanese should force their economies to expand much faster than the governments concerned were willing to risk, for fear of renewed inflation and other counterproductive effects, in order to get in phase with the United States and thus help other countries of the world.

In the United States increases in productivity slowed remarkably after 1968, while in all the other major industrial countries productivity increased relatively rapidly in the early 1970s and then declined abruptly after 1973. Paradoxically one could relate the faster recovery of the United States to this lessened increase in productivity. One can say the United States entered into a malaise period early and had started to recover as the others entered a similar malaise period. More specifically, the United States does not have the huge overcapacity that almost all the other ACNs do, simply because the United States failed to expand its capital base in the late 1960s as fast as the other ACNs did. This was not because the United States had a smarter government or even smarter businessmen, but because capital investment dropped startlingly. The exact cause and effect relationships for the slowdowns in investment are controversial, but we are reasonably certain that these include many acts of the government— both acts of omission (refusal to correct the tax system for the effects of inflation) and acts of commission (active promulgation of many onerous regulations and active interference by regulatory agencies).

Presumably the single most important proximate reason for the slowdown of economic growth in the United States since the mid-

1960s is the sluggish rate of capital investment—again both cause and effect. It resulted in less advanced equipment, less equipment per worker, and a general slowdown in applying new technology. Capital-per-worker failed to rise at previous rates simply because businesses facing unusually large risks with no corresponding prospects of large gains were unwilling to make irrevocable large-scale commitments. (See Figure 7.5.)

The slowdown in productivity growth is probably also as much an effect as a cause of the malaise. From 1965 to 1975 the United States' social climate was characterized by divisions over the Vietnamese war, race riots, loss of confidence in United States institutions, growing feelings of powerlessness and alienation. In addition, the Fourteen New Emphases emerged so rapidly and intensely that the social limits-to-growth psychology pervaded and even dominated—at least temporarily—much of the governmental bureaucracy. Environment, ecology, and health regulations are particularly stark examples, but there were also many others.

An important factor that was much more prominent in the United States and Canada than in the other countries was an unusually large increase in labor force since the mid-1960s, as more women participated in the labor force (see Table 7.1) and the "baby boom" children came of age. While there was a rise in female labor force participation throughout the OECD, the change was particularly rapid in the United States and Canada and was not counterbalanced by other changes in the labor force. As a result, the growth in employment in the United States was far more rapid than in other major OECD countries (Table 7.2). The United States added about five million jobs to the system in the two-year period from early 1976 to early 1978—an unprecedented increase. Canada also had high birth rates throughout the 1950s and rapid growth in female participation in the labor force. Therefore, Canada also showed a very strong rise in employment.

Because United States employment growth was so high, the slower growth of capital per worker was less an actual slowdown in investment than a failure of capital investment to rise correspondingly. This change reflected the shift toward greater use of labor relative to capital, a shift that accounts for the extraordinary gains in employment in the United States through the 1975 recession and into 1978. The rise in labor demand appears to have been a direct response to conditions that made increasing labor relatively less expensive and risky than investing more capital. The increase in energy costs was one such condition. The rise in environmental, health, and safety costs was another. (Both tended to raise the costs of capital-intensive

TABLE 7.1
Labor Force Participation Rates of Women Aged 25-64, 1960-74

Country	1960 or 1961	1965	1970	1974 or 1975
Canada	30.1%	—	38.4%	44.4%
United States	40.4	45.0%	48.0	58.6
Belgium	26.5	—	30.6	33.0
Denmark	35.2	40.0	50.4	63.0
Finland	54.8	—	59.2	65.8
France	42.0	43.0	47.0	—
Germany	43.7	45.8	45.9	—
Netherlands	16.1	—	17.9	18.9
Sweden	34.7	—	59.4	68.4
United Kingdom	41.5	—	49.3	52.5

Source: Paul McCracken, et al., *Towards Full Employment and Price Stability*
(Paris: OECD, June 1977) Table A-12. The readers might note the low participation of women in the Netherlands. In this country there is great admiration and respect for women who "keep house" competently. This is
another example of a cultural factor being more important than basic
economic trends—at least for a while.

production more than they did the costs of labor-intensive
production.)

There were also disproportionate effects on capital as a result of the
tax treatment of illusory gains caused by inflation. Illusionary
increases in interest rates, dividends, and profits that only compen-
sated for the loss of purchasing power were all treated as real increases
in income for tax purposes. Depreciation allowances were based on
original rather than replacement costs and capital gains caused by
inflation were taxed as real gains. These higher tax costs had a
particularly distorting effect on the costs of capital relative to labor in
a tax system that relies fairly heavily on revenue from non-labor
income. Also, the growth of the labor supply itself tended to hold
down the relative cost of labor. And finally there was relatively little
of the kind of legally enforced job security that is so prevalent in
European ACNs and many less developed nations that makes it so
risky for an employer to add new workers.

The growth of the United States labor supply was so rapid that it
masked the extent of the loss of productivity that resulted from a
failure of capital investment to keep up with rising employment.
While the growth rates of GNP per employee declined by 1.4 percent

TABLE 7.2
Average Annual Rate of Change of Employment, 1963–1974

Belgium	0.5%
Canada	3.0
Denmark	1.1
France	0.9
Germany	-0.1
Italy	-0.4
Japan	1.2
Netherlands	0.7
United Kingdom	0.0
United States	2.2

Source: John P. Stein and Allen Lee, *Productivity Growth in Industrial Countries at the Sectoral Level, 1963–1974,* R-2203-CIEP (The RAND Corporation, July 1977).

per year between the periods 1947 to 1966 and 1966 to 1973, the growth rate of total GNP declined by only .7 percent. The growth of employment came at the expense of the growth of GNP per worker, rather than in addition to it, as labor was substituted for capital. While high employment growth would ordinarily stimulate demand, no significant increase occurred because the rise in per capita income was smaller because of lower productivity growth.

The growth in employment per capita in the United States will taper off in the 1980s, but the effects of the rapid growth of the female labor force will continue through the entire decade. Women now remain in the labor force for extended periods, are able to accumulate more experience, and will benefit from reductions in barriers to female employment. The skills that women develop and the improvements in utilizing female labor will add significantly to productivity in the United States in the 1980s, offsetting what would otherwise be a further slowdown in growth from labor factors.

To a lesser degree the same may occur, in many other industrialized countries, but the conditions that resulted in slower capital spending are likely to continue and to restrain investment further. Our projections for United States productivity growth are much more akin to the 1966 to 1973 experience than to the preceding years.

The World Trading System

Generally speaking, trade between two countries should be mutually beneficial in the long run. Each one should produce things

TABLE 7.3
U.S. Productivity

| | *Average Annual Rate of Change* | | |
	1947–1966	*1966–1973*	Difference
GNP	4.0%	3.3%	– .7%
Employment	1.3	2.1	+ .8
GNP per Employee	2.6	1.2	–1.4

Source: United States Council of Economic Advisers, *Annual Report,* (Washington, D.C.: January 27, 1978), Appendix A, various tables.

for which it has a comparative advantage and export them to import things for which the other country has a comparative advantage. We mention this only because so much of the current discussion is cast in the language of war or zero-sum games (that is, relationships in which one side's gain is automatically the other side's loss)—for instance, trade offensive and positive balances.[7] Much of the voluminous literature on this subject assumes a long-run equilibrium situation. However, the extensive and rapid introduction of outside commodities can be very disruptive, at least for a time. There are in addition many other *caveats* qualifying the simple free trade argument that we do not wish to go into at this point. We would like to point out, however, that expanding trade among nations can hurt a country when some other country takes away its customers. For example, the United States earns much foreign exchange by selling soybeans to the world, but if the Brazilians take away that export market, the United States does not necessarily gain from increased world trade (although the world as a whole might). This could also be true for the Swedes if Brazilian competition takes away their iron market. It may be partly true for London and New York as the Singapore financial market grows and takes away some of the business generated in the Pacific Basin. In all these situations, as comparative advantages change over time, the expansion in trade may hurt the less competitive country but continue to help the countries that can remain internationally competitive in traded goods. It seems quite likely that while the growth of the NICs will be, on balance, good for almost everyone, their competition might hurt those ACNs that do not adjust to the new conditions.

It is because the benefits from trade can be quite large that the long decline in world trade that accompanied *La Mauvaise Epoque* was so harshly felt in the world economy. In unsettled times such as depression or chronic stagflation some groups of people, especially those earning their livelihood in industries competing with imports but who in better times might accept more passively foreign competition, may turn the attention of the public and lawmakers from the benefits to the costs (lost jobs, for example) of trade; protectionism then threatens. The so-called beggar-thy-neighbor protectionist policies of the Great Depression reflected tragically changed perceptions about foreign trade in bad times from positive to negative. The result was a throttling of world trade to roughly half its pre-depression level (ratio to gross domestic product).

To the extent that world trade is a contributor to growth (and it has been increasing its share in world output) it may, in our Guarded Optimism scenario, reinforce respectively the slowing and stable growth patterns of the ACNs without affecting much the rapid, sustained growth of most of the Middle Income and Poor countries. Most trade is among the ACNs. Should protectionism rise in response to a long-run slowing of the ACNs' growth, declining or stagnating trade will tend to reinforce the slowdown—a not-insubstantial effect, given the present relative openness of the world economy. It is thus entirely plausible, given the extreme precedent of the Great Depression and the growing wave of protectionistic sentiment among the ACNs, that slow growth in world trade and GNP would mutually reinforce each other to moderate the growth of the ACNs' economies. Only recently did the industrialized nations reach the peak of world trade in relation to GNP that they had prior to World War I. But the very aggressiveness of the Middle Income and some of the Poor countries—and their increasing comparative advantages (discussed below)—enable them to exploit them fully.

Trade in the Emerging Super-Industrial World Economy

We will mainly consider in our discussion of trade in the emerging super-industrial world economy three groups of countries: ACNs, NICs, and the Poor. The other MIs have characteristics between the NICs and the Poor. By and large, these three groups tend to have comparative advantages as Tables 7.4, 7.5, and 7.6 show.

While there is nothing startling on these lists, examining them provides some sense of the likely trends during the rest of this century. The big market of the world, of course, will continue to be the ACNs. However, the ACNs will increasingly price themselves out of certain activities. In many cases they will not let economic considerations dominate but will choose to subsidize these activities or protect them

TABLE 7.4
Areas in Which Poor Countries Tend to Have a Comparative Advantage

---

1. Tourism, second homes, retirement
2. Exported labor
3. Cheap consumer electronics
4. Cheap shoes and clothes
5. Cheap bicycles and toys
6. Many commodities
7. Many spare parts
8. Cheap sporting goods
9. Souvenirs and bric-a-brac
10. Other national resources
11. Some rip-offs
12. Esoteric activities (e.g., importation of archeologists, Peace Corps, missionaries, international officials, and commission development experts, etc.)
13. And a gradual (or sometimes rapid) movement into the area now being exploited by the Middle Income countries

---

rather than allow them to be replaced. Such protection could involve the hope of preventing or deferring structural adjustments due to excess capacity, such as those that the Japanese and the European economies in particular seem to have to make in a period of lackadaisical economic activity. In fact, the United States seems to be moving toward a labor-intensive and away from a capital-intensive emphasis.

This paradoxical situation is not completely understood. However, to the extent that either the Rostow-Kondratieff, or the Forrester-Kondratieff interpretation is accurate for Western Europe and Japan, they will be under enormous pressures not to accept the full force of the necessary adjustments but to increase protectionism more than they would normally like to do. The major stabilizing element in this situation is the great fear of repeating something like the Smoot-Hawley tariff in particular and large-scale beggar-thy-neighbor policies in general.

Everybody knows that most countries are now engaging in "salami tactics"—increasing their protectionism one thin slice at a time. The hope in the current salami tactic situation is that no individual slice will provoke great retaliation or destabilize the system, while at the same time each slice taken will relieve internal pressures to go much

TABLE 7.5

Areas in Which New Industrial Countries (NICs) Tend to Have a Comparative Advantage

---

1. Mass market quality consumer electronics
2. Conventional ships (including super large ships)
3. Ordinary steel, other basic metals
4. Motor vehicle parts (very soon motor vehicles)
5. Some petrochemicals
6. Medium priced textiles (natural and synthetic)
7. Many machine tools, expensive but conventional tool and die components, etc.
8. Simple motors, engines, generators
9. Medium quality bicycles, toys, golf carts, motor scooters, and motorcycles
10. Low-priced shoes, ordinary mass-produced clothes
11. Typewriters, simple office machines, some modern small calculators
12. Sewing machines, chinaware, silver, cookware, many other household appliances
13. Ordinary and some precision optical equipment, some quality cameras (under license)
14. Ripoffs: patent and copyright infringements, cheap copies of popular goods, etc.
15. And almost all of the items on the Poor countries list.

---

further. The hope may well be realized. If one has a growing salami and the slices are thin enough, the situation can be basically stable—perhaps more stable than if there are no cuts at all, so that the pressures to make large cuts by adding extreme protectionist policies become overwhelming.

The interests of the New Industrial countries in particular and Middle Income countries in general are no longer identical with those of the Poor countries. The former are interested in rapidly growing markets, rapidly growing trade among themselves and with the ACNs, and easy access to substantial commercial credit. All this implies great interest in having and abiding by rules of the game (e.g., in reassuring and encouraging traders, creditors, and investors). The NICs and MIs are no longer interested in one-time profits to be obtained by nationalization or by changing the rules, but rather in a continuous process likely to lead them to great wealth in the near future.

TABLE 7.6

Areas in Which the Advanced Capitalist Nations Tend to Have a Comparative Advantage

1. Services—Human and Organization (e.g., technical skills, managerial capability, systems design, and systems implementation, etc.)
2. Investment (in having or getting capital and in the tactics and strategy of using capital)
3. Other Knowledge (and knowledge-related, e.g., publishing, training, etc.) Industries
4. Advanced Technology (e.g., big airplanes, big computers, complex electronics, nuclear power, construction, and other high quality scientific, technological equipment)
5. In many cases Advanced Agriculture (e.g., dairy products, in Denmark and New Zealand; corn, wheat, soy beans, poultry in United States, etc.)
6. In many cases Raw Materials (e.g., uranium, forest production in Canada; coal in the United States, etc.)
7. Specialized, Proprietary and/or Esoteric or Fashionable Consumer Goods (e.g., high fashion, wine, perfumes, cheese in France; children's clothes, soft drinks, bourbon, and blue denim in the United States; scotch and woolens in the United Kingdom; California and Italian sport clothes, etc.)[a]
8. Some Heavy Industry, Petrochemicals, and Specialty Steels—particularly those which are capital or technology intensive—or which can be made so.
9. Perhaps Large Construction Jobs, Oil Exploration, Prospecting, Computerized Analysis of above, etc.
10. Pop and Mass Culture and Entertainment
11. A long, but declining, tradition of attitudes and motivations conducive to economic growth as well as entrepreneurial environments, stable and fair laws, relatively honest and competent governments, etc.
12. The relatively large market size of the ACN has enabled them to develop new products earlier and achieve the competitive cost advantages of long production runs.

[a]But there is much licensed (or "value added") production in NICs—e.g., 50 percent of United States leisure wear is produced in Mexico in so-called "Border Industry Ventures" (which need not pay tax on the total value they export to the United States, but only the value they added to materials obtained from the United States). Roleii cameras and Texas Instrument computers are now produced in Singapore, Hewlett-Packard small computers in Malaysia, and so on.

The Poor countries, on the whole, do not have quite such a short-run stake in cooperating with the system, although more and more the Coping Poor do. India, for example, while it often tries to act like a spokesman for the Poor countries, is finding that its own interests lie in encouraging and obeying the rules. On a recent trip to India, I was startled by the extent to which Indian officials were conscious of the differences between their national interest and the national interests of many other Poor countries. India at the moment has a $4 billion surplus in foreign reserves, record levels of surplus grain stored, and rapidly expanding manufacturing exports.

Fortunately, while many officials have a clear-cut understanding that their interests have changed, the implementation of this understanding is very incomplete. It is now increasingly understood that this trillion-dollar market of the Middle Income countries, especially the capitalist Middle Income countries, is enormously important to the ACNs. It is therefore equally important that they not wreck this market. More than one-third of the exports of such nations as Japan and the United States now go to the capitalist Middle Income nations other than the big OPEC importers. This is a much more rapidly growing market than any other except for some of these big OPEC importers.*

We did not use any special category for the capitalist Middle Income nations, but just listed the comparative advantages of the NICs. The comparative advantage of the NICs lies in standardized, price competitive, manufactured goods, in which the lower cost and relatively productive labor of the NICs provide them with a quite substantial advantage. As the NICs increase their standard of living and their wage costs and upgrade their products, most of the other

---

*Prime Minister Lee Kuan Yew of Singapore stated the point well in his October 1978 speech to the International Chamber of Commerce meeting in Orlando, Florida. "The irony is that just as the truth is becoming apparent to the leaders of the developing countries, the new models for growth—South Korea, Taiwan, Hong Kong, Singapore, and two others in Latin America—face the danger of protectionism in the industrial countries. Plagued by high inflation and high unemployment, for which no easy solution has been found since the oil crisis, I sense a loss of nerve in some leaders in government and in industry, and amongst some academics in the West. Their confidence in working the free-market system has been shaken. . . . The crux of the problem is whether leaders in both industrial and developing countries have adjusted intellectually and emotionally to this being one interdependent world," (pp. 25-26).

Middle Income nations should be able, at one point or another, to compete with them. The Middle Income countries share the characteristics of both the Poor and the NICs. In fact, in all the NICs one still finds a large part of the activities focused on what we identify as areas in which the Poor countries often have an advantage.

The Role of the Gap: NIEO versus NIEFD

In 1974 the United Nations General Assembly adopted a declaration establishing the New International Economic Order (NIEO). The preamble to the NIEO Declaration reads, "The gap between the developed and the developing countries continues to widen." The NIEO argument for international redistribution of wealth rests on this statement, which has to be accepted largely without argument.

We think this is surprising in view of the facts. If the NIEO and similar issues (e.g., the north-south dispute) continue to dominate discussions of development as they have so far, the effects will range from innocuously misleading to counterproductive. We now present some pertinent reasons why the gap idea is misconstrued and discuss how the gap can be productively used in future development policies.

Probably the most important engine of economic development has been the gap. Stated simply, a number of civilizations have appeared on earth, flourished, and then waned. Many of these civilizations were in a good position to launch an industrial revolution, but none did. Today every culture in this world is on its way to industrialize in whole or in part for a simple reason: the West showed them how to do it and in many cases provided the wherewithal and examples.

The Advanced countries of the world, whether Western or not in culture, still play this role. Table 7.7 shows how the gap helps trade.[8] In particular, the ACNs contribute heavily to establishing what we call the New International Environment for Development (NIEFD). We believe NIEFD is a much more valid and important concept than NIEO, which we consider mostly an occasion for and exercise in rhetoric. We do not disparage the earnest and sincere people who are trying to improve the lives of their own people and of others, but we feel much anger and some contempt toward those whose efforts are— or provide cover for—the worst forms of hypocrisy, demagoguery, and confusion.

One pernicious current motivation behind the declaration of the NIEO is the often explicitly stated and widely accepted belief that the poverty of the many has been directly caused by exploitation by the

TABLE 7.7
Why and How the Gap Helps (i.e., The New International
Environment for Development)

1. Secular Increase in Scale of Operations and of Gross World Product
   A. Demand for Resources
   B. Expanding Markets for "Low Technology" or Labor Intensive Producers
   C. Other Demand for Labor
   D. Tourism—Case of Spain
   E. Capital Availability
   F. Importing of "Polluting" Industries
   G. TNCs—More, Bigger, and More Skilled
   H. Extraordinarily Complex and Flexible World Economy

2. Acculturization and Momentum of Economic Development
   A. Examples and Experience Accumulate
   B. Institutions are Created and Gain in Capability
   C. Existing Infrastructure Grows
   D. Improved Communications and Transportation Capabilities
   E. Learning Curves

3. Increased Productivity and Technological Capability
   A. New Industries and Technologies
   B. Many Transferable Technologies—Almost All from User Perspective, Many from Producer Perspective As Well
   C. Above includes: (1) Education, (2) Agriculture, (3) Medicine, and (4) Entertainment

4. From Relative Dependence to Relative Independence
   A. Exploit Various Options Created by 3 Above
   B. Import Substitution
   C. Internal Education, Training, and Research
   D. Changing Patterns of Foreign Aid and of Development Institutions
   E. Other Indigenization of Many Activities

5. Relative External Stability and Freedom from Aggression and Conquest

few. Such a belief is firmly seated on a childish notion of blame (my problem is your fault) and postpones or begs the important questions about what to do. Even if we were to accept the premise of blame and make "retribution" by redistributing wealth, there is increasing evidence that mere aid has not accomplished by a long shot what the world hoped it would in the thirty years since Truman's Point Four program began. Even larger transfers of wealth, therefore, are unlikely to insure future growth, technological advancement, or prosperity in the Third World.

Bauer and Yamey make the point exceedingly well:

> Economic achievement and progress depend primarily on favorable domestic factors, including government policies. The presence of favorable factors cannot be taken for granted anywhere, and indeed are singularly absent in many Third World countries. While wealth transfers would reduce income differences between the West and the Third World, they would do so principally by reducing incomes in the West rather than by increasing productivity, and hence *sustainable* [our italics] incomes, in the Third World.[9]

This is exactly the point. Are we to be satisfied with band-aid or cosmetic solutions, or do we want to do the difficult work and face the realities involved in creating sustainable incomes through higher productivity and more jobs? The cliché *helping people help themselves* has become banal, often a euphemism for plain old redistributive aid. Yet the original meaning of the phrase still applies with a remarkable clarity and simplicity. People must, in the end, *do it themselves*, just as children learning to walk cannot walk by themselves except by walking by themselves. But, just as there are ways in which adults can help children, so nations can and must help each other in ways which are actually constructive and not just rhetorically, ideologically, or emotionally satisfying.

First, we argue that a rethinking of the current gap of ideology is necessary, a rethinking we believe fits well with the concept of New International Environment for Development. NIEFD recognizes that continued growth and sustainable incomes are good things for all nations—both the so-called Rich and the so-called Poor. The role of the gap, therefore, is not productive as long as it is conceived of as demarcating in pernicious terms the distance between the two. A more appropriate role for the gap rests on its conception as a stimulus to further growth rather than as a symptom of ill health and inequity. In particular, it is plainly incorrect to think of the Third World as composed of "have-not" nations whose interests are homogeneous and opposed to the "have" nations. As a stimulus to growth, recognition of the successes of the NICs specifically, of the Middle Income countries generally, and even of many of the Coping Poor, and an analysis of their success in economic growth would be much more productive than tirades and lamentations.

The usual description of the world economy as a "three worlds" economy is grossly inadequate for most purposes. Lumping all the Middle Income countries and the Poor countries together as the Third World shows a failure to recognize the emergence of a genuine middle class. This group of nations is where the dynamism of the world is located; it is growing at about twice the rate of the ACNs. It has almost a fifth of the gross product of the ACNs, but its annual increment is more than a third of that of the ACNs. Very soon this annual increment will be greater than that of the annual increment of the United States. For this and other reasons, the entire concept of a simple gap is rapidly becoming meaningless.

The continuous distribution of income capabilities, productivity, technology and the use of advanced technology and capital-intensive industries now ranges from the extremely Poor countries such as Bangladesh through the very wealthy but sluggish economies of Switzerland and Sweden. The Fourteen New Emphases are also inordinately important at the high end of the curve. This implies that the center of mass of this distribution will rapidly move towards the wealthy end of the spectrum and that increasingly the curve will have a situation where the median is quite close to the uppermost two or three centiles. In this significant sense the gap is closing. Nevertheless, interest in the gap concept is now greater than ever before.

Despite abundant gap rhetoric, the relative improvement of much of the Third World has now come to be understood. A useful, clear, and even eloquent expression of the new understanding appeared in the 1977 report of Robert McNamara, president of the World Bank. Perhaps we may be forgiven for contrasting his 1977 position with a major address he gave in February 1970 at a conference convened by Columbia University to consider the results of the first development decade.

> In the first Development Decade, the primary development objective, a 5 percent annual growth in GNP, was achieved. This was a major accomplishment. The 5 percent rate exceeded the average growth rates of the advanced countries during their own early stages of progress in the last century. But this relatively high rate of growth in GNP did not bring satisfactory progress in the development. In the developing

world, at the end of the decade:

- Malnutrition is common . . .
- Infant mortality is high . . .
- Life expectancy is low . . .
- Illiteracy is widespread . . .
- Unemployment is endemic and growing . . .
- The redistribution of income and wealth is severely skewed . . .
- The gap between the per capita incomes of rich nations is widening rather than narrowing, both relatively and absolutely. At the extremes that gap is already more than $3,000. Present projections indicate it may well widen to $9,000 by the end of the century. In the year 2000, per capita income in the United States is expected to be approximately $10,000; in Brazil, $500; and in India, $200.

Just how much worse these conditions are at the end of the decade than they were at the beginning is difficult to determine. For most of them, even today, we lack satisfactory indicators and data. The result is that trying to plan to improve these conditions, in the absence of such measures and indicators, is like trying to plan price stabilization without price indices. It is an impossible task.[10]

Notice that the problems listed by McNamara in this talk are still going to be troublesome in the year 2000. No matter how successful economic development is, between a fifth and a third of the world's population will still have the characteristics he stated. It is quite correct that very likely the malnutrition will not be as bad, the mortality will be much lower, life expectancy will be much higher, the illiteracy rate will not be quite as high and so on. But anybody who wishes to argue that these problems will still exist has a good case.

The address goes on to point out that from almost every essential viewpoint the First Development Decade was a failure. In doing so, McNamara pointed out such obvious things as that on the average the Poor countries and the less successful ones did not do as well as the more successful ones. But in doing so, and without himself realizing it, he made clear that in fact the decade was much more successful than most people believed. Thus, he explained that the very Poor countries did not do as well as the Affluent countries and had increased their per capita income less. But this showed that it was not true that the rich get richer and the poor get poorer; it was only true that the poor got rich at a slower rate than the rich. He did not point out the emergence of these extraordinarily successful New Industrial countries or even that the Middle Income countries in general were beginning to do well—though both phenomena were obvious.

It can be difficult to maintain or create morale and commitment unless one knows how well one is doing. It is important to understand that if one has a situation where the poor average $200 per capita and the rich $3,000 with a gap of $2,800 and both numbers triple ($600 and $9,000 respectively), the poor are not worse off because the gap has increased to $8,400. The change in the quality of life of the poor will be qualitative and much more dramatic than the marginal and quantitative change in the quality of life of the rich. Universally, the poor seem to recognize this, but the rich do not. Therefore, we think of this as a problem of the rich and not of the poor.

Increasingly there will be a situation similar to that in the United States during the Depression when President Roosevelt pointed out that one third of the country was ill-fed, ill-housed, ill-clothed. In the present world this is more like 50 percent, but both the percentages will go down and the meaning of being poor will be changed. This is all that we can expect to happen in the next two or three decades. We should not make the mistake that Robert Kennedy made when he visited Rio de Janeiro and remarked that the *favelas* (shanty towns) were worse than the slums of Calcutta. Actually at that time the *favelas* in Rio de Janeiro housed some of the most upwardly mobile groups in Latin America. While the wages per employed worker were quite low, most of the families had two or three people working. They had meat two or three times a week or more. As soon as television became available they were able to purchase sets, and so on. On the other hand, at that time people went to the slums of Calcutta to die. They were at the end of the line.

It is terribly important not to confuse success and failure; it is equally important not to project one's own problems as those of the poor. Robert Kennedy was not the worst offender; we quote him because his position was so dramatic, so wrong, and so easy for someone from a rich country to take.

Some More on Middle Income Countries (Including Some NICs)

The People's Republic of China

We begin with the People's Republic of China, the largest Middle Income country, where the current leadership has decided to modernize rapidly, has set new and apparently practical goals, and intends to join the international world system financially and economically as well as politically. In late 1978 many exciting events were taking place in China. It appeared that China might no longer rigidly hew to the Maoist slogans of "ideology and production, but ideology before production" and "Red and expert, but Red before expert." It emerged as a distinct possibility that the Chinese might turn their backs on the old concepts of independence and self-reliance and follow a path similar to those already followed by South Korea and Japan. Specifically, it seems quite plausible that the Chinese will roll up debts of more than 100 billion dollars by 1990, and that they will become major exporters.

It is interesting to indicate just how big the effects of China taking such a path may be. We start with some optimistic numbers and make some optimistic assumptions, but all are quite plausible. Extrapolating and modifying the World Bank data, we conclude that in 1978 China had about 900 million people, about $500 per capita income, and a total GNP of about $450 million. We assume two possible sets of figures for growth rates, and give the results of assuming both in Table 7.8, based on moderately optimistic and optimistic assumptions respectively.

We assume that the population growth rate between 1978 and 1990 averages between 1.2 and 1.5 percent, and then drops as shown in the tables. More observers are willing to accept these figures, although a few believe them to be too low. We assume that GNP per capita grows between 5.5 and 6.5 percent in the future. Although these figures may seem high, the first is more or less equal to what the World Bank estimates was the growth rate of China from 1970 to 1976. We assume that because of the current reforms, the growth rate will increase by about 20 percent. We also assume a slight slowing down in these numbers from 1990 to 2000, but in fact the change might be in the other direction.

It is clear that whether one makes moderately optimistic or optimistic assumptions, China will be a very large and rather modern nation by the end of the century. However, it will still be China.[11]

Brazil

Brazil is the largest country in Latin America. It is increasingly likely that Brazil will become one of the great nations of the western hemisphere and of the world. The only issue is whether it will take twenty-five or a hundred years. This prediction reminds us of the well-known joke that used to be told in Brazil: "Our country has a great future and always will." There is an even more recent joke that, "Our country grows at night while the government sleeps. The great virtue of the current government is that it sleeps a lot." But both of

TABLE 7.8
Some Basic Chinese Indices

A. Moderate Optimism

Variable	1978	Annual Growth Rate %	Year 1990	Annual Growth Rate %	2000
Population (millions)	900	1.5	1080	1.2	1200
GNP/CAP (1978 dollars)	500	5.5	950	5.0	1550
GNP (billions)	450	7.1	1025	6.3	1880

B. Optimistic

Variable	1978	Annual Growth Rate %	Year 1990	Annual Growth Rate %	2000
Population (millions)	900	1.2	1040	1.0	1150
GNP/CAP (1978 dollars)	500	6.5	1065	1.0	1910
GNP (billions)	450	7.8	1110	7.1	2200

these jokes are now very out-of-date indeed.[12]

Brazil has important regional problems. South and southeast Brazil are probably two of the most dynamic areas in the world. We fully expect that region to achieve low to medium European standards of living by the end of the century. But northeast Brazil is very likely to be more like south Italy than north Italy, with the possibility of even greater difficulties than south Italy has. We do not believe that outsiders have any right to blame the Brazilians if they cannot solve this problem; nor do they have any right to ask them to jeopardize either their political or economic future because of this difficult problem—although this is exactly what many outsiders are asking the Brazilians to do. Brazil has a great history before it, and I am personally very pleased that they contradicted the depressing future that was suggested in a previous book, *The Year 2000*.[13]

There is clearly wide-scale violation of human rights and great police brutality in Brazil. These were not introduced by the post-1965 governments but have been characteristic of Brazil for many generations. It is not that the Brazilians are a cruel people; the exact opposite is true. As in Portugal, the bull is not killed in the Brazilian version of the bullfight, at least not in the ring. For that matter, in the Brazilian version of Ali Baba and the Forty Thieves, instead of killing the thieves by boiling them alive in hot oil, they roll the barrels into the river and the police come and take the forty thieves away. Despite numerous exceptions, the Brazilian culture is basically gentle, attractive, pleasant, empathetic, and *simpático*. But it most likely would not work well with fully democratic and parliamentary institutions—at least not in the near future. This does not mean that Brazil will never have a democracy, or more legality and civil rights than currently displayed. The government now in power has promised a full restoration of parliamentary government in a few years. I would be delighted if this turns out to be true, but I am not holding my breath. However, as governments go in much of the world—not to speak of the Third World—the Brazilian government is, if anything, far superior to the average. It is certainly superior to the average for Latin America as judged from the viewpoint of the institutions of Western Europe and Anglo-America.

This is no reason to condone certain excesses of the Brazilian government and system, but it is certainly cause to applaud the good things they have done while continuing to publicize and condemn some of the bad. The Brazilian economic miracle was largely overlooked by the general press of Anglo-America until the pollution problems began to get quite severe. Then the main points mentioned were the pollution problems, the protection of the Amazon, and the hardships inflicted on the indigenous Indians. It is also often pointed out that the minimum wage laws have not kept pace with the ravages of inflation, but it is almost never mentioned that a longitudinal study of these workers would reveal that few of them stay at a minimum wage for very long. Most of them move up very rapidly. The minimum wage is largely earned by people who have just entered the labor market or who have unfortunate problems so that they cannot join the general upward movement (particularly the aged, the infirm, or others who normally do not make minimum wages even when they are working). For most of the people working at minimum wages, this represents a sharp increase in the income they have been getting—that is, in other parts of Brazil or in being unemployed or underemployed.

Mexico

Mexico is the next great success of Latin America. Despite some recent poor prognostications, many believe it may rival Brazil. We believe that it is much more likely to have a great future than not. It is already known as the "colossus of the north" to countries in Central America (having replaced the United States in that dubious role).

During the past several years many concerned and intelligent observers developed strongly pessimistic feelings about the future of Mexico. They asked how a nation with its vast economic and social problems could cope with the population crisis that appears to be approaching. In 1978, the Mexican population stands at 65 million; by the year 2000 it is likely to more than double. However, we believe there is greater cause for optimism than for pessimism. Despite recent problems caused by short-term economic contraction, we expect Mexico to become a major power in the coming years and perhaps the recognized dominant Latin American power, wresting this title from Brazilian and Argentinian competitors. Indeed, in Mexico, per capita income is already 60 percent higher than in Brazil.

Mexico's problems in the 1970s are the growing pains of success. Many problems with the United States, such as illegal immigration, currency devaluation, and cross-border smuggling dominate the headlines. While not necessarily transitory, these are relatively easily handled. Problems between nations with common borders have always existed and always will.

The Mexican economy has been growing at a real annual rate of 6 percent since 1950. It has been one of the most stable high-growth economies in the developing world. This growth has had a dramatic side effect; average Mexicans are much better off than their parents or grandparents. Table 7.9 shows the national poverty index since 1910.

We view the future of Mexico so optimistically because of the following factors responsible for past and future growth:

1. *The demographic transition.* Mexican birthrates are now quite high, averaging 38 births per 1000 population in 1974. However, most other Latin American nations have experienced sharp fertility declines and Mexico can be expected to follow suit. Mexico now has one of the most comprehensive

TABLE 7.9
Percentage of Mexican Population with Poverty Characteristics

Year	Percentage
1910	56.9
1921	53.1
1930	50.0
1940	46.6
1950	39.4
1960	33.1
1970	24.8

Source: James W. Wilkie, *The Mexican Revolution: Federal Expenditure and Social Changes Since 1910,* (2nd Ed.; Berkeley: University of California Press, 1970).

family planning programs in the world and the effects of this and the increased urbanization, affluence, and secularization should be observed in the near future.

2. *Availability of capital, markets, and technology.* The fact that the United States is Mexico's neighbor is, unfortunately, often emphasized from the perspective of certain problem areas. But most effects are much more positive. The United States is the world's largest economy and this cannot but help Mexican growth—indeed, in the past it has provided one of the main driving forces. Over 60 percent of Mexico's trade and 75 percent of the direct investment came from the United States. Many specific examples of the effects of this could be given. One of the best is the development of a large-scale agricultural industry in the coastal areas of Sonora. This region is now the leading wheat producer in Mexico, and was developed mainly with United States capital. Cultivated area has grown from 20,000 hectares to over 120,000 in thirty years.

3. *Import of export-oriented industry.* The movement of labor-intensive industries to border regions has been under way for a considerable period of time. In Nogales, Sonora, about forty factories employ 10,000 Mexicans. Near Douglas, seventeen factories employ 7,500 Mexicans. All told, nearly five hundred factories in the United States–Mexican border zone employ 80,000 Mexicans. Over half of the casual wear trousers and slacks worn in the United States are now produced in the

Juarez-El Paso area. The trend of sending raw material to the workers for production and assembly is likely to expand even more in the years ahead. Of course, when recession hits the United States, these factories are especially hard hit. The growing interdependence of the two nations is thus not without risk to Mexico.

4. *Tourism.* In recent years American tourism to Mexico has declined somewhat. We expect this to turn around, particularly as European vacations become increasingly expensive. But it should be realized that tourism is still very much a growth industry for Mexico. By many standards, few people travel there. While Spain attracts 35 million tourists, Mexico receives only about 3.5 million each year. This is really a small number for a nation so close to a market of almost 250 million affluent North Americans.

Closely related to this area of development is the likely expansion of American, Canadian, and even Japanese vacation home ownership in Mexico. Despite some legal complications, we expect this to be a growth area. The beautiful Sonora coastline certainly has high development potential for this.

5. *Oil and gas.* New oil and gas discoveries have proved much larger than anyone expected a few years ago. By early 1978 the numbers being used were 16 billion barrels of "proven" reserves, and as much as 100 to 200 billion to be found eventually, and equivalent amounts of gas. It should be understood that much of Mexico is still unexplored for oil and gas. People haven't even started to look very hard in such areas as the Baja, where new finds are expected.

It is often said that oil discoveries will not "solve" Mexico's development problems. True enough, but it is not likely to hurt development all that much either. What it is likely to accomplish, with merely a modicum of semi-competent management, is to put Mexico on an economic growth track of 7 percent or greater in real terms. This will have a number of effects. First, more jobs will be provided, not only in the oil producing regions, but also for infrastructure expansion. Current plans call for a pipeline construction project linking the fields of Chiapas and Campeche to the existing pipe network in Monterey. This is likely to require American capital, technology, and material. By the early 1980s a great deal of Mexican oil and gas will be flowing to the American Sunbelt. A second important consequence is the resurgence of a booming border economy. As the peso is stabilized, border towns can look to increased prosperity as demand increases for American goods and services.

Some More on the Poor Countries

We will now discuss what some of the problems of the Poor countries are and some of the things that might be done that could help or hurt them. We will confine our remarks to the Ivory Coast, India, Bangladesh, and Haiti as examples of success, coping, and two kinds of disasters respectively. We are not able to devote as much space and care to these topics as they deserve and would receive in a broader study and a larger book. We believe that the following relatively simple observations are essentially correct. Some of the remarks are based on serious study and background, but others depend on my judgment and that of people I trust rather than on hard, documented information. I am even more prepared than usual to admit possible errors in some of the interpretations. In any case if I am wrong, and even more if I am not,* I would like to apologize in advance for any remarks some people in the nations discussed may find annoying or aggravating.

The Ivory Coast

The Ivory Coast's economic progress has been largely led by export agriculture. In remarkable contrast to the experience of many other LDCs, the government does allow the profits from export sales to trickle down to even the smallest farmers, promoting grass-roots economic initiative and integration into the mainstream of the nation's economic development. In many countries the government appropriates these profits for more "urgent" governmental uses and projects—at a great cost to agriculture and the nation's prospects generally.

I believe that the Ivory Coast illustrates how much can be done if a country has sensible leadership. I am not arguing that the Ivory Coast, any more than any other country, should—or could—be slavishly copied, or that it has no serious defects. But I do point out that the Ivory Coast has few resources and that the indigenous population has one of the lowest labor participation rates in the world, but it has a very intelligent government. President Hou-phouet-Boigny has used French advisers freely throughout the

---

*My position is consistent with English libel laws as explained earlier.

government. Both at the senior, middle, and sometimes even lower levels, officials often have a French colleague who works in the background and actually runs the office, while the Ivorian is basically a public relations front or trainee. In other cases, the Ivorian runs the office and the French colleague is simply an adviser or assistant.

The Ivory Coast government has also allowed almost free immigration from neighboring black nations (about a million immigrants in a total population of 7 million comprise about a fourth of the work force). This means that projects that otherwise would not be done efficiently, if at all, are completed.

Ordinarily, one might expect that a bureaucracy that depends so much upon foreign advisers would exploit the public. This does not seem to be true in the Ivory Coast, partly because they have first-class foreign civil servants, including young Frenchmen who are allowed to work in the Ivory Coast in lieu of their military service. All this could also be called neo-colonialism, based on France's paternalism. But there is no reason to object seriously to this kind of expression of enlightened self-interest by France. It almost certainly means that the Ivory Coast is progressing much more rapidly towards true independence than it would if these ties were greatly weakened and the people were completely on their own. Possibly if they had to rise to the task of becoming more self-sufficient, they might be better off in the long run, but the country is unlikely to do that soon. It should not surprise us that a period of tutelage and growth is necessary before the Ivory Coast can be successfully independent. Many other good things are happening. The Ivorians are gaining experience, sophistication, and technical abilities, and even some affluence—qualities that they can build on in the future. They also seem to be taking some of the reins from the French advisers, an expected development. All of this can help sustain the growth rate.

In summary, an efficient, relatively honest bureaucracy and government has a development strategy that matches the natural economic fabric and strength of the society (e.g., agriculture) and a realistically gradual policy toward self-sufficiency and Africanization. This policy has succeeded in turning the Ivory Coast from one of the most neglected French colonies into the most economically-advanced state in West Africa.

India

In our Guarded Optimism and Moderate Optimism Scenarios we assume that the Very Poor and Coping Poor Countries would grow about 4 and 5 percent respectively in the near future on a more or less sustained basis. Both assumptions are optimistic, but not extremely so. The Coping Poor countries, as already noted, are best typified by India (which contains two-thirds of the population of the Coping Poor). We believe that a 5 percent growth rate—or more—for India is quite reasonable in any optimistic scenario.

The obstacles to achieving such growth are formidable: India supports an oppressive concentration of humanity—a current population of about 650 million people. At the present birthrate, the population will double in three and a half decades, and we are not optimistic that the population problem will be controlled in the foreseeable future. Perhaps 40 percent lives below subsistence level, and 25 percent is unemployed. There are as well seemingly insurmountable internal obstacles in the way of economic progress, chief among them the splintering of the nation geographically, ethnically, and linguistically. Fifteen languages frustrate intranational communications, religious conflicts as well as caste hinder mobilization of a common spirit, discipline and unity of purpose toward social and economic progress, and most of the population is dispersed beyond the reach of voice or print. These and other serious reasons could be given in objecting to the plausibility of growth at the 5 percent rate argued for India in our optimistic scenario.

I do not discount or underestimate them by any means. But at the same time I notice real signs of a renewed momentum toward economic and social progress. Things are improving: life expectancy has increased by 60 percent in the last three decades; India has developed an infrastructure, especially in transportation facilities (India has the second largest railway system in the world); and electrification is proceeding rapidly. These will surely bring with them the more progressive influences and models of the urban centers. The literacy rate has, in fact, climbed in thirty years from 12 to over 30 percent. Perhaps of critical importance, the strength of India's democratic institutions has remained intact, and India has recently tested and repudiated the idea that human liberty must be sacrificed to the task of development. New policies have improved the performance of the economy, and at the same time the government has restored political freedoms that were suspended only recently as incompatible with economic progress. In 1976, for example, foreign exchange reserves rose to $3 billion, grain reserves approached 20 million tons. Along with several good crop years from 1975 to 1978, India has displayed a marked improvement in agriculture. The Green Revolution is no longer restricted to the Punjab and Utter Pradesh. All the bullock carts now have ball bearings—and many have rubber tires. Such things may not seem exciting to visitors but they are terribly important to Indian peasants. In the long run, the economic picture is also not without encouragement: there exist a substantial base of natural resources (large agricultural capacity, mineral deposits, and fisheries, for example); a solid industrial sector (India is today the world's tenth largest industrial nation); an expanding communications, power, and transportation infrastructure upon which to grow further; and a democratic political structure to generate the economic leadership and ideas that are starting to succeed.[14]

Although not intended as a complete statement of our case, these few points do indicate that on balance there are indeed grounds for the optimism of our 5 percent growth rate scenario. One can probably argue that 60 percent of India is in some sort of a take-off stage, while the remaining 40 percent is about the same as it has always been, or, in some cases, a little worse.

Bangladesh

Bangladesh is often described as a "basket case." I believe the phrase is both offensive and inaccurate, even though Bangladesh has recently had almost as many problems as a country could have. Most threatening is its population growth of over 3 percent a year, which has already made Bangladesh a big importer of grains, whereas it once had a net export balance. There are 2,300 people per square mile, making it one of the world's most densely populated rural societies (the vast majority of the population live outside the urban centers). Bangladesh agriculture, suffering from insufficient irrigation, has one of the world's lowest yields per acre. It has been largely foreign aid that has kept the country from economic collapse. Since independence it has suffered food shortages brought about by a surging population, political upheaval, floods, and cyclones.

Some of these problems may well be behind them. There have been positive developments, most notably in agricultural output and political calm. Because of recent record harvests, mass starvation has been avoided. Food imports have actually been reduced, allowing the government time to stabilize itself, to reduce debilitating inefficiency and corruption, and to give high priority to population control. Some successes in these areas would allow progress through exploiting the natural agricultural potential of the country. Half of the 22 million acres now cultivated are suitable for double or even triple cropping, although at present only one crop is able to be harvested per year due to the lack of adequate irrigation. It is estimated that only a 20 percent increase in crop yield would make Bangladesh self-sufficient in grain and allow vital export earnings to flow in again. The United Nations Food and Agricultural Organization has estimated that Bangladesh could become self-sufficient in food in five years.

My colleagues and I estimated a very high growth rate of about 8 percent or so for FY 1978. Of course, with a 3 percent growth in population, the increase in PCG would be only about 5 percent. I hope Bangladesh managed to achieve this, but even if it did not, it clearly did much better than it did in previous years, when it actually had a negative average growth rate. However, this high growth rate represents a catch-up from the negative growth years, not a sustainable rate. The higher growth rate not only reflects good prices for jute and rice, but also better management of the economy and increased investment and other improvements in agriculture.

The most important thing about Bangladesh today is that the government seems to be relatively stable and reasonable about economic issues and about using what resources it has. If this can continue and the confidence of the country can be built up, I believe we could expect increasing investment in the rest of the country from the outside as well as increased foreign aid because the foreign authorities will feel that this is money that can be well-used. It is difficult to make projections for this troubled country, but I do not feel it is overly optimistic to argue for at least a 4 percent growth rate. I am willing to apologize to those who in turn argue that I am being pessimistic. They may well be right.

Haiti

Haiti is a much more depressing example. The people live in pitiable poverty: annual income, $70; urban unemployment, 60 percent; illiteracy, 90 percent; life expectancy, 33 years. The country was run for almost a quarter of a century by one of the most despotic governments in the twentieth century, that of François Duvalier and his *tonton macoutes*.[15] During his regime Haiti not only suffered under a very repressive and rapacious regime; it stagnated economically. When Duvalier died in 1971, his son Jean-Claude Duvalier and an informal regency took over the government. Though many—ourselves included—would criticize the new government severely, it is clearly an enormous improvement politically and economically. One can only feel moderately encouraged that there has been at least some improvement for the Haitian poor.

At the moment, Haiti is the poorest and most densely populated country in the Western Hemisphere, but under the new government it has made modest economic progress. The current government—strongly authoritarian but not as totalitarian as was the preceding regime—has managed to bring the political stability that is so critical to the attraction of foreign capital and tourism and the prerequisite for foreign aid. Even through the worldwide economic crisis of the mid-1970s, the GNP has improved nicely, tourism has been increased, and foreign investment inflows are growing. Over 150 companies have set up assembly operations in Haiti. Haiti has clearly begun to successfully attract offshort manufacturing investments with its chief resource—low-cost labor. Haiti also exports an enormous amount of legal and illegal labor to other islands of the Caribbean and areas in the Western Hemisphere. (The Bahamas alone send back about 40,000 illegal immigrants per year.) At some point there will probably be enough of a labor shortage in these countries so that these Haitians will be welcome. This should force an enormous increase in the growth rate, just as it did in southern Europe and much of North Africa.

I would argue that eventually the gap between the rich and poor will work as an engine for development even for countries such as Haiti. In the long run such countries will do quite well economically and perhaps politically, at least compared to their historic pasts. However, the standard of living is likely to be regarded by many as intolerably low. With any bad luck or even more inadequate management, Haiti is very disaster-prone.

Conclusion

I believe the foregoing arguments comprise a persuasive case that the world is in fact entering a new era in which the Affluent nations get richer, the Middle Income nations get richer, and the Poor nations get richer, but the Middle Income nations get richer at a much higher rate than either the Poor or the Affluent. In particular, the capitalist Middle Income nations, with about a billion people and a trillion dollars gross product, promise both to facilitate and to hinder the further growth of the Affluent nations. The Middle Income nations will facilitate the ACNs' growth by providing opportunities for investment, for trade, and for careers for the increasing numbers of highiv educated people who are having difficulty finding satisfactory careers in their own countries. To the extent that these capitalist Middle Income countries take away customers from the ACNs, they may cause problems. Even when they export goods that were formerly produced domestically, and thus provide opportunities for both sides to reap the benefits of comparative advantage, they may also force somewhat more "creative destruction" than the ACNs involved like.

The latter situation would be especially likely during a period of recession. However, even without a recession, it seems to us that Western Europe is likely to resist strenuously making the required adjustments. As a result, there are serious possibilities for increasing protectionism, but we do not think it is likely to go to an extreme. The sorry experiences of the Great Depression are still remembered vividly, either first hand or vicariously.

Barring a breakdown of the system, the end of the twentieth century is likely to see a very effective decrease in the level and character of poverty in the world, measured by the standards that were applied up until the middle of this century. By the end of the twentieth century, the United States and Japan will together produce more than one-third of the gross world product within their own borders—a condition that will continue until well into the twenty-first century. As long as Japan and the United States work together, they will have not a domination of the world economy but a kind of predominance that could be extremely useful. Given likely policies and developments, the Japanese could conceivably take the lead from the United States in furthering world trade and worldwide investment.

In sum, we suggest that while *L'époque de Malaise* may be quite real for the Affluent countries, it need not be terribly uncomfortable even for them. Indeed, by any reasonable historical standard except that of *La Deuxième Belle Epoque* it might be judged another *Belle Epoque*. However, the period will likely also be one of increasing strains and stresses, which could result in drastic and violence-prone confrontations and changes. Although the Hudson Institute spends about one-third of its research time examining the prospects for such confrontations, they are not a central focus here and are therefore omitted. Hence these conclusions have a more optimistic tenor than would a more comprehensive approach.

Caveats, qualifications, and qualms aside, we are confident that from a narrow economic, financial, and technological perspective the future looks good. Always barring bad management or bad luck or both, the next two or three decades should be good if not great ones for the majority of the world—and great ones for many. Considering the institutional issues as well, the future does not look quite so good. But—again excepting bad luck and bad management—the approaching decades should bring a general improvement of living standards and of other prospects for many of the less privileged people and countries. Even if the century does not end in glory, it will likely end well enough.

Notes

1. Angus Maddison, "Phases of Capitalistic Development," *Quarterly Review*, Banca Nazionale del Lavoro, June 1977.

2. Peter F. Drucker, *The Age of Discontinuity* (New York: Harper & Row, 1968), Chapter 1. Drucker argues, however, that this continuity is now breaking down.

3. When we say these are "Italy-type" societies we understand, of course, that their cultural origins are Spanish. But to a great degree these two societies now look much more like Italy than they do like Spain and have many citizens who were born in Italy or are of Italian descent. Peter Drucker commented in 1968 about Argentina as follows: "An example is Argentina, which for the last fifty years has wasted substance as if by malice aforethought, and turned herself from a highly developed and rich country into an underdeveloped and poor one." Peter F. Drucker, *The Age of Discontinuity* (New York: Harper & Row, 1968), p. 120.

4. The percentages of the labor force in agriculture for major ACNs are as follows:

Low	*1960*	*1974*
United Kingdom	4.1%	2.4%
United States	8.3	4.1
Canada	13.5	6.3
Germany	14.0	7.3
High		
Italy	32.8	16.6
Japan	30.2	12.9
France	22.4	11.6

Source: OECD Labor Force Statistics

5. Japan has had higher growth than would be expected from increases in business capital per worker for many reasons, including rapid importing of technology, large and rapid shifts of workers out of agriculture, and use of relatively austere facilities for most private business investments.

6. John P. Stein and Allen Lee, *Productivity Growth in Industrial Countries at the Sectoral Level, 1963-1974,* R-2203-CIEP (The RAND Corporation, July 1977).

7. Most readers will be familiar with the argument. For those who are not, it goes like this. Assume both countries manufacture both A and B gidgits and are self-sufficient—that is, do not trade. Assume also that the first country has

three hundred man years available and can produce ten A gidgits using 10 man years/gidgit and 10 B gidgits using 20 man years/gidgit, while the second country only has 20 man years available and can produce 10 A gidgits using 2 man years/gidgit and 10 B gidgits using 1 man year/gidgit. Both countries produce 10 A and 10 B gidgits. But it pays the second country not to produce A gidgits (even though it produces them at one fifth the cost of the first country in man years per gidgit) but only B gidgits and trade with the first country for A gidgits and vice versa. If this is done, both countries together will produce 30 A gidgits and 30 B gidgits, an increase of 50 percent. How they get distributed will depend on the bargaining. Both sides should gain.

8. Many of these points are discussed in *The Next 200 Years*, especially Chapters 8 and 9.

9. P. T. Bauer and B. S. Yamey, "Against the New Economic Order," *Commentary* 63, no. 4 (April 1977):31.

10. Robert S. McNamara, Columbia University Conference on International Economic Development, February 20, 1970.

11. South Korea and Taiwan, and to a lesser degree, Singapore and Hong Kong, also have this ability to remain culturally unchanged. Many Americns who meet American-educated South Koreans think of them as almost totally Americanized. They are surprised to learn that most of these South Koreans, if they have returned to South Korea to live, think of themselves as still South Koreans. They do not think of themselves as being Americanized and are not flattered if others think so. However, they are so sure of the Korean heritage, nationality, and identity that they can afford to look American to the Americans without feeling overly defensive or insecure. Some of them do feel slightly defensive and insecure, but to a remarkably lesser degree than members of almost any other culture we have seen which has the same problem. And, as far as we can judge, they are less defensive and less insecure today than they were five years ago.

Recent American human rights criticism may have accelerated this Koreanization—a sense of increased identification with Korea. The Koreans note what they consider a lack of discipline in America—excessive use of drugs, promiscuity, lack of family ties, and a lack of respect for authority. They tend to exaggerate the decadence of America and say, "Is this what these people want us to do? No thank you. We would just as soon do without." This is as true of most Christians in South Korea as of "right wing" supporters of President Park, because the Christians take their Christianity seriously, feel much the same way, and are thus somewhat ambiguous about their American support.

Furthermore, these Christians have been dismayed by their supporters in such organizations as the World Council of Churches, who have been in favor of American withdrawal from South Korea. The South Korean Christians, being sensible and patriotic people, have not allowed their animosity against President Park to influence their position on the defense of their country. They are quite clear what would happen to them if North Korea invaded

South Korea and completely convinced that South Korea should not run any greater risks than necessary. Many of them are aware of what happened to the Buddhists who opposed the Thieu government in South Vietnam, and who are now suffering under a much more oppressive communist government. They have no intention of repeating this mistake.

12. There is another joke that the Brazilians tell about themselves. Colombians, Argentinians, and sometimes even Chileans and Mexicans also tell it about themselves. The Brazilian version indicates both how great Brazil's future may be and how pessimistic the Brazilians used to be about their future. It seems that when God was creating the world He discussed His plans with the Angel Gabriel. God told Gabriel that He would give Brazil the greatest rivers of the world. (About 20 percent of all the water that goes through all the rivers of the world goes through the Amazon. Its electric power potential is greater than all of the electricity generated in the United States.) He added that He would give Brazil the greatest minerals in the world. (We would not be at all surprised if it did not turn out that Brazil has as many or more minerals as Canada plus Australia put together.) He would give them the greatest pampas in the world, the greatest forests, some of the greatest harbors, etc. At this point the Angel Gabriel interrupted, saying, "These people will take the world over." God smiled a wry smile and said, "Wait till you see the people I put there."

The point of the story, and one now well understood in Latin America, is that even a very great endowment of natural resources will not do the trick. And it was true that until relatively recently the Portuguese in Brazil did not show any extraordinary talent at developing their country. However, whether this was necessary or not, they did show an extraordinary talent in allowing outsiders to come in and help them get the process started. However, there was never any question among either of them about who was in charge. As a result, even today many of the big companies and enterprises are still transnational or are enterprises headed by people with names clearly not Portuguese. The people themselves are thoroughly assimilated families. As far as the country is concerned there is no way to tell the difference between them and those with more Portuguese-sounding names. Further it is now quite clear that the Portuguese themselves are beginning to dominate the process or are already doing so.

13. In that book we suggested that Brazil had the largest range of possible growth rates of almost any country we knew. In fact, it could probably range between 3 and 8 percent (a low estimate). Looking at the government that was in charge in 1964, we suggested that it was much more likely to be 3 percent than 8 percent. But, fortunately for the Brazilians, they changed the government and instituted one that has been extraordinarily successful at economic development and that therefore deserves some credit for this achievement. Herman Kahn and Anthony J. Wiener, *The Year 2000* (New York: Macmillan Co., 1967), p. 196.

14. Many of India's problems derive from counterproductive acts of the government. For example, it is almost the only country in the world that

refuses to let IBM operate without entering into joint ventures. It is extraordinary that what such countries as Japan and France have allowed, albeit quite reluctantly, the Indians are not willing to. Similarly, they have asked Coca-Cola not only to enter into joint ventures, but to give the local people information about the special formula (which, for whatever reasons, is so carefully guarded that fewer than a dozen people know it). This surely indicates that the Indian government is basically impractical in its approach to foreign investment and is almost exactly the opposite of the Ivory Coast. We believe that with minimally sensible measures, India's growth rate could be increased enormously.

15. It is not often remembered, but Duvalier was nicknamed "Papa Doc" because he originally gave the world the impression of being a kindly physician who was very successful in eliminating smallpox in two provinces. His emergence in politics as governor of Haiti was received with genuine enthusiasm by many both there and in the United States, which helped engineer his achievement of power.

8

Recommendations, Observations, and Parting Polemics*

If this were a better world, or at least this were a better book, or perhaps even if I were a better author, I would depart with the traditional academic flourish and roll of scholarly drums: succinct recapitulation of major issues and problems; orderly recommendations and systematic solutions flowing inexorably from the identification of issues and problems; and an uplifting peroration. Such a final chapter is, of course, impossible. My colleagues and I are ourselves often confused by some current trends, although in many instances (perhaps more than some readers will find plausible) we believe our suggestions and recommendations are reasonable despite our incomplete understanding of the trends. Even when we believe we comprehend the trends in some depth and detail, we are often not sure what, if anything, can be done about them.

The result is a concluding chapter that presents *seriatim* points I believe are useful but that are not the final words or complete treatments. Some of my comments are frankly speculative because I am convinced there are many issues that demand more systematic and deeper discussion than they are now accorded. If my speculations widen and enrich the terms of current debate, I will be well pleased.

This chapter is divided into three broad topic areas: modernization and planning, cultural and political influences on economic development, and futurology and the future of economic development. The section on modernization and planning includes observations on modernization as a value; the concept of moderniza-

---

Polemic is used in the sense of arguing a position vigorously. We hope to avoid tirades and ideological banalities. This chapter attempts to sum up or drive home some of the important "lessons" to be derived from the entire discussion.

tion; the invisible hand of the market; planning in Japan, South Korea, and Taiwan; and political influences on economic decisions. The more frankly polemical section on cultural and political influences on economic development presents my views on the need for high morale and commitment in developing nations (and how not to meet that need); the importance of a "good" culture and "good" management; development and political stability; poverty and moral imperatives; the impact of the liberal New Class on economic development (South Korea and Taiwan as abused exemplars); environment and ecology; and two personal notes—one on the hunting culture and the raising of children in the United States and one on educated incapacity. Finally, the third section on futurology and the future of economic development describes some uses for scenarios and images of the future, presents a bourgeois (industrial) growth-oriented ideology based on futurology, and sums up the viewpoint that has informed this book.

MODERNIZATION AND PLANNING

Modernization as a Value

An intense discussion of the preferred meaning of the concept *modernization* is taking place in academic and professional circles as well as in New Class circles generally. Some of the basic assumptions and tenets of modernization as traditionally construed are being challenged. Some critics emphasize the need to include various characteristics such as aid to low income groups and meeting civil or human rights as part of the meaning or at least among the goals of modernization. Others challenge the traditional goals—for example, the small-is-beautiful, limits-to-growth, voluntary-simplicity, and joy-love-and-spontaneity movements. In some groups, including certain terrorist or adversary culture groups, the challenge is virtually nihilistic. They want to wipe out all traces of this evil, bourgeois, capitalist hell and assume that something good will thereby emerge.

Even if we restrict ourselves to the traditional approaches to modernization, there are still many roads leading to it, and many mountains to choose from. Selecting the right mountain and the appropriate road can be most difficult, but fortunately society can often hedge or compromise the choice. For example, much lip service is paid to the concept of the free market in certain societies, yet in practice there is plenty of room for exceptional situations. Many of these societies probably compromise too easily. The converse is also true; many socialist systems are run capitalistically and some are closer to state capitalism than socialism in the sense that the state exploits the workers as much as any capitalist system ever has.

In these confusing situations it is important to have objective measures of performance or at least objective criteria that can serve as surrogates for perfect measures and make up in objectivity what they lose in exactness. We believe that GNP and GNP per capita are often useful in this role, although at no point can we rely solely on them, nor do these criteria work even moderately well at all times and in all places. We find them useful for most countries in the second half of the twentieth century—a usefulness that derives as much from accidental factors as from general principles.

The importance and relevance of GNP and GNP per capita have recently come under renewed attack, partly because the concepts were misused in the immediate post–World War II period to justify an overemphasis on modern sectors and on the short run. The attack also is a result of various faddish overreactions: to the intense political difficulties that many countries faced, to the sudden "discovery" that for most countries, development initially and for some time results in greater inequality of income, and to the realization that it would take many decades to eliminate absolute poverty. The attack on the GNP/CAP criteria has greatly intensified with the emergence of influential neo-liberal and humanist left New Class thinkers, writers, and development professionals.

Hostility to GNP and GNP/CAP can also stem from an ignorant, partisan, or emotional hostility to capitalism or from sympathy with various limits-to-growth concepts. Even among many serious professionals, there is an exaggerated awareness of the admitted weaknesses and problems of the GNP concept, an awareness sometimes combined with sentimental, romantic, or excessively utopian expectations about development.

In addition to attacks stemming from the small-is-beautiful movement, some of the limits-to-growth movements, and other ideological movements, there are technical attacks on the customary use of GNP per capita. Many of the latter focus attention on what they call "meeting basic human needs." Most of these officials will admit, if questioned, that GNP does meet human needs, but they argue that there are more urgent human needs that are not being met by the normal development programs, particularly the urgent needs of those at the bottom of society. Some of these officials take the perfectly reasonable position that opportunities for economic development are being overlooked. Others argue the equally reasonable position (if taken in moderation) that one might be perfectly willing to decrease the rate of economic development to increase the amount of justice and equity in the society—for example, by focusing more attention on the current consumption needs of the lowest income groups whether this helps the country as a whole or even the poor themselves develop more rapidly or not. This position is perfectly reasonable in both principle and practice, but it also easily leads to jeopardizing important programs for the medium and long run.

A related concept—the trickle-down effect—has also come under heavy attack. In fact, it is disbelief in this mechanism that is one of the main reasons for the current emphasis on "meeting human needs." The concept of "trickle down" is definitely valid in the sense that if the top of the society becomes richer, almost always some of the increased income trickles down to poorer people. In all the relatively affluent and homogeneous societies we know about, under modern conditions the trickle down gets very close to the bottom. However, this is much less true in non-homogeneous societies where additional income often does not reach the bottom of society until very late in the development process, if at all. This difficulty has been characteristic of many countries. Examples include the North-South difference in the United States after the Civil War and the much greater difference between north and south Italy.[1] Similar problems will characterize much of the Third World. Little can be done except to alleviate some of the worst aspects, and even this will be difficult. This is, of course, a part of our neo-culturist position, and one that we believe is fully jusified both by the data and by much theory. It does not justify apathy and indifference. One must do what one can. But one must also understand that we should not be disillusioned or paralyzed by a certain lack of success, particularly if the programs are designed according to emotional or political criteria and not by criteria of cost effectiveness, practicality, and workability.

Elsewhere in the world, for example, almost a third of the people of Brazil and India and about a fourth of the people of Mexico have scarcely gained at all from modernization. However, from two-thirds to three-fourths *have* gained—and the possibility for gain is increasingly open to the others. On the other hand, if equality of income is used as the basic criterion, incorrectly in our view, then the groups at the bottom actually lost. Their income may not necessarily have gone down absolutely compared with their previous standard of living (except for a few), but it has gone down relatively in the sense that the income of others increased. This situation is almost inevitable. If one region of a country is especially well endowed with talent, resources, or luck, it will move ahead faster than the rest of the country; if there are important cultural differences among various groups within a country, this will also make a difference. It is unreasonable to assert that an economic process is fatally defective because some people move faster than others, or because some people lose or do not make progress while others gain.

Eventually, any increased income will trickle down to the bottom, and the wealth of the richest areas will pull up the poorer areas. This has been observed in all the Affluent countries, even though the inequality itself may or may not diminish greatly over time, and even though in many Poor countries the groups at the very bottom seem likely to stay there for a relatively long time. It does seem possible, at least in some cases, to do a lot for the poorest people through appropriate policies and "appropriate technology." However, in practice one often finds that the policies being pressed are actually counterproductive and should be corrected.

This is especially important because the problem of poverty in the world is increasingly going to be less of an issue among nations than within individual nations. Even today, there are almost as many poor people among the 2 billion people living in Middle Income nations as there are among the 1.25 billion people living in the nations that we have called the Poor countries. However, this should not disturb our perspective on the genuine successes that these Middle Income countries are enjoying.

We are convinced that it would be wrong if not immoral to jeopardize the early prospects of a talented or lucky minority—and the eventual prospects of the great majority—to preserve a relatively egalitarian income distribution or to prevent the existing income distribution from being further distorted. It is even less justifiable to preserve existing inequalities in an otherwise static society on the grounds that any innovations may not rapidly correct the old inequalities, but only create new ones.

People in developed countries tend to exaggerate the increase in envy and hostility that occurs in developing countries when income distribution becomes less equal because of uneven economic development. The poor do envy or hate the rich in some countries, but much less in others. We know of no countries where these emotions seem to be greatly affected by the actual size of the gap separating the rich from the poor, although they may be affected or created by the emergence of new gaps. Among the non-communist countries, it is only in the relatively rich such as Sweden and Denmark that egalitarianism has emerged as a dominant political issue.

People tend to be most upset if they are failing or being replaced.

They also tend to be very upset if they see their socio-economic peers rise in income while they do not, especially if it is neighbors, friends, or relatives who surpass them.[2] They feel much less envy when people who are socially, culturally, or geographically remote surpass them. Rural sectors often gain less during modernization than urban sectors. This characteristic, common to many modernizing cultures, should be distinguished from deliberate draining of rural sectors. Peasants may resent foreigners or their urban fellow citizens because they seem rich and rapacious, but they do not get upset because the city modernizes more rapidly than the countryside. Nor do they seem to feel that they are being drained to support the modernization— unless they are obviously being exploited (as they often are).

This draining process has been typical of some socialist countries. The USSR, for example, modernized by forcibly "collecting" the necessary economic surplus from the collectives. Similar exploitation of rural areas to help the cities often occurs in countries that are not doing well economically. For example, the price of food is often kept artificially low to keep the cities quiet politically, at great cost to the countryside. This has sometimes been called the "high price of low prices."[3] Government control of the export market almost invariably milks the agricultural sector. Also, the tax burden and government spending may be unfairly distributed.

Few democratic or authoritarian (non-totalitarian) countries are able to develop rapidly before their agriculture is in good condition. In most developed or developing non-totalitarian societies, therefore, surplus resources and manpower are first generated by a successful agricultural sector and then used to modernize the rest of the country. In any case, successful industrialization is usually preceded by a successful agricultural program that benefits most rural residents, even if it creates some "surplus labor" and makes the cities still richer. This was true in Great Britain, the United States, Japan, and to some degree Taiwan. There are exceptions—especially among the resource-rich countries—yet even they are rarely able to industrialize entirely on the basis of resources. It now appears that some oil-producing nations will succeed in doing so, but the verdict is not yet in.

Other countries that have managed to industrialize without first putting agriculture in order were able to do so partly because of the unique opportunities available today. Spain, Greece, and Turkey were greatly aided by importing tourists and exporting their citizens to other countries as guest workers. These two factors have often brought in as much income as oil has for most of the OPEC countries.

Further, both tourism and foreign labor are labor-intensive and therefore involve many people in the process in a constructive way.

Many of the neo-Confucian countries that have been so successful with their development efforts have also been successful with their agriculture, at least in the sense that the income of city workers and rural people is about the same. Mainland China is much admired for this achievement, but the Japanese, South Koreans, and Taiwanese are actually doing about as well or better and at far less human and economic cost. (This comparison is not intended to denigrate the admittedly great achievements that have taken place in the People's Republic of China, but simply to put them into perspective.)

The Concept of Modernization

Several times we have defined modernization as the transformation of an entire society from pre-industrial to post-industrial—a transition that involves almost all aspects of society and culture. In some ways this is a slightly circular definition, since both pre-industrial and post-industrial are defined by not being industrial. This also equates modernization with industrialization. We think of industrialization or its equivalent as one among several integral parts of the modernization process. Thus, when Commodore Perry opened up Japan he found a society that had gone a great distance toward modernization but had not gone any distance at all toward industrialization. Nevertheless, because Japan had many characteristics of a modern society, the Japanese industrialized rapidly and relatively easily. Even before Perry arrived, Japan had a strong state, an elaborate commercial structure (including commodity markets), a fairly high level of literacy, and other modern features.

A similar observation applies to some of the resource-rich countries. Having and developing resources may not involve much industrialization, but it can supply income, education, and infrastructure—and these can be important steps toward industrialization. One can imagine a modern society that largely lives off the income of investments that were gained by the exploiting of its resources without engaging in much industrialization. However, none of the OPEC countries is yet officially choosing such a strategy.

The meaning and characteristics of modernization clearly vary over time, place and other conditions. Similarly, post-industrial societies will probably also differ radically. Indeed the first step toward post-industrialization was the original Industrial Revolution. This was a "Western" phenomenon, although it drew heavily from other cultures—technology from the Chinese, the zero from India, mathematics from the Arabs, and the like. Nevertheless, no other culture was able to industrialize even when conditions seemed favorable. The peculiar combinations of factors preceding the Industrial Revolution were distinctly Western. As a result, Westernization and modernization were once largely synonymous. Today, however, sustained economic growth is characteristic of all major cultural areas and of most nations. The Great Transition has become truly global in scope.

Modernization still involves industrialization (at least at some stages), but it is no longer accurately described as Westernization. It remains useful to view modernization as involving an unprecedented increase in human technological knowledge and control over the inner and outer environments. However, from this perspective modernization may not be generally judged to be beneficial. If the process leads to a Malthusian disaster (a catastrophic collapse of the world economic order from population pressures, resource shortages, or environmental abuses), as some believe likely if not inevitable, then a positive connotation of the word *modernization* would obviously be inappropriate (as would also be true in the event of a very destructive thermonuclear war or other catastrophic misuse of modern technology). Even if modernization is successful from a narrow economic and technocratic point of view, if it destroys the "inner environment," or undermines precious human values, many would judge the process to have too high a cost. Nonetheless, it would still be modernization.

Measuring modernization—even in broad terms of "more or less" modern—is difficult because of the many dimensions involved and their associated intangible factors and cultural values. Ambitious efforts are underway in the United States and Western Europe to establish social indicators of progress. Essentially, these studies seek to determine whether material progress results in greater human happiness and fulfillment, or simply in "meeting human needs." Except at the most elementary level (health, longevity, education, etc.) these efforts are not likely to be successful because there is little agreement on what constitutes a useful indicator of happiness or on how to measure it. There is not even any agreement on what happiness is, nor is there any obvious correlation between happiness and wealth or technology or any other reasonable definition of modernization. On the contrary, the world's greatest philosophers and religious leaders basically agree that wealth, material possessions, and technological progress are not key ingredients of human happiness.

The concept of fulfillment raises even more complex and uncertain questions than happiness, but it is doubtful if any of these issues is relevant to a discussion of economic growth. We tend to agree with the following comment by W. Arthur Lewis:

> We do not know what the purpose of life is, but if it were happiness, then evolution could just as well have stopped a long time ago, since there is no reason to believe that men are happier than pigs or than fishes. What distinguishes men from pigs is that men have greater control over their environment; not that they are more happy. And on this test, economic growth is greatly to be desired.[4]

We believe strongly that greater control over the environment (which may or may not lead to greater happiness) is a good indicator of modernization. We also believe it is greatly to be desired. Economic affluence and technological advancement are essential to modernization. They have—at least up to now—reduced day-to-day misery and suffering, helped avoid or alleviate potential catastrophes, and met a variety of human needs. One cannot claim that affluence and technology have always contributed to human welfare. The attempt to achieve them has great human and cultural costs and risks. Their attainment itself can involve or create misery, suffering, and even disaster. But we believe that one of the most important reasons for seeking affluence and technology is that they have the potential for bringing about greater safety and greater freedom of action—of offering more and better choices. They can add to the toughness and resiliency of a society by increasing its ability to survive disaster and to solve problems. Until recently, this survival orientation has been the most important objective and characteristic of modernization.

The West need not apologize for industrialization, even if industrialization on occasion produced or made possible aggression. Almost all successful societies have been aggressive at one time or another. The West more or less abandoned aggression after World War II.[5] Industrialization is often maligned, either as a process itself or because of some of its allegedly inherent properties such as Marxist alienation of the person, aesthetic "plasticization" of material goods and the "quality of life," or the "imperialistic" way industrialization is transmitted to developing countries.

The critics of industrialization have been unwilling to acknowledge such resounding successes as Taiwan, South Korea, Brazil, Mexico, Venezuela, the Ivory Coast, Spain, and Greece. Many other countries are also success stories. East Asian cultures in general perform well according to our criteria of modernization, although except for Japan they almost totally failed to do so before World War II. Given the increasing prevalence of anti-growth sentiment in recent years, it is important to note that there is at least as much to gain from a study of the successes of some as there is from the failures of others.

For the twentieth century, it is reasonable and appropriate for many purposes and for almost all countries to narrow the discussion of modernization to economic affluence and technological advancement or both. This does not discount or underestimate the importance of other factors and characteristics that constitute the "outer and inner environment" of people and institutions. Cultural factors affecting individual and social motivation (attitudes towards work, family relationships, business and governmental practices, organizational loyalty, and discipline) are centrally important. However, in their effects on cultural adaptation to modernization, these factors are best understood and evaluated by how well they contribute to economic growth and technological advancement.

Problems of distribution, quality, and measurement diminish but do not negate the value of such indices as the GNP and GNP/capita. In practice, any attempt to classify nations by using a single number would seem to require simplifications and distortions so drastic as to render the result useless, but empirically this turns out not to be true. In principle, most nations can be placed on a numerical scale of progress by using the simple index of GNP/per capita to measure both economic affluence and technology advancement. To a lesser but still useful degree, comparisons of GNP and GNP/CAP provide an interesting estimate of the "distance" between two nations. This relative measure can not only be used to compare nations, but also to trace an individual nation's progress over time.

GNP/CAP is probably a better index today than it would have been a hundred years ago, or than it will be fifty years from now in any predominantly post-industrial economy.[6] If most of the GNP in a post-industrial society is in services and everybody lives by "taking in each other's washing," or something similar, it may be difficult to use the concept of GNP and GNP per capita as we use it today. However, we do not want to exaggerate the value of this measurement to characterize either the welfare or the modernization of a nation's people; it is obviously far from perfect. Any number of anomalies can be cited, from the slums of New York City to the vast disparities between Brazil's northeastern provinces and the booming cities of Sao Paulo and Rio de Janeiro. But these are, after all, anomalies and not indications of the norm.

The Invisible Hand of the Market

An important aspect of modernization in the non-socialist world has been the introduction of market concepts and mechanisms such as the use of money, prices, and impersonal, financially motivated exchanges and activities. Many primitive communities have little or no conception of a pure economic exchange. They tend to think of exchanges, whether of gifts or labor, as integral parts of hierarchic, familial, or even feudal relationships and frameworks. Individuals may give gifts without any expectation of immediate return. Observers oriented to Western concepts would interpret the actions of these gift-givers as in effect building up credit (or even making loans or deposits). If they need something later on, the recipients will gladly make them a "gift" of what they need—or at least the return gifts are comparable to the gifts received. If one records all the transactions over the long run, the "reciprocal gifts" probably average out much as they would have through commercial trading and bargaining—at least if some correction is made for the relationships involved.

Implicit bargaining may also be carried on in the guise of gift giving. After a while, genuine bargaining may occur but the basic concept remains: "I give you a gift because I like you (or am obligated to you because of our relationship). You are my friend (ally, vassal, or lord). You give me a gift back because you like me (or because it is a custom or your duty)." It is usually considered bad form (adjusting for the relative social, economic, and hierarchic situations) not to exchange gifts of at least equal if not higher value. This is not so very different from gift-giving customs and relationships in the United States or Europe, although we do not ordinarily think of these as market-oriented or akin to normal commercial transactions.

The concept of doing business with an impersonal individual whom one may not even know is basically absent or very limited in many pre-industrial cultures. The ability of modern business to operate worldwide without being involved in strong, enduring, personal, familial, or social relationships is an enormous asset. This is not to say that all primitive trade should be taken at face value or involves only mutual gift giving. Indeed, reciprocal gift giving among primitive peoples may fulfill much the same function and take much the same form as normal barter and trade—intense and "impersonal" bargaining can occur. But, to an extraordinary degree, this gift-giving represents social and symbolic exchanges as much as commercial exchanges.

Similar kinds of exchanges are common in contemporary South

Korea and Japan, where people often give gifts and do not expect any immediate *quid pro quo*. Gifts are exchanged to establish and maintain good psychological atmosphere. They are not thought of or intended as graft or bribes. Specific payments are not made for specific acts, nor is there any expectation of immediate reciprocity. Koreans (and Japanese to a lesser extent) are often startled when foreigners react negatively to such gifts. They are not necessarily intended to influence the recipient, but rather are matters of courtesy, custom, respect, friendship, or admiration. (There is a good deal of bribery and corruption going on as well but the distinction is not sharp.)

In the contemporary United States, and to an even greater extent in Western Europe, there remain extensive remnants of traditional personal relationships in business and commerce. So many persist that Americans often cannot understand the common accusation that they do not value human relationships, that everything in America is business. Yet, to a great degree, the accusation is correct. In the United States, if a man gives his incompetent brother-in-law a good job in his organization, we call it selfishness. If the job goes to a competent stranger, it is unselfish. The rest of the world often reverses the judgment and believes that one has an obligation to hire an incompetent brother-in-law. Indeed, the less competent the brother-in-law, the greater the obligation—for if this relative will not hire him, who will? The fact that it is bad for business, career, or profits is secondary. On the other hand, employing a competent stranger is good for one's business or career and thus is selfish behavior.

In the long run we expect the world to return to intimate "human" rather than impersonal "business" relationships. But for the short run we tend to believe that the American approach is probably better for the world because it makes possible the current global market with all of its efficiencies. Even in domestic affairs, it may be better for the society as a whole if a corporation lays off workers and forces them to find other jobs than if the corporation bears the salary costs for years.[7]

Modernization and Planned Versus Free Market Economies

Neither a planned nor a "free market" economy exists in pure form. The freest market in the world will have some rigidities, controls, and collaboration. No matter how controlled a market is there are a certain number of unplanned, unofficial, gray, black, or illegal transactions that occur and often greatly increase the flexibility of the system and its general smooth operation. (One reason we do not believe the common criticism of the Advanced Capitalist nations that their markets are so managed or otherwise restricted that the model of a free market is wrong is that we find that in many socialist countries the model of the free market holds better than one would have expected.) We believe that under current conditions a greater degree of freedom of market choices, market orientations, and market prices would improve the operation of most economies, whether they are nominally socialist or free market.[8] As a practical matter, we believe that a relatively free market economy is based on the correct fundamental assumption that, if culturally acceptable, self-interest and personal involvement are the most efficient incentives for rational and highly motivated behavior.

In addition, using market forces more, even if it works only halfway well, can relieve the government and society of much of the enormous and difficult burden of staffing the many administrative and planning positions that are needed in a planned society. Precisely such capabilities are in desperately short supply in most developing countries. This shortage may be one of the most relevant reasons for emphasizing the use of price mechanisms. In any case, many socialist countries are also moving toward greater use of market mechanisms and overall strategies.[9] Yet we believe that the development of South Korea and Taiwan would not have been much altered had their overall planning process consisted of nothing more than a somewhat detailed "image of the future," a list of projects to carry out, and a choice of development strategies (e.g., export oriented). The image of the future would provide coordination, create shared expectations, and give useful planning contexts. Projects, of course, have to be planned in detail, although much "muddling through" remains inevitable and desirable. It is useful to use specific numbers to illustrate "images of the future," but it can be terribly dangerous to take the numbers literally and rely on them. What is usually called for is "planned muddling through," with as much emphasis on the "muddling through" as on the planning.[10]

National plans are often less reliable in developing overall economic and social indices than are skilled forecasters who simply predict the future from what they see happening and who modify these *a priori* projections according to those announced intentions of the government that seem most relevant. In most countries, a competent objective outsider with access to most of the available information should do better than a government bureaucrat whose partisan emotions and political fortunes are involved and whose first priority is to maintain face, preserve or enhance morale, and kowtow to special political rhetoric. Thus, in the United States, the Council of Economic Advisers did not predict any of the six postwar depressions, although many private forecasters did quite well.

The planning processes in South Korea, Taiwan, and Japan, discussed in more detail in the next section, have been similar. In all three, comprehensive planning has been devoted more to setting guidelines than to prescribing details. This provides a sense of direction while permitting flexibility and encouraging planned muddling through. This contrasts sharply with centralized planning in many socialist states and with socialist-inspired planning elsewhere that turns goals and targets into moral issues—"the plan must be fulfilled at all costs." In addition to the burden of moral imperatives, socialist economists have to allocate resources as the government—composed of politicians, bureaucrats, and technicians—wishes. The socialist planners must resist popular and special interests who are being successful in ways not envisaged by the plan. Indeed, they may be "interfering" with the plan. There is no room for people "who go around getting things done without permission," to use Lewis Lapham's felicitous phrase.

Socialist governments make centralized planning decisions. To do so, they need a plan. Under these conditions, a poor plan may indeed be better than no plan, since the latter situation produces chaos. This is the weakness of any system that requires the society to take seriously comprehensive plans made many years ahead. In capitalist economies, however, those components of the society that are successful, whether planned or not, automatically attract resources from the more or less "private" financial and labor markets and from the internal profits and cash flow generated by successful firms. No such process exists in most socialist economies.

A clear distinction is seldom made between centralized planning and "flexible planning" (a more graceful phrase than "planned muddling through," although I really prefer the latter). Flexible planning allows for *ad hoc* responses to changing conditions and for the efficient and rapid exploitation of unplanned successes—often occurring long before the central authorities and professionals even know about the success.

Modern industrial economies are far too complex to permit details to be efficiently planned from the top down. In effect, societies (and sometimes projects and organizations) grow. They are not really constructed. The growth process has a dynamism and direction that cannot always be easily influenced or guided to please the theorist— or even the "driver." Rigid and comprehensive planning methods produce serious bottlenecks, extensive rigidity, and superficial and uninformed decisions. Such methods discourage individual or private initiative, minimize the importance of creative but decentralized sectors, and encourage setting ill-chosen goals.

India's second five-year plan (1955 to 1960), sometimes known as the Mahalonobis Plan, is a classic example of such counterproductive centralized planning. Consistent with the socialist thinking of the time, it shifted the emphasis of India's growth strategy from labor-intensive, small-scale production to capital goods and heavy industry. The transition was prompted by the idea that growth designed to increase employment would only lead to greater wage payments, which in turn would increase consumer demand and divert resources from the production of capital goods. The plan therefore downplayed job creation and, even more important, de-emphasized the agricultural sector. On balance, the plan probably significantly retarded India's potential growth.[11]

The capitalist system, which depends so much on the "invisible hand" of the market, can effectively use "marginal input organizations (MIOs).* This is especially significant in relatively pre-modern cultures. Their capability reflects the fact that capitalism makes fewer demands on administrative, leadership, decision making, and management resources than does socialism.

To a remarkable degree, the same allocation problems must be solved in a private free-enterprise capitalist system and in a centrally directed socialist state. Aside from efficiency and competence, it may not make much difference who makes these decisions and calculations. The answers, in principle, will often be the same. However, experience and theory both show that if the basic economy is properly structured and managed, a decentralized private system run by a competent, highly motivated administration is far preferable to an

---

*We use the term, "MIOs" to refer to organizations that tend to use marginal employees, marginal employers, and marginal capital to produce a good deal of product. MIOs range all the way from the typical pre-modern farmers to "sweatshops," to other organizations that are not using modern, high quality equipment or personnel. Until quite recently, about half of the manufacturing production in Japan came from such organizations. They also played a central role in the United States until World War II.

equally competent and motivated centralized government bureau-cracy for doing the analysis, implementing the decisions, and creating and maintaining efficient, resilient, and responsive organi-zations. One reason is that a centralized planning organization has to devote an enormous amount of time and other resources to ensure the political and bureaucratic survival, defense, and influence of the organization and its functions. By contrast, in a capitalist system, businessmen (often including managers of publicly owned enter-prises that operate as businesses), contractors, buyers, and consumers devote much more intense study to particular problems than to overall schemes. The number of planning hours is probably greater, and the quality and intensity of the planning is also almost automatically higher. The important issue is not planning versus chaos but rather who does the planning, at what level, from what perspectives, with what motivation, and how rigidly or flexibly.

Centralized planning remains popular despite its relatively consistent record of more failures than successes and despite the awareness of this record by most development economists, especially those in such international organizations as the World Bank. Its persistence is partly because of the tremendous enthusiasm of early advocates such as Gunnar Myrdal, who romanticized and idealized the planning process. Myrdal described planning as an all-important ideology that becomes the "intellectual matrix" of "modernized ideology":

> The basic idea of economic planning is that the state shall take an active, indeed the decisive, role in the economy: by its own acts of enterprise and investment, and by its various controls—inducements and restrictions—over the private sector, the state shall initiate, spur, and steer economic development. These public policy measures shall be rationally coordinated and the coordination be made explicit in an over-all plan for a specified number of years ahead.[12]

Given this kind of thinking, the plan can become an almost sacrosanct document in a developing country.

It is easy to see why the glorification of the national plan appeals to government officials and academic advisers. It offers a rational, logical, even a "scientific" blueprint justifying the central role of bureaucrats and economists in the development process. It ratio-nalizes strong action; promises (at least on paper) measurable results; provides a pseudo-scientific facade of responsibility and prudence; and gives a completely misleading appearance of neatness and order.

Unfortunately, there is no guarantee that the objectives are appropriate, the implementation practical, or the resource allocation efficient.

It would probably be useful if development economists began to de-emphasize national planning. They should point out that while national planning is important, it is not essential. P. T. Bauer, one of the few distinguished economists to deplore the emphasis on planning, has pointed out that none of the contemporary developed countries, including Russia, utilized national planning during the initial stages of its development.[13]

Planning in Japan, South Korea, and Taiwan

Japan, South Korea, and Taiwan offer excellent examples of successful flexible planning. This kind of planning is particularly applicable to developing countries whose growth effort essentially requires catching up rather than pioneering. The industries, infrastructure, technologies, and methods already exist. The problem for many developing countries is not to anticipate what will come next, but to apply appropriately what already exists. In this light, planning is probably more relevant for developing countries than for advanced economies that are still pioneering their ways toward the emerging post-industrial society. It is hard to plan for goals that have not been clearly articulated, much less accepted or even widely understood.

The planning methods of Japan, South Korea, and Taiwan cannot simply be copied. Their methods are products of the culture, traditions, and unique capabilities of each country. We do believe, however, that both specific aspects and general principles of their experiences can be widely adopted and implemented.[14] The excellence of the planning in South Korea and Taiwan (and—until the late 1960s—in Japan) makes it appropriate and useful to elaborate on and to illustrate their approaches. Discussing these examples also will add some realistic details.

Modern economic planning was first instituted in both South Korea and Taiwan by outsiders (the United States) and it was used mainly for outside consumption. It would not be entirely unfair to say that the primary purpose of the initial plan was to please American advisers. More recently, the plans have been more used to provide credibility and justification for potential lenders and investors as to guide internal decision making.[15] This situation is

typical when foreign experts, particularly those from the World
Bank, assist new nations in developing national loans and grants.

In both countries, economic planning also strengthened and
legitimized the government by explaining to private citizens what it
expected to accomplish. To some degree this is a key function of
planning in any developing country. However, it is obviously
important that over time, achievements should match promises.
Equally important is that promises should not limit achievements.
Japan, South Korea, and Taiwan have consistently performed better
than their economic plans projected. In fact, sometimes the
government deliberately understated potential results to maintain
credibility for goals that would have otherwise been unbelievable.
Often the governments themselves were pleasantly surprised at how
the official goals were surpassed.

As these countries continued to maintain very rapid rates of growth
during the 1960s, the importance of looking toward the longer term
future became increasingly apparent. Japan led the way with the
famous "income-doubling plan" prepared by Prime Minister Ikeda's
cabinet. This set as a target the doubling of Japan's per capita GNP
between 1960 and 1970. In actuality per capita GNP jumped 2.8 times
in real terms (and 4.5 times in nominal terms) during that period.
Osamu Shimomura, often credited as one of the plan's principal
architects, has made some revealing statements about how this
occurred.

> Strictly speaking, the word "plan" as used by the government does not
> have the form of a plan. The free economy has surpassed it. If it is a
> plan, then any excess should be controlled. Hence, in the debates in the
> National Diet and in comments in the newspapers, it is pointed out
> that it is strange that the economy should surpass the plan. They argue
> that it is irresponsible not to hold down growth. But that is against the
> very core of free economy.
>
> The Economic Planning Agency for the past twenty years has been
> describing economic activities under the heading of "Planning," and
> moreover, it does not appear to feel any contradiction. When
> conditions change, free enterprise has always been able to adapt itself.
> That is the mechanism of a free economy. If the question is what the
> government should do, it can take supplementary measures, for
> instance, improving the living environment, public works programs,
> and other measures to meet the conditions. It is not of a nature to be
> called "economic planning."[16]

The shift toward long-range planning (which might better be

called "long-range thinking") is very important. Several countries, including Indonesia and Malaysia, are now setting guidelines for ten years or more, at least informally. In 1973, the Republic of China government in Taiwan produced an outline of national goals for 1990; in the same year the Republic of South Korea came up with a comprehensive set of goals to be achieved by 1981. As futurists we believe that the long term is an appropriate focus for thinking things through and for what might be called "romantic" or "literary" planning by generating images of the future (including quantitative ones). A country's long-range plans should include a vision of what economic growth will mean for the living standards and improved quality of life of the average citizen.

The national economic planning branches of the Republic of South Korea and of the Republic of China government in Taiwan concern themselves with macro-economic factors and integration. Each ministry essentially constructs its own detailed plan. The national plans are constructed from the bottom up; they are the agglomeration of many different plans that are continually being revised. The national "plan" provides perspective without imposing restrictions.

The governments of both South Korea and Taiwan focus on projects that represent the largest amount of government expenditures, mainly infrastructure that supports the development of the private sector. The plan thus provides the private businessman with a sense of where railroads or dams will be constructed and where electrical power will be installed over the next few years. The most important point is that the projects are presented to the people as a comprehensive, flexible package that emphasizes a goal. Because the projects are large and visible, they lend themselves to glamorization.

We strongly believe that the development process should be glamorized. South Korea in particular has done so with its targets for the 1990s. It is useful to celebrate these achievements with dedications of factories, roads, and schools, for example. Comprehensive planning also justifies national celebration like a national holiday— including presidential speeches and pageants—to mark the completion of an important project.

In recent years, the Japanese especially have neglected this aspect of planning. Perhaps the last attempt was the Comprehensive National Development Plan in 1967.[17] The distinguishing characteristic of that plan (in contrast to Japan's overall economic plans) was its treatment of the whole country—the society as well as the economy— as a single unit. It included cultural and social objectives while still focusing primarily on the development of the physical infrastructure—roads, railroads, pipelines, harbors, and communications systems—needed for continued economic growth for the next decades. Unfortunately, there was great disillusionment with this plan and with former prime minister Tanaka's management. Today, Japan's comprehensive plans are treated more as educational and inspirational literature that need not be taken even moderately seriously.

Political Influences on Economic Decisions

One trouble with a centrally managed economy is the political nature of much economic decision making. For example, the government may tell some people to use less and tell others to use much less of some resources. Those with political clout argue that they do not want to make the adjustment being asked of them. Those without such clout resent the government's "tyranny" or "political decision making" and try to evade the regulations. These political discussions—or the revolts against such discussions—can be very wasteful and counterproductive. The market place has the great virtue of being self-enforcing. Those with the economic power generally give full weight to economic considerations and command the necessary resources to implement the decisions made on such grounds.

In socialist or other governmentally controlled economies, this behavior does not occur. There is usually no genuine comparison from the viewpoint of the user of the best way to do something, but rather a judgment by a remote governmental bureau about what is best for the country, the ruling political party, or the bureaucrats concerned.[18] These bureaucratic judgments are usually based on limited knowledge and concern, the prejudices of the decision makers, and the political and economic power of the recipients of the largesse.

Many years ago I wrote, "I have attended many committee meetings of governmental advisors in which decisions involving hundreds of millions of dollars were taken or recommended. In most cases, many of the people present, perhaps all, spent less time and effort on the decision than they would on buying a new suit. And very few of them were well-dressed."[19] The attention given to various decisions is likely to be proportional to the personal stake that the individuals who are making the decision have in its consequences.

While the central planners have an overall view that the individual planners lack, private individuals and organizations have a variety of local and personal perspectives that are at least as important as the special knowledge and perspectives of public officials. One moral is that central planners should rely as much as possible on the intelligence and understanding of the individuals personally concerned about what is best for them. But what if these individuals are perverse, ignorant, dumb, or just do not know what is good for them? Even planners who appear competent and professional can be perverse, ignorant, dumb, and not know what is good for others—and also be more prone to "educated incapacity."

Complexities in the real world sometimes contradict these elementary concepts of planning and economic decision making. Nevertheless, the concepts are usually sufficiently correct to be put into practical use—and to put the burden of proof on those who would violate them. We stress these simple ideas because some of our readers may have been overly exposed to elegantly argued ideological polemics that ignore the fundamental logic of practical experience. No system works perfectly. However, we should normally be willing to risk mistakes by allowing individuals to pursue their own judgments of their own interests. We know of many counterexamples but these exceptions do not occur nearly as often, nor are they as important, as most advocates of central planning believe. Of course, "professional" information and analysis should also be provided where useful.

We believe that a market free enough to communicate useful information through prices, and to utilize that information through decisions made by highly motivated and knowledgeable people (at least at the margin), is likely to operate relatively effectively and smoothly. This concept has been dimmed by a flood of anti-growth, anti-business, anti-middle class, and elitist attitudes. Members of the New Class usually lack the practical experience that good planning needs so badly.

The operation of the "invisible hand of the marketplace," reflected in the structure of prices and the decisions of various personally involved individuals and groups, produces a more satisfactory result than can normally be obtained by centrally managed economies. The market does not have to be very free nor individuals very well informed for this use of prices and price-motivating actions to work extraordinarily well—on the average and over the medium run and perhaps over the long run as well.

The marketplace is flexible, effective, and efficient in making realistic adjustments. A government planner who had to decide where adjustments would best be made simply would not have the information or calculating ability—even with current computing techniques—to do so as quickly or effectively as market forces. Thus, if there is a decrease in the availability of copper or an increase in its demand, the market tells every user of copper overnight that copper has become a little more scarce (i.e., expensive), and therefore should be used more economically. It communicates precise and usable information to users as to how much more economical they should be without any political influence and without involving any personalities. The signals are quick, sure, unequivocal, and unarguable. The price is what the price is.

Basic and general principles are not destroyed just because they do not hold precisely and universally in every single instance. They are not supposed to. Their function is to give general guidance about and perspective on the world. The law of supply and demand may not have the validity of the first or second laws of thermodynamics, but it does express strong tendencies that exist in almost all societies, especially societies with any kind of a market orientation. The concept of economic man may be incredibly shallow as a description of human personality, but it is a useful abstraction for understanding most modernizing countries or as an objective to be achieved in less successfully modernizing countries.

This does not mean that if people actually were "economic men" modernization would be successful. In fact, we believe the opposite and agree with the historian, Christopher Dawson, and with the later remarks of Alexander Solzhenitsyn, that much of modern society works well because it still has a number of virtues and qualities inherited from the medieval period.[20] To the extent that these virtues and qualities disappear (more or less along the lines of the Multifold Trend) certain essential social cements and lubricants become dangerously absent.

In a society where the basic human relationships are taken care of by more or less traditional means, the additional activities stimulated and modified by economic considerations of the sort described by the abstract model of an economic man can be extremely useful in analysis, in policy making, and in practice. One should not decry conventional wisdom just because it is conventional or just because it recognizes realities that some perceive as unpleasant.

CULTURAL INFLUENCES
ON ECONOMIC DEVELOPMENT

On the Need for High Morale and Commitment
in Developing Nations—And How Not to Meet That Need

We have already pointed out that businessmen, government leaders, and cadre of almost every country where rapid economic development has occurred have been characterized by an impressive degree of commitment and unity of purpose. This was as true in Holland and England in the eighteenth century as it is today in Japan, South Korea, and Taiwan. Evident in such seemingly trivial matters as sobriety of behavior and dress, these attitudes can, in both the socialist and capitalist worlds, be more important than material resources and technical aid.

If resources are copious, impressive visible changes in the physical aspects of a developing country can easily be created: new roads, dams, skyscrapers, telephone systems, airports, modern factories, and so on. Such activities are not only useful in themselves but can help to create an atmosphere conducive to development. However, if overemphasized or done inefficiently or incompetently, they can hurt. Such undue emphasis can lead to counter-reformation by traditionalists, to waste, or to excessive inflation. Simply creating opportunities for participation in the modernization process and demonstrating that things are happening is important but insufficient and can be counterproductive. People must eventually *want* to take advantage of these things and have the motivation needed to sustain commitment and effort. And the effort should itself be economically productive and self-sustaining or be a basis for eventual economically productive and self-sustaining activities. Premature attempts by poor countries to leap into ultramodern activities because of a desire to gain the appearances of modernity are usually wrong. It is often what we called in Chapter 3 a talismanic or semi-talismanic synthesis and is not necessarily rational or useful.

Showy projects such as four-lane highways and modern aircraft for national airlines may emphasize the wrong symbols. They furnish good jobs and useful facilities for elites and are admired and used by them, but most developing countries have a much greater need for dirt roads from the farms to the village and secondary highways from the villages to the cities. One of the problems with many governments is that they furnish the kind of public goods they and their friends want and not what the general public needs and wants.

Joseph Schumpeter has pointed out that it is much easier,

politically, to "sell the socialist case" than the capitalist, despite the obvious superiority of capitalism for most developing nations, at least until now. Actually it is not easier to sell unity and commitment in a socialist society to the average person but usually only to politicized elites and young idealists. Effective unity and commitment are more likely to arise from useful economic activities which the people or community concerned own, manage, and gain from than when they work for a state-owned and state-directed organization, do not gain much directly for their labors, but are told that the nation has gained. Propagandists, ideologists, and intellectuals generally find the socialist terminology and the socialist arguments more compelling, whether or not the people concerned are actually benefiting from development or even feel they are benefiting. This can lead to genuine confusion.

A striking example occurred in India. India did well economically during the emergency (from 1975 to 1977).[21] The upper 60 percent of the population were rising relatively rapidly; however, the bottom 40 percent were standing still or losing slightly. The average progress was rapid—and was widely if not completely shared. However, many socialist or welfare-oriented Indians (especially, it seemed to many observers, the affluent ones with good jobs), found it difficult to justify such a situation. These people argued that development should be judged, even in the short run, according to its effects on the bottom 40 percent of the population. While one may question this position, its rhetorical acceptability is clear.

Many of these people were doing very effective work and helping India to modernize, but the official rhetoric was socialist. And one big advantage of socialism over capitalism is clearly a matter of rhetoric and argumentation rather than performance. It simply appears too self-serving when an individual who has profited greatly from the system says, "My labors *also* improve the country as a whole." In a socialist system, where all are presumably working directly for the common good, the fact that the elites in most Third World socialist countries are uncommonly well rewarded is overlooked. Some perceptive and witty scholar has observed, "Those countries devoted to freedom have done more for equality than those devoted to equality have done for freedom or equality."

Capitalism should be defended by intellectuals who are not gaining so much from the system as well as by businessmen. But businessmen should still play a larger part in the ideological battle than they have. While it may be too simple to say that if businessmen do not defend their own interests nobody will, this remark is still cogent. But businessmen should not claim to be totally altruistic. Nothing annoys many Americans more than a glossy ad in a popular magazine claiming that oil company XYZ is going to the farthest reaches of the earth to find oil for them. This is true but misleading. The company should say instead: "Our business takes us to the farthest reaches of the earth, and this is good for both you and us." While many American and foreign businessmen are as altruistic as anybody, they are not excessively so. Indeed, Adam Smith, an admirer of business, once observed that when two businessmen get together, even for social reasons, they tend to start plotting restraint of trade.

It is important for people to believe in, admire, and respect "the system" even if they are not completely satisfied with it. They should sense that good things are happening and that one is not selling out by committing oneself personally to the system. If a truly viable change that is pervasive, orderly, survivable, and persistent is to be attained, most of the people in a nation must become "involved." It is not necessary that everyone understand the development process, but many must accept some of the often unpleasant realities associated with development. This kind of acceptance and understanding usually occurs after takeoff, when the good results are visible to all— or when the nation is under a clear and present danger.

A cogent anecdote about two Israeli Jews, one of Yemenite, one of European descent, makes the point. The Yemeni Jew said, "I don't like your European culture and I have no intention of accepting it. You have no right to try to force it on me. In fact it is cultural aggression to do so." The European Jew said quietly, "We are surrounded by a hundred million Arabs." The Yemeni Jew thought about it for about 30 seconds and then said even more softly, "Where is the electrical engineering school?"[22]

One of the real difficulties that many developing nations labor under today is that they have no clear and present danger which they must face up to. While being developed is still desirable even if there is no clear and present danger to surmount, it is difficult for idealistic young upper-middle class people to believe this if they happen to be under a barrage of propaganda challenging the concept of development that is being carried out in their country. This is a particularly important problem with young people who are being educated outside their nation and find that their nation's government is severely criticized for one reason or another by various groups in the school or country in which they are being educated.

At least initially, development is often carried forward by relatively small groups, but they at least must be committed to their task. This is often a necessary precondition for a more pervasive national approach. Such spearhead groups are normally at least as motivated by private gain as by the public interest. It is important to have the two largely overlap—and to understand that they overlap—even if the group motivated by private gain could hardly care less.

This process is increasingly difficult in the modern world because so many of the signals emanating from the developed world tend to be misleading, counterproductive, and even destructive, often to some of the very elites who should be the vanguard—e.g., the offspring of the middle and upper classes. These signals often confuse, obscure, and even block the messages that the development authorities should be trying to get across. More than anything else, these negative signals highlight the need for the kind of consciously thought through and carefully implemented process of education, information, and indoctrination we suggest below.

We are not saying that people everywhere are obligated to support all the choices and tactics adopted by their leaders; quite the contrary. It is often constructive to have a genuinely free and open discussion of these issues, but less so to have a barrage of propaganda undermining morale and commitment. Furthermore, the current tendency for elites in the developed world to send the wrong messages to the less-developed world is often as much a matter of self-indulgent propaganda as the result of serious thought and discussion. Since the personal and community commitment to modernization is still very fragile (if it exists at all) in many areas in the world, anything that weakens this commitment can be terribly counterproductive for the future of the people concerned.

We especially deplore the activities of self-appointed missionaries who want modernizing nations to return to their supposedly noble state of innocence and ignorance. Among these missionaries are many outsiders who want to prevent important economic development projects in order to "protect" the environment. In reality, most developing nations are long on environment and extremely short on economic development. In many cases these nations are taking "appropriate" precautions to minimize the environmental impact of the disputed projects. (The quotation marks are intended to emphasize that the word appropriate includes full weight being given to economic needs.) While outsiders can play an important role in making people aware of environmental issues, excessive zeal and self-righteousness can be destructive and, we would argue, often willfully and callously so.

The literature of development contains at least three important counterproductive—or at least problem-creating—views. First is the traditionalist who, in Reinhard Bendix's phrase, "fears a loss of harmony among men." People correctly fear a loss of traditional sources of meaning and purpose; of the familiar and comfortable; of status and power; of religious, ethical, and aesthetic values. This viewpoint is created, in part, by a protective reaction against a second group of concepts—that development should "break with the old" and create wholly new individuals and societies. Sometimes these are conceived of as faithful imitations of the early European development process and sometimes as similar to the "creation of a new man" in Maoist China. The third group of views more or less assumes that the post-industrial world—or its equivalent—is already here. Some of these variations of small-is-beautiful and limits-to-growth thinking that hold that traditional industrialization is a mistake, others just want to "knock off" or have less hassle. These approaches can be labeled "excessively pro-traditional," "*tabula rasa*," and "preemptive post-industrial." In our view, they all are misleading, irrelevant, or counterproductive. A modernizing society should build as much as possible on its old traditions but be willing to modify or reject many aspects of the past.

The medium-term goal should be increased affluence and technological capability. The long-term goal should be the post-industrial society in one form or another. We believe the latter can be achieved within a century or two by almost all cultures and societies, but not in a decade or two. We also believe that there are "many mountains leading to heaven" (the post-industrial society goal) and many roads up each mountain. Not only must a mountain be chosen, but also a road must be found that avoids molehills, wandering in the foothills, and other dead ends. And there must be some degree of unity and commitment about the particular mountain and road that are chosen. Two reasons for trying to build on the old as much as possible are that it makes it much easier to create this unity and commitment, and that it reduces the hostility of the traditionalists.

We agree with the attitude expressed in the 1973 UNESCO report that developing nations should find, use, and adapt their indigenous forms of education to the needs of modernization. Few earlier reports recognized the importance of relying upon a nation's own past as an integral part of a design for the future. Fortunately, it is now increasingly understood that better roads to modernization can often be found than slavish imitation of the West—or even of Japan, China, or the Soviet Union. No one doubts that the West provides exemplary development; so do South Korea, Taiwan, Singapore, Brazil, and

Mexico. But none should be slavishly imitated, just as none should be totally rejected.

We include not only the recent past, but also the distant past in the concept of the "old society." It can be useful to suggest that the indigenous people had extraordinarily admirable qualities in ancient times—at least to the extent that history allows such suggestion. A certain charisma is often associated with the people of long ago. If a nation can use them as a model, it may well wish to do so. It may even "resurrect" certain elements that may have been "forgotten" in recent years.[23] This process must of course be selective and adaptive—and, of course, should not be abused to divert too much attention and effort to romantic or outmoded historical concepts.

This line of thought runs counter to the superficial cosmopolitanism of much current discussion. Stressing one's own national and ethnic background is a general virtue and by no means needed only by minority groups in the United States (e.g., many approve of the "black-is-beautiful" movement in the United States but deplore nationalism in developing countries or pride in the achievements of Western culture). We expect that many countries will eventually create textbooks and other literature that help to create and sustain ideologies and systems of beliefs and values that can give governmental authorities and various elites—and even many of the masses—in the Third World countries the self-confidence needed to enter into open and realistic dialogues with the rest of the world. Such material might also be used for internal discussion by the various indigenous groups to explain the rationale of what they are doing.

There is an interesting parallel from our own history. For most of the last 200 years, the United States system worked incredibly well in terms of American values. This resulted in part from the superb system designed by the founding fathers at the Constitutional Convention in 1789. Americans did not have to be particularly aware of the advantages of this system, since it was obvious to almost all that it worked. As a result, Americans are usually inept at defending their system against its critics. Indeed, the ability of most Soviet officials to defend their system more ably than their American counterparts can be taken as indicating the weakness of the Soviet system. A patriotic Soviet citizen traveling abroad is in real trouble if he is not a skilled debater and dialectician.

Despite *L'époque de Malaise*, most Middle Income and some Poor countries are doing rather well now, partly because of good luck and partly because of relatively good management by business and government. We doubt that most citizens of Third World countries could easily explain the advantages of their current system over alternatives, although many can make good points if pressed. In short, there is no overwhelming need to create esoteric or new ideas to justify the policies of the more successful developing countries; such justifications already inhere in the hard facts of present growth. The problem is instead to construct an arena for internal and external debate that will bring these arguments out into the open, where they can be seen and understood. This, of course, is one objective of this book. One of the surprising characteristics of the modern world is the need to provide a defense for the generally constructive character of the governments of many currently successful Middle Income countries, particularly as opposed to their likely alternatives.

On the Importance of a "Good" Culture and "Good" Management*

Some readers may feel that our general culturism and our use of such phrases as "the Atlantic Protestant culture area" involve not only unwarranted generalizations, but also reveal some sinister habits of mind, perhaps even crypto-racism. Many may be even more annoyed at the pervasive idea that culture and national character have often been crucial for economic development. We have also made many remarks about the importance of good leadership and good management.

We are indeed convinced that the world environment for development is still so felicitous that any country that enjoys adequate leadership or management should be able to develop rather rapidly, if it can get access to the modern world. This should be possible unless the cultural background itself prevents "good" leadership or management from emerging. We also believe that worldwide economic and technological trends will make it easier for

---

*The quotes remind the reader that our criterion of good and bad is whether something helps or hinders economic development; no absolute standard is implied. Even by this criterion, judgments of whether a culture is good or bad depend on time and place. At one time, almost all Mediterranean cultures and the Chinese culture would have been judged "good," and northwest Europe "bad." The tide turned in the opposite direction for a long time, but at present the Far East—and to a lesser extent southern Europe—seem to be in ascendance. And of course, for about 1,500 years Europe considered India to be the richest area in the world. Much of India's current plight can be blamed on the explosion of population, which occurred under the British and continued in the post-war period world, simply because famine and war were controlled and were not the killers they once were.

most countries to exploit their assets and to alleviate their weaknesses. Even if there are grave cultural or other deficiencies, it should become increasingly easy to cope with these deficiencies—unless unwise policies or side effects of the less beneficial aspects of the new environment for development either exacerbate the problems or otherwise make solutions more difficult.

The experience of the United States can serve as a prototype for some aspects of this concept. Wave after wave of immigrant groups came in at the bottom, moved up, and were then replaced by later waves. While there are some hard core poor groups among United States blacks, almost half the black population can be judged to be lower-middle or middle class, and another sixth or so to be relatively well off. Most blacks are now well above the poverty line; they think of themselves as middle class and are thought of in this way by their neighbors. (An American with a regular job is normally considered to be middle class rather than working class in attitudes and life style.) Furthermore, less than half of the poor in the United States are now black. Although extensive poverty exists among female-headed families, black females as a whole now earn as much as white females with similar education. Puerto Ricans and Mexican-Americans, while hard hit by the recent recession, are responding to a large degree to economic opportunities like the traditional immigrant groups. Poverty in the United States is now mostly associated with old age and sickness, voluntary intermittent employment, withdrawal from the system, some kind of pathology or special circumstances, or extreme isolation. Within a century something similar should be true of the world as a whole; to a startling degree, it holds today in mature economies.

Another analogy can be made with recent trends in the United States. At present the United States is in the midst of a rapid reversal of roles between the Northeast and the South and the Southwest. Traditionally, before World War II, the Northeast was the technologically advanced, dynamic, industrializing, rapidly growing region; the South was the most lethargic. Since the war these two roles have been basically reversed. The Northeast has grown about 2.5 percent per year and the South and Southwest about 5 percent a year. This is often called the sunbelt shift, but this is only partly correct. First and foremost, while there is much movement of people, there is little or no movement of industry. Rather, the new industries that are starting in the United States are overwhelmingly started in the South and Southwest, partly because of the availability of a relatively hard-working and dedicated workforce. This includes such places as

Alabama and Mississippi that are scarcely thought of as part of the normal sunbelt (vacation-oriented) areas.

The continued existence of traditional American values seems to be as important as climate. We believe that the subculture of the South and, to some degree, the Southwest, which was once thought of as relatively inimical to industrial development, is now far superior in this respect to the subculture of the northeastern United States. This position can be maintained even if full allowance is made for the additional problems of the Northeast in having aging cities and the impact of the automobile in making it much easier for living and developing in open areas of the South and Southwest.

Something much like this is also occurring worldwide, where the currently Affluent countries are playing the role of the Northeast and the Middle Income countries the role of the South and Southwest.

Development and Political Stability

It used to be a cliché among students of development, anthropologists, and sociologists that rapid economic change meant turbulence, internal strife, disorder, and revolution. Economic development not only destroyed the old ties that held people together, but also destroyed regional, class, and other bonds and relationships. In a situation of rapidly changing status, income, and power, the major surprise was the survival of even a modicum of stability.

Today, however, the rapidity of economic development may create as much stability as instability. In a rapidly developing country people see that the process works and has great short and medium-term rewards. They understand that all (or at least most) will benefit, despite much propaganda to the contrary. And many if not most of the costs of the process of breaking the old and changing relationships among various groups have already been paid.

This is clearly the situation on Taiwan. If Taiwan were following the traditional mode of slow economic growth, an army of Chinese carpetbaggers would be living moderately well and suppressing indigenous competition. But the homogeneity of the culture and fantastic rate of economic growth have permitted reasonably equitable distribution of income. Opportunities for all are plentiful and everybody can rise. Competition for the best positions is inevitable, but this competition is not nearly as destructive as it would be if the process of economic development had been slower.

Some groups that either lose or gain little may not be as pleased with the new arrangements. In such countries as Brazil, Mexico, Italy,

India, and Malaysia, where the bottom 20 to 40 percent scarcely gain at all even though the top 60 to 80 percent do, the most intense disaffection usually comes not from the bottom of society, but from those classes that used to be reasonably high up but are now being passed by or relatively reduced in status, power, or wealth. Such a change can arouse the most intense frustration, opposition, and hostility.

In South Korea, for example, two of the most powerful opponents of the Park government are the Christians and the old educated Mandarin class. The first represents an old modernizing elite with a fundamentalist religious attitude towards life, both now being rejected. The status, privileges, power, and income of the previous Mandarin educated class (often Japanese-educated) have also been greatly shaken. Rather than fight the development process (the true cause of their discomfort), they focus on a much more acceptable target—the real or apparent political defects of the "ruling party" (a phrase normally used in the South Korean press).

The potential for democracy is much greater in India than in many developing countries. India is so diverse that it is hard to imagine any system working that was neither relatively democratic nor totalitarian. However, significant participation in the social system as a whole still tends to be limited to a small middle and upper-middle class elite. While the defeat of the Indira Gandhi government was an expression of the will of the people, this was less an expression of a love for democracy than a defensive reaction—an almost desperate uniting by the opposition party. They felt that if they did not unite on this one occasion, they were likely to spend a good deal of their future in jail or at least out of things.

Equally important, many Indians were hostile to the excesses of the birth control campaign. While Indira Gandhi's government did a rather creditable economic job during the emergency, it behaved quite badly from the viewpoint of human rights and the most elementary human privacy.[24] Democracy, of course, has both costs and benefits, but the historical record for the last 200 years suggests that it has worked relatively well only in what we have called the Atlantic Protestant culture areas of Europe, North America, Australia, New Zealand, and, of course, Switzerland—areas where factionalism, confrontation, and conflicting interests have not precluded joint efforts and a basic consensus.

A major difference in political freedom between totalitarian states of the left and authoritarian states of the right resides in the openness of the latter group of societies to international criticism at home and abroad. Over half a million tourists every year visit South Korea and

Taiwan, and thousands of foreign businessmen and government officials reside there. Under these circumstances, the government cannot isolate the local people from the outside world. This difference is extraordinarily important for the preservation and strengthening of the most elementary human rights and often civil rights as well.

Countries tied to the outside world through international financing, investment, foreign aid, and tourism are vulnerable to external pressures and influences. When those pressures are unfair, however, their only alternative may be to restrict the intellectual elites within their own countries, who would otherwise seek to exploit worldwide attention—often to further their own power or financial interests as much as to gain rights for all. Serious leaders of those countries may want to reduce restrictions but feel inhibited by outside pressures.

The problem of intellectuals in developing countries is much broader than that associated with the press and with opposition political parties. Nor is it limited to the neo-Confucian culture areas. Intellectual elites, particularly university professors and students, have always been a major source of unrest and a principal pressure group for change, both for good and for bad. Student riots brought down the Syngman Rhee government in South Korea, and students have played key roles in many other coups.

The role of the intellectual in the student movements in pressuring for change has often been constructive in both expanding individual freedom and promoting modernization. But it has also often displayed impracticality. Students, professors, and other intellectuals seldom emerge as leaders after the unrest. Rather, practical persons assume leadership and use them for their own purposes. The end result is as often greater restriction of freedom as it is expansion of freedom. More important, students have no more moral authority than non-students; they are just in positions of greater visibility and are easily mobilized.

On Poverty and Moral Imperatives

We believe that the developed world everywhere has a moral responsibility to help the poor of this world to become reasonably well off (or at least what we have called "middle income"—neither affluent nor poor). We do not believe that the developed world bears any overwhelming moral imperative to decrease gaps, the large differences in the average incomes of nations. It is probably desirable to do so, but only as a relatively low-priority objective. We see extreme poverty as an evil that should be decreased and perhaps eliminated as soon as possible. We do not take anywhere near as strong a moral position of achieving relative affluence, except as it helps reduce absolute poverty. We view reducing inequality as the least important moral objective, if it is a moral objective at all.

Unfortunately, we do not have three words for degree of poverty— say poverty$_1$, poverty$_2$, and poverty$_3$. Poverty$_1$ could refer to extreme material deprivation; poverty$_2$ to the psychological deprivation that many feel who have relatively adequate access to material goods but possess fewer amenities than their neighbors; and poverty$_3$ how very affluent observers believe that lower income people should feel, even if they do not. Thus, everybody is aware that many people in the United States with an income below $5,000 per year for a family of four are officially judged to be poor by the government, although in many parts of the world this income would place them firmly in the middle or upper-middle class. Indeed, many families in New York City received in services and cash the equivalent of about $10,000 in 1978 from public assistance and welfare authorities.

All three variants of the word "poverty" may be legitimate and useful, but the last two are very different from the kind of desperate material poverty we normally mean when we refer to poverty in this book—i.e., poverty$_1$.

The problem of poverty and wealth is quite complex. Each of the more than 150 different nations in the world has a more or less inegalitarian distribution of income. Furthermore, average income varies widely among nations. Equally important, how people react to this varying income varies widely. An income of $300 per capita has meant very different things in the United States in 1800, in Colombia in 1960, in either of the two Chinas, or in South Korea or Japan at the stage of their development when those nations had that as their per capita income. The differences time and culture make are enormous; so are the variations associated with families and individuals.*

---

*In the original versions of many tables in this book "relatively" appeared in parentheses as part of the classification of Poor, Middle Income, or Affluent to remind the reader that there are rich people and groups even in the Poor countries, and there may be many people in the Affluent countries who are poor even absolutely. We decided not to repeat this reminder but assume that the reader cooperates with us in our use of various generalizations and categories by fully understanding that these can sometimes be partly misleading as well as usefully orienting; they should always be taken in a "by and large" sense relative to other groups.

The Impact of the Liberal New Class on Economic Development: South Korea and Taiwan as Abused Exemplars

Had the economic achievements of South Korea and Taiwan of the last decade taken place fifty or a hundred years ago, they would have been regarded with awe by the advanced nations of the world as almost superhuman feats meriting the highest praise by all civilized persons. Even ten or fifteen years ago, when Japan's economic growth was being commonly referred to inside and outside of Japan as a "miracle," Taiwan's already remarkable achievements were being accorded much less favorable worldwide attention. Since then, except within economic and business circles, these countries' increasingly impressive achievements have received relatively little international praise other than from businessmen.

Both have come to be thought of as more or less pariah states, singled out for criticism in the Advanced Capitalist nations as well as in the socialist states and socialist-oriented developing nations. This political criticism is grossly unfair. It reflects both a political double standard and ignores not only their economic accomplishments but also their relative political success as well. Contrasted with most other nations in comparable positions, they are models of free expression, political tolerance, and the rule of law. Such international criticism is by no means leveled only at these two countries (although they may well be the most unfairly treated) but is more or less directed at all authoritarian "right wing" governments in the developing world, many of whom are the most successful examples of rapid economic growth. This criticism distorts understanding of the development process and creates a counterproductive environment. It adds an unnecessary additional burden both on the countries that are doing an exceptional job of "catching up" and on those that would otherwise admire and perhaps emulate them and improve their own efforts.

There are several reasons for this major shift in international opinion. Perhaps the most important derives from the new opposition to growth. The anti-growth movement has not only made realistic and efficient policies more difficult to perceive and implement in the advanced countries, but it has also confused the situation in developing countries, with the added disadvantage of seriously undermining internal morale and external support. Perhaps it is not necessary to have high morale in the developed world, at least for setting and achieving economic targets. Indeed, a blind adherence to the achievement of purely economic goals, to a single-minded pursuit of "growth for growth's sake," is neither appropriate nor desirable for the advanced countries, where the New Emphases have to be taken seriously. However, the New Emphases are not the key problems for the developing countries. Their first priority must inevitably be to catch up or at least to attain an acceptable level. But the developed countries dominate the international discussion, so mounting opposition to growth has inevitably spilled over into the developing world.

There is some indication that appropriate distinctions are beginning to be made, but the discussion is still badly distorted. There is as yet no sign that widespread recognition will be given to the success stories. Nowhere in the reporting in the United States on the recent "Korea-gate scandal," for example, does one find even a *caveat* in the criticism (as, for example, "Of course we recognize the magnificent achievement that the South Korean government has made in improving the welfare of the Korean people, however much we deplore their political actions").

The double standard is a peculiar phenomenon which, along with the anti-growth movement, must be accorded a major share of the responsibility for this situation. South Korea and Taiwan are excellent examples because they can be directly contrasted with their communist counterparts. The mass media, in the so-called "free world" (but which might better be known as the non-totalitarian world—or perhaps the democratic-and-authoritarian world), heap criticism at "abuses of power and human rights" allegedly committed under President Park Chung Hee, while hardly mentioning the conditions of North Korea under Kim Il Sung, which are more oppressive than in any other communist state except Cambodia. The great majority of critics have few illusions about what is happening in South Korea and North Korea. Why then do they act as they do?

There are several reasons. First, there is a natural tendency to be more critical of friends, associates, allies, and even oneself than of adversaries. This can be healthy if the existence of a double standard is acknowledged. Abuses are easier to document, and protests may have a greater effect on regimes that are less than totalitarian, especially if they depend on the good will of their critics, their own citizens, or others. Discussion by Americans of domestic abuses of power and limitations on individual freedom, even when grossly exaggerated, can be constructive. But accusations sometimes become so intense that people forget that by any reasonable political standard, the United States is one of the freest societies in history, as the criticism itself demonstrates.

Another argument suggests that while nothing can be done about conditions in communist states, we have some responsibility to encourage or even insist on "acceptable levels of behavior" in countries where the United States has some leverage through military or economic assistance. The blatant use of such leverage, however, can be perceived as a cynical form of imperialistic bullying because it is used mainly against those who cannot retaliate. Liberal New Class spokesmen of the Atlantic Protestant culture area who feel a need for causes of some sort tend to press intractably against those who are not in a position to strike back. They seek psychologically satisfying causes that will not disturb détente or some other worthwhile goal. They believe that agitating for what they consider to be human rights in South Korea and Taiwan has a useful positive effect on world affairs, giving no thought to whether or not it is counterbalanced by any particular costs or negative consequences—or at least any that they care about.

Many of these critics are high-minded and idealistic, yet they would feel little guilt if their political pressures hurt the economic development of either country or emboldened either's enemies. Additionally many, while not pro-communist, are very "anti-anti-communist"; that is they retain a sense of cynicism about attacks on communist excesses or atrocities as automatically reflecting an exaggerated and extreme "cold war mentality," particularly as exemplified by the excesses of the McCarthy era. Such skeptics tend to suspect "admirers" of South Korea's or Taiwan's economic achievements of being either dogmatic anti-communists, or simplistic worshipers of GNP.

Along with this, in many prestigious intellectual circles in the West, the point has been reached where it is poor form to laud the accomplishments and advantages of big business, free enterprise, or the capitalist system anywhere, including, of course, in such countries as Taiwan or South Korea. At the same time, it was regarded as perfectly reasonable to speak in glowing terms about mainland China's "heroic efforts" to create a "New Man." This was so even though there was no question about the absence of any attempt to preserve human rights (which, of course, these people vehemently support) in the People's Republic of China, let alone any comparison of relative economic performances.

We concede something awe-inspiring, even admirable, in an attempt to create a "New Man." That this endeavor is necessarily brutal, ruthless, and destructive of certain precious human rights (such as individuality and personality) is simply overlooked or accepted as a natural characteristic of Maoist communism rather than as something that should be condemned or judged abhorrent. In this respect, "Maoism" resembled a religion, and a religion is not often condemned for practicing its own rigid tenets, unless they are totally abhorrent such as cannibalism, suttee, or incest. Perhaps the most important consequence of these attitudes is the loss of morale, faith, commitment in and admiration of our own economic institutions and the culture in which they developed and exist. For example, many people who would ridicule heroic art in the United States admire the ten-foot workers on twenty-foot tractors one finds on Chinese posters.[25]

Certain emotional, political, and psychological needs of Western intellectuals seem to be served by participating, however remotely, in what appears to be an enormously disciplined, homogeneous, monolithic, unitarian movement. Eric Hoffer has called people who participate in such movements "true believers." These uncritical admirers of Maoism or uncritical opponents of almost every right-wing authoritarian government, especially if it is also successful economically, are not otherwise "true believers" in anything; their personal lives are often shallow and lack genuine meaning, purpose, direction, and achievement. To compensate, they applaud movements that have these qualities and can therefore fill some very important personal psychological needs, if only vicariously. Or they get their kicks, or intellectual reciprocal support, by accepting almost any movement, no matter how trendy it is. Such applause and the parallel criticism of currently fashionable targets does not entail courage or require serious study.

Both the admiration and the criticism are partly fads, even though they may have deep roots in group and individual psyches. Nazi Germany, Fascist Italy, and Stalinist Russia had much the same impact on many observers and visitors; things were happening; history was being made (e.g., Lincoln Steffen's remarks on visiting the Soviet Union, "I have seen the future and it works!"). A sense of being part of "a wave of the future" invariably attracts many adherents. To a remarkable degree, visitors from democratic countries who are extremely intolerant of anything undemocratic or violent in their own societies have often found themselves powerfully attracted to the discipline and purposiveness of fascism and bolshevism. Japanese visitors to the People's Republic of China sometimes remark: "We have many criticisms of mainland China, but at least the Chinese have lean, hard, purposeful faces."

Finally, and most important, the communist idea "from each

according to his ability; to each according to his need" has a deep appeal, even if only as an ideal. We must remind ourselves that most societies have been hostile to individuality and egoism—especially in the form of personal selfishness—as a basic engine of society. These traits have usually been thought of as threatening and disruptive to social cooperation and harmony. In almost all religions, the communist ideal would be judged a far superior moral principle to Adam Smith's "invisible hand of the market," with its emphasis on individual self-interest and economic reward as major motivations.

As we discussed in Part I, there are many reasons for the loss of belief in the inherent worth of our economic institutions and the value of economic growth. Whether or not one agrees with the many self-criticisms of capitalism heard in all the Advanced Capitalist nations, they have resulted in extremely unfair standards and criticism for countries such as South Korea and Taiwan. Both countries have been deprived of credit for their humanitarian achievements. In a very poor country, economic growth can fulfill the most basic of all rights and freedoms—the right to life and freedom from starvation and grinding poverty.

In a rapidly growing economy, such as that of South Korea or of Taiwan, change is tangible and visible. It is much more dramatic—qualitatively and even quantitatively—than changes in the People's Republic of China, however different the scale may be. In both South Korea and Taiwan, life expectancy is half again what it was two decades ago; children are usually taller than their parents; and almost everybody shares in the many products and benefits that modern science and technology provide. Because of the exceptionally egalitarian distribution of income, even the poorest families are better educated, better fed, healthier, better housed, and able to acquire more material possessions and live freer lives than all but a handful of families a generation ago.

We do not imply that no valid criticisms can be made of life in South Korea and Taiwan. Some defects of both can be legitimately regarded as serious. However, the benefits of their economic progress are in no way minor—and it is outrageous for citizens of affluent countries to stand in judgment and denigrate them or overlook them by taking their achievements for granted. The expansion of "life, liberty and the pursuit of happiness" has been greatly facilitated by changing per capita income from a few hundred dollars to about a thousand dollars in South Korea and to twelve hundred dollars in Taiwan. When proper account is taken of the serious security issues facing both countries, which necessitate some authoritarian measures, it is clear that an impressive level of personal and political freedom has been maintained in both nations. It is grossly unfair that the world press so rarely acknowledges these realities.

Many specific principles and programs from these two nations can be copied or adapted to other nations and circumstances. Some of these seem potentially very useful. It is not that we believe that most other cultures are likely, in the near future, to do as well as Korea and Taiwan, even with good leadership. Nor do we think it desirable for others to try slavishly to follow their examples. Exact copies do not fit well. But we do believe that others can partake of South Korean or Taiwanese experience and examples and still be creative on their own. Despite the many changes, the South Koreans and Taiwanese (as well as the Japanese) have been true to their own cultures, while borrowing freely from the West, from each other, and elsewhere. Other countries can do the same. It does not show weakness or lack of confidence to borrow successfully. Indeed, the opposite is more likely to be true. Nor does such borrowing—or the recommendation to do so—imply a blanket endorsement of any nation's policies.

Environment and Ecology

For practical reasons as well as for conceptual clarity it is important to distinguish two different kinds of increasing environmental costs. The first reflects the increased size of many enterprises. The bigger they are, the more likely they are to affect the environment significantly. In general, it is understandable that Americans tended to ignore the impact of their activities on the environment before World War II. The impact was relatively small and the environment was very big. However, the super-industrial society has now emerged, and the impact of major projects on the social and physical environments becomes very large and apparent. Under these circumstances, this impact should be explicitly included in the planning process. Furthermore, the law of increasing returns begins to operate on certain surviving elements of the pre-industrial environment and ecology, as they begin to disappear. Those remaining may be more highly prized and are almost certain to require more protection.

The law of diminishing returns also operates. As we get richer or more polluting, our standard of pollution control rises. More and more must be spent to protect the environment and higher levels of pollution abatement are necessary. It has, however, been the history of technology that, until recently, increasing costs did not occur for this reason. Improvements in technology and in management techniques have more than negated the effect of diminishing returns for greater efforts, sometimes called the Ricardian effect. However, something quite different is happening today. Standards for the environment are much higher than they were. Despite this, the diminishing returns issue is not so serious if the higher standards make sense.

The higher standards can become completely unreasonable if they are applied after investments have been made and the various processes frozen in concrete and steel structures. For example, current United States law requires that there be no water pollution from open sources by 1985, an absolutely impossible requirement. The Sierra Club was perfectly willing to block exploitation of 10 to 20 billion barrels of oil in Prudhoe Bay, valued say at something between $50 and $200 billion, and deny that resource to the United States (plus the additional resources that would have come with further exploration of Alaska). They maintained this position even after it became clear that the oil involved would play a critical role for the nation.

We have already mentioned the legislation before Congress that would put aside about a third of Alaska as national parks of one sort or another. Most of them would then not be available for any kind of development except by permission of Congress. The United States can probably afford to do this even if these areas contain resources worth many hundreds of billions of dollars that will now never be found. But it should be clear that few if any less developed countries can afford to do this.

There are two kinds of pollution, one involving such things as dangerous heavy metals. Presumably every country should be careful with these. The other kind of pollution is represented by dirty air and less than pure water or less than the most aesthetic landscapes. We simply do not know how bad normal dirty air and normal impure water are for human health. We are reasonably sure, particularly when these are very bad, that the death rate of vulnerable people is increased, but it would be difficult to show that such pollution took off more than a month or two of average life expectancy. Extreme poverty tends to take off between twenty and forty years of life expectancy. On this ground alone there is no question which most people prefer to choose. They want the increased wealth and affluence created by industrialization, even if it comes temporarily at the cost of dirty air and less than pure water.

At least twice, members of the Brazilian cabinet made speeches in which they in effect said to the rest of the world, "Please send us your pollution." Each time outraged reactions by foreign environmental groups forced them to retract. This itself is an outrage—the rich telling the poor that they should accept poverty so as not to hurt the feelings of the rich. It is hard to imagine a less moral position.

A proper effort to protect the environment should be supported only if costs and benefits are reasonably assessed. There is little doubt, as the world continues to increase its productivity, that it will also manifest increased concern for the environment and ecology, both social and physical. Such increased concern is basically justified, so long as it does not lose contact with reality and common sense.

Personal Note 1: The United States Hunting Culture and the Raising of Children

Personal Note 1 draws on one of many available examples that illustrate how ignorant and even bigoted many members of the American upper-middle class intellectual elite are about the family customs of American rural and lower income groups. It also makes an even more important point about how to raise children. The hunting culture within which these rural and lower income families rear their children is not the bloody, sado-masochistic pastime of latent homosexuals that so many in the elite take it to be, but rather a good way to live and an excellent setting for raising children. The example also illustrates some of the ambiguities that accompany affluence.

This Personal Note and Personal Note 2 on educated incapacity suggest that we simply are not raising the kind of elites that will provide the leadership American society and the other techno- logically advanced societies need to succcessfully cope with the future. We seem to be systematically "spoiling the children" or making them into impractical, unrealistically idealistic persons. There is a pronounced tendency in the American upper-middle class to raise its offspring on a steady diet of illusions and theory and to have them interact only with children similar to themselves. As a result, many of these children cannot distinguish book-learning from practical experience and are totally unaware of the importance of the latter for developing good judgment.

Both Personal Notes discuss some complex, subtle, and badly understood issues that are the technical province of psychology, sociology, and other behavioral sciences but that bear directly on the problems and prospects for economic development and social stability. I do not claim to understand these issues completely, nor do I know of anyone who has achieved such understanding, but I am convinced that they are critical. I believe, for example, that educated incapacity may well be the single most important problem facing the developed world. There are ongoing Hudson Institute studies on the topics of both Personal Notes. Because the data I adduce and the arguments I advance are anecdotal and tentative, I have labeled these notes "personal" and used the first person singular throughout.*

During the middle and late 1960s and to a lesser extent the early 1970s, I customarily gave two or three talks a year at seminars or forums at Berkeley, Brandeis, Columbia, Harvard, Princeton, or Yale. These talks gave me contact with young people and faculty at leading universities during a most interesting and challenging time.

I almost always started my discussion by asking some questions. One common question was, "How many of you have three guns of your own?" About 30 percent of the audience usually did.[26] I then asked those who did not have guns at home why they thought the others owned so many weapons. Most of the non-gun-owners were absolutely perplexed. They looked at the gun-owners in total bewilderment. What in the world would anybody be doing with three guns? How could it be that they were not an isolated minority of one or two, but a significant proportion of the group. Their answers ran from a confused "to protect yourself" to "for defense against attacks by blacks."

I would then proceed. "How many of the gun-owners were given a .22 rifle at the age of twelve?" Generally from 90 to 100 percent received one on their twelfth birthday. "How many of you got a shotgun at the age of fourteen, give or take a year?" The overwhelming majority. "How many got a .30-caliber rifle at sixteen, give or take a year?" Again an overwhelming majority. Back to the non-gun-owners, "What's going on?" Again, they did not know.

They did not realize that they lived in a hunting culture, that these were in effect rites of passage, and that even some students at a seminar in an elite university could have been raised in such a culture.

---

*These Personal Notes were among the appendices for the special ICC edition. Both have been drastically shortened for presentation here. We plan to present them in expanded form in a forthcoming book tentatively entitled *Things to Come: The 80s and 90s,* which will focus on cultural, social, and political issues as opposed to the economic issues that are at the center of this book. However, as we have already made clear, economic issues cannot be separated from social and cultural issues. We believe that Personal Notes 1 and 2, while seemingly a little digressive, are so absolutely central to the main points we are making that we decided to include them in abbreviated form.

Then I would ask, "What happens to a twelve-year-old young man if he and every other twelve-year-old in town is given a .22?" I had deliberately given them a hint by saying "young man" rather than "child." In almost all cultures the age of twelve or thirteen is taken as the onset of manhood. This is the age of the Bar Mitzvah, the Confirmation, the recitation of the Koran, and so on. (The reason these young adults were not allowed to vote until they were eighteen or twenty-one is that the authorities concerned believe that voting should be restricted to mature adults, not that they were too young to assume adult responsibilities.)

A boy who is given a .22 rifle becomes a young man almost overnight. He will not be allowed to play around with a .22 because he can kill somebody or injure them severely, particularly if every other young man in town has a .22. In small-town rural America, where this culture is strongest, everybody will insist that these young people take care in handling firearms. It is similar to a custom that used to be prevalent in much of France. If a young child misbehaved, every adult present would admonish him whether or not the adult was related to the young child. People in our hunting culture areas feel free to admonish any young person who appears to be careless with a gun. If he points the gun at somebody, even in horseplay, he will be severely criticized, even punished. It is obvious that firearms are a serious matter and simply should not be used as toys. In fact, the firearms accident rate for these young people is very low.

Young persons who are given guns go through an immediate maturing experience because they are thereby given a genuine and significant responsibility. A relative or family friend teaches them how to use the gun, how to get along and survive in the wilderness, how to make a camp or break it, and so on. Since they are older and more responsible at the age of fourteen, they are given a weapon that is even more lethal. By the time they are sixteen, boys in this culture are permitted to own a .30-caliber weapon, which is extremely dangerous if used carelessly or malevolently. This hunting culture gives young men a sense of meaningful identification with his pioneer ancestors, with traditional American history, and a chance to participate with other young men in activities which are both pleasant and maturing.

Upper-middle class urban Americans generally regard this hunting culture as perverse or perverted. The liberal press frequently treats the gun as a kind of violent pornography. At one point the head of the New York Board of Education succeeded in having all rifle clubs banned from the school system. Why? "The gun is a phallic symbol, it ejaculates." One can imagine the reaction of a typical American who hears this kind of remark on television. The response to this kind of observation helps to increase the loss of confidence discussed in Chapter 5.

I believe that it is terribly important to give young people (whom we call "children" in our culture) adult responsibilities early in life— to give them experiences that are enlarging and maturing. It is a serious mistake to have them always carefully supervised and treated in ways that keep them from growing into mature adults who accept serious responsibilities and bear the result on their own shoulders. The whole concept of a child is rather recent in our culture, and the notion of adolescence is even more recent. Previously, children were considered to be young adults.

Henry the Fifth was his father's general at the age of fourteen, and at fifteen was in complete command of the campaign against Wales. Romeo and Juliet were fourteen and twelve, respectively; one rather suspects that Shakespeare's dialogue reflects their language reasonably accurately. At the age of sixteen Alexander Hamilton was master of a ship that took a voyage from New York to the Caribbean and back through an area infested with pirates; he asserted authority as master of the ship, and accomplished some very sharp—and very successful—trading in Cuba. At the age of nineteen George Washington was in charge of a party surveying Virginia, and a year or two later was in sole charge of an assault on a French fort.

In a presentation I used to make to university seminars, I often asked the upper-middle class students if they had ever had to wait a year for something reasonable. I explained my concept of "something reasonable" as follows. If you were a young American in a middle-class family and you wanted a bike at the age of six, that is unreasonable; if you wanted one at age ten, then that is reasonable. If you want a car at the age of fourteen, that's unreasonable in most parts of the country; if you want one at nineteen or twenty, that is usually quite reasonable. If you want a trip to Paris at the age of sixteen, that is unreasonable; if you want to go at twenty-one— particularly if you have earned the money or if somebody gives it to you—that is usually reasonable. Now, obviously, if you want a yacht or to change your parents or even to change your height or sex, that is almost never reasonable.

After searching through their entire lives, most of these young people were unable to identify a single situation when they had had to wait more than a year for something reasonable. One explanation has to do with the social customs surrounding birthdays and Christmas—

particularly in upper-middle class families, to some degree in middle class families as well, and to a lesser degree among the rich. Twice a year the two parents get together and say, "What can we buy that little bastard that he or she doesn't already have?" And of course, whatever the parents do not buy, the grandparents do. As a result the unfortunate child is over-indulged—is given presents one, two, or three years ahead of any "reasonable" desires. The child never goes through the experience of understanding that life is not fair, that one does not always get what one is entitled to. Every upper-middle class American will recognize the foregoing as a common experience. In an incredibly large number of American families today, both Christmas and birthdays involve a veritable orgy of gift-giving; the children really get drunk with gifts.

We would argue that the lower-middle class American family is often somewhat more restrained, particularly if it feels it cannot afford such orgies; however, it often follows the upper-middle class example. Many wealthy families, however, are desperately afraid of spoiling their children. Very often at Christmas and New Year's these children get a small number of durable toys, and their closets are not filled with fancy clothes.

This is not to say that the rich raise their children well in America. They probably do not, but on this particular issue they perhaps err less than the American upper-middle class. These youngsters miss the most important lessons that a young person can learn. Everybody should have the experience of wanting something badly for a long time, perhaps working and striving for it, and then sometimes getting it and sometimes not. That is a terribly important experience for a mature individual to have behind him that many young children in the United States simply do not receive.

The children of the academically oriented upper-middle class are even worse off. We have already noted this in Chapter 2, which discusses how different the school atmosphere is from the real world. Very often these young people literally have no contact with the real world that affects their thinking greatly, nor do any of their friends. Their only experiences are a warm family life, a protected social life, and a paternalistic school system. Everything is neat and tidy in all these environments; everything has a beginning, a middle, and an end. Problems are always resolved (as in an hour-long television program—which may also reinforce this particular attitude—everything is complete and finished during the program).

By contrast, a hunting ethic, where responsibility, self-reliance, and mature behavior are necessary is a very reasonable social milieu for child rearing. The fact that this way of raising children is strongly criticized by many upper-middle Americans shows more about their ignorance of their own country than about their supposedly superior values and sensitivities.

Personal Note 2: Educated Incapacity

I have referred many times throughout this book to the concept of educated incapacity, which I believe particularly affects the Atlantic Protestant culture area and, to a lesser degree, Japan. The basic notion is that, since World War II, there seems to be an amazingly high correlation in these cultures between having a better education, or at least more education, and a certain lack of reality testing and common sense. This problem is striking, particularly for younger people in many upper-middle class *milieus* and many New Class people.

Some readers may assume that these observations simply represent a more or less vulgar accusation of "book learning," a phrase which was commonly heard in the United States before World War II, but is now rare. I do not deny the similarity. However, I argue that while the problem existed at that time, it has now become totally pervasive. We noted in the discussion of the agnostic use of information and concepts in Chapter 1 the sixth level of belief called "general acceptance"—beliefs that are so pervasive, quick, and automatic that people tend not to realize that there could be any controversy about such issues. To the extent that the older concept of book learning is akin to educated incapacity, we argue that the problem so pervades the groups affected that they literally do not know there is an issue. For example, they either do not realize how different the "school situation" is from the "real world," or they argue for what they call "relevance" in the school situation. (By relevance they often mean something quite irrelevant to most real needs: e.g., a focus on such issues as nuclear war, ecology and environment, poverty, racism, and so on. While important, these issues are not likely to be at the center of the day-to-day problems and lives of most people.)

A good example of the disasters that educated incapacity has inflicted on American society is provided by the effects during the middle and late 1960s and early 1970s of the lack of understanding of what we called "Middle America" issues in Chapter 5. We turn now to some less documented, more controversial, and more complex aspects of educated incapacity to give perspective on our thesis, before discussing further these social issues.

Perjury, Lies, and Social Lies[27]

Every culture needs a certain number of good examples—even
saints. Saints are individuals who take society's ideals seriously and
literally—perhaps even to the limit. Although they are thought of as
impractical extremists, these persons are often valued highly precisely because of this impracticality. They are a special class of people
who publicly exemplify the ideals of the culture in their own lives.
Society does not expect the average person or even most of its leaders
to live up to these ideals quite so literally and perfectly, but it does
expect them to do so to some degree, and even more, to pretend to do
so as an example for children, for each other, and perhaps for the
"lower classes." As a result, most cultures make a distinction between
everyday life, in which all kinds of compromises must be made, and
the ideals to which people should aspire.

One example is telling the truth. In the United States, everybody is
expected to tell social lies. Adults who do not do so are considered
boorish, boring, and egoistic. If somebody asks, "How are you?" you
are not supposed to supply a detailed report but merely respond that
things are "all right." This custom does not mean, as young
Americans sometimes think, that the questioner is not genuinely
interested in how the person feels, merely that the questioner is less
interested than, say, the person's mother. A greeting such as "good
day" implies, "I sort of like you, I even care about you, but I have no
great intense interest in you—at least not today." There is no
implication of unfriendliness or hypocrisy, but only a kind of
benevolent neglect: "I have nothing against you; I am even a bit in
your favor, but I am also deeply concerned with my own affairs at the
moment and know of no reason to be otherwise."

Lying is also allowed in the United States for reasons of state. This
is why public officials are not usually under oath when they testify
before Congress, as opposed to a court or grand jury. Although they
are supposed to tell the truth almost all the time, every now and then
they need the freedom to lie. Hence, they are not expected or required
to perjure themselves. If the United States is involved in the
overthrow of a foreign government and the secretary of state is asked
about it, he is not supposed to say, "I prefer not to discuss the
subject," or "I'm glad you asked that question, here's a list of our
agents." Instead, he is expected to look the Congressman right in the
eye and say, "No!" It is understood that every country has to do a
certain number of secret things that its officials do not talk about.

But it is also understood that the officials concerned must limit themselves very strictly. The idea is to keep this custom under control. In addition to the conscience and good sense of the officials concerned and their colleagues (an important source of good behavior), this control is enforced in two ways. First, the official is punished if caught, not because he or she did it, but because he or she got caught. Under these circumstances, there's no alternative to punishment. For one thing, a failure to punish cannot be explained to children. And the proposition that public officials are above the law cannot be defended explicitly and publicly. Nevertheless, almost everybody, including most political opponents (but not necessarily most political enemies) would regret that the official was caught lying and would not want to exploit his or her predicament. Thus, under normal circumstances, almost no one is vindictive. If, however, an official is caught and it turns out that he or she has abused the privilege, then the punishment is severe. Such abuse might involve lying for personal reasons, confusing one's self-interest with the national interest, or pure cynicism. When abuses of this kind occur, most people want to make an example out of the culprit, for the best of reasons. However, this ability on the part of officials to lie disappears when they have taken an oath. Perjury in the United States is a very serious crime unless it is committed in a divorce case, where—unless it involves financial issues—it will not be punished. I believe there is almost no case where an individual was jailed for perjury in a divorce case.

Graft Versus Corruption

We sharply distinguish graft from corruption: "graft" is a more or less legitimate fee or "tip" for services rendered; "corruption" is an excessive fee or a payment to an official for something that he or she should not do. In the graft situation, the government official is doing what he or she is supposed to do and being paid by the person who benefits from the action, but the latter is not supposed to have to pay. The basic situation is much like a commercial service by a waiter or porter who is paid to do what he or she is doing, but still expects a tip. The graft case also resembles that of a justice of the peace or a notary public: both have a job to do and both expect to be paid for doing it. In most parts of the world, a public official will not do what he is supposed to do without getting an appropriate tip.

The question is not one of being underpaid. Indeed, it is almost the opposite—the fee is proportional to the salary. The larger the salary, the larger the fee. Americans misunderstand graft if they think that its purpose is solely to make up for an inadequate salary. It is simply considered a perquisite of the office. For example, before World War II, a big oil company in Shanghai fired their office manager when they discovered that he had bought his office from the previous office manager and was taking a rake-off on all office supplies. The reaction of the Chinese community was absolute outrage. In their view, the manager had bought a legitimate business in a legitimate way. They felt that the oil company should have reimbursed him for his costs plus an extra amount to make up for his lost income and the embarrassment he had suffered. The oil company was eventually forced to agree and did so.

Our lack of understanding of this issue contributed appreciably to our problems in Vietnam. We poured billions of dollars into the Vietnamese governmental system that we usually did not audit, partly on the grounds that we were guests and partly on the grounds that we didn't think auditing would do any good.

The Americans soon learned that if somebody paid the Vietnamese worker or peasant ninety-five piastres and asked for a receipt for a hundred piastres, it was given. What the Americans did not understand was that if you paid the Vietnamese ninety-four piastres and asked for a receipt for 100 you would not get it. Vietnamese peasants and workers are very tough; they feel you are entitled to five piastres and not to six—and that is all you get.

In any country where they have a phrase for graft that indicates that it is a tip (to insure prompt service) the graft is usually recognized as legitimate. Thus, in China the word is *cumshaw*, in India it is *baksheesh*, in Mexico it is *mordida*, in the United States it is *honest graft*, and so on. Ethical, careful American companies have learned how to live and operate effectively in this kind of atmosphere in the past. One way was to retain one of the most ethical law firms in the country where the company wished to operate, pay the law firm a substantial fee, and say, "Please handle each problem for us." Because the law firm was ethical, it was careful not to do anything wrong; but because it knew the ropes, it was able quickly to obtain all the licenses, or permits, or whatever else was needed. Today, this is called a questionable payment and can lead to very serious trouble. In effect, it is exactly as if you were asking people to deal regularly with waiters and porters but not permitting them to give tips. Clearly, the service will deteriorate quickly under such restrictions—and should.

The Expert and Educated Incapacity

Educated incapacity often refers to an *acquired or learned inability to understand or even perceive a problem*, much less a solution. The original phrase, "trained incapacity," comes from the economist

Thorstein Veblen, who used it to refer, among other things, to the inability of those with engineering or sociology training to understand certain issues which they would have been able to understand if they had not had this training.[28] The training is essential to gain the skill and society wants these people to have the skills, so I am not objecting to the training. But the training does come at some costs by narrowing the perspectives of the individuals concerned.

I also often use the phrase to describe the limitations of the expert—or even of just the "well educated." The more expert—or at least the more educated—a person is, the less likely that person is to see a solution when it is not within the framework in which he or she was taught to think. When a possibility comes up that is ruled out by the accepted framework, an expert—or well-educated individual—is often less likely to see it than an amateur without the confining framework. For example, one naturally prefers to consult a trained doctor than an untrained person about matters of health. But if a new cure happens to be developed that is at variance with accepted concepts, the medical profession is often the last to accept it.* This problem has always existed in all professions, but it tends to be accentuated under modern conditions.

Large organizations have the tendency to proliferate new forms of expertise and specialists who are drawn largely from a very special social and cultural milieu. Bureaucracies in our technological society depend heavily upon members of the New Class—or at least recruits from graduates of universities that emphasize liberal and progressive, ideologies and viewpoints, almost to the exclusion of hard or tough perspectives. Even the practice of business seems to be in danger of becoming a professional specialty. I would guess that the more prestigious the business school and the more academically difficult the training, the more likely that the graduate will be both ideologically oriented and a narrow technician, rather than a decision maker in contact with the pressures and insights of the real world.

Educated incapacity in the United States today seems to derive from the general educational and intellectual milieu rather than from a specific education. This milieu is found in clearest form at leading universities in the United States—particularly in the departments of psychology, sociology, and history, and to a degree in the humanities generally. Individuals raised in this milieu often have difficulty with

---

*Examples are the introduction of antiseptic procedures for childbirth, vaccination against smallpox, and the use of penicillin.

relatively simple degrees of reality testing—e.g., about the attitudes of the lower middle classes, national security issues, national prestige, welfare, and race. This is not to say that other groups might not be equally biased and illusioned—only that their illusions are generally reflected in more traditional ways.

Educated incapacity is becoming a worldwide problem; in many ways, the post-industrial culture is likely both to cause and to further this "malady," though all cultures have relatively general and deeply held educated incapacities. (In addition, we are all more or less the prisoners of our individual perspectives.)

For example, we have often found in examining projects for less developed countries that the perspective imposed by North American viewpoints or North American perspectives can be very misleading. We therefore developed a concept for what might be called "appropriate technology," though at the time (early 1960s) we used the term "sideways in technology" or sometimes "sideways to technology." The idea was to use whatever technology was actually appropriate to the special conditions involved. In most cases we found appropriate options by approaching the situation from one or more of the following perspectives:

1. By increasing the size, scope, or intensity of some typical activity of the developed world
2. By decreasing the size, scope, or intensity of such activity
3. By seeking socially and politically acceptable devices
4. By changing some primary characteristics of the local area— e.g., through topographical engineering
5. By scanning leverage devices or projects to establish a list of modifiable options
6. By looking for high leverage projects in general
7. By scanning exploitable resources to establish new requirements and possibilities
8. Through new fixes
9. Through overlooked items
10. By exploiting any differences in perspective, requirements, or the performance of individuals and materials
11. By looking for high visibility projects
12. By finding, increasing, or modifying available talent and then modifying techniques or technologies to fit it[29]

On Making Necessary Distinctions

A person has to be reasonably bright to understand the difficulty in drawing a sharp line between day and night. There is a twilight zone, a zone of uncertainty which makes the reality of artificial division between day and night difficult to define precisely. The normal way a sophisticated person handles this kind of problem is to make additional distinctions. He or she defines a certain range of conditions as being twilight or grey. While the person now has a similar problem at the new boundaries, the dramatic character of the problem has been sharply alleviated; the boundary between day and twilight or night and twilight is less significant.[30]

This phenomenon began to be critical in the United States somewhat before the early 1960s. In the late 1950s, at one end of the political spectrum were members of the John Birch Society, who could not distinguish between advocates of relatively moderately progressive or internationalist-minded people and "card-carrying Communists." On the equally far-out left were people who could not distinguish between the Taft-Hartley Labor Relations Act and Soviet slave labor camps, or who felt that authoritarian practices in the United States were such that they overlapped appreciably with those in the Soviet Union. They sometimes based their belief on the correct observation that Soviet authoritarianism was not as total as some advocates held.

Many of these same people later believed that the role of the United States in world affairs was such that it had replaced that of Germany in the late 1930s and early 1940s. Thus, the United States intervention in Vietnam was often compared with the Nazis' genocidal policy toward the Jews—a wildly inappropriate analogy.

The Vietnamese war was not the only public issue that had a particularly low level of discussion in the 1960s. The "Middle America" issues described in Chapter 5 were of the greatest importance in the United States, yet all were largely misunderstood in literate and educated circles here and in most of the rest of the world. Between mid-1965 and mid-1969 these were among the most important problems bothering the so-called Middle American, the middle class or lower-middle class "square" American. These Americans knew what each of these issues meant to them; they understood what was bothering them and could express their concerns in practical terms. But almost without exception, liberal and progressive press columnists, writers in scholarly journals, academicians, TV commentators, and even politicians and government officials, misunderstood the nature of these grievances and the nature of the issues. I am not saying that if they had understood they would all necessarily have agreed with Middle Americans. But I think many would have, and I am certain that almost all would have been more sympathetic.

I believe that if one read the influential American newspapers, consulted the most distinguished academicians, or watched the better TV programs, one would have been completely misinformed as to the nature of these issues and their likely impact and effect. In fact, the ignorance of upper-middle class progressive Americans was almost as complete as that of the European and Japanese press.

Consider the so-called backlash. We were told during most of the 1960s—and are still sometimes told—that the ethnic minorities of the United States and other middle class individuals have a growing racism born out of resentment and anger against blacks. This resentment was allegedly stimulated by race riots, the law and order problem, excessive reverse discrimination, and by black pressure on white jobs and schools and neighborhoods. In fact, all these issues do bother ethnic minorities, but are not normally translated into sweeping anti-black or racist attitudes. Rather, a distinction is made between the "briefcase-carrying *white* liberal" who advocates certain policies, and those who are supposed to benefit from the policy. The backlash is against the white. Another very important distinction is made between relatively poor, uneducated blacks (now less than one-third of the black population) and relatively educated, middle class blacks (now more than two-thirds of the black population). The latter are quite acceptable neighbors.

One of the remarkable things that has happened in America is that in 1960 this was a very racist country, and by 1970 the country had become not very racist at all, though still very conscious of class distinctions. Indeed, it became almost non-racist, at least by comparison with 1960. We have looked at a great many polls which all tell much the same story. It does not seem to matter who took the poll, how the questions were asked, or who was asked. All point to the hypothesis of a very sharp decline in actual racism among middle Americans. There is no question that lower-middle class or ethnic white Americans tend to have more racist attitudes than upper-middle class and progressive people. But they are not manic in their racism.

Coping with Educated Incapacity

How, then, do we deal with the problem of educated incapacity? Most important is to find individuals with good judgment. This seems to be begging the question, because one next asks how to measure or even recognize good judgment. There are many ways, none of which is infallible. One method is simply to look at the record and see if the person has shown good judgment in the past. A better method is to see if an individual has clearly shown bad judgment, which is often easy to discern. One can often observe that someone is either over-emphasizing the wrong information and perspectives, or worrying about trivia, or simply not understanding a problem. It is desirable in analysis to allow many different perspectives to be used—often including views sometimes thought of as fanatic, crackpot, or basically unskilled or uneducated—all to help increase insight, but not necessarily to prepare conclusions and recommendations.

An ounce of an interesting or proper perspective is often worth many pounds of brains or analysis in gaining insight. In particular, a hostile insight is often a very good way to find defects in a proposal. One simply gives a proposal to people who will be very hostile to it, and asks for comments. Political liberals and anti-militarists are very good at detecting "plots" and incompetence in corporations and the military, while political conservatives are often good at spotting flaws in social service and welfare programs.

Similarly, the friendly insight is often a good way to discover the good parts of a proposal. This is exactly the perspective of adversary proceedings in American courts. One hires two partisan lawyers; the investigation conducted by each lawyer is likely to be more thorough than if the state hired a "neutral" investigator. This technique of adversary proceedings can often be used in a research organization. Hudson Institute's members hold a large range of positions from the extreme right to liberal, from pacifism to views that are close to advocating preventive war. We find being able to consult this range of positions very useful and practical. It can help enormously in uncovering seemingly obvious points and issues which most members of an ordinary team or study group might not notice.

FUTUROLOGY AND THE FUTURE OF ECONOMIC DEVELOPMENT

Some Uses of Scenarios and Images of the Future

Our basic thesis is that the medium- and long-range prospects for successful economic development for all nations from the desperately poor to the most affluent are much brighter than commonly perceived, and that probably the single most important way to improve the prospects further would be for this to become widely recognized. We realize that changing world opinion is extremely difficult, and we hardly expect that this book by itself will have much impact. We hope, that it will inspire studies and progress that cumulatively may have an impact. The suggestions we make below are for programs that we think of as possibilities for refocusing the discussion of economic development.

First, we recommend developing various long-range scenarios to replace the essentially negative, pessimistic view based on such dubious concepts as physical limits to growth, the widening income gap, the eroding quality of life, and the like. We think that individual countries or major world organizations looking at economic development regionally or worldwide could construct scenarios of what they can realistically expect to achieve in the next 25, 50, and 100 years. These scenarios could center around specific *targets* of improvements in living standards that can be easily measured. Such targets might include: better health leading to the elimination of protein deficiency and to the increase of life expectancy; the elimination of illiteracy; education at all levels; improving housing conditions; increasing the number of households with electricity or telephones; making modern goods and services available; and so forth. Other purposes could include: providing a sense of inspiration and vision; encouraging greater efforts; giving a useful perspective for setting realistic goals; and explaining to the population, especially indigenous intellectuals and elites, that modernization can be achieved by virtually any nation but only over many years with sacrifices and hard work.

Many people find writing, reading, revising, or suggesting scenarios stimulating and enjoyable. It is generally easy, if it is considered advisable, to involve many people in some stages of the process. In most countries, many people at almost every level would voluntarily participate in producing scenarios with modest official support or encouragement. Most of those who feel uncomfortable with the exploration of images of the future need not participate, nor is there any need for a serious organizational commitment to the results unless there is a decision to promulgate some of them systematically.

One useful possibility for developing scenarios is from the vantage point of a mythical historian in the year 2000 or 2025, looking back over the events of the preceding 25 or 50 years. This is not only a dramatic device, but it also places many discussions into a perspective that can be much more objective and creative than one that focuses on current issues from today's perspective, with all the anxieties, hopes and politics normally involved in such a discussion.[31] The mythical historian of 2025 could round out his story by attempting a scenario projecting the next 50 or 100 years. If a country wished to exploit such scenarios and related images of the future, it could begin with an official or unofficial conference discussing and elaborating them. Such a conference could be casual and off-the-record, or it could be a full-blown production shown live on TV.

At this conference, many medium-run and long-run possibilities for development could be described and elaborated dramatically and informatively. If desired, a much broader public than those present could be reached through the media and subsequent publications or presentations. One result might be a variety of useful materials such as books, pamphlets, films for schools and educational television (and perhaps for wider distribution), illustrated wall charts, and video tapes of part of the proceedings. Some of the materials might be created during the meeting and some through a follow-up. Other information programs and various independent and semi-independent products might be stimulated by the conference or its ancillary activities.

Second, the proposals are intended to de-politicize discussions and to separate political issues from development issues by focusing on the importance of increasing GNP and GNP per capita rather than on worldwide north-south issues or internal income distribution. The double standard used for comparing non-communist and communist nations; the various forums that have given worldwide prominence to outspoken critics of the developed world from the developed nations (such as The Non-Aligned nations and the Group of 77); and the terminology used (north-south problems, widening gap, neo-colonialism) all politicize and distort the real issues. Individual nations would counter these by developing their own growth scenarios or ideologies and advertising their long-range visions.

These could be used to make the point at international meetings that while left or right wing demagogues are still blaming their nations' problems on everything but their own incompetence, other countries are successfully accomplishing the Great Transition. In contrast to those who dwell on problems inherited from former colonial rule, some leaders could say, for example, "I don't know about you but we are going to make it. In ten years 70 or 80 percent of our people will be literate or will have electricity in their houses, and in twenty or thirty years our people will enjoy a standard of living comparable to France or England after they had recovered from World War II."

Another way to make this point would be to create new organizations that would refocus world attention. We discussed in Chapter 5 the possibility of a Pacific Free Trade and Investment Area that would include developed and developing countries and emphasize the mutual benefits of continued growth in this the world's most rapidly growing region. It might also be possible to create an organization of New Industrial States (NIS) made up of the NICs and other rapidly growing Middle Income countries that are on the verge of becoming fully industrialized. Such an organization might become an openly pro-growth lobby comprising the world's most dynamic countries.

It might also be tied in with the OECD. The OECD could set target dates for anticipated entry of new countries. Becoming a member of the OECD or NIS club could be seen as a symbol that successful development had been achieved and could draw attention to the fact that economic development is no longer an exclusive club of former Western great powers and early starters. Hopefully, this might change the over-simplified rich-versus-poor view of the world to a more constructive image of a complicated and mutually beneficial interdependent world economy. It would emphasize that development is a step-by-step process. As Poor countries take off and enter the transitional stage, transitional countries are entering the fully industrialized stage.

Third, our suggestions are intended to give greater attention to the more successful developing countries by drawing attention to their accomplishments. One way of doing this would be to have an international school for economic development in some NIC countries that would give visiting students a sense of what can be done as well as practical insights into how to do it.

A Bourgeois (Industrial) Growth-Oriented Ideology Based on Futurology

The development of the classic industrialized Western world has frequently been linked to the ideology called the Protestant Ethic, encompassing a belief in the virtue of hard work and a willingness to defer the material rewards of that work. As the West has grown progressively richer, this ethic has weakened considerably, first among the intellectual elite and more recently throughout the population. The phenomenon heralded a decade ago as the end of ideology is now seen more appropriately as a loss of faith in the old ideology.

The late 1960s brought with them a need for a new or renewed faith. This need has been met for many Americans by a movement toward traditional doctrinaire, dogmatic evangelical sects and away from the increasingly transcendental mainstream Protestant religion. Other parts of the population found some fulfillment in such disparate phenomena as the new youth culture, a return to religious enthusiasm, various Eastern and mystical or magical sects, the proliferation of groups militantly pursuing self-expression in ethnic, spiritual, or psychological terms, and often in the Fourteen New Emphases generally.

We have argued that humanity will soon be entering a new state of development—the post-industrial society. We believe that the transition to this stage is likely to cause serious stresses and that it is very important to have some kind of overall concept to help organize thinking, program action, furnish a supportive moral and political philosophy, and provide a framework for the creation and analysis of programs. Such a concept would also provide, where justified, high morale to better cope with what might be called the current failure of nerve among upper-middle class elites in much of the free world and the increasing movement toward the Fourteen New Emphases.

We believe all this can be done by taking a reasonable perspective on how we got where we are today, and where we may likely be in the year 2000, particularly if sensible programs are adopted. We are suggesting that a new kind of ideology is needed that we tentatively label a *Year 2000 Ideology*. As ideologies go, this one is relatively weak, but it can meet all our needs. Table 8.1 below explains the functions and characteristics of an ideology. Table 8.2 points out some of the reasons why an ideology of development based on futurology could help with rational planning for a peaceful and affluent world in the future—in particular by setting achievable goals and avoiding unnecessary conflict.

Many persons suggest that we need much more intense or serious ideology that can bring such benefits as:

1. Disciplined and dedicated cadres
2. Legitimacy and appeal
3. Mass movement (or mass acquiescence)
4. Recruiting
5. External allies and sympathizers
6. "Wave of the future" charisma

We argue that this is not needed. For one thing, intense ideologies also frequently bring many disadvantages, including:

1. Foreign axes to grind
2. Extremist programs
3. Excessive use of terror
4. Crackpot theories

TABLE 8.1
What Is an Ideology?

---

1. It emphasizes certain values and attitudes
2. It contains a theory of the past, present, and future (all theories generally have emotionally held normative elements)
3. It provides a rationale, spur, and guide to action
4. And a theory of success and justice (i.e., high morale)
5. In sum, it provides a context and content for overall policies, for applications, for coordination of criteria and expectations, and for meaning and purpose in life
6. In effect, the ideology should promise some combination of God, gold, and glory (or, if you will, honor, glory, and riches)

---

5. Crackpot administration
6. Excessive attention to foreign intervention and proselytizing
7. Excessive wastage of tangible and intangible assets and resources

Intense ideologies are also much more difficult to manufacture and to control. We argue that once it is accepted and believed, the area under discussion and the world in its various parts can be placed on a more or less reasonable course. The crucial issues then become to avoid derailment and catastrophe and to improve current programs. This entails a sound, moderate, businesslike approach to development programs and reasonably high morale, assurance, and commitment.

We believe this perspective can be made persuasive. It may then be possible to take a very different attitude towards a number of currently perceived problems from those of many neo-Malthusians and catastrophists—provisional or otherwise.[32] It then becomes possible to envisage and set in motion an era of great human improvement in material standards of living and hopefully in other ways as well.

The Year 2000 Ideology provides a justification for such an approach. It offers a conception of how successful this approach might be and where we might be able to go. No doubt the projections will turn out to be inaccurate in important details, and perhaps even in certain basics, but it is still likely that its fundamental direction and programs will be useful and will promote humane adjustment to

TABLE 8.2
"Futurology" Perspective (Ideology)

Does:
1. Put population growth, GNP growth, impact of R&D cultural changes, and other long term and compound interest issues in perspective
2. Enable realistic criteria to be set

Should:
3. Energize elite groups—in part to set example
4. Persuade late beneficiaries to "wait"
5. Relieve "ancient regime morale" stigma from current programs and institutions
6. Enlist alienated and frustrated groups
7. Energize whole society

---

material change and growth.

This is very different from the attitude typified by the following from Robert Heilbroner:

> Development will fall into the hands of dedicated revolutionary groups. Mild men will not ride the tigers of development, neither will mild political or economic systems contain or impel it.[33]

The Heilbroner view argues that rapid development can only be brought about by violent revolutions and by elites willing to incarcerate, or kill if necessary, a relatively high percent of the population to achieve their goals. We believe that many of the strains that tend towards crisis or violence can be alleviated without great cost to material and spiritual progress and that a milieu can be created that supports and enhances movements and institutions of human justice and progress. For this reason it is most important to give many groups, nations, and people a stake in a future that is to be achieved by peaceful means and not by a violence and disruption. It may well be necessary—or at least desirable—in many situations to turn to authoritarian methods, perhaps even for a time to some violence and repression, but none of this need be as severe as Heilbroner indicates, and in many cases it need only be temporary.

We think of the Year 2000 Ideology as more or less a Western capitalist ideology that is made trans-ideological by our approach. However, it can easily be fitted into almost any culture. Table 8.3 compares our suggestion with some alternatives.

TABLE 8.3
Futurology Compared with Alternative Ideologies

"Futurology" Ideology	Marxist and Related Ideologies	Gap Ideology	New International Order
Can appear super-modern	Less modern than it used to be	Modern	Super-modern
Secular (non-religious)	Secular (anti-religious)	"Humanistic" and paternalistic	Justice and revenge
Economic and Technological	Scientific and technological	Egalitarian	Egalitarian
Western, capitalist	Anti-Western, anti-capitalist	Anti-rich	Anti-rich
Compound interest	Revolution and class struggle	Charity, aid, subsidy, illusion	Recompense and status
Uses leverage, individuality, tradition, hierarchy	Uses "true believers" and tight organizations		Uses currently fashionable sentiments and rhetoric

The socialist countries can participate in much the same way without significant conflict with the capitalist societies so long as they give up the concept of mass warfare and armed conflict with the West, at least by not letting these concepts dominate day-to-day programs.

Giving people a sense of their stake in the future emphasizes the importance of developing a valid vision of the future. It is critical because peoples' visions of the future, although often unarticulated, dominate their responses to current issues. Giving people a new vision of the future depends on two things. First, there must be an intellectual understanding of the issues that is technically sound, psychologically relevant, and dramatically imaginative. Second, there must be organized efforts to get people to accept or use the new vision of the future communicated to scholars, opinion leaders, and directly to the public.

A SUMMING UP

If this book has made a persuasive case for the *feasibility* of world economic development, we believe this also constitutes an argument for the desirability and morality of such development. To introduce the words *desirability* and *morality* is, of course, to make the argument for economic development turn explicitly on questions of values. I believe that the arguments in favor of continued world economic development—given all the likely human, ecological, environmental, and material costs and risks—are close to if not fully overwhelming.

Arguments in the already developed countries that continued growth is harmful to the world are largely accepted only by relatively small esoteric and elite groups or reflect the narrow self-interests of the already rich countries, or of the already rich sectors of the developed countries. If economic development were not feasible, it would be immoral as well as undesirable to argue in favor of it. Many critics of further economic development truly believe it to be unfeasible, but their moral and intellectual positions are weakened because their beliefs rest on loose reasoning and analysis.

Indeed, they are so shallow that they suggest what have been called "elective affinities," the concept that it is easy for people to accept assumptions, characterizations, or analyses that happened to entail conclusions that did not interfere with their self-interests or values—and even easier if the acceptance tended to further these self-interests and values. We argue that much of the current strength of the various limits-to-growth movements and of the self-perceived moral superiority of the various voluntary simplicity movements is grounded in elective affinities and not in objective facts or analyses. That is one reason for the high correlation of all of these concepts with upper-middle class membership in the Affluent Capitalist nations generally, and with membership in the neo-liberal New Class in particular. We argue that rapid worldwide economic development is feasible and desirable; we believe that a position of indifference or hostility to such economic development is callous and immoral by any standard of Judeo-Christian ethics.

We distinguish between benign indifference and benign neglect. One may be deeply concerned about the economic development of the Poor countries and still support a policy in some cases of benign neglect because one fully recognizes that they really have to do it themselves. Outside interference can sometimes be counterproductive. We do not favor benign neglect for all the Poor countries; in fact, we are very much in favor of certain aid programs. But we would like these aid programs to limit their objectives, to be careful not to do more harm than good, and especially to avoid forcing social and political concepts on the Poor countries that they can neither afford nor really want. The object of the aid is to help the countries concerned, not to satisfy various needs of the rich.

In this age of malaise, when there is more instability than usual and trends can literally go in one direction or another on a roughly fifty-fifty basis, the argument for continued world economic development must be moral. The choice in favor of continued development should be made not only by those countries who are seeking to get to the top but also by those countries who are already there. I believe continued world economic development is so important that it is a moral imperative as well as a practical *desideratum*. It is certainly more moral than current attempts to stop world economic growth at roughly the point it has now reached—or even to make it retrogress. This is true even if one dresses up such retrogression as part of a voluntary simplicity movement or an attempt to protect the environment. I have nothing against people making choices for themselves or against reasonable protection of the environment for use or admiration by society—but I do object to protection of the environment at the expense of humanity.

Continued world economic development may be so feasible that it could proceed even with the opposition of people in the United States and other Advanced Capitalist nations. No doubt it would take longer and involve greater costs, but the process is so well underway, particularly in the Asia-Pacific region, and in the NICs generally, that it is more likely than not that countries who wish to proceed with economic development would find a way to do so with or without the support of the Affluent Capitalist countries. This raises the fundamental question that opposition to such development may be what is unfeasible, not the development itself.

Americans and others in the Affluent Capitalist nations may be unusually depressed in the wake of the United States failure in Vietnam, but this is their problem, not the problem of the majority of the world who continues to wish for and seek economic development.

To attempt to stop economic development and to contend that the world is already rich enough when this is patently not true is to assert what has always been described in Western history as an immorally conservative position. It is one of the ironies of our time that Americans who normally identify themselves as favoring the advancement of Third World countries are also identified with policies at home and abroad that would put a stop to the very progress they so strongly say they favor. To oppose economic development today is literally to stand in the way of progress, and to do so in a manner that is contradictory to Western Judeo-Christian traditions.

Those nations that successfully participate in the process of world economic development will impose their own standards of equity and morality on political and social affairs. The opposition of the West or the Affluent Capitalist countries to this process would hardly endear them to the newly developing countries. The political and social attitudes and norms that these countries will eventually come to impose on the rest of the world will have an anti-Western tinge. If people in the Affluent Capitalist countries wish to continue to affect political and social values in the world, they have no choice but to participate more positively than they have in the last few years in the process of world economic development.

There is also the possibility that the opposition to growth will gain even further ascendancy during L'époque de Malaise that we foresee the world currently entering. But as our discussion of long cycles seeks to show, nothing is permanent. This era of malaise is also not permanent, and will be replaced at some point by an upward slope of a new long cycle. Doubtless, the new cycle will be directed by countries committed to economic development. Possibly, because of the opposition to development of the contemporary advanced countries, their views will not be given much weight, to put it mildly. Alternatively, for the Affluent Capitalist countries to participate in, not to say make more feasible, world economic development is at the same time to make much more likely a synthesis of attitudes toward political and social affairs among all countries. This would not only be consistent with Western traditions, but would also be much more likely to produce a unified and peaceful world than would the alternative.

Notes

1. In Italy, the northern and southern cultures are really quite different. Northern Italy was part of the Charlemagne's Empire and was originally Roman in culture; southern Italy was basically a Greek cultural area and for many centuries was occupied by the Mohammedans. The combined cultural and economic disparities pose an extraordinarily intractable problem. In fact, Italian society has done many extraordinary things to alleviate the problem, from making a high proportion of jobs in the national government available to southern Italians to massive development projects focused on the south. However, the problem persists and in recent years has probably gotten worse rather than better.

2. In most cultures one model of almost total unhappiness is to have a successful brother-in-law whom one does not like—and to be unsuccessful oneself.

3. Unfortunately, concessionary food programs administered under U.S. PL 480 often greatly facilitated this process. PL 480 provides many examples of counterproductive administration and programs. However, on balance, it probably did more good than harm.

4. W. Arthur Lewis, *The Theory of Economic Growth* (Homewood, Illinois: Richard Irwin, 1955), p. 421.

5. Some readers may believe that the Vietnam War was an example of Western imperialism. Few, however, really believe that the United States coveted South Vietnamese territory in an imperialist sense. If there was aggression, it was more psychological or political than directed to material or territorial gain.

6. An excellent illustration of the usefulness of GNP/CAP as an index may be found if the reader turns back to our categories of nations presented in Chapter 2. These nations were more or less ordered on GNP/CAP. If the reader considers the nations in the groups we labeled Very Poor, Coping Poor, Middle Income, and Affluent Market-Oriented it should become clear that except for some of the OPEC nations, the groups are ordered on both affluence and technological capability; that Communist Asia belongs roughly between Coping Poor and Middle Income; and that Affluent Communist belongs roughly between Middle Income and Affluent Market-Oriented.

7. This may seem very harsh from the social point of view, but in countries such as the United States the average dismissed worker finds work within three months, even during a recession, and generally manages to live off unemployment compensation and savings in the interim. While the company can reduce expenses, it cannot cut back nearly as much as a worker, and it normally has no equivalent of unemployment insurance. If a firm has

to maintain workers on more or less a full salary for a long period of time, it can easily go bankrupt or weaken itself so severely that it can no longer function effectively. Excessive legally enforced labor stability is one cause of the European Malaise discussed in Chapter 5.

Excessive programs for job security are also often good examples of what we have called "ins versus outs." The "ins" are those already working. The "outs" are those who are not working. The "outs" find it much more difficult to get jobs because employers are afraid to hire them unless they can let them go when business is bad or they don't turn out to meet expectations. We would also argue that even if there are strong arguments to enhance security and stability to the extent that these measures make it difficult or expensive to discharge employees, they favor the "outs" over the "ins," less in terms of direct competition than because such measures discourage employers from risking hiring new employees.

8. Prime Minister Lee Kuan Yew of Singapore has noted that, "Those countries in Asia that have allowed free enterprise have done comparatively better than those that have tried nationalization and socialist state-corporations. And this is so even where free enterprise has been shackled by legislative and administrative regulations which require the entrepreneur to give a portion of the equity and part of the management to indigenous shareholders and managers." (Orlando: Speech to ICC Convention, 1978.)

9. We do not totally reject socialist, centralist, or mixed planning. Even in capitalist nations, we believe that more attention should be given to generating relatively detailed "images of the future" such as those we outlined in Chapter 2. These can be used by various private groups—and to some degree by governmental bureaus and departments. We are also in favor of indicative planning if it is done properly. However, indicative planning is easily abused, sometimes becoming a vehicle for special groups (e.g., the New Class and input-output theorists), or being taken too seriously or done so badly that it is often better to forego its considerable potential to avoid likely disutilities.

10. The need to rely on "muddling through" and rising to the occasion exists even in highly planned technical projects with crucial deadlines. Thus, for example, one RAND study showed that in the early postwar years almost no fighters flew successfully with the engines they were designed around. In almost all cases, the fighters used subsequently improved engines. Forced and hasty marriages had to be arranged between the fighters and the engines. These studies also found that when people tried to avoid the extreme costs, annoyance, and aggravation of this last minute muddling through and hasty marriage by systematic and detailed planning, they lost enormously in flexibility and the ability to use late developments and significant but unexpected improvements. Even more important, the effects of any failure to meet deadlines were multiplied. The best strategy seemed to be to have a very large menu of research and development projects carried through without worrying too much how they might be used, just seeing to it that they were in the right general area. On the other hand the people trying to build practical equipment did limited R&D for that particular project and on the whole

depended on the rich menu of offerings from the broad general program. It was extraordinary how often last-minute developments were used and completely new equipment appeared that could be modified or adapted. This experience in the military planning area as much as any ideological preference convinced me of the great virtue of having overall conceptions with relatively little detail except that needed for serious planned muddling through.

11. See *The New Economics of Growth* by John Mellor (Ithaca, N.Y.: Cornell University Press, 1976).

12. Gunnar Myrdal, *Asian Drama* (New York: Pantheon & Twentieth Century Fund, 1971), p. 31.

13. P. T. Bauer, *Dissent on Development* (Cambridge, Mass.: Harvard University Press, 1972).

14. In many cases, of course, it may be better for a developing nation not to have *any* overall comprehensive plan. Unfortunately, most international aid programs insist on a comprehensive plan before they will assist a country. For many years it was said in Brazil that "the country grows while the government sleeps"—in other words, much progress is made simply relying on the free market mechanism.

15. See David Chamberlin Cole and Princeton N. Lyman, *Korean Development* (Cambridge, Mass.: Harvard University Press, 1971), pp. 203-221, and Neil H. Jacoby, *U.S. Aid to Taiwan* (New York: Praeger, 1966).

16. Interview with Mr. Osamu Shimomura, "Consistency of Economy Should be Core of Thinking," *Business Japan*, August 1975, p. 47.

17. However, France has also been doing similar planning for a number of years. For the Japanese plan, see *Nihon Retto Kizoron*, published in English under the title, *Building a New Japan, a Program for Remodeling the Japanese Archipelago*, by Kakuei Tanaka. Both editions were published in 1973 by Simul Press, Tokyo.

18. In the same sense, the prospect of 90 percent federal funding has been a strong argument for those who favor the Westway highway project on Manhattan's West Side, since it is doubtful that equivalent federal funds would be made available for any competing project. Similarly, very few current irrigation projects in the United States would be approved if the beneficiaries really had to pay the opportunity costs or even the budgeted costs.

19. Herman Kahn, *On Thermonuclear War* (Princeton: Princeton University Press, 1961).

20. Christopher Henry Dawson, *The Making of Europe* (New York: Meridan, 1956).

21. Declared by Mrs. Gandhi on June 26, 1975. For a discussion of the Indian emergency, see Lloyd Rudolph and Susanne Rudolph, "To the Brink and Back: Representation and the State in India," *Asian Survey* 18 (1978):380.

22. The situation need not be so dramatic to be important. We have a phrase around the Institute that goes, "but it involves the Erickson contract." This phrase is supposed to galvanize the recipient into instant and

enthusiastic cooperation. The phrase comes from a story told to us by an Australian. It seems that the Swedish Erickson Company was competing for a very important contract with the Australian telephone system. This Australian happened to visit Stockholm while the competition was going on and was startled to find that almost every Swede he met knew about the competition and was enthusiastically plugging for the Erickson Company. He told the following possibly apocryphal story. At one point when the Erickson Company was preparing some material for the competition a couple of the staff members were working late in a hotel. Around 1:00 A.M. they went down to the desk and said that it was important for them to have some material photocopied. The desk clerk said it was absolutely impossible. The people who ran the copy machine were not present, and he was not authorized to use it or to let them use it. They said but it is for the Erickson contract. He said, "For the Erickson contract! Well that's different!" and immediately offered to do all the photocopying needed.

Sweden is not known today as a society that cares that much. In fact it tends to feel overly big and overly confident as opposed to the way it felt about fifteen years ago when it had the attitude, "We're not big enough to 'fool around.' " But it seems clear that a good deal of the old spirit is still left.

We should also point out that when we told the story to many people in Australia they felt that it was impossible for that kind of attitude to occur in Australia. This was one reason why the Australians would find it difficult to have a competitive export manufacturing industry. For a small country to be competitive in the export market it has to be very quick on its feet and have the kind of general backing and commitment illustrated by the Erickson story.

23. It has been pointed out, for example, that the Persians had really forgotten their history and only revived it as a result of the researches and scholarship of Western historians and writers. The Shah of Iran emphasized Persia's 5,000-year history, but unfortunately overdid it. He aroused great opposition among the traditional by changing the calendar from the Muslim calendar to one based upon the old Persian calendar. The result was an unnecessary annoyance in the day-to-day life of the Muslims because it was necessary to use the calendar the Shah revived. It is not generally realized in the West how much the internal opposition to the Shah was based on the opposition of the mullahs and stemmed from traditional Muslim attitudes.

24. For example, local authorities were under great pressure to meet their quota for "voluntary vasectomy." As a result local government authorities literally sent trucks into villages to round up any available men. Sometimes these were put under verbal pressure to undergo vasectomies; sometimes they were simply forced. There are reasonably well-documented stories that some villagers had vasectomies performed two or three times, and there were also a number of cases of men over seventy being forced to undergo the operation. It is quite likely that the central government did not know how badly its policies were being abused. Even weak and uncertain democracies can still supply outlets and channels for fury and retaliation when the government's behavior transcends reasonable boundaries as in this case.

25. In this respect, one can perhaps describe these people as "cultural

racists" since they would never accept such standards for themselves. These attitudes actually do not significantly differ from those of "radical chic" in the United States where upper class intellectuals have happily embraced revolutionary and quasi-religious movements for blacks as being appropriate "for them" and they would never have accepted such blatantly separatist, racist, and extremist sentiments as appropriate for themselves or their colleagues.

26. Probably about half the families in America own guns. It has been estimated that there are about 140 million firearms in private homes in the United States; this would be more than four firearms per family of gun-owners. (See B. Bruce-Briggs, "The Great American Gun War," *Public Interest*, Fall, 1976, pp. 37-62.)

27. The relevance of this section to the post-Watergate morality should be obvious.

28. Thorstein Veblen, *Instinct of Workmanship* (New York: Kelley, 1922), p. 347.

29. This list is mainly from Robert Panero, formerly of the Hudson Institute staff. Today, many of these items would be referred to under the rubric "appropriate technology," but because this term is so loaded with ideological nuances of the small-is-beautiful and the anti-advanced technology varieties we prefer to continue to use our original term: sidewise in technology. The latter term also has the advantage of making clear that we do not care whether the technology is "hard" or "soft," primitive or advanced, just so long as it is the best available solution to the problem at hand.

30. Indeed, if the person makes enough distinctions, defines enough shades or colors, the problem vanishes for practical purposes. I would add, more or less parenthetically, that a person has to be intelligent to recognize the necessity for several—or even many—shades and colors, thus correcting for the inadequacy of the simple dichotomies of black and white or day and night in all situations. Our discussion of the six degrees of belief in Chapter 1 exploited this principle.

31. For a detailed discussion of the use of futurology to deal with these and related issues, see Herman Kahn, "On Studying the Future," in *Handbook of Political Science, Volume 7: Strategies of Inquiry*, eds. Fred I. Greenstein and Nelson W. Polsby (Reading, Mass.: Addison-Wesley Publishing Company, 1975), pp. 405-442.

32. A catastrophist believes that current trends and events inevitably lead to some kind of catastrophe. Provisional catastrophies agree but add, ". . . as long as we continue current policies, but if we change policies [presumably according to their recommendation], this is not necessarily so."

33. Robert L. Heilbroner, *The Great Ascent* (New York: Harper & Row, 1963), pp. 134-5.

Appendix:
Quantitative Scenario
Contexts—Exponential
versus S-Shaped Curves

We find it very useful to generate quantitative scenarios but seldom intend the reader to take the actual numbers very seriously. There is no way for anyone to be accurate about what will happen in the distant future. Rather, as we have already suggested, a scenario often has a role analogous to that of a diagram in mathematics. The diagram may be precise, but that precision is incidental to its main purpose—visualization of an idea. We would like in this appendix to make—or reinforce—the five points below:

1. Even conceptually, it is usually a mistake to think of growth in terms of straight lines or exponentials. One should normally think instead in terms of S-shaped curves as the typical case. The key issue is when and why the S-shaped curve turns over.
2. In many phenomena, including economic and population growth, the turnover from increasing to decreasing slope of the S-curve usually occurs because of internal dynamics, not because of external pressures. The burden of proof should be placed on those who think that external pressures are decisive.
3. By using the simple curve-generating formulas below, S-shaped curves can be used flexibly to fit sufficiently accurately (and often quite accurately), either current data or the results of complex models as well as to show the long-term influence of different plausible asymptotes. (We show some examples below, though not as adequately and completely as we do in more detailed studies.)
4. Many of these quantitative scenarios may have some predictive value, but only in a surprise-free sense; in most cases it is difficult, if not impossible, to assess their predictive value.
5. These scenarios are important in informing the analysts' judgment, in creating *a fortiori* arguments, in demolishing

certain hypotheses, and in creating useful and interesting images of the future. In general, they are a versatile educational and analytical tool.

Most often, the name *logistic* is given to S-shaped curves having the descriptive properties in 1 above. Table A.1 and Figure A.1 show a range of possibilities. (Equations (1) and (2) do not product S-shaped curves but are included for comparison.) Each of these equations can be generalized by introducing parameters to fit the particular case of interest and the appropriate initial and limiting or asymptotic conditions. The constants incorporated in the equations as given in Table A.1 are chosen simply to start each curve with an initial value of 0.5 at t=0 and an initial slope or rate of increase of 0.5. Only equation (1) has a constant rate of growth. Equation (2) has a growth rate proportional to the instantaneous value of y_o. This defines the distinctive characteristic of exponential growth: the quantity grows at a rate proportional to the amount already present. Equations (3) through (7) produce various S-shaped curves that level off asymptotically.

For the growth curves in our present study we use generalized forms of equations (4) and (6) with appropriate parameters. For growth curves in which the relative (or percent) growth rate *declines steadily* in the future, we write equation (4) in the form:

$$y = \frac{N}{\{1 + \exp[-\alpha(t-t_0)]\}^\beta}$$

where y is the value of either population, GP or PCG at the time (year)t, N is the asymptotic value of y, t_0 is a convenient time (1978 in

TABLE A.1
Examples of Seven Growth Equations

(1) Arithmetical (A):	$y_1 = .5 + .5t$
(2) Exponential (E):	$y_2 = .5 \, \text{Exp}\,(t)$
(3) Simple logistic (S.L.):	$y_3 = 1/[1 + \text{Exp}\,(-2t)]$
(4) Generalized logistic (G.L.):	$y_4 = 2/[1 + \text{Exp}\,(-t)]^2$
(5) Simple transitional (S.T.):	$y_5 = (1/2e)\,\text{Exp}\{2/[1 + \text{Exp}\,(-2t)]\}$
(6) Generalized transitional (G.T.):	$y_6 = (1/2e)\,\text{Exp}\{4/[1 + \text{Exp}\,(-t)]^2\}$
(7) Gompertz (G):	$y_7 = [-\ln 2\,\text{Exp}\,(-t/\ln 2)]$

FIGURE A.1
Examples of Seven Growth Curves

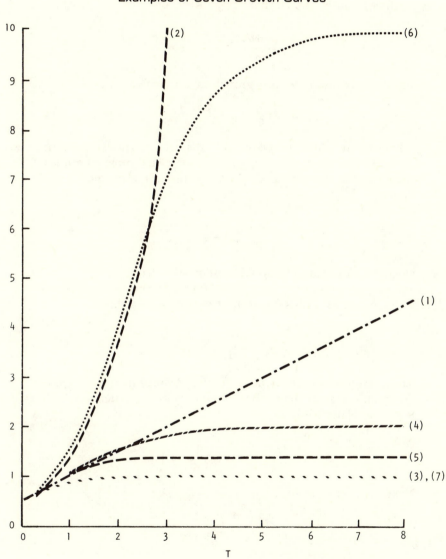

our present scenarios), and α and β are constants which depend on the initial and asymptotic values of y. If y_0 and r_0 are the values of y and r (the *relative* or proportional growth rate) respectively, when $t = t_0$, then it can be shown that:

$$\beta = \frac{Ln(N/y_0)}{Ln2} \text{ , and } \alpha = \frac{2r_0}{\beta} \text{ ,}$$

and the maximum *absolute* growth rate occurs at

$$t_m = t_0 + \frac{Ln\beta}{\alpha} \text{ .}$$

For cases in which the relative growth rate, r, *increases* at some time in the future, we are obliged to use a somewhat more complicated equation. For these cases we write equation (6) in the more general form:

$$y = N_{-\infty} \exp\left(\frac{\gamma}{\{1 + \exp[-\alpha(t-t_0)]\}^{\beta}}\right) \text{ ,}$$

where $N_{-\infty}$ and γ are additional constants which depend on the initial and asymptotic values of y, r_{∞} , and on r_m (the maximum value of r in the future). For this equation it may be shown that:

$$\frac{r_m}{r_0} = \frac{2^{\beta+1}}{\beta(1+\frac{1}{\beta})^{\beta+1}} \text{ .}$$

This permits us to determine β (for ease, by reading it from a plot of the equation rather than solving explicitly for β). Then we obtain γ from the relationship.

$$\frac{y_0}{N_{\infty}} = \exp\left[\gamma(\frac{1}{2^{\beta}} - 1)\right] \text{ .}$$

Next, we find α from:

$$r_0 = \frac{\alpha\beta\gamma}{2^{\beta+1}} \text{ .}$$

And finally we find $N_{-\infty}$ from:

$$N_{\infty} = N_{-\infty}e^{\gamma}$$

(It may be noted that $N_{-\infty}$ is the minus infinity asymptote of the S-shaped curve.) For this equation the maximum *relative* growth rate, r_m, occurs at time:

$$t_m = t_0 + \frac{Ln\beta}{\alpha} .$$

Just to indicate how well these kinds of formulas can reproduce data and to give the reader a sense of how arbitrary we can be in our decisions about some details, let us see if we can reproduce with the formula a United States Census Bureau projection of the United States population from 1975 to 2020 using a simple logistic equation (type 3).

Let us assume that the asymptotic value of the population is 400 million and see if we can not use a simple formula:

$$y = \frac{400}{[1 + e^{-\alpha(t-t_0)}]} .$$

When $t = t_0$, y will equal 200, about the value of United States population in 1968, when it also had a growth rate of 1 percent. (Actually, we use $t = 1969$ rather than 1968 merely because it gives us a better fit to the census projection between 1975 and 2000—the period we are most interested in fitting.) We now use the following simple equation for United States population at any time t:

$$y = \frac{400}{[1 + e^{-.02(t-1969)}]}$$

Table A.2 gives the results using this formula (Col. 3) and the differences with the census projections (Col. 4). Note that the census projection assumes a leveling off of United States population early in the twenty-first century, while our projection continues to rise. We prefer our projection because we believe that the census model's leveling off will not occur, even if the birthrate stays under 2.1 children per woman. There will likely be more net immigration to the United States than the Census Bureau takes account of, and this should lead to a continued but slow increase in population of, say, .5 percent or so.

A further interesting comparison may be made using equations of the form of (4), the generalized logistic model. For example:

$$n_1 = \frac{8}{\{1 + \mathrm{Exp}[-\alpha_1 (t-1975)]\}}$$

$$n_2 = \frac{16}{\{1 + \mathrm{Exp}[-\alpha_2 (t-1975)]\}^2}$$

$$n_3 = \frac{32}{\{1 + \mathrm{Exp}[-\alpha_3 (t-1975)]\}^3}$$

Each of the above logistic equations starts out with the world population $N = 4$ billion at $t = 1975$ and they approach 8, 16, and 32

TABLE A.2
Comparison of U.S. Census Bureau Projection of U.S.
Population with Logistic Equation (A)

Year	U.S. Census Population (in millions)	Logistic Eqn. (A)	Difference Col. (3) - Col. (2) (in millions)
1968	200	198	- 2
1975	213	212	- 1
1980	220	223	+ 2
1990	242	241	- 1
2000	259	260	+ 1
2010	274	278	+ 4
2020	289	294	+ 5
2050	315	334	+19

TABLE A.3
U.N. Population Projections in Billions

Year	Low	CASE Medium	High
1975	4.000	4.000	4.000
1980	4.372	4.409	4.435
1985	4.757	4.855	4.930
1990	5.154	5.323	5.471
1995	5.543	5.809	6.053
2000	5.915	1.305	6.670

TABLE A.4
Comparison with the Low U.N. Population Projection

Year	U.N.	$\alpha_1 =$ .04171	DIFF (%)	$\alpha_2 =$ .01756	DIFF (%)	$\alpha_3 =$ .01122	DIFF (%)
1975	4.000	4.0000	0.0	4.0000	0.0	4.0000	0.0
1980	4.372	4.4156	1.0	4.3587	1.3	4.3460	1.6
1985	4.757	4.8223	1.4	4.7313	0.2	4.7109	2.3
1990	5.154	5.2120	1.1	5.1161	1.9	5.0944	2.3
1995	5.543	5.5779	0.6	5.5114	1.2	5.4962	0.6
2000	5.915	5.9150	0.0	5.9150	0.0	5.9159	0.0

billion respectively as t goes to infinity. But depending upon how we choose α_1, α_2, and α_3, we can get very different population histories between these two "points." We would like for this purpose to fit one of three United Nations cases (Table A.3).

If we choose $\alpha_1 = .04171$, $\alpha_2 = .01756$, and $\alpha_3 = .01122$, Table A.4 shows the resulting comparison with the low United Nations cases. (In each case we chose α_i so as to make n_i (2000) = 5.915. We may do the same for the medium and the high cases. (For the medium case, $\alpha_1 = .05255$, $\alpha_2 = .0209$, $\alpha_3 = .01322$); for the high case, $\alpha_1 = .0645$, $\alpha_2 = 1.024$, $\alpha_3 = .01504$.)

We are trying to indicate by the above mathematical experiment that it is often possible to reproduce the output of very complex models in very simple formulas. Furthermore, these formulas allow a great deal of freedom in their long-term projections. Thus in low, medium, or high cases, we can have sets of projections which have asymptotes of 8 billion, 16 billion, 32 billion people or anything between these numbers. This illustrates another point: one can fit short-term projections without prejudicing the ability to have a very smooth curve, yet have extremely large degrees of variation in asymptotic values. One can either choose the asymptotic values by the information that comes out of these relatively short-term models, or one can introduce other assumptions for a much larger range of choice. We have chosen in our current study to use 10 billion because this is reasonably close or equal to a relatively large number of current models including the United Nations model. And it is a nice round number, so that it does not give any impression of spurious accuracy—an impression that does exist unless one sticks to round numbers as much as possible.

Index

Acceptance as degree of belief, 44, 46, 49-50

Advanced Capitalist nations (ACNs), 13, 14, 17, 31, 81n, 139, 143, 202, 207, 232, 276, 385, 400; growth phases of and factors influencing, 184-92, 222, 223, 386-93, 394-95, 396-400, 428; identified, 184; inflation and, 294, 321; malaise in, 192-93, 222; synchronized business cycles in, 400; world trade, projected trends in, 405-7. *See also* Affluent Market-Oriented countries

Affluent Communist countries, 81; identified, 84-85; malaise in, 192, 222, 290-93; projected growth of, 89, 90. *See also* Communist Asia; Comecon

Affluent countries, 61-65, 219. *See also* Advanced Capitalist nations; Affluent Communist countries; Affluent Market-Oriented countries

Affluent Market-Oriented countries, 81; identified, 85; New Emphases affecting, 140, 153-77; projected stabilization of, 88, 89, 90. *See also* Advanced Capitalist nations

Africa, 136-37, 254; Coping Poor countries in, 83; Middle Income countries in, 84; Very Poor countries in, 82, 119

Afro-Asian socialism, 135, 137

Age and Aging, 375

Agnostic use of information, 39-43

Agnosticism, 44, 45, 48

Agriculture and industrialization, 438-39. *See also* agriculture under names of countries

Agricultural revolution, 7, 18, 181

Alaska: pipeline, 160-61; wilderness preserve, 58, 204, 473

Algeria, 84, 353

American Indians, 133

Amerindians, 129

Amerindian culture areas, 119

Anti-growth movement. *See* Anti-Growth Triad; Limits-to-growth movement

Anti-Growth Triad, 106, 149n, 202, 232; components of, 54-55, 146-48; and New Emphases, 146, 152, 153-77; view of society, 235-36. *See also* New Class, neo-liberal members of

Argentina, 84, 253, 390

Aristotle, 36-38

Arts, Fine, 32, 35, 150

Asia: Affluent Market-Oriented countries in, 85; Coping Poor countries in, 83; Middle Income countries in, 84; Very Poor countries in, 82. *See also* Communist Asia

Atheism, 44, 45, 47-48

Atlantic Protestant culture area, 131, 169, 174, 191, 216, 249, 387, 388, 479; defined, 61

Augustinian view of man, 39

Australia, 38, 55, 61n, 85, 184, 202, 253

Austria, 85, 184

Autos and auto industry, 204; impact of on society, 234-35; in the future, 23, 23n, 75, 235

Bangladesh, 81, 82, 413; economic growth of, 425-26